Thomas L. Clingman

Thomas Lanier

Clingman

Fire Eater from the

Carolina Mountains

Thomas E. Jeffrey

The University of Georgia Press   *Athens & London*

© 1998 by the University of Georgia Press

Athens, Georgia 30602

All rights reserved

Set in Ehrhardt by G & S Typesetters, Inc.

Printed and bound by McNaughton & Gunn

The paper in this book meets the guidelines for
permanence and durability of the Committee on
Production Guidelines for Book Longevity of the
Council on Library Resources.

Printed in the United States of America

02   01   00   99   98   C   5   4   3   2   1

Library of Congress Cataloging in Publication Data

Jeffrey, Thomas E., 1911–

  Thomas Lanier Clingman : fire eater from the Carolina
mountains / Thomas E. Jeffrey.

     p.   cm.

  Includes bibliographical references and index.

  ISBN 0-8203-2023-4 (alk. paper)

  1. Clingman, T. L. (Thomas Lanier), 1812–1897.
2. Legislators—United States—Biography.   3. United
States. Congress. Senate—Biography.   4. Politicians—
North Carolina—Biography.   5.   North Carolina—Politics
and government—1865–1950.   I. Title.

E415.9.C63J44   1998

975.6′03′092

[B]—DC21   98-23103

                                                                                      CIP

British Library Cataloging in Publication Data available

For

Helen M. Jeffrey

and

Maurice F. Jeffrey

Contents

Acknowledgments

I first became acquainted with Thomas Lanier Clingman almost twenty-five years ago as a graduate student at the Catholic University of America. Although I published a brief account of his antebellum career a few years later in the *North Carolina Historical Review*, not until 1987 did I decide to undertake a book-length biography. Two stimulating articles by John C. Inscoe and Marc W. Kruman, published that year in *Civil War History* and the *North Carolina Historical Review*, challenged my own interpretation of Clingman and renewed my interest in the man. Over the summer, I did some preliminary research into Clingman's post–Civil War career and discovered a surprising number of references to the political activities of a man who supposedly had "studiously avoided politics" after the war.

Words cannot adequately acknowledge my debt of gratitude to John Inscoe, who encouraged me to pursue the Clingman project ten years ago and who has supported it enthusiastically ever since. Thanks in part to his glowing letter of recommendation, I was able to secure a fellowship from the National Endowment for the Humanities (NEH), which allowed me to take a six-month sabbatical from the Thomas A. Edison Papers in 1991 to complete the research and write the first eight chapters. My work has also benefited greatly from John's own writings on Clingman and on Appalachian North Carolina. Even in those cases where I do not entirely agree with his interpretations, his careful research and cogent reasoning have forced me to evaluate my own arguments and evidence more carefully. In addition to his numerous other kindnesses, John read the penultimate draft of the manuscript and offered his usual insightful criticism.

Jerry L. Cross also read an earlier version of the manuscript and provided numerous suggestions for revisions, most of which were subsequently incorporated into the manuscript. Paul B. Israel, my colleague at the Thomas A. Edison Papers, read the three chapters on Clingman's inventive and scientific career. I thank him for his helpful comments and also for steering me away from some misconceptions and errors. Numerous other colleagues at the Edison Papers, including project director Robert A. Rosenberg and former director Reese V. Jenkins, have provided information and insight. I am grateful as well to Jeffrey J. Crow and Paul D. Escott, who wrote letters of recommendation to the NEH and who have remained supportive throughout the years, and to the North Caroliniana Society, which helped defray my research expenses with two Archie K. Davis Fellowships.

Space requirements and a faulty memory prohibit me from enumerating all the archivists, librarians, manuscript curators, and others who have assisted my research over the years. The following is only a partial list. At the North Carolina Collection, University of North Carolina at Chapel Hill: H. G. Jones, Robert G. Anthony, Harry W. McKown, Alice R. Cotten, Eileen McGrath, Jeffrey T. Hicks, and Pam Cross; at the North Carolina Department of Cultural Resources, Division of Archives and History: Jeffrey J. Crow, Jerry Lee Cross, Jesse R. Lankford Jr., and Stephen E. Massengill; at the Southern Historical Collection, University of North Carolina at Chapel Hill: Richard A. Shrader, John White, and Donna King; at the William R. Perkins Library, Duke University: Linda McCurdy, Nelda L. Webb, and Jason Tomberlin; at the Iredell County Library, David A. Bunch; at Western Carolina University, George Frizzell, Sue Dietz, and Laura Chapman.

Some of my research on Clingman has appeared previously as articles in the *North Carolina Review* and Carolina *Comments*. Parts of the following articles are reprinted with the permission of the North Carolina Department of Cultural Resources: "'Thunder from the Mountains': Thomas Lanier Clingman and the End of Whig Supremacy in North Carolina," *North Carolina Historical Review* 56 (October 1979); "Thomas Lanier Clingman and the Invention of the Electric Light: A Forgotten Episode," *Carolina Comments* 32 (May 1984); "'A Whole Torrent of Mean and Malevolent Abuse': Party Politics and the Clingman-Mitchell Controversy," *North Carolina Historical Review* 70 (July 1993; October 1993); "An Unclean Vessel: Thomas Lanier Clingman and the 'Railroad Ring,'" *North Carolina Historical Review* 74 (October 1997).

I am indebted as well to Malcolm L. Call of the University of Georgia Press, who has supported and encouraged the Clingman project since its inception, and to numerous others at the press including Jennifer M. Rogers, Karen K. Orchard, Kelly Caudle, Courtney Denney, and Tricia Stuart. I am especially thankful to Anne R. Gibbons, who copyedited the manuscript, for her excellent work and her kind words of support. For more than two decades, the editors at the *North Carolina Historical Review* have been highly supportive of my research on North Carolina politics. I am deeply grateful to all of them: Jeffrey J. Crow, Memory F. Mitchell, Joe A. Mobley, Marie D. Moore, William A. Owens Jr., Robert M. Topkins, and Kathleen B. Wyche. Finally, I owe a special debt of gratitude to my wife, Pamela, for proofreading the manuscript and for tolerating the presence of Thomas L. Clingman in our household far longer than I had any right to expect.

Thomas L. Clingman

1

A Compound of Incongruities

The weather in the nation's capital was cold, damp, and blustery on 4 March 1893, the day Grover Cleveland took the oath of office as twenty-fourth president of the United States. A storm had swept through the city the night before, and by the time dawn arrived the streets were a mass of mud. The temperature continued to drop during the day, and biting wind and sleet greeted the spectators who lined the streets to witness the president-elect and the outgoing president, Benjamin Harrison, ride together in an open barouche from the Executive Mansion to the Senate Chamber of the Capitol, where Adlai Stevenson was to be sworn in as vice president.[1]

For the sharp-eyed reporter of the *New York World,* the harshness of the weather and the solemnity of the occasion were palliated by a dash of unexpected levity. At the conclusion of the Senate ceremony, as Cleveland and Harrison walked out of the chamber arm-in-arm on their way to the east portico of the Capitol, the journalist noticed sauntering immediately behind them

> a quaint figure in a rusty black overcoat, carrying a
> rustier black umbrella, poised upon the top of which was

a still rustier high hat. Reverently and with almost touching dignity this figure trod past the attendants, who would have pulled him from the ranks, but feared to make a scene. It was ex-Senator Clingman, once a man of national prominence, now a harmless crank, who delights to hang about the scenes once familiar to him and imagines that he is an important participant in every great function.[2]

For more than two decades, Thomas Lanier Clingman had spent practically every winter in Washington, where he could be seen "haunt[ing] the Capitol . . . like a ghost." When Congress was in session, he would often exercise the privilege accorded to former members of taking a seat on the floor, "always serene in unshakable confidence that he was yet a power." Indeed, "not even the busiest or roughest members would disabuse the old man's failing mind of this belief, for his history was known." Visitors to the nearby Corcoran Gallery of Art frequently found him there, gazing intently at his portrait, "painted with his favorite pose when speaking in the Senate." Passers-by who recognized that the curious-looking character standing before them was the subject of the painting could only wonder "why this gentility run to seed should have been so honored with a place in one of the great art galleries of the land."[3]

How he supported himself nobody knew. Rumor had it he kept afloat through a succession of "little places and temporary employments" tendered by sympathetic patrons in North Carolina. There were also stories of a failed romance—an affaire de coeur from long ago—that had kept him a bachelor all his life.[4] Cleveland's inaugural proved to be the aging statesman's last public appearance in the city that had charmed and fascinated him even more than the majestic mountains of his native state. Returning to North Carolina a few weeks later, he lived his remaining years under the care of relatives. He died in the Morganton Hospital for the Insane on 3 November 1897 at the age of eighty-five.

Thomas Lanier Clingman was the last of those Southerners who had served in the U.S. Senate before the Civil War to pass from the scene. In his prime, he was one of the most powerful figures in Congress and one of the few North Carolinians to attain a national reputation. Elected seven times to the U.S. House of Representatives, he was not content with accolades from his own constituents in the mountain district. Instead, he aspired after higher honors. "The two great desires of his life," his niece Jane Puryear Kerr recalled, "the prizes for which he strove in every act of his political career [were] . . . to be United States Senator and to be President. . . . Clingman obtained one, and he at least, never doubted that, but for the war, he would have gained the other also."[5]

In his single-minded pursuit of those goals, Clingman eventually abandoned the political party that had nurtured him. As much as any other individual, he was responsible for the transformation of North Carolina from a Whig bastion into a Democratic state during the 1850s. The editor of the *North Carolina Whig,* writing at the end of that decade, remarked with considerable justification that "no man has done as much as Mr. Clingman to break down the Opposition party in North Carolina." Not surprisingly, Clingman's enemies denounced him as an unscrupulous schemer—an "inveterate office-seeker . . . [whose] whole life has been a continual chase from one office to another." Despite a constant barrage of such accusations, he continued to carry his district by lopsided majorities until his elevation to the U.S. Senate in 1858. "No matter . . . what principles he advocated," recalled his friend John Hill Wheeler, "the people were his devoted supporters and never deserted him."[6]

The source of Clingman's appeal among the "unlettered men of the mountains" remains elusive. Entirely lacking the folksiness and earthy sense of humor that so endeared his rival Zebulon Baird Vance to the people, Clingman was uncharismatic, cerebral, egotistic, and pugnacious. Some considered him to be good looking; while in Congress, he reportedly acquired the nickname "Handsome Tom." Others regarded him as a "strange-looking man." His eccentricities and mannerisms—particularly his habit of talking to himself (a trait he acquired from his mother)—invited sarcasm and ridicule, especially among those who were already predisposed to criticize.[7]

Richard Benbury Creecy, one of nineteenth-century North Carolina's preeminent journalists, aptly characterized his former university classmate as "a compound of incongruities." According to Creecy, Clingman's claim to greatness lay primarily in his "great intellectuality & boundless ambition." At the same time, "his manner was his burden. . . . He was without personal magnetism. He had Caesar's ambition & will & ability, but without his adaptability & his personal charm." Indeed, said Creecy, "his personal characteristics would have ruined him but for his indomitable will & ambition."[8]

Great intellectuality, boundless ambition, and an indomitable will. Those attributes were recognized in Clingman by friend and foe alike. Although not an original thinker, he was a voracious reader with an analytical mind, a retentive memory, and an amazing variety of intellectual interests. "His intellect," remarked one contemporary, "was omnivorous; it devoured everything that came within its reach. He invaded the domaine of science art and literature, and culled the choicest treasures of each." Another North Carolinian considered Clingman to be "the best informed man on all questions that we ever had in public life. He was a brilliant, eloquent writer, accomplished gentleman, historian, well versed in chemistry, astronomy, geology and theology and a fine belles-letters scholar."[9]

Friends, as well as enemies, acknowledged Clingman to be a man of "high aspirations and far-reaching ambitions." Early in life, according to family tradition, he was overheard to remark that "I can marry and be a happy man, or not marry and be a great man. I will be a great man." Having thus "deliberately made his choice of ambition for his mistress, and fame for his reward, he loyally adhered to it" and remained a confirmed bachelor until the end of his life.[10] Although family tradition exaggerates Clingman's commitment to bachelorhood (toward the end of his life, he tried desperately to find a wife), it accurately delineates his priorities. Above all other concerns, Clingman devoted his energies toward promoting his own reputation as an important player on the national scene. As journalist Alexander K. McClure recalled, "his desire to be remembered as a great factor in the affairs of the nation was something stronger than even that which is felt by most men of ambition." [11]

Egotism, self-confidence, and indefatigable determination were the driving forces behind Clingman's ambition. Jane Puryear Kerr remembered her uncle as "a strong man in every way. A strong body . . . a strong mind, a strong character, and a will that was strongest of all. That will was his only master. When once it had determined upon a thing the man's whole existence strove for it." Acknowledging that Clingman had been "criticised as possessing 'overweening vanity and colossal conceit,'" she admitted that "his opinion of himself was not a small one." Bettie Puryear Gibson, writing privately to her sister, was less tactful. "I have never before conceived of such utter, absolute, invincible selfishness in a human being," she complained. "And his vanity is, as you well know, a match for it." Risden Tyler Bennett, a North Carolina congressman who saw Clingman frequently during the early 1880s, recalled that "*his vanity was stupendous.*" William H. S. Burgwyn, who served with him during the Civil War, agreed that Clingman's "egotism was colossal" but added that his tremendous self-confidence often "disarmed criticism, even inspired respect." [12]

Admired by some as a talented and principled statesman while denounced by others as a scheming opportunist, Clingman was a controversial figure in his own time. In recent years he has also engendered debate among historians. In both cases, much of the controversy has centered on the factors behind his startling transformation from a disciple of Henry Clay into one of the South's most outspoken "fire eaters." Clingman himself attributed his change of sentiment to his growing alarm at the strength of the antislavery movement in the North. Several recent scholars have endorsed that viewpoint, while at the same time depicting his growing militancy as, at least in part, a response to constituent pressure.[13] Others have portrayed Clingman as an opportunist who put on the mantle of Southern Rights in order to secure Democratic support for a seat in the U.S. Senate.[14]

Conceding the strength of Clingman's own power of self-persuasion, this study will not challenge the sincerity of his eventual conversion to militant Southernism. At the same time, it will reveal that his estrangement from the Whigs began several years before his metamorphosis on the Southern Rights issue. By 1849, after two failed attempts to win the Whig nomination for U.S. senator, Clingman had convinced himself that his party was controlled by a clique of unscrupulous "central managers" who callously promoted their own favorites at the expense of aspirants from remote parts of the state. Moreover, his inability to secure lucrative patronage appointments for his political allies alienated him from the Taylor administration even before the Thirty-First Congress met in December 1849 to discuss the status of slavery in the territory recently acquired from Mexico. The refusal of the Northern Whigs to abandon the Wilmot Proviso was merely the last in a succession of events that had left Clingman frustrated and embittered against the Whig party.

In most respects, Thomas Lanier Clingman was an unlikely fire eater. As his opponents repeatedly pointed out, he never owned a slave himself. Nor did his constituents have a compelling economic interest in the peculiar institution. The rugged and underdeveloped farmlands of the mountain district were unsuitable for plantation agriculture, and Clingman's congressional district contained by far the smallest percentage of slaves in the state. The paradox of a leading advocate of Southern Rights arising out of, and thriving within, an environment where slavery was at best a marginal institution is a phenomenon that cries out for further analysis.

Although political considerations had a profound influence on Clingman's changing course on the slavery issue, his increasingly militant behavior was not motivated by pressure from his Whig constituents, as some historians have argued. Indeed, their overwhelming rejection of disunion during the convention election of February 1861 lends support to the argument, made repeatedly by Clingman's political opponents, that he misrepresented the sentiments of his district. Still, if the congressman really was out of step with his constituents on the Southern Rights issue, why did they continue to reelect him over opponents who presumably were more in tune with their real sentiments? The answer to that intriguing question can shed considerable light on the political culture of antebellum North Carolina and on the divergent positions of the two parties on the slavery issue.

Clingman's success in the mountain district was due, in no small part, to his adeptness at tempering his fire-eating rhetoric to accommodate the unionist sensibilities of his predominantly Whig constituency. In his recent study of the "fire eaters," Eric H. Walther makes an important distinction between genuine secessionists who had no attachment to the Union and those "southern radicals" who "vigorously promoted southern interests but did not necessarily advocate secession." That dichotomy was not so clear-cut during the 1850s. Instead, the term "fire eater" was used "indiscriminately by both northerners and southerners to condemn anyone believed to be too far out of the political mainstream." Until the secession crisis forced Southerners to take a definitive stand on the issue of union or disunion, the distinction between "radicals" and "secessionists" was, at best, a blurry one in the public mind.[15]

Clingman's strident rhetoric and his vigorous promotion of Southern interests justify the appellation of "fire eater." However, his reputation among historians as a "persistent and consistent advocate of secession" is undeserved. Throughout the 1850s Clingman argued that a forceful stand on Southern Rights was the surest means of preserving the Union. By that logic, he was "a better Union man" than his more moderate opponents, whose submissive attitude was merely encouraging Northern aggression. Clingman took pains to dissociate himself from those extremists in the lower South who were advocating immediate secession, and during the crisis of 1860–61 he worked hard to broker a compromise between the sections. Even after endorsing disunion in February 1861, he regarded secession as a bargaining chip in future negotiations for a reconstructed Union rather than as a means of achieving an enduring Southern nation.[16]

Long before he gained national notoriety as the "Champion of the South," Clingman had attained renown in his own state as the "Champion of the West" through his advocacy of railroads and other transportation improvements that would link the products of the mountain counties with seaport market towns in North Carolina, Virginia, South Carolina, and Georgia. The community that Clingman represented in the state and national legislatures was a far cry from the antibourgeois society portrayed by Eugene Genovese and other historians who contend that the antebellum South embodied a distinctive, precapitalistic culture. While some Americans during the Jacksonian Era may have viewed the emerging market economy as a threat to their individual autonomy, Clingman and his constituents in western North Carolina welcomed the establishment of trade and commerce as the surest means of attaining wealth and prosperity.[17]

Well before Henry W. Grady began hailing the arrival of a "New South," Clingman was functioning as a "one-man chamber of commerce," publishing letters and articles that extolled the beauty and natural resources of the Carolina mountains in order to attract the Northern capital that he believed was crucial to the region's economic development. Clingman has accurately been characterized as western North Carolina's "first great booster"—one of its "first and most prolific individual publicity men."[18] Western North Carolinians appreciated Clingman's tireless efforts to promote their economic welfare, and certainly that is one of the reasons why they continually returned him to Congress.

Clingman's political success during the 1850s was also a product of his carefully cultivated image as a political independent whose actions were governed by his own autonomous judgment and not by the dictates of party. Contrary to the claims of some historians, Clingman did not publicly embrace the Democratic party until long after he had abandoned the Whigs. Despite his endorsement of the Democratic presidential candidates during the 1850s and his indifference or outright opposition to the Whig candidates for governor, Clingman remained nominally a Whig, albeit an independent one, until the party collapsed in 1855. Not surprisingly, his enemies denounced him as "a Democrat calling himself a whig," who had donned "the robes of whiggery simply that he may thereby injure the party more successfully."[19] Even after formally joining the Democrats after the presidential election of 1856, Clingman continued to pursue an independent course, breaking with the Buchanan administration over a host of domestic and foreign policy issues.

Historians of antebellum American politics have frequently commented on the tenacity with which the voters clung to the two great parties. Their tendency to view the political issues of the day from partisan perspectives has been aptly described as the "partisan imperative." Ironically, at the same time that they were worshiping at the "shrine of party," many Americans remained deeply distrustful of the constraints that party loyalty and discipline placed on individual autonomy.[20] Unable fully to reconcile the exigencies of nineteenth-century politics with their yeoman ideals and with the tenets of classical republican ideology, antebellum North Carolinians were susceptible to appeals by self-styled independents like Clingman, who professed to disdain "mere devotion to party" as "a reproach to a statesman."[21]

Despite a spate of recent articles about Clingman's antebellum career and a comprehensive investigation of his role as a Civil War general, almost nothing has been written about his political activities after the war.[22] In the absence of solid documentary evidence, two competing—and equally misleading—generalizations about his involvement in postwar North Carolina politics have been expounded. The first is that Clingman self-consciously chose to eschew politics and focus his energies, instead, on lecturing, business ventures, and scientific activities. That viewpoint was expressed in several obituaries published immediately after his death and in a biographical sketch written a few years later by Jane Puryear Kerr. Many twentieth-century scholars have uncritically adopted her argument. It appears most recently in the entry for Clingman in the *Dictionary of North Carolina Biography.*[23]

There is a kernel of truth in that interpretation. Freed from the onerous and time-consuming tasks of a congressman, Clingman did have considerable opportunity after the war to indulge his wide-ranging intellectual and business interests. Until advancing age and poor health finally put an end to his activities, he wrote widely on scientific, literary, and religious topics and was a popular figure on the lecture circuit. A would-be business associate of Thomas A. Edison, he developed his own system of electric lighting and received two patents on his inventions. An aggressive exponent of the medicinal properties of tobacco, he established the Clingman Tobacco Cure Company to promote his poultices, ointments, and other tobacco products. He also engaged extensively in mining ventures and land speculation.

However, Clingman's thirst for fame and power was too insatiable to be quenched by his undeniable scientific and literary achievements. That he failed to hold elective office after the war (except briefly as a delegate to the Constitutional Convention of 1875) was not due to any lack of effort on his part. From the moment he reappeared in Washington in December 1865 seeking reinstatement to the seat he had vacated at the beginning of the war until he presented his claims for the last time to the North Carolina General Assembly in 1889, Clingman never abandoned the hope of returning to the U.S. Senate. Indeed, his postwar political activities consisted, in large part, of a succession of failed schemes to regain his Senate seat. It is, perhaps, understandable that sympathetic contemporaries should gloss over the resulting humiliations and embarrassments and pretend, instead, that he had studiously avoided politics since the war.

A second viewpoint, of more recent origin, holds that Clingman remained a "power in the state Democratic party" after the Civil War, despite his unwillingness or inability to hold public office.[24] That interpretation disregards his tumultuous relations with postwar North Carolina's leading Democrats, most of whom had been Whigs during the antebellum era. Except for a brief period during the 1870s, Clingman persistently remained on the fringes of power. Regarded as an outsider by most Democrats and overshadowed by younger and more popular rivals such as Zebulon B. Vance, he never came close to wielding the political influence he had exercised in the Old North State before the war.

Clingman's political impotence in post–Civil War North Carolina resulted largely from his unwillingness to subject himself to party discipline and his insistence on maintaining the image of an "independent"—ironically, the very traits that had served him so well before the war. A master at the game of politics during the antebellum years, Clingman failed to recognize that the enfranchisement of the former slaves and the organization of a biracial Republican party had drastically changed the rules of the game. During the postwar years defenders of the status quo repeatedly made the argument that the perpetuation of white supremacy (and, incidentally, of upper-class rule) depended on the maintenance of Democratic hegemony and the preservation of party discipline. In such a political environment, independent candidates like Clingman, instead of being admired for their courage, were regarded by most white voters as mere stalking horses for Republicanism.

Even while denouncing his political course, however, North Carolina's postwar leaders praised Clingman for his literary and scientific accomplishments, for his efforts to promote the wealth and reputation of his native state, and for his defense of the tenets of traditional Christianity against the teachings of Charles Darwin and other proponents of evolution. Despite his unorthodox political views and the unfortunate circumstances of his final years, Clingman was respected at the time of his death as one of the Old North State's greatest sons.

Today, however, he is best remembered (when remembered at all) as the explorer who gave his name to Clingman's Dome, the highest peak in the Great Smoky Mountains. No full-length study of his life has ever been published. His career as a congressman, along with his numerous other endeavors, has been relegated to a few specialized studies that are consulted mainly by students of North

Carolina history. In more general scholarly works dealing with the antebellum, Civil War, and Reconstruction eras, he is frequently ignored altogether.[25]

Douglas Southall Freeman once remarked that "a man's place in history depends, in large part, on care and good fortune—care in preserving essential records, and good fortune in having a biographer who uses those records sympathetically."[26] Unfortunately, Clingman did not leave a large collection of personal papers for potential biographers to examine. In light of his intense desire to be remembered as a major player on the national scene, it is ironic that he did not take greater pains to preserve his papers. No doubt, he intended his compilation *Speeches and Writings*, which he edited and published in 1877, to stand as the "essential record" of his career—a more fitting testimonial than any collection of manuscripts, most of which would necessarily consist of incoming letters written by others.

Other factors also militated against the retention of a sizable number of personal papers. Living exclusively in hotels and boarding houses and traveling extensively between Asheville, Raleigh, Washington, and New York, Clingman could not afford to be encumbered by an unwieldy number of personal possessions. Since he had no immediate family with a sentimental interest in preserving the memorabilia of his career, not surprisingly a substantial part of the historical record has been lost.

Fortunately, some of Clingman's papers have survived. A modest quantity of his correspondence can be found in the collections of Clingman and Puryear family papers at the University of North Carolina and Duke University. Letters by Clingman are also scattered among the papers of his political and business associates; other individual items are in archives and repositories across the United States. Because he was continuously in the public eye, contemporary newspapers provide the single most important source for this study. The Raleigh and Asheville presses, in particular, contain an abundance of speeches, letters, and editorials by Clingman, his political allies, and his political enemies. Those newspapers, as well as others published in Washington, D.C., New York, and in various North Carolina towns, also provide significant contextual information and constitute a valuable source for understanding public perceptions of Clingman.[27]

What emerges from an examination of those sources, together with a perusal of Clingman's published speeches, military correspondence, and other official records, is an image of the public man as he presented himself to others and as he was perceived by them. In the absence of diaries and intimate personal correspondence, the private Clingman who lay behind the public persona remains elusive.

Nonetheless, a few tantalizing bits of evidence suggest that Clingman's vanity and arrogant self-confidence, which became even more pronounced as he grew older, may have served as a mask, concealing the unpleasant truth that his life had, by his own standards, been less than fully successful. Speaking before the Alumni

Association of the University of North Carolina in 1889, he probably told his listeners more than they wanted to hear when he remarked that for many years he "did not feel much happiness in life."[28]

Sixteen years earlier, in an address before the graduating class at Davidson College, he had observed that

> we imagine great men to be happy, because we see only their prominent features, which glare before the public eye, while their inner life is hidden from us. Their brightness is but the enchantment which distance lends. On a near approach it fades away as the blue of the mountain becomes rugged rock, its smooth and green slopes are converted into thickets of tangled shrubs and brambles, and its cloud, so white in the sunlight as to dazzle the eye, is seen to be only dark mist.[29]

Perhaps Clingman eventually came to realize that eminence and power had not brought him personal fulfillment. A man who aspired to the presidency and under different circumstances might have attained it, he ended his life penniless, friendless, and a burden to his relatives—"a lagging loiterer on the stage of life." If Clingman did, indeed, deliberately choose ambition for his mistress, he ultimately found her to be a fickle and uncaring one. "In full manhood" (as Richard Benbury Creecy recalled), she brought him "a big slice of the world's bounty. He was honored, feasted, feted, and the world's best was his." But ambition also estranged him from those who had nurtured him in his youth, cajoled him into sacrificing private gratification for public esteem, and denied him the wife and children who might have offered emotional support in his old age. Thus when the advancing years finally took their toll on his physical strength, his mental abilities, and his financial resources, he found "he had not under him in his age and helpless condition its natural props and supports."[30]

2 *A Promising Young Man*

In his later years, Thomas Lanier Clingman liked to boast that he could trace his pedigree all the way back to Julius Caesar. "As Gen. Clingman's grand mother bore the name of Caesar," the *Asheville Citizen* explained, "and was of German descent, and as Julius Caesar had several German wives, Gen. Clingman claims to be one of his descendants."[1] Apart from professing her relationship to the great Roman general, Clingman seems to have said little about his paternal grandmother, Elizabeth Kaiser. According to some accounts, she was already living in the North Carolina backcountry at the time she met her future husband, Alexander Clingman. Others claim that they both grew up in Pennsylvania and traveled together down the Shenandoah and Yadkin river valleys to the fertile lands bordering Dutch Second Creek in southeastern Rowan County.[2] Alexander signed his first deed in German script, and he and Elizabeth both spoke English with heavy Teutonic accents. Nonetheless, it is unclear whether either was actually born in the Old World.[3]

According to Thomas Clingman, his paternal ancestors derived their name from their traditional occupations as blacksmiths and metal workers. In their home country, he said, they were armor makers to the royal family and were known as "Klinkermen" or "great big noisy men."[4] Most likely, the Clingmans came to America during the first half of the eighteenth century for the same reasons that inspired thousands of other Germans to travel to the New World—to improve their economic condition and to escape the destructive wars and religious persecution that had ravaged Europe since the beginning of the Protestant Reformation. The earliest settlers, including numerous collateral branches of the Clingman family, took up choice farmlands in Lancaster and adjoining counties along the Susquehanna River in Pennsylvania. By the 1730s, however, land prices in that area had become high enough to induce newcomers, along with many children of the original settlers, to migrate farther south into the Shenandoah Valley and the Carolina Piedmont.[5]

By the late 1740s a few venturesome settlers had already moved into the country between the Yadkin and Catawba Rivers in what later became Rowan County, North Carolina. Alexander Clingman was among the first to arrive, securing a warrant (an intent to purchase) for 620 acres on the northwest corner of Rowan Court House (present-day Salisbury) in 1754. He never paid for the land, and he may even have returned for a while to Pennsylvania, since his name disappears from the Rowan County records after 1761 and does not reappear until 1772. In February 1774, Alexander acquired 281 acres of land along Dutch Second Creek, the first of many such purchases that would eventually make him one of the largest landholders in the district.[6]

Compared to more established areas, life on the Carolina frontier was primitive. Still, a few backcountry farmers like Alexander Clingman were able to make a comfortable living transporting their grains and meat products overland to markets in Fayetteville, North Carolina (at the headwaters of the Cape Fear River), and Charleston, South Carolina. Alexander supplemented his farm income by trapping animals and making hats from their fur. The money he received as a hatter enabled the Clingman family to improve its standard of living, despite an increasing number of children. George, the eldest child, was probably born shortly after Alexander and Elizabeth established their home on Dutch Second Creek. A daughter, Esther, arrived soon afterward, followed by five other children who lived to become adults—Peter, Henry, Alexander Michael, Jacob (Thomas's father), and Catherine.[7]

The coming of the American Revolution proved only a temporary impediment to the family's growing prosperity. Many Germans remained neutral in the quarrel between Britain and her rebellious colonies, but Alexander joined the Rowan militia and was probably among the eight hundred men who journeyed from Salisbury to Charleston in November 1778 to repel a rumored British invasion. Early in 1780 Alexander again marched to Charleston and was among those captured when Gen. Benjamin Lincoln was routed by the British in May. Many Carolinians died of fever that spring in the overcrowded ships that held the American prisoners in Charleston harbor. Although no longer a young man, Alexander was fortunate enough to return home in good health.[8]

After the war Alexander took advantage of his status as a veteran to acquire land that had been confiscated from the Tories, as well as unclaimed property formerly owned by Lord Granville. By the time of his death in 1803 his estate comprised more than one thousand acres—the second largest in his tax district.[9] Indeed, he had acquired sufficient wealth to leave each child a generous allotment, while at the same time allowing his widow (who lived until at least 1827) to live comfortably on the home farm.[10]

By 1803 most of the Clingman children had already left home. George, the eldest sibling, moved to Charleston, married a woman of Huguenot descent, and became a shipbuilder. Alexander Michael subsequently followed his brother to South Carolina to begin a career as a shipbuilder and merchant. Esther, the oldest daughter, married a ne'er-do-well named Killian Jarratt who abandoned her not long after their son, Isaac, was born. Henry, according to family tradition, migrated to Kentucky, never to be heard from again. Peter moved to Huntsville, thirty-five miles up the Yadkin River, to open a general store. Only the two youngest children—Jacob, age sixteen, and Catherine, age thirteen—were still living on the family estate at the time of their father's death.[11]

Some time in 1810 or 1811 Jacob also moved to Huntsville, purchased the large red building on High Street that Peter had been operating as a general store, and went into business with his brother. The aspiring merchants could not have chosen a more propitious location. A stagecoach road, which traversed the state from Wilkesboro to Fayetteville, ran down one of the town's main streets. Several other important roads also converged at Huntsville. In addition, Shallow Ford, which was located about one-half mile from the store, offered one of the few all-weather crossings of the Yadkin River.[12]

The Red Store provided a prosperous livelihood for its two proprietors. Farmers throughout the Yadkin Valley brought their whiskey, furs, pork, grain, and other products to the store and exchanged them for clothing, tea, sugar, farm implements, and other manufactured goods purchased in Philadelphia. Like his father, Jacob had acquired the valuable skill of making hats, which could be sold at the store for as much as five dollars apiece. The Clingmans supplemented their store business with a blacksmith shop on the other side of High Street just east of the store. That enterprise was probably managed by Peter's two slaves, Boston and Ellick.[13]

The Clingman brothers added status and respectability to their wealth by marrying into one of the most prominent families in the Shallow Ford community. A few years after arriving in Huntsville, Peter married Anne Poindexter. On 10 August 1811 Jacob married her sister, Jane.[14] The Poindexter sisters were exceptionally well connected. Thomas Poindexter, their paternal grandfather, was descended from a long line of churchmen and public figures on the Channel Island of Jersey.[15] Henry Pattillo, their maternal grandfather, was a famous Presbyterian divine who played a prominent role during the early days of the Revolution.[16]

The Poindexter sisters were also connected to several other influential families through their mother's first husband, Robert Lanier. Jane Pattillo was only fifteen years old when she married Lanier, the scion of a large landholding family from Virginia. Lanier's brother-in-law, Joseph Williams, sired a family of twelve children that included a future U.S. senator (John Williams), two congressmen (Robert and Lewis Williams), and a chancellor of Tennessee (Thomas Lanier Williams). Another brother-in-law, Joseph Winston, was Surry County's first member of the House of Commons after independence; he subsequently was elected to the state senate and the U.S. Congress. During the Revolution, Lanier and Winston served as justices of the peace, while Williams was clerk of the court—positions that enabled each man to acquire considerable quantities of choice farmland. After Lanier's death in 1785, his extensive land holdings devolved to his widow and her second husband, Francis Poindexter.[17]

Thomas Lanier Clingman was born in Huntsville on 27 July 1812, the first child of Jacob and Jane. He was named after his mother's half-brother, a promising young physician who had died twelve years earlier at the age of twenty-four. Two other children soon followed—John, born on 14 May 1814, and Elizabeth Ann, born on 21 February 1816. Meanwhile, Peter and Anne Clingman were raising a family of four children.[18]

Despite the onset of the War of 1812 and the pecuniary demands of their growing families, these were prosperous years for Jacob and Peter Clingman. A tax list from 1812 reveals that Peter, with 765 acres of land, was the sixth-largest landowner in the Huntsville district. After 1818 he also enjoyed a modest but steady income as town postmaster, a position in which he served until 1835. Jacob was also steadily adding to his real and personal holdings. In July 1813 he purchased two lots in Huntsville and began constructing a house for his family, who until then were probably living above the store. In January 1817 he acquired two slaves, a twenty-nine-year-old woman named Winny and a child called Judy.[19]

Even as they were advancing in wealth, however, the families of Peter and Jacob Clingman were being devastated by a succession of personal tragedies. In 1814 Elizabeth, the only daughter of Peter and Anne, died suddenly. A few months later, Anne herself passed away. Early in 1817 the house into which Jacob's family had recently moved burned to the ground. Then on 8 May 1817 Jacob himself expired "after a painful illness of nine days," leaving a pregnant wife and three small children.[20]

Shortly afterward, Jane and her family moved into the White House, the spacious new home of her widowed brother-in-law. From an economic standpoint, the arrangement made considerable sense. With the merger of the two families, Peter could focus on managing the store and increasing his personal fortune, while Jane became mistress of the White House and its seven small occupants—a number that would shortly increase to eight when Thomas's cousin, Sarah Mitchell, moved in with the family. At the same time, Jane maintained a degree of financial independence through the rent that Peter paid on Jacob's store and through her other property holdings.[21]

By all accounts, Jane Clingman's relationship with her brother-in-law was a stormy one. Both were headstrong personalities, and they quarreled frequently over a variety of issues ranging from the children's education to what should be planted in the garden. On more than one occasion, the possibility of a separation was discussed. However, financial considerations and the opposition of the children precluded that course of action.[22]

Jane Clingman, who has been characterized as a woman "remarkable for her Christian life, and all the graces that adorn the noblest specimens of female character," seems to have been an affectionate, and perhaps overly protective, mother to Thomas and the other children in her family.[23] An exceptionally well-educated woman by the standards of the early nineteenth century, she was successful in instilling in her eldest son a lifelong love of learning.[24] She was less effective in her efforts to curb his hot temper, a trait he shared with his mother and his uncle. Thomas's fiery personality frequently embroiled him in fights with the other neighborhood boys, and repeated whippings failed to break him of the habit.[25]

Although Jane Clingman more than adequately filled the role of mother, it is doubtful whether Peter Clingman ever managed to replace his brother in the affections of young Thomas. According to Richard C. Puryear, who worked for Peter at the Red Store and later married Thomas's sister, the elder Clingman was stubborn, irascible, and frequently "extravagant and unreasonable in his remarks." "When he is mad about one thing," complained Puryear, "he is mad about everything." A man who had risen to a position of affluence and respectability primarily by his own efforts, Peter never fully understood Thomas's desire for a university education or his unwillingness to follow in the family mercantile business. Those differences, exacerbated by their combative temperaments, must have led to innumerable clashes between uncle and nephew.[26]

As a youth, Clingman "entered as readily into boyish sports as any of his playmates." The woods surrounding Huntsville had a profusion of deer and other game, and hunting was a popular pastime for the Clingman boys. The nearby Yadkin River with its abundant supply of shad and other fish also offered numerous opportunities for Thomas to engage in his "favorite sport." The swift currents and rocky bottoms of the Yadkin presented their share of dangers as well. On two occasions, Thomas came very close to drowning.[27]

Even in those youthful endeavors, Clingman demonstrated the authoritative presence and talent for command that would characterize his adult career. According to his niece, he easily managed to transform his three cousins and two younger brothers into "his willing subordinates." Together "with the village boys, [they] constituted a following of such unquestioning loyalty that traditions of their exploits under the leadership of 'Tommy' have come down in the neighborhood to the present day."[28]

Early in his childhood, Clingman also "gave evidence of an intellect far superior to that of the ordinary individual." He received his earliest education from his mother, who taught him to read and instructed him in the rudiments of composition and mathematics. As he grew older, Thomas, along with the other children, frequently spent part of the year with the Poindexters, attending the subscription school that their uncle Francis had established on the family plantation.[29]

During the antebellum period, education beyond the bare elements of reading, writing, and arithmetic was a luxury reserved only for the affluent. Fortunately for Thomas, his family had sufficient financial resources to send him to Ebenezer Academy, a one-room log schoolhouse located northeast of Statesville in Iredell County. Chartered by the general assembly in 1822, the academy was run in succession by three members of the Hall family: Robert Sloan Hall; his nephew, William Alexander Hall; and Robert's cousin, Hugh Roddy Hall, who took charge in 1828 (the year Clingman matriculated) and continued until his death in 1856. The Clingmans may well have been attracted by the institution's newspaper advertisements, which promised that "all branches of education required for college will be taught . . . in a rural situation . . . [where] students will be measurably free from temptations to vice."[30]

Although its curriculum was largely that of the typical antebellum academy, Ebenezer Academy was distinctive in the attention it paid to the sciences. James Hall, the uncle of Hugh Roddy Hall, was an amateur scientist and inventor who is generally regarded as the first teacher of science in North Carolina. Hall's nephews (some of whom probably studied under him) also offered courses in various branches of what was then called natural philosophy. It is likely that Thomas Clingman's own lifelong interest in the sciences was first nurtured by the teachings of Hugh Roddy Hall.[31] Certainly, his year at the Ebenezer Academy prepared Clingman well for the rigorous entrance examination that awaited him at the University of North Carolina. Indeed, his performance proved so impressive that he was allowed to enter the university as a sophomore.[32]

When Thomas Clingman arrived in Chapel Hill during the summer of 1829, the town consisted of a few dozen houses, several stores, a blacksmith shop, and a tavern. The campus itself contained only a handful of structures, the most prominent of which was the South Building, a three-story edifice that housed the classrooms, the library, and the headquarters of the two literary societies. The student body was diminutive by modern standards. In 1829 there were eighty-one matriculates and a mere fourteen graduates. The faculty was proportionately small.[33]

Since 1804 (with only a brief hiatus), the president of the university had been the Reverend Joseph Caldwell, who also held the position of professor of moral philosophy. A Yale graduate who had joined the faculty in 1796, the austere and dignified Caldwell was a capable administrator who had been responsible for placing the institution on a firm financial footing and effecting what one scholar has called "a renaissance at Chapel Hill." During the later years of his administration, the university had begun moving away from its traditional classical curriculum toward a more balanced program by acquiring some expensive scientific apparatus and appointing several faculty with training in the sciences.[34]

One of those appointees was a burly young man by the name of Elisha Mitchell. Educated at Yale under the tutelage of the renowned scientist Benjamin Silliman, Mitchell had taken a position in 1818 as professor of mathematics and natural philosophy. By the time Clingman arrived a decade later, he was professor of chemistry, geology, and mineralogy. "Old Mike" (as he was affectionately called by the students) was a popular instructor. Students enjoyed his witty and stimulating lectures and relished even more the field trips, which "while ostensibly a scientific, geological and botanical exploration . . . [were] in fact a social festival in which preceptor and pupil unbent, and, waiving the formalities of dignity, had a good time." Mitchell's erudition, amiability, and enthusiasm undoubtedly had an impact on young Clingman.[35]

Clingman's academic record at the University of North Carolina was outstanding. He consistently placed among the highest-ranking scholars in the oral examinations the students took at the end of each semester. His final examination proved to be his most impressive performance. After being queried by a committee of the board of trustees in the fields of philosophy, rhetoric, chemistry, mathematics, and languages, Clingman was ranked first in all categories—"an honor not before achieved and not often afterwards."[36]

According to his classmate Richard Benbury Creecy, Clingman acquired notoriety among his peers not only for his "scholarship [and] intellectuality" but also for his "eccentricity and gawkiness." As a student, he manifested "the same absentmindedness and fondness for talking to himself that characterized him in after life. His voice was harsh and rasping and his gait ungainly."[37]

Despite his eccentricities, Clingman earned the lasting respect of his classmates as the result of an incident that occurred shortly after his arrival at Chapel Hill. Proudly appareled in a cow-colored suit of Surry County homespun, the young student was walking around campus "in absorbed contemplation at the majestic proportions of the old south buildings, his mouth wide open, talking to himself . . . a fit object for derision and practical jests." A nattily dressed upperclassman began ridiculing the newcomer for his odd mannerisms and unfashionable attire. Clingman responded in characteristic fashion with fists swinging, leaving his older compatriot "a wiser and bloodier man." Clingman's fearlessness and self-confidence, together with his refusal to brook any insult, won him "a reputation for pluckiness . . . that caused him to be respected afterwards." Indeed, "with all his awkwardness, Clingman was the most conspicuous man in his class, and his associates were proud of his companionship."

Clingman also acquired a reputation on campus as an "untiring bandy player" and a "noted gourmand." His abundant energy and sinewy physique—he stood

5′ 10″ and weighed about 160 pounds—suited him well for bandy, "a rough and dangerous game" similar to field hockey. He had a voracious appetite and was especially fond of flapjacks and turnovers. According to Creecy, "his gastronomic feats in twirling flannel cakes down his oesophagus excited our wonder and amazement," as did his ability to spin more flapjacks on his fork while grace was being said "than was the case of any student on the hill."[38]

During the early nineteenth century, the state university played an important role in training the children of North Carolina's elite for a career in public service. That task devolved primarily on the two literary societies. Despite their differing sectional orientation—the Philanthropic Society was composed primarily of students from the counties east of Raleigh, whereas the Dialectic Society was dominated by westerners—both organizations had an identical mission: to develop their members' debating skills and improve their writing style; to instruct them in the rules of parliamentary procedure; to inculcate a sense of responsibility and proper conduct; and, most important, to provide instruction and experience in self-government. In order to accomplish those goals, each society established elaborate rules of conduct and levied fines on those who transgressed them. Though violators could be impeached and even expelled from the university for grave offenses, members apparently did not lose caste for less serious breaches of discipline, as long as they took responsibility for their actions and paid the penalty.[39]

As a member of the Dialectic Society, Clingman incurred his share of penalties. On three occasions, he was assessed one dollar—the amount levied for infractions such as casting personal aspersions on a fellow member.[40] Those occasional transgressions did not prevent him from holding a number of important offices and winning several high honors. Before the end of his first year, he won election to the position of censor morum, or disciplinarian. In his senior year, Clingman was honored by being twice elevated to the presidency. In each case, he was awarded the additional distinction of having his presidential address filed in the archives.[41]

Clingman also played a major role in the weekly debates conducted by the Dialectic Society. During his years at the university, the society discussed a wide range of political issues that Clingman and his peers would soon have to deal with in a more serious fashion as legislators. Among the topics that elicited debate was the issue of slavery. In October 1830 Clingman was appointed to open the discussion on the intriguing topic, "Is It Possible That the Slaves of the Southern States Will Ever Be Emancipated by Their Own Exertions?"—a question that was ultimately decided in the negative. During his senior year, Clingman's colleagues acknowledged his forensic skills by choosing him to open the debate on at least six occasions.

The high point in Clingman's college career was the commencement ceremony in June 1832. As the highest-ranking student in his graduating class, he was given the honor of delivering the salutatory address in Latin before the visiting dignitaries who thronged the ordinarily quiet village of Chapel Hill to witness the closing exercises. Clingman was also chosen by the Dialectic Society as its representative to wait upon visiting orator William Gaston and escort him to Person Hall, where he was to deliver the commencement address. A former congressman who would soon become a justice of the North Carolina Supreme Court, Gaston was one of the Old North State's most prominent citizens.[42]

On the appointed day, the procession formed at the Old South Building with the Richmond Cornet Band in front, followed by Gaston, his massive frame adorned in a black silk gown. On one side of the distinguished speaker was Thomas S. Ashe, the representative of the Philanthropic Society. Scion of one of the state's preeminent families, Ashe walked (in the words of Richard Benbury Creecy) "with the trained step of an English grenadier." On the other side was Clingman. Dressed in a fashionable new waistcoat and summer pantaloons—a far cry from the homespun clothing that had inspired ridicule a few years earlier—he no doubt fancied himself a dashing figure. According to Creecy, however, the proud young scholar walked with a gait that was as "awkward and gawky as a plowman's prentice boy . . . throwing out his legs right and left like he was stiff-kneed, and looking for all the world like he thought all the crowd was looking at him, and that Gaston and Ashe were mere small kites dangling at his tail, to give pomp to his pageantry." On arriving at the speaker's platform in Person Hall, Clingman inadvertently knocked over the table on which Gaston had placed his manuscript. Had it not been for Ashe's quick thinking and even quicker hands, "the table, and perhaps Gaston himself, would have gone sprawling on the floor below."[43]

Despite its inauspicious beginnings, Gaston's commencement address proved to be one of the most memorable orations ever delivered at Chapel Hill. Speaking in the midst of the nullification crisis to a gathering that was strongly unionist in sentiment, Gaston struck a responsive chord among his listeners with his eloquent denunciation of disunion and his praise for the U.S. Constitution. Nor did the audience seem to object when he arraigned the institution of slavery as the source of the South's problems. Although Clingman's salutatory address has not been preserved, the young scholar apparently made good use of his opportunity to address the leading politicians, planters, and businessmen of the state. According to David L. Swain, Clingman and his classmate J. H. Parker, who delivered the valedictory, both demonstrated themselves to be "promising young men."[44]

Well before his graduation, Clingman had made up his mind to pursue a career in law. During the antebellum era there were no formal prerequisites for admission to the North Carolina bar. Instead, any individual who passed an examination by the Supreme Court was admitted to practice, regardless of his prior training. While some aspiring practitioners read law by themselves or studied at one of the few private law schools, most served a preceptorship in the office of an established attorney.[45]

Despite Clingman's sterling record at the university, his search for a suitable instructor proved to be long and frustrating. In January 1832 his uncle Henry P. Poindexter had asked Judge Thomas Ruffin, one of the state's most popular law teachers, to allow Clingman to study under his direction. Although the judge accepted the high-born Thomas S. Ashe as a student, he turned Clingman's application down on the grounds that "my family is too large to allow of any addition to it, without subjecting both the student & ourselves to much inconvenience." [46]

After a summer vacation in the North Carolina mountains, Clingman resumed his search for a legal mentor. In November he journeyed to Williamsboro in Granville County to make a personal plea to the eminent jurist Leonard Henderson. When Henderson declined to take him on, he approached Judge Frederick Nash in Hillsborough, who also rejected his entreaties. [47] Finally, he prevailed upon William A. Graham, a young Hillsborough attorney who had received his own license just six years earlier. Then at the beginning of a distinguished political career that would eventually carry him to the governorship and the U.S. Senate, Graham was a brilliant courtroom lawyer and an accomplished scholar. Although too busy to direct Clingman's studies personally, he did allow the young aspirant free use of the books in his law library. [48]

Early in January 1834, while still feeling the effects of a recent illness that had left him "very unwell," Clingman appeared before the North Carolina Supreme Court and received a license to practice in the county courts. Returning to the family home in Huntsville, he presented his license to the justices of the Surry County Court, took the requisite oath, and was admitted to the bar. Clingman was now a full-fledged attorney, but his opportunities for making money were severely limited because North Carolina law required a second examination before a lawyer could practice in the more lucrative superior courts. Moreover, at least a year had to elapse before the second examination could be administered. [49]

Clingman decided to go back to Hillsborough to prepare for the superior court examination. "In fact," he told his cousin Isaac Jarratt on 4 February, "I should have been there now if I had not been sick a couple of weeks since I came home." "Most of the family," he added, "have been sick of the scarlet fever." Clingman's own health had been precarious for several months, and by early spring he was suffering from an inflammation of the eyes that made reading an excruciatingly painful experience. By May he was back in Huntsville under the care of the family physician, Pleasant Henderson. [50]

Unable to provide any relief to his young patient, Henderson wrote to a specialist in Philadelphia, who advised that Thomas come to that city for diagnosis and treatment. A lack of funds and a reluctance to call on Peter Clingman for financial assistance militated against that course of action. The malady continued for many months, during which young Clingman "suffered 'many things of many physicians' in the way of treatment for his eyes." Meanwhile, with a green silk shade bound over his eyes, he listened as his sister read aloud from the various legal texts that had to be mastered for the second bar examination. [51]

The discovery that reading had become a source of torment rather than plea-sure must have been disquieting for Clingman. Even worse than the physical pain was the possibility that the disease might result in a permanent loss of sight. The "awful calamity of blindness" would have been an ominous prospect for any young man coming of age in the 1830s. For Clingman, it must have been espe-cially foreboding. The ambitious lad who had dreams of becoming "a great man" was now confronted with the possibility of spending the remainder of his life as an invalid, totally dependent on the care of relatives. As the affliction continued month after month, with a succession of physicians providing more pain than re-lief and no hope offered for recovery, the despondent Clingman might under-standably have come to the conclusion that a quick death was preferable to a long life of suffering.[52]

Quite possibly, Clingman did attempt to end his life in 1834. Many years later, Mary Boykin Chesnut reported the widely circulated rumor that he had once tried to "cut his throat." "Made a failure then, too," she sarcastically added, "for it was sewed up—and he lives still." By themselves, Chesnut's remarks can be dismissed as mere gossip. Not so the views of Richard Benbury Creecy, who knew Clingman as a youth and, unlike Chesnut, was genuinely fond of him. In a letter written shortly after Clingman's death, Creecy accepted the attempted suicide as an established fact. His only doubts pertained to the motives that lay behind it.[53]

Fortunately for himself and his family, Clingman's life did not come to a pre-mature end in 1834. Late in the year he took a trip to the North, where he may have consulted the specialists who had earlier been recommended to him. Whether be-cause of the ministrations of his physicians or simply as a result of the recupera-tive effects of nature, Clingman's health gradually improved after his northern visit. By January 1835 his vision was sufficiently restored to enable him to take the bar examination and receive his superior court license. However, several more months would elapse before he recovered his eyesight completely. A less ambi-tious man might have been satisfied with remaining at home, regaining his health, and cultivating a law practice. But Clingman at the tender age of twenty-three had fixed his convalescing eyes on a seat in the North Carolina General Assembly.[54]

Long before he formally announced his candidacy for the House of Commons, Clingman had decided to link his political fortunes to the Whigs. In the presi-dential election of 1832 Democrat Andrew Jackson had swept the Old North State, defeating Henry Clay, his National Republican opponent, by a margin of five-to-one. By 1835, however, Old Hickory's forceful response to the nullifi-cation crisis and his controversial removal of the federal deposits from the Bank of the United States had given rise to a powerful new opposition party, which stood ready to challenge the election of his hand-picked successor, Martin Van Buren.[55]

The North Carolina Whig party was a coalition of two disparate groups. On the one hand, there were the "original Jackson men"—politicians like George E. Badger, Edward B. Dudley, Willie P. Mangum, and John M. Morehead, who had supported Old Hickory until they became convinced he had fallen under the control of Van Buren and other "malign influences" from the North. That faction tended to be strongly pro-Southern in its rhetoric, accusing the Democrats in general and Van Buren in particular of lacking "sympathy or . . . interest for the South." [56] The other group consisted of the National Republicans—leaders such as Governor David L. Swain and congressmen James Graham and Lewis Williams, who had long denounced Jackson as a military chieftain unfit for the presidency. Although professing allegiance (as did all North Carolinians) to the principles of limited government and states' rights, the National Republicans looked to Henry Clay for leadership and adopted his nationalistic stance on issues such as the Bank of the United States.

Most of the Whig leaders in the Shallow Ford community where Clingman grew up were National Republicans. The hostility of the powerful Williams family toward Old Hickory went all the way back to the Creek Wars of 1814, when Jackson had accused John Williams's troops of cowardice. By the 1830s John's brother Lewis was the most powerful political leader in the Yadkin Valley. First elected to the U.S. House of Representatives in 1815, his hold on his district remained unbroken until his death in 1842. Lewis Williams was related to Thomas Clingman through the Laniers—indeed, his twin brother was also named Thomas Lanier. The congressman was a regular customer at the Clingman store, particularly during election season when he would purchase the whiskey, brandy, and other liquor to which aspiring candidates were expected to "treat" the voters. On more than one occasion, young Thomas probably witnessed his relative warn the voters at the nearby muster grounds about the evils of Jacksonianism. [57]

Political, as well as personal, considerations propelled Clingman in the direction of the Whigs. During the 1830s the two most important public policy issues confronting the leaders of the Old North State were education and internal improvements. For two decades, reformers like Archibald D. Murphey and David L. Swain had promoted comprehensive programs for public schools and state-financed internal improvements, but their plans had inevitably foundered on the reluctance of the general assembly to raise taxes or create a large public debt. Most of those who felt strongly about such issues eventually joined the Whigs, largely because of Henry Clay's proposal to distribute federal land revenues among the states—a policy that would enable North Carolina to build roads and construct schools without an increase in state taxes. The Kentucky senator's championship of distribution made him a hero to North Carolina reformers, whereas Jackson's veto of Clay's land bill in 1833 enabled the Whigs to portray the Democrats as enemies of state development. [58]

Clingman's own interest in state reform dated from his university years. In June 1831 he became one of the charter members of the North Carolina Institute of Education, an organization whose objective was "to diffuse knowledge on the subject of education, and . . . improve the condition of common schools and other literary institutions."[59] Clingman also played a prominent role in the movement for publicly financed railroads. In November 1833 he took time off from his law studies to serve as one of Surry County's representatives at a convention that assembled in Raleigh to memorialize the general assembly on the subject of state aid. On the second day of the session, he introduced a resolution demanding that "North Carolina . . . adopt without delay a liberal system of Internal Improvements" and supported his position with a "thundering speech" that reportedly impressed even the reactionary Nathaniel Macon.[60]

Clingman's interest in politics and public affairs was further piqued by his visit to Washington, D.C., in December 1834. That year proved to be a critical one in the reemergence of national parties. In March the opponents of Old Hickory, led by Clay, Webster, and Calhoun, pushed through the U.S. Senate a series of resolutions censuring Jackson for removing the federal deposits. Among those voting in favor of the resolutions was North Carolina senator Willie P. Mangum, who had previously been regarded as a supporter of the president. Mangum's defection shocked the Jackson loyalists in the North Carolina General Assembly, who quickly passed resolutions instructing him either to vote for the expunging of the censure resolutions or to resign.[61]

Thus the political atmosphere in both North Carolina and the nation's capital was charged with unprecedented partisan rancor when Clingman witnessed the opening of the second session of the Twenty-Third Congress in December 1834. With the Whigs in control of the Senate and the Democrats holding a majority in the House of Representatives, there was little prospect of any constructive legislation. Instead, opponents of the administration, under the leadership of South Carolina senator John C. Calhoun, occupied much of their time conducting an investigation into Jackson's alleged abuse of the federal patronage. While the investigation was under way, Clingman had a long conversation with Calhoun. "We can beat the one man power," the senator reportedly told him, but "if the *money power* should ever be combined with that of the government, our liberties will be in great danger."[62]

During his sojourn in Washington, the ambitious young Whig also cultivated the acquaintance of Senator Mangum. Back in Huntsville a few weeks later, with the recollections of the "music and beauty" of the nation's capital "still green in my memory," Clingman initiated a correspondence with the veteran politician. A recent visit to Raleigh, he remarked, had given him the opportunity to "form a tolerably accurate idea of the feeling of the people on political topics." Clingman assured the embattled senator that "the intelligent part of the community . . . [is] very generally dissatisfied with the conduct of the last General Assembly . . . and doubt alike the propriety of their instructions to you, and the right of the body to pass them." Although a novice in politics, Clingman was not averse to offering advice to the seasoned politician. "Your friends," he told Mangum, "are rather too inactive. . . . [Since] you are the person most interested in the result . . .

you ought to set a good example by exerting yourself to the uttermost on your return." [63]

While Clingman's communication to Mangum dealt exclusively with political matters, the affectionate letter he wrote William A. Graham a few weeks later was replete with neighborhood gossip and playful references to the "charms" of their various female acquaintances. Clingman also provided his mentor with the latest news about his health, law practice, and political ambitions. It was not his intention, he remarked, to reside permanently in Surry County. Instead, he would remain there just long enough "to give my eyes such partial rest as may prevent a return of the disease, . . . to acquire a habit of speaking without premeditation, and to become better acquainted with men by taking some share in the politics of the county." The young Whig evidently had mixed feelings about embarking on the sea of politics, for he asked Graham whether he thought the advantages of such a course would outweigh "the mental dissipation invariably attendant on political pursuits in this country." [64]

That ambivalence did not prevent Clingman from announcing his candidacy for the House of Commons at the May 1835 meeting of the Surry County Court. The canvass was certain to be difficult. Although the Whigs were strong in the Shallow Ford area south of the Yadkin River, the Democratic majorities north of the river made the overall party balance in Surry County precarious. Fortunately for the Whigs, the fractious Democrats were unable to unite on a single ticket for the House of Commons. Instead, four Democratic aspirants found themselves vying for Surry County's two seats in the lower house. The split in the Democratic ranks enabled the Whigs to win both seats by narrow majorities. Clingman was the leading vote getter, running just twenty-three votes ahead of the strongest Democrat. [65]

On 13 November 1835 Clingman left Huntsville en route to Raleigh, where the general assembly was scheduled to convene three days later. The legislature in which the young Whig made his political debut was the last one to meet under the provisions of the constitution of 1776. Earlier that summer, a state convention had adopted a series of amendments providing for the popular election of the governor, the elimination of the county method of legislative apportionment (which discriminated against the more populous counties of the west), and its replacement by a system based on population and wealth. A referendum in early November had approved these and other constitutional changes. [66]

Thus the legislators who assembled at the state capital in November 1835 did so with the knowledge that they were the last vestiges of a system that the voters had now deemed outmoded. Not surprisingly, the session lasted a bare five weeks—one of the briefest in the state's history—and no important measures of public policy were enacted. Instead, the session was characterized by a series of rancorous and highly partisan debates in which the twenty-three-year-old Clingman would play a conspicuous role.

The legislative session offered Clingman his first opportunity to speak publicly on the issue of slavery. Although not a slaveholder himself, he was by no means a stranger to the peculiar institution. At the time he entered the general assembly, his mother owned four slaves and his uncle Peter possessed ten bondsmen. Moreover, his cousin Isaac Jarratt, who roomed over the family store when he was in Huntsville, was a slave trader—an unsavory, yet profitable, business in which Clingman's brother-in-law Richard C. Puryear also participated as a silent partner. If young Clingman shared any of William Gaston's doubts about the morality or expediency of slavery, he kept those opinions to himself.[67]

Regardless of whether they considered slavery to be a curse or a blessing, North Carolinians agreed that it was a Southern institution in which Northerners had no business meddling. That position was embodied in a series of resolutions that passed the general assembly by a nearly unanimous vote shortly before its adjournment. Even before the passage of these proslavery declarations, Clingman had articulated his own position by introducing a resolution to make the circulation of incendiary publications a capital offense.[68]

Judged by the standards of the antebellum South, Clingman's attitude toward slavery was quite orthodox. Unlike many defenders of the institution, however, he refused to allow an exaggerated concern for its protection to dictate his course on all measures of public policy. Thus when one anxious legislator offered a proposal to require licenses and regular examinations for all Northern booksellers, Clingman spoke out against the measure, calmly informing his fellow assemblymen that he personally "feared no danger from booksellers selling improper publications to slaves." Although quite willing to levy the harshest penalties against anyone actually convicted of "attempting to excite our slaves to rebellion," he "was against . . . meeting that question in an indirect manner" through the adoption of restrictive measures that would penalize the innocent as well as the guilty. Implicit in Clingman's common-sense approach to the slavery issue was the belief that Southerners who overreacted to abolitionist provocations ran the risk of jeopardizing their own interests. As he would learn a few years later during the controversy over abolitionist petitions, his position was one that could easily be misrepresented and distorted.[69]

From the viewpoint of the Whigs, the most important issue confronting the general assembly was not slavery (on which there was a bipartisan consensus) but rather the public lands. Believing that their plan of distributing federal land proceeds among the states was popular with the voters, party leaders were eager to put the Democrats on record in opposition to that policy. The Whig strategy was a clever one. Resolutions expressing the opinion of the general assembly would be introduced, ostensibly for transmittal to North Carolina's U.S. senators and congressmen. The Democrats, many of whom had been equivocating on the land issue, would then be presented with a choice of either opposing a popular policy or voting against the position of their own president.

Clingman must have been elated when the Whig leaders chose him to introduce the resolutions in the House of Commons and lead the debate. On 19 November 1835 the freshman legislator put forward a series of propositions almost identical to those considered at the previous session of the general assembly.[70] The first resolution declared that any attempt by Congress to give away the public lands to the states in which they were situated or to lower their minimum price "would seriously affect the prosperity of all the old States, and do great injustice to those states." The second, more controversial, resolution stipulated that "the public debt having been extinguished," the federal lands "or the proceeds thereof" ought to be distributed among the states in proportion to their population.[71]

After several postponements, the resolutions finally came before the Commons on 30 November. Clingman opened the debate with a lengthy speech expounding the position of the Whig party on the land issue. Citing the acts by which North Carolina and the other eastern states had ceded their western lands to the federal government, he argued that the proceeds from their sale were intended to be used as a common fund for the benefit of all the states. To deny North Carolina a share of that bounty would be "unjust and directly at variance with the terms of the cession acts." On the other hand, an equitable division among the states would, by Clingman's calculations, provide the Old North State with an additional $275,000 each year—"a sum nearly four times as great as our entire present revenue"— that could be used to extend "the benefits of general education [and] Internal Improvement." Distribution would also serve as an effective means of "arresting the rapid progress of our Government to despotism" by eliminating an overflowing federal treasury that had led to the creation of unnecessary offices, the abuse of executive patronage, and extravagant government expenditures.[72]

Clingman's first major address as a legislator was not distinguished by its originality. The specific arguments had been made many times before by Clay, Calhoun, and other opposition leaders. Still, it was tightly organized, well argued, and ably supported by an impressive array of facts, statistics, and citations from presidential messages, congressional reports, and other public documents. The speech was deservedly praised by the Whig presses. Nowhere, exclaimed the *Raleigh Register,* had it "seen the subject more lucidly treated. . . . We speak but the general sentiment, when we say that, throughout, Mr. C. sustained his Resolutions with marked ability." The publication of the address in the Whig newspapers gave it an audience far beyond the chambers of the House of Commons and made Clingman a familiar name to party leaders throughout the state.[73]

Clingman's speech was merely the opening salvo in a debate that would occupy the attention of the legislators for the remainder of the session. During the course of the following week, Democrats in the House of Commons introduced a number of motions to amend Clingman's resolutions or to postpone them indefinitely. In view of the embarrassing surplus accumulating in the federal treasury, many Democratic legislators were willing to endorse distribution as a temporary expedient, though not as a permanent policy. Other members, however, opposed Clingman's propositions in any form, arguing that the state legislature had no business passing resolutions on federal land policy. The lack of a unified strategy worked against the Democrats in the Commons, and one by one their substitute resolutions were voted down.[74]

When Clingman's original resolutions finally came to a vote on 5 December, they passed the House of Commons by comfortable margins. Their author could justifiably take pride in the outcome. Four times within the space of a week, he had spoken ably on their behalf, rebutting the Democratic arguments as "ingenious attempt[s] to give the real question at issue the go-by." Although other Whigs such as William A. Graham and Kenneth Rayner also gave effective speeches in support of the resolutions, it was Clingman who dominated the debate. For a first-term member just three years out of college, that was no small accomplishment.[75]

Clingman's resolutions faced tougher going in the senate, where Democratic leaders were more successful in keeping their members in line. Even before their final passage by the House of Commons, Harrison M. Waugh, the Democratic senator from Surry County, had introduced resolutions endorsing distribution as a temporary expedient but calling for a reduction in tariff duties as the permanent solution to the problem of the federal surplus. Late in the session, the senate Democrats managed to substitute Waugh's resolutions for those passed by the Commons.[76]

On 21 December 1835 the senate propositions were formally presented to the House of Commons for concurrence. Clingman moved immediately to strike out everything after the word "resolved" and insert his original resolutions in their place. By a vote of fifty-one to forty-seven, the Commons approved the motion to strike out. Unable to pass their own resolutions on land policy, the Democrats next moved that Clingman's resolutions be indefinitely postponed. Ten Democrats who had supported his resolutions on 5 December now switched their votes, and the motion to postpone passed the Commons by a vote of fifty-four to forty-three.[77]

Although Clingman's resolutions ultimately failed to win approval by the general assembly, the Whigs had, in fact, accomplished their main objective. They had prevented the Democrats from passing their own land resolutions and had forced that party to go on record in opposition to the Whig plan. By rejecting the only practical means of financing public schools and internal improvements, the Democrats had provided their enemies with powerful campaign ammunition for the upcoming state and national elections. As one Whig editor put it, "the supporters of Mr. Van Buren will no longer have the effrontery to deny that they are opposed to the State's having her just and equal portion of the proceeds of the Public Lands." As he made his way back to Huntsville to join his family for the Christmas holidays, Clingman must have felt considerable satisfaction at his achievements as a legislator.[78]

Unfortunately, Clingman's law practice was not progressing as successfully as his legislative career, and once again the ambitious young attorney was harboring thoughts of moving his shingle to a more remunerative location. Writing to Graham in April 1836, he remarked that he had been "much inclined some weeks since to have left this county and settled in Rutherford or Buncombe from either of which counties I could form a much better circuit than I can do here." But the political climate in Surry was again heating up with the approach of the August legislative elections, and Democrat Harrison Waugh had raised Clingman's dander by charging that Graham had secretly authored his speeches. "The attacks of my enemies have made me feel a little *bull-dogish,*" he told Graham, "and I am disposed to give them another battle."[79]

Perhaps with encouragement from Graham, Clingman decided to remain in Surry County and seek election to a second term in the general assembly. Unfortunately for the Whigs, who had won the previous election because of an excessive number of Democratic candidates, the opposition managed this time to unite behind a single ticket. Even though Clingman proved to be the top Whig vote getter in Surry County, outpolling gubernatorial candidate Edward B. Dudley by sixty-four votes, he still fell nineteen votes short of election. The outcome confirmed Clingman's inclination to find a more hospitable environment for pursuing his political and legal careers. A few weeks later, he started across the mountains en route to the village he would call home for the remaining sixty years of his life.[80]

3 *Champion of the West*

Clingman's arrival in Asheville in October 1836 was somewhat less than auspicious. A few days earlier, a freak storm had swept through the town and the surrounding French Broad Valley, covering them with several inches of snow and making travel extremely difficult. The inclement weather did not deter the young traveler from continuing his journey. As he rode south from Yancey County, through lush forests that shortly before had been in their full summer green, he marveled at "the full foliaged trees . . . bowed down with the weight of snow" and the "beautiful contrast between the vivid green and the immaculate white." [1]

Situated on a high plateau in the Blue Ridge about two miles east of the juncture of the French Broad and Swannanoa Rivers, Asheville was a small town, even by antebellum standards. Little more than a dozen families resided within its limits. The surrounding community was served by half a dozen stores, the courthouse, an old church, a blacksmith shop, and two hotels. There were also a modest number of slaves, many of them owned by James W. Patton, the proprietor of the Eagle Hotel. [2]

Despite its unimpressive population, Asheville's strategic location made it "the hub of western North Carolina's trade and commerce." Since the beginning of the nineteenth century, merchants in Kentucky and Tennessee had used the French Broad Valley as a natural thoroughfare along which their hogs and cattle were driven to markets in South Carolina and Georgia. The town's favorable trade prospects had been considerably enhanced by the completion of the Buncombe Turnpike in 1827. Running along the French Broad and connecting Greenville, Tennessee, with the town of the same name in South Carolina, the turnpike had quickly brought a wave of prosperity to all the farms and villages along its path, and especially to Asheville. From the viewpoint of the town's boosters, the possibilities for additional growth and development seemed almost limitless.[3]

For an ambitious young man like Clingman, this little village with big dreams must have seemed an attractive location in which to begin a law practice. Still, there was not enough business to keep even one attorney profitably engaged, let alone the three or four others who resided in Asheville. Like his colleagues, Clingman spent much of his time riding the circuits, attending the county and superior courts in the other counties of his judicial district. Even for a young man in good health, circuit riding in the mountain district was an arduous and frequently unremunerative endeavor. Roads were often rough, sometimes impassable; during the winter term, the bad weather made travel even more difficult. Hotel accommodations were crude, and fees, when they could be collected from the penurious clients, were usually small. Beginning practitioners often earned less than one hundred dollars per year, and probably few attorneys received annual fees amounting to more than three hundred dollars.[4]

Unlike most of his fellow lawyers, Clingman was able to supplement his private practice with a lucrative patronage position. In 1837 the general assembly authorized the governor to appoint two agents to collect overdue bonds owed by purchasers of Cherokee lands. Those agents were to secure writs from the county courts in Haywood and Macon, where most of the purchasers resided, ordering the arrest and trial of each delinquent. A commission of 5 percent would be paid on all monies returned to the state.[5]

Clingman, who had served with Gov. Edward B. Dudley in the general assembly, received the appointment as agent for Haywood County. By October 1837 he had collected more than $1,000 in overdue bonds—money that he promptly turned over to State Commissioner John L. Smith for use in constructing a road from Macon County to the Georgia line. During the next several years, he continued to file suits against delinquent debtors, and by January 1841 he had returned more than $9,000 to the state, on which he received a commission of $466. By that time, a new series of bonds issued in 1836 had also begun falling due, enabling Clingman to turn in an additional $2,000 before the end of 1841. Although the pace of collections diminished considerably thereafter, as late as October 1845 the aggressive attorney continued to supplement his income with occasional collections.[6]

Beginning in December 1838 Clingman also augmented his earnings by practicing before the North Carolina Supreme Court. During the antebellum period most Tar Heel lawyers contented themselves with riding the circuits in their own districts, "leaving the appellate work to the more adventurous and ambitious members of the group." The majority of cases decided by the highest court were civil suits pertaining to disputed land titles, debt recoveries, and the settlement of estates, and its decisions usually turned on arcane points of legal procedure. For that reason, few local practitioners dared match wits against George E. Badger, Duncan Cameron, Thomas Ruffin, and the other distinguished attorneys who specialized in appellate practice. Clingman's enormous intellect and supreme self-confidence suited him ideally for the challenge. During his brief career as an attorney he argued twenty-two cases before the high court, winning all but five of them.[7]

The case with the most far-reaching implications originated in a land dispute between two settlers named Sutton and Moore. Its significance lay in the fact that Sutton's wife was a Native American who claimed title under the provisions of treaties negotiated between the Cherokee nation and the U.S. government. The case, which was argued before the North Carolina Supreme Court in December 1842, revolved around the relationship of the Treaty of New Echota, concluded in December 1835, to the treaty negotiated in 1817. According to the terms of the earlier treaty, the Cherokee nation had ceded a portion of its North Carolina lands in exchange for a guarantee that homesteads of 640 acres in the ceded territory would be provided to any family that wished to become U.S. citizens. The lot registered by Sutton and his wife in 1817 was not situated on the ceded territory, but rather on common land reserved to the Cherokee nation. In 1835 the Cherokees ceded the remaining portion of their common land, including the lot registered eighteen years earlier by Sutton, to the State of North Carolina. When the lot was subsequently purchased from the state by John C. Moore, Sutton instituted suit.[8]

Clingman, representing the defendant, challenged Sutton's claim that the homesteads guaranteed by the Treaty of 1817 applied not only to the territory ceded that year but also to any "lands that . . . may hereafter be surrendered." He also pointed out that the Treaty of New Echota had specifically provided that the newly ceded lands would be "unincumbered by reservations, or promises of reservations." The Supreme Court sustained Clingman's argument, ruling that "the right to a reservation of land granted by the Treaty with the Cherokees in 1817 . . . does not attach to the land ceded by the Treaty of 1835." By ensuring that the recently ceded Cherokee lands would not be encumbered by claims made under earlier treaties, the decision of *Sutton v. Moore* facilitated the movement of white settlers into western North Carolina.

Neither Clingman nor the court was willing to look behind the Treaty of New Echota and acknowledge that it had been fraudulently negotiated and that the

Cherokees had been forcibly evicted from their ancestral homes. The removal had been carried out during the spring of 1838 by the U.S. Army, assisted by a regiment of state militia temporarily mustered into federal service. Gov. Edward B. Dudley had been empowered to appoint the field and staff officers of the North Carolina contingent, and a number of westerners had vied for those positions.

Clingman, who sought the office of major, persuaded several prominent citizens to endorse his candidacy. John E. Patton, postmaster at Warm Springs and scion of one of Buncombe County's leading families, recommended the young attorney as a man who in addition to his "other claims to high standing" happened to be a "substantial Whig." Former governor David L. Swain also wrote Dudley on behalf of the "late commoner from Surry," reminding the chief executive that the aspirant "is personally known to you." Although his lack of military experience prevented Clingman from receiving the appointment, the episode indicates the high regard in which he was held by the leading men in western North Carolina.[9]

Clingman's standing among the merchants and other entrepreneurs who dominated the politics and society of the mountain region was further enhanced by his vigorous championship of internal improvements. The economic boom that followed the completion of the Buncombe Turnpike had underscored the commercial benefits of improved transportation facilities. In the minds of its boosters, Asheville had the potential to become an important link in the trade network connecting the rich agricultural hinterland of the Mississippi Valley with the seaports of the Atlantic Ocean—a thriving commercial center rivaling Cincinnati, Louisville, and the other great inland cities. The one obstacle preventing the realization of that bright future was the lack of adequate transportation.[10]

By the time Clingman arrived in Asheville in 1836, the town was abuzz with talk about a projected railroad that would run from Charleston, South Carolina, across the mountains to the Ohio River. Promoted by Charleston merchants with ambitions of transforming their town into the "New York of the South," the Louisville, Cincinnati, and Charleston Railroad (LC&CRR) was chartered by the South Carolina legislature in December 1835 with a state appropriation of $1 million. At their first meeting in January 1837, the stockholders rejected John C. Calhoun's proposal to run the road through Georgia and voted, instead, to run it across the French Broad Valley of North Carolina.[11]

For Clingman and other residents of the mountain region, the attractiveness of the proposed railroad was further enhanced by the willingness of its promoters to build it without an appropriation from the North Carolina legislature. Its supporters asked only for the grant of a charter and for the right to operate a bank whose capital would be used to help finance construction. Although merchants in eastern North Carolina towns were adverse to any railroad that would siphon trade to South Carolina markets, their opposition was assuaged by a provision in the charter allowing a North Carolina railroad to intersect the LC&CRR at Asheville or at any other point along its route.[12]

The establishment of transportation connections to the west was an important topic at the internal improvements convention that met in Raleigh on 10 December 1838. With 155 delegates representing thirty-seven counties, the convention was the largest such gathering to assemble in the Old North State up to that time. Clingman, who was one of the members from Buncombe County, played a central role in the proceedings. On the first day of the meeting, he was chosen by the other delegates from his congressional district to serve on the Committee of Thirteen, which had responsibility for evaluating and prioritizing the numerous, and perhaps conflicting, plans that would be offered on the floor of the convention. He was also appointed to the Committee of Five, which prepared the rules of order.[13]

During the second day of deliberations a variety of resolutions were introduced, embracing "every scheme heretofore agitated, with some never before heard of." The committee report, issued on 12 December 1838, identified five high-priority projects that were "so magnificent and costly as to be beyond the reach of individual enterprise," along with three other "minor works" that also merited immediate state support. In the discussion that ensued, Clingman spoke on behalf of the Fayetteville and Yadkin Railroad, the high-priority project of greatest interest to the residents of western North Carolina. Even though the proposed terminus of the road lay considerably east of the Blue Ridge, its proponents regarded it as the first link in a trunk line that would eventually extend from the Cape Fear Valley all the way through the mountains.[14]

The convention ultimately adopted a series of resolutions recommending a state loan of $3 million to support three "first class" projects, including a state subscription of four-fifths of the stock in the Fayetteville road. A resolution requesting the general assembly to order a survey "to ascertain the practicability of extending the Fayetteville & Yadkin Road to the Blue Ridge" was also approved. On the last day of the convention Clingman was appointed to the Committee of Seven, which was instructed to draw up a memorial to the general assembly.[15]

The address prepared by Clingman and the other committee members was an eloquent and powerful plea for the use of government power to promote the public welfare. A state loan of $3 million would be a wise investment, they argued, since the money would be "mostly expended among ourselves" and since the eventual increase in land values and other forms of wealth would yield revenue more than sufficient "to meet the claim which has been entailed." The memorialists challenged the legislators to rise above the "mounds of local prejudice" and "to elevate our beloved State to her proper rank . . . [in] this great confederacy."[16]

The advocates of state assistance, who dominated the internal improvements committees in both houses, gave vigorous support to the entreaties of Clingman and the other memorialists. Once the bills reached the floor of the general assembly, however, the parochial interests that the legislators had been urged to surmount again asserted themselves. One by one, the grand schemes proposed by the convention were either defeated outright or vitiated to the point of insignificance. The only recommendation that received the endorsement of the legislature was a guarantee of the bonds of the Raleigh and Gaston Railroad—a measure that would cost the state nothing as long as the road remained solvent. Even that modest proposal passed the House of Commons by a margin of only two votes.[17]

Clingman and the other proponents of western development must have been bitterly disappointed by the seeming indifference of the general assembly to the interests of their section. The unwillingness of the legislators to support even a survey of a railroad route to the far west gave irate citizens in that region an additional incentive to rally behind the LC & CRR. Whether the grain and livestock of the Mississippi and Ohio Valleys ultimately found an outlet in Charleston or in a North Carolina seaport was of secondary concern to the residents of the mountain region, as long as those products passed through Asheville and the other towns of the French Broad Valley along the way.

Unfortunately, the Panic of 1837 and the ensuing depression were having a disastrous impact on the prospects of the LC & CRR. Despite the continued generosity of the South Carolina legislature, existing resources were scarcely sufficient to build the road as far as Columbia. The original plan to extend the road to Louisville and beyond could not be accomplished without substantial financial assistance from North Carolina, Tennessee, and Kentucky. Despairing of such support, some stockholders began reconsidering Calhoun's earlier proposal for an alternative route that would connect with Georgia's ambitious network of railroads.[18]

Matters finally came to a head at a stockholders' meeting at Columbia in December 1839. Although Clingman personally owned no stock in the road, he attended the Columbia meeting as a proxy for the North Carolina investors and served on the Committee of Fifteen, which was established to determine the future policy of the company. Within the committee competing sets of resolutions were offered by Christopher G. Memminger, the brilliant South Carolina financier who was a proponent of the Georgia route, and B. T. Elmore, who supported the North Carolina connection. The resolutions reported by the committee represented a victory for the Memminger faction. Although Clingman and like-minded members managed to tone down some of the most stringent aspects of Memminger's original resolutions, Elmore's pledge to continue the road through the French Broad Valley did not find its way into the committee report. That a majority of stockholders no longer supported the original route became even more apparent when the Memminger faction pushed through a resolution calling for the election of James Gadsden, a proponent of the Georgia route, to the presidency.[19]

The committee report engendered considerable discussion among the stockholders. Memminger took the lead by denouncing Elmore's resolutions as "a bone of contention thrown in to disturb the harmony of our deliberations." Instead of centering his fire on his fellow South Carolinian, however, Memminger reserved most of his wrath for Clingman, who the day before had unsuccessfully tried to prevent Elmore's resolutions from being buried in committee. Clingman, for his part, seemed eager "to take up the glove" thrown down by Memminger. "I have no such love of contention . . . as would induce me voluntarily to seek the contest," he told the delegates, "yet I have too little dread of the gentleman's powers to get out of his way."[20]

In a lengthy address on the floor of the convention, Clingman denied Memminger's claim that North Carolina bore a large share of the responsibility for the problems besetting the LC&CRR. Indeed, he declared, "she has done all that was asked of her." The state had generously provided the company with banking privileges and a right of way, and the stock subscribed by Buncombe County was "quite as large in proportion to its wealth as that of any of the upper Districts of South Carolina." According to Clingman, Memminger and his supporters were the ones who had acted in bad faith, first by proposing to change the route specified in the charter and then by offering the presidency to "a gentleman who has long favored the route through Georgia . . . [and who] has staked his reputation on the failure of this road." Such a breach of faith, he said, would "give a heavy blow to the cause of internal improvements at the South."

In Clingman's view, far more was at stake than the future of the LC&CRR. Memminger had accused North Carolina of failing to do its duty. But it was the reputation and honor of the Palmetto State that truly hung in the balance. Speaking directly to Memminger, he asked "the gentleman from Charleston . . . who seems so learned in matters of finance . . . how much is the character of a State worth in dollars and cents? . . . Can it be calculated? . . . I regard South Carolina as a noble State; I trust she will remain so. But remember you may lose in an hour what it has taken fifty years to acquire. Put it to your own hearts to say how much her honor is worth."

Clingman's stirring appeal to Southern honor did not prevent the directors of the LC&CRR from abandoning their plan to locate the road along the French Broad Valley. However, his memorable encounter with Memminger did much to establish Clingman's reputation as "a fiery, fearless, and brilliant speaker" and as one of the "foremost champions" of western North Carolina.[21] According to his admirers, the twenty-seven-year-old North Carolinian had more than held his own against an older and more experienced adversary. As the *Fayetteville Observer* put it, "Mr. C. has bearded the lion in his den, and has given such a lashing to the magnificent State of South Carolina, and her magniloquent representative, Mr. Memminger, as they will not soon forget. . . . If there is any North Carolinian who can read the speech . . . without a thrill of pride and exultation, we do not envy him his feelings."[22]

To Whig leaders eager to wrest the mountain district's seat in the state senate from its Democratic incumbent, Clingman seemed an ideal candidate. Even before his confrontation with Memminger, he had taken steps to satisfy the property requirement mandated by the state constitution for members of the upper house by signing a deed with Zechariah Candler, a local landowner, for a three-hundred-acre tract at the top of Mount Pisgah. Located fifty-seven hundred feet above sea level on the Buncombe-Haywood county line, the property offered a spectacular view of five states. Over the next fifty years, Clingman would occasionally visit his mountain estate to partake of the magnificent scenery and enjoy its wild huckleberries.[23]

By the time the Whig district convention met in Asheville on 15 April 1840 to nominate a presidential elector "pledged to the support of Harrison and Tyler," party leaders had already determined upon Clingman as their choice to oppose Democratic incumbent Hodge Rabun. The eighty-one-year-old Rabun, who enjoyed a reputation as "one of the most distinguished figures in Western North Carolina," had first won election to the state senate in 1812. Although a man of "strong character, decided convictions, and noble mind," his advanced age prevented him from mounting an active campaign. Running against a weak opponent two years earlier, Rabun had won by a mere six votes. Now in 1840, he was confronted by a more aggressive adversary and handicapped by a severe depression that many North Carolinians blamed on the Democratic administration in Washington.[24]

Along with numerous other North Carolina Democrats, Rabun found himself buried in the Whig avalanche. Clingman carried all five counties in the district and garnered 1,171 votes, compared to only 561 votes for Rabun. Whig gubernatorial candidate John Motley Morehead also received heavy majorities in most of the western counties. During the three months following the state elections, Clingman remained in the field, addressing the party faithful and urging them to return to the polls for the November presidential election. The citizens of the mountain district responded by giving Old Tippecanoe a vote that surpassed the sizable majorities they had earlier presented to Clingman and Morehead.[25]

When the newly elected general assembly convened in Raleigh on 16 November 1840, Clingman was appointed to serve on the Committee on Internal Improvements and on a special joint committee on Cherokee lands. Those two issues would occupy the time and attention of the legislators for much of the session. Before the general assembly could proceed to the business of governing the state, however, the members had to select their own officers, choose the numerous state officials who were appointed by the legislature, and most important, fill two vacancies in the U.S. Senate.

Bedford Brown and Robert Strange, the Democratic incumbents, had both resigned immediately after their party's defeat in the presidential election, thereby giving the Whigs an unprecedented opportunity to fill both seats. The most formidable Whig contender was former senator Willie P. Mangum, who had resigned his seat four years earlier and was now eager for a comeback. Most Whigs agreed that Mangum was the appropriate choice for the six-year term, and the competition centered on the party's candidate for the two-year term. The strongest aspirant from the eastern part of the state was former congressman William B. Shepard of Pasquotank. The most prominent candidate from the west was David L. Swain, who had become president of the University of North Carolina after leaving the governor's office. Unlike Shepard, who campaigned actively for the nomination, Swain took an equivocal position and refused to come to Raleigh to press his claims.[26]

Like most western legislators, Clingman was initially partial to Swain. Shortly after arriving in Raleigh, however, he became convinced that a bitter sectional contest between Shepard and Swain would present a serious threat to the unity of his party. Accordingly, he urged the distinguished jurist William Gaston to "yield to the wishes of our State" and allow his name to be presented as a compromise candidate. When Gaston declined to enter the contest, Clingman turned to George E. Badger, who had served as the party's chief strategist in the recent campaign. Although Badger proved unwilling to trade his lucrative law practice for a seat in the U.S. Senate, Clingman persuaded the Whig caucus to acknowledge his "great talents" by nominating him for the position of attorney general in the Harrison administration.[27]

Along with a majority of the other members of the Whig caucus, Clingman ultimately voted to bestow his party's senatorial nomination on William A. Graham. The choice of Clingman's former mentor, who lived in the same county as Mangum, must have come as a surprise to many North Carolinians. By blatantly ignoring the concept of geographical balance and unabashedly selecting two men who lived only a short distance from the state capital, the Whigs left themselves open to charges that the party was dominated by a "Raleigh Clique." It was not long before such accusations would surface on the floor of the general assembly.[28]

With the election of U.S. senators behind them, the Whigs could finally turn their attention to matters of public policy. For Clingman and his constituents in the far west, one of the most important issues involved the disposition of the Cherokee lands that North Carolina had acquired through the Treaty of New Echota. Settlers who subsequently purchased this property from the state found their titles challenged by other residents who claimed title under the Treaty of 1817. Arguing that the state had a responsibility to protect the interests of those who had bought the lands in good faith, Clingman introduced a bill authorizing the governor to employ counsel to defend the titles of the purchasers. The measure was approved by the general assembly, and Governor Morehead appointed Clingman as state counsel at a salary not to exceed four hundred dollars. As noted earlier, Clingman eventually brought the claims of the purchasers to the North Carolina Supreme Court, which ruled in their favor in the case of *Sutton v. Moore*.[29]

Another issue of great interest to mountain residents was the construction of improved transportation facilities. During the session of 1840–41 Clingman introduced, and spoke on behalf of, a number of improvement proposals, including a state subscription of $5,000 in the stock of the Hickory Nut Gap Turnpike and an appropriation of $1,000 to open a road across the Blue Ridge into Yancey County.[30]

The most important improvement measure introduced by Clingman was a bill to appropriate $250,000 for the construction of a turnpike between Raleigh and Asheville. On 3 December 1840 he delivered a lengthy speech in support of the proposed road, demonstrating that its route and mode of construction were practical, that it could be financed by existing state resources without an increase in taxes, and that its completion would result in incalculable benefits not only to the mountain region but also to the state as a whole. He concluded with an appeal to the generosity and patriotism of the eastern Whigs, reminding them that improvement measures in their section had been "carried mainly by Western votes" whereas "the western part of the State (notwithstanding her greater need) . . . [has], as yet, [been] given nothing."[31]

Six days after Clingman spoke, William B. Shepard enunciated his position on the western turnpike. The Whig senator from Pasquotank had a reputation as a staunch advocate of internal improvements, and his endorsement of Clingman's bill was essential to its passage. Nonetheless, Shepard proclaimed his intention "to vote against the bill . . . in every form and shape in which it can be presented to this body." The senator followed his startling announcement with a long tirade against the "intense selfishness" of the western wing of the Whig party, which he accused of ignoring the economic interests of eastern North Carolina, particularly its need for an inlet at Nags Head to connect the waters of Albemarle Sound with those of the Atlantic Ocean.[32]

Shepard did not cite votes on specific policy measures to support his assertion that the western Whigs had acted in bad faith. Rather, his entire argument turned on the fact that the Whigs had elected two "westerners" to the U.S. Senate. The west, he said, had lacked "the generosity to yield us on the floor of the Senate of the United States, at least one advocate of our claims." Shepard also pointed to the legislative caucus as the mechanism by which a few determined leaders had managed to impose their will on the party. Although ostensibly governed by majority vote, these caucuses were, he claimed, easily manipulated by "a fraction of a party which, by boldness, intrigue, and cunning, can pass their opinions for the wishes of that party."[33]

Shepard's speech struck the Whigs like a bombshell. The *Raleigh Register* characterized it as "one of the most *extraordinary* Speeches ever heard on the floor of our Legislature." A member who had witnessed the philippic concurred that he had "never known so great an excitement in Raleigh as was produced by the speech of the Hon. Wm. B. Shepard." Even those Whigs who were sympathetic toward Shepard's complaints were not pleased that he had divulged the secret proceedings of their party caucus or that he had provided the Democrats with plenty of ammunition for the next campaign. Nor were critics slow to point out that Shepard had presented his own claims for a seat in the U.S. Senate to the same caucus that he was now denouncing as unjust and unrepublican.[34]

Within a few years Clingman himself would be urging the people of North Carolina to throw off the collar of party discipline embodied in the legislative caucus. On 9 December 1840, however, no man in the general assembly was less responsive to Shepard's arguments. In sabotaging his proposal to construct a turnpike to Asheville, the Whig senator had made no effort to respond to the arguments that Clingman had meticulously presented in his own speech. Instead, he had merely asserted that westerners had behaved badly toward the east and ought, therefore, to be punished. In Clingman's view, Shepard was the one who deserved to be chastised. Twelve months earlier, Christopher G. Memminger had also accused the people of western North Carolina of failing to do their duty. And just as the South Carolinian had been soundly rebuked for his misrepresentations, now Shepard became the recipient of Clingman's scorn.

The following day, Clingman announced his intention to respond to "the most interesting and wonderful speech" of his colleague from Pasquotank. Citing copiously from the legislative journals, he demonstrated that substantially more westerners than easterners had voted in the general assembly for appropriations that would benefit "rail roads, swamp lands, opening rivers, and other improvements in the East . . . [including] the project for opening the Inlet." Clingman also denied that western legislators had been motivated by sectional feelings in their choice of U.S. senators. Challenging the common notion that the "west" comprised all those counties west of Raleigh, he made a distinction between the "middle," or Piedmont region, and the far west. Mangum and Graham, he pointed out, both came from the middle county of Orange. As for the real west— the region that Shepard proposed to punish by sabotaging the turnpike bill—its leaders had "never thought for a moment of what offices and emoluments would fall to our section" but, rather, had voted to bestow such offices on the individuals deemed most qualified to fill them, regardless of their place of residence.[35]

After vindicating his own constituents from the charge of selfishness, Clingman proceeded into a spirited defense of the legislative caucus. While acknowledging that the Whigs were opposed to the congressional caucuses formerly used to make presidential nominations, he claimed that legislative bodies had a perfect right to use caucuses to nominate officials whom they were constitutionally empowered to elect. Had the Whigs failed to concentrate their strength behind the senatorial candidates favored by a majority of their party, the Democrats would have been able to decide the election "by uniting on the individual [Whig] least acceptable to the Whig party generally."[36]

Clingman also challenged Shepard's contention that the interests of eastern North Carolina could be represented only by a resident of that section. Indeed, he argued, the case for Nags Head inlet could be argued more effectively by an outsider who would not be perceived as being motivated solely by "a direct local interest in the matter." The legislators had rejected his colleague's claims to the U.S. Senate, he added, not because Shepard lived in the east but because he was generally regarded as an unreliable Whig. "It was often difficult for us to know how he stood. . . . If not a fence man precisely, as we understand the term, he always seemed so near it, as to be able to leap it." [37]

Clingman's vigorous defense of his party, its two U.S. senators, and the legislative caucus endeared him to the leaders of the North Carolina Whigs. The *Raleigh Register* was ecstatic in its praise for "that young champion of the West, THOMAS L. CLINGMAN, whose effort on this occasion has served to raise him still higher in public estimation." Even the *Fayetteville Observer*, which defended Shepard against the charge of being lukewarm in his Whiggery, conceded that Clingman had answered the easterner's arguments "very ably and 'satisfactorily to the Whigs.'" [38]

Clingman's constituents in the mountain district must also have been gratified by his course in the general assembly. Although he had been unsuccessful in securing state support for the Asheville turnpike, he did obtain legislative approval for more-limited and less-expensive improvements, such as the Hickory Nut Gap Turnpike and the road in Yancey County. He had also steered several relief measures for the purchasers of Cherokee lands through the legislature and, most important, he had defended the honor of the west from the aspersions cast by eastern detractors. Had he been so inclined, Clingman might easily have won election to a second term in the state senate. But the ambitious young Whig now had his sights set on a higher office—a seat in the U.S. House of Representatives.

4 *Ultra Whig*

The contest for the House of Representatives began in the North Carolina mountain district almost as soon as the legislative session of 1840–41 had ended. Congressional elections in the Old North State were ordinarily held in August of odd-numbered years, but President Harrison had ordered a special session of Congress to convene on 31 May 1841 to deal with the ongoing economic crisis. For that reason, the elections were moved forward to mid-May.

Clingman faced an uphill battle in his contest with Whig incumbent James Graham, the elder brother of Sen. William A. Graham. The veteran congressman, who had won the two previous elections without opposition, stood on his long record of service, while Clingman invoked the principle of rotation in office. Although several Whig editors gently chided both candidates for not submitting their claims to a convention, the party presses remained neutral. The Democrats again declined to put forward a candidate. Without any argument against Graham apart from his own desire to fill the incumbent's position, Clingman went down to defeat with only 38 percent of the vote.[1]

The loss did nothing to diminish Clingman's enthusiasm for the Whig cause. During the summer of 1842 he campaigned extensively on behalf of Gov. John M. Morehead, who was running for reelection against Democrat Louis D. Henry. After a debate between Clingman and Henry at Asheville, the self-confident young Whig assured Morehead that he had "used him up utterly" and that the governor need "not be under any apprehension as to his success in this quarter." Indeed, he predicted, "we can beat him farther than we did [Romulus M.] Saunders" in 1840.[2]

The outcome of the election confirmed Clingman's optimistic prognosis. Early returns from the eastern and central counties had indicated a decline in the Whig vote, causing party leaders to despair of Morehead's chances. However, as reports of lopsided Whig majorities began coming in from the mountain counties, it gradually became apparent that the embattled incumbent had won reelection. The jubilant editor of the *Raleigh Register* declared that he was "truly proud of our glorious 'WESTERN RESERVE.' As long as the West thus does her duty, a little defection elsewhere is but a 'flash in the pan.'"[3]

The accolades he received for his prominent role in the campaign of 1842 encouraged Clingman to make another run for Congress against Graham. The Whig incumbent was far more vulnerable in 1843 than he had been two years earlier. During the special session of the Twenty-Seventh Congress, he had voted against three measures sponsored by Henry Clay and the Whig leadership—an increase in the tariff rates, a uniform bankruptcy law, and a distribution of public land revenues among the states. Although the congressman professed his willingness to act "with his party while he believed them in the right," he also claimed that a representative should be "responsible [only] to his constituents, his country, and his God, for his public acts."[4]

Graham's argument that a congressman had an obligation to "always think and act for himself" was challenged by a group of partisans whom he derisively labeled as "ultra Whigs." The ultras were particularly angry at Graham's vote against distribution. Since the formation of the Whig party a decade earlier, the distribution of the public land revenues among the states had been a cardinal tenet in its creed. No matter that the federal government was now deeply in debt or that some Whigs had supported Clay's distribution bill primarily as a pretext for raising tariff rates. For ultra Whigs like Clingman, whose admiration for Henry Clay bordered on hero worship, it was enough that the Kentucky senator had introduced the bill and had worked vigorously for its passage. Anyone voting against it must, *nolens volens,* be less than a true Whig.[5]

The contest between Clingman and Graham was a bitter one, and each candidate issued lengthy public letters blaming the other for the division created within the Whig ranks. As in 1841, Clingman argued that Graham had been in Congress too long and had come to "regard himself as possessing a vested estate in the office." His opponent retorted that Clingman was "the last man in this district who should make that objection," pointing out that his kinsman Lewis Williams had served almost thirty years in the House of Representatives "and Mr. Clingman voted for and warmly advocated his election." "The real cause of his objection to me," concluded Graham, "is not length of time . . . but because he is *uncommonly anxious* to become a Member of Congress himself."[6]

Clingman hammered away at Graham's vote against distribution, arguing that his opponent was out of step with a large majority in his own party, and he attacked the congressman for his alleged inconsistency on the tariff issue. In a joint debate at Asheville, the Whig challenger also brought up the issue of Graham's removal of William Coleman from his lucrative position as Asheville postmaster. Although Whigs outside the district might have regarded the controversy over the postmaster position as a minor matter compared to the great national questions of land and tariff policy, in the mountain counties "this affair produced a greater excitement among the people than any thing that has [ever] taken place here." By antagonizing the influential Coleman and Swain families, Graham had placed his reelection in serious jeopardy.[7]

As election day approached, Clingman expressed confidence that he would emerge victorious. "I expect to succeed in beating my competitor," he wrote his mother in early July, "unless some thing should produce a change in the public sentiment."[8] The outcome fully justified that optimistic expectation. Clingman won the election with an impressive 57 percent of the vote, carrying seven of the district's ten counties and improving on his 1841 showing by more than sixteen hundred votes. While some of those new votes undoubtedly came from Whigs, a sizable number of Democrats who had sat out the previous election also cast ballots for Clingman.[9]

The young challenger thus owed his election to an unlikely alliance of ultra Whigs who were "too good Clay men to permit opposition to . . . [their] favorite measure to go unrebuked" and hard-core Democrats "with the avowed object of getting Mr. Graham out of the way, believing that they could afterwards beat Mr. Clingman with a candidate of their own." William A. Graham attributed his brother's defeat to a "combination . . . such as has been rarely seen in a contest of the kind" and predicted that the unwieldy coalition that had elected Clingman would soon "resolve itself again into its original discordant elements." The events of the next two years would confirm the accuracy of Graham's prognosis.[10]

In the interval between the election and the convening of the Twenty-Eighth Congress, Clingman took steps to secure a newspaper that would give him its unwavering support. Since its establishment in 1840, the *Asheville Messenger* had been the official organ of the Whig party in the mountain region. Editors David R. McAnally and Joshua Roberts, although steadfast in their advocacy of Whig principles, had remained neutral in the factional warfare between Graham and

Clingman. After the election, the two editors found themselves under considerable pressure to resign in favor of a Clingman partisan or face ruinous competition from a rival Whig press.[11]

On 10 November 1843 the embattled editors announced the sale of the paper to John Miller McKee and Thomas W. Atkin. McKee, who had been editing a temperance newspaper called the *Southern Monitor*, brought practical experience to the new enterprise, while Atkin, a native of Knoxville just barely in his twenties, infused it with the exuberance of youth. After McKee's resignation the following summer, Atkin became the sole proprietor of the *Messenger* and one of Clingman's most devoted advocates.[12]

The thirty-one-year-old Clingman arrived in Washington late in November 1843, just a week before the convening of Congress. Also making their appearance at that session were several other talented freshmen who would subsequently go on to long and distinguished political careers. Among them were Alexander Stephens, a diminutive Whig from Georgia whose frail body concealed an extraordinarily strong mind; his attractive, good-natured Democratic colleague, Howell Cobb; the pugnacious Andrew Johnson of Tennessee; Stephen A. Douglas of Illinois, whose nickname "Little Giant" aptly suited both his physiognomy and his ambition; and John P. Hale and Hannibal Hamlin of Maine, two maverick Democrats who would later become leaders of the Republican party. None of those new representatives, however, would make so spectacular an impression on their party elders as the congressman from the North Carolina mountain district.[13]

Only a month after taking his seat in Congress, Clingman won widespread notoriety by his controversial vote against the gag rule. When the abolitionists began deluging Congress in the mid-1830s with memorials demanding the abolition of slavery in the District of Columbia, the House had responded with a rule providing that all such petitions would be automatically laid on the table without being read, debated, or referred to committee. First invoked in 1836, the gag rule had been renewed at each subsequent session of Congress, despite strenuous opposition from John Quincy Adams, Henry Clay, and other defenders of the right of petition. On the second day of the Twenty-Eighth Congress, Adams once again tried unsuccessfully to rescind the rule. Clingman was the only Southerner to vote in favor of his motion.[14]

After being denounced by several Democratic newspapers as a "renegade to the cause of the South," Clingman addressed the House of Representatives on 5 January 1844 to defend his vote. The North Carolinian bluntly told his Southern colleagues that they "have been, on this subject, pursuing a wrong course." Instead of silencing the abolitionists and strengthening the institution of slavery, the gag rule had produced exactly the opposite result, allowing the abolitionists to present themselves to the Northern public as the victims of persecution. The repeal of that obnoxious rule would deprive antislavery zealots of "the powerful lever with which they have operated on the North." Clingman also ridiculed the notion that the abolitionist petitions presented a serious threat to Southern interests. Even if a bill incorporating their views should be reported, no real damage would be done since "there exists no diversity of views [in Congress] on the main question. Nobody thinks of attempting to abolish slavery in the District of Columbia."[15]

While pleading with his fellow Southerners not to unduly magnify the importance of the abolitionist threat, Clingman candidly informed his Northern listeners that if an antislavery majority ever did come to power, "this Union will be at an end. . . . Whenever a large portion of the North should determine that they can no longer abide by the present form of the Constitution . . . the Union must be dissolved." Clingman's ominous warning was not tantamount to a threat of secession, since he also expressed confidence that "there is too much good sense at the North to give up this glorious Union for the sake of abolishing slavery in these ten miles square." The congressman had made it clear, however, that his unionism was contingent on the willingness of Northerners to play fair with the South on the "main question."

Clingman's speech catapulted him into a position of national prominence. The *New York Tribune* extolled him as "a Southern man of enlightened views." The *New York Courier and Enquirer* characterized the "tone and spirit" of the speech as "beyond all praise" and its arguments as ones that "must carry conviction to every candid mind." The *Philadelphia Gazette* described the North Carolinian as "one of the most promising men" in Congress and reported that his speech "was listened to with an attention that might have been flattering even to men of established reputation for talent and sound judgement."[16]

The address was also roundly applauded by the Whig presses in North Carolina. "If we had before a doubt as to the propriety of receiving these petitions," said the *Fayetteville Observer*, ". . . it would certainly have been removed by this speech." The *Greensboro Patriot* found "his argument . . . clear and logical, his tone dispassionate, and his entire remarks abounding in what has rarely been found in speeches on this subject—*common sense*." After noting that "the course of our representative is eliciting praise both at home and abroad," the *Asheville Messenger* announced that "we are the more proud of him because he is a citizen of *Buncombe*."[17]

The Democrats did not share in the enthusiasm. The *North Carolina Standard* denounced Clingman's remarks as "absurd, ridiculous, and dangerous," accused him of being a pliant tool of "the leaders of the *Northern Federal party*," and predicted that "on this question, he will fall like Lucifer, never to rise again." A correspondent of the *Washington Madisonian* cited his vote as "positive evidence of his being an abolitionist." The *South Carolinian* found itself unable to find words "to express satisfactorily our utter disgust . . . for his abominable speech." On the floor of the House, Clingman's speech provided plenty of grist for the Democratic mill. As the congressman himself remarked a few months later, "set speeches have been made against me daily."[18]

The invectives showered on Clingman by the Democrats served only to enhance his prestige among the members of his own party. Later in the session, when Democrat Alexander Duncan of Ohio used a debate over a presidential election bill as an occasion to launch an abusive attack on the principles of the Whig party, opposition leaders chose the young congressman from North Carolina to present their reply. Clingman's speech, "The Principles of the Whig and Democratic Parties," delivered on 7 March 1844, more than lived up to their expectations. Despite its title, the address was not a dispassionate disquisition on the belief system of the two parties but a caustic denunciation of the Democrats and a panegyric on the virtues of the Whigs and their presidential candidate, Henry Clay.[19]

To the delight of his fellow partisans, Clingman lambasted the Democrats as a "spoils party, held together by the cohesive attraction of public plunder . . . [and] united only for the purpose of carrying elections and obtaining office." Indeed, he exclaimed, the only tenets its members held in common were the "seven principles . . . [of] the five loaves and the two fishes." In contrast to the Democrats, who "habitually profess doctrines which they have no purpose of carrying into practice," the Whigs espoused "great cardinal principles which we cherish with entire unanimity." Among those principles were a revenue tariff that would allow incidental protection to manufacturers and artisans, the distribution of the public land proceeds among the states, and a sound currency regulated by a "closely guarded national institution." At the same time, the party opposed Democratic efforts to "convert the office-holders of the country into a mercenary army of electioneerers *[sic]*, commanded by the President" and stood, instead, "for the reduction of patronage, for the non-interference of government officers in elections, and for the rigid supervision of all executive officers by Congress." Clingman concluded his remarks with a lengthy tribute to Henry Clay—"a man whose whole life has connected him with these great principles."[20]

With the presidential election only a few months away, Clingman's address was intended primarily to serve as an electioneering tract that would be reprinted in the Whig newspapers and circulated in pamphlet form among the party faithful.[21] Once again, the Whig presses were lavish in their praise. The Washington correspondent of the *New York Tribune* characterized the speech as a "thrilling discourse, which commanded the profoundest attention from all quarters of the Hall." A communication in the *Baltimore Patriot* noted that Clingman's "spirited and able reply . . . was listened to with great attention" and predicted that its author would "gain reputation by his effort." The Democrats, understandably, were furious at the speech. William W. Holden, the fiery editor of the *North Carolina Standard*, pronounced it "false . . . ungenerous and unfair" and affirmed that "we much mistake the character of the Buncombe District, if Thomas L. Clingman ever represents it again in the National Legislature."[22]

When Clingman returned to North Carolina after the adjournment of Congress, his principal concern was not with his own reelection campaign, which lay more than a year in the future, but with the upcoming gubernatorial and presidential elections. Democratic strategists were well aware that Governor Morehead's image as a "western man" had contributed significantly to his lopsided majorities in the mountain counties, and this time they were determined to steal the Whig thunder by nominating a westerner as their own standard-bearer. Michael Hoke, a popular young lawyer who had served with Clingman in the North Carolina General Assembly, seemed an ideal choice. As one Whig grudgingly acknowledged, "his social swagering [sic] manner is well calculated to captivate & please the unlettered men of the mountains."[23]

The Democrats did not rely on Hoke's personality alone to win over western voters. Party leaders also published a pamphlet entitled *Plain Thoughts for the West*, which they circulated widely in the western counties. Its main argument was that Hoke had devoted his entire career to defending western rights and interests and thus deserved the support of all westerners regardless of their party preference. The circular contrasted Hoke's political course with that of his Whig adversary, William A. Graham, whom it portrayed as an opponent of western interests.[24]

As the preeminent Whig in the mountain region, Clingman had primary responsibility for holding the "western reserve" for Graham. He may well have had mixed feelings about the task, since it was no secret that Graham had expressed regret at his brother's defeat in the congressional election. Despite any misgivings he may have harbored, Clingman exerted his influence "to the uttermost both by political & personal appeals" on behalf of the Whig candidate. Indeed, he later boasted, he had "render[ed] him more service than any one Whig in the state."[25]

Typical of his efforts in the governor's campaign was Clingman's attendance at the great Whig jubilee in Asheville on 4 July 1844. The congressman stood for nearly two hours in front of more than six thousand eager spectators, delivering "a bold, clear, logical and forcible speech" that "was listened to with the most profound attention . . . and elicited the most hearty applause." A month later, Graham carried the mountain district with 62 percent of the vote. Although his margin of victory was considerably less impressive than Morehead's had been two years earlier, Graham's strong showing in the far west proved an important factor in enabling the Whigs to win the gubernatorial election by a razor-thin margin.[26]

Clingman remained in the field after the election, campaigning on behalf of Whig presidential candidate Henry Clay. In late August he journeyed across the mountains to address a mass meeting in Knoxville, Tennessee. The *Knoxville Register* praised the young congressman as "one of the most able and ready debaters we have ever listened to" and remarked that "the mountain district of the Old North State may well be proud of her . . . talented and eloquent son." Shortly afterward, he traveled to Nashville to attend a grand Whig rally that included prominent speakers from eight Southern states.[27]

Clingman continued his exertions until the day of the election. On 11 October he participated in a two-day mass meeting at Rutherfordton, sharing the platform with James Graham, John Gray Bynum, and several other Whig notables. The following week, he spoke at another two-day celebration in Morganton that featured torchlight processions, patriotic songs, and vast amounts of barbecue. As election day approached, the *Raleigh Register* reported that the "utmost enthusiasm is ranging . . . [in] the Western Counties of North Carolina—the GIBRALTAR of Whig principles" and predicted "a tremendous increase of the Whig vote . . . over the Poll for Governor." [28]

That optimistic prediction was not far off the mark. Clay won Clingman's district by more than thirty-four hundred votes—a margin that enabled him to carry North Carolina handily. The Whigs were not as successful in the nation as a whole. Democrat James K. Polk carried most of the South, as well as the key Northern states of New York and Pennsylvania, where Liberty party candidate James G. Birney cut into Clay's vote. The Democrats viewed the outcome as a referendum on Texas, whose annexation Polk and his party had vigorously supported. Ironically, Clay's "Raleigh letter," in which he publicly came out against immediate annexation, probably cost him the election even though it did him no damage in the Old North State. [29]

As soon as the second session of the Twenty-Eighth Congress assembled in December 1844, the Democrats introduced annexation resolutions in both houses. A vigorous debate ensued, with a majority of the Whigs continuing to oppose the measure. When Clingman's turn to speak came on 6 January 1845, he announced that he did not intend to "discuss the constitutionality or expediency of the proposed annexation of Texas." Instead, he would challenge the Democratic claim that the presidential election had been a "manifestation of popular opinion in favor of the annexation" by demonstrating that the opposition had "deliberately entered into a scheme of misrepresentation and fraud" to steal the election from Clay. [30]

What followed was a bitterly partisan diatribe that made his earlier rejoinder to Duncan pale in comparison. The Democrats, Clingman reiterated, were nothing more than a spoils party "held together solely by the love of office, or, in language that has now become classical, 'the cohesive power of public plunder.'" He charged that party leaders had deliberately concealed their positions on controversial issues like the independent treasury during the campaign "in order to deceive the country as to their real intentions." In the Northern states they had misrepresented Polk's position on the tariff and Texas issues by using "phrases [as] indefinite, unmeaning, vague, ambiguous, [and] double-faced as the responses of the old Delphic oracle." [31]

But the Democrats, said Clingman, had not been satisfied merely with lying to the voters. In addition, they had "deliberately formed a widely extended plan for the purpose of procuring a sufficient number of illegal votes to . . . secure the election of Mr. Polk." Citing New York, Pennsylvania, Louisiana, and Georgia as states where fraud had been extensively practiced, he proceeded to back up his charges in excruciating detail. Clingman was especially condemnatory of the Empire Club in New York City—a gang of "gamblers, pickpockets, droppers, thimble-riggers, burners, and the like"—who had been enlisted by the Democratic leaders expressly for the purpose of rigging the election. He characterized Isaac Rynders, the club's president, as a scoundrel who had been "often arrested for thimble-rigging and similar offences" and claimed that other leaders of the organization, whom he did not hesitate to mention by name, had been charged with murder, theft, rape, and burglary.[32]

The North Carolinian reserved some of his choicest barbs for the Southern Democrats. A month earlier the gag rule had finally been rescinded, after being in force for more than eight years. Realizing that they lacked the legislative muscle to prevent its repeal, Southerners had made no attempt to delay the vote as they had done at the previous session. Clingman could not resist twitting his Democratic adversaries for that "extraordinary change in the[ir] conduct." In his mind, their willingness to tamely give up the rule "without a word of objection from any quarter" constituted proof that "all their parade at the last session was a mere humbug—one of the most barefaced political frauds ever attempted to be played off for party purposes." Far from being true defenders of Southern Rights, the Democrats were "false watchmen of the South—traitor sentinels!"[33]

Even in the context of the fierce partisanship that characterized congressional debates during the antebellum era, the roasting that Clingman gave the opposition was truly extraordinary. One Southern Democrat characterized his remarks as "the bitterest things ever uttered on the floor of the House." The Whigs, on the other hand, were ecstatic. One congressman gleefully compared the reaction of his Democratic colleagues to that of "a flock of geese on hot iron." The editor of the *Greensboro Patriot* was equally delighted with Clingman's performance. "If in any case we could enjoy the *torture* of a fellow creature," he exulted, "it would have been in watching the writhings of these political hypocrites, as Mr. Clingman proceeded with the deliberate application of his red-hot pincers to their naked epidermis." Clingman later boasted that his speech had made the Whigs "so indignant, united and resolute" that, had the election been held over again, the party "could have carried the country" for Clay.[34]

The Democrats were determined to return the tongue-lashing administered to them by Clingman. Their opportunity came the next day when William L. Yancey of Alabama took the floor to make his maiden speech. Sparing no punches, Yancey denounced his adversary as "a betrayer of the trust reposed in his hands" and as "one who had given a stab to the institutions of his own land." "Never," reported the *North Carolina Standard*, "was any man so severely castigated as Mr. Clingman was."[35]

And, indeed, Yancey's gibes had hit their mark. Bitter as Clingman's own comments had been, they had not been directed at any particular member of the House. Yancey, however, had gone considerably beyond the bounds of parliamentary etiquette by attacking his adversary personally and casting doubts on his loyalty to the South. From his desk in the House of Representatives Clingman dashed off an angry note, demanding that Yancey explain whether he "intended towards me, personally, any disrespect, or [meant] to be understood that I was deficient in integrity, honor, or any other quality requisite to the character of a gentleman." Yancey replied curtly that he would make "no explanations." [36]

The Alabamian's refusal to disavow his abusive remarks culminated in one of the most memorable duels in American history.[37] On 9 January 1845 Clingman informed Yancey that he did not intend to let the "discussion stop where it was" and challenged his adversary to meet him in Baltimore, where a formal demand for satisfaction would be made. Clingman arrived in the city later that evening and immediately sought the assistance of Charles Lee Jones, the son of a prominent Washington attorney. Jones agreed to do what he could "to bring about an amicable adjustment if such could be done compatible with honor" and to serve as Clingman's second if a settlement could not be obtained.[38]

Knowing that Yancey enjoyed a reputation as a "practiced shot," Jones was shocked to discover that Clingman was "entirely unacquainted with the use and handling of the duelling pistol, never having even fired one." Moreover, the expensive and finely finished pair of pistols that the North Carolinian had borrowed from Sen. William Allen of Ohio were, in his opinion, "too heavy and not well balanced for dropping." Jones hurried back to Washington to retrieve his own weapons, which he considered "better adapted for the purpose." Upon his return, he took Clingman to a house a few miles from Baltimore where "he might be free from arrest, and become familiar with the handling of his pistol."

Yancey and his second, John Middleton Huger of South Carolina, arrived in Baltimore at eight o'clock that same evening and took lodgings at the Exchange Hotel. Jones and Huger spent most of the following day exchanging notes written by the two principals. Clingman continued to demand that Yancey explain his remarks. The Alabama Democrat just as persistently maintained that any explanation would be "superfluous." Unwilling "to close the door to all accommodation," Jones and Huger agreed to meet at Barnum's Hotel the next morning in a final effort to avoid a hostile encounter. After the two intermediaries once again failed to arrive at an amicable settlement, Clingman formally demanded "the satisfaction usual among gentlemen." Jones and Huger then commenced writing out an elaborate set of rules that would govern the proceedings, scheduled to take place the following Monday.[39]

By the time all the paperwork had been completed, the entire nation had become aware of the activities transpiring in Baltimore. The Washington correspondent of the *New York Tribune* characterized the impending confrontation as "the talk of the town" and reported that "all kinds of rumors are floating about." According to one account, the affair had been settled without bloodshed. Another report asserted that shots had already been exchanged and that Yancey had been mortally wounded. Yet another rumor, this one deliberately leaked by Clingman and Jones to put "the authorities . . . on the wrong trail," stated that the two would-be duelists had fled to Delaware.[40]

On Saturday evening Clingman, Jones, and his surgeon Charles Bell Gibson, left Baltimore in a hack and journeyed to the residence of Charles C. Hanson, about eight miles from the site of the duel. On Sunday Jones attempted to give his friend "some practical instructions with the use of the pistol," but the day was "too windy for more than a very little practice." He also tried unsuccessfully to persuade Clingman to use his own pistols instead of the ones borrowed from Allen.

On the morning of Monday, 13 January 1845, Clingman partook of a "luxurious lunch" at the residence of Col. Horace Capron, while Jones rode ahead to meet Huger at Brown's Hotel, about a mile west of Beltsville. To his surprise, Yancey and Huger, along with numerous other friends, were relaxing there with "no expectation of our making an appearance." The rumor that Clingman and Jones had circulated to throw off the police had also fooled Yancey. The Alabamian had read a report in the morning newspaper that Clingman had been arrested trying to cross into Delaware and quite naturally had assumed that the encounter would not take place.[41]

With the duel now back on schedule, Jones and Huger quickly rode off to select an appropriate location. By the time they returned to the hotel, the police had also arrived, their suspicions having been aroused by the crowd descending on Beltsville. Jones rode back toward Capron's and met Clingman and the other members of his party along the way. He informed them that Yancey had most likely been arrested and that, consequently, "no fight would take place." They decided to proceed to the dueling ground anyhow.

Meanwhile back at Brown's Hotel, Yancey, who in fact had been detained, was planning an escape. Two of his friends, A. B. Meek and Reuben Chapman, "entertained the officers, and contrived to have themselves bound over," while the would-be duelist and his second sneaked out the back door and made their way to the meeting place on foot "by a tedious and circuitous route through the woods and fields." In his excitement and haste, Yancey forgot to bring his pistols. Meek, who was holding the weapons, grasped the situation and, together with Chapman, managed somehow to break away from the police. Springing into a nearby carriage, they headed for the field of honor with the authorities in hot pursuit.[42]

With Yancey now in possession of his weapons, the two combatants were hurriedly assigned to position, ten paces apart. Clingman shot first, his ball flying "in to the heav[ens]." Yancey then returned the fire, his shot hitting the ground close enough to Clingman to throw some dirt on him. Although uninjured, the North Carolinian was visibly shaken. According to one observer, "he wheeled about half round, with his mouth open, the muscles of his face completely let down, with a ghastly look." With the police now converging on the scene in full force, a settlement was quickly reached whereby Clingman avowed that he "had intended no personal imputation upon any member of the House of Representatives" in his speech of 6 January, while Yancey agreed to retract "his personally offensive remarks applicable to Mr. Clingman."[43]

Thus an episode that might well have ended tragically was, instead, "turned into a farce." The Democrats could not resist poking fun at Clingman for the duel's "peculiar effect upon his system." On the floor of Congress Andrew Johnson characterized the encounter as one "well calculated to produce a strange distension and convulsive contortion of the muscular and nervous system." Privately, the Tennessee Democrat insinuated that the overwrought North Carolinian had "not only made a copeous *[sic]* discharge of water" as Yancey's bullet passed by him, "but that his Short bread [had] come from him in gr[e]at profusion."[44]

Despite the Democratic ridicule, the encounter with Yancey bolstered Clingman's reputation among the Whigs. Even those who were averse to dueling agreed that the congressman had been left with little choice in the matter. As Sen. Willie P. Mangum explained, "to have declined would have disgraced him here & destroyed his just Weight & influence." By defending his honor, Clingman had regained "confidence & respect," even in the "eyes of the puritan of New England."[45]

The young Whig also received accolades for his willingness to put his own life on the line in his defense of his party's principles. Sounding a theme that would become central to the Whig version of the duel, the *Hartford Journal* charged the Democrats with concocting "a concerted, diabolical plan, *to kill the man* who had dared to be independent of Southern dictation." Reports of almost daily threats on his life by members of the Empire Club and other "irresponsible bullies" further enhanced Clingman's image as a man who had risked his life by daring to expose "the frauds and villainies committed at the recent Presidential election."[46]

Clingman returned to the mountain district in March 1845 as a conquering hero. No first-term congressman from the Old North State had ever attracted so much national attention or made such a favorable impression on his party's leaders. His triumphant reelection to a second term in the House of Representatives seemed a foregone conclusion. According to the *Raleigh Register,* "there is a general and very natural wish not only among the Whigs of this State, but among the Whigs of the Union, that Mr. Clingman should again be returned." Indeed, the Whigs of the mountain district would be ungrateful if they did not "say 'Well done' to a faithful public servant, who by his zeal in behalf of their interests, exposed himself to threats of violence and even assassination."[47]

For a time it seemed that the enormously popular congressman would "walk over the track without opposition" on his way to a second term. Three weeks before the election, however, James Graham, who had just returned from Alabama, announced his intention to enter the race. Clingman's partisan course in Congress had made him anathema to the mountain Democrats, and leading members of that party had assured Graham of their whole-hearted support should he decide to challenge the Whig incumbent. The former congressman had also been approached by a number of his "old Whig friends," who affirmed that they planned to run him against Clingman, regardless of whether he became an active candidate. Enticed by the possibility of avenging his defeat, Graham decided to throw his hat into the ring.[48]

Well aware of his rival's popularity among the Whigs in the district, Graham recognized that his only hope for success was to mobilize the Democrats on his behalf. Clingman's vote against the gag rule seemed an issue well suited for that purpose. In a public letter circulated widely throughout the mountain region, Graham conjured up bloody images of Nat Turner's rebellion and accused his opponent of providing the "fire brand" that the abolitionists would use to ignite the powder keg of insurrection. The former congressman also appealed to Democratic voters by denouncing Clingman's vote against the annexation of Texas.[49]

Clingman's supporters responded with a barrage of circulars and other campaign documents designed to prove that Graham was not a true Whig but merely a stalking horse for the Democrats. A correspondent of the *Asheville Messenger* condemned the "unnatural alliance . . . formed between him and the leaders of the Democratic party." A communication signed by five leading Whigs from Burke County affirmed that Graham had entered the race "without the approbation and against the wishes of the Whigs" and attributed his candidacy to "a combination among the leaders of the Democratic party." Another Whig from Burke County asserted that opposition leaders were fully aware that "no open Democrat can be elected" and were uniting behind Graham in the hope that their support, "together with some of his old Whig friends who have always stood by him," would be sufficient to determine the outcome. Although Graham still claimed to be a Whig, the race had really "narrow[ed] down to a Whig and Democratic contest." [50]

Whig presses outside the mountain district, which normally remained neutral in intraparty disputes, also rallied behind Clingman. The *Greensboro Patriot* condemned "the underhanded manner in which Graham came out" and denounced him as a "demagogue" who "should be sternly rebuked not only at the Polls but every where." The *Fayetteville Observer* categorically asserted that Clingman "is regarded as *the* Whig candidate" and predicted that the congressman "will very probably be elected." The *Raleigh Register,* official organ of the state party, gave its endorsement to Clingman, and even the *National Intelligencer* at the nation's capital broke precedent by announcing its support for him.[51]

At the same time that Graham was invoking the sectional identities of mountain voters by denouncing his opponent's positions on the gag rule and Texas annexation, Clingman and his allies were appealing to the partisan identities of the overwhelmingly Whig electorate. According to a correspondent of the *Asheville Messenger,* the great Whig leader Henry Clay had consistently "entertained and advocated . . . the same opinions and principles [on the gag rule] that Mr. Clingman advocated and voted for during the last Congress." Shortly before the election Clingman issued a public letter designed to demonstrate that "Mr. Clay's views on the subject of receiving Abolition petitions are identical to my own." He also claimed to have a letter from Senator Mangum "concurring entirely with my views on this subject." Could Graham pretend, he asked, that those two sterling Whigs, "both slave-holders, to say nothing of other distinguished gentlemen, are Abolitionists?"[52]

On 7 August 1845 more than ten thousand mountain residents went to the polls—an increase of 52 percent over the previous congressional election. Despite the defection of his 1843 Democratic supporters, Clingman managed to improve on his earlier showing by 1,100 votes, capturing approximately three-fourths of the Whig vote. However, that ringing endorsement on the part of his Whig constituents was not sufficient to enable him to win the election. Adding a corporal's guard of about 1,600 Whig supporters to more than 3,600 Democratic votes, Graham defeated Clingman by a margin of 326 votes.[53]

The cocky young congressman who just a month earlier had seemed destined for a long and brilliant career in national politics had suddenly been forced into retirement. The Democrats naturally pointed to Clingman's defeat as evidence that he had all along "misrepresented the Mountain district in the national councils." According to that viewpoint, his overthrow constituted a "well-merited . . . rebuke . . . to a Southern Representative who dared to outrage the feelings of his constituents by voting with and countenancing the abolitionists." William W. Holden of the *North Carolina Standard* pronounced the vanquished Whig to be "emphatically and totally defunct. No political galvanism can restore him. The people have consigned him to retirement—and there let him remain, to reflect upon his base treachery to the South and to the whole country."[54]

The Whigs, on the other hand, denied that the outcome was, in any sense, a referendum on Southern Rights. The *Asheville Messenger* attributed Graham's victory to a combination of Democrats and Graham supporters who "soured by his defeat two years ago, owed Mr. Clingman a grudge." The congressman's defeat could not be ascribed to "any want of confidence in him, or real objection to his course in Congress by the great body of the Whigs of the District." Clingman himself took a similar view in a letter written to his constituents shortly after the election. It would be "erroneous," he said, to impute his loss "to the public disapprobation of my course in the late Congress." While acknowledging that there had been "much clamor in relation to my opposition to the 25th Rule," he had "no reason to believe that any person voted against me on that ground alone." Moreover, his votes against the annexation of Texas "were approved as far as I could ascertain, by all the Whigs . . . of the district." The result, therefore, "cannot be regarded as a decision of the people against me on any of these grounds."[55]

The true cause of his defeat, Clingman affirmed, was the solid Democratic vote cast against him. Although the leaders of that party "pretended that their opposition to me arose from the belief that I was favorable to the Abolitionists," the real reason for their hostility was "my active exertions in support of the Whig cause, both in and out of Congress." Under the circumstances, Clingman saw no reason to modify any of the positions he had taken in the Twenty-Eighth Congress. "If any one supposes that the result of this contest has induced me to regret any step taken by me heretofore, as a politician, he misunderstands the motives which govern me." Indeed, he defiantly proclaimed, "if I have ever committed errors as a politician, I have not yet lived long enough to perceive them, and would but do again what I have done."

Clingman's unrepentant remarks, together with the overwhelming support he received from the Whigs in 1845, cast doubt on the assertions of those historians who argue that his surprising defeat taught him "an important lesson about his mountain constituency" by demonstrating that "the sectional identities of western Carolinians as southerners ran far deeper than did their partisan identities as Whigs." [56] Far from taking a back seat to sectionalism, partisanship dominated the campaign throughout. Eager to punish the brash young Whig for his vitriolic attacks on their party in Congress, the Democrats in the mountain district successfully combined with a small faction of dissident Whigs to send the congressman into retirement.

The campaign of 1845 did, however, teach Clingman an "important lesson" about politics in the North Carolina mountain district. The lesson, as William W. Holden explained, was that "the democrats hold the balance of power in this District." In 1843 the party had used that power to overthrow the veteran Graham and put Clingman in his place. Two years later, they again employed their strength to oust the ungrateful Whig. Although Clingman was understandably angry at the Democrats for turning him out of office, his defeat ironically served to engender a "remarkable degree of respect toward the Democratic party"—if not for its principles, at least for its latent power. The course of events would soon demonstrate how well Clingman had learned the lesson of 1845. [57]

5 *Renegade Whig*

The congressional campaign of 1845 left a legacy of bad feelings and recrimination among the Whigs of the mountain district. For more than a month after the election, Thomas W. Atkin bitterly assailed James Graham on the pages of the *Asheville Messenger,* denouncing him as "a man who had, Judas like, sold himself and his principles" in order to gratify "a mean spirit of revenge." Although Graham "still calls himself a Whig," Atkin fumed, ". . . he occupies a position from which he might easily and without an effort step into the Democratic ranks." The editor warned his Whig readers to "have nothing to do with any man who is willing to make any sort of compromise with Democracy!"[1]

Ironically, by the end of the decade, the Whig presses in the Old North State would be publishing similar tirades against Clingman. From the perspective of August 1845, however, it seemed that the party had lost a valuable asset in the defeat of the first-term congressman who had already established a national reputation as a bold champion of Whig principles. Party leaders lamented the outcome of the election and chastised Graham for using "discreditable" tactics that ultimately "must react on the head of their author." In a public letter issued a week after the election, Clingman also spoke critically of Graham. At the same time, he declared his readiness "to co-operate with the Whig party of the District and Union" and expressed confidence that the party could "by proper exertion . . . be stronger in the District than ever." Atkin predicted that the former congressman would "wait, without repining . . . [until] the Whig party, mindful of his efforts in its behalf, will again demand his services, and call him from his retirement to the councils of the State or Nation." [2]

While publicly urging the Whigs in his district to close ranks in the face of the Democratic threat, Clingman was privately taking the first step down the road that would eventually lead him into the camp of the enemy. On 5 October 1845 he sent an extraordinary letter to Sen. Willie P. Mangum outlining a Machiavellian scheme to put Mangum in the governor's chair in place of William A. Graham. The thrust of his argument was that Graham was too unpopular in the far west to win reelection. According to Clingman, he had run poorly in the mountain counties in 1844 despite "all the exertion in my power" on his behalf. Since then, his standing had been further eroded by the unpopularity of his brother who "is viewed by the greater part of the whigs . . . in no better light than John Tyler himself." Without the solid support of the mountain district, the Whigs had no hope of winning the election. On the other hand, if Mangum consented to run for chief executive, "the western reserve will come out for you in all its whig strength & give you a larger majority than it would any one else of our party." [3]

The tone of Clingman's letter indicated a deep hostility toward his former friend and mentor, Graham. Undoubtedly, he resented the governor for siding with his brother in the recent congressional campaign, particularly after Clingman had played such an active role in delivering his district to Graham in 1844. The former congressman was also convinced that his support for the unpopular Graham in the governor's race had cost him the congressional election the following year. As he explained to Mangum, "I lost by so doing more votes than I was beaten this year." Clingman had another motive in urging Mangum to run for governor. His election to that office would produce a vacancy in the U.S. Senate—a position to which the ambitious young Whig was already aspiring. [4]

Without waiting for a response from Mangum, Clingman organized a meeting of the Buncombe County Whigs on 7 October 1845, ostensibly to choose delegates to the state convention. Although affirming that "we entirely approve the administration of his Excellency William A. Graham," the Whigs resolved that it would be "inexpedient at this time to express a preference for any one as a candidate for the office of Governor [in 1846]." The coolness of those resolutions stood in sharp contrast to the glowing praise the Whigs usually lavished on their incumbents. William W. Holden of the *North Carolina Standard* grasped the significance of the Asheville resolutions at once. Characterizing the halfhearted endorsement as being "as cold as the summit of Pilot [Mountain] on a January day," the Democratic editor speculated that this attempt to damn Graham with faint praise was an act of "personal vengeance" on the part of Clingman. "We may guess that Mr. Clingman, a defeated candidate for Congress . . . by the Hon. James Graham, cares but little for *Governor* Graham."[5]

The Whigs denied that the Asheville resolutions contained any hidden meanings. The *Asheville Messenger* affirmed that Clingman was "above the mean spirit of revenge and personal ill feeling . . . attributed to him" and promised that the former congressman would "as heartily unite with the Whig party in support of Wm. A. Graham, should he be the nominee, as will any man in the State." Privately, however, some Whigs were considerably less insouciant. John Gray Bynum, a Whig leader in Rutherford County, candidly told Graham that "the conjectures of the Standard are true. . . . Clingman wrote the resolutions, & they were palmed off upon the meeting."[6]

Clingman's efforts to replace Graham with Mangum ultimately came to naught. The veteran senator's unwillingness to trade a lucrative seat in the national Congress for the less prestigious and less remunerative office of governor probably doomed the scheme from the beginning. Equally important, party leaders in other parts of the mountain district refused to go along with Clingman's plan. Instead, Whig meetings in several mountain counties passed resolutions warmly praising Governor Graham and recommending him for a second term. By the time the Whig State Convention met on 12 January 1846, his renomination was a foregone conclusion.[7]

Despite his misgivings about Graham, Clingman campaigned actively on his behalf, debating Democratic gubernatorial candidate James B. Shepard at Hendersonville, Morganton, and Rutherfordton. With perhaps some exaggeration, he later claimed he had rendered the governor more service during "his first and second canvass . . . than any one Whig in the state."[8] Even so, his earlier efforts to derail Graham's nomination provided the Democrats with some powerful campaign ammunition. Their repeated claims that Clingman and his friends would "give, at most, only a cold support to the nomination" put the Whigs on the defensive, obliging them to prove (at least to their own satisfaction) that the "Mountain Boys would do their duty." Fortunately for the Whigs, Clingman's concerns about Graham's electability proved unfounded. Aided by Democratic factionalism and by Shepard's own inept campaign, the party scored a resounding victory in the mountain region and throughout the state, winning not only the governorship but also comfortable majorities in both houses of the state legislature.[9]

Their capture of the general assembly took on added importance for the Whigs because of the sudden resignation of Democratic senator William H. Haywood Jr. shortly before the election. The names of several prominent Whigs were brought forth as suitable replacements, but no one was more eager for the office than Clingman. On 25 August 1846 he wrote a long letter to Mangum soliciting the senator's support. Denying any "wish to be presented merely as a sectional candidate," Clingman justified his claim to the senatorship on the basis of his "zeal in the service of the Whig party" and his "efforts . . . against the democratic leaders in North Carolina & against the Locofocoism of the Union generally." [10]

Clingman's initial strategy of emphasizing his services to the Whig party soon gave way to a more overtly sectional approach. The three main candidates put forward by the Whigs—former secretary of the navy George E. Badger, former governor John M. Morehead, and former congressman Edward Stanly—each could boast of a record of service to the party at least the equal of his own. Stanly was an easterner, while Morehead and Badger both resided in the central part of the state. Thus, it made sense for Clingman to emphasize the claims of the far west to a seat in the U.S. Senate, particularly since that region had traditionally been underrepresented in the distribution of federal offices. [11]

That strategy was embodied in a letter submitted to the *Raleigh Register* in October 1846 under the pseudonym of "Fair Play." Although Clingman did not compose the letter himself, "the material was furnished, and the argument dictated" by him. [12] "Fair Play" justified Clingman's candidacy on the basis of his distinguished record in Congress, his services to his party, and the "flattering commendations" of the Whig presses throughout the nation. After extolling the virtues of his candidate, the anonymous writer then went on to admonish the *Register*'s editor, Weston R. Gales, for overlooking Clingman's strong claims to the senatorship while actively promoting candidates from the central part of the state. He also accused the general assembly of slighting the far west by refusing to advance its most prominent men to high office. "Does it not strike you, Mr. Gales, as a little singular," he inquired, "that West of Guilford, within the memory of man, there has not been one United States Senator elected?" [13]

Put off by the "disrespectful, if not rude and insulting" tone of the letter, as well as by its unabashed appeal to state sectionalism, Gales refused to publish it. Instead, he roundly denounced it in a series of editorials that lambasted the "unfairness and ignorance" of its author and deplored his efforts "to excite the hostility of the West towards the East." The Whig editor could not, however, bring himself to believe that Clingman had personally "countenanced this attempt to forward his advancement at the expense of harmony in the Whig ranks." "We know him to be incapable of such things," asserted Gales. Indeed, "he would be mortified" at such a blatant piece of promotion "written in bad taste and bad temper." [14]

Gales had seriously misjudged the intensity of Clingman's ambition. The former congressman had, in fact, approved the contents of the "Fair Play" letter. He even went so far as to add a glowing encomium to himself, written in the third person, to the version that was eventually published in the *Asheville Messenger*. Reviewing his efforts on behalf of his party during the four previous campaigns, as well as his memorable confrontations with Memminger, Shepard, and Duncan,

Clingman concluded that he had "within the last ten years, met in political debate, a greater number of persons than any man in the State." Not without reason had the Whig presses lauded him as "THE YOUNG CHAMPION OF THE WEST. . . . Whenever a political field is to be fought, those who know him best are always willing to trust the battle to his hands."[15]

Sensing an opportunity to foment dissension within the Whig ranks, Democrats like William W. Holden were eager to fuel Clingman's resentment against the Whig leaders in Raleigh. Just a few months earlier the editor had denounced him on the pages of the *Standard* as an abolitionist. Now he portrayed the former congressman as the victim of a selfish "central clique" and wondered aloud whether his friends would "stand tamely by and consent to see the sceptre of power and the honors of the State conferred *all the time* upon Orange [County] and the East?" According to Holden, "'Fair Play' hit the nail on the head when he said that . . . when the offices were to be distributed, the West was sure to get the bone to pick."[16]

Clingman lobbied aggressively among the legislators at Raleigh and did "not hesitate to declare publicly" that he was "electioneering for one of the seats." Nonetheless, the Whig caucus gave the nomination to George E. Badger, a longtime member of the Whig Central Committee who had not held an elective office in more than thirty years. Clingman was not the only Whig who suspected that Badger owed his election primarily to his connection with the "central clique." The Democrats were quick to add to those suspicions. "The West," snorted Holden, "with its vigorous and growing population, and its overwhelming Federal [Whig] majorities, has *again* been slighted, and that too, with one of its leading champions, Mr. Clingman, upon the ground."[17]

Despite Holden's efforts to stir up trouble among the Whigs, Clingman did not publicly protest the decision of the Whig caucus. Six years earlier, he had vigorously supported Badger for the senatorship, and apparently he bore no ill feelings toward him after his election. Probably he was already making plans to recapture the congressional seat he had lost to James Graham in 1845. Graham's opposition to the Mexican War had eroded his support among the Democrats in the mountain district, and a number of ambitious politicians besides Clingman were convinced that he was vulnerable. By the spring of 1847 Whigs John Gray Bynum and William F. McKesson and Democrat Samuel Flemming had also expressed interest in entering the race. Although eager for a rematch with Clingman, Graham feared that a three- or four-way division among the Whigs would invariably result in the election of Flemming. Unwilling to have "any agency in [such] a contest," the congressman withdrew from the competition. McKesson and Flemming also eventually dropped out, leaving Clingman and Bynum to compete for the seat.[18]

Clingman spent most of the campaign on crutches, suffering from a severe ankle sprain that he had sustained "while carelessly riding a wild horse." Although the injury limited the former congressman's ability to canvass the rugged mountain terrain, his challenger proved unable to capitalize on his misfortune. A Rutherfordton attorney who had known Clingman since their student days at the University of North Carolina, Bynum lacked a substantial popular following or a newspaper to promote his claims. Despite his efforts to make an issue out of Clingman's opposition to the Mexican War, the contest engendered little of the excitement that had characterized the previous campaign. Its dullness was leavened only by the recurrent rumor that Graham might again enter the race at the eleventh hour. With a majority of mountain Democrats sitting out the election, Clingman won handily, receiving 57 percent of the vote.[19]

Contrary to the assertions of some historians, Clingman's defeat in 1845 did not cause him to "temper his partisanship" or to modify his position on the slavery issue after his return to Congress in 1847. Nor did his behavior during the first session of the Thirtieth Congress indicate that "he had learned a lesson from the gag rule controversy."[20] Indeed, only a few days into the session the unrepentant Clingman once again voted against a motion to table antislavery petitions. Again, he was the only Southerner to oppose the measure. This time, however, his vote proved to be the deciding one, since the motion to table was rejected by a one-vote majority. The next day, he defended his position on abolitionist petitions in an address on the floor of the House. Repeating the arguments he had made in his speech of January 1844, Clingman expressed no regrets but, instead, defiantly proclaimed that "experience has given me additional reason to be satisfied with my course."[21]

Nonetheless, Clingman's main purpose on 22 December 1847 was not to expound upon the issue of abolitionist petitions but to enunciate his position on the more volatile question of slavery in the territories. The previous session of Congress had been racked by controversy over the Wilmot Proviso—a proposal that would have prohibited slavery in any territory acquired from Mexico. Shocked by the solid support their Northern allies gave the Proviso, Southerners in both parties did not hesitate to declare that disunion would be preferable to a Union that stigmatized them and the institution of slavery. Clingman's objective, as he later recalled, was to stake out a constitutional "middle ground" on the territorial issue upon which Northern and Southern members of his party might unite for the upcoming presidential campaign—a principle he called "equitable division."[22]

Clingman rejected both the abolitionist argument that the federal government had "no power to establish the institution" of slavery in the territories and the equally militant Southern claim that it "can do nothing to exclude it." Given the absolute nature of Congress's authority over the territories, he reasoned, "it is idle to deny that slavery may either be permitted or forbidden to exist there." At the same time, however, he argued that the constitutional power of Congress to "make all needful rules and regulations" regarding the territories did not give it the right to exclude slavery from *all* the territories. Like other Southerners, he claimed that those lands were held "in trust, for the use and benefit of all the States." Congress could justifiably divide the territories "so as to permit one section to be exclusively occupied by freemen, and the other by those who may hold slaves." But an attempt "to exclude slavery from all the territories of the Union . . . would be a gross violation of the constitution." By his logic, the Wilmot Proviso was unconstitutional not because it interfered with the right of Southerners to carry their slaves into the territories, as John C. Calhoun and the Southern Democrats were arguing, but because it violated the principle of equitable division.[23]

Clingman underscored his moderate position on the slavery issue by denouncing extremist groups in both sections. The abolitionists, he believed, posed the lesser threat. Obnoxious though they were, they had "been able to effect very little mischief . . . hav[ing] been successfully combated by the good sense and proper feeling of the North." More to be feared were Southern radicals like Calhoun, who "ambitious of popularity and influence [had] . . . seized upon the slave question as the means to effect that end." The greatest danger, according to Clingman, was that the two extremes, feeding on each other, might grow in strength at the expense of the moderate center. In that regard, Calhoun's violent and denunciatory rhetoric had provided "food for the Abolitionists just as their fanaticism gave him materials to work with."[24]

The most provocative part of Clingman's speech was his assertion that the passage of the Wilmot Proviso would compel the South to reconsider its relationship to the Union. Although he stopped considerably short of demanding a dissolution of the Union should the Proviso become law, he did contemplate the possibility that the sectional controversy might culminate in disunion. "Should we be forced away," he affirmed, he for one would "stand by the white race, the freemen of the South."[25]

Clingman's reference to disunion, which one historian has characterized as "extraordinary" for its "implied belligerence," was actually no more provocative than the declaration in his maiden speech of January 1844 that the "Union must be dissolved" if the abolitionists ever came into power. Both remarks were brief comments in longer speeches whose main themes were moderation and sectional harmony. Only out of their context do they seem to imply belligerence. Although a majority of Southern congressmen, at least until 1861, professed devotion to the Union, few were unconditional in their expressions of unionism. Like Clingman, most could and did envision circumstances that might hypothetically result in disunion.[26]

Far from welcoming a breakup of the Union, Clingman asserted that disunion would be a "catastrophe . . . the saddest of all partings." In such an event, "it would be vain . . . for us on either side to hope for such prosperity as we have hitherto enjoyed. . . . It would be difficult and most painful." Although fully aware of "the perils which beset us," the congressman expressed optimism that the "strong, clear good sense" of the American people would ultimately prevail and that the memories of "common counsels, common sufferings, common struggles, and common triumphs," together with "a community of interest . . . that no party madness could break up," would prove strong enough to resist the countervailing strains of sectionalism.[27]

Clingman's temperate and balanced assessment of the challenges that Americans faced as they confronted the legacy of the Mexican War won high praise from the Whigs in his home state and throughout the Union. Even the antislavery *National Era* lauded the moderate tone of the speech, characterizing it as "ingenuous, eloquent, sophistical, and good tempered."[28] If Clingman's remarks represented a sharp departure from his earlier position on Southern Rights, as some historians have suggested, that departure went unnoticed by his contemporaries. Moderate Whig newspapers such as the *Raleigh Register* pointed to the address as evidence that the Democrats had all along been deliberately distorting Clingman's position on the slavery issue. The speech, crowed the *Register,* had "given the lie positive and direct to these libellous insinuations" that the congressman's "affinities and sympathies were with the Abolitionists of the North." The paper even demanded that William W. Holden, who had led the chorus of abuse against Clingman, publicly apologize "for the gross injustice he has done him . . . by retracting all he has said, and publishing his Speech."[29]

Neither the *North Carolina Standard* nor the other Democratic presses in the Old North State retracted their previous denunciations or graced their pages with Clingman's lengthy oration. While the speech did not provoke the tirade of abuse that his remarks against the gag rule had produced four years earlier, the Democrats found little to praise in Clingman's assertion of the constitutional power of Congress over slavery in the territories or in his attacks against Calhoun and the Southern wing of their party. According to one Democratic observer, the speech, although "the ablest of his political life," had been fatally marred by the "demagogueism *[sic]* which seems to be an element of his political nature."[30]

An astute Georgia Democrat named Hopkins Holsey discerned a more subtle partisan dimension to Clingman's remarks. Since the introduction of the Wilmot Proviso, leaders of both parties had been searching for a formula that would unite their divergent sectional wings on the territorial issue. Some Democrats like Vice Pres. George M. Dallas and Sen. Lewis Cass were advocating the doctrine of popular sovereignty—the claim that the territorial legislatures should have exclusive control over their local institutions. Other Democrats like Secretary of State James Buchanan were proposing an extension of the Missouri Compromise line to the Pacific. Clingman's plan of equitable division bore a striking similarity to Buchanan's scheme. In Holsey's opinion, the North Carolina congressman was attempting to preempt the Missouri Compromise formula for the Whigs. If

Clingman succeeded in rallying his party behind the plan, he warned, he would cut the ground from under the Democrats in the upcoming presidential campaign *"and kill us off at the South with our own weapons."* [31]

Clingman's strategy of using equitable division as a weapon against the Southern Democrats and a formula for unifying his own party foundered on the refusal of the Northern Whigs to settle for anything less than the Wilmot Proviso. However, the truculence of his Northern colleagues on the territorial issue did nothing to diminish his partisan ardor. Instead, Clingman achieved notoriety during the Thirtieth Congress as one of the party's most vocal opponents of the Polk administration and the Mexican War.[32]

Clingman was especially miffed at the shabby treatment accorded Winfield Scott, the commander of the army that had captured Mexico City in September 1847. Since the beginning of the war, Polk had acted coolly toward the vainglorious Whig general, whose own ambition for the presidency was a matter of record. Despite that lack of cooperation, Old Fuss and Feathers had marched triumphantly from Vera Cruz to the Mexican capital, only to find himself dismissed as commanding general and hauled before a court of inquiry to answer charges arising from a dispute with two unruly subordinates. From the Whig viewpoint, Scott had been berated, hounded, and persecuted by an ungrateful Democratic president who was unwilling to allow a Whig to reap the military glory.[33]

Clingman played a leading role in the efforts of congressional Whigs to vindicate the conduct of Scott. Confident that the general would be completely exonerated if his official correspondence with the War Department were published, the North Carolina congressman introduced a resolution to that effect on 31 January 1848. When the administration failed to provide the documents immediately, he offered additional resolutions demanding to know why the materials were not forthcoming. Polk, who seems to have made a sincere effort to comply with Clingman's request, was deeply angered by the congressman's partisan behavior. His tactics, the president fumed in his diary, were "such as demagogues & little partisans will sometimes resort to."[34]

Contrary to Polk's expectations, the submission of the documents on 20 March 1848 did not "put an end to the party capital" that Clingman "expected to make by his resolution." Over the course of the following month, the Whig congressman repeatedly attacked the foreign policy of the Polk administration on the floor of the House, declaring that the war with Mexico had been "unconstitutionally and unnecessarily begun . . . [and] negligently managed by the Administration." At the same time, he lavishly praised the military exploits of Winfield Scott, sarcastically noting that "General Scott's whole crime consisted in his having made a campaign too brilliant and glorious."[35]

According to the *New York Tribune*, Clingman's "eloquent defence of Scott" and his "glowing eulogy upon his patriotic services" had given "great satisfaction to the Whigs, great discomfiture to the Loco Focos." While the congressman had stopped short of explicitly endorsing Scott for the Whig presidential nomination, it was no secret that he now favored the general over his principal rivals, Zachary Taylor and Henry Clay. Nor was it surprising that when Scott arrived at Port Elizabeth, New Jersey, a week before the Whig National Convention, the North Carolinian was standing on the dock waiting to be the first to shake his hand. By the time the convention assembled in Philadelphia on 7 June 1848, Clingman, who attended as an alternate delegate, had become the most prominent Southerner advocating Scott's claims for the presidency.[36]

Although Zachary Taylor had not been his first choice, Clingman readily endorsed his candidacy after the convention decided to pass over Scott. Old Rough-and-Ready carried North Carolina handily in the November election, winning an impressive 74 percent of the vote in the mountain district. The overall balance of parties in the Old North State was more accurately reflected in the August state elections. Whig gubernatorial nominee Charles Manly squeaked past Democrat David S. Reid by only nine hundred votes, and the two parties won an equal number of seats in the general assembly. The Whigs subsequently picked up two additional seats in by-elections, but their paper-thin majority did not bode well for George E. Badger, who was now seeking a full six-year term in the U.S. Senate.[37]

As the embattled incumbent fully realized, significant opposition to his reelection had manifested itself even within his own party. Badger had alienated many Whigs by his vote against the Clayton Compromise, which would have allowed the Supreme Court to settle the issue of slavery in the territories.[38] As displeasing as the senator's vote on the compromise may have been to some Whigs, the constitutional views underpinning it were anathema to the Democrats. In a speech before the Senate on 26 July 1848, Badger argued that slavery could not exist in the territories in the absence of positive legislation by Congress. While considerations of justice and fairness might dictate that Southerners be allowed to bring their property into the Mexican Cession, Congress was under no constitutional obligation to sanction the institution. Throughout the summer and fall of 1848, Badger was denounced regularly on the pages of the *North Carolina Standard* and other Democratic newspapers as a traitor to the South. In their view, practically any other Whig would be preferable to the hated incumbent.[39]

By the fall of 1848 Clingman had also become a bitter enemy of the senator, though for reasons unrelated to the issue of slavery. Eight years earlier, he had enthusiastically supported Badger for the U.S. Senate, and even in 1846 he had been reluctant to challenge him for the senatorial nomination. As with William A. Graham, however, Clingman's attitude toward Badger changed markedly once he became convinced the politician stood in the way of his own advancement. Shortly after Congress convened in December 1847, Clingman heard (or thought he heard) Badger remark that his cousin, Edward Stanly, should seek the governorship in 1848 to better position himself to take Mangum's place in the U.S. Senate should the veteran senator decide to retire in 1853. As one Whig congressman observed, "this disposing of offices so far ahead was not particularly agreeable to Clingman, who has aspirations himself." When Badger subsequently denied ever making such remarks, his disavowal triggered an angry response from Clingman, and relations between the two deteriorated steadily.[40]

Clingman's growing animosity toward Badger, together with his belief that the incumbent's unpopular views on the territorial question had made him vulnerable, induced him to consider entering the senatorial contest. Stopping at Raleigh on his way to Washington in late November, the congressman sounded out his prospects among the Whig legislators, only to discover that Badger's friends at the state capital had lined up enough votes to secure him the caucus nomination. For that reason, Clingman instructed his supporters not to place his name in nomination and advised them "to act as they preferred individually, with reference to attending the caucus." Three Whigs, including Clingman supporters Thomas W. Atkin and Henry Farmer, abstained from the party caucus and refused to be bound by its decision.[41]

Badger easily won the caucus nomination, but the defection of the three Whigs resulted in a deadlock in the general assembly that continued for more than a week. On the first ballot, taken on 12 December 1848, Badger received eighty-two votes, falling just one vote short of election. Not yet a formal candidate, Clingman garnered six votes, four of them from the Democrats. On the next ballot he picked up eight additional votes from the Democrats, who were probably supporting him in the hope of fomenting dissension among the Whigs. However, seventeen Democrats voted for Southern Rights Whig William B. Shepard, who had received no support on the first ballot.[42]

The Shepard boomlet alarmed one of Clingman's supporters, who wired the congressman that his old rival would certainly be elected unless he came immediately to Raleigh to present his own case. Bayles M. Edney, another Clingman ally, saw opportunity rather than danger in the willingness of so many Democrats to vote for a Southern Rights Whig. He, too, telegraphed Clingman to return to North Carolina, exulting that "we have the game in our own hands."[43] Enticed by the prospect of winning a prize that only shortly before had seemed beyond his reach, Clingman departed from the nation's capital in a state of high excitement. As his colleague David Outlaw reported, he even "spoke of taking . . . a box of pistols with him." While ignoring Outlaw's advice "not to go at all," Clingman apparently did heed his fellow Whig's admonition "to leave his pistols behind." The ensuing battle with Badger for the senatorship would prove to be vitriolic but, fortunately, bloodless.[44]

Three years earlier, Clingman had bitterly denounced James Graham for selling out his party for Democratic votes. Now that his own ambition was involved, he proceeded to engage in the same behavior he had previously condemned. Indeed, Clingman went considerably farther than Graham in accommodating the

Democrats. After the Democratic leaders in the general assembly made it clear that he could win substantial support from their party only by endorsing its positions on the major policy issues, the congressman responded with a remarkable letter that one Democratic editor characterized as "so highly satisfactory" that "it would hardly have been suspected by a stranger that he was a Whig!" [45]

Clingman's letter was actually a masterpiece of evasion and equivocation, meticulously crafted to attract Democratic support for his senatorial candidacy without alienating the Whig voters of his own congressional district. In regard to the economic issues that had traditionally divided the parties, he disavowed any desire to abolish the independent treasury, which the Polk administration had recently established as the fiscal agent for the federal government, or to dismantle the Walker tariff, which had drastically reduced the rates established by the Whigs in 1842. While he believed that "some alterations should be made" in the existing legislation, he was "not prepared to say to what extent these alterations should go." Clingman also equivocated on the issue of slavery in the territories, referring his Democratic interrogators to his speech of December 1847 for a full exposition of his views on that subject. [46]

Anyone familiar with that speech would have realized that Clingman actually shared Badger's belief that Congress had the authority to prohibit slavery in the territories. Unlike Badger, however, his constitutional reasoning also led him to conclude that any effort to exclude Southerners from *all* the territories would violate the principle of equitable division. Thus he was entirely consistent with his earlier position when he told the Democrats that the Wilmot Proviso was "as gross a violation of the Constitution as the Government could possibly commit" and declared that its passage "would justify the Southern States in resisting its execution by all means in their power." Although not entirely palatable to the Democrats, Clingman's stance on the territorial issue was certainly preferable to Badger's. Moreover, his willingness to accommodate the Democrats on partisan issues unrelated to slavery established him as a more attractive alternative than Shepard, whose outspoken Southern Rights views had previously commended him to some members of that party.

While some Democratic legislators remained unpersuaded, a majority threw their support behind Clingman on the third ballot. Badger received eighty-two votes, once again falling one vote short of a majority. This time, however, Clingman garnered forty-eight votes, all but two of them from Democrats. Despairing of Badger's success, a few Whigs advocated the election of an out-and-out Democrat in preference to a renegade like Clingman. Former congressman Edward Stanly, who was now representing Beaufort County in the House of Commons, had a better idea. Although a kinsman and strong supporter of Badger, he placed the name of David L. Swain in nomination and urged those westerners who had previously been supporting Clingman to break the stalemate by elevating one of their section's most distinguished statesmen to the U.S. Senate. While most legislators continued to hold firm for Badger and Clingman on the fourth ballot, Swain received five votes from the Democrats and four from the Whigs.[47]

The smallness of Swain's vote belied its significance. The former governor was the only Whig besides Clingman and Shepard who had thus far received any support from the Democrats. That even five Democrats were willing to break ranks meant Swain would surely be elected if the Whigs finally despaired of Badger's election and united behind his candidacy. In virtually every respect, Swain was an ideal compromise choice. His thirteen-year tenure as president of the University of North Carolina had insulated him from the rough-and-tumble of partisan politics, and he commanded the respect of both parties. Clingman himself had actively promoted Swain for the Senate in the general assembly of 1840–41 and had remained on good terms with him since. Swain's candidacy thus presented legislators in both parties with an attractive way out of the imbroglio in which they found themselves.

Clingman, however, was well aware that the election of his friend Swain would be far more damaging to his own long-term political prospects than would the elevation of his enemy Badger. The principal rationale for Clingman's candidacy was that western North Carolina was entitled to a representative in the U.S. Senate. As one anti-Clingman Whig later pointed out, if Swain had been elected, "the Extreme West would have been fully and for a long time supplied," and Clingman's senatorial ambitions would have been placed indefinitely "on the shelf." Confronted by the likelihood of a massive movement of Whigs toward Swain, Clingman instructed Farmer to switch his vote to Badger, thereby enabling the incumbent to win reelection on the fifth ballot.[48]

That final act of desperation on Clingman's part did nothing to mollify the Whigs. Instead, party leaders were furious at his disloyal and obstructive behavior, particularly after the details of his correspondence with the Democrats became known. "Clingman has rendered himself perfectly odious to the Whigs," wrote one prominent member of that party, "while he has not conciliated the Democrats." Gov. Charles Manly was even more blunt about Clingman's political future, proclaiming that he was "*as good as dead* in No[rth] Car[olin]a."[49]

Those predictions of Clingman's imminent political demise would prove premature. From the perspective of December 1848, however, it seemed that the congressman had taken a bold gamble and had disastrously lost. Clingman had calculated that he might garner enough support as an "independent candidate" to win the senatorship in defiance of the Whig caucus.[50] That calculation had been based on two assumptions: first, that some Whigs who were not initially favorable to his candidacy eventually could be persuaded to desert Badger, and second, that the Democrats would give him virtually unanimous support if the choice were narrowed to him and Badger. Both assumptions proved false. No Whig apart from Atkin and Farmer ever voted for Clingman, and he never came close to re-ceiving unanimous support from the Democrats.[51]

The Whigs were shocked, as well as angered, by Clingman's willingness to sell his political soul to the Democrats for a seat in the U.S. Senate. Until then, the congressman had enjoyed a reputation not only as a loyal Whig but as one of the most partisan of Whigs. What the Whigs did not realize until December 1848 was that Clingman's fidelity to their party was not nearly as intense as his ambition for the senatorship. Up to that point, circumstances had never forced him to choose between party loyalty and personal advancement. Indeed, until then a zealous de-votion to the Whig cause had seemed the surest means of promoting his own po-litical fortunes. Clingman's rabidly partisan behavior during the Twenty-Eighth and Thirtieth Congresses, his vigorous efforts on behalf of his party's guber-natorial and presidential candidates, and even his vote against the gag rule were all designed to demonstrate to party leaders that he was a loyal Whig and, there-fore, a worthy candidate for high office.

After 1848, however, Clingman's ambition took him in a different direction. As long as he remained in the House of Representatives, he would continue to de-pend upon the support of his heavily Whig constituency. However, his hopes for a seat in the U.S. Senate now rested almost entirely on the Democrats. What en-sued over the next several years was a delicate balancing act, in which Clingman intoned the rhetoric of Southern Rights to curry favor with the Democrats, while employing the vocabulary of "western rights" to maintain support among the Whig voters at home.

In his letter to the Democrats, Clingman had based his claims to the senator-ship on his opposition to the Wilmot Proviso and on his belief that "the South will need all the strength in the next Senate of the United States that it can possibly have under the Constitution." However, in the circular he sent to his own con-stituents two weeks after the election, Clingman played down the Southern Rights issue. Instead, he emphasized the same theme that had been sounded two years earlier in the "Fair Play" letter—that he had sought the senatorship in or-der to assert the rights of the west to a "share in the public honors."[52]

Repeating a point he had been making since at least 1840, Clingman reminded his constituents that the massive Whig majorities from the "western reserve" had invariably supplied the winning margin in statewide elections. Yet when the time came to distribute the political rewards, the "central clique" at Raleigh "most modestly make arrangements for dividing among their favorites all the offices in the State." Borrowing the arguments made by William B. Shepard eight years earlier, Clingman pointed to the legislative caucus as the instrument employed by the "central managers" to accomplish their objectives. Through threats, promises, and appeals to the generosity, vanity, and party loyalty of the legisla-tors, the "wire-workers" at the state capital invariably succeeded in nominating the individual of their choice "just as the dullest gamester, when he has the privilege of shuffling the pack to his liking, is able to turn up a particular card."[53]

Clingman did not focus his wrath exclusively on the Whig leaders in Raleigh. He also accused those western legislators who had voted for Badger of deliberately misrepresenting their constituents. The congressman admonished the voters of the mountain district henceforth to choose "such men as will regard themselves as *your* representatives, rather than the servants of the central managers—men, in short, who will dare to tell them that if they want *white slaves* they must look for them elsewhere than in the Western reserve." Should the legislators thus elected subsequently "be cajoled or intimidated into an abandonment of your rights," the voters should "beat them with many stripes, and set earmarks upon them, so that they may be incapable of deceiving again."[54]

Not surprisingly, Clingman's address was roundly denounced by leading Whigs throughout the state, who condemned him for recklessly "fan[ning] the flames of sectional jealousy" in order to gratify his own ambition.[55] The Whig legislators from the mountain district were particularly offended by Clingman's claim that they had misrepresented their constituents. Four of them subsequently published statements asserting that they had openly expressed their preference for Badger before the legislative elections. The lawmakers also denied that they had been manipulated by the party leaders in Raleigh. Instead, they had "acted under a high sense of public duty and were governed throughout by the most patriotic motives and sincerest desire to promote the public good."[56]

Although Clingman's critics might deprecate the vain and self-serving character of his letter, it proved to be a tremendously effective piece of propaganda. Since the emergence of organized parties in the 1830s an undeniable tension had existed between the exigencies of partisan politics, which necessitated the establishment of central committees and other mechanisms of control and direction, and the tenets of traditional republican ideology, which had inculcated a distrust of centralized authority while placing a high value on individual autonomy. Clingman's scathing denunciation of the "central managers" and his invocation of the values of independence and self-respect tapped a vein of sentiment that had deep roots in the political culture of antebellum North Carolina.[57]

Clingman was not the first North Carolinian to charge that his party was controlled by a clique of central managers at the state capital. On the other hand, no Tar Heel would prove more successful in promoting an image of himself as the defender of individual autonomy against the dictates of central authority. Although Clingman's conduct during the senatorial election had alienated many leading Whigs in the mountain district, none dared come forward to challenge him in the congressional campaign of 1849. Despite the lack of organized opposition, turnout declined only slightly from the previous election, and Clingman's own vote increased by an impressive 59 percent.[58]

Clingman's triumphant reelection to a third term in the U.S. House of Representatives demonstrated that his crusade against the "central managers" had struck a responsive chord among his constituents. As long as he presented himself to the voters as the "champion of the west" and the staunch opponent of the "central clique," the congressman remained unassailable in his mountain stronghold. Not until the focus of debate shifted from the rights of westerners in North Carolina to the rights of Southerners in the nation would there be a significant erosion in his Whig support.

6 Champion of the South

The first session of the Thirty-First Congress, which began in December 1849 and continued until October 1850, was, as Clingman later remembered, "not only the longest known in the history of the government, but . . . also the most interesting and eventful." When Congress began its deliberations that fateful winter, the controversy over slavery in the territories was threatening to destroy the nation. By the time it adjourned the following autumn, the outstanding sectional differences had been adjusted, at least temporarily, through the passage of the Compromise of 1850. It was also during that historic session that Thomas Lanier Clingman, who until then had been regarded as a moderate on the slavery issue, acquired a reputation as a fire eater "rival[ing] both Yancey and Calhoun as the most proslavery and prosouthern of antebellum congressmen." [1]

Clingman's first step in the course that would eventually establish him as one of the South's foremost champions had actually been taken a year earlier, after the Democrats in the North Carolina General Assembly had made it clear that their support in the senatorial election was contingent on his willingness to take a sounder position than Badger on Southern Rights. The congressman had immediately risen to the occasion, denouncing the Wilmot Proviso as a "gross . . . violation of the Constitution" and placing his claim to Badger's seat on the ground that "the South will need all the strength in the next Senate . . . that it can possibly have." Understandably, some Democrats expressed skepticism about the depth of Clingman's newfound commitment to Southern Rights. "Looking at Mr. Clingman's course, heretofore, on the slavery question," said the *Fayetteville North Carolinian,* "we are inclined to consider his opinions or pledges volunteered at this juncture, as the promptings of his ambition (which is inordinate) rather than those of his candid judgment."[2]

Clingman's actions after his return to Washington in January 1849 did nothing to allay those Democratic suspicions. Alarmed by the prospect that Congress might move to abolish slavery in the District of Columbia, John C. Calhoun had called on Southerners of both parties to join together to devise a plan of action. Clingman was still in North Carolina when the Southern caucus first assembled on 22 December 1848, but he was present at its next meeting on 15 January. Along with other Whigs, he voted to table the strong Southern Rights address prepared by Calhoun. When that motion failed, he joined the Whigs and a few Democrats in a successful move to refer it back to committee for modification. At the final meeting of the caucus a week later, he supported a resolution by Alexander Stephens declaring it "inexpedient at this time for any Address to be published."[3]

Clingman's behavior in the Southern caucus indicated that he still considered himself a Whig in national politics, despite his break with the North Carolina Whigs. However, even as he was assuring Secretary of State John M. Clayton of his readiness "to give some support to Old Zack if he needs a lift occasionally," Clingman was expressing displeasure with the patronage policies of the Taylor administration. A few months before the presidential election, the congressman had voiced concern that the "central clique" would attempt to secure a cabinet position for Badger and an attractive foreign mission for his cousin Edward Stanly, thus "absorb[ing] about all that North Carolina can hope to receive for her share of the offices abroad." Although Clingman's attitude toward the "clique" often bordered on paranoia, Badger was in fact working hard to obtain an important diplomatic post for his kinsman. After learning in June that the senator was lobbying for Stanly's appointment as minister to Spain, Clingman threatened to "spoil" Clayton as he "had done the central clique at Raleigh" if Stanly received the commission. The eventual selection of William A. Graham for the Spanish mission did nothing to mollify him, since in his mind his former mentor was as closely associated with the central managers as were Badger and Stanly.[4]

Meanwhile, Clingman's efforts to secure a prestigious appointment for one of his own supporters were also proving unsuccessful. The congressman was anxious to obtain the Glasgow mission for Bayles M. Edney as a reward for his services during the recent senatorial contest. Although a competent lawyer, the rough-hewn Edney was considered by many North Carolina Whigs to be unsuitable for an important diplomatic post. Moreover, his efforts to obstruct the election of Badger had done nothing to endear him to party leaders. The eventual appointment of Edney to an insignificant consulate at Pernambuco only aggravated Clingman further. "You have made a great mistake in this instance," he scolded Clayton. "The expectation was so general that he would receive a desirable appointment that much surprise was expressed at the result." During the winter of 1849–50, Clingman continued to lobby on behalf of the Glasgow appointment and even brought Edney to Washington to present his claims personally. Repeated failure intensified his disillusionment with the Taylor administration.[5]

Clingman's growing estrangement from his party was compounded by the intransigence of the Northern Whigs on the territorial issue. The congressman was well aware that most of the votes for the Wilmot Proviso during the previous session had been cast by members of his own party. In 1848 the Northern Whigs had also been instrumental in defeating the Clayton Compromise, which would have allowed the Supreme Court to decide the status of slavery in the Mexican Cession. Clingman himself had supported the compromise when it came to a vote in the House, but Northerners persuaded Alexander Stephens and seven other Southern Whigs to join them in tabling the measure. According to Clingman, the Northern Whigs had promised Stephens and the others that they would "aid us in passing a liberal and just measure" once the presidential campaign was over, only to renege on those promises after the election. Indeed, by the fall of 1849 "the entire Whig delegation from the North were . . . pledged to the abolition of slavery in the District of Columbia, and the application of the Wilmot proviso to all the Mexican territory."[6]

The determination of the Northern Whigs to stand by the Wilmot Proviso did not make Clingman any more favorably inclined toward the Northern Democrats. During an extensive tour of the North in the summer and early fall of 1849, he discovered that the Democrats were just as unreliable on the territorial issue as the Whigs. Demoralized by their showing in the recent presidential election, Northern Democrats had abandoned Lewis Cass's doctrine of popular sovereignty and "were not unwilling that the Wilmot proviso, &c., should be passed and presented to General Taylor for his signature." In Clingman's opinion, the bipartisan support for the proviso among Northern legislators portended its almost certain passage.[7]

Since the beginning of the territorial crisis, Southerners had warned that the prohibition of slavery in the Mexican Cession would be grounds for disunion. In October 1849, while Clingman was still traveling in the North, a convention in Mississippi issued a call for a meeting of all the slave-holding states to take place in Nashville the following June. Five other Southern states subsequently voted to send delegates to the Nashville Convention. Convinced that the enactment of anti-Southern legislation would "dissolve the Union within six weeks after the meeting of Congress," Clingman moved to head off the secessionists "and give a permanent peace to the Union" by issuing a stern warning to the Northern public.[8]

Clingman was joined in that effort by Democratic senator Henry S. Foote of Mississippi. The two legislators agreed to exchange letters for publication in the Washington newspapers. Foote wrote the first communication. After referring to the "erroneous impression widely prevalent in the North that the South is neither in *earnest* nor *united*" in defense of its rights, he asked Clingman as a "prominent member of the whig party" to express his opinion regarding "the probable action of your political associates in the South, should the present sectional contest be pushed to extremities." Clingman responded that the Whigs were just as determined as the Democrats to maintain "an unbroken front . . . in the struggle for the preservation of the rights and liberties of the white race of the South." If an effort was made to exclude slavery from the territories, he was certain that Southerners would resist with an intensity "commensurate with the violence of the attack."[9]

First published in the *National Intelligencer* and the *Washington Union,* the Clingman-Foote correspondence was subsequently reprinted in newspapers across the nation. Antislavery organs such as the *National Era* denounced the exchange as a "declaration of war" against the Union. However, the thrust of the correspondence was moderate rather than extremist. Although unequivocal in asserting that the South would resist any attack on slavery, Clingman was intentionally vague as to the form that resistance might take, and he avoided making any direct threat of secession. In the absence of compelling evidence to the contrary, Clingman's claim that his communication with Foote was intended to preserve the Union, and not to hasten its destruction, must be taken at its word.[10]

Clingman's letter received high praise from the Democrats in the Old North State, who affirmed that the congressman had taken "the true view of this absorbing question." That opinion was not shared by Thomas Ritchie of the *Washington Union.* Mindful of Clingman's partisan behavior during the previous Congress, the Democratic editor wondered aloud whether Clingman's concern for the rights of the South would give way to partisanship once Congress reassembled. In Ritchie's view, his vote in the upcoming contest for the House speakership would provide the answer. Robert C. Winthrop's conduct as Speaker during the previous Congress had conclusively established the Massachusetts Whig as "a thorough-paced Wilmot Provisoist." Should Clingman again be "found voting for Mr. Winthrop . . . we will know where to place him, and that place will be in the front rank of those who have acted falsely and treacherously to the people of the South."[11]

Clingman's course during the first weeks of the Thirty-First Congress seemed to confirm Ritchie's skepticism. At the Whig congressional caucus held on 1 December 1849, the North Carolinian placed himself squarely in the camp of the

party regulars. After Robert Toombs introduced a resolution formally commit-
ting the party to oppose the Wilmot Proviso and the abolition of the slave trade
in the District of Columbia, Clingman spoke against the idea and importuned his
Georgia colleague to withdraw the motion. After the resolution was defeated,
Toombs, Alexander Stephens, and four other Southerners stormed out of the
caucus room. Clingman remained with the other Whigs and joined them in nominating Winthrop for a second term as Speaker.[12]

It would take the House of Representatives three weeks and sixty-three ballots
to elect a presiding officer. Although the Whigs enjoyed a nominal majority, the
refusal of the six "Southern impracticables" and the Whig Free Soilers to support
Winthrop prevented him from winning a majority over Howell Cobb, the Democratic nominee. At the same time, the opposition of the Democratic Free Soilers, along with two radical South Carolina Democrats, frustrated Cobb's own efforts to secure a majority. This pattern of the two sectional extremes combining
together against the moderate center would be repeated numerous times throughout the Thirty-First Congress.[13]

Instead of aligning himself with the "impracticables," Clingman loyally supported the party nominee on the first thirty-nine ballots. After Winthrop's name
was finally withdrawn, he voted at various times for Toombs, Stephens, and several other Southern Whigs. In order to end the stalemate, both parties finally
agreed that a mere plurality would be sufficient to elect. Winthrop's name was
again placed in nomination, and Clingman joined the bulk of his party in voting
for him. Toombs, Stephens, and three other Southern Whigs remained intransigent, and Cobb won the election by a three-vote margin.[14]

During the debates that accompanied the protracted balloting, one Southern
Democrat explicitly called attention to the inconsistency between Clingman's
Southern Rights rhetoric and his actual behavior. In the course of a speech denouncing Winthrop as a friend of the Wilmot Proviso, Andrew Johnson remarked
that North Carolina had not been "so forward as some of the States" in defending the rights of the South. Clingman immediately sprang to his feet, declaring
that "if there should be a necessity for action to protect the rights and liberties
of the South, no State would be more forward than she." Johnson retorted that
Clingman's votes for Winthrop belied that bold assertion. "Why not imitate the
action and example of the gentleman from Georgia," he taunted, referring to
Toombs. The congressman from North Carolina was willing to give lip service to
the cause of Southern Rights, sneered Johnson, "yet when he came to vote, it was
quite another thing. . . . [He] professed one thing and did another."[15]

With his prospects for a Senate seat now in the hands of the Democrats, Clingman could not allow the imputation that he was more interested in serving the
Whig party than in defending the rights of the South to go unchallenged. Ironically, in light of the perception among some Democrats that he was all sound
and no substance, Clingman chose to demonstrate his commitment to Southern

Rights by a brilliant display of fire-eating rhetoric. He apparently began working on his speech shortly after the exchange with Johnson. According to David Outlaw, Clingman was "exceedingly anxious to make a speech, so much so, he can scarcely contain himself." Outlaw wanted to believe that his colleague's decision to stake out an advanced position on Southern Rights "was actuated by patriotic motives." Nonetheless, he could not help concluding that a "desire to promote his aspirations to a seat in the Senate of the U. States, is at the bottom, and that all considerations of the welfare, peace and happiness of the country are subordinate to this grand moving principle." Numerous other Whigs would soon echo that sentiment.[16]

Clingman's opportunity to speak finally came on 22 January 1850, a day after the House received a message from President Taylor recommending that California and New Mexico be granted immediate statehood. The congressman began by expressing "confidence in the judgment, integrity and patriotism of the President," but he then went on to argue that Taylor's plan would not resolve the fundamental problem. Only a short time before, he said, he had also assumed that the admission of California and New Mexico would quiet the agitation of the anti-slavery extremists. However, "a few months' travel in the interior of the North has changed my opinion. Such is now the condition of public sentiment there, that the making of the Mexican territory all free, in any mode, would be regarded as an anti-slavery triumph, and would accelerate the general movement against us."[17]

In his earlier speeches Clingman had pronounced the majority of the Northern people to be sound on the slavery issue, and he had dismissed the abolitionists as an insignificant fringe group. Now, however, he placed his emphasis on the "force and extent of the present anti-slavery movement of the North," and he charged that the actions of both parties in that section were "purely wanton, or originating in malice towards the South." After reciting the usual litany of Southern grievances, Clingman offered some specific remedies that might resolve the territorial crisis. The Missouri Compromise line might be extended through California to the Pacific Ocean, with slavery recognized in all the territory south of that line. Or Congress might allow California to come into the Union as a free state with its proposed boundaries and then adjust the Compromise line to run along the northern, rather than southern, border of Missouri. In any event, the North would have to demonstrate its good faith by making some "substantial" concession to the South and "not cheat us by a mere empty form, without reality."[18]

What made Clingman's speech so memorable was not his enumeration of the options that might bring an end to the sectional controversy but his calm and dispassionate discussion of the possibility of disunion. Already, he said, "many of our people, regard . . . a dissolution of the Union as the inevitable result of this aggression." Although Southerners were willing to remain in the Union "upon the principles of the Constitution," they would not allow themselves to be "degraded and enslaved." "We do not love you, people of the North, well enough to become your *slaves*. . . . Do us justice and we continue to stand with you; attempt to trample on us, and we separate." [19]

The Washington correspondent of the *Richmond Times* was not far off the mark when he characterized Clingman's speech as "the most startling one ever delivered in Congress." Its chilling impact was amplified by the calm and deliberate manner in which it was presented. Avoiding any display of histrionics, the congressman spoke of the dissolution of the Union in a tone of resignation more than anger.[20] The startling contrast "between the calmness of its style and the ferocity of its meaning" gave the address a peculiar force that riveted the attention of the audience. While most congressional speeches were punctuated by a continual chatter from the floors and galleries, in this instance "not a foot fell nor [was] a whisper heard during the time he was speaking." Indeed, marveled one observer, "I [have] never seen any man, Representative or Senator, who so uninterruptedly enchained his listeners." [21]

Another consideration that gave special significance to the address was that Clingman represented a small-farm district in which slavery was only a marginal institution. As the *Charleston Mercury* pointed out, the mountains of North Carolina contained "perhaps fewer slaves than in any other Congressional District in the South." That its representative could take so forthright a stand in defense of the South demonstrated "how baseless are the calculations of those who have supposed that it is only the large slaveholders who care to resist the aggressions of Abolitionists, and only they who would shrink from being placed on a level with emancipated negroes." [22]

Although the *Mercury* proclaimed that "Mr. Clingman represents truly the spirit of his constituents," others were more skeptical. David Outlaw doubted whether the congressman's speech would "be approved by his constituents, about one of whom in thirty is a slaveholder." The *Asheville Messenger,* now under the control of Clingman's political enemies, agreed that the speech was "rather hot for the mountains." Predictably, the address received mixed reviews from the North Carolina presses, with the Democrats praising Clingman's defense of Southern Rights and the Whigs criticizing his candid talk of disunion.[23]

While opinions about the merits of the speech might differ, few would have denied that its author had "acquired for himself by his last speech a National reputation that no man of his age has in this Union." As David Outlaw more cynically put it, Clingman had brilliantly succeeded "in accomplishing one object dear to his heart, notoriety." Indeed, his notoriety now transcended the boundaries of his own country, as European newspapers began taking notice of the South's bold new champion. The *London Chronicle,* for example, lauded the North Carolinian as a "clear-headed Southern politician," commended his speech for its "plain and simple language," and claimed that it was "universally deemed in America to have materially altered the chances of the controversy." [24]

The thirty-seven-year-old congressman's ego, already sufficiently large, received an additional boost from the publicity generated by his address. "Since

Clingman made his speech," remarked Outlaw, "he evidently considers himself a great man." James Cathcart Johnston, a Chowan County planter who was visiting the nation's capital, acidly observed that "the celebrated Mr. Clingman . . . seemed to be full to over flowing of himself, talking as if he were another Sampson who would pull down by his individual strength the pillars that support the Union." Johnston's friend William S. Pettigrew agreed that the congressman, who "no doubt has vanity enough for fifty men," now regarded himself as "an immensely great man among the ultras of the South." [25]

Clingman's new status as Champion of the South did not go unchallenged. Among his most persistent critics was Edward Stanly, the Whig representative from the New Bern district. Although slaves constituted two-fifths of his district's population, Stanly's strident unionism was almost as intense as Clingman's bellicose Southernism. In a long speech delivered on 6 March 1850, Stanly took deliberate aim at the inconsistencies in his adversary's position. He was particularly struck by the incongruity between Clingman's statement that the Wilmot Proviso was unconstitutional and his earlier affirmation that Congress had exclusive jurisdiction over slavery in the territories. "I cannot understand," he exclaimed, "how these views can exist in the same mind at one and the same time. . . . It looks as if one part of the speech was addressed to a Whig Buncombe and another part to a Democratic Buncombe." [26]

Clingman shot back with an angry letter to the *Washington Republic,* in which he accused Stanly of deliberately distorting his position by "selecting parts of paragraphs, and sometimes parts of sentences" and then quoting them out of context. The congressman also challenged the *Republic*'s characterization of him, Toombs, and other militant Southerners as "ultra politicians." The genuine ultras, he affirmed, were those politicians who demanded that the territories be either all slave or all free. "Those men who, standing between these two opposite extremes, are willing that there should be an equitable division of the territory, may well claim to be the moderate men." [27]

Clingman also made an effort in his letter to the *Republic* to put some distance between his own position and that of Robert B. Rhett, William L. Yancey, and other fire eaters who were clamoring for the immediate withdrawal of the South from the Union. While acknowledging the determination of Southerners to resist any infringement on their rights, he emphasized that the preferred method of resistance was parliamentary rather than extraconstitutional. "Under our obligations to support the Constitution of the United States, all means consistent with its provisions should be exhausted before there should be a recommendation to appeal to our rights above it." [28]

By implication, Clingman was also disavowing the argument advanced by Calhoun and other Southern Democrats that the U.S. Constitution was merely a compact among the states and that secession, therefore, was a legally valid remedy. Instead, he based his own case for resistance on an entirely different principle—the South's prerogative, as a last resort, "to appeal to our rights above" the Constitution. That so-called right of revolution, which the thirteen colonies had invoked in their struggle against Great Britain, was acknowledged by all Americans to be an appropriate remedy in cases of extreme oppression.

To modern readers, the debate between the proponents of the "right of secession" and the advocates of the "right of revolution" might seem a hollow controversy about a meaningless abstraction. For antebellum Southerners, however, the practical implications of the two competing viewpoints were quite different. For those who believed that secession was a constitutional remedy, it followed that a state might peaceably withdraw from the Union whenever it believed that the terms of the original compact had been violated. On the other hand, Southerners who invoked the right of revolution regarded disunion as an extraconstitutional option that could be justified only in cases of severe and intolerable oppression. They acknowledged, moreover, that those who resorted to the right of revolution could not expect their oppressors to acquiesce peacefully. Like the thirteen colonies, they most likely would have to fight in order to vindicate their rights. As the events following Lincoln's election in 1860 would graphically reveal, that acknowledgment made the Southern revolutionists considerably more inclined than their secessionist counterparts to search for alternatives to disunion.[29]

Despite his efforts to dissociate himself from more radical fire eaters like Rhett and Yancey, Clingman's strident rhetoric strained his relations with Clay, Webster, and other Whig leaders in Congress. Clay, who had recently returned to the U.S. Senate after a seven-year absence, was displeased by Clingman's correspondence with Foote and by his association with Toombs and the other Whig "impracticables." Nonetheless, the two Whigs, who both resided at the National Hotel, maintained a cordial social relationship and kept a "constant communication" in regard to Clay's compromise efforts. Relations with Daniel Webster were considerably more tense, notwithstanding Clingman's praise for his speech of 7 March. The Massachusetts senator icily informed him that he would not associate "with gentlemen who maintain such extreme views," and the two Whigs remained unreconciled until shortly before Webster's death.[30]

Clingman, in the words of one observer, had now placed himself "on the balancing point between the two great parties," and speculation about his impending defection to the Democrats was rife in the nation's capital.[31] It was by no means certain, however, that the Democrats would warmly embrace the errant Whig. Some party leaders continued to maintain that the congressman was all talk and no action. In commenting on his fire-eating speech of 22 January, for example, Thomas Ritchie could not resist reminding the readers of the *Washington Union* that Clingman had also supported Robert C. Winthrop, a "thoroughgoing Abolitionist," for Speaker of the House. Several influential presses in North Carolina also expressed skepticism about the maverick congressman's enthusiasm for Southern Rights. "We want no hypocrites to join us," thundered the *Fayetteville North Carolinian*. "So far as we are concerned, we have no faith in Mr. Clingman's sincerity in politics. . . . Unless Mr. Clingman can assure the 'locofocos' that he has renounced 'whiggery,' and sees its errors, and is sincerely penitent, we shall oppose taking him into the democratic church." [32]

For many Democrats, the litmus test for Clingman's sincerity would come with his vote on the compromise package being fashioned by Henry Clay. On 29 January 1850 the Kentucky senator had introduced a series of proposals designed to serve as the basis of a comprehensive settlement of the points at issue between the North and the South. Clay's resolutions provided for (1) the immediate admission of California into the Union as a free state; (2) the organization of the remainder of the Mexican Cession as territories without reference to slavery, according to the principle of congressional nonintervention; (3) the cession by Texas of most of the disputed border area to New Mexico in return for federal assumption of that state's outstanding debts; (4) the passage of a more effective fugitive slave law; and (5) the abolition of the slave trade in the District of Columbia.[33]

Within the North Carolina congressional delegation, most of the controversy centered on the first three points of the package. The Democrats and a majority of Whigs opposed granting statehood to California unless its southern border was drawn at the Missouri Compromise line. North Carolina Democrats also opposed Clay's idea of organizing the remaining territories according to the principle of nonintervention. Like popular sovereignty, nonintervention was an ambiguous doctrine susceptible to different sectional interpretations. Its Southern adherents believed that nonintervention meant that both the local and the national legislatures would refrain from interfering with slavery during the territorial phase. Its Northern devotees argued that nonintervention applied to Congress alone and did not preclude a territorial legislature from excluding slavery prior to statehood.[34]

North Carolina Democrats distrusted nonintervention and demanded, instead, an extension of the Missouri Compromise line to the Pacific and an explicit acknowledgment of the right of Southerners to carry slaves into territories south of that line. Most of the state's Whig congressmen also preferred an extension of the compromise line over nonintervention, but they were willing to accept the latter if they could not get the former. The Texas boundary question was closely tied to the territorial issue. Tar Heel Democrats objected to transferring fifty thousand square miles from a slave state to a territory where the status of slavery would be indeterminate. They would consent to an exchange only if they were assured that slaveholders would have the right to bring their property into New Mexico.

During the spring and early summer of 1850, no one could be certain as to how Clingman would vote. Outlaw believed that despite his avowed distaste for nonintervention, his colleague would "probably recover his senses sufficiently to go for" Clay's proposals.[35] Clingman's attitude toward the compromise was probably affected by the outcome of the North Carolina state elections in early August, which resulted in a stunning defeat for the Whigs in both the gubernatorial and legislative races. While the congressman reportedly "exulted" over the outcome, he must have realized that his prospects for winning Democratic support in his next bid for the Senate would not be advanced merely by rejoicing over their victory. Although an election was not scheduled to take place until 1852, the possibility that Mangum or Badger might take a position in the Fillmore administration (Taylor had died on 9 July) meant that the newly elected general assembly might well find itself selecting a replacement. In that event, Clingman's own chances for election would depend upon a clear separation from the Whigs on the compromise issue.[36]

During the first three weeks of August, all the compromise measures except the District of Columbia bill passed the Senate and were sent to the House of Representatives. The Texas boundary and New Mexico territorial bills, combined into a "little omnibus," were the first to be considered. On 29 August Clingman introduced an amendment that would have divided California at the Missouri Compromise line and created a new territory called Colorado consisting of the land south of that line together with the portion of New Mexico lying west of the Sierra Madre. Speaking in support of his proposition, he attacked the doctrine of nonintervention and expressed confidence that Southerners would bring their slaves into the Colorado territory, if allowed to do so.[37]

Clingman's amendment attracted widespread support among Southerners, including seven of North Carolina's nine congressmen. Nonetheless, the House rejected it by a vote of 69 to 130. After failing to secure the adoption of his own plan, Clingman joined the Democrats from North Carolina and the Deep South in voting against the Texas–New Mexico bill. He was the only Southern Whig to do so. Despite their fiery rhetoric, Toombs and the other Whig "impracticables" ultimately cast their votes in favor of the compromise, as did Andrew Johnson and the majority of Democrats from the upper South. By his vote against a key provision in the compromise package, Clingman had clearly aligned himself with the most extreme defenders of Southern Rights.[38]

According to the Whigs, Clingman and the other opponents of the compromise had voted "against the wishes of a large majority of the People of North Carolina." The congressman's former "ultra Whig" allies in the mountain district led the chorus of abuse, lauding the compromise as a victory for the South and characterizing his vote against it as a vote against the Union.[39] After the adjournment of Congress, Clingman responded to those charges in a series of debates with compromise supporters in Asheville, Rutherfordton, Marion, and other locations in the mountain region. Lambasting the compromise proposals as "bills of surrender," he claimed that the settlement would only stimulate the North to further aggression.[40]

Growing indications that many Southerners were willing to accept the Compromise of 1850 as a "final settlement" of the sectional differences did nothing to modify Clingman's intransigent attitude. Speaking to the House on 15 February 1851, he denounced nonintervention as a measure that would exclude slavery from the Mexican Cession just as effectively as the Wilmot Proviso, and he laid the blame for the passage of the compromise on "the action of Southern men, who by their votes consented that this section of the Union should be excluded" from the territories. Once again, the congressman raised the ominous specter of disunion. "Heretofore," he noted, "our people had been accustomed to think of the Union with a sort of religious reverence. . . . The agitation here, and the discussions attendant on it, have produced a great revolution in the sentiments of our population. . . . They no longer rest on the Union as the solid rock of safety. I rejoice that it is so."[41]

Clingman's nemesis Edward Stanly refused to allow those belligerent remarks to go unchallenged. On 3 March 1851 he confronted his colleague on the floor of the House and bluntly announced his intention "to controvert your opinion" just as he had done during the previous session. An angry exchange of words ensued, after which Clingman sprang upon Stanly's desk, struck him on the forehead with one hand, and grabbed him by the back of the neck with the other. Friends intervened and separated the two men. An adjustment was later reached, whereby both members agreed to retract the "offensive and insulting expressions used by them in the order in which they were spoken."[42]

Stanly's "scrimmage" with Clingman proved to be the first move in a concerted effort on the part of the North Carolina Whigs to oust the recalcitrant congressman from his seat. In May 1851 Burgess Gaither, a former Speaker of the state senate, announced himself as a "Union Whig" candidate for Congress in opposition to Clingman. Gaither received the endorsement of the *Asheville Messenger* and virtually every other Whig newspaper in North Carolina.[43] The one exception was the *Asheville News*—a newspaper Clingman himself had set up in 1849 under the editorship of Thomas W. Atkin, the former proprietor of the *Messenger*. Although nominally Whig in its politics, the *News* devoted itself primarily to promoting the political fortunes of Clingman and to advocating radical changes in the state constitution. Atkin was ably assisted by Marcus Erwin, a young lawyer who had served briefly as coeditor of the *Messenger* and who temporarily took over the editorship of the *News* in May 1851.[44]

Clingman and Gaither waged a vigorous campaign, debating each other at numerous locations throughout the mountain district. Gaither presented himself to the voters as a staunch supporter of the Union, accused Clingman of misrepresenting his district on the compromise issue, and tried hard to pin the secessionist label on him. The congressman refused to retreat from his opposition to the compromise settlement, but he cunningly distanced himself from the more extreme fire eaters in the lower South by insisting that his strident rhetoric on the floor of the House had been merely a "pious fraud to alarm Northern men" and to prevent them from driving the South to drastic action. In fact, said Clingman, "he heartily concurred with his opponent" on the necessity of preserving the Union.[45]

Gaither was also unsuccessful in drawing Clingman into a debate over the power of the federal government to coerce a seceding state back into the Union. The Whig challenger unequivocally enunciated his own position, avowing that if "South Carolina attempted to secede, he would vote for giving the President men and money to force her back into the Union." Clingman, however, refused to swallow the bait. Declining either to repudiate or to endorse Gaither's views, he asserted that "he would leave that an open question until the event happened, and that his course would then be governed by circumstances."[46]

Gaither proved no match for his seasoned antagonist. Notwithstanding his solid support from the Whig establishment, the challenger won a disappointing 30 percent of the vote and failed to carry a single county. The secret of Clingman's stunning triumph was his ability to capture the entire Democratic vote while holding on to a substantial number of the Whigs. Despite the lopsided nature of his victory, Clingman did not receive overwhelming support from his Whig constituents. Instead, the election of 1851 split the Whig party in the mountain district down the middle, with about half its rank and file remaining loyal to Clingman and the remainder defecting to Gaither. Clingman thus owed his election less to the Whigs than to the Democrats, who had held the balance of power in the district since the early 1840s. Hundreds of members of that party who had voted for Graham in 1845 and then had sat out the next two congressional elections returned to the polls in 1851 to cast their ballots for Clingman.[47]

Clingman's opposition to the Compromise of 1850 and his strident speeches on behalf of Southern Rights guaranteed him the backing of the Democrats in the mountain district. As the *North Carolina Standard* had noted before the election, Clingman could be "sure of the entire Democratic vote" in the district, since "his course has been such as to identify him, out and out, with the Democratic Union State Rights men of the South." It cannot be assumed, however, that those Whigs who voted for Clingman in 1851 necessarily did so for precisely the same reasons. The most perceptive analysis of Clingman's continuing appeal among the Whigs came from Edward J. Hale Jr., editor of the *Fayetteville Observer*. According to Hale, three factors accounted for Clingman's decisive victory: first, his "repudiating in full his disunion sentiments"; second, his "representing himself [to be] as good a Whig" as his opponent; and third, his self-cultivated image "as the sole defender of the West against Eastern usurpation." According to Hale, "these causes, and not . . . any feelings of hostility to the Whig party or the Union" were responsible for Clingman's success.[48]

On Hale's first point, the evidence is overwhelming that Clingman adroitly crafted his Southern Rights rhetoric during the campaign to accommodate the unionist sensibilities of his Whig constituency. Whigs in the North Carolina mountain district were by no means insensitive to the issues of slavery and Southern Rights. Although blacks comprised only 10 percent of the population, the peculiar institution had a far greater impact on "the structure, attitudes, and values of antebellum Appalachian society . . . than the numerical proportion of slaves would suggest." A disproportionate number of the political elite were slave own- ers, and even those residents who did not own slaves resented Northern interfer- ence in their social institutions. Indeed, Clingman's defense of slavery probably mattered less to his constituents "than his defense of southern liberty against northern despotism."[49]

Still, most mountain Whigs were deeply devoted to the Union, and many took Clingman at his word when he told them that the most effective way to "avert the evil" of disunion was for Southerners to unite in a firm determination to resist Northern aggression. As he explained to one group of voters in Henderson County, the real enemies of the Union were not "those Southern men who have [been] . . . standing up boldly in defence of the rights of their section" but, rather, "those men among us, who, by their language and conduct, have induced the people to the North to believe that the South will submit to whatever they may choose to impose." Throughout the campaign, Clingman's supporters continu- ously hammered away at the theme that their candidate was "a stronger Union man than Gaither." By "shamefully abandon[ing] . . . the rights of their own section," they claimed, Gaither and his "submissionist" allies were "stimulat[ing] the Northern spirit of aggression . . . to a point which will render a collision inevitable."[50]

Clingman also avoided the mistake made by Southern Rights candidates in other Whig districts who endorsed the constitutional right of secession. In Ed- ward Stanly's district, for example, Democrat Thomas Ruffin acknowledged "the right of a state to withdraw from the Union for adequate cause"—a tactical error that allowed Stanly to pin the disunion label on his opponent and win reelection by an increased majority.[51] Clingman was careful not to fall into that trap. When- ever he spoke about the prospect of disunion, he made it clear that he was not em- bracing the South Carolina doctrine of secession but, rather, was invoking the same right that the colonists had exercised in resisting the tyranny of Great Britain.[52] The *Raleigh Register* lamented after the election that if the Whigs had "been able to make the issue in this [mountain] District, which was made in the Third and the Eighth, there could have been no doubt . . . of Col. Gaither's elec- tion." Instead, Clingman had "invariably denied that he was an advocate of the right of *Secession!*"[53]

Secondly, as Hale pointed out, Clingman retained the support of many moun- tain voters by proclaiming himself to be "as good a Whig" as Gaither. Well aware that a clean break with his party would cost him more votes than he would gain, Clingman contested the election not as a Democrat but as an independent "South- ern Rights Whig." Incumbency alone gave him an enormous advantage. In 1851 the congressman was canvassing the mountain district for the sixth time, and there were hundreds of Whigs who had already voted for him on four or five pre- vious occasions. At the same time, not a few Whigs regarded Gaither, who was making his first run for Congress, as "a political aspirant . . . merely desirous of Mr. Clingman's seat in Congress . . . for the sake of personal advancement." [54]

Finally, as Hale astutely observed, Clingman's reputation as Champion of the West enabled him to retain the loyalty of a substantial number of his Whig constituents. According to Hale, the congressman had "so zealously fostered feelings of jealousy and distrust of the Eastern section of the State . . . [and] identified himself with the cause of his section" that he had "induced many to believe as *he* most certainly does, that Thomas L. Clingman *is* the West." [55] To understand the impact of state sectionalism on the congressional election of 1851, one must recognize that the campaign for the U.S. House of Representatives coincided with a strenuous effort on the part of westerners to amend the state constitution to provide for a more equitable apportionment of seats in the general assembly and to secure other reforms favorable to western interests. Through his editorial spokesman Thomas W. Atkin, Clingman played a leading role in the movement for constitutional reform. Moreover, the congressman adroitly managed to link the campaign for western rights in his home state with the issue of Southern Rights in the nation, cultivating an image as a crusader battling against the "abuses inflicted on his constituents by the governments in both Raleigh and Washington." [56]

Although he continued to call himself a Whig and was accepted as one by many of his constituents, Clingman had, over a period of less than two years, transformed himself from one of the most moderate of Southern Whigs into one of the most radical. Undoubtedly, his dissatisfaction with the Taylor administration and his unhappiness at the antislavery tendencies of the Northern Whigs played a part in that transformation. At the same time, however, there is substantial evidence that most Southern Whigs were displeased with their president and with the Northern members of their party. Those considerations cannot by themselves explain why Clingman, alone among the Southern Whig members of Congress, chose to break with his party over the compromise issue and take a position on Southern Rights even more radical than that of many Democrats. As one contemporary perceptively remarked, the most important "clue to the intricacies of his present position" was his "ambition . . . to be elected to the Senate of the U. States by the aid of the Democratic party." In December 1851, when Clingman returned to Washington to attend the opening session of the Thirty-Second Congress, he was still a long way from achieving that goal. [57]

7 *A Sort of Filibuster*

During the early 1850s Thomas Lanier Clingman moved steadily in the direction of the Democrats, opposing the Whig candidate for president in 1852 and the party's gubernatorial nominee in 1854. Democrats who had denounced him during the 1840s as an abolitionist now hailed him as a champion of the South. At the same time, Whigs who had previously heaped encomiums upon the congressman now derided him as an unscrupulous opportunist and a traitor to his party. Most frustrating for the Whigs was Clingman's seeming invincibility in his mountain stronghold. Despite its large Whig majorities (which became even larger as a result of redistricting in 1852), he won reelection to a fifth term in the House of Representatives in 1853 by a comfortable margin. Ironically, the man who had waged his first campaign for Congress on the principle of rotation in office would ultimately distinguish himself as one of North Carolina's longest-serving representatives.

The principal factor behind Clingman's political success during the early 1850s was his carefully cultivated image as an independent. Despite his constant denunciations of the "central clique" and the antislavery Whigs of the North, Clingman did not formally abandon the Whig party or unequivocally embrace the Democrats. Instead, he presented himself to the voters as an independent statesman whose course had consistently been "dictated by his own conscience . . . unfettered by party ties or shackles"—a man of integrity who "always acted fearlessly and independently . . . thoroughly disenthralled from sectional prejudices and party animosities." As Clingman explained to a congressional critic in January 1856, "the gentleman . . . does the Democratic party injustice in holding them responsible for what I do, for I am considered a sort of independent, or a fillibuster *[sic]*."[1]

When Clingman returned to Washington in December 1851 for the convening of the Thirty-Second Congress, the mood in the nation's capital was quite different from the crisis atmosphere that had pervaded the halls of Congress during the previous session. Although many Southerners remained dissatisfied with the specific terms of the Compromise of 1850, the decisive defeat of the secessionists in off-year elections in Alabama, Georgia, and Mississippi revealed that a majority of voters, even in the Deep South, were willing to accept the settlement as "a permanent adjustment of this sectional controversy" provided that the North agreed to do likewise.[2]

Clingman, on the other hand, remained unreconciled to the compromise. In April 1852 he was one of only two North Carolina congressmen to vote against a resolution recognizing the "binding efficacy of the Compromises" and deprecating "all further agitation" of the slavery issue. He was the only Southern Whig to oppose the resolution, again joining that incongruous combination of "ultra States Rights men and ultra Free Soil men" who had resisted the passage of the compromise during the previous Congress.[3]

Despite his lingering reservations about the compromise and his avowal to take an "independent" position on the issues, Clingman attended the Whig caucus that assembled immediately prior to the convening of Congress in December 1851. Although he refused to support a procompromise resolution adopted by that caucus, he also distanced himself from the Democrats by casting his ballot in the Speaker's election for David Outlaw, the North Carolinian who had presided over the Whig caucus. When the caucus met the following April to determine the time and place for the Whig National Convention, Clingman was again among those in attendance.[4]

The session proved to be a contentious one. Southerners like Humphrey Marshall of Kentucky and Meredith P. Gentry of Tennessee demanded that the Whigs formally commit themselves to support no candidate for president who had not "publicly and unequivocally pledged" himself to endorse the compromise as a final settlement of sectional differences. Clingman went even further, introducing a resolution requiring both the convention and its nominee to affirm "in unequivocal and plain language" their intention to carry out the provisions of the Fugitive Slave Act. After Chairman Willie P. Mangum ruled the resolutions of Clingman, Marshall, and Gentry to be out of order—a decision that the

Northern majority readily sustained—thirteen Southerners, including Clingman, walked out of the meeting.[5]

In a letter published in the *Washington Republic* on 10 May 1852, Clingman defended the conduct of the insurgent Southerners. The object of their resolutions, he said, had been to compel the Northern Whigs to abandon their "sectional and *destructive* . . . policy" and to occupy "national ground." Now that the resolutions had been rejected, Southern Whigs should await the actions of the two national conventions and cooperate with the party that proved most willing to "stand upon truly national ground." Like John C. Calhoun, whose political course he had once so vehemently condemned, Clingman was calling upon Southerners to abandon their old party allegiances and join together in resisting the encroachments of the antislavery North. Unlike the South Carolinian, however, he envisioned a new party that would encompass not only Southerners but also "the national men of the North"—Democrats and Whigs who would renounce the antislavery elements contaminating both parties and join their fellow Southerners in defense of the Constitution and the Union.[6]

Although he claimed to be "neither the advocate nor the opponent of any named candidate" for president, Clingman was decidedly partial toward Daniel Webster, who was now serving as President Fillmore's secretary of state. The Massachusetts Whig had at one time severed social relations with the North Carolina congressman, but the two had subsequently patched up their differences. By 1852 Clingman was convinced that Webster was one of those "national men of the North" on whom the South could safely rely. When the Whig National Convention convened in Baltimore on 16 June 1852, Clingman, though not a delegate, labored diligently behind the scenes on Webster's behalf, endeavoring "to induce the Southern delegations to give him a solid vote."[7]

After five days and fifty-three ballots, the convention passed over both Webster and Fillmore and tendered the nomination to Winfield Scott. Like Zachary Taylor, the previous Whig nominee, Old Fuss and Feathers was a Southern war hero who had spent much of his life in the North. Unlike his predecessor, who had been a political novice at the time of his nomination, Scott was a seasoned politician who had been campaigning for the presidency since the 1830s. There was another important difference between the two Whig generals. Whereas much of Taylor's initial support had come from Southern Whigs like Robert Toombs and Alexander Stephens, Scott was the preferred candidate of New York senator William H. Seward and most of the other antislavery Northern Whigs.[8]

Although suspicious of Scott's free-soil supporters, Southern Whigs were delighted at the party platform, which not only endorsed the finality of the Compromise of 1850 but also committed the party—as Clingman had earlier demanded—to the "strict enforcement" of the Fugitive Slave Act. To further buttress their Southern support, the Whigs nominated North Carolinian William A. Graham for the vice presidency. For the first time since 1828, both candidates on a major party ticket were native-born Southerners. Despite his Southern pedigree and his party's unqualified approval of the compromise, Scott "studiously avoided endorsing the platform" in his letter of acceptance.[9]

Most Southern Whigs acquiesced in the nomination of Scott and "ran up the Whig flag for another encounter with the Democrats." However, a number of important party leaders refused to fall in line. A few weeks after the convention, an ominous "manifesto" signed by Toombs, Stephens, and seven other Southern congressmen appeared in the *National Intelligencer.* Denouncing the Whig nominee for his silence on the compromise and branding him as "the *favorite* candidate of the *Free-Soil* wing of the Whig party," the signers concluded that "we cannot and will not support Gen. Scott for the Presidency."[10]

Clingman's name was noticeably absent among the signatories. While other influential Southern Whigs were publicly announcing their opposition to their party's nominee during the summer of 1852, the forty-year-old congressman from the North Carolina mountain district remained silent. On 3 August he casually informed his colleagues that he did not "feel any great interest in the present presidential election." Three weeks later, when he delivered his only set speech of the session, he said nothing about the presidential contest but, uncharacteristically, confined his remarks to the topic at hand—a bill to reduce the tariff duties on railroad iron. The following day, he confided to his mother that he probably would not "take any part at all" in the campaign. "I consider Pierce the better man," he wrote, "but as he has been nominated by the democrats I do not feel under any particular obligation to support him nor to oppose actively the Whig candidate. It is therefore most likely that I shall not take any part in the canvass leaving the friends of each candidate to fight as best they can."[11]

Indeed, Clingman was far more concerned about the August legislative elections than he was about the November presidential contest. Senator Willie P. Mangum's term would expire the following March, and the newly elected general assembly would be responsible for choosing a successor. Fully aware that he was not "the first choice of either party," the congressman nonetheless hoped he might "with the aid of some personal friends" emerge as the winner "after the several parties had failed to succeed with their favorite candidates." To that end, he sought to elect a sufficient number of "Southern Rights Whigs" in the mountain district to hold the balance of power in the legislature.[12]

Clingman was less certain about what course to follow in the gubernatorial campaign, particularly since John Kerr, the Whig candidate running against Gov. David S. Reid, was a distant relative whom he had known since boyhood. While Clingman remained publicly silent, his mouthpiece, the *Asheville News,* proved less reticent. Although stopping short of explicitly endorsing Reid, editor Thomas W. Atkin denounced Kerr for his opposition to constitutional reform and urged his Whig readers to voice their disapproval by withholding their support. In order to bolster his shaky standing in the mountain district, Kerr spent the final month of the campaign in the far west. Fearing that he might direct his barbs against the Southern Rights legislative candidates as well as against Governor Reid, Clingman's supporters urged him to break his silence and publicly repudiate Kerr.[13]

Two weeks before the election, Clingman responded by writing a private letter to J. F. E. Hardy, a prominent Asheville physician and banker. The congressman enclosed a second letter that he authorized Hardy to publish in the event Kerr "assails me in any of his speeches . . . [or] my friends because they sustain my views." The enclosed communication contained a scathing denunciation of Kerr as a tool of the "central managers." According to Clingman, the principal objective of the managers was not to elect Kerr but rather to defeat "the supporters of Western rights and the true Republican Southern rights men" who were running for the general assembly. Should they accomplish that goal, the managers would "feel it a triumph even though they should fail in the contest for governor."[14]

Clingman's letter apparently was not published, but rumors quickly spread that the congressman was "writing numerous letters to his friends in the District" taking ground against Kerr "and for the re-election of Gov. Reid." The Democrats exuberantly predicted that "Kerr's prospects in the far west are blown to the skyes [sic]." That prediction proved only slightly off the mark. The Whig nominee did manage to carry Clingman's district, but his 56 percent of the vote was a far cry from the overwhelming majorities his party had commanded at the height of its power during the 1840s, and it was not sufficient to overcome the Democratic majorities in the eastern part of the state. Reid won the election by a margin of more than five thousand votes.[15]

Despite their loss in the governor's race, the Whigs succeeded in recapturing the House of Commons, and they came within a few seats of winning back the state senate. In the mountain district, all but one of the Southern Rights candidates were defeated by regular Whigs.[16] When the legislature convened on 4 October 1852, the balance of parties remained uncertain because of a disputed election in the Camden-Currituck senatorial district. If the Whigs were awarded the contested district, the parties would have an equal number of legislative seats. Moreover, the absence of one Democratic member due to a "severe personal injury" would give the Whigs the effective majority on joint ballot and enable them to elect a U.S. senator. On the other hand, if the Democrats gained the disputed seat, they would have a two-vote majority.[17]

The defeat of the Southern Rights Whigs did not bode well for Clingman's chances of winning the senatorship. Nonetheless, he did not abandon hope that he might rally some Whig legislators behind his candidacy. Arriving in Raleigh two days before the opening of the session, he immediately began buttonholing the western members. The legislators were naturally anxious to learn about his position in the presidential contest. When one member bluntly asked whether he "intended to take the stump for Pierce and King on his return to the mountains,"

Clingman reportedly replied that "Pierce and King had never done any thing for him," and for that reason "he did not feel called on to do any thing for them."[18]

Unfortunately for Clingman, his already slim prospects for garnering Whig votes for his senatorial candidacy were completely shattered by the inept and indiscreet behavior of his associate, Bayles M. Edney. While attending to some business affairs in Louisville, Kentucky, Edney had written to John A. Fagg, a Whig member from Buncombe County, urging the legislator to "stand by Clingman for Senator" and to use his influence to persuade other westerners to boycott the Whig caucus. Should Clingman win the senatorship, Edney promised, the grateful congressman would "get any office for you that you desire," including "his place in Congress."[19]

Although Edney marked the letter "confidential" and cautioned his correspondent that "*all* this is *between* us," Fagg immediately apprised his other Whig colleagues of its contents. The letter itself eventually fell into the hands of John Baxter, one of Clingman's most bitter enemies, who published it in the *Raleigh Register* after first leaking its contents to the *Asheville Messenger*. Not surprisingly, Baxter professed outrage at Edney's bold-faced attempt to "bribe and corrupt the integrity" of the general assembly. The Whigs were further angered by Clingman's own role in the affair, since he had personally presented Fagg with the unsealed communication. The congressman subsequently denied that he had read Edney's letter or had even been aware of its contents, but many Whigs found his disavowal preposterous.[20]

At the same time that it was becoming apparent Clingman could expect no support from the Whigs, the state senate awarded the disputed Camden-Currituck seat to the Democratic claimant. With a clear majority on joint ballot, the Democrats now had the power to elect a U.S. senator. Clingman's own prospects for advancing to that position would be considerably enhanced if he could swing North Carolina into the Democratic column by obtaining a large vote for Pierce and King in the mountain district. It was probably no coincidence that on the day after the Democrats gained control of the general assembly, Clingman broke his long silence and publicly endorsed the Democratic presidential candidate.[21]

Four years earlier, Clingman had been Scott's most prominent Southern supporter. Now, in a public letter addressed to Southern Rights legislator Ladson A. Mills, he lambasted the Whig nominee as a politician thoroughly "identified with the anti-slavery party of the North" who had put the rights of the South "for sale in the political market for anti-slavery votes." While affirming his belief that "Franklin Pierce should be elected rather than General Scott," Clingman did not formally declare himself a Democrat. Indeed, as the *Washington Union* noted, the "peculiar emphasis and force" of Clingman's letter derived from its Whig antecedents and viewpoint. The thrust of his argument was that a Whig could vote for Pierce in good conscience since there were no longer any policy disagreements "of sufficient magnitude to require us to sustain the Whig nominee at all hazards."

Moreover, by repudiating "an unworthy nomination," the Whigs could send a salutary message to their leaders that "may prevent the recurrence of a similar nomination by any future convention, and greatly contribute to ensure the future quiet of the country."[22]

Not surprisingly, the Whig presses denounced Clingman as a traitor who had "deserted the colors of his ancient faith . . . [and] betrayed his friends who have heretofore stood by him and promoted him."[23] Far from expressing regret at his defection, however, Whig loyalists rejoiced that their adversary would "no longer be able to subject the Whig Party to the humility of being preyed upon and assailed under its own flag." At the same time, they predicted that the Democrats would never bestow the senatorship on a man whose conduct had forfeited the respect of both parties. "They love his treason," intoned a correspondent of the *Greensboro Patriot,* "but . . . despise in their inmost hearts the traitor, and laugh at his vanity and ambition." Clingman's detractors were also confident that his efforts to transfer the Whig voters of the mountain district "like sheep in the shambles, from one party to another" would prove unsuccessful. "It remains to be seen," scoffed the *Patriot* correspondent, "whether the honest people of the Mountain District are such asses as to follow T. L. Clingman wherever he goes and do just exactly as he may bid them."[24]

The presidential election of 1852 proved disastrous for the Whigs throughout the nation. According to one historian, it was "the most one-sided victory since the Era of Good Feelings." Pierce captured the electoral votes of all but four states, and the Democrats carried the Old North State for the first time since 1836.[25] Clingman was willing to take full credit for the outcome, boasting that "no man can fix upon me a greater share of responsibility for General Scott's defeat than I am ready to take." Some of the Whigs also attributed Pierce's victory in North Carolina to Clingman's defection. The *Fayetteville Observer* grudgingly acknowledged the congressman's "power to accomplish so much of evil" and opined that "as Clingman has done the work for the Locos, he should have the Senatorship." The *Asheville Messenger,* on the other hand, took a different view of the results, sarcastically pointing out that "Mr. Clingman's influence was so overwhelming at Asheville (his home) that Scott's majority was 10 more than Kerr's! And it is so . . . throughout the District."[26]

There was some validity in both viewpoints. Throughout the 1840s the lopsided Whig majorities in the mountain district had provided the winning margin in statewide elections. As Clingman himself had remarked at the end of that decade, "when . . . as a party, we are beaten in the central and eastern parts of the State, the West, by its heavy majorities, neutralizes and overcomes the partial success of our opponents, and gives us the control of the State." Although Scott garnered 60 percent of the vote in the mountain district in 1852, his showing was considerably less impressive than the 74 percent captured by Taylor in 1848 or the 68 percent won by Clay in 1844. Moreover, Scott received about twenty-two hundred fewer votes in Clingman's district than Kerr had obtained in the governor's election just three months earlier—a decline substantially greater than that in any other congressional district. Had Scott been able to retain the support of even a third of those Whig absentees, he would have carried the state. These factors indicate that Clingman's defection did have an impact on the outcome of the election.[27]

On the other hand, Clingman's contribution to Scott's defeat becomes less impressive when the decline in the Democratic vote is also taken into consideration. Franklin Pierce received about forty-six hundred fewer votes in the mountain district than David S. Reid had won the previous August—a drop in turnout more than twice that of the Whigs. Even though Scott did not receive as many votes in the far west as did Kerr, his 60 percent share of the two-party vote in the mountain counties compares favorably with the 56 percent won by the Whig gubernatorial candidate. Ironically, the Democrats fared better in the state election, in which Clingman had not played an active role, than in the presidential contest, in which he had campaigned aggressively for their candidate.

Under the circumstances, it is not surprising that the Democratic caucus bypassed Clingman and tendered the senatorial nomination to former congressman James C. Dobbin. A few days before the caucus met, Duncan K. McRae, a leading supporter of Dobbin, had cautioned Clingman not to throw any roadblocks in the way of Dobbin's election. It was in his own best interests, he told the congressman, "to prevent any action by your friends *at this time* which may injure your prospects *hereafter*." To sweeten the bitter pill, McRae acknowledged his party's "obligation to you for the fearless and successful stand you have taken in the late contest," and he assured Clingman that the Democrats would "stand by you to a man" in 1854, "unless *something* should *occur now* to injure you with the Democratic party." Clingman, who had realized all along that he most likely would not be the first choice of the Democrats, had no option but to follow McRae's advice. Accordingly, he did not permit his small cadre of legislative supporters to press his claims for the senatorship on the floor of the general assembly.[28]

Fortunately for Clingman, the Democrats lacked the discipline to rally en masse behind their caucus nominee. Instead, supporters of Dobbin's principal Democratic rivals, Romulus M. Saunders and James B. Shepard, defied the caucus and voted for their own favorite. Thirteen ballots over the course of the next four weeks failed to produce a winner. On the fourteenth ballot, the Whigs, who had previously been supporting former congressman Kenneth Rayner, nominated Nicholas W. Woodfin, the senator from the Asheville district, in the hope of attracting the support of a few mountain Democrats. As Clingman had hoped, the Democratic leaders, having repeatedly failed to elect their "favorite candidate," were now willing to give him a chance. Dobbin's name was withdrawn, and Clingman was "recommended" in his stead. The choice of words was significant, because—unlike a caucus nomination—the recommendation was not considered to be binding on party members.[29]

With many Democrats throwing their votes away on other candidates, Clingman received a disappointing fifty-three votes. He fell twelve votes behind Woodfin and twenty-seven votes short of Dobbin's total on the previous ballot. Although he managed to pick up another eight votes on the next ballot, Woodfin also made gains, falling just three votes short of a majority. Meanwhile, the balance of parties in the general assembly was becoming increasingly unpredictable, as one legislator after another departed for the Christmas holidays. Apparently preferring to see the Senate seat remain vacant rather than risk having it filled by someone from the opposition, both parties decided to abandon the contest. For the next two years, North Carolina would have only one member in the U.S. Senate.[30]

Clingman was furious at his failure to win the senatorship. Characteristically, he placed the blame squarely on the Whig central managers. "Sooner than permit another balloting, which would have most probably resulted in my election," the managers had, he claimed, threatened to "defeat all the public business, including the important districting bills." In reality, however, the decision to discontinue the balloting had been bipartisan. Moreover, it was the Democrats—and not the Whig central managers—who had withheld the crucial votes needed to secure his election.[31]

Clingman may well have been as concerned about the upcoming congressional campaign as he was about his failure to win the senatorship. In the recent presidential election three-fifths of the voters in his district had cast their ballots for Scott. It remained to be seen whether those Scott Whigs who had voted for Clingman in 1851 would continue to support him now that he had officially repudiated their standard-bearer and contributed to his defeat. Moreover, Clingman had to wage his campaign in a district quite different from the one that had previously sent him to Congress. As a result of reapportionment, the populous, heavily Democratic, and strongly pro-Clingman county of Cleveland had been removed, and the even more populous, but staunchly anti-Clingman, county of Wilkes had been substituted.[32]

Clingman fired the opening salvo of the congressional campaign in January 1853 with the publication of a long letter to his constituents. His arguments were directed specifically toward those Whigs who had voted for Scott in 1852. With characteristic immodesty, he asserted that "I attach no blame whatever to those who supported him." Throughout the district, "honest and intelligent men were . . . misled" by the misrepresentations appearing in the *Asheville Messenger* and other Scott organs. Indeed, he acknowledged, "if I had been at home with no other means of information than the newspapers afforded, I might have been deceived possibly, and induced to sustain General Scott." From his vantage point in Washington, however, he "had been placed in a position to get a better knowledge of the issues involved than many others." Knowing that the election of

Scott would have constituted a triumph for "the anti-slavery party, headed by Mr. Seward," he would "have been false to the trust reposed in me" had he supported the Whig nominee merely "out of deference to the general feeling of the party."[33]

Clingman's opponent in 1853 was Burgess Gaither, the man he had decisively beaten two years earlier. Gaither realized his only hope for success lay in convincing a sizable number of Clingman's Whig supporters that the congressman was no longer worthy of their vote. In a lengthy campaign circular that exceeded even Clingman's in verbosity, the challenger reminded the voters that his opponent's "course upon the compromise question was . . . adverse to the opinions of the most of the leading whigs," while "his notions of secession and disunion . . . are in direct conflict with one of the cardinal principles of the Whig party." Indeed, his entire political course since 1848 provided indisputable proof of his "alienation from the Whig party and his connection with the Democracy." According to Gaither, Clingman was not a Whig but rather "a Democrat calling himself a whig," who had donned "the robes of whiggery simply that he may thereby injure the party more successfully."[34]

The diligence with which Gaither attempted to pin the Democratic label on Clingman attests to the congressman's success in evading that designation. Confident that "the Democratic party will support him anyhow, let him call himself any name he pleases," the congressman toned down his Southern Rights rhetoric and focused his efforts on shoring up his Whig support.[35] Claiming that "any person [who] charged him with betraying the whig party" was a prevaricator, he presented himself to the voters as a Whig, albeit an independent one, who was waging a campaign on behalf of "the right of private judgment in public men, against the corrupt and tyrannical dictates of cabals, caucusses [sic] and cliques." In that regard, his refusal to support Winfield Scott constituted "no abandonment of principle" or betrayal of Whiggery, as Gaither was claiming. Indeed, "a large number of the most talented and influential Whigs" in both sections of the country had gone on record in opposition to their party's presidential candidate.[36]

While the Whig loyalists boasted that "Col. Gaither's election . . . is absolutely certain," the congressman's supporters retorted that "Clingman will beat him worse than he did before."[37] The outcome belied both predictions. Clingman won the election with 60 percent of the vote, receiving majorities in all of the mountain counties except Wilkes. On the other hand, Gaither improved on his share of the vote in the previous election by ten percentage points. Some of those gains were the result of redistricting, but even in the older parts of the district, the challenger's vote increased substantially. Gaither apparently did succeed in convincing many of Clingman's erstwhile Whig supporters that he was a traitor to their party. Nonetheless, enough Whigs remained unpersuaded to allow the forty-one-year-old congressman to coast easily to a fifth term.[38]

Although he owed his election primarily to the Democrats, Clingman refrained from openly aligning with that party in the Thirty-Third Congress. While the

Democratic members were casting their ballots for Kentuckian Lynn Boyd in the contest for the speakership, Clingman threw his vote away on fellow North Carolinian William S. Ashe. Later in the session, the congressman acknowledged himself to be "rather out of all regular party organizations, and . . . regarded, I believe, as an independent."[39]

Even though Clingman had moved from the Committee on Territories, where he had served since January 1850, to the Committee on Foreign Affairs, his one set speech during the session pertained to the major domestic policy issue confronting Congress—the establishment of a government for the Nebraska Territory. Late in the previous session, a Nebraska bill had passed the House of Representatives by a comfortable margin, only to die in the Senate. Since slavery would be excluded in the new territory according to the terms of the Missouri Compromise, the vast majority of Southerners had voted against the earlier bill. Despite his image as a strong supporter of Southern Rights, Clingman had expressed no interest at that time in the expansion of slavery into Nebraska. His only objection to the original bill related to the rights of the resident Native Americans, and once those concerns had been resolved to his satisfaction, he had been one of the handful of Southerners who voted for the measure.[40]

When Sen. Stephen A. Douglas again presented the Nebraska bill to Congress in January 1854, Archibald Dixon, a Kentucky Whig, offered an amendment that would open the territory to slavery by explicitly repealing the Missouri Compromise. Correctly anticipating that the repeal would weaken the position of the Northern Democrats, Clingman met privately with Dixon and his Tennessee colleague James C. Jones and urged them to withdraw the provocative amendment. Understandably, the two Whigs were more concerned about their own political fortunes than about the fate of the Northern Democrats, and they refused to retreat from their position. Despite the outcry from the Northern antislavery forces, a bill containing the repeal provision passed the Senate on 3 March 1854.[41]

By the time the bill reached the floor of the House, Clingman had swallowed his initial doubts and was prepared to speak publicly on its behalf. In a wide-ranging address delivered on 4 April 1854, he accused the antislavery men of the North of being the first to repudiate the Missouri Compromise during the debates over the Mexican Cession, and he defended the proposal to allow the residents of the territories to determine the status of slavery as "a better bill than the Utah and New Mexico bills of 1850." In customary fashion, much of his speech consisted of an attack on the Northern Whigs, whom he accused of treachery, hypocrisy, duplicity, and numerous other political crimes. According to Clingman, the Northern Whigs were feigning outrage at the bill simply "to obtain party strength in the North" at the expense of their Democrat opponents, "who are more liberal to us on these questions."[42]

After another six weeks of speech making and legislative maneuvering, the Kansas–Nebraska Act passed the House of Representatives by a vote of 113 to 100.[43] Although Clingman worked closely with Alexander H. Stephens and other

Southern leaders in shepherding the bill through the House, his speech of 4 April probably persuaded no one who was not already predisposed to be convinced. As opposition leaders were quick to point out, Clingman's address was intended primarily to serve as a campaign document "to defeat the [North Carolina] whig party at the ensuing August elections." Whig congressman Richard C. Puryear reported that his brother-in-law planned to circulate eight thousand copies of the address throughout the mountain district, and he predicted that it "will injure us greatly as he don't profess to be a democrat and what he says is to go out as coming from a Whig."[44]

As Puryear perceptively observed, Clingman had once again stopped short of formally declaring himself a Democrat. While some prominent Southern Rights Whigs like Thomas W. Atkin and Marcus Erwin were announcing their conversion to the Democracy during the early months of 1854, Clingman refused to take the final step. The Whigs were disappointed, since they realized that the congressman presented a far greater threat as a quasi-Whig than as a full-blooded Democrat. With considerable justification, Puryear characterized Clingman's strategy as "a sort of Guerrilla warfare much more dangerous than open assault from an avowed enemy."[45]

Notwithstanding his growing estrangement from the Whigs and his opposition to Winfield Scott, Clingman had thus far refrained from openly endorsing a Democrat for state office. Two years earlier, he had remained officially neutral in the governor's contest, and as late as May 1854 the *Asheville News* declared that it was "not prepared to say what his course in the approaching canvass would be." Clingman had privately expressed disapproval of Whig gubernatorial nominee Alfred Dockery in March, and the *News* had placed the name of Democrat Thomas Bragg on its masthead in mid-May. However, a similar endorsement from Clingman did not immediately follow.[46]

Even if Clingman had wanted to remain neutral in the governor's contest, practical political considerations militated against that course. With Badger's term in the Senate about to expire and Mangum's seat still vacant, the general assembly would have two senators to elect when it convened in November. Barring a Whig landslide, Clingman had reasonable expectations of securing one of those seats, particularly if he could lure the mountain district away from its Whig moorings and deliver a solid vote to Bragg. At the end of June the congressman finally broke his silence and issued a public letter opposing the election of Dockery. In an effort to link the Whig candidate with the unpopular Northern wing of the party, Clingman accused Dockery of "having adopted the opinions of the most ultra federalists and consolidationists of our day." He also cited the candidate's support for Scott in 1852 as conclusive evidence that his "sympathies . . . [were] with the Northern or anti-slavery section of the Whig party."[47]

The outcome of the legislative elections was even more important to the realization of Clingman's ambition than the result of the governor's contest. As early as March, the congressman had emphasized the importance of getting out "the right sort of men" for the legislature, and Marcus Erwin (who had temporarily replaced Thomas Atkin as editor of the *Asheville News*) made it clear that the "right sort" consisted only of those candidates who would support Clingman for the U.S. Senate. If Whig loyalists like Nicholas W. Woodfin were sent to Raleigh, Erwin warned, they would "again stifle the voice of a majority of the people, should Mr. Clingman be a candidate." The people should keep in mind that "every vote they give for N. W. Woodfin is a vote against Thomas L. Clingman for the U.S. Senate. . . . If you elect Nick Woodfin, you defeat Tom Clingman for the United States Senate." [48]

Many of the pro-Clingman legislative candidates were not professed Democrats but "Southern Rights Republicans"—"gentlemen who were formerly out and out Whigs, but who have had the independence and manliness to prefer the rights of their section . . . to continued alliance with the Abolition Whigs of the free States." Clingman actually preferred those independent candidates to avowed Democrats who might be pressured into supporting the nominee of their party caucus. As in 1852, his goal was to elect a sufficient number of Southern Rights legislators to hold the balance of power between the two parties. [49]

In the closest gubernatorial election since 1848, Bragg edged past Dockery by a margin of two thousand votes. Despite his defeat, Dockery's support for the westward extension of the North Carolina Railroad enabled him to garner 63 percent of the vote in Clingman's district—a substantial gain over Kerr's showing two years earlier. In the legislative elections, on the other hand, Clingman's supporters were considerably more successful than they had been in 1852. Although the Southern Rights candidate in Buncombe County lost to a twenty-four-year-old newcomer named Zebulon B. Vance, four Southern Righters did manage to win election. In the Asheville senatorial district, moreover, Democrat David Coleman unseated five-term incumbent Nicholas Woodfin, while in Madison County another Democrat ousted veteran Whig legislator John A. Fagg. Overall, the Democrats won ten-seat majorities in both the House of Commons and the state senate. [50]

Those comfortable Democratic majorities meant that Southern Rights legislators from the far west would not hold the balance of power in the upcoming general assembly. Also working against Clingman's chances for winning election to the U.S. Senate was his inability to deliver his district to Bragg—or, indeed, even to hold the Whigs to their lackluster 1852 showing. Shortly after the August elections, several eastern Democratic presses came out openly in opposition to his candidacy. While expressing admiration for Clingman's "independent course as a Southern rights Representative," the *Wilmington Journal* attributed Bragg's victory to the party's "own intrinsic strength [rather] than to Whig defections in Mr. Clingman's district," where Dockery's majority was "actually larger . . . than that obtained either by Mr. Kerr or by Gen Scott." The *Journal* also challenged

Clingman's Democratic credentials, characterizing him as a "man who has not even assumed the party name." The *Fayetteville North Carolinian* likewise noted that "he has never yet canvassed his District for Congress as a democrat, and up to a very late period has been regarded as an outsider." According to the *North Carolinian*, the Senate seats should go to "none others but *good, known, acknowledged* Democrats."[51]

It was no coincidence that the most vocal opposition to Clingman's candidacy came from the east. Underlying the battle for the senatorial nomination were the long-standing divisions within the North Carolina Democratic party between its conservative eastern wing and its more progressive western wing. Those divisions had been exacerbated by the railroad legislation recently enacted by the general assembly, which had necessitated a substantial increase in state taxes. Outgoing governor David S. Reid, whom many Democrats believed should be rewarded with the senatorship for redeeming the state from fourteen years of Whig rule, was a westerner associated with his party's progressive wing. The concept of political balance seemed to dictate that the other seat should go to an eastern conservative.[52]

As Clingman watched the coveted Senate seat slipping from his grasp, he was understandably furious. Two years earlier, Democrats like Duncan McRae had promised that the party would stand by him "to a man" in 1854 if he patiently waited his turn. As recently as June, Reid and state treasurer Daniel W. Courts had assured him that "if the West does but do her duty that your election is certain." In his own mind, Clingman had in fact "done his duty" by opposing the popular Dockery. In so doing, he had placed his standing among his western Whig supporters in serious jeopardy. But now that the elections were over, leading Democratic presses were pronouncing him an unsuitable vessel for the senatorial honors.[53]

Late in September the congressman dashed off an angry letter to Reid, warning about the consequences of thwarting his ambition. Denying him the senatorship, he averred, would "be fatal to the democratic cause [in the mountain district] probably for some time to come." Even if he remained "ever so quiet myself," many of his allies were "saying that if certain matters do not go to please them, they will never vote with the democratic party again." Clingman asked Reid to use his influence with William W. Holden to put in a good word for him in the *North Carolina Standard.* "I do not like these attacks [by the eastern Democratic presses] and if Holden were to do anything to rebuke them, it would not hurt him."[54]

Clingman's threats and entreaties failed to persuade either Reid or Holden to actively promote his candidacy.[55] With the Democrats comfortably in control of the general assembly, the congressman concluded that "his only chance for success" lay in winning the nomination of the party's caucus. Despite his carefully crafted reputation as a crusader against caucuses, he instructed his Democratic supporters to enter the caucus and take part in its deliberations. Although the western Democrats "battled manfully and nobly for his election," Clingman never received even half the requisite number of votes. Instead, the eastern-dominated caucus awarded the nominations to Reid and former congressman Asa Biggs.[56]

After the Democrats had made their choice, the Southern Rights legislators (who were nominally still Whigs and had not participated in the Democratic caucus) entered the Whig caucus and suggested an arrangement whereby Clingman's supporters would combine with the Whigs to elect Badger to another six-year term and Clingman to the open seat. Not surprisingly, the Whigs reacted to the proposal "with loathing and disgust."[57] When the general assembly began balloting on 24 November 1854, one of the Southern Rights members, in a final act of desperation, placed Clingman's name in nomination. The congressman failed to receive a single vote—not even from the legislator who had nominated him.[58]

Clingman, who had been at the state capital throughout the proceedings, abruptly left for Washington the following morning. The Whigs were unable to conceal their glee. "Rejected by those who had profitted [sic] by his treachery, and spurned by his old [Whig] friends, what better could he do," jeered the *Carolina Watchman*, "than—*take his hat and leave!*" The *Watchman* could not help wondering whether Clingman, after having been so "badly treated by . . . the naughty Locos . . . [would] *cling* to them any longer?" The *Milton Chronicle* also offered mock condolences to the unsuccessful aspirant. "Alas, poor Clingman! . . . While the democracy love your treason they hate the traitor." Another Whig commented that "both parties seem to look upon him, as the Czar did upon Turkey—as a sick man, politically." Although Clingman may not have been in the best of spirits as "the cars whisked him off to Washington" to attend the second session of the Thirty-Third Congress, he would soon demonstrate that those predictions of his impending political demise were premature.[59]

8 *Not "Locofocoised," but "Clingmanised"*

Clingman's landslide victories in 1851 and 1853, juxtaposed against the Democrats' disappointing showing in the far west in the elections of 1852 and 1854, seem on their face to substantiate the conclusion of one historian that the congressman from the North Carolina mountain district was "a remarkable politician, but one with equally unremarkable political coattails."[1] Contemporary observers also commented upon Clingman's seeming inability to transfer his personal support to other candidates. In 1854, for example, Richard C. Puryear remarked that in the mountain district "we loose *[sic]* votes where we have not real[l]y lost Whigs." The voters there, he said, "are not Locofocoised but Clingmanised . . . [and] act with the Whigs in all elections except that of Mr. Clingman himself."[2]

By the mid-1850s, however, Clingman's "coattails" had grown considerably longer. In 1856 Democratic governor Thomas Bragg polled a handsome majority in the mountain district, which also sent a solid phalanx of Democrats to the general assembly. A few months later, the party scored an equally impressive victory in the presidential election. In 1857 Clingman contested his district for the first time as a Democrat and easily

won election to a seventh term. Even after his conversion to the Democracy, however, the congressman continued to chart an independent course. As a member,
and later chairman, of the Foreign Affairs Committee, his eagerness to take the
initiative in matters that had traditionally been the prerogative of the executive
branch constantly placed him at loggerheads with the Buchanan administration.

During the 1840s Clingman had opposed the Democratic policy of territorial
expansion. Like most Whigs, he had voted against the annexation of Texas and
had denounced the Mexican War as an unjust war of aggression. As he grew increasingly estranged from the Whigs over the following decade, Clingman's attitude toward expansion changed accordingly. By 1851 he was proclaiming that
slaveholders were "destined to . . . fill up all the country around the gulf [of Mex-
ico], including the peninsula of Yucatan, and perhaps the northern portion of the
South American continent." Three years later, he articulated an even more
grandiose vision of expansion, predicting that "all the country between Cape
Horn and the Polar ocean of the north" would one day be "united in one empire."[3]

The difference between those two statements was more than simply one of
magnitude. Speaking at the height of the sectional controversy in 1851, Clingman
had specifically linked the issue of territorial expansion to the protection of slavery. Like many Southern sectionalists, he had also raised the possibility that this
great slave-holding empire might be established outside the existing Union. The
concept enunciated by Clingman in 1854 was much more in keeping with the notions of the Young America movement, whose leaders were not Southern radicals
but nationalist Northern Democrats like Stephen A. Douglas. Indeed, by 1855
Clingman was explicitly identifying himself with "what is called the party of
progress, or . . . Young America."[4]

The proponents of Young America justified an expansionist foreign policy on
national, rather than sectional, grounds. In their view, the United States was di-
vinely ordained to spread its republican institutions throughout the Western
Hemisphere. That nationalistic vision was closely connected with Douglas's doctrine of popular sovereignty or congressional nonintervention. As Clingman explained in the speech announcing his conversion to the principle he had opposed
so vehemently in 1850, if the residents of each community were allowed to determine for themselves the character of their local institutions without interference
by Congress, the United States would continue to expand in territory without
being "disturbed with agitations about slavery."[5]

The Young Americans were vague regarding the means by which the nations
of the Western Hemisphere might eventually gravitate into the American orbit.
That was particularly true in the case of the coveted island of Cuba. While radical Southerners like John A. Quitman organized filibustering expeditions to take
control of the Spanish colony, more moderate expansionists like Franklin Pierce
and Secretary of State William L. Marcy hoped to acquire it by purchase. Another

alternative, which Clingman vigorously pursued, was to foment a conflict with Spain that would serve as a rationale for seizing the island. In February 1854 the Cuban governor-general offered a convenient pretext for aggressive action when he confiscated the American merchant vessel *Black Warrior* in Havana harbor and placed its captain under arrest. Shortly afterward, Pierce sent a message to Congress affirming his intention "to obtain redress for injuries received, and to vindicate the honor of our flag."[6]

The incident led to a heated discussion in Congress. In order "to induce the government to take decided action," Clingman, along with John Perkins of Louisiana, drafted resolutions authorizing the president to use the army and navy to protect American interests and providing for the enlistment of fifty thousand volunteers. Clingman hoped to bring his resolutions directly before the Foreign Affairs Committee, but Perkins insisted they communicate them first to Pierce and Marcy. Clingman's apprehensions that the administration "would endeavor to strangle the proposition" proved well founded. The cabinet informed Perkins that "nothing would be more embarrassing to them than such a movement in Congress" and urged him and Clingman to drop the matter. The subsequent release of the *Black Warrior* defused tensions, and Marcy's policy of patient negotiation eventually resulted in an amicable resolution of the crisis. From Clingman's point of view, however, the cool reaction of Pierce and Marcy toward his efforts to impose a military solution on the controversy provided evidence that the Democratic administration was "not . . . really in earnest" in its call for an aggressive defense of American interests.[7]

Ironically, in light of his bellicosity toward Spain, Clingman's next confrontation with the Pierce administration arose from his efforts to help Great Britain and the other belligerent nations extract themselves from a bloody war in the Crimea. By the time the second session of the Thirty-Third Congress met in December 1854, the initial hopes of Britain and her allies for a quick victory over Russia had given way to a protracted land war. Early in the session, Clingman introduced a resolution requesting the president "to tender to the belligerents . . . the mediation of the United States." On 3 January 1855 he spoke to the House on behalf of his proposal, arguing that mediation would increase the popularity of the American republic among the European masses, counter "the impression . . . that we are a grasping and rapacious people," and guarantee that the governments of Great Britain and France "would not . . . quarrel with us in opposition to the wishes of their subjects."[8]

Clingman's effort to bring an end to the war in the Crimea and his attempt to provoke a conflict in the Caribbean, although seemingly aimed at opposite objectives, were both manifestations of his belief that the United States could best promote its national interests by abandoning its traditional isolationism and adopting a more assertive foreign policy. The response of the Democratic leadership to his mediation proposal was less than enthusiastic. No sooner had the North

Carolinian concluded his first major speech on foreign policy than Thomas H. Bayly, the chairman of the Foreign Affairs Committee, stood up to voice his opposition to Clingman's resolution. Admonishing his colleague that mediation "was a very delicate matter, with nations as well as with individuals," the Virginia Democrat announced that he had learned from his own "sources of information" that overtures had already been made "from the proper quarter . . . on the part of this Government . . . [and] it was thought advisable for this country not to interfere." Bayly did not elaborate, but the story quickly spread that the State Department had raised the possibility of mediation with the French government, which had peremptorily declined the offer.[9]

In a "personal explanation" to the House three days later, Clingman asserted that he had not been aware of the ongoing negotiations when he had presented his mediation proposal. While of the opinion that "the information does not . . . change at all the propriety of making the movement I suggested," he nonetheless had decided to "decline taking any steps at this time." Although he tried to put the best possible gloss on the matter, Clingman must have been deeply embarrassed by Bayly's unexpected announcement. Undoubtedly, he was also miffed by the Virginian's reminder that the "proper quarter" for foreign policy initiatives was the executive branch and not Congress. At the same time, the incident underscored the power and influence of the committee chairman, who had been privy to "sources of information" beyond the ken of the other members. Only by becoming chairman himself could Clingman expect to play a major role in foreign affairs. Within a few years, he would succeed in achieving that goal.[10]

From the perspective of 1855, however, Clingman's top priority was to hold on to his seat in the House of Representatives. When the congressman returned to Asheville in March 1855 at the close of the session, the political climate in the mountain district was quite different from what it had been only a few months earlier. By early spring, the Whig party in North Carolina was rapidly giving way to a new and potentially more powerful organization—the American, or Know-Nothing, party.

At first glance, the North Carolina mountain region might have seemed infertile soil for a party dedicated to curbing the political influence of Catholics and foreigners, both of whom were practically nonexistent in Clingman's district. Nonetheless, many westerners proved susceptible to dire warnings that their democratic system of government was being threatened by hordes of immigrant criminals and paupers who owed primary allegiance to the Pope. With their rallying cry of "Americans should rule America," the Know-Nothings made impressive gains not only among the Whigs but also among clergymen and others who had not previously been involved in politics.[11]

In order to attract Democratic support, Know-Nothing leaders self-consciously dissociated themselves from the Whigs and boasted that their party had "arisen upon the ruins, and in spite of the opposition, of the whig and democratic parties." Outside the mountain region, opponents of the Know-Nothings challenged that statement and accused them of being merely Whigs in disguise. Clingman, on the other hand, was happy to take the new party at its word, hoping to convince his Whig constituents that Know-Nothingism was not the legitimate offspring of Whiggery and, therefore, was undeserving of their support.[12]

Almost immediately after his return to North Carolina, Clingman formally announced himself as a candidate for reelection and commenced a canvass of the mountain region, speaking to large crowds in practically every county in the district. In his first public address at Franklin on 13 March 1855, he outlined the themes he would emphasize throughout the campaign. Declaring himself to be an "independent outsider" rather than a Democrat, he condemned the Know-Nothings for their secrecy, their irresponsible appeals to religious prejudice, their unconstitutional attempts to combine church and state, and their affiliations with the Northern abolitionists.[13]

Clingman had the field entirely to himself until 14 May, when a Know-Nothing convention in Asheville chose Leander B. Carmichael of Wilkes to run against him. A three-term member of the House of Commons, the strikingly handsome Carmichael was a decade younger than the forty-three-year-old Clingman and was reported to be an effective stump speaker. His amiability and courteousness provided a sharp contrast to his hot-tempered antagonist, and even his opponents acknowledged him to be "a clever man." However, Carmichael was little known outside his own county, whereas Clingman, a five-term incumbent, was a familiar figure throughout the district. The two candidates conducted their first joint debate at Murphey in Cherokee County in early June, and they canvassed the district together for the remaining two months of the campaign.[14]

As in the two previous campaigns, both sides asserted that their candidate was a "better Union man" than his opponent. The Know-Nothings routinely dubbed Clingman with epithets like "disunion traitor," while portraying themselves as the "great American, Union saving party." Avoiding any threats of disunion, the congressman countered with the same argument he had used earlier against Burgess Gaither. According to Clingman, his record as a strong supporter of Southern Rights made him the better choice for stemming the tide of Northern fanaticism that was endangering the Union. As he explained to the voters of Macon County, "all depends on what kind of stuff the representatives we shall send are made of." If Southerners expected to "repel the [antislavery] attack," it was important that they "send to Congress men of the right sort . . . [with] the proper spirit and firmness to represent us." The *Asheville News* likewise admonished its readers that "the only hope of the South in that God-forsaken assemblage" lay in the election of "such men as Mr. Clingman—men of nerve, before whom the hordes of fanaticism quake and tremble. . . . An error here may be fatal."[15]

The Know-Nothings did not rely exclusively on issues that the Whigs had failed to exploit effectively against Clingman in 1851 and 1853. Party newspapers such as the *Herald of Truth* also made an appeal to the "prejudices of church members" in the mountain district. They depicted the congressman as "a *wicked* man" who did not belong to any church himself, who "quotes from the bible 'irreverently,'" and who was in "sympathy with Roman Catholicism"—perhaps even a Catholic himself. Clingman's supporters took those accusations quite seriously and made strenuous efforts to rebut them. They pointed out that "Mr. Clingman is a protestant in principle, as are all his family and relatives," at the same time reminding the voters that he "is not before the people for a church office." In his speeches on the hustings and in a campaign circular issued two weeks before the election, Clingman repeatedly invoked "the great doctrine of religious toleration" and condemned efforts "to proscribe and persecute others on account of their religion." [16]

East of the mountains, the Know-Nothings made a respectable showing in the congressional elections of 1855, carrying the three traditionally Whig districts and garnering almost half the popular vote. In Clingman's district, on the other hand, the veteran congressman easily won election to a sixth term. The *Asheville News* hailed the "triumphant re-election of Hon. T. L. Clingman" and pronounced "K[now] Nothingism Spurned by the People." Nonetheless, Clingman's 55 percent of the vote was substantially lower than his majorities in the three previous elections. Especially embarrassing was his showing in Buncombe County and his home town of Asheville, both of which he lost for the first time since 1841. The Know-Nothings could derive some comfort from the knowledge that their enemy had been "repudiated at home, whatever may have been his success elsewhere." [17]

Clingman's supporters in the mountain district were careful not to characterize his election as a triumph for the Democrats or as a repudiation of Whiggery. The *Asheville News* designated the victorious congressman as an "Anti-K. N. Independent" and claimed that the voters had endorsed "the cause of true Republicanism . . . without regard to former party prejudices and divisions." In his private correspondence, Clingman underscored the importance of emphasizing the discontinuity between the Know-Nothings and the Whigs. In "a region formerly strongly Whig but now dead against the Know-Nothings," he explained, it was essential that "the lines of division should be kept [as] wide as possible." Although the congressman interpreted his reelection as a victory for "Republican principles," it remained to be seen whether the outcome really constituted a rejection of Know-Nothingism or whether, instead, it was simply another personal triumph for Thomas Lanier Clingman. [18]

When Clingman returned to Washington to attend the convening of the Thirty-Fourth Congress in December 1855, the various parties were in a state of confusion and disarray. As a result of their staggering losses in the North in the wake of the furor over the Kansas-Nebraska Act, the Democrats no longer controlled the House of Representatives. But neither of the two opposition parties that had sprung up after the demise of the Whigs—the Know-Nothings and the Republicans—was strong enough by itself to command a majority. The ensuing contest for the speakership exceeded even the 1849–50 imbroglio in duration. Republican Nathaniel Banks consistently outpolled his various competitors, but his vote fell considerably short of the requisite majority. Understandably, the Republicans introduced numerous resolutions to elect the Speaker by a plurality vote—a proposition that the Democrats and Know-Nothings strenuously resisted.[19]

After more than one hundred fruitless ballots, the Republicans found an unlikely ally in the maverick congressman from the Old North State. On 30 January 1856 Clingman astounded his fellow Southerners by offering a plurality resolution of his own. Unlike the Republicans, he did not believe that such a course of action would result in the election of Banks. Instead, he expected that the Know-Nothings would vote for Democratic nominee James L. Orr "as a lesser evil," if forced to choose between him and a Republican. The Democratic leaders did not share Clingman's optimism, and they urged him to withdraw his motion. After failing in that effort, the Democrats combined with the Know-Nothings to defeat his resolution by a four-vote margin. Three days later, Samuel A. Smith of Tennessee introduced another plurality resolution, and this one passed by a nine-vote majority. Clingman and Smith were the only Southerners who voted in the affirmative.[20]

As Clingman had anticipated, most of the Know-Nothings, including the three in the North Carolina delegation, were willing to support the Democratic candidate once the plurality rule was invoked. Contrary to his expectations, however, six Know-Nothings continued to throw their votes away on other candidates, while several others refused to vote at all. Banks won the election by a three-vote margin. After the vote had been announced, a few die-hard Democrats protested that "Banks could not be declared Speaker, as he had not received a majority of the votes." In order to erase any doubts about the legality of the election, Clingman offered a supplementary resolution affirming that the Massachusetts Republican had been "duly chosen speaker, and is hereby so declared." The battle-weary House approved his resolution by an overwhelming majority.[21]

The opposition presses in North Carolina were furious with Clingman for his role in elevating a Republican to the speakership. Noting that he had been "found standing, side by side, with . . . the whole abolition crew, in opposition to the *entire South*," the *Asheville Spectator* accused him of trading his vote for "the Chairmanship of some important committee—that of Foreign Affairs, for instance." According to the *Raleigh Register,* even the Democrats were muttering epithets about "Clingman's 'last move.'" One member of that party allegedly exclaimed that the congressman had "never been right since he voted to receive those infernal abolition petitions," while another reportedly predicted that his behavior in the speakership controversy "will kill him politically." As usual, the prophecies of Clingman's impending demise would prove groundless.[22]

Now the third-ranking member of the Foreign Affairs Committee, Clingman continued to steer an independent course, much to the consternation of the Pierce administration. In May 1856, after several Americans had been killed in disturbances in Panama, he introduced a resolution authorizing the president to use troops in order to protect the railroad route across the isthmus and to provide for the safety of American citizens. Although ostensibly a defensive measure, the real purpose of Clingman's resolution, as he indicated to Secretary of State William L. Marcy, was to pave the way for an American occupation of Panama.[23]

The response in Congress was less than enthusiastic, particularly since it was clear the administration was not supporting Clingman's initiative. Democrat George W. Jones of Tennessee ridiculed his resolution as a "proposition authorizing the President to take possession of Central America." Alexander H. Stephens could see no reason for the House to suspend its rules to consider it. A motion to suspend the rules was defeated by a vote of fifty-three to seventy-four. Clingman later remarked that a pusillanimous Congress had hesitated out of fear that "the President might . . . involve us in war."[24]

Clingman was aware that an aggressive movement in Central America might well provoke a reaction from Great Britain, whose aim was to prevent the United States from extending its power in that region. Far from fearing a confrontation with the former mother country, the congressman seemed eager to foment one. He believed that Britain was giving aid and encouragement to the American abolitionists in order "to keep us in an eternal agitation about this question of slavery to the neglect of great national interests." In light of that hostile attitude, the United States "had a perfect right to interrupt her movement against us, if necessary, by going to war with her." In Clingman's view, an aggressive anti-British posture would also serve to mitigate sectional hostilities by directing "the public attention . . . to foreign questions rather than to a domestic controversy."[25]

The cautious diplomacy of Pierce and Marcy (which Clingman privately characterized as "irritating and weak") prevented the differences between the two nations from escalating into a full-scale war. Clingman proved more successful in exploiting anti-British sentiment for domestic partisan purposes. Twisting the lion's tail was a favorite pastime for American politicians during the antebellum era, and the congressman from the mountain district proved to be an adept practitioner. As the presidential campaign of 1856 commenced, Clingman was also eager to discredit the Republicans by linking them to the alleged British conspiracy to undermine the American republic. In March 1856 he published a lengthy circular with the avowed purpose of "exposing the injustice of the [American] Abolitionists toward us, and at the same time rendering their great ally odious to our people." Although ostensibly directed at his own constituents, the pamphlet was, according to Clingman, "intended for general circulation, and . . . in fact was used to some extent in other States."[26]

Clingman began by accusing the British of engaging in a deliberate plot to destroy the economy of "her great commercial rival . . . [by] forc[ing] the United States to emancipate her slaves." He then pointed to the "complete understanding between our enemies in Great Britain and their allies in this country" and denounced the "abolition managers" of the North as "unprincipled . . . cowardly, mean, and malicious." Their object, he claimed, was nothing less than "the total abolition of slavery, the raising of the negroes to equality with us, and the amalgamation of the white and black races." Should they succeed in electing their candidate to the presidency, "it is hardly to be hoped that our system would long survive." On the other hand, "should the party of the Constitution triumph, it is probable that the anti-slavery feeling of the North . . . will subside, and allow the government to move on in the even tenor of its way."[27]

Clingman left no doubt as to which party in his mind constituted "the party of the Constitution." "The great antagonist . . . of the anti-slavery party," he affirmed, "must be the nominee of the Democracy." Once again, however, the congressman stopped short of professing to be a Democrat himself. As in 1852, the thrust of his argument was that a conscientious Whig could support the Democratic presidential nominee "with propriety, and without any loss of self-respect." The Democrats of the 1850s, he explained, were no longer the "spoils party" against whom he had railed during the 1840s. "That party has been essentially modified within the last few years." It had not only "thrown off the free-soilers in the North" but also "gotten rid of some bad elements in the South" and gained added respectability from "the assistance of patriotic Whigs who have marched to its support." Standing "firmly on the principles of the genuine Republican party of the olden time," the Democracy was "entitled to the support of all conservative and patriotic men."[28]

Although Clingman had kind words in his address for "Franklin Pierce and the granite Democracy of New Hampshire," he refrained from explicitly endorsing the president for reelection. Pierce was popular among North Carolina Democrats because of his efforts on behalf of the Kansas-Nebraska Act, and he enjoyed the solid support of the delegation from the Old North State at the Democratic National Convention, which met in Cincinnati during the first week of June. Clingman, though still nominally an independent, attended the convention and participated in its proceedings. As expected, North Carolina held firm in support of Pierce until his name was withdrawn after the fourteenth ballot. The Tar Heel delegates gave a unanimous vote to Stephen A. Douglas on the next two ballots before joining the other states in bestowing the nomination on James Buchanan.[29]

A seasoned politician and a veteran of many party battles, Buchanan had been out of the country during the controversy over the Kansas–Nebraska Act—an absence that undoubtedly strengthened his candidacy in the North. At the same time, the former minister to Great Britain was popular among Southern Democrats as the author of the Ostend Manifesto, a controversial document that had advocated the acquisition of Cuba, even at the cost of a war with Spain. While nominating a Northerner for the presidency, the Democrats bowed to the wishes of their Southern wing by adopting a platform that endorsed an expansionist foreign policy designed to promote "American ascendancy in the Gulf of Mexico."[30] Two weeks after the adjournment of the convention, Clingman issued a circular endorsing the Democratic nominee as "a statesman admirably fitted for the station of chief executive" and commending the platform as both "sound and national."[31]

The congressman was considerably less outspoken in regard to the state elections. Perhaps mindful that his involvement in the governor's race two years earlier had produced no benefits for the Democrats, he remained behind the scenes in 1856 and allowed his lieutenants to direct the campaign. Marcus Erwin, who was hoping to succeed Zebulon Vance in the House of Commons, traveled extensively throughout the mountain district during the spring, organizing meetings of the "Democratic and Anti–Know Nothing party" and speaking on behalf of Thomas Bragg, who was seeking a second term as governor. At the same time, Thomas W. Atkin hoisted Bragg's name atop the editorial page of the *Asheville News* and vigorously assailed his Know-Nothing opponent, John A. Gilmer.[32]

Erwin and Atkin faced a seemingly uphill battle. Although the Democrats had been gaining strength in the mountain district during the 1850s, Bragg had polled only 37 percent of its vote in 1854. State sectionalism also appeared to work in favor of the Know-Nothings in the far west. Bragg was a resident of the east, whereas Gilmer was a westerner with a long record of support for internal improvements and constitutional reform. To counteract Gilmer's appeal among voters who had previously supported the Whigs, Erwin and Atkin adopted the same strategy Clingman had employed against Carmichael a year earlier, emphasizing the discontinuity between the Know-Nothing party and its Whig predecessor and calling for "a union of the conservative men of the old parties—Whigs and Democrats" as "the only means . . . of preventing the dangers to the South and the Union." In counties where the Whigs were particularly strong, they downplayed Bragg's Democratic pedigree and referred to him, instead, as the candidate of the "Anti Know-Nothing party."[33]

The outcome of the election demonstrated the wisdom of that strategy. Bragg's vote in the mountain counties increased by eighteen percentage points from the previous election, enabling him to become the first Democrat ever to carry that district. Even more impressive were the Democratic gains in the legislative elections. In Clingman's district the party elected four of the five state senators and captured ten of the sixteen seats in the House of Commons. For the first time since the advent of organized parties in the 1830s, the Democrats were the majority party in the mountain district.[34]

Despite the low profile kept by Clingman during the campaign, his supporters did not hesitate to give him the lion's share of credit for the outcome. According to the *Asheville News,* the congressman's crusade against the Know-Nothings a year earlier had paved the way for Bragg's triumph in 1856. "The K.N.'s built their hopes that Gov. Bragg would not be able to obtain Mr. Clingman's majority. He could not have obtained it twelve months ago, but the seeds of truth sown by Mr. Clingman have taken deep root in the soil. He did his work well."[35]

Undoubtedly mindful of the substantial drop in Democratic strength during the three-month interval between the state and national elections of 1852, Clingman returned to North Carolina in September and undertook a thorough canvass of the mountain district. The congressman continued to focus his efforts on persuading Whig voters to "forget past party prejudices and bickerings" and support the Democratic nominee. In effect, that meant convincing them that Millard Fillmore, the Know-Nothing candidate, was not a viable alternative to Buchanan. Clingman refrained from any personal criticism of the popular former president, acknowledging that he "would no doubt administer the Government fairly . . . were he President." At the same time, he asserted that Fillmore "cannot in any possible contingency be elected." Thus, it would be "folly . . . for southern men to throw away their votes upon him, especially as the contest between Buchanan and Fremont will be close and the vote of one State may decide the fate of the South and the Union."[36]

Like numerous other Southern leaders, Clingman warned that the election of Republican John C. Fremont could very well result in a dissolution of the Union. As early as March, he had predicted that "if beaten, we may be forced to declare independence, to maintain equality and honor." In June he reiterated his belief that "the success of the black republican candidate . . . will most probably be fatal to the existence of the government."[37] Inherent in those statements, as well as in the pronouncements of other Southerners who warned of the dire consequences of a Republican victory, was a calculated ambiguity that would not be completely resolved until the secession crisis of 1860 – 61. If the "black republican candidate" should in fact be elected, an attempt would probably be made by Southern radicals to dissolve the Union. In that case, how would politicians like Clingman, who hoped that Southern Rights might be maintained within the Union, respond? Would they join the secessionists? Would they remain on the sidelines and simply allow events to take their course? Or would they actively resist disunion?[38]

In a letter to a group of Southern militants at Charlotte, written three weeks before the presidential election, Clingman addressed that issue but, in the process, raised more questions than he answered. After first expressing confidence that Fremont would not be elected, he then went on to discuss how Southerners should react to a hypothetical Republican victory. He dismissed as "an absurdity" the notion that Southern leaders should limit their resistance merely to refusing to hold federal office under a Republican administration. He also characterized the belief that Southerners "ought to wait for an *overt act* before taking action" as "the height of fatuity." Clingman had hard words as well for those "few traitors" who might urge submission to Republican rule, boldly proposing that such men should "receive *swift attention* from our Committees of Vigilance, until the State governments could take the necessary steps to insure tranquility."[39]

On their face, those inflammatory statements seem to confirm one historian's conclusion that Clingman had, by October 1856, "revealed unmistakably his secession views."[40] However, a more careful examination of his letter indicates that it was riddled with ambiguities and contradictions. On the one hand, Clingman compared his correspondents in Charlotte to the Revolutionary signers of the Mecklenburg Declaration of Independence.[41] On the other, he branded as "preposterous . . . the idea . . . that we are threatening to *revolt* against the government." In one breath, he seemed to be threatening a bloody confrontation by daring Massachusetts and New York to respond "by force of arms . . . *if they can.*" In the next, he predicted that his "line of policy" could be carried out peacefully "without any real sacrifice."

A close reading of the Charlotte letter reveals that Clingman was not calling upon the slave states to establish an independent confederacy in the event of Fremont's election. Instead, as he later recalled, he was urging Southerners "to hold the government, and make the fight in the Union" by purging the nation of its antislavery elements. He explained to his correspondents in Charlotte that only those states that had "stood by the Constitution are entitled to hold the organization of the government." Those "who refuse to obey the Constitution, are to be held as having gone out of the Union." While he was vague on the specifics, Clingman—like some Southerners during the crisis of 1860–61—seemed to be contemplating a confederacy bereft of the troublesome states of New England, which would not be readmitted into the fold until they had acknowledged the error of their ways and agreed to respect the constitutional rights of the South.[42]

Clingman's enemies ignored the ambiguities and fine distinctions and branded his letter as a disunion document. His supporters interpreted the communication quite differently. Declaring that the Union was "such an unmixed good that the worthless and faithless should not be permitted to participate in its measureless blessings," the *New York Day Book* characterized Clingman's proposal as "a capital idea" and asserted that his plan could be accomplished simply by "withdraw[ing] the federal functionaries from the defaulting or faithless States . . . [and] refusing a seat to their delegation at Washington." The *Asheville News* also denied that Clingman's letter "convict[ed] him of being an enemy to the Union" and claimed that he had sought only "to warn his countrymen of the probable consequences of Fremont's election." Indeed, it remarked, many prominent members of the Know-Nothing party, including Fillmore himself, had "expressed opinions similar to those advanced by Mr. Clingman." [43]

Clingman did not have an opportunity to elaborate on the ideas contained in the Charlotte letter since, as he had predicted, Fremont lost the presidential election to Buchanan. Although the Pennsylvania Democrat carried only five Northern states, his majorities in North Carolina and all the other slave states except Maryland gave him enough electoral votes to outdistance both his competitors. In the weeks following the election, Clingman took steps to cement the alliance he had forged with the Democrats during the campaign. On 18 November he was a featured speaker at a Democratic rally held in Raleigh to celebrate Buchanan's victory. A week later, he was one of the guests of honor at a large and enthusiastic Democratic meeting at Tammany Hall. Standing on the same platform as Isaac Rynders of the Empire Club—a man whom he had once denounced as a cheat and a swindler—Clingman announced to his former adversary and to the cheering crowd that "it was now his pride to avow himself a member of the Democratic Party, which was the only party that could be called national." [44]

Now a full-fledged Democrat, Clingman returned to Washington in December amid speculation that he would be appointed to a cabinet position in the Buchanan administration. During the lame duck session of the Thirty-Fourth Congress, he once again focused his energies on steering his adopted party toward a "bolder foreign policy." Having long since given up on Pierce, Clingman approached President-elect Buchanan, only to find that the aging statesman "had weakened greatly" and was now "disposed to qualify" the bellicose language he had used two years earlier in the Ostend Manifesto. Still, he hoped the new president might be "strengthened in his feelings and induced to maintain bold American ground." [45]

On 5 February 1857 Clingman himself staked out that ground in a vituperative speech on British policy in Central America and Cuba. A considerable part of the congressman's animus was directed toward the treaty that Whig secretary of state John M. Clayton had negotiated with Sir Henry Bulwer in 1850. Designed to forestall a potentially explosive rivalry between the two powers for control of a canal or railroad route across Nicaragua, the Clayton-Bulwer Treaty prohibited either government from exercising exclusive control over such a route or from "assuming or exercising domain" over any Central American country. Clingman roundly denounced the Taylor administration as "feeble and imbecile" for allowing itself to be "entrapped by British diplomacy" into signing the treaty, and he condemned Britain for systematically violating its provisions by extending its protectorate over the Mosquito Coast and annexing the Bay Islands. A treaty that blocked American expansion in the Caribbean while doing nothing to prevent British incursions there would, he said, inevitably result in "Central America . . . becom[ing] one of her possessions as completely as Canada is at this day." For that reason, it was important that the Clayton-Bulwer Treaty "be got rid of" and not simply modified, as Pierce and Marcy were proposing.[46]

Like most Southern Democrats, Clingman believed the United States was destined eventually to control the entire "parcel of territory which lies between us and the Isthmus of Panama." By 1857, however, he was basing his argument for American expansion into the Caribbean on broad national interests and not on the South's need for additional slave territory as he had done during the early 1850s. Clingman's effort "to present these considerations . . . as national questions" and to eschew "those sectional issues with which . . . the country is already wearied" was far more in keeping with the position of national Democrats like Stephen A. Douglas than with the notions of Southern sectionalists like John A. Quitman.[47]

The growing congruence between Clingman's views and those of Douglas and the national Democrats was underscored by his vote on the bill authorizing Minnesota to enter the Union as a free state. Clingman was one of only a handful of Southerners who supported the bill. The irony of "this most ultra of Southern Rights extremists" voting against a majority in his own section was not lost on Clingman's enemies in the Old North State. The *Wilmington Herald* bitterly denounced him for "play[ing] into the hands of the Black Republicans" and reminded its readers that Clingman was the same congressman who had introduced "the motion, by the operation of which Banks, the Black Republican, was elected Speaker of the House of Representatives."[48]

Clearly, the course Clingman was charting in the late 1850s was quite different from the one taken by fire eaters like Robert Barnwell Rhett and William L. Yancey. The North Carolinian had not abandoned his commitment to Southern Rights, but like other Southern Democrats who affiliated with the national wing of the party during the late 1850s, he had come to the conclusion that the best hope for protecting those rights lay in the preservation of the Democratic party as a national institution. That attitude naturally led him to oppose any move that would weaken the Democratic party in the North without significantly advancing the interests of the South. As the *Asheville News* explained in defending his vote on the Minnesota bill, if Southern Democrats refused to admit a territory to statehood simply because its residents chose to prohibit slavery, "our Northern allies . . . *cannot* stand up before a Northern constituency, and advocate the admission of new slave States."[49]

Clingman's move toward a more national orientation was not without risk. Indeed, under different circumstances his vote on the Minnesota bill and his pivotal role in electing Banks to the speakership might have provided powerful campaign ammunition to the opposition. But as the congressional elections of 1857 approached, the Know-Nothings—seemingly so formidable just two years earlier—now found themselves "weak, broken down, and scattered." The party had been thoroughly demoralized by its abysmal showing in 1856, and many Democrats predicted that Clingman would return to Congress unopposed.[50]

Those predictions underestimated the tenacity of Clingman's enemies in the mountain district. After unsuccessfully trying to persuade Democrat William H. Thomas to enter the race against Clingman, opposition leaders (who were now calling themselves "American Whigs") put forward the name of Zebulon B. Vance. Although he allowed his name to be placed on the ballot, Vance never formally accepted the nomination, and he refused to undertake an active campaign. Even the rabidly anti-Clingman *Asheville Spectator* acknowledged that there was "no chance" of Vance's election and that "the vote is intended merely as a compliment for his integrity and faithfulness to his principles."[51]

Clingman won the election handily, garnering almost eighty-seven hundred votes, compared to about thirty-two hundred for Vance. Despite the one-sided nature of the outcome, voter turnout exceeded that for the presidential election held the previous November, and Clingman improved upon Buchanan's showing by more than twenty-five hundred votes. The Democrats interpreted the result as a victory for both the South and the Union. According to the *Asheville News,* Clingman's triumph demonstrated that "the freemen of this District are Southern and States Right men to the backbone." It also proved that "they know the value of the Union . . . and while it continues to be a Constitutional Union they will defend it at every hazard and to the last extremity."[52]

As he commenced his seventh term in the U.S. House of Representatives, the forty-five-year-old Clingman enjoyed the distinction of being one of North Carolina's longest-serving congressmen. His stature as one of the most powerful men on Capitol Hill was further enhanced by his appointment to the chairmanship of the Foreign Affairs Committee.[53] His tenure as chairman would be brief. A few weeks after the convening of Congress, a notice appeared in the North Carolina newspapers announcing the death of Judge Henry Potter of the U.S. Circuit Court. Probably few besides Clingman could have anticipated that this seemingly unrelated occurrence would finally provide him the opportunity to achieve his long-standing ambition for a seat in the United States Senate.[54]

9 *The Bubbling Cauldron*

On 7 May 1858 Thomas L. Clingman resigned his seat in the House of Representatives in order to accept an appointment to the United States Senate. In a formal letter of resignation addressed to Governor Thomas Bragg, he remarked that he was "acting in accordance with what I believe to be . . . the general wish of the Democratic party in our State." Opposition spokesmen (who were once again beginning to call themselves Whigs) were considerably more cynical. They claimed that Bragg had appointed the veteran congressman to fill the vacancy occasioned by the recent resignation of Asa Biggs in return for Clingman's promise to support the governor for the other Senate seat. Clingman did, in fact, lobby aggressively and at times unscrupulously for the senatorship. His relentless efforts at self-promotion alienated a considerable number of North Carolina Democrats and left a legacy of bitterness and recrimination within the party.[1]

When the Thirty-Fifth Congress had commenced the previous December, Clingman had been appointed chairman of the House Foreign Affairs Committee. Democratic presses throughout the nation hailed his appointment to "one of the most important positions in the House" and predicted that "he will exert a favorable influence on the policy of the Government." Despite those predictions, Clingman's bellicose expansionism and his irritation at the failure of President Buchanan to adopt "a vigorous American policy, with reference to . . . controversies with Great Britain" created constant friction with the Democratic chief executive.[2]

Much of that friction resulted from Clingman's persistent efforts to pressure Buchanan into abrogating the Clayton-Bulwer Treaty. Ostensibly designed to secure American transit rights across Central America, the treaty also bound both Britain and the United States not to seize territory or establish protectorates in that region. Like other expansionists who viewed the agreement as an obstacle to U.S. hegemony in the Caribbean, Buchanan took a dim view of the Clayton-Bulwer Treaty. In his first annual message to Congress in December 1857, he explicitly called for its abrogation. But the former ambassador to the Court of Saint James hoped to accomplish that objective through patient negotiation, avoiding any precipitate action that might needlessly complicate relations with Great Britain. Like his predecessors in the executive office, Buchanan considered the negotiation of treaties to be the prerogative of the president. Clingman's determination to play a major role in the diplomatic process inevitably placed him on a collision course with the new administration.[3]

After "many rather disagreeable conversations" with the president on the subject of Anglo-American relations, Clingman became convinced that Buchanan had "been completely won over to England" by British envoy Sir William Gore Ousley, who also happened to be a personal friend of the chief executive. Clingman certainly did the president an injustice in attributing his behavior to his "boundless . . . admiration for the British government." Indeed, Buchanan's cautious and nonconfrontational approach would eventually result in substantial British concessions. However, the impatient North Carolinian was not willing to wait for the president's quiet diplomacy to produce results. Instead, he decided to "entirely disregard his wishes" by introducing a resolution denouncing the Clayton-Bulwer Treaty as "an entangling alliance" and an "entire surrender of the rights of this country . . . [that] ought therefore to be abrogated."[4]

On 5 May 1858 Clingman spoke on behalf of his resolution in a wide-ranging address that touched on a variety of subjects in addition to the Clayton-Bulwer Treaty. The congressman denounced the agreement as "a Wilmot proviso imposed by a foreign government against the growth not only of the South, but likewise of the North, and of the whole United States." Its abrogation, he said, would open Central America "to the occupation of citizens of the United States." On the other hand, if the United States failed to exert its influence in the region, the British would inevitably fill the vacuum. "The real question," according to Clingman, "is, 'Shall Great Britain or the United States control this Central American country?'"[5]

Despite "the persistent opposition of the President's especial friends," Clingman's resolution passed the House of Representatives on 6 May 1858 by an eleven-vote margin. Five days later, however, Democrat Daniel Sickles of New York persuaded his colleagues to strike out its key provisions "on the ground that it would embarrass pending negotiations, and tend to initiate a war policy." Clingman was not on hand to oppose Sickles's motion since by then he had moved up to the U.S. Senate. The opposition presses could not resist pointing out that he had received that choice political plum "whilst in open rebellion . . . to the will of the administration . . . [and] to the foreign policy of the Government."[6]

The news of Clingman's elevation to the Senate came as no surprise to informed observers of North Carolina politics. For months, rumors had been circulating that Asa Biggs would leave the Senate to become a federal judge and that Clingman would be appointed in his place. Still, there was nothing inevitable about Biggs's decision to resign just a few weeks before the adjournment of Congress or about Governor Bragg's choice of Clingman as his replacement. Indeed, Clingman himself played the central role in orchestrating the complicated series of events that would culminate in his promotion to the position he had coveted for more than a decade.[7]

Since 1846, when he had tried to persuade Willie P. Mangum to resign his Senate seat to run for governor, Clingman had been maneuvering to create a vacancy that he might subsequently be appointed or elected to fill. Early in 1857, when it appeared that Sen. David S. Reid might be named to a cabinet position, the congressman had requested his trusted ally William H. Thomas to sound out Bragg about "what he would be likely to do in the event of there being a vacancy in the Senate." Since the dictates of propriety prohibited Clingman from lobbying directly on his own behalf, he instructed Thomas to approach the governor "without of course intimating that I have any connection with your asking the question."[8]

No record exists of Bragg's response, but Clingman's subsequent behavior suggests he was probably given assurances that the governor would react favorably in case of a vacancy. It is also likely that Bragg received at least an indirect promise that Clingman would support him for the other Senate seat, once it became vacant. Contrary to the predictions, Reid did not resign from the Senate in early 1857. However, the death of Judge Potter in December presented Clingman with the prospect of another opening should Biggs be appointed to take his place on the bench. By January, rumors were already circulating in the Whig presses of "a bargain made by and between our . . . democratic Senators and Representatives at Washington and 'the Raleigh Clique,' by which one is to be Governor, another U.S. Senator in place of Reid, still another Senator in place of Biggs, and the last and least, U.S. Judge." By spring, the identity of the various parties to the bargain had become public knowledge. As the *Fayetteville Observer* explained, "Biggs [was] to be U.S. Judge, Clingman to be Senator in his place, Holden to be Governor, and Bragg to be Senator in place of Reid."[9]

The eventual outcome of that complex scenario depended on Biggs's willingness to trade his Senate seat for a federal judgeship. Although more inclined toward the law than politics, the senator did not immediately jump at the opportunity to take Potter's place on the bench. Several of his closest political allies advised him against such a move. Moreover, there was no guarantee that President Buchanan would nominate Biggs, even if he were willing to serve. Numerous other aspirants, including former congressmen Romulus M. Saunders and Abraham W. Venable, were also vying for the position.[10]

Neither Saunders nor Venable, however, had an advocate as tireless and determined as Clingman. Within a week after Potter's death, he had already drafted a letter to Buchanan recommending Biggs for the vacant judgeship, which he subsequently persuaded Reid and three of his fellow Democratic congressmen to sign. When Biggs returned to Washington after the Christmas recess, Clingman went to work on the senator himself, using Thomas as an intermediary. Those assiduous efforts did not go unnoticed. Congressman Henry M. Shaw, who had been urging Biggs not to leave the Senate, marveled at the "zeal and energy" that Clingman had "brought to the work." Indeed, said Shaw, he was inclined to believe "that, like Macbeth, he has sought out some weird sisters, who have predicted over their bubbling cauldron, that he shall have it all. . . . He seems to work at the business as tho' he was fully persuaded that if Biggs come[s] out he will go in."[11]

By mid-February, the bargain was ready to be consummated. Biggs agreed to resign from the Senate as soon as Buchanan formally nominated him to the court. Yet, despite assurances from the president that Biggs was his choice, no official announcement was forthcoming. Buchanan's inaction "has created much suspense," Biggs wrote Reid on 21 February, particularly since "the reason for delay is not satisfactorily accounted for."[12]

Buchanan's hesitation in filling the judicial vacancy was a product of the complex legislative maneuvering over the seemingly unrelated issue of Kansas. Early in February, a bill to admit Kansas into the Union as a slave state had fallen four votes short of a majority on its first test in the House of Representatives. Clingman could be counted on to support the statehood bill in the House, and Buchanan, who had staked his prestige on a satisfactory resolution of the Kansas issue, could ill afford for him to resign his seat before the bill was passed. As the debate over Kansas dragged on through March and April, the judicial appointment continued to languish. On 30 April 1858, a compromise measure known as the English bill finally passed both houses of Congress, with Clingman and the other members of the North Carolina delegation voting in its favor. By the end of the following week, Biggs was a U.S. judge, and Clingman was the junior senator from North Carolina. Within a few months, Bragg would join Clingman in the U.S. Senate.[13]

Only one part of the scenario failed to unfold in the manner the Whigs had predicted. A few weeks before Biggs's resignation, William W. Holden, who had allegedly been offered the governorship in return for supporting the senatorial aspirations of Clingman and Bragg, presented his claims to the Democratic State Convention. Although county meetings and Democratic newspapers throughout the state began taking sides in the contest between Holden and his principal rival John W. Ellis as early as February, Clingman remained publicly neutral. The Whigs were unconvinced by the congressman's seeming impartiality. In March the *Greensboro Patriot* reported the existence of a "combination" between Clingman and Holden "to defeat the nomination of Judge Ellis." The Democratic editor, whose strong advocacy of internal improvements identified him with the progressive western wing of his party, received the votes of all but two of the mountain counties at the state convention. However, those votes were not sufficient to overcome the overwhelming support Ellis secured from the conservative eastern counties. One cynical Whig claimed that Clingman had deliberately double-crossed his erstwhile ally by "marshaling . . . his mountain men for Holden, but [leaving] just enough deficient . . . to defeat him."[14]

If Holden placed any blame on Clingman for his failure to win his party's gubernatorial nomination, he gave no hint of it on the pages of the *North Carolina Standard*. Indeed, in announcing the congressman's appointment to the U.S. Senate, the editor had nothing but accolades for him. Comparing the new senator to John C. Calhoun, Holden predicted that "he will at once take and maintain the front rank among American Senators." Other Democratic editors shared that enthusiastic assessment. The *Washington Union* characterized Clingman as "a man of ability and great usefulness, whose capacities and experience fit him for almost every department of public business." The *Richmond South* remarked that he had obtained "an enviable reputation . . . during his twelve years' service in the House of Representatives" and asserted that he "will greatly enhance his reputation" in the Senate.[15]

The opposition presses retorted that Clingman had been rewarded not for his abilities as a legislator but for betraying his former party and delivering the mountain district to the Democrats. Edward J. Hale of the *Fayetteville Observer* acknowledged that the new senator had performed "most efficient services to the Democratic party" but added that "they were Benedict Arnold services." "Nearly four years before he ceased to be a Whig," Hale reminded his readers, ". . . he was working, as a Whig leader, to undermine the principles of the Whigs of the Mountain district; and finally, as a Whig, he succeeded. . . . To reward such an act is monstrous." The *Greensboro Patriot* agreed that "Clingman has been rewarded for betraying the confidence of his early friends," while the *Raleigh Register* opined that Bragg would have done better to have "appointed an old sinner instead of a renegade."[16]

Even the Whigs, however, grudgingly gave Clingman "credit for considerable ability." Not since the days of Nathaniel Macon had a North Carolinian made such a mark on the House of Representatives or achieved such prominence outside his own state. "His position as one of the leading men of the country," said the Democratic *Wilmington Journal*, "will hardly be questioned by friend or foe." Indeed, asserted the *Washington Star*, "no other member of the House fills a larger space in the public eye."[17]

Still, Clingman's legislative record had been singularly barren. Despite his almost two decades of service in Congress, no major piece of legislation bore his name. His major domestic policy initiative—the elimination of the tariff duties on railroad iron—had been repeatedly voted down, while his efforts to pressure the Pierce and Buchanan administrations into adopting a more aggressive foreign policy had proven equally unsuccessful. It is difficult to disagree with the assessment of one historian that the "belligerently self-assertive" Clingman was "unfit to handle . . . sensitive issues of major scope." His bellicose attitude toward Great Britain, whose government was increasingly inclined to acknowledge the hegemony of the United States in Central America, was, at best, misguided and, at worst, irresponsible.[18]

Nor had the new Democratic senator distinguished himself as a party loyalist. For most of the 1850s he had self-consciously styled himself an independent, and he continued to steer his own course even after he formally joined the Democrats. Most of his foreign-policy initiatives had been made contrary to the wishes of the Pierce and Buchanan administrations. On matters of domestic policy, Clingman also proved to be a thorn in the side of the Democratic leadership. Throughout the 1850s he complained incessantly about corruption and extravagance in the federal bureaucracy and voted repeatedly against congressional appropriation bills. Opposition leaders were quick to point out that his appointment to the Senate had closely followed his vote against the administration-sponsored deficiency bill, which had been designed to provide for the shortfall in government revenue occasioned by the Panic of 1857.[19]

Clingman's reputation as a legislator rested not on specific measures of statecraft or on a record of party regularity but on his prowess as a speaker and debater, his indefatigable energy, and his undisputed skills as a parliamentarian. At first glance, the North Carolinian seemed to lack the attributes of an effective rhetorician. Far from being mellifluous, his raspy voice was characterized by a somewhat unpleasant twang that, according to one observer, could invariably be heard rising "above all the [other] nasal voices of the House." Avoiding the histrionics in which many of his colleagues habitually indulged, he delivered his prepared speeches at a "quiet and deliberate pace" in a tone that some considered to be overly "cold and calculating." Nor did Clingman gain notoriety in Congress as an original thinker. His denunciations of the protective tariff, his exposés of abolitionism, his calls for Southern unity, his warnings about British designs on Central America—the changes on all those themes had been rung many times before by John C. Calhoun and other Southern Democrats.[20]

On the other hand, few of Clingman's colleagues could match his "strong, cogent reasoning," "his remarkable fluency," or the impressive array of facts and statistics that he used to buttress his arguments. A voracious reader blessed with an enormous intellect and a highly retentive memory, he was regarded as one of the best-informed members of Congress. Newspaper accounts, government reports, census returns, memorials from lobbyists, scientific treatises, classical literature—all provided grist for his mill. That abundant storehouse of information, along with his "superior powers of analysis," made Clingman a formidable opponent in the extemporaneous debates that frequently occurred on the floor of Congress. Noting that he was "quite at home on all the subjects that come into daily attention," one observer doubted whether there was "a single member less liable to be taken by surprise upon any unexpected point." Another eyewitness characterized him as "one of the most effective debaters in the Hall. . . . His adroitness in such scenes is proverbial—no one ever gets the better of him in any such encounter of wits." [21]

Clingman's reputation as a "fearless and merciless" debater rested on more than deep research and quick wits. The calmness with which he delivered his prepared speeches concealed a fiery temper that sometimes manifested itself during more spontaneous exchanges. At such times, the North Carolinian could display a "savage vindictiveness . . . which spared no feelings," and on several occasions he actually came to blows with fellow members of Congress. Although Clingman did not necessarily seek out controversy, his "extreme sensibility" sometimes led him to misconstrue inoffensive behavior as personal insult. [22]

Occasionally, Clingman's "sensibility" crossed the border into paranoia. In March 1856 Sidney Webster, the young private secretary of President Pierce, learned firsthand just how thin Clingman's skin could be when he received an angry communication demanding to know why he had not returned the congressman's greetings during church services. The flabbergasted Webster, who apparently had committed no impropriety, responded that he found it difficult "to believe that your note was written in seriousness. . . . But for your note, it would not have occurred to me that there had been anything unusual either in my manner or your own." Clingman's readiness to take offense at the slightest provocation—real or imagined—alienated potential allies and made him an unpredictable and somewhat fearsome figure on Capitol Hill. [23]

Despite his hot temper, Clingman earned the respect of his colleagues for his tireless devotion to his congressional duties. One commentator marveled that "he seems to go daily through a quantity of business which would be sufficient to wear down an ordinary constitution." Frequently staying awake until two or three o'clock in the morning, he invariably was back at his desk when Congress assembled the following day. [24] Clingman's comprehensive understanding of the intricate rules of the House also made him an astute parliamentarian. One contemporary considered him to be "the most competent on the floor" in his knowledge of "the technical details of Representative business." Veteran journalist Alexander K. McClure regarded him as second only to Alexander H. Stephens in his ability to guide a bill through the complicated maze of House procedures. According to McClure, the passage of the Kansas-Nebraska Act over fierce Northern opposition in 1854 could be attributed primarily to the shrewd "parliamentary movements" of Clingman and Stephens.[25]

Clingman's renown in the capital city was not confined to the halls of Congress. Particularly during the Buchanan administration, Washington enjoyed a vibrant social life, and the congressman from North Carolina was a familiar figure at the receptions, balls, and formal dinners hosted by the wives of the legislators and cabinet members. As one of the few bachelors in Congress, Clingman acquired a reputation as "a person of mark in ladies society . . . said to exercise much influence in drawing rooms." From a distance at least, the congressman must have presented an impressive sight to the ladies of Washington society. Fashionably dressed and looking younger than his forty-plus years, he had a trim figure, a strong-featured face complemented by a full head of chestnut brown hair, and piercing blue eyes. He was particularly fond of ballroom dancing and, like several of his colleagues, regularly went to "dancing school" to improve his style. Yet despite almost two decades of residence in "one of the most marrying places of the whole continent," Clingman remained the "gallant bachelor."[26]

Some Washington observers claimed the congressman was "so wedded to politics that he has no taste for other matters." But the evidence belies their argument that this "great admirer of the ladies" remained a bachelor by choice. During the late 1850s, two capital socialites caught his fancy. One was Harriet Lane, the beautiful and charming niece of President Buchanan who acted as official hostess at the White House. During the first session of the Thirty-Fifth Congress, Clingman and Representative Lawrence M. Keitt of South Carolina were both "looked upon as rival suitors for the hand of Miss Lane."[27]

An amusing anecdote related by Mary Boykin Chesnut suggests why the "queenly and gracious" Miss Lane may have been less than impressed by the congressman from North Carolina. Upon being introduced to the First Lady at one social occasion, Clingman bowed his head so low that his nose began to bleed. Trying to make the best of an awkward situation, he held his nose firmly and excused himself, remarking stiffly that "I will retire now. I may come back and make a few remarks." Chesnut surmised that even the stately Miss Lane "must have laughed then." Another humorous story recounted by Chesnut involved a young lady who made the mistake of trying to engage in conversation while dancing with Clingman. "Pray withhold all remarks," he reportedly told her. "It puts me out. I cannot do two things at once. If you will talk, I shall have to stop dancing." As Chesnut wryly observed, "dancing is a serious business with him."[28]

Clingman may have considered himself a lady's man, but if Mary Chesnut can be believed, the eccentric behavior of "the staid and severe-of-aspect Clingman" generated laughter more often than admiration among women. "Stories of Clingman abound," she gleefully noted in her diary. The acerbic Chesnut was not the only one who regarded the North Carolinian as a strange and somewhat comical figure. Lawrence O'Bryan Branch, who represented the Raleigh district in Congress during the late 1850s, remarked that his colleague had been "the subject of general ridicule" as he danced his way through a dinner party hosted by the postmaster general.[29]

Congressman David Outlaw, who had considerably more respect for Clingman than either Chesnut or Branch, characterized him nonetheless as "an enigma." "I am very much inclined to believe he is crazy," he told his wife. "Some of the mental balance wheels, necessary to regulate properly the machine, [are] either absent, or out of order." Outlaw also called attention to the congressman's most conspicuous idiosyncrasy—his "habit of talking to himself." "His lips are generally moving," he noted, adding that the "habit has grown upon him" over the years. Clingman's eccentric mannerisms invited ridicule, particularly among those already predisposed to criticize, and undoubtedly triggered a defense mechanism that contributed to his "extreme sensibility."[30]

Those eccentricities—combined with an overly formal manner of relating to women and a glaring age difference—made Clingman no match for the courtly and urbane George Eustis Jr. when both men vied for the hand of Louise Corcoran, the lovely teenage daughter of Washington banker William Wilson Corcoran. Corcoran enjoyed a reputation as "the prince of entertainers," and the weekly dinners he hosted at his magnificent residence across from the White House became "an institution in Washington life." Most likely, it was at one of those dinners that Clingman first made the acquaintance of Louise. When she finally decided to marry the former congressman from Louisiana, who was sixteen years younger than his rival, Clingman was reportedly "generous and hearty in his congratulations." Yet according to Alexander K. McClure, the rejection left a "wound . . . too deep to be healed." Years later, after the Corcoran affair had been forgotten, others would speculate upon the "hidden romance that has kept him all his life a bachelor."[31]

Although the first session of the Thirty-Fifth Congress was nearing its end when Clingman took his seat in the upper house, the new senator quickly made his presence known. With the Kansas issue now settled, the main question before the Senate was Andrew Johnson's homestead bill. The idea of providing western settlers with 160 acres of free land was unpopular among both parties in the Old North State, who regarded federal land sales as an important source of public revenue.[32]

Clingman responded to Johnson's proposal with a stratagem he had used against a similar bill six years earlier in the House. Instead of opposing the measure outright, he introduced an amendment to provide a homestead to every head of family in the United States. The motion to amend gave Clingman a convenient pretext for launching into a long speech against the bill, and even the Whig presses applauded him for opposing a measure that would discriminate against the citizens of older seaboard states like North Carolina. After forcing his western colleagues to go on record against the extension of the homestead principle to all Americans, Clingman moved successfully to kill the original bill.[33]

Congress adjourned on 14 June, and well before the end of the month Clingman was back in Asheville "in the enjoyment of fine health" and eager to participate in the summer election campaign. The contest promised to be an exciting one, since the voters of the mountain district would be choosing not only a governor and members of the general assembly but also a congressman to fill the seat that Clingman had occupied for most of the 1840s and 1850s. Shortly after resigning his House seat, Clingman had published a "valedictory address" in which he extolled his own record "as an independent American Representative," endorsed the principal policy measures of the Democratic party, and lauded its leaders as "national men [who] are willing to do justice to all sections of the Union." The valedictory was not so much a farewell message as an effort to shore up support for the Democrats in a region that until recently had been a Whig stronghold.[34]

The governor's contest pitted John W. Ellis, the regular Democratic nominee, against Duncan K. McRae, an insurgent Democrat who was actively soliciting Whig support by campaigning for the distribution of federal land revenues among the states. Distribution was the last of the cardinal Whig principles to be sacrificed on the altar of Clingman's ambition. In 1853 he had voted with the Whigs in favor of Henry Bennett's land bill, and two years later he had publicly denied reports that he was opposed to distribution. During the campaign of 1857, however, Clingman had publicly renounced his earlier position on the land issue, and in his valedictory address of May 1858 he reaffirmed his opposition to distribution, using the standard Democratic argument that it would necessitate an unacceptable increase in tariff duties.[35]

The debate between McRae and Ellis over distribution mattered less to Clingman than the legislative campaign, since the newly elected general assembly would have responsibility for choosing a permanent successor to Asa Biggs. In several of the mountain counties the regular Democratic candidates were being challenged by Distribution Democrats whose allegiance to Clingman was questionable. Recognizing the potentially damaging impact of the distribution issue, the senator's supporters admonished the voters that a candidate's loyalty to Clingman must take precedence over his position on land policy. Moreover, said the *Asheville News*, "it is not enough that a candidate should not profess to be hostile to him. . . . [Unless] a man intends to go into the Democratic caucus and there vote for Mr. Clingman, it matters not what he may say on the subject." [36]

The state elections resulted in an overwhelming victory for the Democrats. Ellis easily defeated McRae in the governor's race, and the party retained its fifty-six-seat majority in the general assembly. In the mountain district the Democrats captured fourteen of the twenty-one assembly seats, thus guaranteeing Clingman a large bloc of votes in the Democratic caucus. Nonetheless, the mountain Democracy suffered a major disappointment when William W. Avery lost the congressional election to Zebulon B. Vance by a substantial majority. Vance's triumph provided the North Carolina Whigs with their one bright spot in an otherwise dismal campaign.[37]

Vance's election took the Democrats completely by surprise. Thomas Atkin of the *Asheville News* admitted that he "never dreamed that there was a possibility of the defeat of Mr. Avery." The explanation offered by the Whig editor of the *Greensboro Patriot* was that Clingman had not campaigned very hard on behalf of his would-be successor. "Before Clingman returned home from Congress," he noted, "there was great enthusiasm in the district for Avery. . . . The all powerful Clingman returns home, and lo! and behold! his friend Avery . . . is beaten over 2,000." According to the *Patriot,* the senator's "over-weening ambition" and "intriguing disposition" had taken precedence over his desire to see a Democrat succeed him in the House. "Mr. Clingman has no idea of elevating any democrat in the West, who from his position or talents, might become a rival, and who might some day be ready to unseat him. Mr. Clingman wishes it to be understood, that he, and he alone, is King among the mountains." If Clingman did in fact view the Burke County Democrat as a rival lying in wait to unseat him, his political instincts proved correct. Within a few years, Avery's ambition for high office would play an important role in bringing an end to Clingman's career in politics.[38]

From the perspective of 1858, however, the outcome of the state elections seemed to augur well for Clingman's prospects of remaining in the U.S. Senate. The Democratic general assembly was entrusted with responsibility for electing two senators—one to fill the two remaining years of Biggs's term and the other to fill the seat held by David S. Reid, whose term would expire in March 1859. Although Reid, who was actively seeking reelection, was popular among the rank and file in the North Carolina Democracy, the Whigs were convinced that Clingman and Bragg had the inside track as a result of the bargain allegedly made the previous winter. As the *Greensboro Patriot* sarcastically explained, "Bragg is to transfer the Eastern democracy to Clingman, and, as one good turn deserves another, Clingman can hardly do less than give Bragg a bill of sale of the Western democracy."[39]

Reid's precarious health was another consideration working against his chances for reelection. In January 1858, he became violently ill on his way to Washington and was detained for several months in Richmond before recovering sufficiently to be moved to North Carolina. Although he returned to his Senate seat in late May, lingering questions about his health—many of them circulated by friends of the rival aspirants—still plagued him. Yet another complicating factor was the decision of William W. Holden to enter the senatorial contest. The Democratic editor conceivably could have challenged Clingman for the party nomination, but he decided instead to go after Reid's seat. Since both Reid and Holden were associated with the progressive wing of the party, much of Holden's support came from legislators who might otherwise have been backing Reid.[40]

Still, as one of Reid's advisers astutely pointed out, it was Clingman—and not Holden or Bragg—who presented the most serious obstacle to his reelection. "Depend upon it," he warned, "Mr. Clingman will endeavor to get the advantage of you." The junior senator, who controlled a large bloc of western votes, had no incentive to assist his colleague and several reasons to oppose him. Four years earlier, Reid had spurned his entreaties for assistance, whereas Bragg had recently bestowed the coveted Senate seat upon him. Even though the two senators were not in direct competition, Clingman's residency in the far west militated against Reid's chances of winning his party's nomination, since the eastern-dominated caucus would be loathe to award both Senate seats to men regarded as "westerners." For that reason, Reid's supporters urged him to form an alliance "with the strongest eastern man who will go before the Legislature for Senatorial honors" in order to derail Clingman's candidacy. Unfortunately for Reid, the "strongest eastern man" was Governor Bragg, who was already irrevocably committed to Clingman.[41]

By the time the Democratic caucus assembled at Bain's Hotel on the evening of 22 November 1858, even the Whigs acknowledged that Clingman had "managed matters so well as to be without any opponent." After nominating the junior senator to fill the remaining two years of Biggs's term, the caucus turned its attention to the other seat. On the first ballot, Bragg fell one vote short of the requisite majority, while Holden and Reid divided the votes of the other legislators. On the second ballot, seven of Reid's supporters switched to Bragg. The two Democratic nominees easily won election by the general assembly the following day.[42]

The secret of Clingman's success was his adroit manipulation of the legislative caucus—an instrument he had earlier derided as the tool of unscrupulous "central managers." The senator worked the system to his advantage by ensuring that the Democrats voted on his candidacy before his legislative supporters had to commit themselves on the various aspirants for the other seat. Once he had been safely nominated, some of his friends who had earlier promised to vote for Reid or Holden apparently switched to Bragg. As one Democrat remarked after the election, "Clingman was cunning. He secured the support of *all* the opposing candidates, and when secure himself, poured his strength into the scale of Bragg—down it went, and Reid and Holden stood aghast."[43]

Nonetheless, the election left a bitter taste in the mouth of many Democrats. William J. Yates of the *Charlotte Democrat* told Reid that he had "been badly treated . . . by scheming politicians." "For my part," said Yates, "I feel disgusted, mortified, and almost angry." Incoming governor John W. Ellis assured the defeated senator that "*the people* were certainly for you. In my own County of Rowan, there would not have been a dissenting voice to your election among the people." The *Wilmington Journal* expressed regret at "the bitterness of feeling" produced by the election, professed itself to be "heartily sick of the whole affair," and warned that the infighting among the Democrats posed a threat to "the ascendency of their principles . . . [and] the unity of their party." Without doubt, the acrimonious contest for the senatorship left scars upon the North Carolina Democratic party that were never completely healed.[44]

Shortly after the election, Clingman returned to Washington to attend the second session of the Thirty-Fifth Congress. Although brief, the session proved tumultuous. The fireworks began the first week, when the Democratic senators met in caucus to select committee members. With the support of President Buchanan, Jefferson Davis moved to oust Stephen A. Douglas from the chair of the Committee on Territories as punishment for opposing the Lecompton Constitution, which would have admitted Kansas into the Union as a slave state. Seven Democratic senators, including Clingman, attempted unsuccessfully to block that move, arguing that such a vindictive action would be "suicidal to the party."[45]

The intraparty debate, which lasted from ten-thirty in the morning until late in the afternoon, underscored the growing divergence between the national wing of the Southern Democracy, led by Clingman and Robert Toombs, and the sectionalist faction, led by Davis and John Slidell. The sectionalists, as a correspondent of the *New York Tribune* remarked, were determined "to tolerate no diversity of opinion upon any measure which the South demanded." That attitude led them to demand that Northern Democrats accept their definition of popular sovereignty. Clingman, on the other hand, regarded the territorial question as "a dead issue" now that the Kansas controversy had been settled and, thus, was willing "to ignore the difference in opinion" between Northern and Southern Democrats over the meaning of popular sovereignty.[46] Clingman's defense of Douglas earned him the lasting respect of the Illinois senator, and rumors of a Douglas-Clingman ticket in 1860 soon began making their rounds among the North Carolina presses.[47]

Clingman's willingness to defy the Buchanan administration also manifested itself in the realm of foreign policy, as he continued to press hard for the abrogation of the Clayton-Bulwer Treaty. On 13 December 1858 he introduced a series of provocative resolutions accusing the president of reversing his earlier opposition to the treaty and demanding that he explain "the reasons for this change to the country." The resolutions were opposed by James M. Mason of Virginia on the grounds that they would interfere with the ongoing negotiations with Britain. Mason succeeded in quashing a motion to proceed immediately to their consideration. Clingman refused to let the matter drop and tried unsuccessfully on several occasions to bring his resolutions to the floor. Rebuffing the senator's efforts to provoke a confrontation with Britain over Central America, the administration managed to resolve the differences between the two countries the following spring without formally repudiating the Clayton-Bulwer Treaty.[48]

Shortly after Congress adjourned in early March, Clingman announced his intention to spend the spring and summer touring Europe. According to the *Asheville News*, his impending vacation was well deserved. "No public man in America has devoted himself more assiduously to the interests of his constituents than Mr. Clingman. And now that he has for a brief season left business and care behind, he has our best wishes for a safe and pleasant visit to the 'old world.'" Clingman was not the only member of Congress who decided to go abroad at the conclusion of what one historian has characterized as "a runaway session." Republicans like Charles Sumner and William H. Seward were as eager as Clingman to trade the "business and care" of statecraft for a protracted sojourn in Europe.[49]

Clingman left Boston on 23 March 1859 aboard the steamship *Arabia*. The voyage proved far from pleasant and relaxing, however, as the senator became violently seasick. He was still in feeble health when he arrived in England on 2 April and was presented to Queen Victoria by George M. Dallas, the American minister to the Court of St. James. Indeed, throughout his month-long stay in that country, the North Carolinian complained of "a nausea resembling that produced by the motion of a vessel."[50]

Clingman crossed the English Channel in early May en route to Paris with a trunk full of dispatches from Secretary of State Lewis Cass to the U.S. minister, John Y. Mason. Immediately upon his arrival in France, an amusing incident occurred that caught the attention of the opposition presses back home. Apparently expecting that his quasi-diplomatic status would allow him to pass through customs unencumbered, Clingman officiously remarked to a traveling companion that he would "wait while they examine your trunks, which I suppose, will require a considerable time." To his surprise, the customs officer merely opened and shut his companion's trunks. However, the ostentatious sealing wax on Clingman's dispatches aroused the curiosity of the French official, and the senator suffered the indignity of seeing his own baggage ransacked, with almost every article being dragged from the trunk.[51]

Still in poor health, Clingman continued his journey to Rome by way of Marseilles. By the time he arrived in the Eternal City, Italy was embroiled in war. A few weeks earlier, Emperor Francis Joseph of Austria had issued an ultimatum to the tiny kingdom of Piedmont—an action that prompted Piedmont's powerful ally France to declare war. The outbreak of the conflict quickly triggered popular uprisings throughout the duchies of northern and central Italy, although Rome itself, garrisoned by French troops, remained impervious to the disturbances.[52]

Clingman remained in Italy through the beginning of the summer, enjoying the company of former president Pierce and numerous other visiting Americans and traveling extensively through the southern half of the peninsula. He was impressed by the richness and variety of the vegetation as well as by the well-kept farms, unmarred by fences and resplendent with "the greatest abundance [of] grain and grass, tree and vine." The North Carolinian celebrated his forty-seventh birthday in Paris, and he was still in that city on 14 August when the Army of Italy, fresh from its triumph over Austria, paraded through the Place Vendôme. The eighty thousand soldiers with "their glittering bayonets, gilded by the sunbeams" reminded him "of a field of ripe grain gently waving in the breeze." As he witnessed the splendid array, he felt "confident that that day's pageant surpassed any that had hitherto been presented to the eye of man." [53]

Clingman concluded his seven-month tour with a visit to the Rhineland and northern Europe. During his stay on the continent, he made the acquaintance of several heads of state. Reportedly, his favorite was the King of Belgium, to whom he later sent "several kegs of the best whiskey the Old North State could produce." Clingman returned to New York aboard the *Vanderbilt* on 7 November 1859. After resting a few days at the Fifth Avenue Hotel, he traveled to Washington where he expressed his opinion that the peace again prevailing in Europe was "likely to be of short duration." By the middle of November he was back in North Carolina. Stopping at Raleigh on his way to Asheville, he enjoyed a "long and interesting conversation" with William W. Holden on the subject of "European matters, manners, customs, &c." The editor of the *Standard* informed his readers that Clingman, "a close and most intelligent observer," had "learned much during his sojourn in Europe which will be useful hereafter." [54]

Undoubtedly the two Democrats also talked about other, less pleasant, topics during Clingman's stay in Raleigh. While the senator from North Carolina was marveling at the wonders of Europe, the Whigs had made a dramatic comeback in his home state, ousting two Democratic congressmen while holding on to their own two seats. One of the victorious Whigs was Zebulon B. Vance, who easily won reelection to a second term. The Whigs claimed that Clingman had seen the handwriting on the wall and had left the country in order to escape responsibility for his party's impending defeat. Even some Democrats were attributing their party's disappointing showing in the state elections to popular dissatisfaction at "the promotion of the Janus-faced Clingman—a tricky politician . . . who only come[s] to the democratic party to *bargain* for *place*." [55]

Another subject undoubtedly on the minds of Clingman and Holden as they conversed in Raleigh was the daring raid John Brown had made into Virginia on 17 October 1859. In an address before the North Carolina Agricultural Society the previous October, Clingman had assured his audience that the black race was "instinctively so sensible of the superiority of the white man, and so docile in their disposition" that there was no reason "to apprehend resistance, or rebellion, among the negroes on any large scale."[56] After Brown's raid, no Southerner would ever speak with such insouciance about the impossibility of a slave insurrection. Indeed, the widespread fear that a Republican president would unleash hundreds of John Browns against the slave states would soon provide radicals with a powerful argument for forming an independent Southern nation. The resulting crisis of the Union would bring a premature end to Clingman's brief career in the United States Senate.

B-4265

Thomas Lanier Clingman, ca. 1850s. Courtesy of National Archives.

Above left: Thomas Lanier Clingman in his Confederate Army uniform. After serving as colonel of the 25th North Carolina Infantry, Clingman received a commission as brigadier general on 17 May 1862. From Clement C. Clay Papers. Courtesy of Special Collections Library, Duke University.

Above right: Thomas Lanier Clingman, ca. late 1860s. From Clingman and Puryear Family Papers. Courtesy of Southern Historical Collection, University of North Carolina Library at Chapel Hill.

Left: Thomas Lanier Clingman, ca. 1870s. From Clingman and Puryear Family Papers. Courtesy of Southern Historical Collection, University of North Carolina Library at Chapel Hill.

Promotional brochure issued by the Clingman Tobacco
Cure Company in 1885. North Carolina Collection,
University of North Carolina at Chapel Hill Library.

T. L. CLINGMAN.
INCANDESCENT ELECTRIC LIGHT.

No. 276,133.   Patented Apr. 17, 1883.

Fig.1.

Fig.2.

Fig.3.

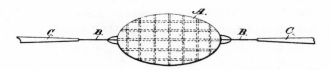

WITNESSES:
Jas. E. Hutchinson.
Henry C. Hazard.

INVENTOR.
Thomas L. Clingman

Drawing accompanying U.S. Patent 276,133, issued to Thomas Lanier Clingman in 1883. A indicates the zirconia incandescing element; B indicates the platinum pins or wires; C indicates the copper electrodes. Courtesy of Edison National Historic Site.

10 *A One-Man Chamber of Commerce*

In announcing Clingman's appointment to the U.S. Senate in May 1858, Democratic newspapers were quick to remark upon his seemingly invincible hold on "the affection of the citizens of his district." According to the *North Carolina Standard*, "the secret of his influence" could be attributed in part to factors not directly related to partisan politics. "Amid the pressure of his public duties," the congressman had also found time "to turn his attention to scientific subjects, and to the condition and natural resources of the State." Indeed, the *Standard* pointed out, "no man is better acquainted than he is with the topography and geological formation of Western Carolina, and no one has contributed more to set before the world the resources and the characteristics of that portion of the state." Subsequent commentators on Appalachian North Carolina have shared that assessment, characterizing Clingman as "the pioneer 'press agent' of western Carolina"—its "first great booster"—a veritable "one-man chamber of commerce." [1]

In recent years, the traditional image of Appalachia as a remote and isolated region has been challenged by scholars who have emphasized the "essentially bourgeois nature" of antebellum mountain society. Although some residents did adhere self-consciously to "a pioneering lifestyle of subsistence farming," the majority of westerners "had some stake in the market economy of their region." Moreover, the "entrepreneurial elite" who dominated the society and politics of the mountain region had "strong capitalist propensities" and functioned as "active promoters of their region's economic development."[2]

Clingman's tireless efforts to publicize the resources of western North Carolina accurately reflected the entrepreneurial spirit of the region's leadership. For him, the ideal was a diversified economy in which agriculture, commerce, and manufacturing would all play important roles. Despite his increasing estrangement from the Whig party during the 1850s, Clingman never abandoned the Whiggish notion that industry and agriculture were complementary rather than antagonistic interests. Nor did he ever lose faith in his belief that western North Carolina had the potential to become a great manufacturing center. As he pointed out numerous times in his publications, the region was rich in iron ore and other natural resources and blessed with sufficient waterpower "to move all the machinery in the civilized world." At the same time, Clingman recognized that industry could not develop without a solid agricultural base. "From the nature of things, agriculture must prosper . . . before manufactures can flourish [since] it is only when the products exceed the wants of the community, that the surplus can be devoted to manufacturing."[3]

In Clingman's mind, the main obstacle preventing westerners from realizing their economic potential was the lack of adequate transportation facilities. As he explained to his fellow legislators in 1840, "from the great cost of getting our productions to market . . . we are advancing but slowly." If transportation costs could be reduced, "no country would improve faster than ours, [and] in none would manufacturing establishments spring up more rapidly." Another impediment to economic development was the chronic lack of capital. According to Clingman, the dearth of adequate venture capital had inhibited the exploitation of the region's mineral resources, since "the process by which the ores are reduced, is tedious, and requires much capital." In addition to "throwing open the whole western country to the world," the construction of improved transportation facilities would, in Clingman's opinion, "tend directly to transfer capital there."

Clingman initially expected the infusion of capital to come from wealthy easterners in his own state. However, the prospect of eastern investment failed to materialize, and as the nation emerged in the mid-1840s from a long depression Clingman began looking toward the North as a potential source of financial support. A major deterrent to Northern investment was the lack of adequate knowledge about the Appalachian region. Indeed, as one historian has noted, even in North Carolina "only a small segment of the population . . . outside the immediate area . . . had any substantial familiarity with the mountain region." When outsiders did think about the southern Appalachians, they were likely to view the region as barren, rocky, and inhospitable.[4]

In order to dispel those negative stereotypes, Clingman published a series of articles during the 1840s that extolled the beauty, climate, and natural resources of the North Carolina mountains. The first essay appeared in February 1844 in the form of a letter to the agricultural reformer John Stuart Skinner. It was published in Skinner's *New York Albion* and in the *National Intelligencer* and later was reprinted in Charles Lanman's widely read *Letters from the Alleghany Mountains.*[5]

Much of the letter focused on the potential of the mountain region, with its "delightfully cool" climate and "uncommonly fertile" soil, for agriculture and animal husbandry. Far from being "so much covered with rocks as to render it unfit for pasture," most of the surface consisted of "elevated table-land, *undulating,* but seldom too broken for cultivation." Clingman also called attention to the region's rich mineral deposits. The variety of its resources, together with "water power enough . . . to move more machinery than human labor can ever place there," gave western North Carolina the potential to "one day become the manufacturing region of the South." Clingman concluded by urging prospective capitalists not to allow that "great *bugbear*" slavery to serve as a deterrent to investment, pointing out that "the number of slaves in those counties is very small in proportion to the whole population."

Clingman's interest in the natural resources of the mountain region was a product of his scientific curiosity, as well as his zeal for economic development. His fascination with the sciences had first been aroused by Hugh Roddy Hall at Ebenezer Academy. He had continued his studies at the University of North Carolina under the direction of Elisha Mitchell, whose area of specialization lay in the fields of geology and mineralogy, and after graduation the two men had remained in close contact. Mitchell's own acquaintance with the southern Appalachians dated from 1827, when he had visited the region in connection with his work on North Carolina's first geological survey. A frequent contributor to the *American Journal of Science and Arts* (popularly known as *Silliman's Journal*), he gained a national reputation as the discoverer of Mount Mitchell—the highest peak east of the Mississippi. By the early 1840s Clingman had also developed a personal and professional relationship with Charles Upham Shepard, an eminent mineralogist who taught at the South Carolina Medical College in Charleston. Like Mitchell, Shepard was a transplanted Yankee who had worked with the renowned scientist Benjamin Silliman before accepting an appointment at a Southern university.[6]

Clingman eagerly enlisted the services of Mitchell and Shepard in promoting his vision of economic development. In 1845 Mitchell wrote two public letters to Clingman, which were initially published in the *Asheville Messenger* and *Raleigh Register,* then reprinted by Skinner in the *New York Albion,* and subsequently "copied into many other papers." The letters focused on the agricultural and mineral resources of the mountain region, its natural beauty, and its potential for "the rearing of cattle and sheep and the making of butter and cheese." The scientist also repeated Clingman's argument that decent roads and an outlay of capital were all that were needed to convert vast tracts of lands "now almost waste and worthless" into luxuriant meadows and pastures that would "amply repay an outlay of capital upon them."[7]

The following year, Clingman and Shepard published a joint communication in the *Asheville Messenger,* which was later reprinted in Lanman's *Letters from the Alleghany Mountains.* Clingman directed the attention of his readers to the "mineral wealth, which now lies unobserved in their very midst," while Shepard lauded the mountain region as "a country of the highest mineralogical promise" and "a fertile source of prosperity." Both writers called for the initiation of a comprehensive geological survey. According to Shepard "the entire outlay required for carrying forward the work would in a very short time be many times over returned to the people."[8]

Clingman and Shepard also emphasized the "knowledge, wealth, and happiness" that they believed would ensue from the exploitation of the mineral resources of western North Carolina. According to Clingman, "opening valuable mines . . . would attract capital from abroad and furnish a good home market to the farmer." Shepard likewise remarked upon "the indirect results to the neighborhood in which the mines are situated . . . flowing from the increased demand for farming produce, from the free circulation of capital, the improvement of roads, and the general stimulus which is always imparted by successful enterprise to the industry of a country."

Mitchell and Shepard were exemplars of a new type of scientist who had come to dominate the field by the middle of the nineteenth century. The part-time "gentleman amateur" had now been superseded by "the trained specialist—the professional whose sole source of support was his scientific employment." Despite his own interest in scientific inquiry, Clingman was fully cognizant of his nonprofessional status, and he readily acknowledged specialists like Mitchell to be "my superior vastly in all matters of science." Nonetheless, the line of demarcation between professional and nonprofessional was not as sharply drawn in mid-nineteenth-century America as it is today. Antebellum science continued to be dominated by the tenets of the seventeenth-century British philosopher Francis Bacon. And Baconian science, as practiced by Americans like Mitchell and Shepard, explicitly acknowledged a role for talented amateurs like Thomas Clingman.[9]

In the view of the Baconians, the work of the scientist primarily involved "collecting particulars and grouping them into classifications." From the careful observation of those facts, the "laws of science" could then be deduced. That emphasis on the systematic accumulation and analysis of an abundance of factual evidence led professional scientists to place a high value on the contributions of industrious and inquisitive nonprofessionals. Shepard, for example, justified a state geological survey not only on the basis of the specific information that it

might uncover but also on the grounds that it would stimulate "the spirit of inquiry" among the people and produce "an efficient band of native mineralogists
and geologists whose services . . . would, in a few years, greatly outweigh all that
had been achieved by the original explorers." [10]

In North Carolina, Thomas Lanier Clingman was foremost among those citizen geologists whom Shepard believed were indispensable to the accumulation of
scientific knowledge. A charter member of the American Association for the Advancement of Science (AAAS), he remained active in that organization from its
establishment in 1848 until well into the 1850s. Both the AAAS and its predecessor, the Association of American Geologists and Naturalists, attracted numerous
amateurs like Clingman "who could and did contribute as fieldworkers in geological and meteorological investigations." Like other such fieldworkers, Clingman attained his reputation in the scientific community as a result of explorations
and discoveries that were subsequently analyzed and publicized by professional
scientists. [11]

By his own account, Clingman's interest in exploring the mountains of western
North Carolina was stimulated during the spring of 1839 by a chance encounter
in Asheville with the botanist Thomas Nuttall, who "had come down to examine
the zircon locality in what was then the south end of Buncombe, now Henderson
county." While Nuttall and Clingman were examining the mineral collection of
Asheville physician J. F. E. Hardy, the scientist "suddenly paused and examined
for some moments one of the specimens. He then . . . said, 'I at first thought that
might be a specimen of cinnabar, which it resembles, but I see . . . [it] is not.' He
then stated that he had seen two specimens of cinnabar (the principal ore of mercury) from the French Broad in Buncombe." [12]

Knowing that cinnabar, "though found in few localities in the world, was usually abundant where found and a very valuable mineral," Clingman decided to
undertake a systematic search of the French Broad River in present-day Madison
County. Although he failed to discover any cinnabar, he soon extended his investigations to include other minerals as well. As residents of the mountain region
became aware of Clingman's growing interest in mineralogy, "minerals were
brought to me, during my circuit through . . . the judicial district." Clingman sent
the most promising specimens to Shepard for analysis, and he later recalled, his
scientific curiosity "enabled me to make many discoveries of interest."

During the winter of 1845–46 Clingman made what he considered to be "the
most important of my discoveries" among the gold washings at Twitty's mine in
Rutherford County. There he found "a small crystal which . . . was hard enough
to scratch every thing to which I applied it." Shepard's analysis confirmed Clingman's hunch that the mysterious stone was a diamond. Valued at between fifteen
hundred and two thousand dollars, it was the first diamond discovered in North
Carolina and one of the few ever found in the United States. Shepard publicized

the find in *Silliman's Journal,* concluding that "there can scarcely remain a doubt, but that the diamond is to form a part of the available mineral wealth of the country."[13]

A year later, Clingman made another significant discovery in a gold mine in the northern part of Rutherford County. He suspected that the metallic grain might be platinum, even though no specimen of that metal had ever been uncovered in the United States. Shepard's analysis corroborated his suspicions, and the scientist reported the event in the September 1847 issue of *Silliman's Journal.* In that same issue, Shepard also published a letter from Clingman noting that numerous other miners "had seen just such specimens, but they had supposed them to be fragments of steel or iron that had been broken from the edges of the mining tools." Shepard heralded his friend as "the discoverer of the diamond and platinum in North Carolina"—a title that Clingman later characterized as "the proudest of my life."[14]

Shortly before he returned to Congress in 1847, Clingman made another important find when Col. Chunn (probably A. B. Chunn) of Buncombe County presented him with some curious rocks of "intense blue color." Chunn believed the rocks might contain some type of lead ore, but they ultimately "proved to be corundum . . . so remarkable as to excite the wonder and admiration of the scientists" to whom Clingman showed the mineral at the September meeting of the Association of American Geologists and Naturalists in Boston. The discovery attracted worldwide attention after a block of the corundum was displayed at the London Crystal Palace Exhibition in 1851. A fragment was subsequently exhibited in the British Museum, and other pieces "were extensively distributed over the world."[15]

By the 1850s Clingman's reputation had far transcended the realm of politics and statecraft. As the journalist Benjamin Perley Poore put it, he had also "distinguished [himself] among the savants as a mineralogist." His contributions in that field were publicly recognized not only by personal friends like Shepard and Mitchell but also by other influential scientists such as Benjamin Silliman Jr. and James Dwight Dana.[16] In light of his intense "desire to be remembered as a great factor in the affairs of the nation," Clingman must have been especially gratified when Silliman attached his name to a brittle, micalike mineral that the North Carolinian had found among the corundum deposits in Buncombe County. Although "Clingmanite" is no longer recognized as a distinct species of mica, it was regarded as one throughout most of Clingman's lifetime.[17]

The untapped mineral wealth of the mountains offered Clingman the promise of fortune as well as fame. During the two decades before the Civil War, he invested heavily in land and mineral rights in western North Carolina and in nearby Georgia. In addition to his personal investments, he acted as a broker for other landowners desiring to sell or lease their properties to Northern investors. Clingman's efforts to bring Northern capital into the South continued until the outbreak of the Civil War. Indeed, some of his most intensive activities coincided with the secession crisis of 1860 – 61, as the ensuing financial panic encouraged proprietors in Jackson and Macon Counties to unload their copper mines and other properties at low prices.[18]

Although Clingman was not oblivious to the economic potential of the rich copper deposits that had been discovered in western North Carolina and Tennessee during the 1850s, his personal investments centered in the potentially more valuable realm of gold mining. During the 1820s and 1830s North Carolina had acquired a reputation as the "golden state" as a result of the substantial number of deposits discovered in the western Piedmont and in the mountain counties of Burke, McDowell, and Rutherford. Most of the early extractive activity had been in the form of placer, or surface, mining along the streams and stream beds. By the end of the 1830s, those mines were exhausted, and the focus of activity shifted to vein, or underground, mining. However, that method required a considerable investment of capital, machinery, and skill. As a result, gold mining in North Carolina declined substantially during the 1840s.[19]

The most important factor contributing to its revival during the 1850s was the introduction of hydraulic hose mining, a type of placer mining that was first used in the California mines where high labor costs made the traditional pick-and-shovel method prohibitively expensive. Clingman, who had been "reading carefully [the] reports of operations in California," was one of the first to recognize the potential of hydraulic mining in revitalizing the seemingly exhausted goldfields of North Carolina and Georgia. In January 1857 he provided a succinct description of the hydraulic method in a public letter to Joseph Henry of the Smithsonian. "The hydraulic hose process," he wrote, "consists simply in conveying the water in canals or ditches, and over valleys in flumes supported on tressel [sic] work, to the place where the gold deposits lie. . . . Under a pressure of fifty or sixty feet, the water shoots out [from the hose pipes] with great force, and with surprising rapidity cuts down the most compact clay . . . leaving the gold along the sluices, where it settles, from its superior specific gravity, and from which it is easily taken out."[20]

Although the goldfields of North Carolina and Georgia were not nearly as rich as those in California, Clingman believed that lower labor costs and more abundant waterpower would make the hydraulic system just as profitable in the Atlantic states. Indeed, he argued, there was enough gold in the mountains of North Carolina and Georgia "to yield a dozen millions [of dollars] annually, probably for the next half century." An investment of a few thousand dollars might thus "be made to yield enormous profits by this operation."

Enticed by the possibility of those enormous profits, Clingman entered into a partnership in October 1856 with Dr. Marinus H. Van Dyke, "a practical and expert mining engineer." The two men agreed to lease property and make contracts for water rights in order to engage in mining operations "with what is called Van

Dyke's Hydraulic Hose Power." After successfully trying out the hose oñ some Burke County mines owned by Benjamin Hamilton, they decided to extend their activities into Georgia. Together with a group of investors from New York City and Boston, they received authorization from the Georgia legislature to form two companies—the Chestatee Hydraulic Company with a capital stock of $2.5 million and the Yahoola River and Cane Creek Hydraulic Hose Mining Company, capitalized at $500,000. Clingman received thirty-five thousand shares of Chestatee stock with a face value of $350,000 on his own account and another ten thousand on his partnership account with Van Dyke. In addition, he was named as one of the company's nine directors. Together with Hamilton, the partners also controlled half the shares of the Yahoola company.[21]

In March 1858 the Chestatee company hired William P. Blake, "a noted geologist, mineralogist and mining engineer," to conduct a survey of the gold region. Blake reported in May that the lands along the Chestatee River were "very favorable for washing by the hydraulic method." Encouraged by that favorable report, the company began leasing mining tracts from local owners and commenced construction of a twelve-mile canal from the river to the gold belt. During the fall of 1858 Blake conducted another topological survey for the Yahoola company. His investigations confirmed that the ridge between the Yahoola River and Cane Creek was "traversed with gold-bearing veins." Blake proposed the construction of a twelve-mile aqueduct from the river to the goldfields and affirmed that "with proper management the yield of gold would be enormous, and sufficient to return the whole cost of the ditch in a short time."[22]

Unfortunately, the enormous profits that Blake had so confidently predicted failed to materialize. Van Dyke, who took responsibility for constructing the canals, proved to be an inept businessman. That ineptness was compounded by technical problems that would have proven challenging even to an adroit manager. "Unexpected delays in the completion of the ditch" prevented the Chestatee company from commencing operations on schedule, while the high trestle proposed to be erected above the river proved to be the "chief difficulty" for the Yahoola company. By the time Clingman returned from Europe in the fall of 1859, both companies were in a precarious financial position, and the senator was eager to divest himself of them.[23]

With considerable difficulty, Clingman finally managed to transfer his interest in the Yahoola company to George H. Gordon, a Boston lawyer, for the sum of ten thousand dollars. Although the Bostonian purchased the stock at considerably less than par value, Clingman probably recovered most, if not all, of his investment.[24] The senator also made an arrangement with C. P. Culver, a Washington broker, to dispose of his Chestatee stock (by now reduced to a mere thirty-one hundred shares) "at the best possible advantage." By April 1861, Culver had managed to trade two hundred shares for 430 acres of land in North Carolina and another four hundred for 145 acres in Manassas, Virginia. A few months later, the first major engagement of the Civil War would be fought on the property that Clingman had recently acquired in the Old Dominion.[25]

Although Clingman's antebellum mining ventures ultimately proved unprofitable, they are nonetheless indicative of the role he believed Northern capital and technological expertise would play in the development of the economic resources of the South. Unlike other fire eaters such as Edmund Ruffin of Virginia, Clingman was entirely devoid of anti-Yankee animus in his business relationships. He willingly entered into partnerships with Northerners like Van Dyke and served on the board of directors for Northern-controlled corporations. Even as it became evident that the nation was splitting apart over the slavery issue, Clingman continued to maintain a national vision of economic development. Regardless of whether the South remained in the Union, the key to its future, in his view, lay in Northern investment.

While it is convenient for purposes of analysis to separate Clingman's role as "the most avid of the region's many commercial boosters" from his career as a politician, his achievements as an explorer, scientist, and propagandist undoubtedly redounded to his political benefit. As John C. Inscoe has pointed out, Clingman's long-standing goal of "creating a new south by developing both untapped natural resources and commercial prospects" was one that all "entrepreneurially oriented mountain residents would recognize as desirable" regardless of their opinions on partisan politics or Southern Rights. Clingman's hold on the voters of the mountain district thus rested on factors that proved to be even more tenacious than party loyalty. In the words of one admiring contemporary, he "stole the affections and hearts of the people and kept them . . . in his explorations for mineral[s] and lofty mountain peaks." [26]

Although Clingman's endeavors as one of "western North Carolina's first and most prolific individual publicity men" won him many admirers, not all westerners gave unqualified approval to his efforts to develop the region's rich mineral resources. Some, at least, were concerned about what today would be called "environmental impact." With a passion that compensated for his infelicitous grammar and spelling, one mountaineer in Cherokee County complained that Clingman and his associates were "destroying all of the timber & a digging up all the small flats that might be made tolerable good little farms. . . . They are a doing great damage to the Lands & to myself. . . . If men that holde a hig[h]er office than I do are allowed to do as they do, some of us will have to leave the State." [27]

Clingman's political enemies were not averse to exploiting such issues for partisan advantage. As his editorial spokesman Thomas W. Atkin indignantly complained, "Mr. Clingman cannot even pursue a scientific investigation—measure a mountain or test a gold mine—but it brings down upon his head a whole torrent of mean and malevolent abuse." Clingman's protracted debate with Elisha Mitchell over who had been the first to identify, ascend, and measure the highest peak in the Black Mountains of Yancey County provides the most cogent example of how partisanship could transform a seemingly nonpolitical issue like "measuring a mountain" into a controversy with important political ramifications.[28]

The dispute, which culminated in Mitchell's death in 1857, was doubly tragic insofar as it destroyed the friendship of two men who had been close for more than twenty-five years. Accounts of the Clingman-Mitchell controversy have typically portrayed it as a needless and "unmannerly" debate between a "gentle, shy scientist" and a "congenital disputant" envious of the "fame [that] came to Dr. Mitchell" as the discoverer of the highest mountain east of the Mississippi.[29]

There is a grain of truth in that assessment. Clingman's large ego and disputatious personality sometimes did embroil him in needless controversy, and his unfortunate break with his scientific mentor Mitchell in some ways paralleled his earlier estrangement from his political mentor William A. Graham. In this case, however, Clingman did not go out of his way to stir up controversy. Indeed, he entered into a public debate with his former professor with great reluctance and only after he felt compelled by political necessity to do so.

Mitchell's claim to have ascended the highest peak in the Black Mountains rested on two visits to the region made nine years apart. During the summer of 1835 he had taken measurements confirming that the range contained several peaks higher than those in the White Mountains of New Hampshire, which had previously been regarded as the highest mountains east of the Mississippi. Accompanied by two guides, he ascended what he then considered to be the highest point. Mitchell returned to the Black Mountains in 1844 and measured another mountain that he believed was even higher than the one he had climbed nine years earlier. His claim remained unchallenged until September 1855, when Clingman ascended a peak that he calculated to be almost two hundred feet higher than the one three miles to the south known as Mount Mitchell.

Clingman related his findings to Joseph Henry of the Smithsonian Institution, who submitted the congressman's communication to the *Washington City Spectator,* along with some introductory remarks in which Henry referred to the point as "Clingman's Peak." The following year, the communication was published in the Smithsonian's annual report. A new introduction by Henry cited recent measurements by Arnold Guyot substantiating the claim that Clingman's Peak was more than one hundred feet higher than Mount Mitchell.[30]

Mitchell never challenged Clingman's assertion that the mountain he measured in 1855 was in fact the highest point east of the Mississippi. Rather, the controversy centered on the identity of the peak that Mitchell had ascended in 1844. The scientist denied that he had ever "measured, ascended, or even approached nearer than two miles" the point local residents had named Mount Mitchell. Instead, he claimed the mountain he had visited in 1844 was the same one Clingman had ascended in 1855.[31]

Mitchell was correct in contending that he had preceded Clingman to the highest peak. However, he did not reach it in 1844, as he believed, but during his earlier visit to the Black Mountains in 1835. The mountain he measured nine years later was most likely Mount Gibbes—part of a three-knob complex that also included the point known as Mount Mitchell. Ironically, the difference in the physical features and vegetation of the two mountains he had ascended led Mitchell to conclude, mistakenly, that his guides had led him to the wrong peak during his first visit. Thus, when the controversy began in 1855, he focused his arguments on the 1844 visit, thereby setting himself up for Clingman's successful rebuttal.[32]

At the time he wrote his public letter to Henry, Clingman did not realize Mitchell would take exception to his claim to have discovered a mountain even higher than the one his former professor had ascended a decade earlier. Instead, he was proceeding on the common-sense assumption that the peak at the southern end of the range, which by then was generally called Mount Mitchell, was the same point Mitchell himself regarded as the highest. He must, therefore, have been flabbergasted to read the letter Mitchell wrote Henry in November 1855, in which the scientist declared that local residents had made "a mistake" in attaching his name to the peak three miles south of the highest point.[33]

Mitchell had requested Henry to show the letter to Clingman and secure his consent prior to its publication. The scientist evidently expected that his friend would withdraw his claim to priority once he realized that his central premise—that Mitchell had ascended the peak known as Mount Mitchell—was invalid. Indeed, had Mitchell been content merely to assert that Clingman's account of the mountain he had measured in 1855 was consistent with the location and features of the one he had ascended eleven years earlier, the congressman might have relented. However, Mitchell presented Henry with a detailed description of the mountain he had climbed in 1844 that came much closer to fitting Mount Gibbes and the other peaks in the three-knob complex than it did the mountain Clingman had recently measured. Wishing to avoid embarrassing his friend, Clingman urged him to revisit the range and refamiliarize himself with its features before pursuing the matter further.[34]

Until the spring of 1856, Clingman and Mitchell both hoped that their differences would not evolve into a public quarrel. Yet each also apparently expected the other to retreat from his position once all the facts were fully understood. Mitchell decided not to publish his November 1855 letter to Henry and told Clingman that he intended, instead, to write an article for the *North Carolina University Magazine*. The congressman evidently found that plan acceptable, and Mitchell sent the new manuscript to him for examination. Although the scientist modified some of the details of his argument in light of Clingman's criticisms, he refused to back down from his central claim. Moreover, for reasons that he never explained, he announced his intention to publish his article in the rabidly anti-Clingman *Asheville Spectator*. Clingman tried unsuccessfully to dissuade his friend from that course of action. If Mitchell persisted, he warned, he would be obliged to respond in kind, since he expected to "be attacked by my political enemies probably, to operate on the canvass . . . going on in the State."[35]

Even under the best of circumstances, Mitchell's decision to bring his quarrel with Clingman to public attention might have generated ill feeling between the two men. But it was his determination to publish his side of the case in the partisan *Spectator* that transformed a scientific controversy into a bruising political "bear fight."[36] The political ramifications of the controversy between Clingman and Mitchell become more salient when it is remembered that their newspaper debate, which began in June 1856 and ended in November, coincided exactly with the presidential election campaign. Clingman realized that his chances of winning the Democratic senatorial nomination in 1858 would be greatly improved if he could deliver the mountain district to Buchanan in 1856. Any issue that impaired his own credibility and standing among his constituents would necessarily have an adverse impact on the outcome and, consequently, on his prospects for political advancement.

The controversy began in earnest on 19 June 1856 with the publication of the first of four communications by Mitchell. The letter, which differed substantially from the draft he had shown to Clingman, recounted the details of his first visit to the Black Mountains in order to demonstrate that he had correctly located the peak that was "rediscovered by Mr. Clingman last year, and represented by him as being before unknown." Mitchell's communication proved, at best, that he had identified the highest point from a distance in 1835. He did not discuss his 1844 visit, which was his central bone of contention with Clingman. In an ill-conceived follow-up published a week later, the scientist (who had not visited the Black Mountain region in twelve years) demonstrated shocking ignorance of its geography by claiming that the highest peak lay on the Buncombe-Yancey line—a statement Clingman had no difficulty refuting.[37]

The unpublished rebuttal Clingman had prepared the previous winter in response to Mitchell's letter to Joseph Henry had been respectful, even deferential, in its tone. Once the congressman's political survival instincts had been aroused, however, he came out with both fists swinging. In a long and densely argued communication to the *Asheville News,* which was also published as a sixteen-page pamphlet, he made a compelling case that Mitchell's own evidence "in publications made by him, and in articles *written for publication,* but subsequently withheld," demonstrated that the scientist had actually ascended Mount Gibbes in 1844. He reprinted and summarized passages from Mitchell's letter to Henry and subsequent unpublished letters to make the point that the scientist had repeatedly backtracked from his initial position to meet the succession of objections raised by Clingman. With more than a tinge of sarcasm, he concluded that "these mountain peaks stand boldly and stubbornly, and will not change their outlines to accommodate themselves to his *shifting representations.*"[38]

Most likely, Mitchell was as much put off by the tone of Clingman's pamphlet as he was by its substantive arguments. Although intent on vindicating his claims, the professor had entered the controversy in the spirit of a scientist trying to arrive at the truth, rather than a politician attempting to score debating points against an opponent. Clingman's pamphlet, on the other hand, more closely resembled a campaign tract than a scientific disquisition. While he stopped short of accusing Mitchell of deliberate prevarication, his reference to "shifting representations" did suggest that the scientist was playing fast and loose with the truth. And he certainly gave Mitchell no credit for his willingness to admit to his mistakes and modify his initial hypotheses in light of new evidence presented to him.

Nonetheless, Clingman's strictures were mild compared with the torrent of abuse Mitchell unleashed against his former student in his third communication to the *Spectator,* which was subsequently published as an eight-page pamphlet. The scientist placed the blame for initiating the controversy squarely on Clingman, who had been "inclined to yield" the points at issue until "the apprehension of what his political enemies would say or do, seemed to overcome every other consideration." He also accused Clingman of distorting his own argument by printing letters that had been explicitly withdrawn from publication, by quoting their passages out of context, and by resorting to "the most dishonorable of all methods, *a falsification of the documents on which his argument rests.*" In Mitchell's opinion, such "tricks . . . which correct men scorn to employ" constituted sufficient evidence that Clingman had shown himself "unworthy of being trusted." "The words old friend," he snarled, "do not harmonize with the malignity that characterizes . . . your pamphlet. It is likely to be said in view of the whole, that you do not know what friendship is; that whatever you may claim to feel of that kind, is hollow and pretended, or, if real, is unreliable and worthless."[39]

Mitchell's pamphlet, written in August 1856 after a return visit to the Black Mountains, was the first to deal directly with the crucial 1844 ascent. In support of his claims, he cited the authority of William Riddle, the Yancey County guide who had accompanied him that year. Mitchell, who had not seen Riddle in more than a decade, had hoped to speak to him before returning to Chapel Hill, but poor health forced the scientist to cut short his visit. Thus it was Clingman who had the first opportunity to interview the guide. Riddle's testimony, which the congressman published in the *Asheville News* in October 1856, proved devastating to Mitchell's case. Not only did the guide provide a detailed description of a route of ascent leading directly to the top of Mount Gibbes, but he explicitly denied ever accompanying Mitchell to the summit of the higher peak three miles to the north.[40]

In a communication published in the *Spectator* in November, Mitchell expressed dissatisfaction with Riddle's account but conceded the main point to Clingman by retreating to the position that he had correctly identified the highest peak from a distance in 1835 "though I [may have] failed to reach its top either on that or any following year." Clingman made no reply to Mitchell's communication, nor did the scientist attempt another publication. Their public debate was over, and Clingman had emerged as the victor. Even Mitchell's colleagues at the university grudgingly acknowledged that "Dr. M. is getting the reputation of being a *'singed cat'*."[41]

The tragic epilogue came in June 1857, when Mitchell once again set out for the Black Mountains. By now the scientist had begun to reevaluate his earlier belief that he had failed to reach the highest peak in 1835, and he intended to interview William Wilson, one of the guides who had accompanied him that year. Setting out alone for Wilson's house on 27 June 1857, he failed to arrive there. A week later, a search party led by "Big Tom" Wilson of Yancey County discovered Mitchell's body in a clear pool at the base of a waterfall. He had apparently lost his footing and drowned.[42]

The controversy did not end with Mitchell's fall from the mountain. It was renewed almost immediately by Charles Phillips, his colleague at the University of North Carolina, and by Zebulon B. Vance, his former student. Vance secured written depositions from William Wilson and Samuel Austin, the two surviving guides from the 1835 visit, that provided persuasive evidence that Mitchell had in fact ascended the highest peak that year. Their testimony, together with other evidence supporting Mitchell's case, was presented to the public in articles written by Phillips and published in the *Asheville Spectator, Raleigh Register,* and other Whig presses.[43]

Clingman responded through letters published in the *Asheville News, Raleigh North Carolina Standard,* and other Democratic newspapers. By the end of 1857, however, he was clearly on the defensive. Instead of defining the terms of the debate, as he had done with Mitchell, he now found himself reacting to the barrage of statements and accusations brought forward by Phillips and Vance. Thomas Atkin of the *Asheville News* expressed indignation at these attempts "to revive the former controversy . . . by taking advantage of the universal sympathy felt on account of Prof. Mitchell's melancholy death . . . [to] make capital against Mr. Clingman." According to Clingman, "disinterested persons" had long ago become "wearied with the clamor which my opponents have kept up." The controversy continued only because "Dr. Mitchell's friends and my political and personal enemies" had combined "to gratify the vanity of the former and the *hostility* of the latter."[44]

Clingman never faced the voters of the mountain district after 1857, and it is difficult to measure the impact of the controversy on his political reputation. By the end of that year, however, most westerners had apparently been persuaded that the congressman's charges against Mitchell were groundless. According to Vance, "a large majority, embracing many of Clingman's warmest friends, [now] profess themselves convinced that Dr M[itchell] was right." Moreover, thanks to the efforts of his "political and personal enemies," the image of Clingman as a selfish opportunist who provoked a tragic and unnecessary controversy with his former professor had taken hold on the public mind. To some extent, that image has persisted to the present day.[45]

The political repercussions of the controversy became apparent in August 1858 after the special election that was held to fill the congressional seat vacated by Clingman in May. By that time, Zebulon B. Vance, the Whig candidate, had achieved renown in the mountain district as Mitchell's most prominent defender. In addition to securing the testimony that eventually vindicated the scientist's claims, he also played a leading role in the movement to re-inter Mitchell's body on the highest peak. That well-publicized ceremony, which attracted several hundred visitors from across the state, took place on 16 June 1858, just a few weeks before the congressional election.[46]

Nonetheless, Democrat William W. Avery began the campaign as a heavy favorite. The *Asheville News* confidently predicted that his challenger had not "even the shade of a shadow of a chance" of winning. Contrary to that prediction, Vance defeated his rival by more than two thousand votes, carrying two-thirds of the counties and garnering 57 percent of the vote. Since the Democrats won handily in the governor's race and in most of the legislative contests in the mountain region, Vance's victory over Avery must be viewed as a personal, rather than partisan, triumph. Most likely, the favorable publicity generated by his efforts to vindicate the reputation of Elisha Mitchell was an important factor affecting the outcome.[47]

It is impossible to predict whether Clingman himself would have fared any better in a head-on confrontation with Mitchell's champion. Nor is it possible to determine the precise extent to which the Clingman-Mitchell controversy contributed to the decline of Clingman's influence in western North Carolina and to the emergence of Vance as the dominant political figure in that region. The controversy may well have played a role in weakening Clingman's hold on the voters of the mountain district, but the secession crisis of 1860–61 and the resulting Civil War proved to be even more significant factors in bringing about an abrupt end to his remarkable political career.

11 *Almost a Union Man*

Historians have long regarded Thomas Lanier Clingman as one of the South's "most persistent and consistent advocate[s] of secession"—a fire eater who "rival[ed] both Yancey and Calhoun as the most proslavery and prosouthern of antebellum congressmen." As the controversy between the North and South escalated in the wake of John Brown's raid, Clingman, together with his "close associates . . . the fire-eaters from the cotton states," supposedly led the way in preparing the South for disunion. Many of Clingman's contemporaries shared that assessment. According to the *Wilmington Herald,* the North Carolina senator was "as thorough a disunionist as William L. Yancey himself. . . . He goes the extremest length of the fire-eaters." The *Greensboro Patriot* agreed that he "fully sympathizes with Yancey, Rhett, and . . . the leaders of the disunion faction." [1]

Clingman's behavior both before and after Brown's raid raises doubts about the validity of that time-honored viewpoint. During the 1850s he had repeatedly won reelection in his district by assuring the voters that a strong stand on behalf of Southern Rights was the most certain means of preserving the Union. By that logic, he was "a better Union man" than his political enemies, whose submissionist attitudes were encouraging Northern aggression and thus hastening the dissolution of the Union. After formally joining the Democrats in 1856, Clingman had identified himself not with the sectionalist wing led by Jefferson Davis and John Slidell but with the national wing led by Stephen A. Douglas. National Democrats like Clingman differed from the sectionalists primarily in their belief that "the best way to defend Southern institutions . . . was by working with the Northern friends of the South." For that reason, they consistently opposed measures that might weaken the Northern Democrats in their battle against the Republicans.[2]

Clingman's determination to maintain the Democratic party as a national institution led him to oppose Buchanan's efforts to make the Kansas issue a test of party loyalty and to punish Douglas for defying the president. As early as 1859 Clingman had decided to support the Little Giant for the presidency on the grounds that his "strength in the North, and his position on the territorial question might tend greatly to secure the doubtful votes [of Northerners] . . . who were hesitating to join the Abolitionists." Accordingly, he urged Gov. John W. Ellis and editor William W. Holden to "prepare the State to support Douglas."[3]

By 1859 Clingman had also come to the conclusion that the territorial question was "in fact a dead issue" now that the controversy over the admission of Kansas had finally been settled. As he told Douglas in February, most Southerners were now "willing to ignore the difference of op[i]nion [over the meaning of nonintervention], and stand on the old platform [of 1856] as against our common adversary." When Clingman came back from Europe in November, he learned that Douglas had disregarded his advice to let the territorial issue rest and had published an article in *Harper's Magazine* affirming that a local legislature could effectively exclude slavery simply by refusing to enact the enabling laws that the institution needed to exist. The article produced a howl of protest throughout the South. Ellis and Holden bluntly informed Clingman that Douglas had "placed himself in a position where it is impossible to sustain him."[4]

Clingman, however, was not willing to give up on the Illinois senator. He admonished his colleagues that the party must at all costs remain united in "common defense against the Black Republican organization." In his opinion, the best way to prevail against the Republicans in the presidential election was for the Democrats to rally behind the candidate with "the most positive strength in the North." For that reason, he "preferred that if it were practicable to do so, that Mr. Douglas should be made our candidate."[5]

Shortly after returning to the nation's capital in December 1859, Clingman began work on a speech he hoped would "unite the Democracy of the North and South" and, at the same time, warn Northerners of the "danger that seemed to stare us directly in the face." The address, which was delivered on 16 January 1860, began with a review of the territorial issue. Clingman defended the

Democratic doctrine of congressional nonintervention without discussing the conflicting sectional interpretations of that policy. He then drew a sharp distinction between the "wise, patriotic and statesmanlike" position of the Democrats on the slavery issue and the platform of the Republican party, which "has but a single principle, and that is hostility to negro slavery in the United States." With the "fate of the country" dependent "upon the success . . . of those brave and patriotic men in the North, who . . . have so long maintained an unequal struggle against the anti-slavery current," Southerners should do everything in their power to support and encourage the Northern Democrats.[6]

Clingman then proceeded to speculate about the consequences of a Republican victory in the upcoming presidential election. If the antislavery movement "cannot be arrested under the Constitution," then "a temporary or permanent separation of the Southern from the Northern States" might be necessary. The senator warned his Northern colleagues not to underestimate the strength or pervasiveness of disunionism in the South. "In those sections that I am best acquainted with," he remarked, "there are hundreds of disunionists now where there was one ten years ago." Although outright secessionists still constituted the minority in most states, "the majority is ready to unite with them upon the happening of some further causes. In my judgment, the election of the presidential candidate of the Black Republican party will furnish that cause."[7]

After bluntly discussing the possibility of disunion, Clingman ended his speech on a more optimistic and conciliatory note. He explicitly denied that he was one of those individuals who "would willingly to-day see the Union dissolved." On the contrary, he still possessed "confidence in the good fortune of the United States" and had no doubts regarding "the benefits of this Confederacy to all sections, provided justice be done in the administration of the government." The future of the American republic could be a glorious one, he concluded, if Northerners and Southerners would only agree to put aside their differences over slavery. "If the Union of our States continue[s], at no distant day we should control the world."[8]

The Republican presses, whose initial reaction to Clingman's address was based on early telegraphic summaries, curtly dismissed it as a "disunion speech." The senator's supporters disputed that characterization. The *North Carolina Standard* described Clingman as a "steadfast friend of the Union" and argued that his policy of "resistance in advance" might well "induce a majority of the people of the non-slaveholding States to pause in their course and thus perpetuate the Union." That Clingman intended his address to serve as a rallying cry for the Democrats rather than a blueprint for disunion became apparent when the *Washington States* praised the speech as "one of the best campaign papers that could have been prepared for general distribution" and announced its intention to "print many thousand extra copies . . . [and] broadcast [them] throughout the Union." A correspondent of the *New Bern Progress* agreed that members of Congress "will greatly serve the country by employing their franks in its general distribution among our Northern fellow citizens." [9]

At the same time that national Democrats like Clingman were laboring to unify and strengthen their party, sectionalists like Jefferson Davis were working to divide and weaken it. On 2 February 1860 the Mississippi senator introduced a series of resolutions that denied the right of territorial legislatures either directly or in an "indirect and unfriendly nature" to interfere with slavery. Although the resolutions stopped short of explicitly demanding a congressional slave code for the territories, they affirmed that if experience should demonstrate that the federal judiciary lacked the power to insure adequate protection, "it will then become the duty of Congress to supply such deficiency." [10]

Davis hoped to commit the entire Democratic party to his doctrine of federal protection. Clingman understood that such an inflexible position would cripple the Northern Democrats. Privately, he was furious at this "irrational" attempt to "divide and destroy the Democratic party," comparing it "to the conduct of a man about to do battle for his life, who should, as a preparatory step, cut off one arm and one leg, in order that he might march and strike with more efficiency." Publicly, however, he suppressed his indignation and strove "to state my opinions in a manner as conciliatory as possible" in the hope that some of Davis's supporters "might be won back." [11]

Clingman undoubtedly agreed with Robert Toombs that "hostility to Douglas" was the "sole motive" behind Davis's resolutions. The sectionalists hoped to prevent the Little Giant's nomination at the Democratic National Convention in Charleston or, failing that, to force him to run on a platform that explicitly repudiated his own doctrine of congressional nonintervention. [12] The convention, which met on 23 April 1860, proved to be an acrimonious affair. The adoption of a platform affirming the party's support for nonintervention triggered a walkout of delegates from the lower South. When the balloting for presidential nominees commenced, Douglas, as expected, led the field. However, he never came close to obtaining the requisite two-thirds majority. [13]

As the prospect of a deadlock loomed before the convention, some of its members began looking for a dark horse candidate. William W. Holden, who was serving as one of the North Carolina delegates, considered Clingman to be an ideal choice. "Douglas cannot be nominated," he telegraphed the *North Carolina Standard* after the eleventh ballot. "Clingman may be." In an accompanying editorial, the *Standard* hailed "the prospect of Mr. Clingman's nomination" and expressed its hope "before we go to press to receive another dispatch announcing that he has been nominated." With a ticket consisting of "Clingman and some good Northern Democrat," it added, ". . . victory will again perch upon the banner of the great national Democratic party." Instead of tendering the nomination to the senator from North Carolina, the delegates adjourned to meet again in Baltimore in mid-June. [14]

Three days later, Clingman announced his support for the Democratic platform and his opposition to Davis's resolutions in a long address before the Senate. After characterizing nonintervention as "the settled policy of the Democratic
party for the last ten years," he made it clear that his hostility to the doctrine of
federal protection was based on practical, rather than constitutional, considerations. The adoption of Davis's resolutions, he predicted, would "divide our own
party into two sections" and debilitate the Northern Democrats in the upcoming
campaign. In Clingman's view, Southern Democrats should be working to bolster
their Northern allies rather than trying to undermine them. "Instead of throwing
additional burdens on them, by narrowing the platform, I would rather widen it,
and give them all the aid and support possible." The senator also had harsh words
for the Southern delegates who had walked out of the Charleston convention.
The great strength of the Democratic party, he reminded his colleagues, was its
nationality. "Cut it in two, and many patriots and good men . . . who have come
into it recently, will fall off."[15]

Not content with merely speaking out against Davis's resolutions, Clingman
was determined to modify them in order to make them more palatable to Northerners. On 24 May he proposed an amendment declaring that "the existing conditions of the Territories . . . does not require the intervention of Congress for the
protection of property in slaves." The proposal was approved by a vote of twenty-
six to twenty-three. Most of the "yea" votes were supplied by the Republicans—
a fact not lost on the North Carolinian's enemies who charged that his "extatic
[sic] devotion to Stephen A. Douglas" had caused him to desert his own section.[16]

Clingman's victory proved short-lived. After Davis's remaining resolutions
had been adopted, Republican Henry Wilson of Massachusetts moved to reconsider the vote by which Clingman's amendment had been approved. This time the
Republicans abstained from voting on the amendment, thereby ensuring its defeat. In the end, Davis's resolutions passed the Senate in the same form in which
they had been introduced in February. Southern militants could rejoice that the
Senate had gone on record in support of federal protection. Republicans could ex-
ult in the powerful campaign ammunition that Southerners had handed them for
the upcoming Northern elections. Clingman, for his part, expressed no regrets
for having spearheaded "the last fight for the integrity of the Democratic party."[17]

In fact, Clingman had not abandoned his efforts to unify his splintered party
behind Douglas and nonintervention. Two days before the vote on Davis's resolutions, he participated in a mass meeting of Douglas supporters, who rallied under the banner of "the Constitution and the Union" at the Cooper Institute in
New York. A month later, he was also present at the reconvened session of the
Democratic National Convention in Baltimore, where he "labored earnestly to
effect a reconciliation." Clingman probably had another, less altruistic, motive
for attending that gathering. If Douglas did receive the presidential nomination, the convention would certainly choose a Southerner as his running mate.

And what better choice than the Little Giant's most vocal supporter in the U.S. Senate?[18]

By 1860 the two Democrats, who had known each other for almost two decades, were not only political allies but also personal friends. Congressional observers frequently noticed them shaking hands or chuckling together "over something that seems to be highly relished on both sides." Occasionally, Douglas would place his hand affectionately on Clingman's knee. Since early February, rumors had been circulating in Washington that a North Carolinian would be picked as Douglas's running mate. A ticket consisting of the North's most popular Democrat and one of the foremost champions of the South would be a formidable one indeed. It would also bring Clingman one step closer to his ultimate goal—the presidency of the United States.[19]

According to one report, the ambitious North Carolinian "worked" the convention "night and day" in an attempt to secure the vice presidential nomination. Despite those efforts, the delegates ultimately tendered it to a Democrat from the lower South—Sen. Benjamin Fitzpatrick of Alabama. Even if Clingman had received the nomination, it would have been a hollow victory, for the refusal of Douglas's supporters to seat many of the Charleston bolters had triggered another Southern walkout. This time all but four of North Carolina's delegates joined the bolters, who proceeded to nominate a separate ticket consisting of John C. Breckinridge and Joseph Lane. The party that Clingman had struggled so mightily to unite was now in shambles.[20]

By early summer, the vast majority of North Carolina's leading Democrats, including most of the state's presidential electors (who had been chosen before the Charleston convention), had joined the Breckinridge bandwagon. Those few electors who favored Douglas withdrew from the ticket.[21] The rapidity and unanimity with which the North Carolina Democracy swung behind Breckinridge put Clingman in an awkward position, particularly since he would be seeking reelection to the U.S. Senate in November. If he remained faithful to Douglas, he would jeopardize his chances of winning the caucus nomination. On the other hand, if he endorsed Breckinridge, he would lay himself open to charges of inconsistency and opportunism and alienate the Douglas Democrats who, though few in number, might possibly hold the balance of power in the general assembly. Clingman's enemies relished his predicament. The *Wilmington Herald* jubilantly predicted that he would "be 'rotated' out of his Senatorial office by the next Legislature."[22]

For several months after the Baltimore convention, Clingman chartered a tortuous course in regard to the presidential election. While urging North Carolina Democrats "to sustain the Democratic electoral ticket already in the field," he refrained from explicitly endorsing Breckinridge. His principal goal was to prevent the formation of a separate Douglas ticket that would divide the Democratic vote and throw the state to John Bell, the Constitutional Union candidate. In a meeting with the Illinois senator in Raleigh on 29 August, Clingman suggested a plan whereby the North Carolina electors would cast their vote for whichever Democrat stood the best chance of defeating Lincoln. He would "induce the Breckinridge men to assent to the arrangement" by threatening otherwise to "canvass the State against Breckinridge, and thus throw its vote into the hands of the Bell and Everett party." Douglas turned the proposal down, arguing that any efforts to fuse with the Breckinridge Democrats "would lose him strength in the North."[23]

The following day, a convention of Douglas supporters in Raleigh proceeded to nominate a separate electoral ticket. Before a cheering throng of supporters, the Little Giant delivered "an ultra Union speech" in which he avowed that "he would use force, whether as Senator or President, to carry on the government and preserve it from disruption." To Clingman, who was in the audience, that assertion sounded uncomfortably like the Republican "doctrine of coercion." If the South gave a sizable vote to a Democratic candidate standing on that platform and the Republicans won the general election, "that fact would encourage Lincoln to resort to force." Douglas's unwillingness to acknowledge the possibility of peaceable secession convinced Clingman that his "duty [was] to canvass against him, and reduce his vote as much as possible."[24]

Even if the Illinois senator had not taken unacceptable ground on the "doctrine of coercion," Clingman would have found it difficult to support him after the establishment of a separate Douglas ticket. The August legislative elections had once again produced a Democratic majority in the general assembly, and the senator's prospects for returning to Washington were contingent on winning the support of the Breckinridge Democrats, who would dominate the party caucus. Like a chameleon, Clingman had strong survival instincts that sometimes impelled him to change political colors in order to protect himself in dangerous situations. Douglas's "ultra Union speech" provided him with a convenient rationale for disavowing his longtime ally and endorsing the Breckinridge ticket, thus helping to ensure his own political survival.[25]

Clingman formally announced his conversion at a mass meeting in Raleigh on 6 September. Declaring his unalterable opposition to the "doctrine of coercing States to submission—the whipping-in process," he asserted that "no States Rights man could consistently vote for Mr. Douglas after he had enunciated such a policy." Looking ahead to the likelihood of a Republican victory in November, he also argued that "determined resistance" was preferable to "submit[ting] to the practical workings of Black Republican policy." At the same time, he assured his listeners that he was "for maintaining the Union" and remarked ambiguously that "circumstances must determine what course is best to pursue."[26]

Despite his statements to the contrary, Clingman's enemies relentlessly pressed the argument that he was a disunionist. To underscore that point, opposition newspapers reprinted his controversial Charlotte letter of 1856, in which he had stated that the South would be justified in resisting the election of John C. Fremont. According to the *Wilmington Herald,* "this letter clothes Mr. Clingman with a robe of disunion that fits like the shirt of Nessus." In fact, the Whig presses were less interested in presenting an accurate assessment of Clingman's opinions on the sectional crisis than they were in preventing his reelection to the Senate. After affirming that "Mr. Clingman's disunion doctrines wont *[sic]* go down in North Carolina," the *Greensboro Patriot* gleefully predicted he would "soon have leisure to return to his favorite amusement of measuring the mountains of Western North Carolina." Of course, such reports of Clingman's imminent political demise had been made many times before. It remained to be seen whether his remarkable survival skills would once again enable him to defy the predictions.[27]

In North Carolina the election resulted in a narrow victory for the Breckinridge ticket, which polled slightly more than half of the statewide vote. Bell received about 47 percent of the vote, while Douglas garnered a meager 3 percent. The efforts of Clingman and other North Carolina Democrats to unite the party behind Breckinridge had proven largely successful, particularly in comparison with neighboring Virginia where the party split had pushed that strongly Democratic state into the Bell column. Nationwide, however, Lincoln won a comfortable majority in the electoral college, despite winning only 39 percent of the popular vote.[28]

Secessionists in the lower South lost no time in responding to the news of Lincoln's election. Within a week, both of South Carolina's U.S. senators had resigned, and its legislature had formally issued a call for a state convention. The governors of several other states summoned their legislatures into special session. In Alabama, Florida, and Georgia, large and enthusiastic public meetings advocated immediate secession. Before the end of November, secessionists in the Old North State had also organized numerous county meetings, which passed resolutions demanding radical action.[29]

The rapid move toward disunion caught Clingman by surprise. Despite his public declarations that the South should "resist" the election of a Republican president, he greatly underestimated the determination of the radicals in the Deep South to carry through on their threats of secession. Several weeks before the election, he had privately expressed his opinion that "the southern states will *all* submit" to Lincoln's election. Although he did not rule out the possibility that the South might ultimately be driven out of the Union, Clingman expected that the slave states would not act individually or precipitously but, instead, would cooperate in "a united movement" that would not commence until at least "the close of Mr. Buchanan's administration." The decision of the lower South to embark immediately on a course of separate state action was, as he later recalled, "a surprise to most of us, and very unsatisfactory to many."[30]

With the lower South on the verge of secession and the North Carolina General Assembly about to convene, Governor Ellis consulted with Senators Clingman and Bragg and with several other Democratic leaders on 17 November. All except Bragg favored a state convention. In his message to the legislature three days later, Ellis formally recommended that a convention be called to consider North Carolina's relationship to the Union. At a meeting of the Democratic caucus the following evening, Clingman endorsed the idea of a convention that might demand "proper assurances that the rights of our section were not to be invaded," but he stopped short of advocating disunion in the event its "ultimatum" was ignored.[31]

During the first week of the legislative session, Clingman seemed far more interested in returning to the U.S. Senate for another six years than in leading North Carolina out of the Union. Edward J. Hale of the *Fayetteville Observer*, who was reporting events from Raleigh, noted that "Clingman not only does not resign, like Hammond and Chesnut [of South Carolina], but he is working like a beaver to get a re-election." John L. Pennington of the *New Bern Progress*, who was also at the state capital, agreed that Clingman was busily "working the wires for the Senatorship." The irony of the situation was not lost on the Whigs. If Clingman really believed the election of Lincoln to be grounds for resistance, asked the *Greensboro Patriot*, "then in the name of common sense, why does he want to be elected United States Senator?" In a similar vein, the *Raleigh Register* sarcastically observed that the man who earlier had exhorted Southerners not to accept office under the Lincoln administration "is [now] disposed . . . to consent to a re-election for the next six years." Chuckled the *Register*, "he is almost a Union man, just now—*he is*."[32]

Clingman's enemies had predicted that his course during the presidential campaign would seriously jeopardize his chances for reelection. In fact, he did encounter considerable opposition in the Democratic caucus that met on 21 November. Two-fifths of the Breckinridge Democrats deserted him, dividing their votes between William W. Avery, his arch rival within the mountain Democracy, and former Superior Court Judge Samuel J. Person. The Douglas Democrats cast their ballots for former senator Bedford Brown. Nonetheless, Clingman managed to win the caucus nomination with just three votes to spare. According to Hale, his victory was not "evidence of his peculiar fitness, or great popularity" but, rather, "the result of the most assiduous and systematic process of *button-holing* ever seen even in Raleigh."[33]

This time, however, the caucus nomination was not tantamount to election because the Democrats decided not to bring the senatorial question before the general assembly. Some of those legislators who favored immediate secession opposed the election of a U.S. senator "upon the ground that one might not be needed." Party leaders were also concerned that the Douglas Democrats might ignore the caucus decision and combine with the Whigs to elect Brown or some other "submissionist." Under the circumstances, the Democrats concluded that the most prudent course would be to defer the election and proceed to the consideration of the convention bill. The Whigs could not resist rejoicing at the "anxiety" and "surprise" experienced by Clingman upon learning of his party's refusal to elect a senator. The *Wilmington Herald* dubbed him "the worst scared man in America," while a correspondent of the *Fayetteville Observer* opined that "from present appearances, he is not likely to be the Senator." When Clingman returned to Washington in early December to attend the lame duck session of the Thirty-Sixth Congress, his political future was still very much in doubt.[34]

Clingman was the first member to address the U.S. Senate on the sectional crisis, and his remarks set the tone for the discussion that followed. The North Carolinian bluntly informed his Northern colleagues that "a number of States [will] secede in the next sixty days" and that, if left unchecked, "the movement will not stop until they all go." At the same time, he expressed hope that the Union might be preserved "if proper guarantees can be obtained . . . sufficient to save our honor and insure our safety." Although he did not specify the precise nature of those guarantees, he agreed with President Buchanan that they should be woven into the fabric of the U.S. Constitution through the amendment process. He also declared that the initiative for resolving the sectional crisis would have to come from the North. "I do not see how any Southern man can make propositions. We have petitioned and remonstrated for the last ten years, and to no purpose."[35]

Unionists in his home state condemned Clingman's remarks as unnecessarily inflammatory. William W. Holden of the *North Carolina Standard,* who had broken with the Democratic leadership and was now unabashedly promoting the unionist cause, denounced Clingman for advocating "disunion for existing causes" and asserted that "the people of this State are against him by an immense majority."[36] Although regarded by his enemies as a disunionist, Clingman can more accurately be characterized as a conditional unionist or, as Daniel W. Crofts has put it, a "fast ultimatumist." In other words, his unionism, though genuine, was predicated upon prompt and substantial Republican concessions that would protect the rights of the South and offer the seceding states an inducement to return to the Union. That attitude set him apart from the "unconditional unionists," who opposed secession under any circumstances, and the "extended ultimatumists," who were willing to remain in the Union until all reasonable hope for compromise was exhausted. However, it also distinguished Clingman from the immediate secessionists, who had no expectation that the sectional crisis could be resolved through compromise.[37]

The attitude of the immediate secessionists was embodied in a public address issued on 14 December 1860 by a group of twenty-nine Southern senators and representatives. Declaring that "all hope of relief in the Union . . . is extinguished," the address called for "separate State secession" and the "organization of a Southern Confederacy." Two North Carolina congressmen—Burton Craige and Thomas Ruffin—were among the signers. Significantly, Clingman's name was not on the document. Compared to radicals like Craige and Ruffin—not to mention the secessionists in the Deep South who were actively making plans to withdraw their states from the Union—Clingman was, indeed, "almost a Union man." [38]

During the first weeks of December, Clingman had reason to be optimistic about the prospects for sectional reconciliation. As he later remembered, "the desire for a settlement seemed general among the Northern members." Early in the session, John J. Crittenden of Kentucky introduced a series of proposed constitutional amendments, the most important of which stipulated that slavery would be "protected as property" in all territory "now held, or hereafter acquired" south of the latitude 36° 30'. That proposal not only met the demands of Southern Democrats for congressional protection but also offered the possibility that the slave system might expand southward into the Caribbean. [39]

Clingman's hopes that the Republicans would accede to a territorial compromise were quickly dashed. On 31 December 1860 the Senate Committee of Thirteen reported that it had failed to agree on a plan. A week later, the House Republicans refused to consider a watered-down version of the Crittenden compromise proposed by Emerson Etheridge. Even the unionists now acknowledged that the prospects for a peaceful settlement were "gloomy in the extreme." [40]

Still, Clingman had not lost hope that a settlement might be effected if North Carolinians could be persuaded to do their duty. In his view, the key to a successful resolution of the sectional crisis now lay in the passage of the convention bill, which had been languishing in the general assembly since December. In several public letters published in the North Carolina newspapers in middle and late January, Clingman asserted that the legislative stalemate had promoted a belief among the Republicans in Congress that there would be "no resistance outside of the cotton states." Laboring under that false impression, they had taken "a stand against any substantial concession." If the Republicans could be brought to understand that the South was united in the determination to maintain its rights, that understanding might result in concessions that would "prevent a further dissolution of the Union, and lead to its re-construction." In Clingman's mind, the purpose of the convention was not to lead North Carolina out of the Union but "to save the Union . . . [and] to prevent civil war." [41]

Clingman's public letters were aimed at breaking the logjam that had thus far prevented the passage of the convention bill. According to the state constitution, a two-thirds majority of both houses was required to call a convention. That meant that no bill could pass the general assembly without substantial support from the unionists. Many unionists were willing to vote for a convention, but they insisted on incorporating guarantees that would prevent precipitate action. Specifically, they demanded that any measure enacted by the convention be approved by a popular referendum before taking effect. The refusal of the Democratic leadership to accede to that demand prevented a speedy resolution of the convention issue. [42]

Apart from his concern that the inaction of the general assembly was sending the Republicans the wrong message, Clingman had another reason for desiring the quick passage of a convention bill. Early in the session, the Democrats had decided not to proceed with the election of a U.S. senator until the convention question had been settled. The Whigs, on the other hand, were eager to bring the senatorial issue to a vote, believing that they had enough support among Union Democrats to elect Bedford Brown or some other unionist. On several occasions in December and January, the Whigs introduced resolutions to proceed with the election. Until late January, Clingman supporters such as Marcus Erwin and William H. Thomas had joined the other Democrats in voting them down. On 28 January, however, Erwin, Thomas, and five other senate Democrats defied the party leadership and helped pass a resolution calling for the immediate election of a U.S. senator. House Democrats barely managed to defeat the motion.[43]

Erwin and Thomas no doubt expected the legislature to reelect Clingman. Other Democrats were not so certain about the outcome. That uncertainty offered a powerful incentive for party leaders to capitulate to unionist demands on the convention bill in order to avoid sending an avowed "submissionist" to the U.S. Senate. The measure that finally passed the general assembly on 30 January 1861 provided for a popular referendum on any action taken by the convention. It also stipulated that the electorate would have an opportunity to vote for or against the convention itself at the same time they were selecting delegates. In return for those substantial concessions, Union Democrats agreed to abide by the decision of the November caucus. On 31 January 1861 Clingman was reelected to the U.S. Senate by an eleven-vote majority.[44]

Four days later, Clingman stood before the Senate to deliver what would prove to be his last prepared speech. By early February, the prospects for the passage of a compromise bill had markedly improved. The Senate had agreed to reconsider Crittenden's proposals, and the Kentucky senator had telegraphed his North Carolina supporters that "there is yet good hope of success." Moreover, at the behest of Virginia, a Peace Conference consisting of delegates from twenty-one states was assembling at nearby Willard's Hotel to recommend proposals to save the Union. Clingman's conciliatory address reflected that renewed hope for a sectional compromise. Reassuring his Republican colleagues that "the great body of the people of the South do not hate the North," he asserted that most Southerners "would far prefer a union with the North upon honorable terms" than secession. All they were asking was that "full justice be done them on this slavery question."[45]

At the same time, however, Clingman made the point that the Union would not be saved merely by singing its praises. Northerners must agree to constitutional guarantees that would "place this entire question [of slavery] where it cannot be reached." Otherwise, "a large and powerful body of conservative men [in the upper South] will at once go to the side of the secessionists." In Clingman's mind, secession did not necessarily mean the establishment of an enduring Southern nation. The separation might be temporary rather than permanent. If the North subsequently proved willing to "change its views, then there might be a reunion and a reconstruction of the government." Looking back at the record of history, he reminded his listeners that "twice did the Plebians *[sic]* secede, and twice did the haughty Patricians make such terms of conciliation as rendered Rome the foremost empire upon earth."[46]

On the same day that Clingman spoke to the U.S. Senate, the seceding states met at Montgomery, Alabama, to frame a constitution and set up a provisional government. Five days later, Jefferson Davis and Alexander H. Stephens were elected president and vice president of the Confederate States of America. As it became clear that the Deep South was in earnest in its intent to establish an independent nation, the efforts of compromisers like Clingman seemed increasingly futile. As the *Wilmington Journal* explained, the seceding states would not accept the Crittenden compromise "even if Mr. Clingman should agree to do so. Mr. Clingman is not the whole South, and his agreeing to a compromise would not commit even North Carolina to adopt it. It is too late in the day to talk about compromises. . . . The border Southern States must decide to which Confederacy they will attach themselves. . . . There can be no half-way course now."[47]

By mid-February, Clingman's political survival instincts had brought him reluctantly to the same conclusion. The vote in the November caucus had revealed that his moderate course had already cost him substantial support among the Southern Rights Democrats. The criticism of secessionist newspapers like the *Wilmington Journal* indicated that his political base had eroded still further since then. If Clingman continued to resist the secessionist impulse and a majority of disunionists were elected to the state convention, he would most likely have no political future in the Confederate States of America. On the other hand, if the voters of the Old North State decided to remain in the Union, an endorsement of secession would not preclude his bowing to the will of the people and taking his seat in the Thirty-Seventh Congress. From the perspective of February 1861, Clingman had much more to gain than lose by casting his lot with the secessionists.[48]

Ten days before the convention elections, the North Carolina senator came out publicly in favor of disunion. In a series of telegrams and public letters, he announced that "there is not at this time the slightest prospect that any just Constitutional guarantees will be obtained." The "great practical question," therefore, was whether North Carolina "will aid Lincoln in this policy of coercion, or join the Southern States in resisting it." Should the Old North State "take a stand for resistance, her influence, and that of Virginia, may be sufficient to arrest the purpose of Lincoln and his followers . . . and peace may, in that way, be secured." On the other hand, "a vote for submission is in effect a vote for *civil war* and *free negro equality* over the South."[49]

For once, the residents of the mountain district failed to follow Clingman's lead. Although William W. Avery and William H. Thomas squeaked by in the convention election with narrow victories, Marcus Erwin and the other secessionist candidates in the far west were swept away by the Union tide. In addition, almost 60 percent of the mountain voters cast their ballots against the convention despite its endorsement by Zebulon Vance and other prominent unionists. The large anticonvention vote in Clingman's district resulted in a narrow defeat for the proposal statewide. Had the delegates assembled, the opponents of immediate secession would have dominated handily, thanks to their large majorities among non-slave-holding voters in the Piedmont and the far west.[50]

The opposition was quick to point out that the outcome in the mountain district constituted "a very decided repudiation of Senator Clingman's fire-eating proclivities." For more than a decade, Clingman had maintained his political base by assuring his constituents that a strong stand on behalf of Southern Rights was compatible with their support for the Union. Ironically, his enemies prevailed in 1861 by making the same argument. While Clingman was now claiming that voters would have to choose between their desire to uphold their rights and their wish to remain in the Union, his opponents were affirming that those two objectives were not antithetical and that "southern interests, particularly slavery, would be protected under the incoming administration." The overwhelming opposition of the mountain district to secession in February 1861 indicates that the vast majority of westerners continued to believe that their rights as Southerners could best be defended within the Union.[51]

Once the voters of the Old North State had decisively asserted their determination to remain in the Union, Clingman once again demonstrated his adeptness at changing his political colors in order to adapt to new situations. Instead of resigning his seat in the U.S. Senate, he was among the handful of Southerners who returned to Washington in March 1861 to attend the executive session of the U.S. Senate, which met to consider President Lincoln's appointments. The *North Carolina Standard* charged that Clingman had returned to Washington "to destroy the very government he was commissioned to serve and uphold."[52]

Actually, his motives were more complex. Although his hopes for an immediate resolution of the sectional conflict had diminished, Clingman continued to believe that his exertions might avert a bloody war that would destroy all possibility of reconciliation and reunion. On 6 March he warned his fellow senators that Lincoln's determination to hold on to the federal forts and execute the laws, as announced in his inaugural address, was tantamount to a declaration of war. Clingman advised the president to defuse the situation by withdrawing federal troops from Forts Sumter and Pickens and suspending attempts to execute the revenue laws. Two days before the end of the session, he introduced a resolution to that effect, but the Republicans refused to consider it. If his plan had been adopted, he later recalled, "instead of war there would have been an appeal to Congress, to ascertain if an accommodation could not be made."[53]

Clingman's behavior during the secession crisis indicates that his commitment to Southern independence was tenuous at best. He embraced disunion reluctantly and only after the repeated failure of numerous compromise efforts in Congress. Moreover, like an indeterminate number of other Southerners who aspired to reconstruct a Union in which slaveholders might feel secure, he regarded secession as a tactical maneuver rather than an end in itself. A unified South negotiating from a position of assumed independence, he reasoned, would be in a stronger position to extract meaningful concessions from the North than would a helpless and divided minority of border states begging for their rights within the Union.[54]

In retrospect, the strategy of reconstruction through secession might seem quixotic, even foolhardy. Clingman certainly must have been aware of the risks. No one could know for certain whether a unified South making demands from outside the Union would be able to extract significant concessions from the Republicans or whether such concessions would be satisfactory to the states of the lower South. But a united South might at least deter the Lincoln administration from a policy of coercion and prevent the outbreak of civil war. And as long as peace was maintained, the possibility for reunion would remain alive. After all, twice had the Plebeians seceded and twice had the haughty Patricians come to terms with them.[55]

The Confederate attack on Fort Sumter and Lincoln's call for federal troops to suppress the rebellion dashed the hopes of Clingman that war might be avoided. Upon hearing the news of the surrender of the federal garrison at Charleston, he hurried to South Carolina and, in an impromptu speech at the Charleston Hotel, assured his audience that "the Old North State was now ready to imbibe the spirit and energy of South Carolina and . . . resist the infernal treachery of Lincoln." A few weeks later, Governor Ellis dispatched him to Montgomery, Alabama, to negotiate North Carolina's entrance into the Confederacy. In deference to the "high station and reputation" of its representative, the Confederate Congress accorded Clingman the privilege of attending its sessions, "secret as well as public," and participating in the debates. He returned to North Carolina in time to witness the recently elected state convention secede from the Union on 20 May.[56]

Despite his service as a volunteer aide-de-camp to Gen. Joseph E. Johnston at the Battle of Manassas in mid-July and his election a month later as colonel of the 25th Regiment of North Carolina infantry, Clingman had no intention of exchanging his "senatorial robes" for a set of "soldier's clothes." Indeed, at the same time that the troops nominally under his command were drilling near Asheville, their leader was electioneering in Raleigh for a seat in the Confederate Senate. The balloting for North Carolina's two senators began on 27 August 1861, and more than two weeks would pass before the matter was finally settled. The popular demand for a united front against the Yankee invaders had led the state's political leaders to abandon their party labels and proclaim "an era of good feelings in state politics." However, the temporary cessation of partisanship did nothing to quench the desire for political preferment. As the *Raleigh Register* pointed out, it seemed like "about every prominent man in the State is in nomination" for the senatorship.[57]

Without a party caucus to narrow the field of contenders, the legislators found themselves unable to agree upon a choice. Many Democratic members were supporting William W. Avery and Samuel J. Person. Both men had opposed Clingman in the Democratic caucus the previous November, and both had taken more advanced ground on the issue of secession. On the first ballot Person led the field with thirty-one votes, but his total was considerably below the seventy-six votes required for election. Clingman won only fourteen votes and placed a distant fifth. The three ballots taken on the next day also proved inconclusive. On 30 August, the rules were changed to allow each member to vote for two candidates. This time Clingman surpassed all the other contenders with thirty-eight votes. Even so, he fell far short of the requisite majority.[58]

After another inconclusive ballot, the general assembly made no further effort to elect a senator until 10 September. The stalemate continued, as five ballots over a period of four days failed to produce a winner. On the next ballot, however, George Davis of Wilmington easily outdistanced all the other candidates with seventy-nine votes—three more than the required majority. The election of Davis, a Whig attorney who had recently served as a delegate to the Washington Peace Conference, must have come as a surprise to many observers, since he had garnered only twenty-eight votes on the previous ballot. The unexpected outcome resulted from the decision of Clingman's and Avery's supporters to cast their second ballot for Davis in the hope that the selection of an eastern Whig might pave the way for the elevation of a western Democrat to the other seat. Clingman placed second to Davis in the balloting, outdistancing Avery by fourteen votes but still falling twenty-three votes short of a majority.[59]

If Clingman expected to become the leading candidate now that Davis had been elected, those expectations were quickly dashed. On the next ballot, easterner William T. Dortch was elected to the second seat, garnering three votes more than the necessary majority. William W. Holden believed that Clingman would have won the election if he had been the only western candidate. Instead, "the claims of the West, as presented in the person of Mr. Clingman, were embarrassed by Mr. Avery . . . [who] never stood at any time the ghost of a chance of being elected."[60]

Avery's desire to replace his rival as "King among the mountains" undoubtedly did play a role in determining the outcome. The most fundamental cause of Clingman's defeat, however, was the breakdown of the legislative caucus. Earlier in his career, he had denounced the caucus as a mechanism used by a few "central managers" to bestow public offices on their unworthy favorites. By 1861, however, the onetime "independent outsider" had himself become the consummate insider. As the state's senior senator with almost two decades of service in

Congress, he was arguably the most powerful and well-connected Democrat in North Carolina.

At the same time, Clingman had acquired more than his share of political enemies both within and outside his party. In 1858 and 1860 he had brilliantly used the Democratic caucus to neutralize his intraparty rivals, who had bound themselves to abide by the decision of the majority. On two occasions in August and September 1861, he actually received more votes than he had garnered in the Democratic caucus the previous November. Yet without the discipline of the legislative caucus, he could not force challengers from within the party to rally behind his candidacy or prevent them from combining with the Whigs.[61]

Indeed, the main factor behind Dortch's victory over Clingman was the solid vote he received from the Whigs. After the election of Davis, many Whigs apparently felt comfortable in bestowing the second seat on a Democrat. Although Dortch had not acted with the unionists during the secession crisis, there was reason to believe that "instead of encouraging [the secessionists], he labored to restrain them in their headlong course." Thus he was more acceptable to former unionists than either of his main Democratic challengers. On the final ballot, the Democrats scattered their votes in almost equal numbers among Clingman, Avery, and Dortch, thereby allowing the more disciplined Whigs to determine the winner.[62]

Clingman's supporters were furious at the result of the senatorial contest. John Spelman, the editor and proprietor of the *Raleigh State Journal*, characterized his defeat as "a gross outrage on the people of the West." Spelman could not help wondering "how it was that this same General Assembly [that] last winter elected [him] . . . now [has] repudiated him?" Clingman, he concluded, had "been sacrificed on the altar of petty partizan *[sic]* rancour and shameless political intrigue." Despite the hyperbolic language and partisan bias, Spelman's assessment was basically accurate. The Whigs had finally exacted their revenge on Thomas Lanier Clingman for deserting their party and contributing to the breakup of the Union. With his political career at least temporarily at an end, he would now have to exchange his senatorial robes for soldier's clothes and seek new laurels on the field of battle.[63]

12 *A Noble Ambition*

Political necessity forced Clingman into the Confederate army even before his defeat in the senatorial election. With the onset of hostilities, he found himself severely castigated by the former unionists for gasconading about Southern Rights while others were risking their lives in defense of their homeland. "Such a furious secessionist as Clingman ought to have gone to Charleston . . . *before* the fight there," groused the *Fayetteville Observer* two weeks after the Battle of Fort Sumter. "This is no time for politicians to be stumping. . . . Let them go to the forts and *work,* and if a fight comes, let them be there to fight." On the floor of the North Carolina Senate, the sharp-tongued Josiah Turner also took aim at Clingman, deriding him as "a 'carpet knight' of the revolution, who was to be found in the Exchange Hotel in Richmond . . . or the lobby of the Senate [in Raleigh] instead of the battlefield."[1]

In order to deflect such criticism, Clingman volunteered as an aide-de-camp to Joseph E. Johnston, the commander of the Confederate forces guarding Richmond. His first taste of combat came at Manassas on 21 July 1861. There he witnessed a gallant charge against a Union battery by Charles F. Fisher and the 6th North Carolina Infantry—a movement that, in Clingman's opinion, "saved the day to the Confederacy." Unfortunately, Fisher and many of his men were among the casualties. From his own observations and from conversations with other eyewitnesses, Clingman concluded that they had been killed by troops from Alabama, who had mistaken them for Union soldiers.[2]

Clingman urged Fisher's second-in-command, Lt. Col. C. E. Lightfoot, "to make such a report as would do justice to Colonel Fisher and the regiment." However, Lightfoot's company had become separated from the regiment and had not participated in the fighting. Instead of acknowledging his commander's role in turning the tide of battle, Lightfoot "complained very much of Colonel Fisher because he carried the regiment into action by the flank." Clingman appealed to Johnston to make the facts public, but the general replied that "he could only give such statements as come up to him from the reports of his subordinates." Fisher's heroic maneuver was never officially recognized.[3]

Clingman's initial contact with war may well have strengthened his resolve to return to the more familiar realm of statecraft. Although he now had his eye on a seat in the Confederate Senate, he could not afford to create the impression that he was reentering government merely to avoid a fight. An ideal way to demonstrate his patriotism and fighting spirit was to accept command of a regiment of North Carolina troops. Since May, the residents from Buncombe and adjoining counties had been forming volunteer companies and assembling at Camp Patton near Asheville. On 15 August the commissioned officers in the ten companies organized the 25th Regiment and elected Clingman as their colonel. His second-in-command was Lt. Col. St. Clair Dearing, a professional soldier who had recently resigned his commission in the U.S. Army. Dearing most likely accepted a subordinate position with the understanding that he would receive command once Clingman was elected to the Senate.[4]

Under the "skillful training and accurate drill" of Dearing, the raw recruits of the 25th Regiment began learning how to function as a fighting unit. Their nominal leader, meanwhile, was spending much of his time in Raleigh electioneering for the senatorship. In the past, Clingman's personal appeals to the legislators had proven extremely effective. This time, however, they may well have backfired. His enemies were quick to point out the unseemliness of a commander deserting his troops to campaign for office. "The proper place for him," scolded the *North Carolina Standard*, ". . . [is] at the head of his regiment, not in Raleigh, electioneering for the Senator's place."[5]

After failing to win the senatorship, Clingman rejoined his regiment, which was drilling just west of Asheville at "Camp Clingman." A month later, his troops were ordered to Wilmington "to assist in protecting the coast against an apprehended attack." On 29 September the regiment arrived at Camp Davis on Middle Sound east of the city, where arms and muskets were distributed. However, the troops lacked sufficient clothing, and there was "a pressing need of blankets." In

mid-October Clingman published a letter in the *Asheville News* urging mountain residents "to relieve the wants of those volunteers who are risking their lives
in defence of the country" by furnishing them with shirts, socks, drawers, and
blankets.[6]

The anticipated Federal attack against Wilmington never materialized. Instead, the Union fleet sailed to Port Royal at the southern end of South Carolina
and took possession of the forts at Hilton Head and the other sea islands. On 5 November Clingman's regiment was ordered to Camp Beauregard, about twenty
miles from Port Royal. Nine days later, his troops were dispatched to Camp Lee
near Grahamville with orders to guard the Charleston and Savannah Railroad
from enemy attack. The swampy lowlands made a Union advance against the railroad highly unlikely, and disease, rather than any human enemy, presented the
greatest threat to the lives of Clingman and his men. During the first two months
of their stay, measles and typhoid fever swept through the camp. By early 1862,
the worst was over, and the health of the regiment began improving.[7]

Instead of striking the South Carolina coast, the Federals attacked Roanoke Island, captured the two regiments of infantry stationed there, and occupied the
coastal towns of Edenton, Elizabeth City, and Hertford. The debacle caused
"great excitement . . . & much depression" in the Old North State. On 15 February 1862 the state's congressional delegation called on President Davis and demanded that the North Carolina troops stationed in South Carolina be transferred to Wilmington. Davis responded that he could not recall them without
endangering Charleston and Savannah. Not until the Union army began moving
against New Bern in March was Clingman's regiment finally called back to North
Carolina. By then, it was too late to save that town from capture.[8]

The 25th Regiment joined the retreating Confederates in camp at Kinston,
about thirty miles upriver from New Bern. With their one-year term of enlistment about to expire, most of the men were now expecting to return home. The
passage of the Conscription Act in mid-April, which extended their term for the
duration of the war, caught them by surprise. With "disaffection and insubordination" spreading rapidly among the troops, Clingman agreed to go to Richmond
to plead their case. He had gotten no farther than Goldsboro, however, when he
fell from his horse and severely injured his leg and ankle. Unable to travel any
great distance, he returned to Kinston and tried to "restore a better feeling"
among the troops. On 30 April he was unanimously reelected as regimental
colonel.[9]

While recuperating at Kinston, Clingman briefly considered a return to politics. Despite their promises to refrain from partisan politics, the "original secessionists" and the "old unionists" had been at loggerheads since the beginning of
the war. On the pages of the *North Carolina Standard*, William W. Holden bitterly
criticized Governor Ellis and his successor, Henry T. Clark, for neglecting the
state's defenses and discriminating against old unionists in their appointments.

Faced with the prospect of a strong challenge from the antiadministration forces in the upcoming state elections, former congressman William S. Ashe and several other prominent Democrats journeyed to Kinston to urge Clingman to run for governor.[10]

Clingman rejected the invitation for both political and personal reasons. Since the antiadministration forces consisted primarily of former Whigs, he believed the proadministration or "Confederate" party should endeavor to divide the Whig vote by selecting a Whig as their standard-bearer. Clingman's plan was ultimately the one that was followed. The Confederates nominated William Johnston, a Whig businessman who had joined the secessionists after Lincoln's election. The antiadministration or "Conservative" party nominated former congressman Zebulon B. Vance, who was now commanding the 26th Regiment at Kinston. Despite the endorsement of Clingman and other prominent Democrats, Johnston was soundly defeated. Indeed, the 74 percent of the popular vote given to Vance constituted "a dramatic popular repudiation of the Democratic leadership that had controlled the state for more than a decade."[11]

Clingman's disinclination to run for governor also stemmed from his determination to serve in the army "as long as the war might last." By the spring of 1862, the same ambition that had earlier led him to aspire to a succession of high civil offices now induced him to seek advancement in the Confederate army. In November 1861, shortly after his former Senate colleague Thomas Bragg was appointed Confederate attorney general, Clingman dispatched Bayles Edney to the capital to present his case for a promotion to brigadier general. Bragg demurred on the grounds that he "never said anything to the President about Military appointments," but Clingman's persistent lobbying eventually paid off. He received his commission on 17 May 1862. On 4 August—eight days after his fiftieth birthday—he officially assumed command of the District of Pamlico and Cape Fear, a vast area extending from Weldon near the Virginia border to the Cape Fear River.[12]

Reaction to Clingman's appointment divided predictably along partisan lines. William W. Holden, who had earlier pronounced Clingman "a novice in military matters," declared that he had received the promotion "solely on account of his politics." On the other hand, Thomas W. Atkin asserted that Clingman's "great abilities, his sound practical judgment, quick perception, and cool bravery . . . eminently qualify him for the high and responsible position." A correspondent of the *Raleigh State Journal* took a more dispassionate view. While acknowledging that "Gen. Clingman has been reproached in times gone by with being ambitious," he went on to make the argument that ambition was a necessary ingredient in a successful general. "A noble ambition—the desire to excel—the aspiration to soar—the 'thirst for fame'—constitutes an essential element in the character of military greatness."[13]

At the time he received his command, Clingman was literally a general without an army. With McClellan and Pope pressing Lee before Richmond, all available troops had been moved to the Virginia front, leaving the North Carolinian with only two regiments of infantry, one of cavalry, and three of artillery. The situation remained grim until Lee's victory at the Second Battle of Manassas in late August finally relieved the pressure on the Confederate capital. It was doubly fortunate for Clingman that the Union forces in North Carolina confined their activities to small raiding parties, because he was physically incapable of commanding an army. The injury he had sustained in April still troubled him, making it difficult for him to walk or even ride a horse. A trip to Petersburg in early August only aggravated the problem. On 25 August, his foot was operated upon at Goldsboro. Recovery was slow, however, and Clingman secured a leave of absence that allowed him to spend much of his time at the Confederate capital in Richmond.[14]

While Clingman was recuperating in Richmond during the fall of 1862, the four regiments that would eventually comprise his brigade were doing picket duty in the vicinity of Kinston. The 8th and 31st Regiments, commanded by former congressman Henry M. Shaw and John V. Jordan, were composed of troops recruited primarily from the eastern counties. Both units had acquired a somewhat unsavory reputation as a result of their capitulation to Federal forces at Roanoke Island in February. After being exchanged for Union prisoners, the regiments were reorganized in September and dispatched to Kinston in October. There they joined the 51st Regiment, a unit that had been organized in April under the command of John L. Cantwell, a Wilmington cotton broker. The 61st Regiment, organized in August under the command of James D. Radcliffe, was also operating in eastern North Carolina. Although it was formally attached to Clingman's Brigade in early November, it remained in the Kinston area until mid-December to protect the Wilmington and Weldon Railroad.[15]

Clingman arrived at Wilmington, where he had been ordered to take command, on 20 November 1862. The 51st Regiment was already in the city, and it was soon joined by the 8th and 31st.[16] The troops did not remain idle for long. On 11 December Union general John G. Foster left his base at New Bern with a force consisting of ten thousand infantry, forty pieces of artillery, and 640 cavalry. His objective was Goldsboro and the nearby railroad bridge over the Neuse River. Over the next five days, the Federal troops dislodged Confederate defenders at Kinston and Whitehall, a small village about eighteen miles from Goldsboro. Clingman arrived at Goldsboro on the same day Foster attacked Whitehall. Under his command were the 8th and 51st Regiments of his own brigade, along with the 52d Regiment of James J. Pettigrew's Brigade. Nathan G. Evans, the South Carolinian who had overall command of the defensive operations, ordered Clingman to defend both the railroad bridge a few miles south of Goldsboro and the county bridge about half a mile upriver. Clingman stationed the 52d Regiment on the road from Whitehall, about one and a half miles south of the railroad bridge. He placed the 8th Regiment by the county bridge. The 51st Regiment was held in reserve between them.[17]

On the morning of 17 December the main body of the Union army attacked the railroad bridge. Unable to sustain themselves against the enemy's heavy artillery, the 52d Regiment fell back along the river. Confederate artillery continued to defend the railroad bridge from their position on the north side of the river, but the Union troops eventually managed to set it on fire. Later in the afternoon, Clingman, now reinforced by the 61st Regiment and two field pieces, received orders from Evans to counterattack. By then, the bulk of the Federal forces had fallen back toward New Bern, but a contingent remained to form a rear guard by the railroad. Clingman planned to attack the Federal position on both flanks. He moved the 51st and 52d Regiments down the river to a protected location about three hundred yards from the enemy's right flank and ordered them to remain still until they heard the two other regiments attack. He then rejoined the 8th and 61st Regiments and led them down the county road toward the Union left flank.[18]

Before Clingman had time to get the 8th and 61st into position, Evans arrived on the scene and ordered the 51st and 52d immediately to advance. When informed that such a movement "would disconcert all of General Clingman's plans and result in disaster," he curtly responded that he outranked Clingman and then repeated the order. In the face of a heavy discharge of grape and canister from the enemy batteries, the two Confederate regiments charged across an open space of one thousand yards, sustaining heavy casualties before falling back. Upon hearing the sound of cannon, Clingman immediately ordered his own artillery to fire. The Federal batteries responded in kind, and the artillery duel continued until darkness put an end to the contest. The Union troops then retired to Kinston.[19]

Militarily, the engagement had been inconclusive. Although Foster succeeded in burning the railroad bridge, reports of massive Confederate reinforcements dissuaded him from attempting to occupy Goldsboro. The damage to the bridge affected only the superstructure, and Confederate work crews quickly made the necessary repairs. In his first taste of combat Clingman had demonstrated great personal courage. Thomas C. Fuller, who commanded the Confederate artillery during the counterattack, recalled that no man was ever "braver in the hour of fiercest battle than was Clingman on that occasion. He rode up and down the line on horseback, absolutely without fear, giving his commands."[20]

The North Carolina presses regarded the battle as a significant victory. If Goldsboro had fallen, they pointed out, Wilmington, Fayetteville, and even Raleigh would have been exposed to attack. Instead, Clingman's "masterly movement" in the afternoon had "caused the enemy to skedaddle." Some of the South Carolina newspapers were more critical, blaming Clingman for allowing the railroad bridge to be burned. A number of opposition members of the North Carolina legislature were likewise inclined to censure Clingman for failing to hold the bridge.[21]

Clingman was stung by those "unjust imputations." On the day of the battle he had been heard to remark that the bridge could have been saved if reinforcements had arrived in a timely manner. There were, in fact, other Confederate troops in the vicinity, but transportation problems prevented them from reaching the scene in time to participate. In his official report submitted four days after the engagement, Clingman defended his own conduct and blamed Evans for the burning of the bridge. Had he been allowed to concentrate all his forces at the railroad bridge, he wrote, he might have withstood the Federal advance. But it was "impossible with only three regiments to hold both the [railroad and county] bridges and at the same time fight a large army."[22]

Convinced that his report would fully vindicate the conduct of his troops, Clingman asked Secretary of War James A. Seddon for permission to publish it. His request was denied. Seddon's refusal should have ended the matter, but Clingman was unwilling to "allow the brave men whom I commanded to suffer in public estimation from false statements made through ignorance or improper motives." On 28 January 1863 he wrote Governor Vance to solicit his assistance. While acknowledging that army regulations prevented him from publishing the report himself, he reasoned that "the same rules do not apply to you. . . . Like any one else out of the Service, you can in your discretion publish whatever will not be injurious to the public interests."[23]

Vance subsequently published the report in the *North Carolina Standard,* and it was reprinted in several other North Carolina newspapers. Although technically Clingman may not have violated War Department orders, he certainly strained the bounds of propriety by publishing his report through an intermediary. In his mind, however, the need to vindicate himself and his brigade "by the publication of the truth" overrode all other considerations. Once before at Manassas the facts had been suppressed and the heroic conduct of North Carolina's soldiers had gone unreported. This time he was determined that "all the facts should be known."[24]

Clingman's Brigade returned to Wilmington on 2 January 1863 and went into winter quarters at Camp Whiting. On 16 February, in response to reports of Federal naval activity along the coast of South Carolina and Georgia, the brigade was ordered to James Island in Charleston Harbor. Apart from one week in early March when they were dispatched to Fort McAllister near Savannah, Clingman's troops remained in South Carolina until the end of April. During that period, the Federal forces limited their activities to an eight-hour bombardment of Fort McAllister and a two-and-one-half-hour naval assault on Charleston. In neither instance was Clingman's Brigade involved in the fighting.[25]

As one member of the brigade later recalled, going from Savannah back to

Charleston Harbor was "very much the same as dropping out of Paradise into Hell." The encampment at James Island was like "a little Sahara, having plenty of wind; rolling and twisting clouds of sand; millions of black gnats (much greater pests than mosquitoes), and a very scanty supply of devilish poor beef, that a respectable Charleston buzzard would not eat." Once again, Clingman's troops discovered that "swamps and malaria were the most destructive enemies." Early in April, one soldier reported "a good deal of sickness in our Brigade" and noted ominously that "an unusual proportion of the cases terminate fatally." He attributed the health problems to "bad water, short and very bad rations . . . [and] the damp atmosphere." [26]

Their periodic visits to Charleston provided no boost to the men's morale. Prices were exorbitantly high; the merchants refused to accept North Carolina treasury notes; and the supercilious attitude of the local "ruffled shirt, cod-fish aristocracy" rankled the visiting Tar Heels to no end. Clingman's troops felt particularly aggrieved in light of the recent newspaper criticism of their conduct at Goldsboro. One soldier protested that he and his comrades were "getting heartily tired of doing all the fighting, enduring all the hardships, and getting no credit for anything . . . [while] South Carolina [is] getting all the credit." "We wish to be relieved from duty in this State," he concluded. "We don't care where they send us." [27]

As morale within the brigade plummeted, desertion and absenteeism increased sharply. In mid-March Clingman sent Vance a list of absentees, "a portion of whom are doubtless staying at home without reason," and requested the governor to "arrest such as are now able to do duty." A month later, he complained to his commanding officer that a large number of his men were abusing medical furloughs. Clingman understood that these problems would persist as long as his troops remained at Charleston, and he lobbied aggressively to have them transferred to North Carolina. On 29 April 1863 the brigade was finally ordered back to Wilmington. According to Daniel H. Hill, the commander of the Department of North Carolina, "Clingman's troops have been much demoralized and . . . can only be trusted behind earthworks." [28]

Chase Whiting, the commanding general at Wilmington, was less than pleased with the return of Clingman's Brigade. The strategic importance of that city, he groused, demanded that the few soldiers under his command "should be the best possible, not the worst." Whiting resolved nonetheless to "go to work on Clingman's brigade and get it into shape." Clingman and his regimental commanders were equally determined to instill "a little discipline" into the troops. In a general order issued two weeks after their return, Clingman lectured his troops on the virtues of "punctuality and promptness," noting that "many battles have been lost and won because troops failed to move promptly to the positions assigned to them." [29]

If Clingman's troops believed they had seen the last of the Palmetto State, they were bitterly disappointed. On 10 July 1863 the brigade was called back to Charleston in response to a combined naval and infantry assault that had resulted in the establishment of a Federal beachhead on the south end of Morris Island. On the evening of his arrival, Clingman attended a strategy session involving Gov. Milledge L. Bonham, Congressman William Porcher Miles, Gen. Pierre G. T. Beauregard, and several other military leaders. Clingman proposed a frontal attack on the Federal position at Morris Island. Beauregard and the others disagreed. At least four thousand men would be required for such an operation, they pointed out, and it would have to be executed under cover of night to be successful. However, by the time the troops were landed and deployed on the narrow island, it would be daylight, and the Confederate forces would then be vulnerable to fire from both land and sea. Under the circumstances, "the operation could but result in disaster, and ought not to be attempted." The meeting ended with a decision to forego a frontal attack and "defend the north side of the island as long as practicable."[30]

On the north end of Morris Island, guarding the ship channel into Charleston Harbor, stood Battery Wagner, a makeshift structure composed of sand, turf, and palmetto logs. During the fifty-eight-day Federal siege, Clingman's troops alternated with other regiments in doing garrison duty at the fort. One member of the brigade recalled that there was "no place so uninviting as Battery Wagner." The troops were continuously exposed to the sharpshooting and cannonading of the enemy, while "suffering almost beyond endurance from heat and great scarcity of water and rations." The only place of safety was a "bombproof" inside of which the troops stood during the day "elbow to elbow and face to back" in one-hundred-degree heat.[31]

The 51st Regiment was dispatched to Morris Island on 13 July 1863; the 31st joined them four days later. Although Clingman himself was not present on the island during that period, the two regiments from his brigade comprised the bulk of the forces that repulsed a bold night attack on 18 July. The Union assault, which was spearheaded by the black troops of the 54th Massachusetts under the command of Robert Gould Shaw, came after eleven hours of intense and continuous bombardment that had left the Confederate defenders weary and exhausted. Nonetheless, the 51st Regiment, which bore the brunt of the attack, "gallantly maintained their position and drove the enemy back . . . with immense slaughter." Aided by the Charleston Battalion and by reinforcements from the 32d Georgia, the embattled defenders managed to surround the enemy troops inside the fort and force their surrender.[32]

Undoubtedly mindful that his men had not received proper credit for their defense of Goldsboro six months earlier, Clingman was determined that they would now receive their just due. In early August, he prepared two detailed accounts of "occurrences at Battery Wagner" from the time of the brigade's arrival on Morris Island through the conclusion of his own four-day tour of duty there on 1 August. The first account, addressed to Governor Vance, dealt at length with the assault of 18 July. Clingman pointed out that his regiments had comprised about two-thirds of the fifteen hundred defenders and that they had sustained more than two-thirds of the casualties. "I cannot doubt," he concluded, "but they are justly entitled to an equal proportion of the credit of the victory."[33]

Clingman's second account focused on his own experiences as commander at Battery Wagner from 29 July through 1 August. By the end of his tour of duty, he noted, several thousand shells had been fired into the battery by the Federal fleet, some of them weighing over four hundred pounds. The cloud of dust caused by the incessant bombardment was so thick that "for hours the fort could not be seen at all from Charleston." Throughout the siege, his troops had "exhibited a self discipline and courage creditable to the best disciplined troops." Clingman later claimed that the "endurance of our men under such attacks" encouraged the Confederate authorities, who had earlier predicted that the fort would fall in a matter of days, to hold on to it for another month.[34]

After his service on Battery Wagner, Clingman returned to his command post at Sullivan's Island, which lay directly north of Morris Island on the other side of the ship channel leading into Charleston Harbor.[35] With some justification, he characterized that position as "the point of most danger" and, for that reason, "the point of honor." His responsibilities were to prevent the Federal fleet from sailing into the harbor and, at the same time, to protect the island itself against an amphibious attack. Clingman later recalled that the precarious outpost had previously been offered to two other generals "both my seniors in commission . . . but each of these officers, after taking a look at the Island, declined to occupy it."[36]

Clingman was more successful in defending Sullivan's Island than in maintaining morale among his troops. With its various regiments scattered on James, Morris, and Sullivan's Islands, the brigade no longer functioned as a cohesive unit, and "its organization and discipline . . . [were] impaired in consequence of this condition." In addition, there were constant complaints from the soldiers about poor rations, the hot and unhealthy climate, the arduous work assignments, the infrequent rest periods, and the long delays in receiving their pay. Adding to the morale problem was the widespread perception that the South Carolina troops were not bearing their fair share of the burden. Clingman privately complained to Governor Vance that his men were assigned longer periods of garrison duty at Battery Wagner than were other troops. Not surprisingly, desertion in Clingman's Brigade reached epidemic proportions during the summer of 1863. As one soldier remarked, "it is no longer a reproach to be known as a deserter."[37]

As the siege of Charleston dragged on and as sickness, death, desertion, and absenteeism thinned the ranks of his brigade, Clingman became increasingly anxious to return to North Carolina. On 28 September he wrote Chase Whiting at

Wilmington, informing him that Roswell S. Ripley, the commander of the First Military District at Charleston, had become satisfied that the enemy would not attack Sullivan's Island. "I should not be surprised," he added, "... if the [Union] monitors should go up to give you some trouble at Wilmington." Clingman volunteered the services of his own brigade to assist in the defense of that city. "I know your force is small," he told Whiting. "If the enemy attack Wilmington, I should be willing to go there." [38]

Clingman surely understood that he was touching a responsive chord. Since the beginning of the war, Whiting had been fretting that his undermanned garrison would be overwhelmed in the event of a Union attack. Now Clingman was practically telling him that the Federals were on their way. Whiting quickly forwarded Clingman's letter to Secretary of War James A. Seddon, remarking that "it tends to confirm anticipations I have long had." Unless reinforcements were sent immediately, he warned, there might be "a great and irremediable disaster." [39]

Seddon showed both letters to Jefferson Davis, who ordered that Clingman's Brigade be "promptly returned to Wilmington ... if required." The secretary authorized Whiting to call for the brigade upon receipt of "certain intelligence" of an enemy attack and instructed Beauregard to "hold Clingman's brigade so prepared that . . . it may be thrown rapidly to Wilmington." Beauregard protested that "not one regiment can be spared without jeopardizing [the] safety of Charleston." However, he agreed to send the brigade to Whiting "when called for." The call never came, since, contrary to Clingman's predictions, Wilmington was not attacked. [40]

Clingman's Brigade remained in Charleston until the end of November when, again over Beauregard's protest, it was ordered to North Carolina to assist in the defense of the Wilmington and Weldon Railroad against an anticipated Federal attack. After the threatened Union assault failed to materialize, the brigade was transferred to Petersburg. Clingman arrived in that city on the evening of 15 December 1863 "looking war-worn and travel-stained, but healthy and strong." [41]

Meanwhile, Chase Whiting was still pressuring the War Department for an additional brigade at Wilmington. On 8 January 1864 Seddon ordered Clingman's troops back to North Carolina. George E. Pickett, commander of the Department of North Carolina, advised him not to send the brigade into the state. Referring to the widespread war weariness and disaffection that had taken political shape in William W. Holden's peace movement, Pickett warned that North Carolina troops might prove unreliable "in case of internal trouble." Over Whiting's protests, the order was countermanded, and the brigade remained in Petersburg. Clingman did not raise any objections. After more than two years of garrison duty in the swampy lowlands of the Carolinas, he was anxious to join Lee's army in Virginia. [42]

Instead of being ordered to the Virginia front, however, Clingman and two of his regiments were sent back to North Carolina under the command of Pickett as part of an expedition to recapture New Bern. The plan was to attack the Union position from three directions. The 8th and 51st Regiments, along with Robert F. Hoke's Brigade, would advance toward New Bern by way of Bachelor Creek between the Trent and Neuse Rivers. Another force would attack the town from the north, while Seth M. Barton's troops would take the railroad bridge on the south side of the Trent, thereby cutting off any Federal reinforcements from Morehead City.[43]

The Battle of New Bern commenced at one o'clock in the morning of 1 February, when Clingman's and Hoke's troops surprised the Federal pickets at Bachelor Creek. Unfortunately for the Confederates, they were unable to prevent the enemy from retreating across the bridge and burning it behind them. Henry M. Shaw, the commander of the 8th Regiment, was struck in the head by a bullet while watching the battle with Clingman. He died instantly. Hoke and Clingman pursued the retreating Federals to the railroad depot, hoping to capture the train before the enemy could reach it. By the time they arrived there, however, the Union troops had boarded the train to New Bern.[44]

On the south side of the Trent, meanwhile, Barton's troops had failed to cut the railroad and telegraph line to Morehead City. As trainloads of Federal reinforcements were being dispatched to New Bern, Hoke's and Clingman's troops remained in front of the town. Clingman was inclined to dislodge the enemy by a frontal assault, but Pickett and Hoke overruled him. Since the element of surprise had been lost, they reasoned, "it would have been a desperate matter to attempt an attack in front." On the morning of 3 February 1864, the Confederates began withdrawing toward Kinston.[45]

Although some Confederate newspapers faulted Pickett for failing to capture New Bern, others regarded the expedition as an "important and glorious achievement." Several hundred Union troops, along with a quantity of arms and other supplies, had been captured, and Confederate casualties—despite Shaw's unfortunate death—had been light. According to an eyewitness from the *Richmond Dispatch,* "the conduct of Gens. Pickett, Hoke, and Clingman, won my entire admiration." Duncan McRae of the *Raleigh Confederate,* who had joined the troops in front of New Bern, also praised the "soldierly qualities" of Clingman, noting that "under rather a nervous and excited exterior, [he] is remarkably cool and self-possessed." The general "would be sure to make his mark," he added, if he were assigned to a position where he could "act . . . on his own discretion."[46]

Clingman returned with his two regiments to his camp at Petersburg, but he did not remain there long. With the winter weather precluding a major Federal assault, he obtained a two-week leave of absence and left camp on 22 February to visit his relatives in Yadkin County. On his way back to Petersburg in early March, he stopped over at Raleigh, where he most likely talked with Zebulon Vance about the upcoming gubernatorial election. Two days before Clingman's arrival at the state capital, William W. Holden had announced his intention to enter the governor's race as a "peace candidate." Although Clingman had long been a political enemy of Vance, he regarded the governor as preferable to Holden, whose conduct "gives encouragement to our enemies and thus induces them to continue to destroy our brave and patriotic men." Undoubtedly, he was also grateful to Vance for vindicating the conduct of his troops by publishing his account of the Battle of Goldsboro.[47]

Two years earlier, Clingman had turned down an invitation to run for governor. Now rumors were again circulating that he was contemplating a bid for the executive office. Far from wishing to challenge Vance, Clingman was determined to use his influence to prevent the friends of the Davis administration from nominating a candidate of their own and thus dividing the prowar vote. In a communication to the *Raleigh Confederate,* published on 29 March 1864, Clingman denied that he had any inclination "to leave the field for any civil station" and recommended that Vance be "cordially supported by all who are in favor of a vigorous prosecution of the war." Vance won the election by a landslide, garnering an unprecedented 77 percent of the civilian vote and an even more spectacular 87 percent of the army vote.[48]

By the time the ballots were cast in late July, Clingman's Brigade was enmeshed in a sanguinary contest with Federal forces in the trenches around Petersburg. On 4 May 1864 an army of 130,000 men under the command of Ulysses S. Grant had crossed the Rapidan River to begin a major offensive against Richmond. Simultaneously, a Union force of 30,000 men led by Benjamin F. Butler was dispatched to the south of the Confederate capital with instructions to destroy the railroad connections between Richmond and the rest of the South. On the same day that Grant crossed the Rapidan, Butler occupied Bermuda Hundred, a narrow piece of land between the James and Appomattox Rivers, and began advancing toward Petersburg. After several days of skirmishing in which Clingman's Brigade was involved, a major battle took place at Drewry's Bluff, a high point overlooking the James River.[49]

On 16 May Pierre G. T. Beauregard, who had taken command of a Confederate force numbering 10,800 men, launched a full-scale assault on Butler's position, which was defended by about 17,000 Federal soldiers. The 31st and 51st Regiments—the only two units over which Clingman had direct command during the engagement—found themselves "in the thickest of the fights" and conducted themselves "nobly" in their first major offensive operation. Several hours into the battle, the regiments were ordered to assist Bushrod R. Johnson's Tennessee troops, who were being attacked on their right flank and rear. Together with Montgomery D. Corse's Brigade, Clingman's men "went forward in good style and drove the enemy from their front." Although the outnumbered Confederates later fell back to their original positions, the fierce assault eventually impelled Butler to withdraw from the field of battle leaving behind large quantities of ordinance and commissary stores.[50]

The exploits of Clingman's troops did not go unnoticed. Maj. Gen. Robert F. Hoke declared that Clingman's and Corse's Brigades both "did their duty well," particularly since "the strength of the enemy was in front of these two brigades, both in position and forces." The casualties, he added, "were necessarily heavy owing to a front attack." Jefferson Davis, who was present during the later stages of the battle, reportedly characterized the assault by Clingman's Brigade as "the most gallant charge he ever witnessed." With pardonable exaggeration, Clingman boasted that his two regiments had "decided the contest" at Drewry's Bluff and "defeated the entire army of the enemy." Butler would remain bottled up in Bermuda Hundred for the remainder of the year, unable to move against either Petersburg or Richmond.[51]

Clingman's troops remained in the vicinity of Bermuda Hundred until 31 May, engaging in occasional skirmishes with the enemy. The brigade was then ordered to Cold Harbor to support Fitzhugh Lee's cavalry, which was expecting an assault by Philip Sheridan. After a brief encounter with the Union forces, during which a piece of shell sailed through his hat and grazed his forehead, Clingman ordered his troops to fall back. By the following morning, the main bodies of both armies were converging on Cold Harbor. What had begun as a small-scale skirmish would soon turn into one of the bloodiest battles of the Civil War.[52]

Shortly after three o'clock in the afternoon, the enemy artillery opened fire on Clingman's position. Three-quarters of an hour later, the Union infantry began advancing. Unbeknownst to Clingman, Joseph B. Kershaw's South Carolina troops, which had been positioned on his left, had "fled precipitately from the field" upon the Union advance. Meanwhile, Johnson Hagood's Brigade, which was also on his left, had been moved away to the right. The gap in the Confederate lines left Clingman's flank dangerously exposed. The Federals quickly took advantage of the opportunity, moving through the thick brush and smoke to positions behind Clingman and to his left.[53]

With the enemy firing on them from three directions, Clingman's troops were "cut to pieces." As he later recalled, "our men fell so fast that . . . it was impossible for them longer to maintain the contest there." The 8th and 51st Regiments bore the brunt of the Union attack. Clingman, who had been in the trenches with the 61st Regiment, rushed forward and ordered the survivors to form a new line perpendicular to the first. He then ordered the troops from the 31st to leave their entrenchments and form with them. With the help of Alfred H. Colquitt's 27th Georgia, Clingman's men "charged the enemy, and drove them back . . . [to] our original line." The fighting continued for several hours, as Clingman's forces successively advanced, were driven back, rallied, and moved forward again. By the time night put an end to the battle, "we . . . held again our original line intact."[54]

Once again, Clingman's Brigade had acquitted itself well. Although one-third of the troops had sustained casualties, they were "neither panic-stricken or beaten." Instead, as the *Raleigh Confederate* later remarked, they "did their part . . .

with a courage and efficiency unsurpassed by any other troops on that field of blood and carnage." Clingman must have been mortified after reading the account of the battle that was published in the *Richmond Dispatch* and subsequently reprinted in numerous other Confederate newspapers. According to the press association reporter, the Federal assault had "caus[ed] Clingman's North Carolina brigade for a time to give way . . . [but] Colquitt's Georgia brigade quickly came to its assistance, recovering nearly all the ground Clingman lost." Although accurate as far as it went, the report conveyed the impression that the North Carolina troops had fallen back for no good reason and that the credit for regaining the position belonged exclusively to the Georgia troops.[55]

An angry Clingman immediately dashed off a letter to the *Dispatch* protesting against the "great injustice to the gallant and patriotic men under my command." He asserted that his troops had "fought with the utmost coolness, courage, and cheerfulness." Indeed, "no brigade from any State, in this war, or any other war, ever acted better than did mine under such circumstances." He pointed out that a "brigade from another State . . . stationed on our left . . . did give way," which had allowed the enemy to attack his own left flank and rear. Had his own brigade then given way, instead of holding its position, "it might have escaped with much less loss." Indeed, four-fifths of its total losses had been sustained because its flanks had been "left unprotected by the troops which should have been there."[56]

The North Carolina presses praised Clingman for his diligence in correcting "a slander on his Brigade." As the *Fayetteville Observer* ruefully noted, that was "not the first time that our North Carolina troops have been charged with the failure of troops from other States." In his eagerness to vindicate the conduct of his men, however, Clingman had failed to secure permission to publish the letter, and he had included various "statistical details" that some papers deemed "inexpedient for publication." Most likely, the unauthorized publication ruffled some feathers in Richmond, particularly since Clingman had once before published a battle report without permission.[57]

Although the fighting around Cold Harbor continued for another two weeks, Clingman's Brigade did not play a major role after the engagement of 1 June. In mid-June, Grant suddenly shifted his troops to Petersburg in the hope of taking that vital railway center by surprise. Among the first Confederate troops to be rushed to the scene were the 51st and 61st Regiments of Clingman's Brigade. Those two units bore the brunt of the massive Union attack on 17 June, particularly after Henry Wise's Brigade on the right "abandoned its position in a panic." For four hours, Clingman's men managed to sustain their position against two corps of Grant's army until reinforcements finally arrived. "But for their prompt and energetic action," said Clingman, "Petersburg would have fallen."[58]

After a week of heavy fighting, the assault on Petersburg settled down into a protracted siege. Huddled in their entrenchments "amid the hissing of bullets & the roar of Artillery," Clingman and his troops found themselves doing "hard duty" under conditions that rivaled those endured at Battery Wagner. For two months, the brigade "walked in ditches, ate in ditches and slept in pits." When the Federal army exploded a huge mine under the Confederate lines on 30 July, the 8th and 61st Regiments were among those who assisted in repulsing the enemy.[59]

On 17 August 1864 the brigade finally came out of the trenches in response to a Union assault on the Petersburg and Weldon Railroad. On three occasions, Clingman's forces advanced on the Federals and were driven back, only to rally and advance again. After night began to fall, Clingman rode out toward the Federal position to reconnoiter. As he approached the enemy breastworks, about fifty Union soldiers leveled their guns at him. A bullet entered his leg diagonally and penetrated eight to ten inches. "His presence of mind and courage induced him to hold on to his horse" and return to his own lines, where "he fell from exhaustion and loss of blood" and lay for three hours in the heavy rain.[60]

Reports quickly began circulating that Clingman had been mortally wounded. Though severe, his injury proved more painful than life threatening. He was taken to the home of Thomas Branch in Petersburg, where the wound was examined and treated. Avowing that he "prefer[red] death to the loss of my limb," he reportedly told the surgeons that "if I find on my return to consciousness that you have cut off my leg, I'll be damned if I don't shoot you." Fortunately, Clingman did not lose his leg. Early in September, he was moved to the home of Henry King Burgwyn in Raleigh, where he convalesced for almost two months. He spent the remaining months of the war at the plantation of his brother-in-law, Richard C. Puryear, in Yadkin County.[61]

In reporting the news of Clingman's injury, the North Carolina newspapers showered praise on the military record of the fallen general. According to the *Raleigh Confederate,* Clingman had given "his whole heart, soul and body to the war." From "a life of luxury at the Capital," he had "descended to the muddiest and most exposed trench" and had "fearlessly exposed his life in every action to which he or his command was called." Even the antiwar *North Carolina Standard* now wondered "why is not Gen. Clingman made a Major General? He deserves it."[62]

There were many others who shared that sentiment. As early as February 1864, North Carolina's two senators and ten congressmen had signed a letter to President Davis recommending his promotion. In October, former congressman Daniel M. Barringer made the same request on the grounds that "he has greatly distinguished himself in the present campaign." "I am sure," he added, "that the *people* of this State would hear with the greatest satisfaction of his appointment as Major General." Despite such entreaties, the promotion never came.[63]

One factor that undoubtedly worked against Clingman's advancement was his lack of formal military training. Although he had read widely in military history and fancied himself "a student of the art of war," the North Carolinian had "never seen even a regiment maneuvre [sic]" at the time he entered the Confederate army. Like many other brigadier generals in the Army of Northern Virginia, he had initially been given a command because of his political connections. Few such "political generals" ever advanced to the rank of major general unless they also had "extensive prewar military education, experience, or both."[64]

On the other hand, Clingman's lack of experience did not necessarily disqualify him from becoming an effective military leader. As one authority has noted, "nothing prevented a politician with the necessary attributes, and with study and experience, from becoming a capable general." By 1865 the battle-hardened Clingman had come a long way from the nervous young congressman who, two decades earlier, had lost control of his bodily functions as a duelist's bullet passed near him. Indeed, his personal courage and fearlessness under fire were probably his greatest assets as a military leader.[65]

Clingman's impetuousness and unswerving faith in the efficacy of the frontal assault were his most serious liabilities. Although sometimes effective in defensive counterattacks and small-scale offensive maneuvers, the frontal assault was generally unsuitable for large-scale offensive operations. If Clingman's advice had been followed at Morris Island in July 1863 or at New Bern in February 1864, the result could well have been disastrous. Clingman was more effective in holding on to an established position than he probably would have been as a division or corps commander with more wide-ranging responsibilities.[66]

Clingman's limitations as a military leader were not the only factors behind his failure to win a promotion. In the Confederate army, advancement beyond the rank of colonel depended on the favor of the president. Even at the beginning of the war, Clingman was not on the best of terms with Jefferson Davis. As the conflict progressed, their relationship deteriorated. Clingman strenuously objected to the manner in which the administration was conducting the war, and although he did not publicly air his differences until the conflict had ended, it is unlikely that Davis was unaware of his disapproval.[67]

Equally important, Clingman had on several occasions demonstrated a penchant for disobeying orders and bypassing the chain of command. At Goldsboro he had ignored a War Department interdiction by having his official report published in the North Carolina newspapers. At Cold Harbor he had also published an unauthorized account of the battle containing information that might have proven useful to the enemy. While in South Carolina he had tried several times to have his brigade transferred to North Carolina by using stratagems that the authorities in Richmond may have considered devious and improper. Clingman's egotism, together with his long tenure in the seat of power at Washington, made him temperamentally unsuited to adhere unquestioningly to the strictures of civilian leaders whom he undoubtedly considered his inferiors. He ultimately paid the price for that defiant attitude.[68]

Shortly after Lee's surrender at Appomattox, Clingman returned to his brigade, which had joined the remnants of Joseph E. Johnston's Army of Tennessee in their retreat before the forces of William T. Sherman. Still on crutches, he asked for the honor of commanding the rear guard. Johnston turned him down on the grounds that he was physically incapable of performing that function. Clingman then advised the commanding general to "take our stand here and fight the two armies of Grant and Sherman to the end, and thus show to the world how far we can surpass the Thermopylae of the Greeks." Johnston explained that he was "not in the Thermopylae business" and surrendered to Sherman at Greensboro a few days later.[69]

Clingman was still in camp when news arrived of the assassination of Abraham Lincoln. A lively discussion ensued in which about a dozen general officers participated. One of the generals made a disparaging remark about the slain Union president, to which another retorted: "if we had had Lincoln and they had had Davis, we should have subjugated the North." After a moment's silence, Clingman acknowledged that "in that event . . . we should have secured our independence." Instead, after four years of sanguinary conflict, the South had abandoned its efforts to establish an independent nation. It remained to be seen what price would have to be paid for readmission into the Union.[70]

13 Poor Old "Played Out Clingman"

Once the fighting had ended, Clingman had little difficulty adjusting to the realities of defeat. Never quite the fire eater his enemies had portrayed him to be, he readily accepted the abolition of slavery and the repudiation of secession as the necessary consequences of the war. "Having made a fair stand-up fight for our principles," Southerners now had no choice but to acknowledge defeat and "submit to the will of the conqueror." At the same time, he believed that Southerners bore "no moral guilt" for the war and, therefore, did not deserve punishment. To Clingman, as to most of the state's political elite, Reconstruction involved nothing more than an expression of their willingness once again to "support the constitution and obey the laws of the United States." In his view, a radical reorientation of existing power relations was neither necessary nor desirable. Indeed, reunion could best be effected by returning the South's "representative men" to the councils of state.[1]

Clingman considered himself to be one of those "representative men" whose duty it was to lead the South back into the Union. Claiming that the war had vindicated the "theory that the State of North Carolina never was nor could be out of the

Union and that the [secession] ordinance . . . never had any effect," he argued that he was "still United States Senator" and thus entitled to serve the remaining fifteen months of the term to which he had been elected in January 1861. As his enemies were quick to point out, that logic conveniently ignored the fact that he had for the past several years "been in armed hostility to the Government . . . whose officer he was." [2] Moreover, although Clingman never formally resigned his Senate seat, he had been expelled from that body in July 1861. The provisions of Andrew Johnson's amnesty proclamation of 29 May 1865 also made him ineligible to hold any federal or state office. Only a presidential pardon could relieve him of that disability. [3]

Still, Clingman apparently hoped that Johnson and the Republican Congress might be persuaded to acknowledge his claims. In November 1865 he journeyed to Washington to present his case personally to his former colleagues. Shortly after arriving there, he published a letter in the *New York Times,* ostensibly in order to correct "erroneous statements in relation to the condition of affairs in North Carolina and other Southern States." While affirming the loyalty of his home state and urging the federal government to pursue a conciliatory course toward the South, the letter consisted primarily of a defense of Clingman's antebellum career and an attack on the "arrogant and insolent" extremists in each section whom he blamed for bringing on the war. [4]

Ignoring his own strident utterances on the sectional question, Clingman portrayed himself as a moderate who, on numerous occasions, had been "thrown into collision with the extreme men of the South." He denied that he had favored disunion prior to the outbreak of hostilities. Instead, he had "condemned the policy of secession, and insisted that the South would find it advantageous to remain in the Union." Indeed, even after the fighting had commenced, he "still believed that there might be a union of all the States under a common government."

Despite the self-serving character of Clingman's letter, his claim that the vast majority of North Carolinians were reconciled to defeat and were now loyal to the Union met a warm reception in his home state. A notable dissenter to the prevailing viewpoint was the *North Carolina Standard,* the organ of Provisional Gov. William W. Holden. Clingman and Holden had been political allies throughout the 1850s, but they had parted company during the secession crisis and had remained on unfriendly terms since then. While not directly challenging Clingman's characterization of the mood of postwar North Carolina, the *Standard* denied that he was qualified "to speak for the Union men" in the state. In a scathing review of his political career, the paper quoted liberally from his speeches and public letters in order to demonstrate his "secession proclivities." Instead of working tirelessly for compromise and reconciliation during the secession crisis, said the *Standard,* the former senator had been in the vanguard of those "advising North-Carolina to prepare for war and resistance to the federal authority." [5]

In truth, both Holden and Clingman had selectively presented the facts in order to advance their respective political goals. Whereas Holden aimed to discredit his enemies by portraying them as unrepentant secessionists, Clingman's primary objective was to return to the U.S. Senate. In order to do that, he had to dissociate himself from those "extremists" whom a majority in both sections held responsible for the war. It was also to his advantage to put distance between himself and the Confederate administration of Jefferson Davis. Clingman disliked Davis personally, and he had privately criticized his conduct of the war almost from its beginning. In his letter to the *Times,* he publicly announced his disgust with the Davis administration, accusing it of being "utterly destitute of practical talent" and even suggesting that "for some unexplained reasons" it had intentionally tried "to retard our movements and prolong the war." Although no admirer of Davis himself, Holden took Clingman to task for turning on the "benefactor . . . from whose hands his commission as Brigadier General emanated."[6]

Clingman's attempt to regain his Senate seat suffered a double blow when Congress and the North Carolina General Assembly both refused to acknowledge his claims. On 12 December 1865 the U.S. Senate passed a resolution refusing to seat any claimants from the Southern states until a full investigation had been undertaken. A week earlier, the Judiciary Committee of the North Carolina Senate had issued a report declaring that Clingman's seat was vacant as a consequence of "his voluntary withdrawal therefrom . . . [and] his failure for more than four years to apply for admission or to attempt to exercise the functions of his office." The recently elected general assembly, which was dominated by former Whigs, subsequently chose John Pool to fill the remaining portion of Clingman's term.[7]

Clingman was equally unsuccessful in his efforts to secure a presidential pardon. On 4 January 1866 he swore the required oath of allegiance and submitted a formal application. Attaching a copy of his *New York Times* letter as a full statement of his views, he affirmed his intention henceforth "to support faithfully the constitution and obey the laws of the United States." If Clingman hoped that Andrew Johnson would expeditiously grant his request, those hopes were quickly dashed. The two men had served together in Congress for fifteen years, and there was no love lost between them. Clingman regarded the president as "a man of only average intellect," whose "driving forces . . . were selfishness, envy and malice." Johnson was undoubtedly aware of Clingman's low opinion of him. Moreover, he generally refused to approve pardons that were not first endorsed by the governor, and he had no incentive to make an exception for Clingman.[8]

Clingman returned to Raleigh in late January to present his case to Jonathan Worth, who had succeeded Holden as governor a few weeks earlier. Worth complied with a lukewarm endorsement, merely noting that "in view of the pardons heretofore granted in this State, I know no rule of discrimination which should exclude Genl. Clingman." Privately, the governor regretted that he had gone even that far, asserting that Clingman "did more than any body else (except Holden) to foment discord between the South and the North." The recommendation

Clingman received from Holden was considerably more enthusiastic. The former governor expressed confidence that "he is submitting in good faith to the national authority, and will be prompt to avail himself of every suitable occasion to confirm and perpetuate that authority."[9]

In light of the rough treatment the *North Carolina Standard* had meted out to Clingman just a few weeks earlier, the warmth of Holden's endorsement was startling. Indeed, the *Standard* itself was now speaking favorably of Clingman, praising him as a "distinguished North Carolinian" and a gallant war hero who "bears on his person marks of the deadly strife got in the battle." It was no secret that since his return to North Carolina Clingman had been spending long hours in the *Standard* office conversing with Holden about undisclosed matters. The former enemies had obviously achieved a reconciliation, but on what terms? "This looks like the 'lion and the lamb' lying down together," one pundit observed. "But which is the *lamb?*"[10]

There were some like Governor Worth who believed that Clingman and Holden were making arrangements to reconstitute the prewar Democratic party and elevate Clingman to the U.S. Senate.[11] There was probably more than a grain of truth in that belief. At the end of the war, the politics of the Old North State was dominated by the Conservative party, an uneasy alliance of Whigs and anti-administration Democrats that had initially been formed to challenge the pro-Davis Confederate party in the state elections of 1862. In 1864 Holden and many of his allies had bolted the Conservative party in order to establish the Peace party. Holden's decisive defeat in the gubernatorial elections of 1864 and 1865 dramatically revealed that the Peace party (which was now calling itself the Union party) could not compete effectively at the state level with the Conservatives. On the other hand, if Clingman and other Southern Rights Democrats who had been sitting on the sidelines since 1862 combined with the Holden Democrats, together they would constitute a formidable political force.

Clingman probably broached the idea of reuniting the Democratic party during his conversations with Holden. He was certainly angered by the proscriptive policies of the recently elected general assembly, which had not only rejected his own claim to the U.S. Senate but had filled nearly all the state offices with former Whigs, turning out several Democratic incumbents in the process. Holden, for his part, was perfectly willing to accept former secessionists into his party on an individual basis—provided that they acknowledged the errors of their ways and accepted his leadership. But he balked at the prospect of a wholesale amalgamation with unrepentant secessionists who most likely would dominate the reconstituted party. On several occasions, he publicly denied reports that "Mr. Clingman and ourselves were about to form a new party." "We have no sympathy with the . . . secession party," he thundered. "There should be but one party in this State . . . and that is the *Union* party."[12]

On the other hand, Holden did not deny the rumor that Clingman was negotiating with him for the purchase of the *North Carolina Standard*. Disappointed by his recent defeat, the editor was now giving serious consideration to moving to Washington. In addition, Thomas W. Atkin had recently disposed of his interest in the *Asheville News*, leaving Clingman without a reliable editorial spokesman. The idea of controlling "a leading press situated at the capital of the state" must have been appealing to Clingman. Nonetheless, the purchase was not made. Clingman, whose personal finances were in disarray, may have lacked the resources to consummate the deal. In any event, as one observer noted, Holden preferred to sell his establishment to a man "of a more conservative record." [13]

Holden's enthusiastic endorsement of Clingman's pardon application did not prove sufficient to secure the removal of the disabilities that were barring him from making a political comeback. Early in February 1866, the former senator sent his application, together with the recommendations from Holden and Worth, to Washington. He also requested his friend John Hill Wheeler, who resided in the nation's capital, to speak to the president on his behalf. Johnson granted the interview but declined to make any promises. Instead, he told Wheeler "he would do the best he could" for Clingman. In truth, the president had no intention of granting an early pardon to an individual whom he regarded as one of the prime instigators of the rebellion. Clingman would remain unpardoned until 14 June 1867. By that time, the Fourteenth Amendment and the Reconstruction Acts had created new disabilities that effectively prevented him and other former Confederates from holding public office. [14]

Shortly after sending off his pardon application, Clingman returned to the mountain region, probably for the first time since the beginning of the war. [15] Like much of the South, the hills and valleys of western North Carolina bore the scars of four years of brutal warfare. Although there had been no full-pitched battles, Union and Confederate sympathizers alike had been frequent victims of raids by enemy forces as well as by the numerous bands of deserters and outlaws who roamed freely through the mountain counties. In addition to the occasional loss of life, many houses, barns, fields, and orchards had been destroyed, and horses, cattle, foodstuffs, and valuables had been confiscated. Of the thousands of mountaineers who marched off to war, many never returned and others came back hopelessly incapacitated. A shortage of money and a rapid increase in prices, brought about by the repudiation of Confederate bonds and currency, added to the hardships of western residents in the months following the cessation of hostilities. [16]

Clingman believed that Northern capital would provide the key to the revitalization of the mountain economy as well as to his own financial recovery. Cash-poor landowners were eager to sell their gold and other mineral properties to Northern capitalists. The investors, for their part, were just as eager to exploit the mineral resources of the South. As one Philadelphian told Clingman, "gold seems to be the mania now in Northern Cities & particularly in New York. . . . [There are] many parties who are anxious to invest in mines." Even such staunch political enemies of the South as Benjamin F. Butler and Thaddeus F. Stevens found themselves unable to resist the temptation to invest in the Old North State.[17]

Clingman's familiarity with the topography of western North Carolina, together with his numerous contacts with local landowners and Northern businessmen, placed him in an ideal situation to serve as a land broker. He had engaged extensively in such activities before the war, and he resumed them almost immediately afterward. Beginning in February 1866 he executed powers of attorney with several landowners in McDowell County, and in late April he headed North to find purchasers. Over the next two years he traveled continuously between western North Carolina and New York carrying bonds for properties deemed rich in gold or copper.[18]

The results were disappointing. In September 1867 Calvin H. Wiley reported to Governor Worth that Clingman and several other North Carolinians had been operating in New York for many months "without success. . . . The prospect of filling the South with new industrial energy is very discouraging." Indeed, as long as political conditions in the South remained unsettled, the prospects for Northern investment would remain dim. In early 1867 the yearlong controversy between President Johnson and the Republican Congress over Reconstruction policy had culminated in a series of Reconstruction Acts that overturned the state governments established by Johnson and placed most of the South under military rule. The specter of confiscation raised by the Radical Republicans produced a general distrust of Southern land titles and a consequent anxiety on the part of Northern investors. "If it were not for the present political situation," said one North Carolinian, "millions of capital, now idle, would flow in a ceaseless stream to the South."[19]

After the passage of the First Reconstruction Act in March 1867, white Southerners found themselves divided over whether to cooperate with its terms or to resist them. Clingman was among those who favored cooperation. Writing from New York in mid-March, he advised Worth that the best way to "prevent the State from falling into the hands of Holden and Co." was for him to "call the Legislature together so that we may have a Convention at once." By "Holden and Co.," Clingman was referring to the North Carolina Republican party. A coalition of Union party members, newly enfranchised blacks, and a handful of Northern-born carpetbaggers, the Republicans proposed an ambitious program of democratic reform and racial equality that sharply challenged existing power relationships. Holden's steady gravitation toward the Republicans after the defeat of the Union party in the state elections of 1866 ended his rapprochement with Clingman and prompted the former senator, at least temporarily, to ally himself with the Conservatives.[20]

Clingman believed that by taking the initiative and issuing a call for a constitutional convention, the Conservatives might be able to elect a majority of delegates and thereby moderate the Reconstruction process. Most of the party's leaders opposed participating in the convention elections, particularly after the military authorities took control of the election process according to the terms of the Second Reconstruction Act. Worth, William A. Graham, and other prominent Conservatives urged their followers either to vote "no" or to abstain from voting in the referendum scheduled for November 1867.[21]

To Clingman, such intransigence was the height of folly. If the voters of North Carolina rejected a convention, he argued, Congress would simply impose harsher measures. The only ones who would benefit from its defeat were Worth and the other Conservative officeholders, since the Reconstruction Acts had provided that the existing state governments would remain in power until a new constitution was written and ratified. In Clingman's view, the desire to continue in office was the driving force behind the Conservative opposition to a convention. As he later remarked, the prospect of "a new Legislature and new elections to office . . . was more than their intense selfishness could bear."[22]

Despite his belief that resistance to congressional Reconstruction would be futile and counterproductive, Clingman did not publicly announce his support for the convention during the spring and summer of 1867. Even after the *Standard* challenged him and the other "old time leaders" to speak out and give the voters "the benefit of their experience and wisdom," he remained silent. Clingman's strong political survival instincts may have dissuaded him from breaking publicly with the Conservatives over the convention issue. While his fellow North Carolinians were debating its merits, the former senator was away in the North tending to his land business. As he was riding in a hack in New York City in late August, he was struck by the lash from the driver's whip and sustained a severe injury to one of his eyes. The rumor that his eyeball was "completely cut out" proved fortunately to be unfounded, but he did suffer in pain for many weeks. By early October, he was well enough to return to North Carolina, but still he made no effort to drum up public support for the convention.[23]

The Conservative attempt to derail the convention proved unsuccessful. The Republicans succeeded not only in securing its approval by a substantial majority but also in electing all but a handful of the delegates. The convention, which met from 14 January until 17 March 1868, drew up a constitution that extended the suffrage to black males, abolished property requirements for officeholding, democratized the structure of local government, apportioned the upper house of the general assembly according to population rather than wealth, and made most state offices elective rather than appointive. Apart from black suffrage, those were changes for which western reformers like Clingman had been agitating since the 1850s.[24]

During most of the time the convention was in session, Clingman was in Washington and the North, attending to his land business, witnessing the impeachment proceedings against Andrew Johnson, and dealing with tax issues relating to the estate of his recently deceased brother-in-law, Richard C. Puryear. He learned about the details of the new constitution from William Johnston, a Charlotte businessman who was visiting New York City. Clingman considered the document to be "liberal and fair," particularly since its framers had resisted efforts to disenfranchise former Confederates. He urged Johnston "to use his influence to get all parties to acquiesce in it, and endeavor to elect the best men to office." [25]

The most troubling aspect of the constitution, from the viewpoint of North Carolina's political elite, was its provision for black suffrage. Like most white Southerners, Clingman regarded the black race as intellectually and morally inferior. Although the war had "determined that the negroes should all be free," it had not, in his opinion, established "that they are capable of becoming the political and social equals of the white race." Nonetheless, Clingman's views on race relations were more liberal than those of most Southern whites. By 1868 he was willing to extend the franchise to "the most industrious and intelligent of their race." The framers of the new constitution had gone much further, but Clingman was confident that "any objectionable features . . . would in time be corrected by general consent." Thus, he was inclined "to accept any tolerably fair Constitution" that would end military rule and the possibility of confiscation and enable North Carolina to resume its place in the Union. [26]

Clingman's broad-minded view of the constitution was not shared by most Conservatives. In February 1868 party leaders adopted a declaration of principles affirming their unalterable opposition to "political and social equality with the black race." Following the adjournment of the convention, Conservatives such as Zebulon B. Vance and Marcus Erwin worked hard in the mountain district "for the defeat of the nigger-begotten Constitution" in the ratification election. Illness prevented Clingman from returning to North Carolina until a few days before the April elections, but in the short time remaining he privately urged his friends to "acquiesce" in the constitution and "elect the best men to office." [27]

The election resulted in a resounding defeat for the Conservatives. The voters ratified the constitution by a majority of nineteen thousand votes and elected William W. Holden to the governorship by a similar majority. In addition, the Republicans carried six of the seven congressional districts and won commanding majorities in the general assembly. Clingman attributed the result to the "selfishness and folly" of the Conservative leaders, who had not only associated their party with opposition to a popular constitution but had also "boldly proclaimed that they wished for the votes of no colored men." Had they not "declared for the *white* line of division," he later claimed, they might have elected "a set of fair men of moderate views." [28]

After the North Carolina General Assembly ratified the Fourteenth Amendment in July 1868, Congress allowed the newly elected representatives to take their seats. The restoration of civil government also meant that North Carolinians would be able to participate in the fall presidential election. Although they had toyed earlier with the idea of forming a new national party, Conservatives now urged their supporters to participate in the election of delegates to the Democratic National Convention, which was scheduled to convene at Tammany Hall in New York City in July. On 30 May 1868 a district convention composed of leading figures from both antebellum parties met in Asheville and chose Clingman, along with former Whig Samuel McDowell Tate, to represent the mountain counties at the national convention. In his first public address to his former constituents since the end of the war, Clingman admonished those in attendance to lay aside all former party prejudices and cooperate with the Northern Democrats "for the restoration of the Southern people to their Constitutional rights and liberties." [29]

The twenty-member delegation that North Carolina sent to the Democratic National Convention consisted in almost equal numbers of prewar Democrats such as Clingman, Bedford Brown, and John F. Hoke, and Whigs such as Zebulon B. Vance, William N. H. Smith, and Patrick Henry Winston. In order to avoid any appearance of "dictation," the Southern delegates presented no presidential candidate of their own but, instead, expressed their willingness to accept "whatever candidate should be deemed most available by the Democracy of the North." Clingman's own preference was for Gen. Winfield Scott Hancock. As he later recalled, he "worked very hard to secure his nomination, and . . . [almost] brought him to a point when . . . he would have been nominated." Like most Southerners, however, he readily acquiesced in the nomination of former New York governor Horatio Seymour.[30]

Clingman returned to North Carolina confident that "the election of Gov Seymour [is] certain." In September he issued a public letter on behalf of Seymour and his running mate, Francis P. Blair, which received high praise in the Conservative presses. First published in the *Asheville News,* it was subsequently issued in pamphlet form and circulated throughout the state as a campaign tract. Faithfully echoing the plank in the national Democratic platform, Clingman declared the Reconstruction Acts to be "*unconstitutional* and void" and called for "a return to the system of constitutional government." [31]

Clingman's enemies would later charge him with inconsistency for supporting the new constitution in the spring of 1868 and then denouncing the entire Reconstruction process as unconstitutional during the presidential campaign. Although consistency was never one of Clingman's strong suits, in this case the charges were not well founded. Clingman never defended the Reconstruction Acts or claimed they were constitutional. Instead, he had "merely advised acquiescence in them, as we could not resist them." "A man may be willing to submit to a law," he pointed out, "but yet desire to have it repealed and support men for that purpose."[32]

Moreover, opposition to Reconstruction was not the centerpiece of Clingman's indictment of Republicanism. He gave only perfunctory attention in his circular to Reconstruction policy, and unlike the national platform, he said nothing about black suffrage or "negro supremacy." Instead, he focused his attack on the economic policies of the Republican party, which in his opinion, promoted the interests of manufacturers, bondholders, and "a few wealthy capitalists" at the expense of "the Farmers and other classes." The circular ended with an appeal for all North Carolinians, "old Whigs, old Democrats, Secessionists and Union men," to rally on behalf of a "peaceable, cheap, honest and quiet system of constitutional government."[33]

Despite his continuing poor health, Clingman campaigned hard for the Seymour-Blair ticket, addressing large crowds in Asheville, Rutherfordton, and other towns in the mountain region. The Asheville meeting, which reportedly attracted ten thousand "noble mountaineers," was said to be the largest public gathering held up to that time in western North Carolina. According to one eyewitness, Clingman's speech was "delivered in a spirit of great moderation and with singular force, power, and dignity." Indeed, it was "one of the most powerful speeches I have ever heard." The spectator concluded with the observation that "the General is doing much good in these Western counties."[34]

It is unlikely, however, that Clingman's aggressive campaigning did significant damage to the Republicans, for the new party had already built a strong popular following in the far west. Although a majority of mountaineers had supported the Confederacy in 1861, a significant minority had remained loyal to the Union. As the conflict progressed, enthusiasm for the Southern cause had given way to disaffection. The unpopular policies of the Davis administration, combined with the devastation and economic dislocations of the war, led a substantial number of westerners to support William W. Holden's peace movement. Holden also made a strong showing in the mountain counties in his unsuccessful bid for the governorship in 1865, and many of his supporters subsequently followed him into the Republican party.[35]

Playing up to the unionist sentiments of their constituents, the Republicans were quick to seize on Clingman's fire-eating past in order to discredit his present pronouncements. The *Rutherfordton Star* reminded its readers that such "men as Mr. Clingman brought about Secession and are responsible for the present condition of the country." The paper admonished the voters to "spurn everything from such source as unclean, poisonous, and deadly to the touch." Even outside the Old North State, Republicans invoked the name of Thomas Clingman as evidence of the "treason and treachery" of the Democratic party. The election resulted in another victory for the Republicans, as Ulysses S. Grant carried North

Carolina by more than twelve thousand votes and received 52 percent of the vote in the mountain region.[36]

Clingman accepted the result with more equanimity than most supporters of the Democratic ticket. A few months after the election, he assisted Republican legislator James Sinclair, a "warm personal friend" with whom he had served during the war, in drafting a resolution commending the "extraordinary ability and varied talent, as well as exalted patriotism" of President Grant. "I am happy to state," Sinclair told the president, "that Senator Clingman will warmly support your Excellency[']s administration." To less well-disposed partisans like the editor of the *Raleigh Sentinel,* the one positive aspect of the election was that the citizens of North Carolina could now put aside politics "and turn their attention, with greater zeal and energy, to their material wants."[37]

In Clingman's mind, the satisfaction of the "material wants" of western North Carolina depended upon the establishment of railroad connections with eastern market towns. By the end of the war, the state's once-impressive railroad system was in shambles. Both Federal and Confederate armies had destroyed bridges, water tanks, shops, cars, and rails. The Western North Carolina Railroad, which had been chartered in 1854 to run from Salisbury across the Blue Ridge, was in especially bad shape as a result of the depredations of George Stoneman's raiders. Much of the roadbed had been destroyed, and only three engines, one passenger car, and a small number of freight cars were in usable condition. The finances of the various railroad companies were also in a precarious condition because of the repudiation of the Confederate and state bonds in which many had invested. Only a generous infusion of state aid could provide the capital needed for repairs and new equipment.[38]

In 1868 the Republican-controlled general assembly passed a number of acts favorable to the state's railroads. The Western North Carolina Railroad was split into two divisions, each of which would be managed by a separate board of directors. The Eastern Division would construct the remainder of the line between Salisbury and Asheville, while the Western Division would extend from Asheville to Paint Rock and Ducktown on the Tennessee border. The Western Division was capitalized at $6 million, with two-thirds of the stock to be subscribed by the state. At a stockholders' meeting at Morganton on 15 October 1868 the Western Division was formally organized, and George W. Swepson was elected as its president. At his behest, Clingman was appointed to the board of directors.[39]

Within a few years, Swepson would attain a reputation as "one of the greatest rascals of North Carolina history." In 1868, however, he was a successful and highly regarded businessman. Politically, he was a Conservative or, as he liked to put it, an "old line Whig." His friends and associates included such prominent Conservative leaders as Zebulon B. Vance, Matt W. Ransom, and Augustus S. Merrimon. Clingman later claimed that Swepson had appointed him to the directorship because he "wished to have one [prewar] democrat on the board."[40]

Most likely, Swepson also wanted to use Clingman's extensive political connections to secure legislation favorable to the railroad. The act of 14 August 1868, which had authorized the state to issue bonds to the Western Division, had been hastily and carelessly drawn. Indeed, as Clingman pointed out, technically it was unconstitutional since a special tax had not been levied to pay the interest on the bonds. With the assistance of Merrimon and Kemp P. Battle, Clingman drew up two bills, the first authorizing the issuance of new bonds and levying a tax to pay their interest and the second increasing the capitalization to $10 million. While Swepson's associate Milton S. Littlefield worked on the Republican members to secure their passage, Clingman lobbied extensively among the Conservatives. Neither Swepson nor Littlefield was averse to the generous use of money and favors to influence legislation. Clingman subsequently denied having any direct knowledge of such illegal activities, although he did admit to being aware of the allegations against the corrupt practices of the so-called railroad ring that appeared in the Conservative presses during the fall and winter of 1868.[41]

Clingman also played a central role in Swepson's controversial efforts to gain control of three Florida railroads—the Florida Central Railroad, the Pensacola and Georgia Railroad, and the Tallahassee Railroad. In December 1868 Swepson sent him to Georgia to negotiate a deal with Edward Houstoun, a Savannah attorney who was then serving as president of the three railroads. The plan was for Houstoun, acting as Swepson's agent, to buy a controlling share of the stock in the Florida Central, as well as a majority of the mortgage bonds of the two other railroads. According to Clingman, they agreed to keep the arrangement "entirely secret in order that the stocks and bonds then low in the market might be bought in on the least terms." Clingman arranged for the purchase at a cost to Swepson of $843,633. Swepson expected to receive an enormous profit on those investments, and on at least two occasions he promised that Clingman would receive $100,000 for his assistance.[42]

The details of the arrangement were hammered out during the spring and summer of 1869 in a series of negotiations involving Swepson, Clingman, a group of Florida investors, and other interested parties including the governor and attorney general of Florida. Although Clingman had no direct financial interest in the railroads, Swepson relied heavily on his legal advice and negotiating skills. On 5 April 1869, a few weeks before leaving for New York for their first meeting with the Florida investors, they signed an agreement whereby Swepson promised to give Clingman 10 percent of the net profits resulting from his investments in the three railroads—an interest that Clingman later estimated to be worth about $120,000.[43]

The prospect of such enormous profits made Clingman reluctant to ask too many questions about where Swepson was getting the money for his Florida investments. Whenever the subject did come up, Swepson spoke of the Florida deal as "a private transaction of his own," and according to Clingman, he "never once intimated . . . that it was an investment for the N. C. Railroad." On a number of occasions, he specifically assured Clingman that the special-tax bonds issued to the Western Division were still in his hands and that he was waiting for their price to rise before putting them on the market. In fact, Swepson had sold the bonds almost as soon as they came into his possession and had used part of their proceeds to purchase the stock and mortgage bonds of the three Florida railroads.[44]

Swepson's reluctance to settle his accounts at the annual stockholders' meeting on 13 October 1869 finally aroused Clingman's suspicions that the bonds might have been misapplied. At that time, Swepson announced his intention to step down as president of the Western Division. Over the protest of Clingman and two other directors, the Republican majority on the board chose Milton S. Littlefield as his successor. Believing that the election of the notorious carpetbagger "would be disastrous to the company," Clingman threatened to resign. Swepson prevailed upon him to remain on the board for a few months "till Littlefield got under way."[45]

The election of "the prince of the 'Ring'" as president of the Western Division produced an outcry among the Conservative presses. Swepson was also severely criticized for his failure to make a full financial report before leaving office, particularly since it was now widely rumored that he had invested several million dollars of the division's bonds in the Florida railroads. Nor did Clingman and the handful of other non-Republican directors escape criticism. The *Asheville News* wondered aloud "how it is that men who pretend to be opposed to Littlefield and his party . . . can risk their reputation by continuing in their company and acting with them."[46]

When the general assembly reconvened in November 1869, the public demand for a thorough investigation of the railroad scandals became so intense that even the Republicans went along. On 20 January 1870 the state senate set up a special committee to investigate the issuance and disposal of the special-tax bonds. Wishing to avoid the appearance of partisanship, Republican lieutenant governor Tod R. Caldwell appointed respected Conservative leader Thomas Bragg to head the investigation. However, the Republicans in the senate severely limited the scope of the inquiry, and on 7 March they pushed through a resolution demanding a report in three days. The committee found no definitive evidence of corruption, but they did discover enough irregularities to underscore the need for a more comprehensive investigation.[47]

Clingman was well aware that his own reputation and future political prospects were being jeopardized by the outcry against Swepson and the "railroad ring." On the same day that the Bragg Committee issued its report, he moved to preempt his critics by publishing a sixteen-page circular vindicating his conduct as a director of the Western Division. He had accepted the appointment, he declared, because he was "extremely anxious to have the portion of the State where I reside improved." Despite being "politically isolated" as the only Democrat on the twelve-member board, he had "at all times . . . urged a vigorous prosecution of the work on the Road." Upon Swepson's resignation, he had immediately introduced a motion to examine his accounts, had vehemently opposed the election of Littlefield, and had given serious consideration to resigning from the board. However, Littlefield's "declaration that he would press the work vigorously" had induced him to remain on the board "and to give all the aid in my power to advance the enterprise."[48]

Clingman also went into considerable detail regarding "the causes which have destroyed the credit of the State." Although he saw a number of influences at work, he attributed the rapid decline in the price of North Carolina bonds primarily to the machinations of "a set of persons, mostly living in the central part of North Carolina, who act as though it was absolutely necessary that they should control all the offices to be filled." According to Clingman, these unscrupulous individuals had "formed a plan to break down the credit of the new bonds . . . in the hope of making capital on which they might run into office. . . . If they could be foisted into place, it mattered nothing to them what mischief was done."[49]

Readers familiar with Clingman's antebellum career would have recognized at once that the central influences who were now allegedly undermining the credit of the state were, in his mind, the same Whig "central managers" against whom he had railed during the 1850s. Since the end of the war, Clingman had been on uneasy terms with the former Whigs who dominated the North Carolina Conservative party. Now his suppressed resentments came bubbling to the surface. According to Clingman, the "selfishness and folly . . . [of] the so-called Conservative leaders" had allowed the Republicans to take control of the state in 1868 and elect a "Legislature who have proved themselves incompetent to transact business. . . . But not content with the great mischief they have done, these politicians in their insane anxiety for office have formed a deliberate scheme to destroy the credit of the State, and ruin its character."[50]

Clingman also faulted the Conservative leaders for their proscriptive attitude toward old-line Democrats. Although dependent on Democratic voters for most of their popular support, "many of them are as hostile to Democrats as if they were lords of the ascendant in their own right, and by their adroitness and activity they always push their own men forward for office." Only by "forfeiting their self-respect" could Democrats continue to support "a set of persons who evidently intend to use them as convenient tools for their own advancement." Clingman concluded by calling on his fellow Democrats to assert their "manhood and worth" and to unite with "the best elements of the Whig and Republican parties" and with "the adopted citizens and . . . the colored people" in order to establish "a genuine North Carolina party" that would extricate the state from "the perils which menace her welfare."[51]

Not surprisingly, Clingman's circular triggered a barrage of attacks from the Conservatives. His former mentor William A. Graham characterized it as "a wretched piece of vanity, malignity, & effrontery." The sharp-tongued Josiah Turner, who had recently assumed control of the *Raleigh Sentinel,* dismissed it as "nothing but the peevish and churlish jealousy of an old man, who talks more to himself than he does to the world, and sees nothing in government but *office.*" According to the *Asheville Citizen,* Clingman's "present lamentable step excites much disgust and more indignation, but no sympathy. . . . His late circular merely fixes him where many had long believed, and all had suspected was his true place."[52]

And that "true place," in the estimation of the Conservatives, was with Holden and the Republicans. Clingman might still be calling himself a Democrat, said Turner, but he had "showed the cloven foot" by having his address published in the office of the *North Carolina Standard.* Indeed, added a correspondent of the *Hillsborough Recorder,* thousands of copies had been printed there for circulation by the Republicans "as a campaign document for next summer." According to the correspondent, "this address was gotten up for the purpose of creating disensions [*sic*] in the conservative rank and thereby enabling the Radicals to carry the state next August." The *Salisbury Old North State* agreed that the intent of Clingman's letter was "to array the Democrats against their former [Whig] opponents, and thus divide the Conservatives into two organizations, or parties, instead of one."[53]

The Conservative editors had no doubt that the principal objective of Clingman's "North Carolina party" would be to return its self-appointed leader to the U.S. Senate. According to the *Old North State,* Clingman hoped to elect a sufficient number of his supporters to the general assembly in 1870 to enable them to hold the balance of power. He would then "lead them over to Holden and the Radical party" and receive the Senate seat in payment. "The action of Gen. Clingman was taken in concert with Gov. Holden," it concluded, "and was meant to be a diversion in favor of the latter."[54]

Although there is no evidence that Clingman had acted in conjunction with Holden or any other Republican, his detractors were quite correct in affirming that the Republicans would be the principal beneficiaries of a split in the Conservative party. Their assertion that the former senator was maneuvering to reclaim his old seat was also valid. In February, the U.S. Congress had voted to remove the Fourteenth Amendment disabilities that until then had prevented him from holding federal office. Conservatives were understandably angry that a leading "secessionist" like Clingman had received amnesty while Vance, Graham, and other prominent members of their own party remained under the ban. Many perceived a connection between Clingman's newfound affinity for the Republicans and the recent removal of his disabilities. According to the *Greensboro Patriot,* the Republican Congress had pardoned him "for the express purpose of enabling [him] . . . to inaugurate and carry into effect this great political cheat for the benefit of the Radical party in North Carolina." Indeed, added Josiah Turner of the *Sentinel,* it was none other than Milton Littlefield, the notorious leader of the "railroad ring," who had "electioneered for the removal of the General's disabilities."[55]

Although Turner never provided any evidence to back up his charge that Littlefield had engineered the removal of Clingman's disabilities, the editor did publish some damaging revelations regarding Clingman's financial dealings with Swepson and Littlefield. Clingman, he asserted, had profited handsomely from his association with the railroad ring. "He has a written obligation from Swepson to pay him ten per cent on his agency in the Florida affair, besides which he has Littlefield's note, or bond, or check for $15,000 for services rendered, and a promise from the same party for $10,000 in cash additional." Turner would refer repeatedly to "Littlefield's bond for $15,000" throughout the spring and summer.[56]

Clingman never denied Turner's charge. Nor could he, since it was substantially correct. His arrangement of April 1869 with Swepson had guaranteed him 10 percent of the profits on his associate's Florida railroad investments. In December 1869, after acquiring Swepson's interest in the Florida roads, Littlefield had also entered into an agreement with Clingman. Under the terms of that arrangement, Littlefield would pay ten thousand dollars down and another fifteen thousand dollars in six months for Clingman's interest in the railroads. He verbally agreed to provide the cash "in ten days probably, and certainly in twenty days," and he gave Clingman a note for the balance. Littlefield habitually made promises that he had no intention of keeping, and this one was no exception. Clingman never saw any of the money.[57]

Clingman regarded his dealings with Swepson and Littlefield as private transactions having nothing to do with the Western Division. The Conservatives saw matters differently. According to Turner, the substantial fees promised to Clingman had come out of "funds belonging to the Western North Carolina Railroad, to which he had no more right than the man in the moon." When Clingman returned to the mountain district in late spring to begin his campaign for a new party, Turner's accusations about his Florida investments followed hard on his heels. With dripping sarcasm, the editor warned the "people of the mountains . . . [to] look out for Gen. Clingman. He is coming among them on a speech-making expedition with Littlefield's note for $15,000 in his pocket." The general "would be listened to with much more complacency and satisfaction by the mountain people," he opined, "if he would turn over the fifteen thousand dollars to the contractors, or to the State Treasurer."[58]

Clingman's efforts to form a "North Carolina party" met with a lukewarm reception in the mountain district. As the *Rutherfordton Star* sardonically noted after reporting his appearance at Hendersonville, "we did not hear of any converts to the General[']s party." In light of Clingman's own involvement with the railroad ring, he was hardly the ideal person to lead a new party dedicated to honest government. Even if his reform credentials had been impeccable, however, it is unlikely he would have enjoyed any more success. The majority of North Carolinians accepted the Conservative argument that the Republicans with their overwhelming majorities in the general assembly bore responsibility for the railroad frauds. They were also receptive to warnings that a split in the Conservative ranks would "continue the same set in power another term." Conservatives also benefited from popular reaction to Governor Holden's controversial decision to call out the militia and suspend the writ of habeas corpus in order to suppress Ku Klux Klan violence. In the mountain district, according to the *Sentinel,* Holden's actions created "a perfect storm of indignation, in which Republicans and Conservatives participated." [59]

The election of 1870 resulted in a resounding victory for the Conservatives, who won almost two-thirds of the seats in the general assembly. Particularly impressive was their showing in the mountain counties, where thousands of white voters turned away from the Republican party. Their overwhelming legislative majority also put the Conservatives in a position to elect a U.S. senator in place of Republican Joseph C. Abbott, whose term would expire in March. Zebulon B. Vance was the popular favorite, even though he was still barred by the Fourteenth Amendment from holding federal office, but numerous other prominent Conservatives were also mentioned as possible candidates. [60]

The division within the Conservative ranks was a cause of concern to party leaders. If the legislators from the majority party scattered their votes among a number of aspirants, the Republican minority might end up holding the balance of power. "Their policy," warned one correspondent of the *Sentinel,* "will be to unite upon some man, who professing to belong to our party is nevertheless *in heart* for himself alone and will be willing *to owe his election to them.*" There was no doubt in Josiah Turner's mind that Clingman intended to be that man. On 31 October he reported the rumor that "the old gentleman is seeking to secure the Radical vote of the Legislature, for U.S. Senator, assuring them that he can secure [the office] . . . through Democratic votes with theirs." [61]

Although some Republicans might well have been inclined to vote for Clingman in order to prevent the election of Vance, there was never a serious possibility of his receiving substantial support from other quarters. Even Turner acknowledged that the former senator's prospects were hopeless since any Conservative foolish enough to vote for him "would be sure of being cashiered by his constituents." In order to avoid a divisive fight on the floor of the general assembly, the Conservatives finally agreed to abide by the decision of a party caucus. Although Vance received the caucus nomination with only two votes to spare, he was subsequently elected to the U.S. Senate by a huge majority. As many skeptics had predicted, the Senate refused to seat him, and the office remained vacant until April 1872. [62]

Turner's attacks on Clingman did not end with the conclusion of the contest for the senatorship. The editor continued to hammer away at him not only for his connections to the railroad ring but also for his evasive testimony the previous spring before a legislative investigating committee chaired by G. W. Welker. In an editorial of 3 December 1870, Turner returned yet again to the issue of Clingman's testimony, sarcastically attributing his equivocal answers to his belief that it was "bad policy to investigate the Railroad frauds." For Clingman, who had been seething for months under the withering barrage of Turner's attacks, that comment proved to be the last straw.[63]

Later that day, Clingman encountered the editor walking near the capitol on Morgan Street. "Turner, you continue to slander me," he shouted as he struck him over the head with his walking stick, drawing blood profusely. Before he could recover his balance, Clingman hit him a second time. Turner, who was ten years younger and sixty pounds heavier than his antagonist, then proceeded to pay him back in kind, striking Clingman four times on the face with his own walking stick with a force sufficient to break it into splinters. Turner wrestled his opponent to the ground, managed to get Clingman's head between his legs, and for good measure delivered a few more blows to his back with the fragment of the stick. The two men remained in that undignified position until a policeman finally separated them.[64]

The "Morgan Street fight" was widely reported in the North Carolina presses and, indeed, in newspapers throughout the country. The consensus was that "Gen. Clingman seems to have gotten the worst of it." The wounds to his face, though not life threatening, were quite serious. Whereas Turner was able to return to work the next day, Clingman was confined to his room for over a week. On 19 January 1871 both men were arrested. Clingman pleaded guilty and received a fine of five dollars. Turner pleaded not guilty, arguing that he had acted in self-defense. Clingman subsequently testified on his behalf, claiming that he would have acted no differently had he been in Turner's position. The editor was acquitted.[65]

Despised by the Conservatives and regarded with suspicion by the Republicans, the once-powerful Clingman had become a political pariah. As a correspondent of the *Raleigh Sentinel* put it, "truly his condition is now pitiable in the extreme—defeated, politically isolated, forlorn and solitary." Josiah Turner was even more blunt. "Clingman is dead politically," he proclaimed, "not only in the mountains, but everywhere else."[66] On the pages of the *Sentinel*, the former senator was repeatedly characterized as "old man Clingman," "the old gentleman," "the old rotator," and even as "poor old 'played out Clingman.'" Words such as "decrepitude" and "dotage" were also used liberally by Turner and his correspondents to create the image of an aging politician who had long since outlived his usefulness.[67]

Indeed, at almost sixty, Clingman was now well past his prime. Even within the dominant Conservative party, younger men like Vance, Ransom, and Merrimon, along with other politicians who had not been born at the time Clingman first ran for office, were supplanting the older generation of leaders such as Graham, Worth, and Bragg.[68] But age was not the only factor that kept Clingman on the fringes of power in postwar North Carolina. His "secessionist" antecedents, the enmity of the former Whigs who controlled the Conservative party, and his close association with the railroad ring were sufficient in themselves to have consigned a much younger man to political oblivion.

However, even his adversaries acknowledged that Clingman was not the type of man who would "remain in this state of political isolation very long if he can help it." [69] Few politicians had demonstrated such a remarkable ability to come back from the political dead. Time and again, Clingman's enemies had confidently predicted that his days were numbered. And each time, he had defied those predictions. It remained to be seen whether he would do so again. But even those who were now publicly rejoicing at his political demise must have suspected they had not heard the last of Thomas Lanier Clingman.

14 *Endeavoring to Redeem Himself*

The reports of Clingman's political death that appeared in the North Carolina newspapers during the early 1870s did, in fact, prove premature. By the middle of the decade, the onetime outcast had succeeded in transforming himself into a "power in the state Democratic party." Although he held no elective office apart from his brief service as a member of the Constitutional Convention of 1875, Clingman played an important role as a campaigner and strategist, and party leaders came to rely heavily upon his advice and experience. In 1871 few would have predicted such a remarkable political comeback. Probably even fewer would have prophesied that Clingman's chief antagonist, Josiah Turner, would be the one to be permanently cast out of the Democratic party and "end . . . his life as a Republican."[1]

When the Conservatives took control of the North Carolina General Assembly in November 1870, they immediately set about consolidating their power. Party leaders demanded that Gov. William W. Holden be impeached for his unconstitutional efforts to use the state militia to suppress Klan violence. Turner, who had been arrested and briefly imprisoned for his alleged involvement with the Klan, led the forces calling for the governor's ouster. Clingman, along with a few Conservatives like Zebulon B. Vance, opposed making any effort to remove Holden, arguing that such action might well lead to a reimposition of military rule. On 3 December 1870 Turner roundly criticized Clingman for his "tender hearted and forgiving" attitude toward Holden in the same editorial that led to their fight on Morgan Street later that day. Undaunted by the prospect of federal intervention, the Conservatives quickly impeached the Republican governor and removed him from office.[2]

The next item on the Conservative agenda was to summon a constitutional convention that would declare all state offices vacant and order new elections, thus enabling the party to take control of the executive and judiciary branches as well as the legislature. Conservatives in eastern counties with large black populations also hoped to win control of the machinery of county government by making local offices appointive rather than elective. Since Conservatives in the lower house lacked the two-thirds majority required to call a convention, the legislators by simple majority passed an act providing for a referendum on a convention and for the election of delegates who would serve only if the convention were approved. The Republicans denounced the act as unconstitutional, arguing that a convention could not legally be called by means of a referendum. Tod R. Caldwell, the Republican lieutenant governor who had become chief executive after Holden's impeachment, refused to issue a proclamation for the election. The Conservatives responded with supplementary legislation placing the election machinery in the hands of the local sheriffs.[3]

A year earlier, Clingman had publicly characterized the Constitution of 1868 as "liberal and fair," and he had severely criticized the Conservatives for opposing it. In a speech at Hendersonville on 29 May 1871, however, he endorsed the convention movement and declared himself "an ally of the Conservative party in the present campaign of Law and Order vs. Usurpation and Revolution." In announcing "this latest apostasy of the General," the Republican *Asheville Pioneer* wryly observed that "with him consistency has never been a jewel, nor even a pocket piece." In his own mind, Clingman may not have perceived any inconsistency, since he had always acknowledged that the Constitution of 1868 contained certain "objectionable features" that should "in time be corrected by general consent."[4]

Nonetheless, Clingman's course on the convention issue was dictated as much by political considerations as by a desire to remedy the "objectionable features" in the constitution. As one Conservative noted, his recent behavior had "brought upon him much obloquy," and he was "now endeavoring to redeem himself" by crusading on behalf of a popular cause. Clingman's chameleon-like instincts had given him a remarkable ability to change political colors in order to protect himself in dangerous situations. The Conservative victory in 1870, together with the failure of his efforts to organize a third party, most likely convinced him that if he wished to end his isolation and again become a player in the political game, he would have to work as "an ally of the Conservative party" rather than as its avowed enemy.[5]

On 7 June 1871 Clingman explicated his views on the convention issue in a long letter that was published in the *Asheville Citizen* and reprinted in several other Conservative newspapers. He devoted considerable attention to the constitutionality of the referendum bill, arguing that the specific method of revision prescribed in the constitution applied only to the actions of the general assembly and did not restrict "the great inherent right of the people to make and change at their own will their form of government." Clingman also addressed several other objections to the convention that were being made by the Republicans. Their claim that it would repeal the popular homestead provision, which protected the property of farmers from seizure for debt, was in his opinion a "frivolous" complaint because the delegates had been expressly forbidden from touching that subject. Nor, said Clingman, should black voters be concerned that their rights would be abridged, since "the convention act expressly protects all rights guaranteed by the constitution of the United States."[6]

Clingman's letter was warmly received by the Conservative presses. The *Wilmington Journal* praised it as "a manly, bold and dignified paper, just such an one as we expected from one who had rendered such eminent services in the civil and military history of the state." Its editor predicted that Clingman's endorsement of the convention would ensure its success in the far west. "His voice will echo among his native hills and vallies *[sic]*, and as of old he will lead his fellow citizens to a glorious victory." Even the acerbic Josiah Turner called it an "able letter."[7]

The convention campaign of 1871 was hard fought. Although the Republicans were initially inclined to boycott the elections, they decided to enter the canvass in order to vote the convention down or, failing that, to elect a majority of delegates. Both sides sent armies of speakers into the field, and both predicted victory. The Republicans proved to be the better prophets. The convention was defeated by a majority of more than eighty-six hundred votes. It was fortunate for the Conservatives that the convention never met since the Republicans also elected a majority of delegates. Nonetheless, Clingman did succeed in rallying the mountain counties behind the movement for constitutional revision. There, the proconvention forces garnered 52 percent of the vote, winning majorities in twelve of the twenty counties and coming within a few votes of winning two others.[8]

Clingman's efforts on behalf of the convention went a long way toward redeeming him in the eyes of the North Carolina Conservatives. Still, there were troubling questions regarding his involvement in the railroad schemes of Swepson and Littlefield. Shortly after the convention election, Clingman had an opportunity to vindicate his conduct before a special commission that had been established to investigate the charges of fraud and corruption. The three-member

Shipp Commission—so named after its chairman, Attorney General William M. Shipp—began collecting evidence in April 1871 and continued throughout the remainder of the year. Its findings, which were made public early in 1872, revealed a disturbing pattern of bribery, bond manipulation, and financial mismanagement involving Republicans and Conservatives alike.[9]

In a deposition taken on 30 August 1871 Clingman provided the Shipp Commission with numerous details regarding his own role as director of the Western Division and as lobbyist and agent for George W. Swepson. He admitted that he had conversed with members of the legislature, chiefly Conservatives, regarding railroad legislation, but he claimed he had no knowledge of money being used to influence votes apart from what he had read in the newspapers. None of the bonds issued to the Western Division had ever passed through his hands, he testified, nor was he ever consulted regarding their disposition. He had "no apprehension that Mr. Swepson had misapplied any of the bonds" until his failure to settle with Littlefield in October 1869 had finally aroused his suspicions. Clingman acknowledged that Swepson had given him over a period of time approximately fifteen hundred dollars for professional services not relating to the Western Division, but he affirmed that the expenses he had incurred were "more than all I received." In short, he had not profited personally from his involvement with Swepson or the Western Division.[10]

As for Littlefield, Clingman testified that he saw very little of him during the legislative session of 1868–69 and that he had no consultations with him regarding railroad legislation. He stated that he had opposed Littlefield's election to the presidency of the Western Division in October 1869 but that he had stayed on as a director after being assured that the new president would vigorously begin construction. His only direct financial dealings with Littlefield, he said, involved the sale of his interest in the Florida railroads, for which Littlefield had agreed to give him ten thousand dollars down and a note for the balance of fifteen thousand dollars. Neither sum, he added, had ever been paid. In Clingman's mind, the railroad interests he had sold to Littlefield were earnings for services he had rendered Swepson over a period of two years. Thus, he considered his own claims against Littlefield to be just as legitimate as those of the Western Division and Littlefield's numerous other creditors.[11]

Although Clingman was never formally charged with any wrongdoing, his testimony before the Shipp Commission did not exonerate him in the eyes of his critics. Allegations regarding his involvement with Swepson and Littlefield continued to haunt him during the campaign of 1872. This time, however, the accusations would be made by the Republicans. Having made his peace with the Conservatives, Clingman was now ready to assist them in ousting the Republicans from the governor's office. In May 1872 he was a featured speaker at the Conservative Convention that met in Greensboro to nominate candidates for governor and other state offices. Occupying a place of honor on the platform with Vance,

Turner, and other prominent party leaders, he came forward "amidst a general storm of applause . . . [and] entertained the body for nearly an hour." Throughout the speech, he was interrupted by rounds of applause. One Republican observer dryly remarked that "if words could reinstate him, I think he is fully again in the fold."[12]

That an association with the "railroad ring" was not an insurmountable obstacle to advancement within the Conservative party was evidenced not only by the prominent role Clingman played at the Greensboro convention but also by the nomination of Augustus S. Merrimon as the party's candidate to oppose Governor Caldwell. The platform adopted by the convention promised honesty, economy, and a judicious system of taxation; condemned "secret political societies"; endorsed an educational system that would benefit "all classes of the people, without distinction of race or color"; and pledged to "faithfully abide by the constitution of the United States . . . with all the amendments, including emancipation and equality before the law." The platform was ostensibly drawn up by a committee consisting of Clingman and numerous other party luminaries. The Republicans claimed it was actually written by Clingman—an assertion the Conservatives never denied. Certainly, its moderate and conciliatory tone was entirely in keeping with his long-standing belief that Southerners should acquiesce in Reconstruction rather than try to resist it.[13]

Clingman would soon come to realize that moderation was no guarantee of success. From the beginning of the campaign, Republican presses hammered away at his and Merrimon's involvement in the Swepson-Littlefield frauds. To support their claims that both men had served as Swepson's "confidential advisers," the editors presented a generous quantity of extracts from their recent testimony before the Shipp Commission. The Republicans also contrasted Caldwell's vigorous efforts to prosecute Swepson with the alleged attempts by Clingman and Merrimon "to shield him from the penalties of the law." The *Carolina Era* reminded its readers that Caldwell had ordered Swepson's arrest as soon as he became governor. He had also made repeated efforts to secure the extradition of Littlefield after he fled to Florida. Certainly, it pointed out, the governor would not have been "so vigorous in the prosecution of these criminals if he had been implicated in the least degree with them."[14]

On the other hand, it was no secret that Merrimon had served as one of Swepson's defense attorneys after his indictment by the Buncombe County Superior Court. Thanks partly to his efforts, Swepson had been able to make a financial settlement with the Western Division that allowed him to escape criminal prosecution. Clingman had declined a similar offer to serve as Swepson's defense counsel, but he and the other directors of the Western Division did formally approve the financial settlement. Clingman most likely viewed the arrangement as a means of recovering at least some of the money owed to the Western Division. The Republicans, however, insisted that he and Merrimon had "come to Swepson's rescue from motives of personal interest, to cover up and hide their friend's rascality in order to prevent an exposure of their complicity in the matter." [15]

The issue of Clingman's involvement with the railroad ring may well have cost him a seat in the U.S. House of Representatives. With no immediate prospects for returning to the Senate, he had decided instead to seek the congressional nomination at the Conservative Convention that met in Marion on 1 June 1872. The balance of parties in the mountain district was close, and the Conservatives could ill afford to run a candidate with as many liabilities as Clingman. After eleven ballots, the convention gave the nomination to Robert B. Vance, the elder brother of Zebulon B. Vance. Clingman was offered two consolation prizes—an appointment as a delegate to the Democratic National Convention and a commission as elector-at-large to canvass North Carolina on behalf of the party's presidential nominee. [16]

On 9 July 1872 twenty delegates and twenty alternates from the Old North State assembled in Baltimore to attend the eleventh quadrennial Democratic Convention. Clingman was selected to serve on the Committee on Resolutions. According to one observer, the announcement of his nomination elicited "enthusiastic applause" from the delegates equaled only by that bestowed upon the legendary Fitzhugh Lee, a Civil War hero and nephew of Robert E. Lee who was serving as a delegate from Virginia. Clingman's committee reported the same platform that had been adopted in May by the Liberal Republican Convention in Cincinnati. In the balloting for a presidential nominee, the North Carolina delegation unanimously supported Horace Greeley, the former antislavery editor who had earlier been nominated by the Liberal Republicans. Greeley won the Democratic nomination by a vote of 686 to 60. [17]

Shortly after the convention adjourned, Clingman dropped a bombshell on the North Carolina Republicans in the form of a letter ostensibly written by former Democratic congressman James B. Beck of Kentucky. The letter, which was addressed to Clingman, pointed out that the August state elections in North Carolina were widely regarded as a barometer for the presidential election in November. For that reason, the Grant administration had determined to use every corrupt means possible to carry the Old North State. Large sums had been raised for that purpose, including funds illegally drawn from the Justice Department. Indeed, said Beck, he had personally examined the Treasury records and had discovered that Samuel T. Carrow, the U.S. Marshal for North Carolina, had withdrawn an enormous sum of $223,000 over the past year "for pretended judicial expenses." [18]

First published in the *Washington (D.C.) Patriot*, Beck's letter was reprinted in many of the North Carolina presses. According to the Republicans, it was Clingman—and not Beck—who had examined the Treasury accounts and written the letter, which he had then persuaded his Democratic colleague to sign. That accusation is probably valid. Clingman was, in fact, in Washington on the day the Kentuckian had supposedly gone over to the Treasury Department, and he never explicitly denied the Republican charge. Regardless of who actually penned the letter, the initiative almost certainly came from Clingman as part of a plan to put the North Carolina Republicans on the defensive.[19]

The Conservatives seized upon the "startling revelations" contained in the Beck letter to support their claim that "Federal office-holders are using money from Washington to aid the Republican candidates in this State." The Republicans responded with a rejoinder from Carrow denying that any federal money had been used for electioneering purposes. Instead, he asserted, the sizable amounts withdrawn from the Treasury had been expended on court costs resulting from the large number of prosecutions for Ku Klux Klan activity. Carrow claimed that he could support that assertion with "a voucher for every dollar paid out." The charges of impropriety were "slanderous and false," he concluded, and their authors knew them to be false at the time they were made.[20]

Clingman's efforts on behalf of the Conservative ticket were not limited to publishing letters in the partisan presses. During the final three weeks of the campaign, he addressed mass meetings in at least twelve North Carolina towns in addition to participating in a grand procession and barbecue at Raleigh. The national organizations of both parties had sent dozens of speakers into the Old North State, and the Conservative celebration in Raleigh was attended by luminaries such as Gov. Gilbert Walker of Virginia and former senator James R. Doolittle of Wisconsin. Doolittle subsequently accompanied Clingman to Fayetteville, where they spoke to "the largest crowd seen there in years."[21]

Clingman's campaign efforts were greeted with a warm reception by the Conservative presses. The *Goldsboro Messenger* characterized his address in that town as "lucid, bold and thoroughly convincing" and noted that the Republicans in the audience "sat in gloomy silence as his caustic but truthful accusations fell upon their guilty ears." The *Raleigh News* declared that Clingman had attracted "good audiences" throughout his tour of the eastern counties and that "his able and argumentative speeches have been of much service to our cause." In the strongly Republican mountain counties of Rutherford, Polk, and Henderson, where he spent the final days of the campaign, his "telling speeches" reportedly "succeeded in reducing the Radical majorities almost to mere nothings."[22]

As early returns from the governor's election revealed Conservative increases in Republican counties where they had not expected to gain support, the party presses were ecstatic. On 3 August the *Raleigh News* proudly proclaimed that the Old North State had been "Redeemed from Radicalism." Five days later, its editor conceded that Merrimon had narrowly lost the election. The Conservatives did better in the legislative elections, winning majorities of fourteen in the senate and ten in the House of Representatives. Nonetheless, the result was a disappointment considering the lopsided majorities they had commanded in the previous general assembly.[23]

Clingman's prominent role in the campaign probably proved more of a liability than an asset to the Conservatives. His undeniable connections with the railroad ring, together with Merrimon's own reputation as Swepson's "confidential adviser," made it difficult for Conservatives to present themselves convincingly to the voters as the party of "honesty and reform." Even so, party leaders were certain they would have won the governor's race had there not been widespread fraud at the ballot box. Many of Merrimon's supporters called on him to contest the election.

Clingman played a leading role in that movement. In a letter published in the *New York World* and copied by numerous North Carolina newspapers, he presented a cogent summary of the Conservative argument. The election, he said, had been managed by "an army of . . . [federal] revenue officers and deputy marshalls," who had been "liberally supplied with money." Those federal managers had practiced massive fraud, importing black voters from other states into the eastern counties and inducing native blacks to vote several times in different townships. In the white-majority counties of the west, they had mobilized violators of the revenue laws and those under indictment for Klan activity with promises of immunity from prosecution "if they vote the Radical ticket." Others, who refused to cooperate, had been arrested in order to prevent them from voting.[24]

Although Clingman may have exaggerated the extent of the fraud, there was some truth to his accusations. In several eastern counties, the number of voters did exceed the number of adult males reported in the census. Moreover, a large number of indictments for Klan activity were in fact made just before the election, and many of them were dropped soon after the campaign had ended. Merrimon shared in the widespread belief that the Republicans had stolen the election. However, he had informally been promised a U.S. Senate seat if he lost the election for governor, and he probably had no stomach for a protracted fight over an office he never really wanted in the first place. Merrimon made it clear he would not contest the election unless the Conservatives could find enough "positive and indisputable" evidence of fraud to negate the results. The matter was finally turned over to the party's executive committee. Perhaps fearful that a close scrutiny of the election would reveal too many improprieties of their own, the committee decided to drop the issue.[25]

The disappointment of their loss in the governor's election cooled the ardor of the Conservatives for the presidential contest. On 9 October the *Raleigh Sentinel* commented upon the existence of a "fearful apathy" among the voters of the Old North State—an indifference that was not being countered by active campaigning. A few days later, Clingman talked with Horace Greeley in New York, where the candidate reportedly told him that "the chances of his election . . . will turn upon N.C." Clingman most likely understood that that was wishful thinking on

Greeley's part. He did make a few speeches on Greeley's behalf both before and after their meeting, but his efforts did not match the feverish pace of his summer campaign. With thousands of Conservatives remaining away from the polls, the Republicans carried North Carolina by almost 24,000 votes. Nationally, the Liberal Republican insurgency fared no better. Greeley lost the election by more than 763,000 votes and garnered only 66 electoral votes.[26]

The Conservatives could at least take comfort in knowing that their control over the general assembly would allow them to elect a U.S. senator to succeed Republican John Pool. Zebulon B. Vance, who had been elected to the Senate in 1870 only to resign after Congress refused to remove his Fourteenth Amendment disabilities, was anxious to make another run. Vance had recently been granted amnesty, but many in the party were still angry at him for waiting more than a year before turning in his resignation. His chief rival was Merrimon, who believed the Senate seat was due to him as a result of his services to his party in the recent gubernatorial campaign. Other Conservatives such as William A. Graham also coveted the position. In addition, Clingman was reported to be "not altogether out of the race." In mid-November he spent more than a week in Raleigh sounding out his prospects.[27]

Vance received the caucus nomination on 25 November 1872, but unlike in 1870, the nomination did not prove tantamount to election. Nineteen Conservative legislators, primarily Merrimon supporters, refused to participate in the caucus deliberations. When the balloting for senator began the next day, the general assembly found itself deadlocked between Vance, Merrimon, and Pool. After a week of inconclusive voting, the two leading Conservative contenders finally withdrew, and the party presses came forward with the names of a number of "equally worthy" alternatives. Clingman was among the Conservative worthies so mentioned. During the subsequent balloting, he received only two votes—a striking indication of the narrowness of his base within the party.[28]

None of the Conservative alternatives proved able to break the stalemate. On 3 December Vance was renominated by the caucus after a head count seemed to indicate he now had enough votes to win election. The Republicans, however, had decided to resort to a variation of the stratagem the Conservatives had feared they would use back in 1870—"to unite upon some man, who professing to belong to our party is nevertheless . . . willing *to owe his election to them.*" Ironically, that man proved to be Augustus S. Merrimon—the same individual whom the Republicans had lambasted just a few months earlier as the "confidential adviser of Swepson." Although Merrimon made no overtures to the Republicans and had no sympathy with their goals, opposition leaders regarded him as preferable to Vance, whom they were determined to defeat at all costs. Combining their own votes with those of sixteen dissident Conservatives, the Republicans elected Merrimon to the U.S. Senate by a vote of eighty-seven to eighty.[29]

After the election, Clingman refrained from joining the chorus of those condemning Merrimon for his "insubordination to the party mandate and . . . breach of party discipline."[30] There was no love lost between Clingman and Vance. Despite his rapprochement with Vance during the war, by 1872 Clingman had come to regard the former governor as a major obstacle to his own political comeback. Nor had "party discipline" ever been one of his overriding concerns. Indeed, Clingman almost certainly would have accepted the senatorship had it been offered to him under similar circumstances. Unlike Merrimon, however, he lacked the cadre of supporters that would have made a combination with the Republicans a realistic possibility.

A few weeks after the senatorial election, Clingman returned to Raleigh to testify before a legislative committee looking into the circumstances surrounding the recent sale of the Western Division. Despite several threats of resignation, Clingman had continued as a member of the board of directors after the discovery of the Swepson-Littlefield frauds. By October 1870, however, all construction west of Asheville had ceased due to lack of funds to pay the contractors. From the viewpoint of the contractors and other creditors of the Western Division, selling the road seemed to offer the best hope for recovering their money and resuming construction. In 1872 the directors were empowered by the general assembly to negotiate its sale or lease.[31]

Pres. Wallace W. Rollins, along with most of the board, backed the proposal. Clingman and Nicholas W. Woodfin were the only dissenters. But the force of local opinion was strongly behind the sale. As Rollins told Rufus Y. McAden, the Charlotte banker with whom he was negotiating to purchase the road, "the people are all with us. . . . Woodfin and Clingman will be alone to fight." On 25 June 1872 the board voted unanimously to approve a motion that the road "be sold under executions now in the hands of the sheriffs." As Rollins had predicted, Clingman and Woodfin had both succumbed to the "pressure." However, Clingman did not attend the four board meetings in early July that consummated the sale. His official connection with the Western Division had ended.[32]

The long and frustrating delay in the construction of the Western North Carolina Railroad induced Clingman and other proponents of western development to revive the old idea of a rail line through the French Broad Valley that would connect Charleston, South Carolina, with the great inland cities of the Mississippi Valley. That project had remained dormant since the 1830s, but as one enthusiast put it, "piece by piece the survey . . . had been adopted, until now only a small gap was left to complete the whole line. . . . It only remain[s] now for the Gap to Spartanburg to be completed to insure the building of the whole line." To fill that "gap," a proposal was made to construct a railroad that would run from Spartanburg, South Carolina, through Asheville to Wolf Creek on the Tennessee border, where it would connect with the Tennessee rail system. In May

1873 subscription books were officially opened for the Spartanburg and Asheville Railroad Company.[33]

Clingman played an active role in the propaganda campaign that was launched to secure stock subscriptions from the counties along the proposed route. At a railroad meeting in Asheville on 12 June 1873, he told his listeners he had moved to that town thirty-six years earlier in "the hope that we would have a railroad." Thus far, however, he "had been doomed to disappointment." He then offered a resolution affirming that "we will do all in our power" to connect with South Carolina "by the nearest and most practicable route." A few weeks later, he regaled another meeting in Hendersonville with an "enthusiastic" speech designed to "awaken . . . interest in the good cause." Resolutions were passed calling on the commissioners of Buncombe, Henderson, and adjoining counties "to subscribe to the capital stock . . . such sums as are necessary to secure the completion of the Road."[34]

Clingman also participated in efforts to reach out to capitalists in Northern cities. At the Hendersonville meeting, he was appointed to a committee of three that was instructed to visit the boards of trade in Louisville, Cincinnati, Chicago, and Pittsburgh "to bring the importance of this line of Railroad to the attention of those bodies." At a meeting in Asheville on 23 September he was selected to represent Buncombe County at the Chicago and South-Atlantic Railway Convention to be held in Chicago on 9 October. Clingman played a prominent role in the convention, which attracted eighty-nine delegates from seven states, including Cyrus McCormick and other "merchant princes" from Chicago. As chairman of the resolutions committee, he reported propositions endorsing the idea of a "grand trunk railway" from Chicago to "one or more of the South-Atlantic ports" and pledging to "use their best efforts to procure . . . such subscriptions and other aid as may assist the enterprise and satisfy capitalists abroad."[35]

The prospects for an early completion of a line between Chicago and the South Atlantic coast were severely dampened by the sharp economic downturn that began during the fall of 1873. Efforts by Clingman, Congressman Robert B. Vance, and Robert Furman of the *Asheville Citizen* to secure private subscriptions in Buncombe County were largely unsuccessful, despite pleas by Furman that the "one salvation left for Western North Carolina . . . [is] the speedy completion of the Spartanburg and Asheville Railroad." After failing in their attempts to attract private investors, Clingman and the other boosters of the Spartanburg road pushed hard to secure assistance from the county government. As a result of their efforts, the voters of Buncombe County approved a bond issue of one hundred thousand dollars to facilitate construction.[36]

The road finally reached Hendersonville, just north of the South Carolina border, in July 1879. The occasion was commemorated by a "grand jubilee" attended by Clingman, Gov. Thomas J. Jarvis of North Carolina, Gov. W. D. Simpson of South Carolina, former governor D. W. C. Sentor of Tennessee, and numerous other luminaries from those three states. Amid copious quantities of barbecued meats and other delicacies, Clingman opened the ceremonies with a welcoming address in which he recalled the "great effort of the gifted R. Y. Hayne" on behalf of the Louisville, Cincinnati, and Charleston Railroad forty years earlier. Alluding to the biblical story of Jacob, who had to wait seven years before he could marry his beloved Rachel, he told the audience it had taken him "six times as long to get a railroad to Hendersonville." Clingman would have to wait another seven years before the Spartanburg railroad finally reached Asheville. The remaining twenty-one miles were not completed until July 1886—six years after the arrival in Asheville of the much-maligned Western North Carolina Railroad.[37]

However beneficial Clingman's efforts at railroad promotion may have been to the economic development of the mountain region, they brought little financial benefit to him personally. Although the profits from his land dealings enabled him to support his peripatetic lifestyle, he had been without a steady source of income since he had left his seat in Congress. In the spring of 1873, Clingman decided to resume the practice of law. As he explained to one prospective client, he had "practiced somewhat irregularly" since the end of the war but now was ready "to give the necessary attention to such matters." He professed to be particularly knowledgeable in "matters connected with our railroads . . . state debt and bonds" and would, therefore, have "little trouble . . . [with] that class of cases." "Of course," added the former fire eater, "I would just as soon be engaged by northern as southern clients and [will] do my best for those whose business I undertake."[38]

Clingman's most promising client did prove to be a Northern concern. During the Civil War, the Atlantic Mutual Insurance Company, like many other Northern underwriters, had paid out several million dollars in compensation to shippers whose property had been destroyed by the *Alabama* and other Confederate vessels built and fitted out in British ports. In 1871 Britain had agreed to compensate American citizens for their losses, and a tribunal of arbitration in Geneva, Switzerland, had subsequently fixed the amount at $15.5 million. Eighty-nine of the 129 ships for which Britain accepted responsibility had been insured. About one-third of them had policies issued by Atlantic Mutual, which was now claiming a portion of the award equal to the amount previously paid out in compensation. In June 1874 the U.S. Congress created a special court to receive and adjudicate the various claims. However, the law also provided that claims by insurance companies would not be allowed unless the company could prove that the sum of its losses exceeded the sum of its premiums and other gains.[39]

From the passage of the Act of 1874 until the entire Geneva Award was finally expended in the 1880s, the underwriters lobbied strenuously to secure a law authorizing their claims. Ironically, the Atlantic Mutual turned to a Confederate general to help them recoup the losses inflicted by rebel privateers. Clingman argued the company's case before the House Judiciary Committee on numerous occasions during the 1870s. Three of his arguments were subsequently published in pamphlet form, probably in an effort to stir up public opinion in favor of the underwriters. Clingman expected to receive a sizable commission should the claims be allowed, and he reportedly told Pres. Kemp P. Battle of the University of North Carolina he would make a substantial donation to that institution out of his professional fees.[40]

Clingman made a convincing argument that the insurers' claims were consistent with international law and that the Geneva Tribunal itself had recognized their validity by calculating their monetary value as part of the final settlement. Although his legal reasoning may have been sound, it was politics rather than the law that ultimately determined the result. In June 1882 Congress passed an act reviving the Court of Claims and providing that the remainder of the Geneva Award would be used to satisfy claims by owners of "exculpated vessels" (ships that had been destroyed by Confederate privateers not based or outfitted in Britain) and the "war premium men" (shippers who had suffered indirect losses by paying high wartime premiums). No provision was made for the underwriters. Still, Clingman had served his clients well. On numerous occasions, the House Judiciary Committee did report a bill favorable to the underwriters that was subsequently approved by the full House. Each time, however, the measure failed in the Senate. Clingman's law practice did not make him a wealthy man, but clients like Atlantic Mutual apparently did provide him with sufficient business to enable him to live comfortably during the 1870s.[41]

Clingman's effectiveness as a lobbyist derived not only from his long experience in Congress but also from his personal acquaintance with former and current members of that body. As journalist Alexander K. McClure noted, "almost as soon as the first bitterness of the war and of reconstruction began to be less poignantly felt, Clingman reappeared in Washington. During the sittings of Congress the place had fascination for him that he could not resist." Taking full advantage of the privilege accorded to former members, Clingman went regularly to the Capitol each morning and took a seat on the floor of the House or Senate, just as he had done during his days as a legislator. "He likes to be here," his friend John Hill Wheeler remarked in 1873, "the scenes of his former triumphs and fame."[42]

Clingman was also an active participant in the social life of postwar Washington. As in the days before the Civil War, many North Carolina congressmen left their wives and families at home and roomed in hotels or boarding houses. During the evenings, they frequently visited each other's lodgings for conversation about politics, finance, religion, history, science, and literature. Over the years, Clingman had amassed an extraordinary store of information about those and other topics, and he was not shy about flaunting his knowledge. Congressman Risden Tyler Bennett recalled that "he was almost daily in my room at the Metropolitan Hotel. . . . He talked to me on every subject good, bad and worse. . . . He expressed himself to me without reserve and I was as direct with him." Bennett remembered once asking Clingman where he might find the best discussion of the tariff. "In my book" was his answer. "It is the greatest book since the New Testament." After pausing a moment, he then added in all seriousness, "I am not certain that it ain't greater than the New Testament." Bennett's opinion that Clingman's "vanity was stupendous" was no overstatement.[43]

His "colossal egotism" notwithstanding, Clingman had a reputation as an entertaining conversationalist. "To meet him and to talk with him," declared Walter Hines Page of the *Raleigh State Chronicle,* "is one of the pleasantest things his friends can do; and the General will talk about anything." Julius Bonitz of the *Wilmington Messenger* agreed that "he is a pleasant companion, and when he is in the mood can be highly interesting." The opinion of Judge David Schenck, who once roomed across the hall from Clingman at the Eagle Hotel in Asheville, was probably shared by many of the former senator's congressional acquaintances in Washington. "I am very fond of hearing him talk," said Schenck, "and he loves a good patient listener."[44]

According to Schenck, Clingman was particularly "fond of recounting the interesting incidents of his long political life, which has thrown him in contact with nearly all the distinguished statesmen and politicians of this age." For most North Carolinians who served in Congress during the 1870s, Webster, Clay, Calhoun, Mangum, and the other political leaders of the antebellum era were merely names. Clingman had known them all personally, and he brought them to life with his "graphic reminiscences of the giants of politics."[45]

Despite his fondness for reminiscing about the halcyon days of the early republic, Clingman lived very much in the present. When not attending the sessions of Congress, he read the *Congressional Record* and other sources to keep informed on current policy issues. A master of self-promotion, he maintained himself in the public eye through frequent interviews with the Washington and New York presses. As the *Raleigh News* remarked, "when he has gone North . . . [he] never fail[s] to appear in print in such papers as the Washington Republican, New York Tribune and Times." Although no longer a member of Congress, Clingman continued to act the part of "a great factor in the affairs of the nation."[46]

Clingman generally remained in Washington from the convening of Congress in December until its adjournment (in March during odd-numbered years and in midsummer during even-numbered years). His sojourn in the nation's capital was punctuated by periodic trips to New York City to attend to his business interests. While in Washington, he stayed at the fashionable Willard's Hotel. In New York he invariably could be found at the New York Hotel, a favorite gathering place for Southerners. After the adjournment of Congress, he returned to the mountain district, sometimes stopping along the way to visit his nieces and nephews in Yadkin and Cabarrus Counties.

Although Asheville remained his base of operations while in North Carolina, Clingman never maintained a permanent residence there. Instead, he roomed at the commodious Eagle Hotel, a popular destination for "visitors and pleasure seekers from the States of North and South Carolina, and Georgia . . . some of whom are the most distinguished in social and political circles in their respective places." There he would regale the guests with his "ever delightful . . . talks about this region." The "delightful summer climate" of the Carolina highlands also provided Clingman with plenty of opportunity to visit his numerous acquaintances in Buncombe and adjoining counties and to continue his explorations. In the fall he could often be seen in Raleigh, particularly during October, when the annual fair and meeting of the state agricultural society were held, and during the sessions of the North Carolina General Assembly.[47]

Clingman's most extended sojourn in the state capital took place in September and October 1875, when he served as one of Buncombe County's delegates to the state constitutional convention. After the Conservatives (who were now beginning to call themselves "Democrats") won lopsided majorities in both houses of the general assembly in 1874, they passed a law providing for a convention to assemble on 6 September 1875. Despite "repeatedly expressing a wish not to be run as a candidate," Clingman was persuaded to enter the contest after being told that his presence in Raleigh would "give character and weight to the convention . . . [and] give our entire Western section an influence which it has long needed."[48]

The campaign, though brief, was hard fought. The party balance in Buncombe County was close, and the Republicans were determined to do everything in their power to defeat Clingman. As he later recalled, "our adversaries never worked harder, using whisky by the barrel and money freely." Clingman's "connection with the railroad frauds" of 1868–69 made him vulnerable to challenge, and the opposition did not hesitate to assail him at his weakest point. They also charged that he favored reimposing property qualifications on the voters—an accusation the candidate branded as "an infernal lie out and out." Referring to a prior commitment that would keep Clingman out of the county during the final week of the campaign, the *Asheville Citizen* warned the voters to beware of "a new batch of lies" that would be brought out "on the eve of election . . . . too late for him to answer and expose." Despite waging a vigorous campaign that would have taxed the energies of a much younger man, Clingman won the election with only seventy votes to spare.[49]

When the delegates assembled in Raleigh on 6 September 1875, it was still unclear which party would be in control. The Democrats had elected fifty-nine delegates, compared to fifty-eight Republicans and three independents, but the death of William A. Graham shortly after the election had reduced their strength to the level of the Republicans.[50] Moreover, two of the Democratic seats were in dispute. In Robeson County, the Democratic-controlled board of commissioners had declared the candidates from their party to be the winners, but only after throwing out the votes of four Republican townships. The Republicans quite naturally cried foul. When the roll of delegates was called, both sets of claimants presented certificates to Thomas Settle, the Republican judge who was serving as temporary chair. Settle ordered both delegations to stand aside. Had the convention proceeded to organize without the presence of the Robeson delegation, the Republicans would have been in control.[51]

Clingman, along with his old antagonist Josiah Turner, immediately sprang to their feet to protest the ruling. Settle, they argued, had no right to go beyond the sheriff's certificates, which had been issued to the two Democrats. Clingman asked the chairman whether he intended to rule upon the disputed seats before the organization of the convention. Settle replied that he would make a decision after the roll call was completed. In the meantime, he said, all delegates who held sheriff's certificates subject to challenge would be asked to stand aside. The Democrats responded by challenging the certificates of five Republicans who, they claimed, were ineligible on account of being federal officeholders. Settle had little choice but to allow all those with sheriff's certificates to take their seats pending an investigation by the convention itself. The shrewd parliamentary tactics of Clingman and Turner had prevented the Republicans from taking control.[52]

Still, with one independent aligning with the Democrats and another with the Republicans, the Democrats were one vote short of a majority. The balance of power lay in the hands of Dr. Edward E. Ransom of Tyrrell County, a former Republican state senator who had been elected as an independent. The Democrats decided to secure Ransom's support by nominating him for convention president. As one observer noted, "everybody in the hall was thunder struck, except the Democrats who were in the secret." Ransom subsequently won the election and proceeded to appoint Democratic majorities to key committees. The *Charlotte Democrat* singled out Clingman, former governor David S. Reid, and John Manning of Chatham as the leaders who developed the strategy that ultimately gave the Democrats control of the convention.[53]

On 9 September Clingman joined several of his colleagues, both Democrats and Republicans, in eulogizing the recently deceased William A. Graham. Although his relations with Graham had been strained ever since his break with the Whig party in the late 1840s, Clingman spoke of his old mentor with a reverence befitting the occasion. In an unconscious critique of his own confrontational political style, he attributed Graham's enormous influence to "his courtesy and dignity of manner and the fairness with which he presented his views"—qualities that had inspired respect and admiration even among his political enemies. Indeed, "perhaps no man so prominent as he was, made so few personal enemies."[54]

Clingman may have lacked the easygoing manner of William A. Graham, but his unquestionable abilities as a legislator and parliamentarian made him an important asset to the Democrats in the convention of 1875. Those skills were acknowledged by his appointment to two important committees—the Committee on the Legislative Department, on which he served as chairman, and the Committee on Amendments. On behalf of the legislative committee, Clingman presented his first report on 11 September. His proposed amendment, which dealt with the rate of compensation for members of the general assembly, was the first constitutional change to be reported from committee and voted upon by the convention.[55]

The Constitution of 1868 was silent on the issue of compensation. In order to discourage lengthy and expensive sessions, Clingman proposed to add language explicitly fixing the pay at three dollars per diem for the first sixty days and two dollars for the next twenty days. Should the general assembly decide to remain in session longer, its members would have to serve without compensation. In the debate that followed, Clingman spoke on behalf of his amendment and argued against proposals to modify it by raising the per diem, substituting a flat salary, or allowing the legislature to change the rate of compensation. On 14 September the amendment passed its second reading by a vote of seventy-seven to thirty-four. Two days later, a substitute proposed with Clingman's approval raised the per diem to four dollars for the first sixty days but deleted the provision for additional pay thereafter. The substitute passed by a vote of eighty-two to twenty-seven, with a substantial minority of the Republicans voting with the Democrats.[56]

Clingman also participated in the debates over a proposal to remove the disabilities of former governor William W. Holden, who had been disqualified from ever again holding office. An ordinance to that effect was introduced by the Republicans on the third day of the convention. Shortly before the measure was scheduled to come to a vote, Edward Conigland, an attorney who had defended Holden at his impeachment trial, asked Clingman to support it, arguing that the governor was "rarely, if at all the instigator of any of the measures for which he stood impeached."[57]

The amnesty ordinance occasioned a spirited two-day debate, with most Republicans supporting it and most Democrats opposed. On the second day of deliberations, Clingman announced his own position. Declining to pass judgment on the merits of Holden's case, he claimed that the convention lacked the authority to remove his disabilities. He then "went on to illustrate by analogies why the power to pass this ordinance did not reside in the convention." It is unclear whether Clingman's position was a product of genuine conviction or whether he was simply dodging the issue. In either event, he joined the other Democrats in voting down the amnesty ordinance.[58]

Even more contentious than the issue of Holden's disabilities was the proposal to repudiate or drastically scale down the special-tax bonds that had been issued by the general assembly of 1868–69. Anticipating that the debate would divide the Democratic majority, the Committee on Revenue, Taxation, and Public Debt delayed submitting a report until most of the other work of the convention had been completed. On 2 October the committee finally reported a resolution prohibiting the general assembly from paying more than 5 percent of the principal on the special-tax bonds or more than 33 percent on any other bonds without the approval of a majority of the voters.[59]

That effort at partial repudiation did not go far enough for some Democrats. Thomas J. Jarvis proposed an amendment that would forbid payment of any principal or interest on the special-tax bonds unless approved by the voters. According to Jarvis, the bonds "were conceived in fraud, rocked in the cradle of iniquity, born in corruption, and prostituted to the basest purposes." Clingman, who had consistently spoken out against all attempts to scale down the public debt, threw his influence against the repudiators. He announced that he could not support Jarvis's amendment because it would "repudiate the bonds held by those persons who purchased in good faith as well as those . . . who got them by means not strictly honorable." After considerable discussion, the report was referred back to committee.[60]

The issue of the public credit would occupy the attention of the convention during the remainder of its session. On five occasions over a period of ten days, Clingman and a handful of other Democratic delegates bolted their party and joined the Republicans in voting down proposals to repudiate or scale down the debt. Confronted by the prospect of an ordinance that might actually enjoin the state to honor the bonds, the Democratic leadership abruptly adjourned the convention on 11 October.[61]

The adjournment caught most Democrats by surprise. As the *Charlotte Democrat* remarked, "the object or cause of the sudden movement is not exactly understood, though we presume the majority had good reasons for forcing an adjournment *sine die* with only a few hours notice." Josiah Turner, the acerbic editor of the *Raleigh Sentinel*, was not inclined to give his fellow delegates the benefit of the doubt. In the weeks that followed, he repeatedly denounced the convention for its "one great failing error," laying the blame squarely upon "*three* Democrats who, every time the subject [of repudiation] came up, voted with the Radicals to suppress it."[62]

Fortunately for Clingman, few Democrats proved willing to follow Turner in his efforts to make repudiation the "grand test" and "party shibboleth." There was nothing in the revised constitution that specifically obligated the state to pay either the interest or the principal on its Reconstruction debt, and apparently that was enough for most Democrats. Moreover, the party had honored its promises of "retrenchment and reform" by eliminating offices, reducing the pay of the legislators, replacing the annual legislative sessions with biennial ones, and giving the general assembly greater control over the judicial system and the county and township governments.[63]

The *Raleigh News* summarized the prevailing sentiment among Democrats when it remarked that even though a few things had been "left undone," the convention's accomplishments "reflected credit" upon that body. On the other hand, Josiah Turner's intemperate attacks against the convention and against the "rings and bond rogues" within the Democratic party were perceived as divisive distractions at a time when the party was gearing up to redeem the state from

Republican misrule. In 1876 mounting debts forced the editor to sell the *Sentinel*, effectively ending his career as a major player in North Carolina politics.[64]

While Turner's star was clearly on the descent during the mid-1870s, Clingman's seemed to be on the rise. One observer characterized him as "the ablest man in the Convention." His skill as a parliamentarian had played a central role in enabling the Democrats to gain control of the convention, and he had served with distinction on two of its most important committees. By 1875 the former senator had come a long way toward redeeming himself in the eyes of his fellow Democrats. Over the course of the next two years, he would also play a significant role in redeeming North Carolina from the last vestiges of Republican rule. By his own estimation, he had "given more labor and money to the support of the Democratic party than any man in the State, who has not himself been a candidate for any high political office." It remained to be seen how long Clingman would continue to support a party that repeatedly denied him that "high political office" to which he had aspired since the end of the Civil War.[65]

15

Champion of the New South

During the years following the Civil War, Thomas Lanier Clingman enjoyed a reputation as one of the most outspoken champions of the "New South creed." Although the phrase itself did not come into widespread use until the 1880s, "there was no argument made by the 'New South' spokesmen of the 1880s that was not developed at length . . . [in] the 1840s and 1850s."[1] During the antebellum period, Clingman had been foremost among those Southerners who believed that the path to wealth and progress lay in economic diversification, Northern investment, scientific agriculture, and improved education. Implicit in that belief, although rarely admitted explicitly, was a critique of the plantation system and an acknowledgment of the superiority of Northern free labor over Southern slave labor. The war had dramatically underscored the inability of the industrially backward South to hold its own against the modernized North. Once the conflict had ended, Southern reformers were ready to harness that "Northern energy" and "Northern respect for labor" in order to "revolutionize the South and make its desolate places smile again."[2]

Clingman and the other postwar modernizers believed that immigration and investment would provide the keys to unlocking the South's underdeveloped resources. In the years following the war, they pushed hard to attract Northerners and Europeans "with capital and agricultural skill" to settle in the South. "We want the best people from Europe and from all parts of the United States to settle among us," intoned the *North Carolina Standard*. "Let them come with their enterprise and money, their muscle and intelligence, and let us welcome capital and immigration, furnishing, as they will, the indispensable means to the progress and prosperity of our beloved State." By 1867 more than one hundred companies had been established in the South to promote the settlement of immigrants.[3]

Clingman was eager to play a role in that process. Early in 1867 he accepted a commission from Gov. Jonathan Worth to bring the resources of North Carolina to the attention of prospective settlers and investors at the Paris Exposition.[4] He apparently did not go to Europe, but he did lend his pen to the cause of immigration by publishing numerous testimonials and publicity pieces. Advancing many of the same arguments he had made in publications twenty years earlier, Clingman extolled the delightful and healthy climate of western North Carolina, the fertility of its soil, its vast mineral resources, and its suitability for the raising of livestock and the production of grains, fruits, and grasses. An abundance of waterpower, "beyond any demand that can ever exist for it," also made the region ideal for manufacturing. The resident white population was "quiet, industrious, intelligent and moral," while the black population was "not . . . numerous enough to constitute an important element in the whole society." In short, there was "no country more inviting to industrious emigrants."[5]

During the first decade after the war, Clingman was also involved with the North Carolina Land Company, a Raleigh-based organization that was chartered by the general assembly in February 1869 "for the transportation and location of Northern and European Settlers, the selling and leasing of real estate, [and] the purchase and sale of agricultural implements, machinery, etc." Under the direction of George Little, a Raleigh entrepreneur who also served as state immigration commissioner, the company did a steady business in the sale of real estate until the Panic of 1873. Although Clingman did not participate in the day-to-day operations of the company, he lent his prestige to its endeavors by serving on the board of directors and contributing a testimonial to a promotional booklet published by the company in 1869.[6]

For the next two decades, Clingman continued to serve as western North Carolina's foremost publicity man, writing articles and delivering lectures to bring its natural and human resources to the attention of audiences in the North and in his own state. However, his boosterism was not limited to the mountain region. In a communication to the *New York Sun* published in December 1881, for example, he made the point that virtually all the agricultural products grown in the United States could be profitably cultivated in North Carolina. Indeed, he added, "I doubt if there can be found on the face of the globe 50,000 square miles in one body which, when all things are considered, is equal in the production of wealth for humanity to North Carolina." Still, he acknowledged, there were many farmers in his state who "think they must plant cotton or corn, so as to get an immediate return of money," thus avoiding other crops that might eventually yield even larger profits.[7]

Clingman's complaint about the one-crop mentality of Tar Heel farmers echoed the views of numerous other agricultural reformers who condemned the backward attitudes and inefficient methods that had prevented the South from realizing its full potential. In a letter published in the *State Agricultural Journal* in 1875, Clingman presented a detailed critique of contemporary agricultural practices. He attributed this "unwise mode of agriculture" partly to "laziness" but primarily to "ignorance." Mere exhortation alone, he said, would not resolve the problem. "It is not sufficient that an article should occasionally appear in a newspaper, or an essay be read to a small assemblage of people. . . . Earnest and continued efforts are necessary to enlighten the public mind."[8]

The remedy, in his opinion, lay in a systematic program of education modeled along the lines of a political campaign. Speakers should be dispatched throughout the state who "will address the crowd earnestly, like a man who wants an office very much." These lecturers should appeal to the self-interest of their audience, announcing that they will "show the people how to pay their taxes easily, and live comfortably." And just as the leading politicians used sub-electors to spread their message, "these men should have local orators to aid them and distribute documents." "If one half the effort which was made in this State in 1872, to elect Greeley or Grant, could be made to enlighten the people on these subjects," he concluded, "the face of the country would be greatly changed for the better."

Just as the Democratic and Republican executive committees in Raleigh planned and coordinated strategy for the North Carolina parties, so too the North Carolina Agricultural Society served as the central agency for the agricultural reform movement in the Old North State during the nineteenth century. Established in 1852 and revived after the Civil War in 1869, the society claimed among its members many of the state's foremost political, economic, and social leaders. Through its annual meetings and its sponsorship of the North Carolina State Fair, the society hoped to instruct the state's farmers in the ideas and practices of scientific agriculture.[9]

During the 1870s Clingman played an active role in the agricultural society, attending its annual meetings, participating in its discussions and debates, serving on its committees, and helping to expand its mission beyond the promotion of "scientific agriculture." Having never plowed a field himself, Clingman had little firsthand understanding of the agricultural conditions that he was trying to reform. Nonetheless, he had an extensive knowledge of "book farming," and he was not reluctant to express his views. At the 1871 meeting, for example, he offered comments on two papers—one by Colonel Hatch of Buncombe County on wool growing and another by Walter W. Lenoir of Haywood County on the value of timber for mechanical purposes. He also took advantage of the occasion to remind his listeners of the "inexhaustible mineral wealth . . . and other resources" of western North Carolina, which were "lost at present to the consumers of the world for want of cheap and rapid transportation."[10]

Clingman and the other members of the North Carolina Agricultural Society were well aware that the Southern economy would not be reformed merely by making speeches and passing lofty resolutions. Yet, with the meager resources available to them, there was little else they could do. The fifteen hundred dollars the society received each year from the state was barely enough to operate the state fair, and even that modest appropriation was in constant danger of being eliminated by budget-conscious legislators.[11] Speaking at the annual meeting in October 1877, Clingman "congratulated the Society upon the progress of the past few years" but added that "there was still much to do." In his opinion, "what the farmer wanted [i.e., lacked] was concert of action [and] cooperation [to] work for each other's interest in farming."[12]

Unfortunately, cooperation and concert of action were goals that the individualistic farmers of the Old North State found difficult to achieve. In Clingman's mind, the most fundamental obstacles inhibiting reform were attitudinal rather than organizational. The "two vices yet to overcome," he told the agricultural society in 1877, were "ignorance and laziness." Like other champions of the New South creed, he called for a transformation in Southern attitudes toward work and leisure. Instead of regarding manual labor as suitable only for the menial classes, white Southerners must come to "recognize the truth that all honest occupations are equally capable of giving satisfaction to those engaged in them." "Let us teach the rising generations," he admonished the graduating class at Davidson College in 1873, "that industry and frugality are better than riches. . . . If every one of us would, for five years, labor as earnestly as we generally did during the war, and live as economically, we should be, at the end of that period, far in advance of what we now are."[13]

Clingman's solutions to the agricultural problems of postwar North Carolina were too simplistic for the complexity of the situation. His complaints about the one-crop mentality of Tar Heel farmers ignored the fact that many were trapped in an insidious crop-lien system that gave them little choice but to raise cotton and other cash crops. Even those fortunate enough not to be caught up in that system were often impelled by poverty and mounting debt to devote an increasing amount of acreage to market crops. Clingman's notion that North Carolinians were lacking in "industry and frugality" would not have sat well with the majority of the state's farmers, who worked from dawn to dusk, had little hard cash, and were unfamiliar with the meaning of the word "leisure."[14]

In truth, the problems confronting the state's farmers during the 1870s had little to do with laziness or any other character flaw. Falling crop prices, inadequate banking and credit facilities, high transportation costs, and a tax system that weighed more heavily on landowners than on businessmen or corporations—together with the economic dislocation caused by war, emancipation, and the breakdown of the plantation system—were at the root of the troubles that plagued the farmers of the Old North State. Clingman's nostalgic invocation of the sacrifices made by North Carolinians during the Civil War may have been an appropriate motivational technique in a commencement address, but few who had actually experienced the privations of the war years would have regarded a return to that era as a practical solution to their problems.[15]

Clingman was on more solid ground in his strictures against that other "old wrong-doer," ignorance. He was well aware that outmoded and inefficient farming methods were only one part of the problem. Indeed, as he remarked in 1878, "the saddest result of the war . . . [is] the destruction of our system of [public] education. . . . Its full restoration, with added efficiency and advantages, is the most urgent call of the present hour." Clingman must have recognized that the task would be formidable. The collapse of the Confederacy and the subsequent repudiation of the state's war debt had destroyed the value of the bonds comprising the Literary Fund, which had supported the state's public school system during the prewar years. Although the Constitution of 1868 had mandated the establishment of a system of free schools for both races, the provision remained a dead letter because of the refusal of the parsimonious Conservative legislatures to levy the necessary taxes. Illiteracy in North Carolina actually increased during the 1870s. At the end of the decade, only one in three of the state's school-age children was attending school.[16]

Clingman's interest in education was not limited to the public schools. His advocacy of a more "efficient" system of instruction also reflected the views of Southern reformers who regarded the traditional classical curriculum of the academies and universities as elitist and impractical. Instead of preparing a small number of students for a career in politics or law, they argued, those institutions should focus on teaching a broader population the skills necessary to function as engineers, mechanics, skilled craftsmen, and enlightened farmers.[17]

In his 1873 commencement address at Davidson College, Clingman made an eloquent argument for a balanced curriculum that would include practical training as well as theoretical knowledge. Those who aspired "to become really great," he said, should train themselves to be "practically useful." In that regard, "our present systems of education are still faulty. . . . [They] direct the attention of the student too much to the ideas and opinions of men, rather than to things." In order for the new generation "to effect great and useful enterprises . . . their studies must take a wide range, they must investigate material things . . . by acquainting themselves with the forces of inanimate nature, as well as the impulses which move men."[18]

Five years later, Clingman elaborated on that theme in a lecture delivered at the Normal School of the University of North Carolina. Once again, he called for a balance between theory and practice. A man "who depended on the words of others might obtain a wide range of ideas, and yet know nothing thoroughly. . . . To become really wise, men must study both things and the opinions of others also." Clingman also cautioned his listeners against the dangers of overspecialization. The most important advances in human knowledge, he argued, had been made by generalists rather than specialists. "Had Lord [Francis] Bacon passed his life in a laboratory, it is not probable that he would have made the great impression on the philosophy of the age . . . that he actually did produce. His being a great lawyer and statesman gave expansion, clearness and force to his views of science."[19]

Certainly, few North Carolinians exemplified the Baconian ideal of the scientist-statesman more fully than Clingman himself. Introducing his speaker to the students at the University Normal School, Pres. Kemp P. Battle remarked that "the taste of a scholar and a man of letters and the taste of a lawyer are generally considered incompatible." However, "the one who addresses you to-day has become distinguished . . . in the field of scientific and general research as well as in law." Other North Carolinians also regarded Clingman as "a scientist of no mean attainments." The editor of the *Carolina Watchman* opined that Clingman "ought to be at the head of some grand scientific institution or some leading College. His varied learning and great abilities fit him for any position . . . in this or any other country."[20]

Unlike some of his admirers, Clingman never considered himself to be a professional scientist. With uncharacteristic modesty, he denied having any "more scientific knowledge than any gentleman who reads and reflects may possess." Still, Clingman lived in an age when the literature of science was not so vast, esoteric, or highly specialized as to be inaccessible to an interested layman, and his grasp of that literature was encyclopedic. One contemporary recalled a conversation between Clingman and a group of scientists in New York during which "he talked so learnedly on the subject that they were surprised to learn that he had been a politician all his life, and had not made a specialty of the subject he was discussing." At the same time, Clingman had the ability to explain complicated scientific ideas in a manner that the layman could easily comprehend and appreciate. Judge David Schenck recalled an hour-long discussion with Clingman on the subject of mineralogy, during which he "made what is to me an uninteresting subject, quite entertaining."[21]

Freed from the time-consuming tasks of an officeholder, Clingman had considerable opportunity during the 1870s and 1880s to indulge his numerous scientific interests. During those two decades he wrote and lectured about a variety of topics, including astronomy, anthropology, climatology, meteorology, and geology. Although none of his efforts resulted in a profound contribution to science, many of his fellow North Carolinians probably shared the opinion of one enthusiastic admirer, who characterized him as "one of the most accomplished scientists in the United States."[22]

Clingman's most ambitious foray into the sciences was his essay "The Great Meteor of 1860," which appeared in 1871 in *Appleton's Journal,* a popular magazine specializing in scientific news. On the evening of 2 August 1860 numerous residents of the southeastern states had witnessed "a bright glare of light . . . equal in size to the full moon" moving across the sky from the southeast. The object had remained in sight for about ten seconds before finally exploding in the northwest. After collecting the impressions of witnesses from the mountain counties and reading the detailed newspaper accounts from "points widely distant," Clingman calculated the meteor's angle of elevation at two observation points about six hundred miles apart. He then used a surveying technique called triangulation to estimate its height at the time it first came into view.[23]

Based as they were on the notoriously unreliable testimony of eyewitnesses, Clingman's measurements were necessarily rough approximations. Nonetheless, his calculations enabled him to arrive at an important conclusion regarding the height of the atmosphere. From their observations on the refraction of light, scientists had long believed that the blanket of air surrounding the earth could not be higher than forty-five miles. Clingman's deduction that the meteor had been more than one hundred miles above the earth when first viewed called that time-honored notion into question. Accepting "the common opinion . . . that meteors are rendered visible only by passing through the earth's atmosphere," he correctly concluded that the atmosphere "must extend much more than one hundred miles from the earth's surface." The astronomer Simon Newcomb subsequently remarked that Clingman's essay provided "the best evidence of the height of the earth's atmosphere that had [ever] been given."[24]

An essay published two years later in the *Asheville Western Expositor* further enhanced Clingman's scientific reputation. For many years, North Carolinians had been intrigued by a series of ancient excavations in Mitchell County. Most believed them to be the workings of Spaniards looking for silver or gold. Clingman, who had visited the area frequently in his search for minerals, correctly deduced that the excavators were actually searching for mica—a mineral of no interest to the Spaniards—and that they had used metallic tools unknown to the indigenous Native American tribes. He concluded that "a former race of Indians—possibly the 'Mound-builder,' who used copper tools—made these excavations." Subsequent archeological research has confirmed the accuracy of that supposition.[25]

On the other hand, numerous other hypotheses put forth by Clingman have not withstood the test of time. Reacting to a series of violent disturbances on Bald and Stone Mountains in McDowell County that began in February 1874 and continued into the late spring, he speculated that the shocks "were due to a low manifestation of volcanic action" produced by heated gases breaking through the strata immediately above them. The professional scientists who examined the locality quickly discounted the likelihood of volcanic action. The rumbling and shaking, they concluded, were local phenomena caused by the "simple settling of the mountain[s]," while the smoke seen rising from their summits could be attributed to "dust generated by the attrition of the rocks."[26]

Two essays published in the *New York Sun* in the early 1880s also advanced intriguing theories that have subsequently been discounted. Seeking an explanation for "the extraordinary warmth and drought in certain parts of the earth" during much of 1881, Clingman theorized that "the remarkable weather" may have resulted from the earth passing through the tail of a comet. The abnormal heat in the upper atmosphere caused by friction from the particles in the comet's tail might, he speculated, produce a substantial rise in the temperature of the air below and prevent the formation of rain-bearing clouds. Two years later, he cited "the remarkable red sunsets . . . exhibited during the last six months" as additional evidence that the earth may have recently passed through the tail of a comet. In fact, the red sunsets visible throughout the world during the mid-1880s were caused by ash from a volcanic eruption in Krakatau—and not by dust from a comet. Although the earth has passed through the tail of a comet on a number of occasions during the nineteenth and twentieth centuries, those occurrences have never had any discernible impact on the weather.[27]

The evanescent character of Clingman's specific contributions to science does not detract from his importance as one of the handful of devotees who kept the spirit of scientific inquiry alive in the South during the Reconstruction and Redeemer eras. Although "the dream of building a new South inspired calls for higher education in applied science," few proponents of the New South creed gave more than perfunctory attention to the role of science and technology in creating a modern industrial society. Clingman's enthusiasm for science, in contrast, was unbounded. Scientific inquiry, he remarked in 1878, had produced the telegraph, the telephone, the phonograph, and other technological marvels that "would have seemed the propositions of the wildest imagination" to intelligent men a century earlier. Indeed, "so great has been the progress of modern science, and so vast have been the benefits it has conferred on the world, that its genuine devotees can well afford to laugh at the . . . foibles of its weaker brethren."[28]

Nonetheless, Clingman was deeply disturbed by the direction in which science was moving in the late nineteenth century. The publication of Charles Darwin's *Origin of Species* in 1859 had inaugurated a profound revolution in scientific thinking that undermined the traditional harmony between science and religion. Most pre-Darwinian scientists believed that nature was the creation of an omnipotent and benevolent God and that the role of science was to "study . . . the laws by which God regulated the matter of the physical world and directed it for the benefit of his creations." Implicit in that conception was the notion of an orderly and purposeful universe that functioned according to a plan preordained by the Creator.[29]

Darwin's theory of evolution by natural selection completely exploded that time-honored view of God and nature. In place of the traditional idea of a benevolent universe working according to a divine plan, Darwin substituted the notion of a brutish struggle for existence whose outcome was determined by blind chance and random variation rather than cosmic design. Although Darwinism was not necessarily atheistic, it was perfectly consistent with atheism. "By making explicable in naturalistic terms what had hitherto been inexplicable except in religious terms, the theory of natural selection made it possible to dispense with God in organic nature." Moreover, two of the most prominent popularizers of Darwinism—Thomas Henry Huxley and John Tyndall—were avowed agnostics who ridiculed prayers and miracles and regarded Darwin's theory as "a final step on man's road to eliminating metaphysical and theological language from his descriptions of nature." [30]

By the 1870s most of the American scientific community had embraced the theory of natural selection. At the same time, Darwin's work aroused virulent hostility among many Protestant clergymen who "became convinced that Christianity could survive only by taking a firm and long-lasting stand against evolution in particular, and against all of science in general." Occupying the middle ground were certain Protestant laymen like Clingman, who opposed the theory of natural selection but who still adhered to the traditional belief that the findings of science, if properly interpreted, were consistent with the tenets of Christianity. [31]

In Clingman's opinion, the atheistic implications of Darwinism posed a threat not only to organized religion but also to the very foundation of human society. "The sense of obligation and accountability to a higher power," he remarked in 1878, "is just as essential to the existence of a well ordered human society, as the law of gravity is to the material world." Without the notion of an all-powerful Deity who rewarded good and punished evil, men would "more easily give way to temptation and disregard obligations that stood in the way of the gratification of their wishes." In Clingman's mind, the alarming spread of Nihilism in Russia, resulting from "the degraded condition of the Russian church," offered a compelling example of the social consequences "growing out of the dissolution of morals and . . . the complete absence of religious principles." [32]

Through his numerous lectures and publications, Clingman became a leader in the crusade against Darwinism during the 1870s. Initially, he was more concerned about combating the atheistic implications of Darwinism (or "positivism" as he called it) than he was in rebutting the notion of evolution. [33] Early in 1873 he prepared a lecture on science and Christianity, which he delivered in New York, Washington, Raleigh, Asheville, and other cities over the course of the next two years. Clingman did not mention Darwin by name nor did he allude specifically to the theory of natural selection. Instead, his lecture consisted of an able and lucid explication of the sophisticated "natural theology" that American scientists had developed during the first half of the nineteenth century. [34]

Natural theology sought to prove the existence and perfection of God from a careful observation of the facts of nature rather than from the testimony of the

Bible. As Clingman explained, the "character and purposes" of God could be "fairly and necessarily deduced from a thoroughly scientific examination of the material world." In his view, the evidence of nature "fairly interpreted" revealed a universe of intricate detail and vast dimensions infused with "intelligence and system." Such a magnificent and orderly creation presupposed the existence of an intelligent and all-powerful Creator. "Philosophic science indicates no termination to the material universe. And if it is to exist forever, why should not its great Creator be eternal? Is He less than the work of His hands? Have we any reason to suppose that His power to-day is not as great as it was in the dawn of creation?" [35]

Clingman also brought the insights of phrenology and Scottish common-sense philosophy to the defense of Christianity. Phrenologists believed that the human brain was composed of over thirty distinct "faculties." One of them was "spirituality"—the ability to "perceive and know things independent of the senses or intellect." The common-sense philosophy of Thomas Brown provided reassurance that such perceptions were true representations of a real objective order and not merely delusions. As Clingman explained, men of all cultures and all ages had believed in spiritual beings, and that in itself constituted sufficient proof of their existence. Just as "nature would not disappoint the eye . . . [by] fail[ing] to furnish light for its use," it would not have provided man with a spiritual faculty unless there were spiritual beings to perceive. [36]

For anxious Americans hoping to reconcile their faith in science with the traditional tenets of Christianity, Clingman's lecture provided gratifying assurance. According to one account, "it received the flattering comments of the leading journals" in New York City, as well as "the warm encomiums of the press" in the nation's capital. In Raleigh, the lecture was listened to with rapt attention by a distinguished audience that included Republican governor Curtis Brogden, the Democratic Speakers of both houses of the general assembly, other leading men in both political parties, and numerous religious and civic leaders. Shortly afterward, the *Raleigh News* published a testimonial signed by Brogden and twenty-two other dignitaries praising the "purity, precision and elegance of his language, [and] the vigor, clearness and striking arrangement of his thought." The signers urged Clingman to repeat his presentation in other communities, since "this lecture will do much good wherever delivered." [37]

In January 1875 Clingman confronted Darwin and his leading disciples head-on in an essay appropriately titled "Huxley, Darwin and Tyndall; Or, The Theory of Evolution." Once again, he grounded his opposition to Darwin's theories on scientific rather than religious grounds. "Physical science," he reminded his readers, ". . . rest[s] on observed facts, and not on mere suppositions. . . . How, then, can a hypothesis be maintained which not only has no fact to support it, but to which every known fact bearing on the case is directly hostile?" Displaying a thorough knowledge of recent developments in cell theory, embryology, and paleontology, Clingman considered the various arguments for natural selection and dismissed each as absurd and unscientific. "Science, in her sphere," he concluded, "gives us an amount of knowledge that cannot be overestimated, but it has utterly failed to explain the origin of life." [38]

Three years later, Clingman renewed his attack on Darwin, Huxley, and Tyndall in a lecture at the University Normal School entitled "Follies of the Positive Philosophers." This time he centered his fire on the positivists' notion that the orderly and well-regulated universe revealed by science had resulted from chance rather than design. Such a theory, he scoffed, was as absurd as the claim that an accurate edition of the works of Shakespeare might eventually be produced simply by throwing out hundreds of bushels of printer's type. Clingman did not reserve his barbs exclusively for the scientists. He was equally critical of those theologians who "attempt to decide the argument against the positive philosophers by the authority of the Bible alone." In his opinion, a thorough understanding of the theories and methods of science provided the most powerful weapon against the heresies of Darwinism. "By acquainting themselves better than they sometimes do with the arguments of the Scientists, the Theologians would often meet their objections more successfully." [39]

Clingman's lecture, which was widely circulated as a twenty-five-page pamphlet and as a two-page supplement to the *Raleigh Observer,* received an enthusiastic reception in his home state. The *Salisbury Carolina Watchman* characterized the address as "a handsome contribution to science." Richard B. Creecy of the *Elizabeth City Economist* praised "its originality, its learning, and the sensible manner in which he gives out his ideas." According to a correspondent of the *Raleigh News,* Clingman had convincingly substantiated "the common and generally adopted themes relating to the formation of the world" and had "literally dissected Darwin, Tyndall, and those who are dissatisfied because God made them." The one discordant note was sounded by the literary editor of the *Raleigh Observer,* who remarked that "the general opinion of the scientific and literary world will not sustain him in his assertion." [40]

The *Observer*'s editor was closest to the mark. By the late 1870s, Clingman's "scientific" critique of Darwinism was fast becoming an anachronism. While many fundamentalist Protestants continued to adhere to the biblical version of creation, the conviction that natural selection could be refuted on scientific grounds was giving way to efforts by scientists and liberal theologians to demonstrate that Darwin's theory of evolution was, in fact, compatible with the teachings of Christianity. Just as Clingman's views on evolution were out of step with prevailing scientific thinking, his other investigations into the mysteries of nature had negligible impact on the development of science. In retrospect, Clingman's reputation as a scientist clearly had more to do with his skills at self-promotion and his adeptness at playing to a sympathetic audience than with his specific contributions to the advancement of scientific knowledge. [41]

Although he was unable to stem the tide of Darwinism, Clingman enjoyed considerably more success in his efforts to promote the set of traditions that collectively came to be known as the "Lost Cause." In the years following the

surrender at Appomattox, Southerners struggled to come to grips with the meaning of the Civil War and to reassure themselves that defeat was not tantamount to
dishonor. In response to Northern accounts that portrayed the war as a "rebellion" brought about by an evil "slave power conspiracy," Southerners developed
an alternative interpretation that emphasized the justness of the Confederate
cause and the bravery of the Confederate soldier while romanticizing the plantation culture of the Old South. That viewpoint was propounded not only by die-
hard reactionaries who continued to resent all things Northern but also by "New
South advocates . . . [who] affirmed loyalty to the southern past even as they
offered a vision of a very different future."[42]

Clingman's own interpretation of the Civil War was developed in a series of
lectures and articles written during the mid-1870s. In his Davidson College
commencement address in 1873, he assured his young audience that "North Carolina was not as a State, nor were her sons responsible . . . for the great war." Nor,
he added, did its outcome prove "that we were, as a people, less worthy than our
opponents." Instead, "the war was the result of causes for which the people of neither the North nor the South, of this generation, were responsible. . . . Those who
fought on both sides . . . [bore] themselves like brave and honorable men in a cause
regarded as just." According to Clingman, Southerners had "no alternative" but
to fight. Had they quietly submitted to the violation of their constitutional rights,
the destruction of their social system, and the confiscation of one-third of their
property, they "would have been a mark for the finger of scorn." Through their
"manly resistance," Southerners had succeeded not only in retaining their self-
respect but also in winning "the confidence and esteem of all the enlightened
nations of the earth."[43]

Two years later, Clingman sounded a similar theme at a celebration in Charlotte commemorating the centennial of the Mecklenburg Declaration of Independence. After praising North Carolina's contributions to the Confederacy and
"the unshaken courage" of her troops "under the most formidable assaults," he
affirmed that Southerners "regarded the contest as finally settled" and were ready
to resume their place in the Union. "Our citizens are satisfied that they did right
in the late war; but having been beaten, they are willing now to join cordially with
those to whom they were once opposed, in all honest and fair efforts to maintain
sound constitutional government and the true principles of American liberty."[44]

The Charlotte address reached a wide audience through its publication in the
New York Tribune, Raleigh News, Asheville Citizen, and other presses. It was also
reprinted in *Our Living and Our Dead,* a periodical established by Stephen D.
Pool in July 1873 to present "a complete record of the heroic deeds of the sons of
North Carolina upon the battle fields of the Confederacy." In a prospectus announcing the new publication, Pool called upon the "prominent actors in the
war" to lend "the valuable aid of their pens . . . to do justice to the soldiers of my
native State." Clingman was among those who heeded the call. During its brief

existence, the journal published several pieces written by him, including his accounts of the "heroic deeds" of North Carolinians at Manassas, New Bern, and Cold Harbor.[45]

Pool's effort to collect and preserve documentary material relating to the wartime history of the state was part of a more general endeavor by postwar North Carolinians to "rescue the records of the past" so that future generations might be furnished "with the means to understand and correctly appreciate the deeds of those who have gone before." During the 1870s this renewed interest in the history of the Old North State was manifested in numerous attempts to establish a state historical society and to write an "authentic and truthful history of North Carolina" from the earliest settlements to the present.[46]

Clingman played an active role in several efforts to revive the historical society that David L. Swain had established during the 1840s and to regain custody of the substantial collection of books and manuscripts that had passed into the hands of his widow. Efforts were also made to persuade Clingman to write a comprehensive history of North Carolina. In April 1875 Theodore Kingsbury of the *Wilmington Star* publicly called on him to "do the State a great service" by preparing "an elaborate though not necessarily voluminous 'History of North Carolina from the early voyages to the adoption of the Constitution of 1835.'" Clingman, he reasoned, possessed "the general culture, the political insight and knowledge, the practical intellect, the rhetorical ability and the judicial spirit requisite for the great work." Moreover, his "national reputation" would guarantee the work a wide readership. The *Raleigh News, Charlotte Observer,* and several other presses quickly echoed Kingsbury's call. However, Clingman's own historical interests were focused in other directions, and he never took up the offer.[47]

Indeed, his most highly regarded literary effort had nothing to do with either state history or the Lost Cause. Ostensibly a disquisition on religious and popular orators, Clingman's commencement address at the University of the South on 5 August 1875 was actually a series of exquisitely crafted reminiscences of Henry Clay, Daniel Webster, John C. Calhoun, and other antebellum leaders whom he had personally known during his years in Congress. Clingman accompanied his praise of the "heroic self-denial and noble patriotism" of "the great triumvirate" with a lamentation that the quality of American morals and the caliber of its leaders had declined precipitously since the antebellum years. If the "men who are to control the destinies of the country" hoped to "resist the downward tendency," he warned, they "must select these high models for their imitation" and not "be carried away by mere buffoonery, and recitals from the jest book."[48]

Clingman's oration reached a nationwide audience through its publication in the *New York Tribune* and its circulation as a twelve-page pamphlet. Reaction was universally enthusiastic. Theodore Kingsbury characterized it as "an excellent literary performance, alike creditable to the distinguished speaker and to North Carolina." Former senator Matthew W. Carpenter of Wisconsin gushed that "after finishing it, I felt as I often have in reading some splendid passages in Shakespeare." Joseph P. Bradley of the U.S. Supreme Court described it as a "beautiful and instructive oration" and remarked that he had "greatly enjoyed and benefitted by its perusal." According to the *Raleigh News,* "the pre-eminent beauty and power of General Clingman's production . . . has done more to fix universally the fame of the author and the literary claims of North Carolina than any other production with which we are acquainted." [49]

Clingman's address stands as a tribute not only to his literary craftsmanship but also to his powers of self-promotion. That his oration managed to attract "more attention than usually attaches to productions regarded as ephemeral in their character" was not the result of happenstance. Carpenter and Bradley both admitted that they had no idea how Clingman's pamphlet had found its way to them. Its author undoubtedly knew better, since he almost certainly took pains to circulate his publication among the "distinguished men of other States" whom he deemed most likely to respond favorably to it. [50]

Clingman's nostalgic reminiscences of bygone days were not simply the musings of an old man who was more comfortable living in the past than the present. Though now in his mid-sixties, Clingman operated very much in the present, and self-advancement was always at the center of his calculations. If his fellow North Carolinians could be brought to accept his argument that the quality of leadership had declined since the days of the "great triumvirate," they might also conclude that the deficiency could be remedied by returning to the U.S. Senate a man who had rubbed shoulders with those antebellum giants. On the other hand, the interests of the Old North State would not be served by elevating to high office "demagogues [who] attempt to palm off . . . buffoonery for wit"—a not-so-veiled reference to his rival Zebulon B. Vance, whose homespun humor and jocular speaking style were legendary. [51]

The culmination of Clingman's efforts at self-promotion, as well as his desire to present an account of the antebellum era that would be "interesting and instructive to the young men of the country," was the publication in July 1877 of *Selections from the Speeches and Writings of Hon. Thomas L. Clingman.* Although the book included a selection of his postwar writings, it was primarily a compilation of his antebellum congressional speeches interspersed with "explanatory remarks . . . to indicate the condition of affairs which seemed to render such a speech necessary." That Clingman intended the work to serve as an important contribution to the political history of the United States and not merely as a collection of his own writings is clear from his introduction. Since "important results are often produced by events known only to a few actors concerned in them," he explained, only "those conversant with the transactions" could properly recount them. Thus, a firsthand narrative "presenting the prominent points at issue" would be "far more interesting than any subsequent history, prepared as they usually are." [52]

Clingman promised to include all the "important facts" and to strive for "the same impartiality that the Bible manifests," regardless of whether his observations "may be deemed advantageous or hurtful to the reputations of [the] individuals" involved. He largely succeeded in accomplishing that objective. Although his book does not lack opinions or a distinctive point of view, its dispassionate and nonpolemical tone contrasts sharply with the "brief-for-the-defense approach" that dominates most accounts written by the wartime generation. Even an unsympathetic Northern reviewer conceded that Clingman had "brought to the task a degree of candor and of moderation which few of his antagonists in Congress and in the field would be likely to exhibit under the same temptations." [53]

Absent in Clingman's work were the elaborate constitutional arguments that characterized most Southern interpretations of the coming of the Civil War. He included no discussion of state sovereignty, the compact theory, or the right of secession. Moreover, he explicitly rejected the notion that "the late civil war was mainly, if not entirely, owing to a difference of opinion . . . as to whether we should have a consolidated or a federal system of government. Nothing is further from the truth, and no view is more superficial than this." Indeed, said Clingman, "the only issue which directly and necessarily divided the sections" was slavery. "From the beginning of the government slavery was the subject of contention." [54]

According to Clingman, slavery was a highly emotional issue "appealing to feeling as much as to reason," which spawned extreme reactions in both sections. "Though in calmer times the wise govern countries, yet during periods of great excitement, the extreme men always lead the masses." Thus, it was not surprising that "those rather remarkable for violence of feeling than statesmanship controlled the immediate movements which precipitated the struggle on our side [and] . . . in the North." Another factor that militated against a peaceful resolution of the sectional crisis was that each side was "profoundly ignorant of the state of feeling" of the other. "Southern Democrats . . . were deluded with the idea that the people of the North, though they loved the Union . . . would not go to war for it." At the same time, Northerners mistakenly believed that Southerners "could not be induced to secede . . . [and] that even if the South were to attempt resistance, it would make such a feeble fight as to be very easily put down." "Delusions like these on both sides," he concluded, "led to war." [55]

Clingman's willingness to admit that the North was not exclusively to blame for the Civil War distinguishes his account from virtually every other history written by a Southerner of the wartime generation. Another distinguishing feature of his book is its harsh criticism of Jefferson Davis, whom most Southerners had come to revere as the principal symbol of the Lost Cause. Clingman faulted Davis for recklessly dividing the Democratic party in 1860 and for his "executive imbecility" during the war. Together with his "doughface" ally James Buchanan, he was assigned chief responsibility for bringing on the Civil War. Indeed, said Clingman, it was remarkable "that in the same century, and in the same country there should exist . . . two such men as James Buchanan and Jefferson Davis . . . so childishly feeble in action for good, and so absolutely destitute of all administrative ability. . . . So extraordinary was their conduct . . . that we are reminded of the declaration, 'the gods first make mad those that they intend shall be destroyed.'" [56]

Not surprisingly, the centerpiece of Clingman's book is its account of his own role in the events culminating in the Civil War. The image he presented of himself was far removed from the irresponsible "fire eater" portrayed by contemporary critics and subsequent historians. By his own self-estimation, he had been a wise and far-seeing statesman who had consistently sought to preserve the Union and, when that no longer seemed possible, to head off a bloody civil war. His visit to the North in 1849, where he "for the first time realized the extent of the anti-slavery movement," had dictated a change in tactics but not in goals. In Clingman's mind, his strident appeals to Southern Rights were designed not to prepare the people of the South for disunion but, on the contrary, to avert such a catastrophe. [57]

That his strong Southern Rights rhetoric might have further inflamed sectional passions and thereby played into the hands of the more extreme fire eaters was a possibility that Clingman did not consider. Nor did he have second thoughts about the propriety of his course during the crisis of 1860–61. He argued that if North Carolina at any time prior to the attack on Fort Sumter had summoned a convention and "[laid] down propositions in the nature of an ultimatum . . . instead of war there would have been an appeal to Congress, to ascertain if an accommodation could not be made; and, in the event of failure, it is not unlikely that the 'erring sisters' would have been allowed to 'go in peace.'" [58]

Fittingly for a champion of the New South, Clingman ended his account of the events leading to the Civil War with an impassioned plea for sectional reconciliation. "As the only issue which directly, and necessarily divided the sections, has been removed, we ought, on our side, to allow the recollections of the struggle to pass away." Nor, he added, should Southerners "judge the majority of the people of the North by the bad specimens we have seen among us." Indeed, "from my own personal knowledge of the citizens of the Northern States, I am able to say that I have met no better specimens of humanity any where, than I have known in New England, the great Middle States, and in the Northwest." He concluded by urging "every wise and good man, both in the North and in the South" to accept the outcome of the war and "cause all the painful memories of the past to be forgotten." [59]

The North Carolina presses responded enthusiastically to the publication of Clingman's book. The *Raleigh News* characterized it as "a really valuable contribution to the literature of the day . . . a mine of carefully prepared and accurate information on an extensive variety of political, scientific, geological, social and religious topics . . . entitled to a wide circulation." A correspondent of the *Raleigh Observer* agreed that the book was "a valuable contribution . . . [that] supplies a hiatus which has long been felt in our midst." The *Wilmington Star* predicted that "the volume . . . will be prized more and more as men recede from the time in which the distinguished author figured."[60]

The two features of the book most frequently singled out for praise were its vivid "pen-portraitures" of Clay, Webster, and the other leaders of the antebellum era and its depiction of the issues and events that culminated in the Civil War. As the *Raleigh News* put it, "the main interest and value of his book may be traced to his remarkable keenness of observation and accuracy of information, enabling him to present most vividly . . . [the] characteristics of the great men with whom he was thrown in contact during his political career, and to give new insight into the movements that led up to the great civil war."[61]

To Southerners wary of a new industrial order that seemed to place a higher value on the pursuit of profits than on honesty or integrity, Clingman's vivid recollections of "those 'better days' of the Republic, when there were 'giants on the earth'" had enormous nostalgic appeal. At the same time, Southerners anxious to vindicate their motives and actions during the "agitation that led to the great civil war" could find plenty of evidence in Clingman's book to support their viewpoint. Thus, the *Raleigh Observer* lauded the work as "an exceedingly valuable publication . . . showing, as it plainly does, that the South had truth and justice on its side."[62]

The publication of Clingman's book brought forth not only a series of highly laudatory reviews but also a chorus of praise for its author. A correspondent of the *Raleigh Observer* hailed him as "one of the most accomplished scientists in the United States . . . one of the deepest and most original thinkers in the whole country . . . [and] a statesman . . . [with] no superior. . . . It is but truth and justice to say that the people of North Carolina are proud of Gen. Clingman." Remarking that "he has but few equals in the South," Theodore Kingsbury of the *Wilmington Star* predicted that Clingman "will leave a name for general information, ability, courage, patriotism, varied mental gifts, and distinguished public services that will entitle him to be ranked among those North Carolinians who have reflected the most credit upon their mother during the nineteenth century."[63]

By 1877 Clingman's contributions to the fields of science, literature, and history were widely acknowledged in his home state, and his reputation as one of North Carolina's most distinguished sons seemed secure. A less-determined man might have been inclined to rest on his laurels and savor the plaudits of his admiring countrymen. But politics was too much in Clingman's blood for his ambition and ego to be satiated by his undeniable achievements as a scientist and savant. Indeed, even his lectures and writings on seemingly nonpolitical topics had an important political dimension since they were intended, in part, to enhance his popularity and build public support for a return to high office. Although Clingman had mended his fences with the North Carolina Democratic party and was now honored as an elder statesman, he would never be satisfied as long as someone else was sitting in his seat in the United States Senate.

16 *An Old Dog Who Has Lost His Teeth*

The mid-1870s witnessed the apogee of Clingman's postwar career as a "power in the state Democratic party." After playing a leading role in the Convention of 1875, which modified significant aspects of the Republican Constitution of 1868, he was a major participant in the campaign of 1876, which overthrew the last vestiges of Republican rule in the Old North State. As a campaigner and strategist, he now enjoyed the confidence and respect of the Democratic leadership. A less ambitious man might have been content simply to relish the accolades traditionally accorded an elder statesman. In Clingman's case, an insatiable appetite for office would place him on a collision course with other North Carolina Democrats that by the end of the decade would drive him to the fringes of the party.[1]

Although the issues of race and Reconstruction had dominated North Carolina politics during the early postwar years, financial issues became increasingly important, particularly after the Panic of 1873. Like the rest of the South, North Carolina suffered from an acute shortage of capital and the lack of an adequate circulating medium. Those problems had been exacerbated by the monetary policies of the postwar Republican party.

In 1865 Congress had destroyed the antebellum system of state-chartered banks by laying a prohibitive tax on their notes. On the other hand, few national banks were established in the South after the war because most of the $300 million in authorized notes had already been taken up by Northern banks. Legal-tender treasury notes, popularly known as "greenbacks," might have made up for the deficiency in bank notes, except that the Treasury Department had been systematically withdrawing them from circulation in anticipation of a return to the gold standard. Efforts on the part of Southerners and westerners to expand the supply of bank notes and to distribute them more equitably among the sections met with only limited success in the Republican-controlled Congress.[2]

By the mid-1870s Clingman had emerged as one of the South's most vocal critics of Republican monetary policy. His interest in banking and finance was long-standing. In 1849 he had proposed a modification in the banking system to allow local banks to exchange government bonds for U.S. treasury notes that would circulate and be receivable for public debts. The basic features of that plan were later incorporated into the National Banking Act of 1863, although Clingman had envisioned his own scheme as an "auxiliary to the existing system" of state banks rather than as a substitute for them. Indeed, the restriction of banking privileges to "only a few favored individuals . . . the so-called National Banks" lay at the core of his persistent complaints against the "Banking monopoly."[3]

The economic recovery of the late 1860s and early 1870s, together with the modest expansion of banking capital provided by the Currency Act of 1870, had temporarily muted demands for monetary reform. The financial calm came to an abrupt end with the banking panic of September 1873, which threw the nation into one of the longest and severest depressions in its history. During a visit to New York City in the fall of 1873, Clingman had an opportunity to witness firsthand the stagnation in manufacturing and trade that followed in the wake of the panic. His conversations with "a gentleman connected with one of the great dailies of that city" prompted him to write an essay on the causes of the financial crisis.[4]

Although Clingman saw the root of the problem in the enormous destruction of capital during the Civil War, he argued that the hardships had been "immensely aggravated by the action of the [federal] government in withholding a proper supply of currency, and by its aiding monopolies for the benefit of the wealthy, and consequently oppressing the working classes." He also had harsh words for the "gamblers" on Wall Street, who had stockpiled a substantial portion of bank notes for speculative purposes so that "nearly one-fourth of all the money of the country is . . . completely lost for all legitimate business purposes." He was critical as well of the national banks, which were "making enormous profits, and contributing largely to the impoverishment of the people" through their exorbitant rates of interest.[5]

As remedies for the financial distress, Clingman advocated the elimination of the monopoly that national banks enjoyed over note issues, together with a "more liberal" system of "metallic and paper currency provided by the government" similar to the one he had proposed in 1849. He ended the essay with a prediction that "the present panic will greatly strengthen the popular cause," and he expressed optimism that "a combined effort on the part of the people will insure reform . . . [despite] the advantages which the monopolies possess." [6]

Clingman's prognostication that the "popular cause" would benefit from the Panic of 1873 proved on the mark. During the Forty-Third Congress the soft-money forces managed to push through an "inflation bill" providing for a significant expansion of both bank notes and greenbacks. Pres. Ulysses S. Grant's veto of that popular measure gave the Democrats a powerful weapon to use against their opponents in the congressional campaign of 1874, and the party won a majority in the House of Representatives for the first time since the Civil War. Convinced that the tide of public opinion had turned in their favor, Democratic leaders confidently predicted victory in the 1876 presidential election. According to Clingman, only a "great blunder" on the part of the Democrats could block their path to the White House. [7]

In September 1875, while attending the constitutional convention in Raleigh, Clingman sounded some of the themes of the upcoming campaign in an interview with a reporter from the *New York Herald*. Repeating many of the points made in his unpublished essay of 1873, he attributed the financial crisis to the rapid contraction in the money supply initiated by the successive Republican administrations after the war. In Clingman's mind, the ringleaders in the plot to constrict the currency were the bankers, bondholders, and other creditors who had placed their own financial interests above the interests of the people. "The greediness of the money power has thus paralyzed the industry of the country." [8]

Although Clingman's barbs were aimed primarily at the Republicans, he did not attempt to conceal his disappointment at the failure of the Democratic leadership in Congress to exploit popular discontent to full advantage. The Republican losses in the midterm elections would have been even more substantial, he said, if his own party had not been "deprived . . . of the counsel of most of those who should have been [acting as] their leaders." Indeed, "two or three bold speeches in the Senate, setting forth the truth of the causes from which the country was suffering, would have greatly increased the majorities against the administration party." By implication, North Carolina's two U.S. senators, Matt W. Ransom and Augustus S. Merrimon, had failed to do their duty. The Republicans were quick to pick up on Clingman's implied criticism. With tongue in cheek, the editor of the *Raleigh Constitution* wondered aloud about the identity of "the recreants, who lacked 'sagacity, disinterestedness and manliness'" and rhetorically asked, "who, then, and where were 'those who should have been their leaders'?" [9]

The Democratic presses ignored Clingman's critical comments about their party and, instead, praised his "lucid, illustrative and unanswerable arguments" about the currency issue. The *Raleigh News* predicted that his "clear and forcible" exposition would "furnish the text for arguments which are to be used at the South . . . in the approaching Presidential campaign." The interview also attracted the attention of Northerners like Henry C. Carey, the nation's leading soft-money philosopher, and William D. ("Pig Iron") Kelley, "the chief mouth-piece for the inflationists" in Congress. In a testimonial published in the *Raleigh News*, Kelley praised Clingman's ability "to express himself so clearly" on ab-struse financial issues that he could be understood by common laborers in upstate New York as well as by erudite social scientists like Carey.[10]

As the editor of the *News* had foreseen, the "money question" played a sig-nificant role in the campaign of 1876. On 14 June "an immense and enthusiastic body of Democrats" assembled in Metropolitan Hall in Raleigh to nominate their state ticket. As chairman of the Platform and Resolutions Committee, Clingman was responsible for developing the program for the upcoming campaign. The task of coming up with a set of proposals on which all party members could unite was not an easy one. The Democratic party in postwar North Carolina was a hetero-geneous coalition of easterners and westerners, conservatives and progressives, prewar Democrats and former Whigs, who were united only by their hatred of all things Republican. Not surprisingly, the platform submitted by the committee and subsequently adopted by the convention was, in Clingman's words, "made like an old indian rubber shoe to fit everybody."[11]

Apart from affirming support for the constitutional amendments proposed by the Convention of 1875 and promising "judicious legislative aid" to complete the Western North Carolina Railroad, the platform ignored state issues and focused instead on the "unwise and mischievous financial policy" of the Grant adminis-tration. Absent from the platform crafted by Clingman was any specific mention of race or national Reconstruction policy. Those issues had not brought victory to the Democrats in 1868 or 1872. Now the party was admonishing the voters "to ignore all dead issues, to disregard the prejudices engendered by past events, and to unite with us in the effort to restore constitutional, honest, economical and pure administration of the government."[12]

The convention selected Clingman to be one of the four at-large delegates to represent the state at the Democratic National Convention in St. Louis. Accord-ing to the *New York Herald*, the veteran legislator's "distinguished political record and innate force of character [make] him the leader of the delegation." Like the other delegates from the Old North State, Clingman expressed his de-termination to go to St. Louis "entirely unpledged and uncommitted." Despite his predilection for soft money, he was willing to sacrifice his "wishes and . . . in-terests in this respect if it will aid us to obtain a change of government." He viewed financial considerations as secondary to the paramount objective of defeating the Republicans, and he was ready to tender his support to the presidential candidate with the best chance of winning. Increasingly, that candidate appeared to be Gov. Samuel J. Tilden of New York. Although some North Carolinians dismissed the hard-money New Yorker as "a representative of Wall Street and the bondholders," others emphasized the importance of the Empire State to the Democrats and recognized that Tilden was the nominee best able to deliver its electoral votes.[13]

When the balloting for presidential candidates began on 27 June 1876, nine of the twenty delegates from the Old North State voted for Tilden, who fell just eighty-eight votes short of the requisite two-thirds majority. Clingman, along with four other North Carolinians, cast his ballot for Winfield Scott Hancock. On the second ballot, the eleven Tar Heels voting in the minority, together with 120 other Democrats, switched their votes to Tilden to give him the nomination. As many pundits had predicted, the Southerners had ultimately "subordinate[d] the currency . . . issue to the prime object of winning."[14]

Clingman campaigned extensively in the mountain counties on behalf of the Democratic ticket. His most notable efforts were in Henderson and Polk counties, Republican strongholds that had given large majorities to Grant in 1872. Speaking to a crowd at Hendersonville on 12 September, he admonished his Republican listeners to "discard all past prejudices" and ignore those who "seek to divert your minds from the true issue . . . by referring to past events, that in fact, have no connection with the present." Consistency, he said, was not always a virtue in politics. "The present Republican leaders . . . say you voted with us formerly, and that you must do it again, or be inconsistent. You may reply to them that you formerly voted with them for reconstruction, perhaps, but that there is a very different issue now to be decided, and that is whether the country is to be ruined by their oppression and robberies."[15]

Clingman was optimistic about the outcome of the presidential contest. Early in the campaign he had told the *New York Tribune* that Tilden would carry the Old North State by a majority of ten to fifteen thousand votes. A few days before the election, he declared that "everything beyond the mountains [is] bright, and growing brighter every day." His enthusiasm, however, was limited to the national ticket. While praising Tilden as a modern Hercules who would sweep down upon the nation's capital and clean out the Augean stables of corruption, he ignored his party's gubernatorial standard-bearer, Zebulon B. Vance, and "confined himself exclusively to National politics." Two weeks before the election, the *New York Herald* reported that Clingman had "expressed his belief . . . that Vance would be defeated." Although he subsequently disavowed that report, his indifference toward Vance was undeniable.[16]

The outcome of the election confirmed the optimistic expectations of the Democrats. Under the headline "A Glorious Victory," the *Raleigh News* proclaimed that "Vance is our next Governor and Tilden our next President. . . . North

Carolina is redeemed. The nation is saved." Clingman's prediction of a fifteen-thousand vote majority for Tilden proved close to the mark. The Democratic presidential candidate received 125,427 votes in North Carolina, compared to 108,484 for Rutherford B. Hayes, his Republican opponent. Vance, who had waged his campaign for governor largely on the "old issues" of race and Reconstruction, fared less well. Although he defeated Republican Thomas Settle by a margin of more than 12,600 votes, he received 2,000 fewer votes than Tilden. Indeed, all the other candidates on the Democratic state ticket received majorities substantially surpassing Vance's.[17]

The Democratic celebration in the presidential contest proved premature, as Republican returning boards in Florida, South Carolina, and Louisiana threw out the Democratic majorities and awarded those states to Hayes. The Democrats naturally cried foul, charging that the Republican boards had acted fraudulently out of partisan motives. The responsibility for counting the electoral votes lay in the hands of the U.S. Congress. With the Democrats in control of the House of Representatives and the Republicans having a majority in the Senate, a constitutional crisis loomed as the North Carolina General Assembly convened in late November.[18]

The Democratic legislators who assembled in Raleigh were also confronted with the more mundane problem of electing a U.S. senator. It was no secret that Vance was anxious for the seat that had eluded him in 1870 and 1872, while Matt Ransom, the Democratic incumbent, had canvassed the state diligently to promote his own reelection. Other aspirants such as former Confederate senator George Davis and former congressman James M. Leach also had their eyes on the seat. Clingman undoubtedly hoped that a contest between Vance and Ransom might result in a deadlock and give him a chance at the prize. Thus, he made it a point to be in Raleigh when the Democratic caucus met on 22 November. By that time, however, the two leading contenders had reached an understanding. Vance agreed not to contest Ransom's seat in return for the latter's support against Merrimon in 1878.[19]

With Vance no longer a contender, all opposition to Ransom evaporated, and the Democratic incumbent was renominated by acclamation. The doors to the caucus room were then thrown open to the public. After Ransom had formally accepted the nomination, Clingman was called upon to speak. The veteran Democrat addressed the caucus for about half an hour, focusing his remarks on the electoral crisis in Washington. He urged the people of the South to "maintain quiet and let matters take their own course." He also expressed confidence that "the people of the North would do their duty in the great crisis, and that on the 4th of next March Samuel J. Tilden would be inaugurated President of the United States."[20]

Within a few months, Clingman would become severely disillusioned by the failure of Tilden and the other Northern Democrats to "do their duty." By nature cautious and conservative, Tilden lacked "the qualities of a rough-and-ready politician or a fighting man." Remaining quiet in his Gramercy Park mansion throughout the crisis, he rejected suggestions that he "carry his case to the people" by issuing a call for mass demonstrations. With tacit approval from Tilden, congressional Democrats agreed to the creation of a fifteen-member electoral commission, which, contrary to their expectations, awarded all the disputed votes to Hayes.[21]

Like many other Southerners, Clingman laid the blame for the debacle on the timidity of Tilden and his advisers. A year after the crisis had ended, he told the *New York World* that "the presidency was needlessly sacrificed . . . at Mr. Tilden's sanction." The electoral commission, in his opinion, was an "experiment . . . that need not and should never have been resorted to." Instead, Tilden "should have encouraged popular demonstrations" to pressure Congress into acquiescing in "the wish of the people as . . . expressed at the ballot box." According to Clingman, the Democratic candidate "could have been seated without trouble . . . had he shown the firmness and, I might say, manhood that was required of him."[22]

Not surprisingly, the crisis led to a number of proposals to reform the electoral college. One of the most novel came from Clingman himself. In February 1877 he published an "open letter" to Congress, together with the draft of a proposed constitutional amendment, in the *Washington Union*. As a means of preventing "the evils resulting from the present mode of choosing a President," he suggested that the voters of each district should select an elector of not less than fifty years of age, who would hold his office for life. Each December, the electors would meet to choose a president, who would serve for one year and would be ineligible to succeed himself. The terms of all executive officers would be fixed for periods of four years or longer, and the patronage power of the president would be restricted to filling any vacancies that might occur during his term. In Clingman's opinion, a presidency of limited tenure and patronage would eliminate the most glaring abuses of partisanship, since "there would be no adequate inducement for a number of partisans to co-operate to influence the choice of electors."[23]

Clingman's letter met with a tepid response among the North Carolina presses, most of whom gave it only a perfunctory notice. The most positive assessment came from the *Raleigh News*. Without endorsing the specifics of his proposal, the editor characterized it as a "remarkable document" and opined that "nothing more entirely original has emanated from the brain of an American statesman." The letter also attracted some attention in the North. With tongue in cheek, the *New York Tribune* described it as "more fearfully and wonderfully made than its author," while dryly adding that "Gen. Clingman's idea may not bear fruit at once." Indeed, his plan met with no more success than the numerous other proposals made at the time to reform the nation's system of choosing a president.[24]

The Democratic legislators who assembled in Raleigh for the session of 1876–77 had more immediate concerns than reforming the electoral college. For many years, Democrats in eastern counties with black majorities had expressed dissat-isfaction with the system of popularly elected commissioners and justices of the peace, which gave the Republicans control of local government in those counties. Responding to those concerns, the Convention of 1875 had given the general assembly the power to alter the system of county government. Easterners were now demanding changes that would end "the dominancy of ignorant and venal negroes, and of no less ignorant and venal whites." Westerners were considerably less enthusiastic about the proposed changes. The elimination of the undemocratic system of county government had been a principal demand of western reformers during the antebellum era, and many western Democrats had promised during the recent legislative campaign "not to interfere radically with the popular franchise in the townships."[25]

During the early weeks of the legislative session, the issue of county government was widely debated in the North Carolina presses and among ad hoc committees established to present proposals to the general assembly. In response to a solicitation in the *Raleigh News* for communications on "this all important topic," Clingman submitted a letter outlining his own views on county government. He opposed the idea of special legislation that would apply only to the black counties in the east. Such a blatantly discriminatory measure would, he said, "subject us to criticism and denunciation by those opposed to us in the North." Instead, he proposed "to return . . . to our old system and have the Justices of the Peace all appointed by the Legislature." He suggested, however, that the appointment be limited to a fixed term instead of reinstating the antebellum practice of "good behavior or life."[26]

Clingman dismissed the notion that the residents of the west would vehemently object to a change in the system of local government. With "proper explanations," the people would be "wise enough and public spirited enough to be satisfied with what is the best system that can be presented." In an accompanying editorial, the *Raleigh News* reminded its readers of Clingman's "long experience in affairs of State" and his role as "one of the most prominent and influential members of the Constitutional Convention." For that reason, it argued, his views deserved the "highest consideration."[27]

The county government bill that passed the general assembly in February 1877 was identical to the plan that Clingman had proposed a month earlier. By placing the machinery of local government in the hands of the Democratic-controlled legislature, the bill cemented the hold of that party on the politics of North Carolina and completed the Old North State's "redemption" from Republican rule. Contrary to Clingman's prediction, however, the decision to return to an undemocratic system of county government would sow seeds of discontent in the west that would trouble the Democrats for the next two decades.

While the Democrats in the general assembly were deliberating the issue of county government during the winter of 1877, Clingman was in Washington attempting to steer the Hayes administration in a more liberal direction in its policy toward the South. Shortly after the inauguration, he called on former secretary of state Hamilton Fish, "an old friend, and the only member of Grant's cabinet that I kept any social acquaintance with." Fish asked him how the Democrats would react to the appointment of one or two Southerners to Hayes's cabinet. Clingman responded that "such persons would merely be regarded as having been bought up." He suggested that, instead, Hayes could strengthen his position in the South by removing "the corrupt officials, and put[ting] in honest and efficient men." [28]

Fish mentioned the conversation to Joseph H. Defrees of Indiana, "an old congressional acquaintance and personal friend" of Clingman. Defrees approached the North Carolinian a few days later and proposed that he should call on the president "and talk freely with him, for he is disposed to act liberally." As Clingman later recalled, he replied that "it was not necessary for me to see him, but that if he would give us a good set of officials, and issue an order similar to [William Henry] Harrison's [of 1841] forbidding them to interfere in the elections, he would give our people all the satisfaction that could be expected." Defrees subsequently attempted to locate a copy of Harrison's executive order and, failing to do so, he returned to his friend for assistance. Together they went to the Library of Congress, where Clingman found a copy in the files of the *National Intelligencer.*

On 22 June 1877 Hayes issued an order prohibiting federal officials from engaging in partisan activity. With characteristic immodesty, Clingman claimed credit for the outcome. That claim may not have been entirely unfounded. As several newspapers pointed out, Hayes's order did, in fact, bear a remarkable resemblance to the one issued by Secretary of State Daniel Webster at the beginning of Harrison's administration. When Clingman paid a call on the president in the White House on 16 July, he applauded Hayes for his efforts on behalf of civil service reform and mentioned the executive order issued thirty-six years earlier. Looking the North Carolinian straight in the eye, Hayes responded, "you must know that I had that order before me when I issued mine." [29]

Like many other Southerners, Clingman quickly became reconciled to the new administration, particularly after its withdrawal of the remaining federal troops from the South. In an interview with the *New York Star* early in 1878, he remarked that "the course of Mr. Hayes has been gratifying to the best elements of the Democracy in the South," and he urged the Democrats in Congress to "stand by the President and give him sympathy and practical encouragement." On the other hand, Clingman had nothing but scorn for Roscoe Conkling and the other Republicans in the "stalwart" faction, who rejected Hayes's policy of "national pacification" in favor of "the bloody-shirt school of politics." "The country had long been distracted by this class of politicians," he groused. ". . . The war was supposed to have ended in 1865." [30]

The honeymoon between Hayes and the Southern Democrats came to an abrupt end in the spring of 1878 when several Florida Republicans, furious with the president for abandoning them to the Democrats, issued sensational "confessions" admitting that they had stolen the election in 1876 and accusing Hayes of complicity in the fraud. The Democrats immediately called for a congressional investigation. At the suggestion of Montgomery Blair, Congressman William Kimmel of Maryland introduced a bill to initiate proceedings in the U.S. Supreme Court to determine the validity of Hayes's title to the presidency.[31]

Clingman agreed that the confessions had proven beyond doubt that "the electoral vote of Florida was stolen," but he strongly disapproved of the plan to bring the issue to the Supreme Court. "It would be dangerous, very dangerous," he said, to give the court jurisdiction over the matter. "That's a political question. It has been decided as such. That decision is irrevocable and irreversible." On the other hand, he supported a congressional investigation as a means of bringing the facts to public attention. Comparing the embattled president to a "man tried for the murder of his wife and acquitted on suborned testimony," he opined that "you can't try him over, but his infamy should be perpetuated as long as life lasts."[32]

At the same time that the Florida revelations were raising the political temperature in the nation's capital, North Carolina Democrats were finding themselves embroiled in a bitter contest for the U.S. Senate. Supporters of Governor Vance had never forgiven Augustus S. Merrimon for defying the Democratic caucus and accepting Republican votes in 1872. As the legislative elections of 1878 approached, they began making efforts in township meetings and county conventions to require their local nominees to pledge themselves to support Vance in the Democratic caucus. On 1 June 1878 Merrimon announced his own candidacy in a public letter that accused Vance of trying to "pack the legislature" through "new and untried methods of electioneering."[33]

Some Democrats expressed dismay at the internecine warfare between Vance and Merrimon, regarding it as "unfortunate for the party and discreditable to their friends." William J. Yates of the *Charlotte Democrat* raised the possibility of setting aside the two main contenders and nominating a third candidate. "There are plenty of men in the State," he said, "who have worked longer and harder for the Democratic party and Democratic principles than either Vance or Merrimon." Although Yates did not specifically mention his name, Clingman certainly harbored hopes that he might emerge from a protracted contest for the senatorship as the main beneficiary. Refraining from making any direct attacks against Merrimon, he centered his fire on Vance's supporters and condemned the practice of pledging as a violation of long-standing party tradition. That strategy, as one statehouse watcher noted, was based on the supposition that "if Merrimon sees no chance of being elected he may induce his friends to support Clingman."[34]

Clingman formally entered the fray on 20 June 1878 with an interview published in the *Raleigh Observer*. The bulk of the interview consisted of an attack on pledging. "It has heretofore been the custom in this State," he said, "for the people to choose the best members of the Legislature that they could select, and then allow them like an impartial jury to choose such gentlemen as they regarded as most able to represent the State in the Senate of the United States." That time-honored system, he remarked, had produced such notable leaders as Willie P. Mangum, William A. Graham, George E. Badger, and Thomas Bragg. Pledging, on the other hand, would "give an advantage to the least worthy aspirants," because "a high toned, honorable man would scorn to resort to such stratagems to secure his elevation."[35]

After noting that he personally had "never sought to have any one pledged to me before his election," Clingman ended the interview with an appeal to his fellow Democrats to reject any legislative candidate who so declared himself. "If a man pledged should be opposed by a respectable candidate who was not pledged, I should give the preference to the latter upon the same principle that I would reject a man as a Juror who had formed and expressed an opinion." Since Merrimon was discouraging his own supporters from making formal pledges, Clingman's strictures were, in effect, directed against the legislative aspirants pledged to Vance.

Officially, Clingman remained a noncandidate. Although he did not rule out his availability should the Democrats find themselves deadlocked between the two main contenders, for the time being he and Merrimon were allies in their mutual desire to prevent Vance from receiving the party's nomination. Thus, when a large crowd of Merrimon's supporters assembled on 21 June 1878 to greet him upon his return to North Carolina, Clingman made it a point to be on hand. After the senator declined to address the gathering, pleading exhaustion and lack of sleep, Clingman was only too happy to step into the breach, "rehearsing the points in his late interview with the 'Observer' in regard to pledging candidates."[36]

Vance's supporters were not pleased with Clingman's criticism of pledging. One irate partisan privately fumed to the governor that the *Raleigh Observer* had no business "interviewing *old Clingman* and parading his opinion before the public . . . when every school boy in the state knows him to be an enemy of yours." The *Charlotte Observer* agreed that Clingman could not be an impartial commentator since he was himself a "tied-out horse for the Senate." The *Raleigh News* characterized his comparison of the party caucus to a jury as "a ridiculous proposition . . . [that] a plain practical mind cannot understand, however apparent may be the analogy to a metaphysical mind like that of the scientific, philosophic and diplomatic statesman, ex-Senator Clingman."[37]

By far the most devastating rejoinder came in the form of another "interview" published in the *Raleigh News*. Ostensibly a transcript of a telephone conversation between Clingman and the "young gentleman who does the telephoning for this establishment," the piece was actually a clever parody of his interview with the *Observer*. Although its authorship was never conclusively established,

Clingman subsequently claimed that Vance himself had written it. Neither the governor nor the *News* ever specifically denied that claim, and the "interview" does bear unmistakable signs of Vance's legendary wit. Vance, who had been a candidate for the House of Commons in 1854, undoubtedly remembered Clingman's strenuous efforts that year to elect Southern Rights Whigs pledged to support him for the U.S. Senate. Under the circumstances, the former senator's current strictures against pledging must have struck him as more than a bit hypocritical and self-serving.[38]

The Clingman depicted in the telephone interview is an unrepentant old political sinner who sets about educating his young and somewhat naive interrogator in the "ways of politicians." The reporter begins by asking him a series of questions about pledging. "You say, General, that the constitution gives the election of United States Senator to the Legislature alone. . . . Do you mean by that . . . that the people have no right to instruct their representatives at all?" "That is the logical deduction from my statement, of course," acknowledges Clingman, "but it would not do to put it that way exactly; people might not like it."

"Did you not," the reporter continues, "in 1852, 1854, and along there, try to have every member of the Legislature in the mountain district pledged to vote for you for Senator?" "Well," concedes Clingman, "there was something of that kind took place, but that was twenty odd years ago. And besides, circumstances alter cases. . . . I remember very well that in 1854 my friends tried to make Vance . . . pledge himself on the stump, and they succeeded, but he pledged himself to vote against me, and I have never liked him since."

The reporter then inquires why Clingman is "so bitter against Vance and so strong for Merrimon" in the current contest for the senatorship. "Young man," he retorts, "you are wide of the mark. . . . *I ain't for Merrimon* any more than for Vance. Can't you see who I am for? Here's what I am after: When there is a bone to be had, and two stout, able-bodied young dogs are growling over it, and an old dog who has lost his teeth and is a little mangy stands no earthly chance for that bone unless he can get the others to fighting over it—don't you see?"

"I think I do," says the reporter. "You are, then, a candidate yourself?" "Well, I'll tell you how it is," explains Clingman. "I was most anxious for the Senate, or most anything else, just after the war, but my judgment failed me in trying to coquet with Holden and his crowd. And by writing that infernal letter to dissolve the Conservative party by arousing the prejudices of the old Whigs and Democrats against each other, I fell flat between two stools. Since that time I have been mostly like Mark Twain's jack-ass ra[b]bit, sitting about, meditating on my sins; but now that the State is decidedly Democratic, I think I know where I am. If the people would stop declaring for Vance, and I could get him and Merrimon both out of the way . . . why I believe I wouldn't object to trying my hand at the Senatorship for the good of my country."

The *Raleigh News* claimed that its "interview" was meant to be nothing more than a "really good joke." Clingman, however, was not amused at seeing his entire career exposed to ridicule, particularly since some of the barbs had hit too close to the truth. He might have done well simply to have ignored the piece. Instead, he shot back with a splenetic communication to the *Raleigh Observer* that was entirely lacking in the wit that had made Vance's production so effective. Oblivious to the veneration with which many North Carolinians regarded their wartime chief executive, Clingman compounded his miscalculation by launching into an ill-conceived attack on Vance's war record. He accused him of abandoning his regiment in 1862 and running for governor "in order that he might 'get out of the infernal war.'" He then contrasted his adversary's pusillanimous behavior with his own decision to remain in the military, and he claimed credit for preventing Vance and his friends from betraying the Confederacy and joining Holden's peace movement in 1864.[39]

In addition to arraigning Vance for cowardice and disloyalty, Clingman portrayed him as an inveterate office seeker more concerned about his own political advancement than the good of the state. Since the end of the war, Vance had sought one public office after another, "and now he is getting up excitement over the whole State to enable him to get into the Senate." According to Clingman, the Democratic party had already bestowed upon him "more [offices] than any man . . . in the State in proportion to what he was worth or had ever done for the public. Whether this is due to his good luck or his excessive greediness and industrious electioneering I shall not argue." Clingman, who had made his first run for elective office when Vance was only five years old, demonstrated no awareness of the irony in his remarks—that his indictment of his opponent as a political opportunist applied with equal force to himself.[40]

Not surprisingly, the ill-tempered tone of Clingman's communication triggered an immediate response from Vance's partisans. The day after his letter was published, the *Raleigh News* filled an entire page with anti-Clingman editorials, and its onslaught continued for several days afterward. "The people will be surprised to learn," it sneeringly observed, ". . . how absolutely weak, trifling, false, of no account and of bad record, that once popular man, Zeb Vance, really is. It will be news to the old soldiers of his command that Colonel Vance was a skulker out of the war. . . . Their blind infatuation throughout the war, and that of the people since, can only be accounted for by reason of the fact that General Clingman has only lately assumed the role of a personal and political pamphleteer . . . in the preliminary contest for United States Senatorship."[41]

In a more serious vein, Vance's supporters complained about the detrimental impact that Clingman's attacks were having on party unity. His "deliberate assaults upon Governor Vance . . . should not fail to meet with rebuke at the hands of every friend of the Democratic party," said the *Raleigh News,* "for these publications, though aimed at one man, are in the interest of Democratic division and disorganization." The *Asheville Citizen* reported that Clingman's letter had "been struck off in circular form" and was now "being distributed broadcast throughout this section by Independent and radical candidates." Its editor wondered whether he would dare to declare himself "a candidate before the democratic caucus . . . after thus teaching insubordination?"[42]

In truth, however, Clingman's hopes for returning to the Senate rested not on the Democratic caucus but on the same "Independent and radical candidates" whom the *Citizen* was denouncing. It was no secret that the *Asheville Pioneer*, the organ of the Republican party in the mountain district, had "suddenly taken a liking to Clingman" and was predicting that "the republicans [in the general assembly] will go for him." Moreover, the efforts in the Democratic county conventions to pledge the legislative candidates to Vance had produced "a spate of independent candidates" running against the party's regular nominees. Although most of these independents were Merrimon supporters, they could be expected to vote for Clingman over Vance should Republican opposition to Merrimon narrow the choice of senator to those two.[43]

The newspaper war between Clingman and his detractors continued until the end of the campaign. In his earlier letter to the *Raleigh Observer*, Clingman had twitted Vance for his unspectacular showing in the governor's election, claiming that he had been swept "along in the general current" into office. The *Raleigh News* responded by reminding its readers of Clingman's near defeat in the convention election of 1875. According to the *News*, he had been "pulled through" that year only on account of "the united effort of the Buncombe Democracy."[44]

That gibe prompted Clingman to fire back with a blistering attack on the Buncombe County Democratic organization. He accused Vance's cousin Allen Turner Davidson of supplying material to the Republicans during the convention campaign, and he charged that his son Theodore Davidson had discouraged local Democratic activists from making an "exertion" on his behalf. For good measure, he once again launched into Vance's war record in an effort to prove that the governor had secretly supported the peace movement in 1864 and would have "carr[ied] his strength over to the Holden side" had it not been for Clingman's own unremitting efforts to get him to "fall into the strong Confederate current of the State."[45]

Those renewed allegations of disloyalty prompted a stern rebuke from Vance's supporters. "Is there any one in North Carolina who believes these statements?" queried the *Raleigh News*. "Of course there is not, and a man simply renders himself ridiculous who utters them." The *Pee Dee Herald* condemned the "senile peevishness of Gen. Clingman"—an "able and brilliant [man] . . . before old age bereft him of his powers"—and reported that "his best friends view with sorrow his present course against Governor Vance." A correspondent of the *Raleigh Observer* opined that "the General has weakened his own chances [for the U.S. Senate] very much by his uncalled for attacks upon a man the people know to have been true."[46]

By midsummer the heated contest for the senatorship in North Carolina was attracting significant press attention outside the state. Newspapers in Alabama,

Georgia, Louisiana, Texas, and Virginia speculated on the chances of the various candidates, while the *New York Times* brought Clingman's views to the attention of Northern readers by reprinting several paragraphs from one of his anti-Vance letters. Clingman's opinions on the upcoming state election and its implications for the national parties were further amplified in an interview that appeared in the *Washington Post* on 26 July 1878.[47]

Refraining this time from any specific criticism of Vance, Clingman focused on the widespread disaffection that he perceived among the "120,000 independent voters" in North Carolina who had "lost faith in the political integrity of both existing parties." He asserted that "an independent party [is] growing in my state, and I believe all over the South. The Republican party . . . is almost dead in North Carolina, but it is probable that the independent party will take its place." Indeed, he added, "I should not be at all surprised to see a man of independent views elected as Merrimon's successor in the Senate." Clearly, Clingman was positioning himself to become that "man of independent views" to whom the legions of dissatisfied voters in the Old North State could turn for leadership.[48]

The reaction of the Democratic presses to the interview was predictable. The *Charlotte Observer* dismissed Clingman's comments as a blatant attempt to lure the independents away from Merrimon and expressed "hope that Merrimon and his friends will not suffer themselves to be out-generalled by this last convert to the dogma of independency." The *Concord Register* likewise pointed to the self-serving nature of Clingman's remarks. "It all amounts to anything to beat Vance and Merrimon—by the which General T. L. Clingman may succeed in entering Congress as the next Senator from North Carolina."[49]

If Clingman was pinning his hopes on the election of men "of independent views" to the general assembly, the outcome must have been a disappointment to him. Most of the independent candidates fared poorly. Only two were elected to the senate, and only four to the House. Even so, the Democratic victory did nothing to resolve the senatorial question. Despite the outcry about pledging, only fifteen counties had formally pledged their Democratic candidates to vote for Vance, and some of those candidates had been defeated in the general election. With considerable justification, Merrimon could boast that "Gov. Vance's plan of *instructing, pledging,* and packing, is a failure, a signal failure." The *Charlotte Democrat* observed that "there is very great doubt as to who has a majority for the U.S. Senator" and predicted "a good deal of wrangling and bolting" when the members met in January.[50]

Clingman remained noncommittal about his own candidacy. On 21 November he issued a statement disavowing a recent claim in the *Raleigh News* that he had formally entered the race. But he also denied giving "repeated notices in published letters that I was not a candidate." There would be time enough when the general assembly met in January, he said, "for me to decide whether or not I should be a candidate for the Senate." Despite such disclaimers, Clingman was not averse to trying to "bolster himself for the position of 'dark horse'" by mailing the recently published second edition of his *Speeches and Writings*, postage prepaid, to each of the members-elect.[51]

During the late fall, Clingman and Merrimon each surveyed the senatorial terrain in interviews with the *New York World*. Clingman, speaking on 28 November, said that he anticipated "quite a close contest." Although Vance presently had the lead, "a compromise candidate may be called in and win the race." Merrimon, interviewed a few weeks later, was less coy about Clingman's prospects, remarking that "I am told that ex-Senator Clingman feels confident of receiving a large vote." He added, however, that his own friends had "made a canvass of the Legislature and tell me I will be elected."[52]

Based on those optimistic assessments of his own strength, Merrimon made the fateful decision in December "to be governed by the *caucus*." After returning to North Carolina at the end of the month, he learned that his supporters had greatly overestimated his popularity and that Vance was the overwhelming choice of the Democratic legislators. Rather than endure the humiliation of a caucus defeat or the strain of another, possibly unsuccessful, battle on the floor of the general assembly, Merrimon abruptly withdrew from the senatorial race two days before the caucus was scheduled to meet.[53]

The surprise announcement ended all hopes for Clingman's candidacy. The Democrats subsequently nominated Vance by acclamation and easily elected him to the U.S. Senate over feeble Republican opposition. Clingman did not wait for the inevitable outcome. On the same day that Merrimon withdrew from the contest, he left Raleigh, where he had spent the past several weeks, and took the train to Washington. His departure did not go unnoticed. The *Charlotte Observer* could not resist gloating that "the dark horses have abandoned all hope . . . [and] Gen Clingman has quit Raleigh." It went on to predict that "the general will be very inconspicuous in politics during the coming four years . . . [but] he will come up again, smiling and confident of a Senatorship, when Gen. Ransom's term expires in 1882."[54]

A few months earlier, the same newspaper had made light of Clingman's prospects for the Senate, claiming that he had "not the shade of a shadow of a chance" of getting the Democratic nomination.[55] But Clingman's strategy was not premised on winning the caucus nomination. Instead, he hoped for a repetition of the situation that had occurred in 1872, when a substantial number of Democrats had bolted the party caucus and combined with the Republicans to elect a U.S. senator. With many Republicans unwilling to vote again for Merrimon and the anti-Vance Democrats unlikely to support an out-and-out Republican, Clingman had reason to expect that he might be the beneficiary, particularly since he had spent the past six months establishing himself as the state's most vocal opponent of Vance and the pledging system. Still, there is no evidence that a significant number of Merrimon Democrats would have defied the caucus in

1878, even if their leader had urged them to do so. Many of them had promised during the campaign to abide by the caucus decision and thus felt honor-bound to keep that commitment.[56]

The *Charlotte Observer* greatly underestimated Clingman's tenacity when it predicted he would disappear from the political scene after the failure of his bid for the senatorship. Indeed, he would remain prominently in the public eye for the remainder of the decade and well into the next. However, its prognosis did prove quite accurate in one respect. As Matt W. Ransom's second term in the U.S. Senate neared its conclusion in 1882, Clingman would be found in the thick of the battle for the succession.

17 *The Mahone of North Carolina*

Clingman's futile campaign for the U.S. Senate in 1878 antagonized many influential North Carolina Democrats and relegated him to the sidelines of the state party, now firmly under the control of Senators Zebulon B. Vance and Matt W. Ransom. Although he remained nominally a Democrat, for the next four years he would continue to flirt with independentism. As the Old North State's most prominent political gadfly, he denounced both parties as corrupt and unresponsive and called for a realignment that would restore two-party competition in the South. Clingman's mounting disaffection, together with his burning desire to return to the U.S. Senate, would finally lead to a decisive break with the Democrats in 1882.

In March 1879, scarcely two months after his unsuccessful bid for the Senate, Clingman renewed his criticism of the national party system in an interview published in the *New York Tribune*. Sounding the same theme as in his *Washington Post* interview of July 1878, he claimed that "both the old parties . . . have outlived their usefulness and ought to be broken up." The Democrats, he said, had thus far maintained their hold on the South by pandering to popular fears of a return to the corrupt regimes of the Reconstruction era. But thousands of discontented voters would quickly abandon the party if presented with a viable alternative. That would not happen as long as the Republicans remained the main opposition party. "The only way to bring about the disintegration of the white vote of the South," he asserted, "will be to disband the Republican party."[1]

Later that year, Clingman elaborated on those views in a discussion with a reporter from the *New York Herald*. With a tall, spare figure "erect as an Indian chief" and an iron-gray beard that accentuated a "somewhat weather-beaten appearance," the sixty-seven-year-old former senator impressed the journalist as "a venerable connecting link between the present and that era of the past when the utterances of Southern statesmen were all potent in the councils of the nation." Clingman reminisced about his early days in Congress when both parties were truly national organizations—when "my speeches were as well received in the whig States of Vermont and Massachusetts as they were in my own district."[2]

In contrast, he said, both of the postwar parties were largely sectional in their orientation. The Democrats maintained their power in the South by playing on memories of military Reconstruction and carpetbag rule. The Republicans kept their hold on the North by waving the bloody shirt and blaming the Democrats for the Civil War. Both parties, in his opinion, had degenerated into "mere machines for keeping certain men in office." Neither enjoyed "the confidence and support of the majority of the people." For that reason, "a large majority of the people of the South would be willing to enter into a fair and liberal new national organization."

The Democratic presses did not take kindly to Clingman's characterization of their party as boss-ridden and machine-ruled. The *Raleigh Observer* denied that any "ring or junta exists in the Democratic party to-day." The *Asheville Citizen* took exception to his claim that the people of the South were disenchanted with the Democrats and charged that Clingman was agitating for a new party simply as a vehicle to ride back into office. Undoubtedly, the former senator was attempting to revive his own political fortunes by cultivating a public image as a crusader for good government. But with the Democrats firmly in control of the Old North State and the next senatorial election more than three years away, he could do little more than give interviews to the press.[3]

In between his two visits to New York, Clingman allowed himself—for the first time in twenty years—to take a vacation. Although rumor had it that he was sailing to Liverpool, his actual destination was Bermuda. He departed 1 May 1879 on the steamer *Flamborough* and arrived there after a four-day cruise. The one hotel on the island was closed, but fortunately he was able to find lodging at a private boarding house. He remained in Bermuda for four days and arrived back in the States after another leisurely three-day cruise. Upon his return, he spoke "in glowing terms of the delightful sea voyage, and still more of the delightful climate of the island, and the good living which he found there."[4]

According to his friend John Hill Wheeler, Clingman had gone to Bermuda "for health" as well as for pleasure. Until late in his sixties, Clingman had never experienced any significant medical problems. He was blessed with a strong constitution and, apart from a slight limp left by the wound sustained at Petersburg, he was in excellent physical condition. In 1873 Wheeler had characterized the sixty-one-year-old Clingman as being "both physically and mentally as vigorous as at 25." To the reporter of the *New York World* who interviewed him in November 1878, he seemed "as active and sprightly as when he occupied a seat in the United States Senate." The editor of the *Raleigh Observer,* who had seen him a month earlier, agreed that "though in advanced years the General shows few, if any, of the physical infirmities of age, and his vigorous and well stored mind is, if anything, brighter and stronger than in the days of yore." [5]

By 1879, however, age was finally starting to catch up with Thomas Lanier Clingman. "Gen. Clingman is beginning to look old," the *Concord Sun* reported toward the end of that year. "His iron gray is fast turning to snow." Most likely, the problem that led him to seek relief in Bermuda was an early manifestation of a neuralgic condition that would become more severe the following year. After his return from the island, he pronounced himself "improved by his 'sea change.'" In July the convalescing former senator checked into the summer resort at White Sulphur Springs in Greenbrier County, West Virginia. His stay at the springs may have been more for social than therapeutic reasons. Known as the "Saratoga of the South," it enjoyed a reputation as "the great central point of reunion for the best society of the South, North, East, and West." During his visit, Clingman had an opportunity to renew his acquaintance with several of his former colleagues in the Senate, including Simon Cameron of Pennsylvania and Robert Toombs of Georgia, as well as to mingle with other luminaries such as Gen. Fitzhugh Lee and Congressman George C. Cabell of Virginia, Judge John Kerr of North Carolina, and Gov. H. M. Mathews of West Virginia. [6]

Clingman arrived in Asheville in early August "looking well" from his visit to West Virginia. Despite his advancing age, he continued to maintain a peripatetic lifestyle, making frequent trips through the mountains to visit old acquaintances and tend to his various business interests. In late August, he was in Hendersonville near the South Carolina border, negotiating the sale of zircons from a nearby mine that he operated. In early September, he was reported to be in Marshall near the Tennessee border, enjoying "a stay with his many friends." Later that month, he spent a few days in Franklin, about thirteen miles from the Georgia line. [7]

Politics was probably a prominent topic of discussion during Clingman's conversations with his friends in the mountains. Although he had not represented the district in Congress in more than twenty years, many of its residents still respected his opinions on political issues. Indeed, even those who did not share his dim view of the postwar Democratic party acknowledged that his views carried great weight among many ordinary voters. As a correspondent of the *Raleigh News* remarked, "the principal part of the politics of this section of the world, is I think, General Clingman, for the political horizon seems to be high or low, in proportion as the General seems inclined or not, every one feeling an interest in such affairs, consulting him."[8]

Clingman's extensive rambling through western North Carolina during the summer of 1879 suggests that he had recovered from the ailments that had afflicted him earlier in the year. He was reported to be "looking well" during a visit with his niece Bettie Gibson in Concord in mid-November. John Hill Wheeler, who saw him in Washington later that month, characterized him as appearing "very well," as did the Washington correspondent of the *Asheville Citizen* in early December. By the end of January, however, his health had taken another turn for the worse. This time he decided to seek relief in Hot Springs, Arkansas. Apparently, the visit did not have the desired effect. An acquaintance who saw him in Washington in late May reported him to be in "feeble" condition.[9]

Clingman claimed he was suffering from "frontal neuralgia." Probably he was a victim of trigeminal neuralgia, a common form of paroxysmal facial neuralgia that generally occurs in late middle age. It is characterized by intermittent spasms of sharp pain in the areas of the face supplied by the trigeminal nerve. Those attacks are often followed by long periods of spontaneous remission. It is likely that the malady afflicting Clingman early in 1879 had gone into remission later that year only to flare up again in January 1880.[10]

"Having suffered . . . for a long time, and tried many remedies with no advantage," Clingman decided in May to treat his condition with the application of "an old-fashioned blister of flies." When he woke up the next day, he noticed that his face "still had a reddish appearance [and] was somewhat swollen." Unbeknownst to Clingman, his face continued to swell throughout the day. When he went to dinner at Willard's Hotel that evening, some acquaintances there did not even recognize him. Looking into a mirror, he discovered that his face had taken on the appearance of "a large pumpkin." Rejecting the advice of a local druggist to consult a physician, he secured a piece of tobacco at a cigar stand; wet it and placed it, together with four layers of cotton cloth, over the afflicted area; and immersed his face in a bowl of water every ten or fifteen minutes to keep the bandages wet. He continued the treatment until the next morning, by which time the swelling had substantially subsided.[11]

That was not the first time Clingman had used tobacco for therapeutic purposes. He had first tried it in 1847 to reduce the swelling from a sprained ankle. He had also applied it to the leg wound he had suffered at Petersburg in 1864 and to the eye injury he had sustained in New York in 1867. In each case, the swelling had subsided and the pain had diminished. The notion that many afflictions are self-limited and will eventually run their course without benefit of treatment was as foreign to Clingman as it was to most other nineteenth-century Americans. Falling into the post hoc ergo propter hoc fallacy, he assumed that the tobacco treatments had caused the beneficial effects.[12]

By late June, Clingman's health had improved sufficiently for him to return to North Carolina and participate in the presidential campaign. Despite his recent criticisms of the Democrats, he showed no interest in the Greenback movement or in any of the other third parties that were offering alternatives to the traditional parties in 1880. For the time being, at least, the Democracy seemed to him the only viable vehicle for ending the two decades of uninterrupted Republican control of the executive office.[13]

Clingman's choice for the Democratic nomination was Gen. Winfield Scott Hancock. He had supported the Hero of Gettysburg at the national conventions in 1868 and 1876, but he was willing once again to set aside his personal preference in favor of the "strongest man." The only contender he would not support was Samuel J. Tilden. Expressing a sentiment shared by many other Southern Democrats, he maintained that the New Yorker "did not show sufficient resolution and manhood four years ago—a very serious defect in Southern eyes." Although Clingman believed former governor Horatio Seymour, the party's nominee in 1868, might again be the favorite of the convention, he accurately predicted in May that Hancock would be the nominee if Seymour refused to be a candidate.[14]

The front-runner for the Republican nomination was Ulysses S. Grant. Clingman readily acknowledged the former president's popularity in the South. Southerners, he explained, believed that "Grant would be more liberal as a President than such men as Blaine, Sherman, or Conkling, who . . . are constantly repeating malignant calumnies against the Southern people." At the same time, he was among the first to foresee that Grant would not receive the nomination owing to "the opposition among the people to a third term, added to the notorious corruptions of Grant's administration." As for James Garfield, the dark horse who ultimately beat out the former president at the Republican National Convention in Chicago, Clingman pronounced him to be a "poor nominee" who would be "distasteful to a great many republicans."[15]

Clingman did not go to Cincinnati to participate in the choice of the Democratic candidate. At the Democratic State Convention on 17 June 1880, his name had been placed in nomination for one of the at-large seats at the national convention. But party leaders, perhaps to indicate their displeasure at his recent apostasy, relegated him to the less-prestigious position of alternate delegate. Thus Clingman was still in Asheville when the news arrived that Winfield Scott Hancock and William H. English had won the party's nomination for president and vice president. Local Democrats immediately organized a ratification meeting and invited the town's most prominent resident to be one of the featured speakers.[16]

"Upon looking at what the politicians of Cincinnati have done," Clingman told the enthusiastic crowd, "Buncombe pronounces it *good.*" Reminding the audience that he had long been an advocate of Hancock's nomination, he characterized the Democratic candidate as "in all respects a first-rate man." Indeed, "in his action and general bearing, he reminds me more of Washington than any man I have known." As a nonpolitician "under no obligations to any political or corporation rings," Hancock could be trusted to clean out the corruption in Washington and appoint the best men to public office. From a purely political standpoint the choice was also judicious, Clingman argued, because the nomination of a distinguished Union general would neutralize the Republican argument that the Democrats were a party of "copperheads and rebels." Should the opposition continue to "raise the banner of the 'bloody shirt,' and talk about the war issues," Democrats would counter by extolling "the splendid glories of Hancock's military record." In short, "his candidacy spikes the cannon of the enemy." [17]

From late June until mid-September, Clingman stumped the mountain counties on behalf of the Hancock-English ticket. On 9 September, he once again ventured into the Republican stronghold of Henderson County, where he had delivered his most notable address during the campaign of 1876. Drawing a striking contrast between the prosperous condition of the country in 1880 and its bleak situation four years earlier, he attributed the economic recovery to the monetary policies of the Democratic-controlled Congress. In particular, he pointed to the Bland–Allison Act, which had reversed the "narrow contracted policy" of the Republicans by "restoring silver with full legal tender qualities." According to one Democratic observer, the speech was well received and the speaker loudly cheered at its conclusion. Indeed, he asserted, Clingman's argument was so overpowering that "many Republicans left the court-house swearing that they would never again vote a Radical ticket." [18]

Clingman departed for Washington on 13 September to attend to some "business engagements," and he did not return to North Carolina until late November. Thus he did not vote in either the state or national elections, although he reportedly took the precaution of pairing off with "a leading Garfield man" before leaving the Old North State. The day before the presidential election Clingman was in New York City, where he paid a call on Hancock at the candidate's home on Governor's Island. Later that afternoon, he spoke to a Democratic rally on Broad Street. After being introduced to the cheering crowd as the "greatest orator of the South," he repeated the standard themes about Republican misgovernment and extolled the Democratic nominee as "a fine-looking man—the best statesman he ever saw," likening his personal appearance to that of George Washington. [19]

To the end, Clingman remained optimistic about Hancock's prospects. In September, he had predicted that the Democratic candidate would carry New York by 20,000 votes, thereby garnering a sufficient number of electoral votes to win the presidency. Clingman was correct in his assessment of the key role the Empire State would play in the election, but the outcome there belied his prediction. Garfield carried the state by 7,000 votes. New York's 35 electoral votes provided the winning margin, enabling the Republican candidate to beat his opponent in the electoral college by a vote of 214 to 155. The nationwide distribution of the vote underscored Clingman's claim that the Democrats and Republicans had both become sectional parties. Hancock carried North Carolina and the rest of the South, whereas Garfield won majorities in all the Northern states except New Jersey.[20]

Two days after the election, Clingman paid a call on the defeated candidate and found him "placid and possessed under the results of the election." The Democratic presses in the Old North State were considerably less serene about the "mortifying" outcome of the state elections. Although Democrat Thomas J. Jarvis won the governorship by a margin of 6,500 votes, the election returns revealed a disturbing erosion in the party's popular support. The decline in the Democratic vote was particularly pronounced in the mountain counties. As the *Raleigh Republican* gleefully put it, "the whites of that section revolted from the ranks of the Democratic party by [the] thousands."[21]

It would be an exaggeration to attribute the Democratic losses in the far west to Clingman's failure to campaign for Jarvis and the other candidates on the state ticket. Popular dissatisfaction with the undemocratic system of local government and with the recent sale of the Western North Carolina Railroad to a group of Northern investors were the principal factors contributing to the sharp drop in the Democratic vote. Nonetheless, Clingman's denunciation of parties as "mere machines for keeping certain men in office" certainly fanned the flames of discontent in the mountain region.[22]

Clingman's strictures against the party system continued unabated after the election. In January 1881 he told a reporter from the *New York Tribune* that "a majority of the people of both parties are discontented with the existing condition of political affairs." Thus far, he said, the fear of a return to military rule had kept most white Southerners loyal to the Democratic party. But "differences of opinion as to matters of public policy and contests for political positions will, whenever this pressure is removed, produce divisions." A month later, a correspondent of the *Louisville Courier-Journal* overheard him "moralizing upon the great change that has come since the golden days of his prime" when Clay, Webster, Mangum, "and that order of giants" had walked the halls of Congress. In May he complained to the *Raleigh News and Observer* about the poor quality of leadership in the Democratic party, comparing his own efforts to steer it in a constructive direction to those of "a horse behind a wagon trying to push it along with his forehead, while a weak team and an awkward driver were directing it against stumps and into mud-holes."[23]

Clingman's splenetic disposition was not improved by another flare-up of the neuralgia that had been troubling him for the past several years. Toward the end of March, he paid another visit to the hot springs in Arkansas in an effort to obtain relief. This time he remained there for almost two months, returning to the North in late May "apparently without benefit or injury to his health." Later that summer, he spent some time at a resort in Cape May, New Jersey—again without appreciable benefit. According to one of his nieces, "his head is not improved by his trip." [24]

In between his visits to the two resorts, Clingman returned to Asheville, where he worked on a satirical essay about Virginia senator William Mahone. A railroad executive and an unsuccessful contender for the Democratic gubernatorial nomination, Mahone broke with his party in 1877, organized an independent movement based on scaling down the state's enormous debt, and two years later trounced the Democrats in the legislative elections. Elected to the U.S. Senate, which at the time was evenly divided between the parties, Mahone traded his vote to the Republicans in return for prestigious committee assignments and offices for his leading supporters. [25]

Clingman had mixed feelings about the enigmatic Virginian. On the one hand, he regarded him as a crass opportunist and had nothing but disdain for his program of debt repudiation. On the other hand, he was well aware that Mahone had successfully accomplished in Virginia what he had thus far only dreamt about doing in North Carolina. He had organized an independent movement strong enough to hurl the Bourbons from power. [26]

Those ambivalent feelings are clearly evident in Clingman's satire. Purportedly a transcription of a speech made by Mahone in the U.S. Senate, it was issued as a broadside in June 1881 and published in the *Asheville Citizen* a few months later under the title "Senator Mahone's Great Speech as Phonographed by Gen. Clingman." Mahone begins by candidly admitting his intention to overthrow both major parties "so that other and better political parties might spring up in their stead." Having already destroyed the Democrats in Virginia through his manipulation of the debt issue, he is now going after his nominal allies, the Republicans. "To disgrace them before the country . . . I must induce them to do something that would disgust all honorable men, and make the country eject them from its confidence." In order to accomplish that objective, he had forced the Senate Republicans to support Harrison H. Riddleberger, the author of Virginia's debt repudiation bill, for the position of sergeant-at-arms. [27]

According to Mahone, Riddleberger embodied all the traits that Republicans abhorred the most. First, he was "an old original, life-long Democrat." Second, "he had been a Rebel officer who had slaughtered loyal union men." Third, "he was a repudiator so virulent that he insisted on expelling from the Legislature a colored man merely because he was honest enough to wish to pay the debts of his State." In short, "Riddleberger combined all these detestable and loathesome [sic] elements in himself. He was worse than tartar emetic, ipecac and asafoetida all combined in one dose, and I made them agree to swallow him. Is it strange that they thus turned the stomach of the country?" [28]

After Mahone finishes lambasting the Republicans, the Democratic senators burst into gales of laughter in which the galleries heartily join. "I am glad to see my Democratic neighbors in such a good humor," he continues. "I hope you will try to listen pleasantly to what I am next about to say. How have you been behaving in the meantime! Have you been united on any public question?" Mahone then proceeds to castigate the Democrats for failing to make good on their promises to expand the money supply, reduce the tariff, and reform the civil service. "Instead of your showing any statesmanship and public spirit, you have merely been like a body of driftwood, which is forced along by the current." Mahone concludes with a prediction that the people will soon "arise in their majesty and obliterate both these present organizations, sectional and office-loving only as they are, and . . . fall back on the principles and practices of Washington's administration, and give to the country honest, economical and impartial government."

Clingman's "phonographic speech" is less a lampoon of William Mahone than a scathing indictment of both postwar parties. Although the crafty politico who boasts about forcing the unpalatable Riddleberger down the Republican throats is clearly meant to be Mahone and not Clingman, the two persona become increasingly indistinguishable as the essay goes on. By its end, when the speaker declares that "the people are honest and desire good government; it is only the public men who have become corrupt," the sentiments are clearly those of Clingman himself, proposing to lead a popular movement to overthrow the party machines and restore "honest, economical and impartial government."

When Clingman's essay appeared during the summer of 1881, North Carolina seemed ripe for political revolt. A bitter contest over a proposal to outlaw the manufacture and sale of liquor had ended in August with a stunning victory for the antiprohibitionists. The prohibition forces were spearheaded by the leaders of the two main religious denominations, the Baptists and the Methodists. The antiprohibitionists were an incongruous collection of whiskey dealers, saloon keepers, and revenue collectors, who viewed the proposed restrictions as a threat to their livelihood; ordinary country folk, who resented government intrusion into their private affairs; and Republican politicians, who hoped to use the liquor issue to split the Democratic party and ride into office.[29]

In June 1881 the opponents of prohibition had created a statewide organization known as the Anti-Prohibition Association for the State of North Carolina. The association orchestrated the summer campaign against the prohibition referendum, creating "an effective and smoothly operated machine in all the counties." It remained in existence after the election, serving as a potential nucleus for an independent third party. Early in August, rumors also began circulating that the North Carolina Republicans were planning to disband and reorganize as "The Anti-Prohibition Party."[30]

By 1881 the issue of prohibition had become closely connected with the seemingly unrelated issues of county government and public schools. A year earlier, the general assembly had given the unelected county commissioners absolute discretionary power over the licensing of liquor dealers, and some of them had used that authority to close down the saloons. Such arbitrary actions intensified long-standing hostility in the central and western counties to the undemocratic system of county government. Moreover, in many counties the fees from liquor licenses constituted a major source of funding for the local schools. Antiprohibitionists argued that the elimination of those licenses would undermine the very foundations of public education.[31]

Within a few months after the August referendum, the antiprohibition movement would burgeon into a full-scale political revolution. For a time, however, the issue of prohibition was overshadowed by another concern of potentially greater consequence to the future of the republic. On 2 July 1881 a disappointed office seeker named Charles Julius Guiteau fired a bullet into the spinal column of President Garfield. For the next eighty days, the American people waited in anticipation as the president's condition alternately improved and deteriorated, while important matters of public policy that required the personal attention of the chief executive were ignored or deferred.[32]

Unfortunately, the U.S. Constitution provided little guidance on the matter of presidential disability. Article II stipulates that the "powers and duties" of the chief executive "shall devolve on the vice president" in the event of the president's "inability to discharge the powers and duties of said office." But the meaning of the word "inability" is not specifically defined, nor is it clearly stated who has the authority to establish its existence. Two other perplexing questions also lacked clear-cut answers. In the event the vice president did assume the powers of the presidency, would he hold them for the remainder of president's term or only until his health was restored? If the latter, then how would the fact of recovery be established? As those issues were thrashed out in the country's leading newspapers during the summer of 1881, "widespread variation in the opinions of 'experts' . . . revealed itself."[33]

Clingman, who never lost an opportunity to thrust himself into the public eye, was not averse to offering his own "expert" opinion. Late in August, he was approached in the New York Hotel by a reporter from the *New York Express*, who talked with him for about twenty minutes. Unfortunately, the journalist took no notes and, writing up the interview from memory, presented a confused and garbled account that would later cause considerable embarrassment to Clingman.[34]

Clingman's first point was that the powers devolving on the vice president would end with the president's recovery. To argue otherwise would, in his opinion, go against the "logical construction" of the Constitution. In the version of the interview published in the *Express*, he also seemed to be saying that the framers of the Constitution had been influenced by the debates in the British Parliament over the illness of King George III. His second point, which was also expressed somewhat opaquely by the *Express*, dealt with the issue of who had the authority to declare a president disabled. In Clingman's view, "it was a question for Congress to determine." However, since Congress was not then in session, the most expedient course would be for Garfield himself to invite Vice President Chester A. Arthur to assume his duties temporarily.[35]

Shortly after the publication of the interview, former congressman Kenneth Rayner published a letter in the *New York Herald* declaring that Clingman had "committed a decided historical mistake." The debates over the disability of George III had occurred in 1788, whereas the U.S. Constitution was written in 1787. Thus the framers could not have been influenced by the British example. In North Carolina the *Raleigh News and Observer* also took Clingman to task for his "misleading" and "mistaken" opinions, avowing that his "memory was wholly at fault in his assertion." A correspondent of the same newspaper assailed him for suggesting that Garfield should transfer his powers to Arthur, as if "the high office of the Presidency . . . was a piece of private property—to hand . . . over, as a watch, for instance, to be kept till called for."[36]

Clingman, who prided himself on his retentive memory and his encyclopedic knowledge, was incensed by these challenges to his intellectual credibility. "I knew very well when the constitution was adopted, and also the date of the other events," he shot back in a letter to the *Herald*. He explained that the point he had been trying to make was that the debates over the presidential succession bill in 1789 had been influenced by the discussions in Parliament. The *Express*'s reporter "mistook what I said about the act of Congress, and supposed I had been speaking of the adoption of the Constitution." Clingman also defended his recommendation that Garfield temporarily transfer his powers to Arthur, emphasizing that he had made that suggestion only because Congress was not then in session. His main point, which the *Express*'s reporter had missed altogether, was "that there was urgent need of legislation on the subject."[37]

On 19 September 1881 Garfield finally succumbed to his injuries, thus rendering moot the issue of presidential disability. The tragic event offered Southerners an unexpected opportunity to demonstrate their patriotism to those Northerners who still regarded them as unrepentant rebels. Throughout the South, leading citizens organized meetings to give expression to their grief and outrage. Clingman played a prominent role in the memorial meeting that convened in Asheville the day after the president's death to pass resolutions condemning "in the most unmeasured terms the brutal murder" and requesting President Arthur to proclaim a day of fasting and national humiliation. Clingman seconded the resolutions and then addressed the audience with "some remarks suitable to the occasion."[38]

At a meeting of Confederate veterans held in Raleigh on 12 October, Clingman also struck a conciliatory note, remarking that "all true Confederates would stand firmly by their country . . . [in] deploring the death of the President." While admitting to no regrets regarding his decision to cast his lot with the Confederacy in 1861, he added that it was "far better that the people of the United States should be united under one government than divided into two."[39]

Two weeks after speaking at the veterans' meeting, Clingman journeyed to Washington to attend the special session of Congress called by President Arthur. Apart from a brief visit to Asheville in early November, he did not reappear in the Old North State until the following summer. While Clingman was away in the North, dissidents in his home state were making preparations to challenge the Bourbon hegemony. As early as December 1881, newspapers had been commenting upon the impending arrival of the "Mahone of North Carolina"—a dynamic leader who would "repeat the campaign against the Bourbons which has proved so successful in Virginia."[40]

Speculation about the identity of the upcoming Tar Heel Mahone centered on William Johnston, a railroad executive, Confederate candidate for governor, and three-time mayor of Charlotte; and Charles Price, a former Speaker of the North Carolina House of Representatives. Both men had broken with the Democrats a year earlier and had become leaders of the antiprohibition movement. In January 1882 they had consulted in Washington with President Arthur and other Republican leaders. It was no secret that the Southern strategy of the Arthur administration was predicated on the promotion of coalitions between local Republican organizations and disaffected Democrats. That strategy would culminate a few months later in the organization of the North Carolina Liberal party.[41]

Clingman initially viewed the emerging Liberal movement with skepticism. In an interview with the Washington correspondent of the *Charlotte Observer* in late January, he dissociated himself from Johnston and Price and expressed his opposition to a formal coalition with the Republicans. In light of that interview, the North Carolina presses were understandably incredulous when the *Washington Star* announced early in February that "the liberal or anti-Democratic movement in North Carolina has found a leader . . . [in] ex–U.S. Senator Clingman." "It is not likely," said the *Asheville Citizen*, "that he will attempt any revolution, nor advocate any alliances outside of the party." The *Goldsboro Messenger* agreed that "the General is misrepresented." Rather than organize a new party, "he would like to see the [Democratic] party so reorganized or remodeled as to bring him to the front once more."[42]

A communication by Clingman to the *Washington Post*, which appeared on 20 February 1882, seemed to support the conclusions of the Democratic newspapers. As usual, he had harsh words for both national parties, affirming that "each one is sustained, not from affection, but mainly to keep out the other." Although he faulted the Democrats for failing to carry through on their promises to restore silver, abolish internal revenue taxes, reduce the tariff, and reform the civil service, he reserved his severest criticisms for the Republican party, which he characterized as "the most mischievous and most corrupt political organization that has ever exercised power in this country." The North Carolina presses pointed to his letter as evidence that Clingman would continue to support the Democrats. According to the *Carolina Watchman*, "there is nothing either in the words or tone of the General's letter to justify the conclusion that he proposes to join the Republicans in a crusade against the Democratic party."[43]

Until well into the summer, Clingman remained aloof from the insurgency in his home state, playing no part in the movements during May and June to organize the "Liberal Anti-Prohibition party" and to nominate candidates for federal, state, and local offices.[44] However, after returning to Asheville in mid-July and surveying the political terrain firsthand, he evidently concluded that the Liberals stood a reasonable chance of accomplishing his ultimate political objective—the overthrow of the "Vance dynasty." In a twelve-column address published in an extra edition of the Republican *Asheville News* on 18 July 1882, the former senator announced his decision to cast his lot with the Liberals.[45]

Clingman's address contained the familiar strictures against the postwar Republican administrations, along with criticisms of the Democrats for failing to correct those abuses while they controlled Congress. Both parties, he said, were dominated by "bosses" who maintained their power through their manipulation of conventions and other party machinery. Both served the interests "of Wall street, of the national banks, of the great corporations and of the high protectionists." Both were too fundamentally corrupt to be reformed. Change would come only by "overthrow[ing] the boss system and all its machinery." Fortunately, said Clingman, the mass of the people were honest and desirous of good government. Only the politicians were corrupt. The people could "burst to pieces all the present party machinery, break up the rings, and overthrow the bosses" simply by willing to do so. "We have the power to govern ourselves, and we owe it to our manhood and our past record to exercise that power."

Clingman preferred to call the new movement "the Washington party" after the first president, who had been elected to office without the aid of any convention or party platform. What the country needed, he said, was to return to "the sincerity, honesty and purity of the former times"—to "the system and practices of Washington's time." And just as President Washington had been "able to give the country a most excellent administration . . . by having the benefit of comparing opposite and varied views," the Washington party would welcome honest men of all shades of political opinion. Moreover, it was not necessary for a member to serve a long apprenticeship before receiving preferment. "In the Washington party all the seats are in the front. No man is required, as when he joins the old parties, to take a back seat, and wait ten years before any consideration is given to him."

The Democratic presses could not resist the temptation to poke fun at Clingman's Washington party. "A party of Washington!" the *Oxford Torchlight* exclaimed. "Well, that is a happy thought. . . . Washington is a favorite name with the old General. He has an unexpired term in the Senate there and he has been trying ever since the war to form a party to get to it." The *Wilmington Star* agreed that Clingman was "just crazy to go to Washington." The Democrats also made light of his claim that the new party would give "front seats" to its younger members. Certainly, the majority of the leading Liberals were not young men by any definition of that word. Clingman himself had just turned seventy; Johnston was sixty-five; and former congressman James Madison Leach was sixty-seven. And yet, scoffed the *Raleigh News and Observer,* those three "young and progressive ex-Bourbons call on the young men of the State to rally around the flag, boys, and elect them to office."[46]

On 5 August 1882 the Liberals officially launched their campaign with a "grand rally" at Morganton. Clingman was the first to speak, and for once he had nothing negative to say about the Republicans. Instead, he directed his attack toward the Democrats, whom he castigated for failing to keep their promises to reduce the tariff, reform the civil service, and eliminate corruption. He challenged the notion that the party could somehow be reformed from within. "We have tried that for 12 years, and the result has been disappointment." Clingman also had harsh words for the North Carolina Democratic party, which, he asserted, was firmly in the grip of "a half dozen . . . machine politicians" who were proposing "to reform the chicken thief by allowing him to steal more." But fortunately there were two hundred thousand votes in the Old North State that nobody owned. "Let them be cast in the coming election for the best men, and without regard to party shackles."[47]

To the dismay of some of the Liberals, Clingman said nothing about prohibition, and he refrained from endorsing the Liberal call for the restoration of local self-government. Indeed, the various speakers were unable to sound a consistent theme. While Clingman was urging the white voters in the audience to throw off the shackles of party, Republican Isaac Young was assuring the black voters that he was "talk[ing] as a fire-tried Republican to Republicans." As the Democrats were quick to point out, "there was no concert of action—no fixed line of argument, but every man for himself and his own peculiar views." After the rally Clingman reportedly admonished his colleagues that "if we don't have some consultation, and come a little nigher together, we'll have this Vance dynasty on us for the next fifty years."[48]

Although the Democratic newspapers dismissed the Morganton rally as a "failure" and a "fizzle," party leaders took the Liberal threat quite seriously. Breaking with precedent, Governor Jarvis stumped the central and western counties in support of the Democratic legislative and congressional candidates. Senators Vance and Ransom also campaigned aggressively on their behalf. According to Clingman, "all the prominent men they can get into the field are working as we never saw them work before. . . . They tell us that the Liberal movement is dead. . . . Why then this terrible panic?"[49]

Everywhere the Democrats spoke, their message was the same. Liberalism, they claimed, was merely a stalking horse for Republicanism. Should the Democrats lose power, North Carolina would return to the evils of Radical Reconstruction, with its corruption and "Negro rule." Moreover, a general assembly dominated by Republicans and quasi Republicans would certainly revalidate the special-tax bonds that the Democratic legislature had recently repudiated—bonds that Swepson and Littlefield had used to line their pockets at the expense of the honest taxpayers of the Old North State.[50]

Once the Swepson-Littlefield frauds had been raised as a formal campaign issue, it was inevitable that Clingman's name would be dragged into the controversy. The occasion proved to be the heated contest for the congressional seat in the mountain district. Throughout the summer, reports circulated that Clingman was planning to run against Robert B. Vance, the longtime incumbent who had defeated him ten years earlier in the Conservative nominating convention. Although he may have toyed with the idea of avenging that defeat, Clingman ultimately decided to throw his support behind William M. Cocke Jr., whose father had served with him in the U.S. Congress. On 12 September 1882 Cocke issued a broadside announcing his candidacy and assailing the record of Vance. He also alluded to the Democratic attacks on the special-tax bonds, noting that prominent members of that party had lobbied and voted for them in the general assembly and that most of the beneficiaries had been Democratic railroad presidents. The Democrats charged that the broadside had actually been "dictated and prepared" by Clingman—an accusation that neither Cocke nor Clingman ever formally denied.[51]

Two weeks later, an article appeared in the *Asheville Citizen* under the title, "Will Wonders Never Cease? Clingman's Cocke Circular." Although the article was written under the pseudonym of "Truth," word quickly spread that its author was William H. Malone, Vance's close friend and brother-in-law. Malone ignored the circular's nominal author and centered his fire entirely on Clingman. Reviving all the accusations that had been levied against him by the Conservatives in 1870 and by the Republicans in 1872, Malone asserted that, at best, Clingman had been grossly negligent in allowing Swepson to gain control of millions of dollars in railroad bonds and then to squander them on his Florida investments. "As Gen. Clingman is holding up . . . the leaders of BOTH parties . . . for INEFFICIENCY and FRAUD," he concluded, "is it not legitimate to enquire is HE shown by the record to be a SAFE, PRUDENT leader. . . . It does not look like George Washington in the least."[52]

Although Clingman attempted to answer Malone's charges in a broadside published under the title *Reply of Gen. Clingman to "Truth,"* the damage had already been done. In an editorial entitled "The Tainted Candidate," the *Asheville Citizen* gleefully observed that "the Washington idea of Gen. Clingman to create an entirely new party . . . loud in its professions of purity and reform" had hit a snag. "The experiment of purification had not gone very far before it was found that the purifiers were not very clean vessels themselves, that all of them were tarred with the same stick with which they charged others with being blackened; and that it was but a repetition of the old story of the pot calling the kettle black."[53]

While the references in the Cocke circular to railroad frauds raised the hackles of the Democrats, many Republicans were angered by its repeated use of the term "late Republican party" and by its assertion that those Republicans and Democrats who had joined the Liberal coalition had permanently abandoned their old organizations. Like the Readjustors of the Old Dominion, the Liberals of North Carolina were dependent on the support of thousands of Republican voters who were sympathetic to their movement but unwilling to formally join it. Clingman and the other Liberal leaders were never able to resolve the dilemma of how to mobilize the Republican electorate without, at the same time, giving credence to the Democratic charge that they were plotting "to Mahoneize North Carolina and turn over the State to the Republicans."[54]

In their efforts to convince disaffected Democrats that they were not simply Republicans in disguise, Clingman and Cocke alienated the Republican voters whose support they most needed. An irate party member from Asheville wrote that he could "not see how any true Republican can support the liberal movement after Capt. Cocke's declaration that the 'Liberal party intended to destroy both the old parties.'" The Republican editor of the *Greensboro North State*, who earlier had halfheartedly endorsed the Liberal ticket, now claimed that Cocke's circular provided conclusive evidence of a conspiracy "to bury forever the Republican party in North Carolina." The editor predicted that "thousands and thousands of Republicans will stay home" on election day.[55]

Despite his advanced age and periodic complaints about suffering from "lumbago," Clingman worked tirelessly for the Liberal ticket during the fall of 1882. For the first time in ten years, he even campaigned outside the mountain district, addressing a rally in Granville County on 17 October. A week later, he commenced a canvass of the southern Piedmont and mountain counties, speaking on four successive days in Cleveland, Lincoln, and Rutherford. He also addressed a gathering in Morganton in early November before finally returning to Asheville a few days before the election.[56]

On 8 November 1882, almost 225,000 North Carolinians went to the polls. In the election for congressman-at-large, Democrat Risden T. Bennett squeaked past Liberal Oliver H. Dockery by 443 votes. In the mountain district Cocke lost to Vance by almost 3,000 votes. However, Liberals and Republicans captured three of the remaining seven congressional seats and came close to winning two others. In the legislative elections, the Democrats managed to retain control of both houses, but their majority in the lower house was reduced to eighteen votes. In the far west the Liberal-Republican coalition made spectacular gains in the legislative elections, despite Cocke's defeat, winning House seats in nine of the twenty-two counties.[57]

In view of the obstacles under which they had labored, the Liberals had made an impressive showing. Nonetheless, they failed to break the hold of the Democrats on the politics of the Old North State. In the final analysis, the Democrats' skillful exploitation of the race issue was the most important factor behind the inability of the North Carolina Liberals to forge a biracial alliance of lower-class voters. Throughout the campaign, the Democrats hammered away at the theme that "the Democratic party is a white man's party, and recognizes its obligation to protect its members . . . from the curse of negro rule." The unwillingness of most white Democrats to cross the color line, together with the suspicions of die-hard Republicans who viewed the Liberal movement as a threat to their own organization, doomed the efforts of Clingman and other insurgent leaders to organize a successful third-party movement in 1882.[58]

The failure of the Liberal-Republican coalition to capture the general assembly dashed Clingman's hopes of becoming the Mahone of North Carolina. Even if the coalition had won a majority, his chances of returning to the U.S. Senate would have been slim. Nonetheless, it is possible that in a general assembly closely divided between the parties, a handful of pro–Clingman legislators from the far west might have held the balance of power. Three months before the election, a correspondent of the *Raleigh News and Observer* had anticipated the scenario that might return Clingman to the Senate. "Suppose," he speculated, "the Radicals and Liberals combined should have a majority of one in the next Legislature, and that one should be a Clingman man from Graham, Cherokee or Transylvania?" As it was, Matt Ransom was easily reelected to a third term over William Johnston, the candidate of the coalition.[59]

From the perspective of 1882, it seemed that Clingman had permanently burned his bridges with the Democratic party. Upon his arrival in Asheville a few days before the election, the *Asheville Citizen* had commented that "Gen. Clingman has just returned from a work he will be ashamed of after awhile. He looks well, physically . . . but his political corpus is not in a very assuring condition." Two weeks after the election, the *Greensboro Patriot* revealed the disdain with which the Democrats now viewed Clingman by publishing a mock interview with the former senator, accompanied by a drawing of a figure attired in his trademark white pants and black frock coat with the head of a jackass. "And a big head at that," chuckled the *News and Observer*.[60]

By early December Clingman was back in Washington, attending the opening session of Congress and presiding at memorial services for John Hill Wheeler, who had succumbed to Bright's disease after a long illness. In the weeks that followed, he may have turned his mind to more pleasant thoughts to compensate for the failures and humiliations of the recent campaign and the loss of a dear friend. Although Clingman had failed in his effort to become the Mahone of North Carolina, his prospects for attaining fame and fortune as the Old North State's answer to the Wizard of Menlo Park seemed to be growing increasingly more promising.[61]

18

Benefactor of the Human Race

In view of the vehemence with which the Democrats denounced Clingman during the campaign of 1882, it is remarkable how quickly he managed to regain his standing among them. The attitude of the *Raleigh News and Observer* typifies that change. In August 1882 the paper was assailing him for his "insatiable . . . desire for office." A year later, it was praising him as "one of the most extraordinary men ever produced in North Carolina—indeed we may say in the United States." Since the end of the Civil War, North Carolina Democrats had held ambivalent feelings about Clingman. Although they regarded him as an ambitious opportunist and were unwilling to reward him with high political office, they nonetheless applauded his literary and scientific accomplishments and his untiring efforts to promote the wealth and reputation of his state.[1]

In the spring of 1883 Clingman gave the Old North State good reason to feel proud of its native son. After a three-year effort, he had finally succeeded in obtaining a U.S. patent on an incandescent lamp that some predicted could be "produced one-third cheaper than the Edison light." At the same time that he was making plans to illuminate the households of America, Clingman was also promoting a miraculous remedy that would relieve the pain and swelling of sprains, blisters, insect bites, and a variety of other afflictions. Small wonder that an adulating press characterized him as the "benefactor of the human race."[2]

Clingman's involvement in incandescent lighting grew out of his long-standing interest in the exploitation of the mineral resources of western North Carolina. In 1839 the botanist Thomas Nuttall had called his attention to a large deposit of zircon crystals in the southern part of Buncombe (later Henderson) County. Smaller particles of zircon had previously been found among gold washings in other western counties, but never before in North Carolina—or, for that matter, anywhere else in the world—had zircons been discovered in such large crystals or in such massive quantities.[3]

Clingman had subsequently gained control of the Freeman mine, which contained most of the zircon deposits, and had sent samples to Charles Upham Shepard for analysis. However, there were no known commercial uses for zircons at that time, and the discovery of such large quantities had nullified their earlier value as rare minerals. The zircons would remain in the ground until after the Civil War, when two inventor-entrepreneurs named Cyprien Tessie du Motay and Edward Stern finally came up with a potential use for them.[4]

Tessie and Stern proposed to use zirconia (a metallic oxide chemically extracted from zircons) in the construction of improved calcium lights. Popularly known as "limelights," calcium lights had been in use since the 1820s as surveying signals and, later, as stage lighting for theaters. Tessie and Stern believed they could improve the quality of the light by substituting zirconia for the lime or calcium. The two inventors approached Clingman in New York and negotiated a deal for one thousand pounds from the Freeman mine. Early in 1869, the minerals were taken out of the ground and shipped to New York. Unfortunately, Tessie and Stern had more enthusiasm than money, and after paying for and receiving 130 pounds, they asked Clingman to supply the remainder on credit. He refused, and the deal fell through.[5]

It was during that unsuccessful business venture, as Clingman later recalled, that he first "became acquainted with the remarkable qualities of the oxide zirconia." Because it seemed "to possess a greater power of resisting heat than any known substance," he believed zirconia offered a possible solution to the perplexing problem of developing a practical incandescent light. Since the early nineteenth century, scientists had been aware that an electric current could be used to heat a substance to the point where it would begin to glow and produce light. But they had also discovered that most substances either burn, melt, or crack when subjected to the extremely high temperatures required to produce incandescence.[6]

Although the first patent for an electric lamp had been granted in 1841—the year Clingman had made his first run for Congress—the basic technical problems were still unresolved when Thomas Alva Edison turned his attention to incandescent lighting during the summer of 1878. In an interview with the *New York Sun* on 16 September, the Wizard of Menlo Park, who had recently received worldwide acclaim for his invention of the phonograph, announced that he was on the verge of developing a practical system of electric illumination that would make conventional gas lighting obsolete. The *Sun*'s story was quickly picked up by other newspapers, including the *Raleigh News* and *Raleigh Observer.* The intensive publicity continued through the end of October. Six months later, despite occasional optimistic reports in the New York presses, there was still no news of the anticipated breakthrough.[7]

Clingman, who undoubtedly had been following Edison's progress in the newspapers, believed zirconia might offer an attractive substitute for the platinum the inventor had been experimenting with. Most likely, he was also mindful that a commercially successful zirconia lamp would create an enormous market for zircons, of which he controlled most of the known supplies. Clingman broached his idea in a letter to Edison on 26 March 1879. In addition to outlining the advantages of zirconia over platinum, he pointed out that he had several hundred pounds of zircons on hand and that he controlled the locality where additional quantities could be obtained. Edison's initial response was less than enthusiastic. "I do not have the slightest difficulty with my platinum and iridium electric lamp," he told Clingman.[8]

The inventor would soon develop an intense interest in Clingman's zircons, but for a purpose entirely different from what the North Carolinian had in mind. By the spring of 1879 Edison had come to the conclusion that a tightly wound spiral of platinum and iridium (a silver-white metallic element of the platinum group) would provide the most practical incandescing element. In order to prevent the successive winds of the coil from short-circuiting, he needed to coat the wire with an insulator. Around the same time that Clingman was touting the virtues of zirconia as an incandescing element, Edison was coming to the conclusion that it was the most promising of the various insulating materials he had tried.[9]

By mid-May Edison had become quite interested in Clingman's zircons, and he inquired about the price at which they could be obtained in quantity. The North Carolinian responded that he had five or six hundred pounds in New York left over from the venture with Tessie and Stern, which he was willing to sell at two dollars per pound. Edison placed an initial order for ten pounds to "see what I can do with it," adding that "if I am able to work it, [I] will require a great deal of it." On 28 May Edison reported that the sample "tests very well. . . . If I conclude to use it . . . [I] would like very much to know . . . if you can furnish me large quantities without delay." Clingman assured him that he could provide at least twenty thousand pounds by the end of the summer.[10]

After another two weeks passed by without further word from Edison, Clingman took the initiative and wrote to "enquire whether you have made sufficient experiments with the zirconia to enable you to decide as to . . . your being able to use zircons to advantage." In order to dig up a sizable quantity during the summer, he added, "I ought to be apprised at once, as some weeks of work will be necessary in the way of preparation." Four days later, Edison responded that his chemist was still trying to extract the oxide from the crystals and could do nothing "until the experiments are completed." The inventor continued to hedge throughout the summer, informing Clingman at the end of July that he could not commit himself to purchasing additional quantities of the mineral until he had made "a thorough test for the purpose which I intend to use it."[11]

Despite those protestations, by midsummer Edison was eager to acquire a copious supply of zircons. However, he had come to believe he could obtain them at a cost substantially lower than the price quoted by Clingman. He was encouraged in that belief by William E. Hidden, the mineralogist whom he had dispatched to North Carolina to search for platinum. Hidden was convinced he could obtain the crystals at fifty cents per pound or less. Indeed, he boasted, "I may yet get it down so low as to frighten you at its cheapness." Edison's response to Hidden on 5 August was quite different from the noncommittal reply he had given Clingman a few days earlier. He immediately placed an order for five hundred pounds and instructed him to make arrangements for purchasing additional amounts.[12]

Clingman, meanwhile, was becoming increasingly anxious about Edison's reluctance to make a commitment. He informed the inventor on 21 August that the zircons could not be mined during the winter, so the work would have to begin immediately if he was planning to purchase substantial quantities. Indeed, he added, he had already ordered operations to commence. "If you have decided let me know and I will instruct the parties who have been at work for me to suspend or go on." Despite Clingman's obvious concern, Edison delayed responding to the letter and waited for Hidden to report back on his own investigations.[13]

Hidden arrived in Hendersonville on 27 August, expecting to meet John T. Humphreys, the man who had promised to sell him the "dirt cheap" zircons. Instead, he received a message from his would-be supplier that "Gen. Clingman had leased all the Zircon property around here . . . and that *he* could get none." Clingman, who had learned about Hidden's impending visit to Hendersonville, made it a point to be in town when the mineralogist arrived. Together, they examined the zircon deposits at the Freeman mine. Although Clingman at first insisted he would not reduce his price, he finally agreed to provide an additional two hundred pounds at one dollar per pound. Hidden advised Edison to accept the offer. "Unless we can discover some new locality for Zircons, we shall be obliged to depend on Gen. Clingman for our supply. . . . The lot is unusually fine and it is the best you can do."[14]

Edison, who had been willing to pay high prices for platinum, might well have come to terms with Clingman had he not by then arrived at the conclusion that zirconia was unsuitable after all as an insulator for his platinum spirals. He had initially been impressed by its durability and adhesive quality, as well as by the brilliance of the light produced by it. However, he also discovered that the zirconia-coated wires would short-circuit after they had been heated beyond a certain point. At first Edison had attributed that phenomenon to impurities in the wire or oxide, but he later concluded, correctly, that zirconia loses its character as an insulator and actually becomes a conductor when heated to a sufficiently high temperature (about 950°C). When Edison received Hidden's telegram containing Clingman's final offer, he responded with a simple "no." [15]

The inventor was somewhat more diplomatic when he informed Clingman on 3 September that "I shall give up [the] use of Zircon." In fact, Edison had not lost interest entirely. He had expended a considerable amount of time and money developing a process to extract zirconium oxide from the crystals, and he was reluctant to let those efforts go to waste. "As I have expended $1,500 in experimenting to obtain a process for economically extracting the pure oxide," he told Clingman on 10 September, "I thought if I could get the crystals cheap enough, I would go into the manufacture of the basic oxide and make all the application in the arts possible." However, the fifty cents Edison was willing to pay for each pound of crystals would have left Clingman with no margin of profit. "As my zircons have cost me considerably more than I understand you propose to pay," he told the inventor on 13 September, "I must retain them and take my chances for remuneration." [16]

Despite Edison's decision to "give up the use of zircon," Clingman remained convinced that zirconia would provide the answer to the problem of producing a practical electric light. If Edison was not willing to develop a zirconia lamp, then Clingman would have to invent one on his own. On 20 November 1879 he requested an interview with Edison to discuss the idea. The two talked briefly in New York City early in December. A few days later, Clingman provided Edison with a brief description of his proposed invention. In order to avoid the expense of using large quantities of platinum, he would "substitute for the [platinum] spiral coil . . . a hemispherical hollow ball of zirconia . . . supported by two pins or legs of platinum . . . fastened at one end to the copper wire, and the other stuck into the sides of the zirconia cup." Edison, who by then was on the verge of developing a successful carbon-filament lamp, refused to become involved in what he considered an impractical scheme. "It is out of the question to use zircon as you suggest," he replied on 9 December, "therefore I cannot consider the matter." [17]

By the time he received Edison's response, Clingman had already applied for a patent on his "zirconia cup." Although he knew something about electric lighting from his reading of such basic sources as the *Encyclopedia Britannica* and the *American Encyclopedia*, his grasp of the technology was rudimentary at best. His enthusiasm and boundless self-confidence did not prove sufficient to remedy that deficiency. The Patent Office rejected his application on the grounds that it "is informal and fails to properly define what [the] applicant apparently regards as his invention." After several attempts to amend the specifications failed to satisfy the patent examiner, Clingman appealed to the board of examiners, which sustained the initial ruling. According to the board, his specifications were too vague, and even worse, "his drawing reveals . . . a want of practical familiarity with the principles of electrical science." [18]

A less-determined man might have given up after such a rebuff. In Clingman's case, the rejection only stimulated him to further exertion. He realized he had made a mistake in filing his application without first consulting a patent attorney, and with the expert assistance of A. H. Evans and Co., he submitted a new application on 20 March 1880. Although he previously had suggested an incandescing element consisting entirely of zirconia, he now claimed it could be composed of either zirconia by itself or a mixture of "zirconia and carbon, or of zirconia and alumina, or magnesia, or lime, or silica, or mixtures with one or more of these substances together." [19]

The news of Clingman's patent application was published in a New York daily, and from there word spread to North Carolina and other parts of the South. "Gen. Thomas L. Clingman is going to beat Edison," crowed the *Spartanburg (S.C.) Spartan.* "He is applying for a patent for zirconia . . . which he thinks the finest illuminator ever discovered, and . . . the very thing required by Edison." The Patent Office failed to concur with that glowing assessment. On 31 March 1880 the examiner rejected his proposal, noting that his claims were "substantially the same as . . . in his former application." Twice, Clingman amended his specifications to deal with some of the specific points raised by the examiner. Each time, the revised application was rejected. Once again, Clingman appealed to the board of examiners. [20]

Principal Examiner H. C. Townsend presented the board with two objections to Clingman's application. The first related to his proposal to bring a mass of zirconia to incandescence simply by passing an electric current through it. That was not practical, he said, because zirconia was a nonconductor. It could be brought to incandescence only by mixing it with some conducting substance or by heating it with some outside source. Townsend's second objection pertained to Clingman's proposal to mix zirconia with carbon or some other conducting substance. That idea, he argued, had already been preempted by a patent granted to Edison on 16 September 1879. [21]

The Edison patent cited by Townsend bore little resemblance to the carbon-filament lamp perfected later in 1879 or even to the various platinum lamps the inventor had tested during the spring and summer. On 9 December 1878 Edison had filed an application for an incandescing element composed of finely divided particles of platinum, iridium, or ruthenium, in combination with certain oxides such as magnesia or zirconia. Whereas zirconia was a central component in Clingman's invention, Edison had proposed to use it only to increase the brilliance of the light. Clingman must have found Townsend's reference to Edison's patent particularly galling. Just a few months earlier, the inventor had dismissed his proposed zirconia lamp as impractical. But now his own application was being re-jected on the grounds that Edison had already translated the idea into an actual invention.[22]

In a fourteen-page printed argument, Clingman attempted to refute the objec-tions of the examiner, focusing primarily on the patent of 16 September. Edison's application, he pointed out, had been filed the previous December and had "been lying in the [patent] office more than nine months." As late as 10 September, the inventor had told him that zirconia had "no value" as a substitute for platinum. "Why he, six days after his letter to me, so suddenly changed his mind, I leave to the Board to find out." Although Clingman stopped short of accusing Edison of stealing his invention, he did insinuate that Edison's application had been lan-guishing in the Patent Office until he had sparked the inventor's interest in zirco-nia. Then Edison had inexplicably "changed his mind" and pressed forward with the application. Perhaps Clingman was unaware that even successful patent ap-plications are often amended a number of times before finally being granted and that a nine-month delay between application and issuance is not unusual.[23]

Clingman's argument was most persuasive in its discussion of how his own in-vention represented a departure from the work of Edison and others who had pre-viously mentioned zirconia in their patent applications. He conceded that all the materials he proposed to use in his electric light—zirconia, carbon, platinum, and copper—had been suggested at one time or other by various inventors. But that in itself, he argued, did not constitute sufficient grounds for rejecting his ap-plication. Indeed, Edison's own application employed exactly the same metals and oxides proposed in a patent earlier awarded to Tessie and Stern (Clingman's former business partners). Even so, "Edison was adjudged worthy of a patent. . . . Yet, now, the Examiner rejects my application, though I use . . . [zirconia] in a manner essentially different from Edison."[24]

Clingman was on much less solid ground in his response to the other objection raised by Townsend—that zirconia, being a nonconductor, could not be brought to incandescence without being mixed with a conducting substance or subjected to an outside source of heat. The North Carolinian would have done well to have dropped his untenable claim before filing his appeal. Instead, he injudiciously chastised the examiner for his surprising "want of information on this subject." It was an established fact, he said, that electricity can pass through nonconduct-ing substances like air for short distances. Electricity had also been made to pass through glass for a distance of six centimeters. "For the purposes of my patent, it need be passed along the non-conductor only for a fraction of an inch."[25]

Clingman's assertion about air and glass was valid, but his analogy was flawed. That electricity could pass for short distances through nonconductors did not prove it was capable of generating the intense heat necessary to bring a noncon-ductor to incandescence. Focusing on the weakest part of Clingman's argument, the board of examiners rejected his appeal for "want of practicability." Indeed, it compared his proposal to the numerous applications received by the Patent Office for perpetual motion machines. In such circumstances, where the would-be invention seemed to defy the known laws of science, some "practical demonstration of . . . utility" was required. In response to Clingman's insinuation that Edison had acted improperly, the board asserted that he had an "unquestionable right as a true inventor" to patent "the means which his experiments led him to regard as conducive to practical success."[26]

The board's characterization of Edison as "a true inventor," along with its intimation that Clingman was a novice unfamiliar with the basic principles of electricity, certainly must have rankled the North Carolinian. On 8 May 1880 he appealed to the commissioner of patents to reverse the decision of the board. The tone of his four-page printed argument was more suitable for a campaign tract than a brief in a legal proceeding. Clingman's main point was that he had been treated unfairly. The examiners, he said, had repeatedly recognized zirconia as a practical element in the production of electric light. "When they allowed Edison's patent, which they say anticipated mine, the matter was so plain that they required no proof of practicability. . . . Now, when I propose to use it, [they] say that the suggestion is as absurd as would be a proposition to patent a machine for a perpetual motion."[27]

The commissioner was unpersuaded. On 5 June he upheld the decision of the board on the grounds of both practicality and prior invention. He ruled that Clingman's proposal to use zirconia by itself was untenable. Indeed, the examiner and the board had both "so fully considered this point as to render further discussion upon my part unnecessary." As for his proposal to mix zirconia with powdered carbon or some other conducting substance, the commissioner concurred with the examiner and the board that the idea was "substantially anticipated by the patent to Edison." The use of carbon in place of the platinum and other metals mentioned in Edison's patent "does not appear, under the familiar doctrines of law relative to the substitution of material, to require in any degree the exercise of invention."[28]

The commissioner's rebuff did nothing to dissuade Clingman from pursuing his invention. Although he had now exhausted all avenues of appeal within the Patent Office, he still had recourse to the civil courts. A week after the commissioner's decision was issued, Clingman filed an appeal with the Supreme Court of the District of Columbia on the grounds that the commissioner had erred "in holding that my device was inoperative," as well as "in holding that the references [to Edison] cited by the Examiner anticipated my invention." The court placed the case on the calendar for its September term.[29]

By the summer of 1880, Clingman's quarrel with Edison and the Patent Office had become common knowledge in North Carolina. He had sent copies of his printed arguments to leading newspapers in the Old North State, and those that commented invariably took the side of Clingman. According to the *Wilmington*

Star, his argument before the board "very clearly establishes two points: first, that he has not been fairly dealt with by the Examiners; second, that he has made a valuable discovery as to the remarkable qualities of oxide zirconia. . . . Gen. Clingman shows up the Examiner's ignorance and unfairness in a way that must be refreshing to that person." A correspondent of the *Asheville Citizen,* after taking Edison to task for stealing Clingman's invention, predicted that "Gen. C. will get after him in his usual style, and we trust successfully." [30]

Indeed, Clingman did "get after" Edison in the four-page answer he presented to the court on 27 September 1880. "It would seem," he said ". . . that the case is narrowed down to a comparison of Edison's patent and mine. Let them, then, be compared." After briefly pointing out that Edison had proposed to use zirconia for a completely different purpose (merely to increase the brightness of the light), Clingman went on to argue in detail against the practicality of Edison's patent. For one thing, the platinum and other metals he proposed to use were costly and easily susceptible to melting. In addition, Edison had never explained how he planned to accomplish the difficult task of reducing the metals into small bits. Finally, his proposal to mix the metallic salts with the oxides was "too absurd for consideration." Clingman concluded by explaining the advantage of carbon over the platinum and other substances that Edison had proposed to combine with zirconia. "Carbon is . . . next to the metals, the best conductor; . . . [it] may easily be reduced to the most impalpable powder, and can thus readily be mixed with the zirconia likewise in powder." Best of all, carbon—unlike platinum—was "abundant and cheap." [31]

Clingman must have experienced a feeling of vindication when Chief Justice David K. Cartter delivered the unanimous opinion of the court in late October. The court overruled the commissioner's decision that Edison had priority of invention, and it declined to take sides in the debate over whether zirconia by itself could be brought to the point of incandescence. The court did, however, agree with the commissioner that Clingman had not convincingly demonstrated that he had come up with a practical invention. In order to avoid encumbering the Patent Office with yet "another experiment under letters-patent with a failure ahead of it," Clingman would have to "furnish the evidence that his invention will do that which he says it will." [32]

The decision of the court was reported in the *Washington Post* and from there was copied by the North Carolina presses. Those papers that commented on the decision regarded it as a victory for Clingman. A correspondent of the *Charlotte Democrat* asserted that the case "has not been finally decided against him but only delayed for practical tests which he will render in due time." The *Asheville Citizen* pointed out that the court's ruling "does not prevent him from obtaining a patent upon making the loop and proving its efficiency, which he is confident of doing." By the end of the year, Clingman could also take satisfaction in knowing that his claims had been recognized abroad. A British patent for which he had applied on 5 May 1880 was granted in November. A few weeks later, his invention was also patented in France.[33]

Another two and a half years would elapse before Clingman was finally able to produce a functional prototype of his zirconia lamp. During that time, he must have experimented with numerous spheres of varying sizes and shapes, some composed of zirconia by itself and others containing various amounts of carbon and perhaps some of the other substances mentioned in his specification. In early 1883, he finally managed to develop a suitable mixture of zirconia and carbon, which he had pressed at the Washington Navy Yard "into pencils of different proportions."[34]

Shortly thereafter, Clingman brought a sample of his "pencils" to the Smithsonian Institution, where they were tested by an electrical engineer named William J. Green. After a current was passed through one of them, Green testified, "it became highly incandescent and continued to give a very brilliant light as long as I submitted it to the current." In his opinion, there was no doubt that "such a pencil could be thus kept luminous a long, and perhaps indefinite period." On 17 April 1883, Clingman was granted U.S. Patent 276,133 for "a new and useful means of producing electric light."[35]

The news was received in North Carolina with predictable enthusiasm. "Gen. Clingman made a brave fight and has at last secured patents," raved the *Greensboro North State*. "It is seldom that we meet with men possessing genius so versatile as Gen. Clingman can boast of." The *Raleigh News and Observer* ranked his accomplishment as commensurate with "the inventions of the wizard Edison" and praised him for his dogged determination. "Gifted with a strong, clear mind, he has that faculty of application to a single purpose which accomplishes results usually ascribed to the highest genius."[36]

As early as 1880, enthusiasts in the Old North State had predicted that Clingman would "doubtless make a good pile of money to leave his posterity" should he succeed in his patent suit. Although he had subsequently "spent several thousand dollars in getting letters-patent," he did not yet have a lamp that could be marketed commercially. Thus far, Clingman had managed only to bring a pencil of carbon and zirconia to incandescence for a few minutes in an engineer's laboratory. To obtain the financial resources and technical expertise necessary to translate his invention into a commercial success, he would need support from outside investors.[37]

Despite his earlier strictures against Edison, Clingman was not averse to seeking the inventor's cooperation and assistance. Shortly before his patent was issued, he wrote to request an interview. Edison declined even to acknowledge the letter. Undaunted, Clingman went to New York in October 1883 "to meet a party of capitalists who desire to purchase his Electric Light." Two months later, he entered into an agreement with Benjamin H. Willis, a Wall Street lawyer who was acting as trustee for Manhattan banker Edward H. Potter, to organize a manufacturing company. For the rights to his patent, Clingman would receive an initial sum of five thousand dollars, an additional twenty thousand dollars to be paid later, and one-third of the profits realized from the sale of his lamps. In return, he would provide the company with advice and assistance "in the preparation of the pencils . . . and in the conduct of necessary experiments."[38]

It is not clear whether the company was ever organized or whether Clingman ever received any money from Willis. In an interview with the *New York Tribune* in March 1884 he talked optimistically about a series of experiments then being conducted by his chemists. In an interview with the same newspaper a few months later, however, he spoke about efforts being made to form another company "to take hold of . . . my electric light," thus implying that the deal of the previous December had fallen through.[39]

On 1 January 1885 Clingman assigned his patent rights to two electrical engineers named Andrew J. Baldwin and John H. Miller. According to the agreement, he would receive an initial eight hundred dollars, with an additional seven thousand dollars to be paid prior to the organization of the company. Again, there is no evidence that the company was ever actually organized or that Clingman received any remuneration for his invention. In an interview with the *Raleigh News and Observer* early in 1886, he noted that he had employed an electrician in New York, who after long investigation, had reported unfavorably on his invention. He had subsequently "employed another party skilled in this department of science, and with similar results."[40]

While conducting their tests on zirconia in 1884, Clingman and his associates also extended their inquiries into the field of arc lighting. Whereas an incandescent lamp produces its illumination by heating a substance to the glowing point, the light of an arc lamp is created by the passage of an electric current between two carbon electrodes. First employed in Europe during the 1840s for the illumination of theaters and public halls, arc lamps came into widespread commercial use in the United States during the 1870s.[41]

One of the major technical problems that had delayed the development of a commercially successful lamp was the tendency of the carbon electrodes to burn rapidly and unevenly from the intense heat. Over the years, inventors had experimented with a variety of regulators and other devices to improve the performance of the lamps, but none had proven totally satisfactory. Clingman believed the answer lay in zirconia. In March 1884 he announced that his "chemists" had just completed a series of experiments "with zirconia as the base of carbon points." He characterized those experiments as "highly successful" and predicted that he would soon "be able to make a point two inches in length that will last a year under ordinary usage." Clingman was unable to keep that promise, but in 1887 he did receive patents for his improved arc lamp in France and Germany. A U.S. patent, which substituted the mineral serpentine for the zirconia, was granted the following year.[42]

Although his serpentine arc lamp fared no better than his zirconia incandescent lamp, Clingman never abandoned hope that he might eventually turn his inventions into commercial successes. In November 1888 he offered to sell the rights to his British, French, and German patents to the International Patent Company in return for one thousand dollars and half of all the profits. In March 1890 he sought the assistance of William Hadden, an acquaintance in New York, in marketing his inventions in the United States. Hadden responded that "things are very dull here in a speculative way" but that he hoped to have better news from some business associates in Chicago. "I shall see," he promised, "whether any of the brisker men there will take hold of the best Electric Light system extant."[43]

Despite his persistence, Clingman certainly must have realized by the end of the 1880s that his immediate prospects of gaining fame and fortune through his electric lighting system were not promising. Characteristically, he was unwilling to assume personal responsibility for his disappointments. Just as he had earlier attributed his political failures to the machinations of the "central managers" and "bosses," he now accused the monopolistic electric light companies of engaging in a deliberate conspiracy to boycott his invention. The electricians whom he had first brought in to test his inventions, he asserted, were "paid by electric light companies to report the plan impracticable." Other experts were then consulted, "and in every instance the interference of parties interested in electric lights had been discovered." Even though his own system of lighting was "superior to the systems now in use," a "combination of existing companies" had thus far prevented its introduction.[44]

Ironically, Clingman proved a better prophet than Edison in predicting that zirconia had a place in the future of illumination. By the late 1880s, the Austrian inventor Carl Auer von Welsbach had perfected a gas lamp composed of a mixture of zirconia and oxides of various rare earth metals that "heats white-hot and glows like an electric light." The zircons Welsbach used to manufacture the oxide for his lamp came from the Freeman mine in Henderson County, North Carolina. As the *Atlanta Dixie* explained, the "success of Gen. Clingman in mining zircons came to Carl Auer's notice, and the sequel was that a contract was given for the unheard of quantity of twenty tons, which was subsequently increased to 50,000 pounds." Had Clingman been able to hold on to his zircon property, he might have profited handsomely from Welsbach's invention. Unfortunately, economic necessity had forced him to sell his mine to Marion C. Toms and Hamilton G. Ewart shortly before orders began pouring in from Europe for "unlimited quantities" of zircons.[45]

By the mid-1890s the Welsbach lamp had significantly reduced the cost of gas lighting, making it a strong competitor to electricity for interior illumination. Welsbach's success with zirconia also inspired inventors in their search for better filament materials to improve the efficiency of the incandescent lamp. In 1897—

the year of Clingman's death—a professor of electrochemistry at the University of Göttingen named Walther Nernst, who had been studying the Welsbach lamp, hit upon the idea of mixing powdered zirconia and several rare earth oxides into a paste and molding them into a small rod. Once perfected, Nernst's zirconia lamp had a life and efficiency considerably greater than Edison's carbon-filament lamp. It was widely used in the United States and Europe until 1912, when it was superseded by the ductile-tungsten lamp that is still in use today.[46]

Clingman did not live long enough to witness the triumph of the zirconia lamp. Rather than fame and fortune, his costly and unsuccessful venture into electric lighting brought on a host of financial problems, which increasingly plagued him during the 1880s. Another enterprise that ultimately proved expensive and unremunerative was his effort to promote the curative powers of tobacco. Clingman was by no means the first person to extol the miraculous healing properties of the tobacco plant. Indeed, by the end of the sixteenth century, tobacco had already "taken its place in the materia medica of Europe as God's greatest gift to man," and a considerable literature on the subject had developed. During the course of the next two centuries, scientists who analyzed the plant gradually came to recognize the dangerous properties of nicotine. By the mid-nineteenth century, most physicians no longer believed in tobacco's therapeutic qualities.[47]

Nonetheless, the use of tobacco persisted as a folk remedy long after it had disappeared from the materia medica. Clingman himself had employed it since at least 1847 to relieve the pain and swelling resulting from sprained ankles, gunshot wounds, head and eye injuries, sore throat, and neuralgia. His faith in the healing power of tobacco was further enhanced after he suffered a "terribly painful attack of sciatica" in the spring or early summer of 1883. After consulting two physicians, whose treatments only aggravated his condition, Clingman finally found relief through the application of several large poultices of tobacco to his hip. By the end of July he was well enough to take a trip to Boston, and a month later he was reported to have "nearly recovered his health." A newsman who saw him in Raleigh on 15 October judged him to be "in remarkably good health and . . . in the best of spirits."[48]

Inspired by that experience, Clingman published an essay on the "advantages of wet tobacco as a poultice" in the May 1884 issue of the Washington monthly *Health and Home*. He began by making the point that he had "never chewed, smoked, nor snuffed tobacco." Nonetheless, he added, on several occasions it had "saved my life." Clingman went on to present a detailed account of his various experiences with tobacco, with particular emphasis on how quickly a poultice of wet tobacco had relieved pain and reduced swelling from a variety of ailments. He also mentioned a few other individuals who had successfully used tobacco. One of them was his brother John, a physician in Farmington, who had employed it to treat sore throats. Another was the Asheville lawyer Allen Turner Davidson.

Although a bitter political enemy of Clingman, Davidson apparently was not averse to accepting medical advice from him. After Clingman suggested that he apply tobacco on his red and swollen eyes, the problem had quickly cleared up.[49]

Clingman's essay attracted widespread attention. According to W. H. Hale, the editor of *Health and Home,* it had been republished in full in more than three hundred major newspapers and had appeared in synopsis in more than fifteen hundred country weeklies. In the following weeks, testimonials flooded into *Health and Home* and other papers that had printed the essay, all written by individuals who claimed to have personally benefited from the therapeutic powers of tobacco. Even Clingman's longtime enemy Zebulon B. Vance joined in the chorus of praise, asserting that a tobacco leaf had quickly eliminated the pain and swelling caused by a severe contusion on his leg.[50]

Perhaps inspired by the dramatic increase in the sales of his magazine following the publication of Clingman's essay, Hale filled successive issues of *Health and Home* with letters attesting to the curative powers of tobacco. Among the afflictions that were reported cured or relieved through the application of the tobacco remedy were boils, cuts, piles, scabies, stomach irritation, and dog, snake, and insect bites. Mindful of the town's growing importance as a tobacco market, the *Asheville Citizen* also aggressively promoted the tobacco cure. "Tobacco! Tobacco! Tobacco!!!" it thundered in August 1884. "As General Clingman sounds its uses and praises, when will the market stop?"[51]

In an era of flamboyant medicine men and miraculous cure-alls, Clingman's tobacco remedy struck a responsive chord. As the excitement mounted, the claims became increasingly extravagant. In September, *Health and Home* published a letter from Clingman promoting tobacco as a remedy for hog cholera. He also suggested it might well provide a cure for the epidemic of Asiatic cholera that had killed thousands in France and Italy. Indeed, he added, he had already furnished the health departments of Toulon, Marseilles, and other stricken cities with information, and he hoped that Hale would continue those efforts "by sending out printed slips or otherwise, to bring it to notice in Europe."[52]

Small wonder that the North Carolina presses characterized Clingman's remedy as "an almost universal panacea" and anointed its discoverer as "the benefactor of the human race." J. S. T. Baird, an Asheville physician who had effected a number of cures with tobacco, told Clingman his discovery would "mark an era in the history of medical service and stamp you as a benefactor of the race." Baird went on to predict that a thankful public would bestow "such testimonials of appreciation . . . as will be more grateful to you than even the 'applause of listening senates.'" W. H. Hale of *Health and Home* suggested a more tangible form of appreciation—"a well-filled pocket book." The editor urged all his readers, and particularly those who had directly benefited from the tobacco remedy, to send a contribution to the banking house of Riggs and Co. in Washington, D.C., where it would be credited to Clingman's account.[53]

Although contributions to the "Clingman Fund" of twenty-five, fifty, and even one hundred dollars were reported in the North Carolina presses, it is unlikely that those donations were sufficient to defray the expenses involved in the production and distribution of the forty-two-page pamphlet Clingman believed would "reduce human suffering 90 per cent." Published in January 1885, *The Tobacco Remedy* was a compendium of the letters and testimonials that had appeared in *Health and Home* during the previous year, along with additional commentary by Clingman. While the pamphlet failed to live up to Clingman's promise to dramatically reduce human misery, it does enjoy the distinction of being one of the last works on the curative properties of tobacco written in the English language.[54]

In the concluding paragraphs of *The Tobacco Remedy*, Clingman urged manufacturers of cake tobacco to refrain from using additives to improve its flavor, since that would render their products useless for medicinal purposes. He also suggested that ointments, plasters, and liniments might be prepared for cases where it would be impractical to apply the leaf directly, and he referred to "experiments" in that direction being made by himself and others. While in New York arranging for the publication of his pamphlet, he tried to interest a number of druggists in manufacturing such ointments and plasters. They told him that unless the products were protected by a patent, there would not be a sufficient margin of profit. On 10 January 1885 Clingman applied to the Patent Office for a trademark consisting of a tobacco leaf stamped with the name "CLINGMAN'S." The trademark was issued a month later.[55]

In April 1885 Clingman assigned exclusive rights to his tobacco remedies to the recently established Clingman Tobacco Cure Company. Located in Durham, the enterprise was capitalized at ten thousand dollars. The three officials of the company, each of whom owned one-third of its stock, were all leading figures in the North Carolina tobacco industry. The president, Edward J. Parrish, owned a large tobacco warehouse in Durham at the corner of Mangum and Parrish Streets, which probably served as the company's headquarters. The treasurer, William T. Blackwell, had until recently been president of W. T. Blackwell and Company, manufacturers of the enormously successful Bull Durham smoking tobacco. After retiring from the tobacco business, Blackwell had established the Bank of Durham, which kept the accounts of the new company. The secretary, Julian S. Carr, had succeeded Blackwell as president of his tobacco company, now renamed Blackwell's Durham Tobacco Company.[56]

Clingman was, indeed, fortunate to secure the backing of three such influential capitalists. Whether any of them actually believed in the curative powers of tobacco is uncertain.[57] However, Clingman's timing could not have been more opportune, for he approached them at a point when the burgeoning tobacco industry seemed threatened by ominous reports linking tobacco use with cancer. In the spring of 1885 it was reported that former president Ulysses S. Grant, an inveterate smoker, was dying from a cancerous growth at the root of his tongue.

Opponents of tobacco were quick to seize upon his unfortunate condition as a "terrible warning to smokers." By mid-April the *New York Sun* was reporting that "many veteran smokers [have] . . . already discarded the use of tobacco." [58]

To the embattled tobacco manufacturers, Clingman was offering a positive image of their product. Indeed, he and other proponents of the tobacco cure were claiming that the plant, under some circumstances, might actually serve as a cure for cancer. Clingman had initially been cautious in his assertions about the powers of tobacco over cancer. "Persons have told me that cases of cancer have also been cured," he wrote in December 1884, "but the sores may possibly not have been really cancers." Other advocates of the tobacco remedy were less reserved. According to the *New York World*, "Gen. Clingman offers affidavits of the positive and permanent cure of this dread disease by the application of tobacco poultices." W. H. Hale of *Health and Home* asserted that a foot cancer that had been troubling him for a year "dropped off like a large dead wart" after being treated with tobacco. The *Greensboro Patriot* reported that "Clingman's tobacco cure has made a marvelous cancer record in this county." [59]

The officials of the Clingman Tobacco Cure Company may have believed that ten thousand dollars was a small price to pay to dispel the negative view of tobacco promulgated by "those religious bodies in yankee-land." A thirty-two-page promotional brochure issued by the company in June 1885, which was probably put together by Clingman, contained new testimonials regarding the curative powers of tobacco in addition to numerous ones previously published in *The Tobacco Remedy*. Included was a statement from Vice Pres. Thomas A. Hendricks, who after applying the remedy to a boil that had been troubling him for two months had been "completely relieved in a single night." Unfortunately, the remedy was not powerful enough to prevent the Indiana politician from dying a few months later. [60]

The company's advertising brochures also provided a detailed description of the three preparations offered for sale. Clingman's Tobacco Cake, which retailed at twenty-five cents, was simply a cake of tobacco unadulterated by the additives found in most manufactured tobaccos. Clingman's Tobacco Plaster, prepared "according to the most scientific principles and Gen. Clingman's formula, of the purest seadtive *[sic]* compounds," was recommended for children and others whose systems were too delicate to handle the stronger tobacco cake. Each plaster, bearing the distinctive tobacco leaf trademark, sold for fifteen cents. Clingman's Tobacco Ointment, "prepared after the most careful and exhaustive experiments, with Gen. Clingman's formula," was designed especially for maladies such as piles, anal ulcers, ringworms, pimples, and insect bites. The most expensive of the three remedies, it retailed for fifty cents. [61]

Initial reports of the company's prospects were invariably positive. The ubiquitous Dr. Hale predicted that the tobacco remedies would "exceed the combined sales of all patent medicines." A Durham druggist claimed he had sold "more of the Clingman Tobacco Ointment than . . . all other Ointment and Salves combined." The *Asheville Citizen* reported in April 1885 that the remedy "is now manufactured on a large scale . . . and is meeting a large sale." In August the *News and Observer* announced that the company had just received a huge box of advertising cards and was now "getting ready to push things."[62]

Despite a promising beginning, the Clingman Tobacco Cure Company never managed to meet those initial expectations. During the period January 1886 to March 1887, total sales from the cakes, plasters, and ointments amounted to less than $700. Although the three stockholders invested $9,620 in the company over the same period, it had a bank balance of only $1,912 as of March 1887. By the end of the year, its account at the Bank of Durham had been closed and the Clingman Tobacco Cure Company had taken its place on the long list of defunct American enterprises.[63]

One of the most formidable obstacles confronting Clingman's company was the inability of his products to live up to the extravagant claims that had been made for them. Simply put, there is no scientific evidence that tobacco is an effective remedy for any affliction or disease. For every individual who swore that tobacco had produced relief from a complaint, there must have been many others who tried the remedy without success. The tobacco cure failed to bring about a measurable reduction in human suffering, and after the middle of 1885 the number of miraculous cures reported in the North Carolina presses dropped sharply.[64]

Still, ineffectiveness is not necessarily an insurmountable obstacle for a patent medicine. During the last decades of the nineteenth century, the drug stores of America were cluttered with remedies with names like Dr. Pierce's Pleasant Purgative Pellets, Dr. Prosanko's Cough and Lung Syrup, and Darby's Prophylactic Fluid—none of which were probably any more effective than Clingman's preparations. Most of them did, however, contain an ingredient lacking in Clingman's remedies—alcohol. Whereas the high alcoholic content of many patent medicines had great appeal among Americans living in "dry" communities, an ordinary cake of tobacco could be purchased at a drug store for a lower price than any of Clingman's products. In rural areas of North Carolina and other parts of the South, leaf tobacco was also readily available to cash-poor residents inclined to experiment with the tobacco remedy.[65]

Despite the failure of his tobacco cure company, Clingman never lost faith in the healing power of tobacco. As late as 1891 he was extolling the remedy in the Asheville newspapers as a cure for "cases of grip . . . [and] cancer." In conversations with his friends and acquaintances, sooner or later the topic would inevitably turn to tobacco. The journalist Alexander McClure recalled that "it was a source of much chagrin to him, that his friends seemed to grow tired of his expatiations relative to the virtues of the immortal weed."[66]

According to McClure, Clingman's unsuccessful effort to promote his tobacco cure cost him "much of the remnant of his fortune." There is considerable evidence to substantiate that statement, although it is likely that his electric light endeavors were equally costly. Prior to the mid-eighties, Clingman seems to have had little difficulty financing his peripatetic lifestyle or paying for the numerous pamphlets he published. In 1875, at a time when the country was racked by a major depression, he had enough liquid assets to pay off two thousand dollars of a debt owed by his cousin Isaac A. Jarratt. Indeed, Clingman's nephews, nieces, and cousins in North Carolina habitually looked to him not only for pecuniary support but also for advice on handling their financial affairs.[67]

The first indication that Clingman was experiencing serious financial difficulties came in a response to yet another request by Jarratt for a loan in March 1885. Writing shortly after the publication of *The Tobacco Remedy*, he protested that "I am not in a condition to assist you. Though for the last two years I have worked to get money, harder I think than I have ever done previously, yet I have had no success." In May 1885, a few weeks after the organization of the Clingman Tobacco Cure Company, he told Jarratt he thought he would "in a few months be able to help." By August the prospects seemed less promising. "I have less money," he wrote, "than I have had in fifteen years." The following July, after another of Jarratt's notes had fallen due, Clingman told his niece he had "no money now" but would sell some of his property and possibly be able to provide assistance "in less than a year." For the remainder of the decade, Clingman managed to support himself by periodically selling his mining property and other investments. It would be only a matter of time, however, before the money finally ran out.[68]

Although Clingman's electric light and tobacco ventures did not bring him financial success, they did enhance his reputation as a "scientific statesman" and "public benefactor."[69] By the mid-1880s most North Carolinians were probably ready to forgive his earlier political heresies as long as he was willing to focus his undeniable talents in more acceptable directions. But even while preoccupied with other matters, Clingman never completely lost interest in politics. Indeed, by the end of the decade, he would once again be a candidate for the U.S. Senate seat that thus far had eluded him.

19 *A Candidate for Matrimony*

Despite his advancing age and increasing financial problems, Clingman's routine changed little during the 1880s. He continued to maintain a peripatetic lifestyle, generally spending the winter and spring in Washington and New York and returning to North Carolina after the adjournment of Congress. His constant moving about did not allow for an extensive collection of personal possessions, nor did it offer him the opportunity to raise a family. Clingman enjoyed the company of women and, toward the end of his life, even tried hard to find a wife. However, he waited too long to become a "candidate for matrimony." Ultimately, his efforts to find a suitable partner would prove as fruitless as his endeavors to reclaim the Senate seat he had given up at the beginning of the war.

Although preoccupied with the patenting and marketing of his electric light system and the promotion of his tobacco cure, Clingman did not eschew politics during the mid-1880s. Indeed, he remained prominently in the public eye, promulgating his views on the tariff, civil service reform, and other political issues in letters to the newspapers and discussing them with reporters from the Washington, New York, and North Carolina presses. Shortly after his return to the nation's capital at the end of the 1882 state campaign, he spoke to a meeting of currency reformers at the National Hotel. Two days later, he published an exposition on the protective tariff in the *Washington Post*. Presented in the form of an imaginary conversation between an old lady and a country merchant, his essay made the familiar point that the tariff was an unfair "bounty" paid to domestic manufacturers, since it shielded them from foreign competition and thus allowed them to charge much higher prices.[1]

Nor was Clingman reticent in regard to the Civil Service Act that Pres. Chester Alan Arthur signed into law in January 1883. Passed by a lame-duck Republican Congress after that party's disastrous defeat in the midterm congressional elections, the so-called Pendleton Act established a merit system administered by a bipartisan civil service commission. The act also outlawed the practice of compulsory assessments, which had required federal officials to return a certain percentage of their income to party coffers. Although the Pendleton Act addressed some of the most salient demands of civil service reformers, Democrats were well aware that the Republicans had pushed the bill through Congress in order to freeze their partisans in office in the likely event their opponents won the next presidential election.[2]

Echoing the views of many Southern Democrats, Clingman denounced the Pendleton Act as a "mere sham." Since the act did not prohibit "voluntary" assessments, he claimed it would have little effect on electioneering practices. In January 1884 the former senator presented his own views on civil service reform in an open letter to the U.S. Congress. He suggested that a law be enacted making it a felony for any government official to call upon his subordinates to contribute money. According to his proposed bill, anyone making such contributions would be guilty of a misdemeanor and liable to a civil suit for twenty times the amount contributed. According to Clingman, congressional Democrats were "highly pleased" with his proposition and would soon introduce a bill to that effect. He predicted that if the bill were enacted into law, it would destroy the Republican party in those states where the organization was "maintained by contributions from office holders." Clingman was undoubtedly referring to the situation in North Carolina and other Southern states, where revenue officers and other federal appointees constituted the mainstay of Republicanism.[3]

Clingman's remarks about the potential political impact of his civil service bill indicate that in the aftermath of the Liberal defeat of 1882, he was again coming to the conclusion that his own best interests lay in working within, rather than outside of, the Democratic party. Perhaps his attitude was affected, in part, by Gov. Thomas J. Jarvis's decision to appoint Clingman and James Madison Leach, another disaffected Democrat, as state attorneys to argue North Carolina's cotton claims before the U.S. Congress. Certainly, the cash-strapped Clingman must have appreciated the additional income. Still, he continued to chastise the Democrats for failing to keep their campaign promises, particularly in regard to tariff reform. "The Democrats must do something more than talk," he told a reporter from the *New York Tribune*. "I tell them it is all talk and no action so far. There are plenty of good professions, but no fulfilment *[sic]*."[4]

Clingman's growing rapprochement with the Democrats brought into question his relationship with the North Carolina Liberal party. During the early spring, rumors again circulated that he would run for Congress as an independent against Robert B. Vance. Clingman waited until the Liberal and Republican Conventions met on 1 May before announcing his plans. Undoubtedly, he was disappointed by the nomination of Congressman Tyre York, a longtime opponent of the Western North Carolina Railroad, as the Liberal-Republican candidate for governor. Nor could he have applauded the provision in their platform calling for a tariff that would "give all needed protection to American industries and labor." And he was, at best, indifferent to the key plank in the coalition platform—the abolition of the existing system of county government.[5]

Early in May, Clingman announced he would not be a candidate for Congress. At the same time, he expressed his willingness to support "good nominees of the Democratic party" if the choice were limited to a Democrat or a Republican. While his remarks constituted something less than an enthusiastic endorsement of the Democracy, one observer noted that "he talks now rather like a Democrat than a sore head." Clingman's participation at a Democratic rally at Tammany Hall later that month also encouraged speculation that he had decided to "stand by his first love."[6]

When Clingman returned to North Carolina in mid-July, the *Asheville Citizen* reported that "we hear from him nothing of the Washington party, but a great deal of the . . . now world famous tobacco cure." Indeed, by that time he had already decided to endorse the national Democratic ticket of Grover Cleveland and Thomas A. Hendricks. Clingman did not accord Cleveland "a very high order of talent," but he did regard him as a man of firm character, patriotic purpose, and thorough honesty. In his opinion, the New York governor would, if elected, "prove the best President the country has had for the past twenty-five years." By the end of the month, Clingman had also announced his support for Alfred M. Scales and the other candidates on the Democratic state ticket.[7]

Clingman gave Cleveland and Scales little more than a perfunctory endorsement, however. He addressed no public meetings, even in his own county, preferring to devote his energies to promoting his tobacco cure. By the mid-1880s those energies were beginning to diminish. Shortly after returning to Asheville, Clingman celebrated his seventy-second birthday. Few of his contemporaries had lived that long. The ladies at the Eagle Hotel honored the occasion by presenting him with a beautiful bouquet of flowers they had gathered from a nearby field. Even though he was reported to be "in unusually good health and spirits," advancing age probably made him less inclined than in previous years to engage in a vigorous political campaign.[8]

Clingman was not entirely oblivious to politics during the summer and fall of 1884. In August he attended a debate between the two gubernatorial candidates in Madison County, after which he opined that "Scales did admirably." Shortly before the election, he offered his predictions about the outcome to the *Raleigh State Chronicle*. He was "sure" of Scales's election and "hopeful" of Cleveland's. "The national election," he observed, "is a treacherous thing to bet on," particularly since several third-party candidates would be siphoning off votes from the major parties. Moreover, the Democrats lacked a charismatic leader—"a man of resolution like Clay or Benton."[9]

The result in North Carolina, as Clingman had predicted, was a landslide victory for the Democrats. The endorsement of the national Republican ticket by Tyre York, William Johnston, and other Liberal leaders clearly identified them with that party and undermined their claim to "independentism." Scales beat York by more than twenty thousand votes, while Cleveland carried the state with an eighteen-thousand-vote majority. The legislative elections were even more catastrophic for the Liberal-Republican coalition, as the Democrats won a majority of more than one hundred seats in the 170-member general assembly. The debacle of 1884 sounded the death knell for the Liberal party in North Carolina. For some leaders, like York, Johnston, and Charles Price, Liberalism proved merely a way station on the road to Republicanism. Other erstwhile Liberals like Clingman and William M. Cocke drifted back into the Democracy.[10]

Clingman returned North in December eager to meet the first Democratic president since the Civil War. On 5 February 1885, he called on Cleveland at the Fifth Avenue Hotel in New York City, where the president-elect was receiving numerous fellow partisans seeking appointments or offering advice about the makeup of his cabinet. The cantankerous former senator protested loudly when the doorkeeper insisted he present his card before being admitted, but ultimately he did gain entry. A few weeks after the inauguration, Clingman had another opportunity to pay his respects to the president, this time at the White House. Possibly, he used the occasion to present the chief executive with the copy of his *Speeches and Writings* that today sits in the Princeton University Library.[11]

Clingman returned to Asheville on 30 April 1885 "looking healthy and in good spirits." A few weeks later, he received a letter from Lyman Draper of the Historical Society of Wisconsin. The previous summer, Draper had written in regard to his book on Daniel Boone—a project on which he had been working for more than thirty years. Clingman had presented him with an account of his visit to Grandfather Mountain in 1832, when his guide Jim Riddle had pointed out the place, near the present border of Watauga and Mitchell Counties, where Boone had once made camp. Draper had twice asked him for additional details, but Clingman could remember only that the camp was supposed to have been "a little to the South East of Grandfather Mt." Now the historian was inquiring about the origin of the name "Yadkin." On 2 June Clingman wrote back explaining that he had tried to obtain the information but had not been successful. He had no doubt, however, that the name was of Indian origin.[12]

Three days later, Draper wrote again, this time about Peter S. Ney, the enigmatic North Carolina school teacher who in his less sober moments had claimed to be Marshal Michel Ney of Napoleon's army. Clingman answered on 11 June that he had seen Ney only once—at a hotel in Mocksville "during the Jackson canvass." He told Draper that he took no side in the controversy over the teacher's relationship to the French general. "Some people believed he was really Marshal Ney, others doubted." Again, the persistent Draper pressed for additional details. Clingman remembered that he was not tall, but "rather a large man" with a large forehead. Draper seemed satisfied, at least for the moment.[13]

Clingman was still in Asheville when the news arrived that former president Ulysses S. Grant had passed away after a long illness. Grant's death, like that of James Garfield four years earlier, offered Southerners an opportunity to demonstrate their patriotism by joining their Northern brethren in expressions of mourning. On 24 July the citizens gathered at the Asheville courthouse to pay tribute to the departed statesman. Clingman called the meeting to order and was the first to speak. He characterized his Civil War adversary as having "been more liberal toward the South than his party generally were." To illustrate that point, he referred to an occurrence during the early part of Andrew Johnson's administration, which he had recounted eight years earlier in his *Speeches and Writings.* While Johnson was anxious to court-martial Robert E. Lee and other prominent Confederates, Grant had repeatedly insisted that such vindictive behavior would violate the terms of surrender. "I am satisfied," said Clingman, "that but for Gen. Grant's firm resistance, Johnson and Stanton would have attempted to execute prominent Confederates in this mode."[14]

Three days after delivering his eulogy on Grant, Clingman turned seventy-three. By now he was sufficiently advanced in years that his birthday had become a news event in itself. The *Asheville Citizen* playfully noted that he was still "younger than Moses" and "not as old as Methuselah." Referring to the presence of the State Guard in town, it jokingly added that his birthday had been celebrated that year "by a parade of the military." The *Tarboro Southerner* speculated that "the old gentleman, perhaps, has found the elixir of life in his now famous tobacco cure" and expressed hope that "he [may] long be spared to his State."[15]

Clingman remained in his native state, and very much in the news, until early December. In August he was reported "luxuriating . . . [on] huckleberries, from his plantation on the top of Pisgah"—in his estimation, "the finest huckleberry plantation on the continent." In early October the *Asheville Citizen* announced that he had been "contributing to the pleasure of guests of the Eagle Hotel . . . by singing the 'songs of his youth.'" According to the *Citizen,* "he attributes his

success in vocalism to his Tobacco Remedy." Later that month, he was a conspicuous figure at the Asheville fair, visiting the exhibits and cracking jokes with local reporters.[16]

In mid-November a resident of Asheville recorded his impressions of Clingman in a letter to the *Greensboro North State.* "Gen. Clingman is quietly resting
here," he reported, "thinking of the good old times and wondering what will happen next. He is in good health and ascribes it principally to the use of his tobacco
cure." As for his views on contemporary politics, the correspondent remarked
that "he had not much to say on the subject. . . . He seems quite jubilant about
democratic prospects; but deplores what is reported as the Senatorial-Satrapical
Division of North Carolina."[17]

Clingman returned to Washington on 3 December 1885 in time to witness the
opening of the first session of the Forty-Ninth Congress. By the time the session
ended eight months later, his opinion of the Cleveland administration had soured
considerably. Clingman was by no means the only Southerner to experience disillusionment. Democrats who adhered to soft-money views were angered by the
call in Cleveland's first annual message for the repeal of the Bland-Allison Silver
Coinage Act. On 13 January 1886 Senator Vance responded in a celebrated "silver speech," in which he "poured a merciless torrent of sarcasm and raillery at the
magnates of Wall street, their agents, associates and abettors." Though no admirer of the junior senator from North Carolina, Clingman was obliged to admit
he had made "a very fine effort."[18]

The slow pace of removals by the Cleveland administration also disappointed
those Democrats whose idea of civil service reform consisted primarily in the replacement of partisan Republicans with equally partisan Democrats. On 25 March
1886 Democratic senator Daniel W. Voorhees of Indiana called for the "absolute
repeal" of the Civil Service Act of 1883, characterizing it as a "violent and odious
obstruction to the will of the people and a stumbling-block in the way of a ratio-
nal and successful administration." No friend of the Pendleton Act himself,
Clingman was "among the first to congratulate Senator Voorhees at the conclusion of his speech."[19]

When Clingman returned to Asheville after the adjournment of Congress on
5 August 1886, his mind was not on politics but rather on the preparation of an
essay for *The Land of the Sky*—a monthly periodical "devoted to immigration,
real estate, and the development of our Western section of the State." Again, he
called attention to the existence of gold, silver, zircons, mica, corundum, iron,
nickel, and other metals and minerals in the western counties. Although much of
the essay simply repeated the themes presented in his previous publications,
Clingman did provide an engaging account of how his own interest in mineralogy
had developed during the late 1830s and early 1840s. He concluded with the standard paean about the prosperous future awaiting the residents of the mountain

region. Indeed, he predicted, "the day is not far distant when this will be probably the most productive region of the world." [20]

For a time it seemed that Clingman would not live long enough to witness that
day. In late October he had been healthy enough to travel to Raleigh, where he
"took [a] conspicuous and useful part in the discussions before the State Agricultural Society." On 14 November, however, while attending the Sunday morning
service at the Episcopal church in Asheville, he suddenly became ill and had to be
taken back to his room at the Eagle Hotel. On the twenty-seventh he claimed to
be "feeling better," but early in December he suffered a relapse and his condition
steadily deteriorated. On 4 December, the *Raleigh News and Observer* announced
that he was "lying critically ill." The onset of his second attack coincided with the
arrival in Asheville of the worst snowstorm in fifty years. The storm continued
unabated for more than sixty hours, leaving twenty-eight inches of snow and
drifts from six to ten feet. [21]

To all appearances, the seventy-four-year-old Clingman was "in his last illness." The Raleigh correspondent of the *Richmond Dispatch* went so far as to write
an obituary, noting that although "in later years he has been somewhat eccentric,"
he was a "kindly, courteous gentleman, full of pleasant reminiscences [and] . . . an
inventor of no mean ability." "One of his special discoveries," he added, "is the
'Clingman Tobacco Cure.'" There is no record of the nature of his illness or of
whether Clingman attempted to treat it with his tobacco preparations. If he did,
in fact, put the healing power of the "immortal weed" to the ultimate test, it fully
lived up to his expectations. By 7 December, he was well enough to leave his hotel room, trudge through the snowdrifts, and pay a call on the editor of the *Asheville Citizen*. Four days later, the paper reported that "Gen. Clingman continues
to improve, and speaks of going North in a few days." By 14 December he was
back in the nation's capital on the floor of the House of Representatives. [22]

According to the Washington correspondent of the *Charlotte Chronicle*, the
"old gentleman" was as garrulous as ever and seemed none the worse for wear.
"He speaks of Webster and Clay . . . with the utmost familiarity, quotes poetry by
the yard, sings a song sometimes, and always regrets that the average man is not
as great as he was about half a century ago." "I expect," the correspondent wryly
added, "he will say that tobacco cured him and enabled him to return to his accustomed haunts in this city." As further "evidence of his restoration to health,"
the *Asheville Citizen* pointed out that the general had visited New York City and
had given a "bright interview with the New York Sun." [23]

The interview was vintage Clingman. Once again, he made it clear that the
Cleveland administration had failed to provide satisfaction on the most pressing
political issues of the day. After cavalierly dismissing its civil service policy as
"unconstitutional," he went on to note that "there are two other questions of
vastly more importance. . . . On one of them the President is palpably wrong; as

to the other he is feebly right." The issue on which he was "palpably wrong" was the currency. Clingman staunchly disagreed with Cleveland's opposition to the remonetization of silver and his determination to repeal the Bland-Allison Act. In his opinion, "silver and gold bullion should be alike received by the government and coin certificates issued thereon, receivable by the government for all dues to it." With such certificates in circulation, it would be "almost impossible that any serious money panic could occur."[24]

The issue on which Cleveland was only "feebly right" was the tariff. In his first annual message to Congress, the president had called for a revision in the tariff system that would reduce the cost of "necessaries" while taking into account the just claims of labor and industry. A moderate tariff reduction bill introduced in the House of Representatives had received Cleveland's support, but Democratic protectionists had combined with Republicans to defeat it. In his interview with the *Sun*, Clingman made the familiar point that protective tariffs were merely bounties paid to "the wealthy monopolist and manufacturing bosses." He spoke favorably about a return to the ad valorem system that had prevailed during the late antebellum years, but he acknowledged that such a tariff would be a "better tariff than any we are likely to have."[25]

Shortly after presenting his views to the *Sun*, Clingman returned to North Carolina to spend the Christmas holidays with his niece Bettie Gibson and her family in Concord. Reporting his visit, the *Concord Times* noted that "his health is much improved." After the holidays, he turned his attention once again to electric lighting, spending the spring and summer of 1887 in Washington in an effort to get his application for an improved arc light through the U.S. Patent Office. He returned to Asheville on 19 October, in time to greet President Cleveland when he stopped in town after a tour of the Midwest. Later that month, he spoke at a mass meeting in support of a county subscription of four hundred thousand dollars in the capital stock of three railroads that were proposing to extend their lines through Asheville.[26]

By January 1888 Clingman was back in the North, making the final revisions in his patent application and looking for investors for his lighting system. In April he finally secured a patent on his improved arc lamp, and in late November he entered into a tentative agreement with the International Patent Company on the foreign rights to his patents. When Clingman returned to North Carolina in mid-December, his mind was very much on the electric light. As he explained to the *Asheville Citizen*, his experiments had demonstrated that his own system of lighting was decidedly "superior to the systems now in use." Thus far, a "combination" of major electric light companies had successfully blocked its introduction, but he was still hopeful that "some companies which aver that they do not belong to the combination" might take an interest in it.[27]

Although his efforts to promote his electric lighting system had occupied much of Clingman's attention for the past two years, he had by no means abandoned hope for returning to the U.S. Senate. The term of Matt W. Ransom was due to expire in March 1889, and the Democratic caucus would be meeting in January to nominate a successor. The three-term incumbent, whose record in the Senate had been unimpressive, was more than willing to spend another six years in Washington. However, a number of prominent Democrats, including former governor Thomas J. Jarvis, former congressman Alfred M. Waddell, and Sydenham B. Alexander of the recently established Farmers' Alliance, were openly vying for the seat. According to one report, Ransom's opponents were crowing "that it is about certain that he will be defeated; that he is, in point of fact, already defeated." With Ransom appearing increasingly vulnerable, the seventy-six-year-old Clingman decided to throw his hat in the ring.[28]

Three days before the convening of the general assembly, Clingman appeared in Raleigh to buttonhole the incoming legislators. He reminded them that he had been elected to a six-year term in the Senate in 1861 but had served only a few months when the war began. All he was asking was to be allowed to complete his term. One legislator characterized it as "a queer argument," but it was probably as effective as any other he might have put forward. When the Democrats assembled in caucus on the evening of 15 January 1889, Melvin E. Carter, a member from Buncombe, asked that Clingman be permitted to address them. The request was regarded as "most unusual" and initially was voted down. After discussion, the former senator was finally given twenty minutes to present his case.[29]

Following the completion of Clingman's presentation, which one observer described as "a covert attack upon Senator Ransom," nominations were declared to be in order. J. S. T. Baird, the Buncombe County physician who had once attested to the tobacco cure, announced that "by request, he presented the name of Thomas L. Clingman." After the other nominations had been tendered and speeches made on behalf of the candidates, the vote was taken. Ransom received sixty votes—one short of the requisite majority. Clingman received only Baird's vote. On the second ballot, several supporters of Waddell and Jarvis switched to Ransom, thereby giving him a nomination that was tantamount to election. Dr. Baird remained loyal to the discoverer of the tobacco remedy.[30]

If Clingman found the experience humiliating, he never publicly admitted it. Indeed, his subsequent behavior suggests that he might have been grateful to the legislators for giving him an opportunity to formally present his case. Two months later, when sixty Democratic assemblymen took a train excursion to Asheville, Clingman was among those who feted them at a banquet with toasts and "entertaining addresses, which were applauded and received with much good will." Although he was undoubtedly disappointed that the Democrats had not seen fit to acknowledge his claims, he probably could take comfort in knowing he would have another opportunity in two years when Vance's term expired.[31]

In the meantime, other interests took his mind off his political failures. One of the most important related to the plight of the thousands of indigent and disabled

Confederate veterans. Despite pleas for support by Gov. Alfred M. Scales, the penurious general assembly had provided only a pittance for relief. In January 1889 the veterans took matters into their own hands by organizing a convention to present their demands formally to the legislature. The meeting, scheduled for 22 January, was preceded by a march to the capitol and a reception in the office of incoming governor Daniel G. Fowle. That evening, the convention assembled in the hall of the House of Representatives, and a resolution was presented calling for a 5 percent tax increase in order to provide pensions for soldiers and their widows. Clingman was the first to speak in support of the resolution. In a few "happy and facetious remarks," he "warmly endorsed the movement to increase the pensions of the wounded soldiers." [32]

As one of North Carolina's oldest living veterans, Clingman also took an active part in the Confederate Veteran's Association, which was organized in Raleigh the day after the convention. In August he participated in a three-day encampment near Waynesville, which attracted fifteen hundred veterans and several thousand spectators. In what one observer characterized as "a brief, very felicitous, entertaining, and somewhat facetious speech," Clingman recalled the exploits of his brigade, as well as the several wounds he had to remember them by. Referring to those wounded veterans who had dutifully preserved the bullets and other relics of their misfortune, he jokingly remarked that "all the balls had passed through [him] and left no such abiding memento." [33]

Clingman also played a conspicuous role in the alumni reunion that was held in Chapel Hill on 5 June 1889 to commemorate the centennial of the University of North Carolina. The aging statesman occupied a place of honor on the rostrum, along with Governor Fowle, the justices of the state supreme court, other prominent North Carolinians, and representatives from Harvard, the University of Virginia, and other institutions of higher education. Walter L. Steele, the president of the alumni association, called the meeting to order and then proceeded to call the roll of classes according to the year of graduation. As a member of the class of 1832, Clingman was one of the first to come forward to speak. [34]

In a wide-ranging and somewhat rambling address, Clingman reminisced about his days at Chapel Hill and about a chance conversation in New York twenty years earlier that had inspired him to join the Episcopal Church. Moving from the spiritual into the realm of the material, he proceeded to recount the marvelous technological advances of the age—telegraphs, telephones, phonographs, and electric street cars—inventions so fantastic that if he had mentioned them to Pres. Joseph Caldwell fifty years earlier, the professor would have told him, "young man, no one will ever beat you in the expression of absurd ideas." Yet, all of those fanciful ideas had since become reality. He expatiated upon the enormous agricultural, mineral, and timber resources of the Old North State and upon his own contributions in calling the attention of the world to the existence of corundum, mica, diamonds, and platinum—not to mention the zircons that would soon furnish "the best light to the world." He concluded with a reference to his favorite topic, the tobacco remedy, predicting that once men learned how to put it to proper use, it would dispel "at least nine-tenths of the bodily sufferings of humanity."[35]

Although Clingman's public address focused on the undeniable material advances of the past half century, privately he could not help lamenting that politics had not kept pace with scientific and technological progress. During his sojourn at Chapel Hill, he was overheard expounding to a group of interested young men about the "decadence of the times" and about "how far behind the past in statesmanship were the Congressmen of to-day." Clearly, the times had changed—and, in Clingman's opinion, not for the better.[36]

Clingman generally left for Washington in early December, but he was still in Asheville on 6 December 1889 when the news was announced of the death of Jefferson Davis. Clingman's opinion of the former president of the Confederate States of America had never been high. Indeed, as one acquaintance remarked during the 1870s, "he despises Mr. Davis and cannot mention his name without excitement in his manner and bitter words of reproach." Possibly, his views had mellowed somewhat with the passage of time. Certainly, when the citizens of Asheville gathered at the courthouse to mourn his passing and to pass resolutions of respect, it would have been entirely unfitting to have expressed any negative sentiments.[37]

Because of his long association with the deceased statesman, Clingman was selected to be the first speaker at the memorial service. To his credit, he managed to rise to the occasion, presenting "a short, but eloquent sketch of some of the more prominent characteristics and public services of the dead chieftain." Afterward, he joined the other attenders in support of resolutions lauding "the patriotism which he exhibited during the long years of struggle to establish the glorious, but lost cause." On 11 December Clingman walked at the head of the one hundred silver-haired veterans who marched from the courthouse down Patton Avenue and Church Street to the Central Methodist Church, where another memorial ceremony was conducted. As he listened to the services, the seventy-seven-year-old Clingman must certainly have been aware of his own mortality. Two years earlier, it had been noted that he and Davis were the only Southerners serving in the U.S. Senate on the eve of the great war who were still among the living. Now there remained only one.[38]

Clingman was not ready to relegate his own career to the pages of history. There was still plenty of work to be done in the present. The hard-money policies pursued by the federal government for the past twenty-five years had greatly increased the Southern farmer's burden of indebtedness. But now a new wind seemed to be blowing through Washington in the person of the recently elected chief executive, Benjamin Harrison, who reportedly was a friend of silver. Although he had failed to come out forthrightly in support of free silver in his recent message to Congress, Harrison did seem inclined to favor additional leg-islation. A large number of silver bills were introduced into both houses of Congress in January 1890, and inflationists were hopeful about the possibility of passage.[39]

It was within that context of optimism that Clingman invested what little re-mained of his financial resources in the eight-page *Message to the Senate and House of Representatives.* The pamphlet, which was published on 7 March 1890, con-sisted primarily of extracts from his Hendersonville speech of September 1876, in which he had denounced the demonetization of silver as "a great fraud and crime against the American people." In the remainder of the pamphlet, he as-serted that nobody except Great Britain and the "Wall Street buzzards" had benefited from demonetization, and he dismissed the arguments against silver as "so absurd that they seem amazingly ridiculous."[40]

Although Clingman's pamphlet probably had negligible impact on the passage of the Sherman Silver Purchase Act a few months later, it was generally well re-ceived in his home state. The *Raleigh News and Observer* noted that "the General is . . . one of the ablest men this State has ever produced and he possesses such a wide range of information as to entitle him to high rank in any circle of savants. His views will always command the attention of the people of North Carolina." The *Asheville Democrat* agreed that "like everything emanating from him," his ar-gument on behalf of silver "is able, and strongly presents the interests of the people in their demand for more currency."[41]

The day after publishing his pamphlet, Clingman talked with the Washington correspondent of the *Raleigh State Chronicle.* The journalist was impressed that the years had taken so little toll on his intellectual powers. "He seems not to have lost the mental vigor that characterized him during his long public life before the war." He added that the general seemed as much interested in tobacco as in silver and had boasted of inventing "an elixir of youth, mainly composed of tobacco, which has made a young man of him." The reporter also noted that the "sprightly gentleman from Buncombe" had been quite "attentive of late to two wealthy wid-ows at the Riggs House" and that he expected Clingman would soon announce "that he is opposing 'Our Zeb' for the U.S. Senate."[42]

Clingman was not yet prepared to formally declare his candidacy for the Sen-ate. As he explained to another reporter a few months later, he "never works for a thing so far ahead." However, by the spring of 1890 the seventy-seven-year-old bachelor had definitely become a candidate for matrimony. Thirteen years earlier, when he had been confined to his hotel room in Washington because of illness, he had lamented to John Hill Wheeler about his "lonely condition in life—no one to comfort and minister to him." His loneliness had not dissipated in the interven-ing years, as Wheeler and most of his other friends and associates from the ante-bellum generation had, one by one, passed on. On occasions when he had re-marked to acquaintances that he "did not feel much happiness in life," he had generally been told, "it is because you have never married."[43]

There was another, equally compelling, reason why Clingman needed to make a "lucky strike"—and soon. By 1890 he had just about run out of money. His unsuccessful electric light and tobacco ventures had depleted much of his resources. The publication of his silver pamphlet had consumed still more. He had property in North Carolina that could be unloaded for cash, but buyers were difficult to find and his creditors were beginning to dun him for unpaid obligations. "Don't you think it about time you paid me the $20 I loaned you . . . two *years ago*," one angry creditor wrote in May 1890. Marriage to a wealthy widow would provide the ideal solution to his financial problems.[44]

Thus when Clingman visited the White House on 19 May 1890 to pay his respects to President and Mrs. Harrison, he made it a point to shake hands not only with the Chief Executive and First Lady but also with "about twenty-five elligible [sic] ladies, to all of whom . . . he was very attentive." He told the president, and probably most of the ladies as well, that two senators had recently complimented him for being "the best looking man in the Senate Chamber at [James B.] Beck's funeral." According to one report, "Harrison didn't seem to like it! Our statesman thinks Cousin Ben is a little jealous of him!" Apparently the eligible ladies were not impressed either, for Clingman was still a bachelor when he returned to North Carolina in the summer.[45]

Lacking the financial resources to make his customary winter trip to Washington, Clingman spent the next sixteen months as a resident of Asheville. By 1890 the town had come a long way from the tiny hamlet in which the ambitious young lawyer had hung his shingle fifty-four years earlier. As Clingman had predicted, the coming of the railroads had provided the key to growth and prosperity. During the 1880s Asheville's population increased from twenty-six hundred residents to almost twelve thousand inhabitants. The town could now boast of ten schools, ranging from the elementary to the college level; sixteen churches; a public library; gas, electric, and telephone systems; four miles of electric street railway; a large shoe factory; a cotton factory; and numerous tobacco factories and warehouses.[46]

Along with that phenomenal growth had come the typical urban problems. The water and sewage systems that had been constructed during the mid-1880s had become inadequate to support the rapidly increasing population. Early in 1891, heavy torrents of rain that continued from January until March had made the streets almost impassable. Largely through the intercession of Mayor Charles D. Blanton, the general assembly had authorized the town to issue five hundred thousand dollars in bonds to pave the streets and extend the sewage system and water mains. The bonds could be issued, however, only if approved in a referendum.[47]

The contest was a "bitterly hot" one. Clingman threw the weight of his prestige behind the bond issue, informing his fellow townsmen at a public meeting on 17 April 1891 that he "heartily favored the bill." He appealed especially to the black residents to support the measure, arguing that the construction work would put a large amount of money into circulation and offer numerous employment opportunities. Moreover, the improvements, once completed, would "build up

Asheville," thus allowing its black population "to secure permanent employment." The bond issue was approved, and the town's rapid growth continued unabated.[48]

During his protracted stay in Asheville, Clingman participated actively in local politics. Despite his criticisms of the Democrats over the past decade, party leaders in Buncombe County apparently welcomed his reentrance into the fold. On 23 August 1890 the former senator made his first appearance at a county convention in more than a decade, regaling his listeners with "an old time Democratic speech" about the "scarcity of money" and the "obnoxious tariff laws." Four days later, he spoke at the district convention that nominated William T. Crawford as the Democratic candidate for the U.S. House of Representatives. Later in the fall, he was a featured speaker at the conventions that selected Buncombe County's Democratic candidates for the state House of Representatives and senate. Clingman was also given the honor of introducing Sen. Matt W. Ransom when he made a campaign speech in Asheville on 10 October.[49]

Two years earlier, with Clingman's criticisms of President Cleveland and the Democratic Congress ringing in their years, the voters of the mountain district had elected Republican Hamilton G. Ewart to the House of Representatives and had given a majority to Benjamin Harrison in the presidential contest. Now, as if to atone for his earlier apostasy, Clingman centered his fire on Congressman Ewart. Speaking at a Democratic meeting on 13 October, he accused the Republican of using outside money in an attempt to buy the election. In the old days, he said, if it were known that a candidate had accepted money from outside his district, "he would have been sent to Jericho with a whirl."[50]

Clingman cleverly played to the sentiments of the blacks in the audience, reminding them that before the war an able-bodied slave sold for fifteen hundred dollars. "If you sell yourself for less than $1500 now," he admonished them, "you will put yourself below what you were as a slave. . . . Had you not all better vote against Ewart than have it thought that you had sold yourselves." Ewart, who lost the election by more than one thousand votes, reportedly remarked afterward that Clingman's speech "did him more harm than any other, and that it had caused his defeat."[51]

Clingman remained prominently in the public eye after the election. In December he attended a three-day convention of the Southern Interstate Immigration Association, which was held in the Grand Opera House in Asheville and attracted about six hundred representatives from fourteen states. The following May it was announced that Gov. Thomas M. Holt had appointed him as a delegate to the Scotch-Irish Convention in Louisville. In June his name appeared at the head of a list of signatories calling for a meeting to plan for the upcoming centennial of Buncombe County. In July he published a letter in the *Washington National View* advocating "the free coinage of silver and a large supply of greenbacks" and expressing hope for a return to "the pure systems of government that we had in our earlier days." Later that month the *Asheville Citizen* acknowledged the occasion of his seventy-ninth birthday. In October he was reported attending a banquet in honor of the Philadelphia journalist Alexander K. McClure, sitting at the head table with McClure, the mayor and aldermen of Asheville, and other local dignitaries.[52]

By November, Clingman had become weary of his stay in Asheville and was anxious to return North. Speaking to the editor of the *Asheville Democrat* a few days before he left town, he said he planned to spend some time with his relatives and friends and then go to New York "to look after his electric light patents which are now being tested with a view of putting them to use." Clingman spent almost four months in Concord with his niece Bettie Gibson and the other members of her family. Shortly after his arrival, he contacted businessman James Turner Morehead and offered to sell his share in a baryta mine he owned. Negotiations over the terms of the sale dragged on until early February, when Morehead agreed to purchase the property for five hundred dollars. With instructions from Clingman, Bettie Gibson drew up the deed of sale, and her husband, James, the Cabarrus County clerk, had it acknowledged, witnessed, and sent off to Morehead.[53]

Even though Clingman remained in reasonably good physical condition, an obvious decline in his mental abilities was now causing concern among his relatives. Bettie Gibson confided to her sister that "his mind is undoubtedly impaired to a considerable degree and his memory less good on many subjects than it used to be." However, she quickly added that "he never forgets anything he wants to remember—nor allows any one else to forget it." Indeed, although "it is certainly impossible to exaggerate his unreasonableness and absurdities . . . the Genl does and says all those thing[s] because he chooses to do and say them and not because he is crazy." His most irritating characteristic, in the opinion of Bettie Gibson, was his incessant talk about marriage. "His mind is fully made up to get married," she told her sister. Provided, she sarcastically added, "he can find a woman with the requisite amount of money whom he can make up his mind to honor with his name and the care of his personal comfort."[54]

Finally, the money from Morehead arrived, and on 9 February 1892 Clingman took the night train to Washington. The Gibsons and several of their friends accompanied him to the depot. One of the friends helped him get his ticket, assisted him onto the train, and escorted him to his seat. Clingman appeared not to recognize the man, even though he had seen him on numerous occasions throughout the winter. Bettie Gibson expressed mixed feelings about her uncle's departure. She understood his desire for "a few weeks relief from the dreariness of his life" in Concord. However, she feared that "his hopes of 'making a lucky strike'" would prove futile and he would "come back here just as destitute and even more disappointed and discontented than he is now."[55]

Once in Washington, Clingman returned to his familiar haunts. Although he occasionally still listened to the congressional debates, he now spent most of his time on the leather lounges in the cloakrooms of the House and Senate, "talking in loud, strident tones to the younger members of the grandeur of the old institutions and the degeneracy of modern times." With hair and beard as white as snow and dressed antebellum style in a long frock coat and soft thin-soled shoes, he moved about the cloakrooms "like a veritable ghost of departed times." Needless to say, he remained "a 'crank' on the subject of tobacco." [56]

Clingman's hopes for a "lucky strike" now centered on his long-departed friend Stephen A. Douglas's widow, who was visiting the nation's capital during the winter of 1892. Indeed, his interest in the Widow Douglas became a subject of Washington gossip after an amusing incident in a streetcar in March. An acquaintance who ran into Clingman on a trip uptown surmised that he must be calling on a lady. "How did you guess that?" Clingman asked. "Why," responded the acquaintance, "you look so spruce and your expression is so very pleasant. Am I right?" "You are right," Clingman shouted back in a voice that had become increasingly loud as a result of the onset of deafness. "I am on my way to call on a lady and a very charming one she is. . . . She is now a widow, and as I am a bachelor . . . my call may set the gossips to talking. But I can't help that. I am not to be denied the pleasure of seeing her simply because people will talk about matrimony." [57]

Clingman returned to Asheville still a bachelor on 21 July 1892. A few days later, he celebrated his eightieth birthday—an event that, as usual, was duly noted by the town press. The *Asheville Journal* pointed out that few men ever reached their eightieth birthday with "the remarkable physical and mental powers that still attend Gen Clingman" and expressed hope that "he may continue to appreciate and enjoy them for many a long year." Although those remarkable powers were already beginning to fail him, Clingman's major concern was an acute lack of money. In September the *Asheville Citizen* called on the legislators from the mountain district to introduce a bill granting him a state pension. Despite its entreaties, no aid was forthcoming. [58]

Meanwhile, Clingman managed to come up with an additional eight hundred dollars by selling his choicest property—his "plantation" on Mount Pisgah. By December he was once again thinking about returning to Washington. He told the *Asheville Gazette* he would be leaving sometime after the new year. He had been favored with very good health throughout the fall, he remarked, and "did not feel over forty years old." He also wanted the readers of the *Gazette* to know that "he is still a candidate for matrimony." [59]

On 8 February 1893 Clingman left Asheville en route to the nation's capital, where he remained until 22 March, witnessing the final days of the Fifty-Second Congress and the inauguration of Grover Cleveland. At the inaugural ceremonies, he showed unmistakable signs of disorientation, as he tried to appropriate for himself the scarlet chair in front of the clerk's desk that had been reserved for outgoing president Benjamin Harrison. At the end of the ceremonies, he also created a stir by taking a position at the head of the procession that followed Cleveland and Harrison out of the Senate Chamber. His eccentric behavior and old-fashioned, threadbare attire caught the attention of a reporter from the *New York World,* who ridiculed him as "a harmless crank" who had once been "a man of national prominence."[60]

The North Carolina presses howled with indignation. The *Asheville Citizen* reminded the *World*'s reporter that "it is not yet a crime, outside of Washington at least, to wear either a rusty hat or a coat or both." As a former member, Clingman had a right to the floor of the Senate, and if the arrangements for the ceremony "had been more carefully ordered and generally understood, we feel sure that the General would not have intruded on them." The *Wilmington Messenger* was more terse in its response to the "cruel caricature." Noting that Clingman had "passed his eightieth year," the paper said it was "brutal to make game of any eccentricity that might appear."[61]

Fortunately, as one contemporary pointed out, Clingman "had few humiliations. He was too confident of his own powers to feel them, too sure of his own position to be ashamed." Besides, he had other concerns more compelling than the boorish remarks of an ill-mannered reporter. His most recent trip to Washington had exhausted his remaining liquid capital. By the summer of 1893, the once-powerful statesman had been reduced to borrowing small sums from his relatives in order to pay his hotel bills. Still, he remained optimistic that by selling his mineral properties and other assets "I will be able not only to become free from all debts, but be able to aid my friends."[62]

At the end of November, Clingman left Asheville to visit his niece in Concord. He had frequently spent the Christmas holidays with the Gibson family, and he probably did not realize he had taken his last look at the town he had called home for almost sixty years. Clingman remained in Concord until July 1894—just long enough to exhaust the patience of Bettie Gibson. He was then brought to the home of Bettie's sister Jenny Kerr, who lived on the plantation she had inherited from her father in Yadkin County. Another sister and several brothers also resided in the vicinity, and collectively they took responsibility for their aging uncle.[63]

Much of the day-to-day care was provided by Henry Augustus ("Hal") Jarratt, the grandson of Clingman's late cousin Isaac Jarratt. Then in his midteens, Jarratt remembered Clingman as "a very provoking and difficult old man to have in the house." On the other hand, he acknowledged that he "got clearer and more understandable explanations of the then important political questions of the day from him than I was ever able to get from several of the younger and supposedly better balanced male members of my family." Clingman remained with his relatives until September 1897, by which time his mental and physical condition had deteriorated to the point where specialized care had become necessary.[64]

The State Hospital for the Insane at Morganton, which enjoyed a reputation as a "model of care and management," seemed the most appropriate location. In a clinical sense, Clingman probably was not insane. As Hal Jarratt put it, "he was no more insane than the people who had him so declared; but was simply in his second childhood." The family based the claim to insanity on the head injury inflicted by Josiah Turner twenty-seven years earlier. On that pretext, the hospital committee approved the application for his admission. Accompanied by his nephew Thomas Lanier Puryear, Clingman departed in mid-September for what would prove to be his final destination.[65]

During his six weeks at Morganton, Clingman seemed "more interested in eating than anything else." Despite a rail-thin physique, his appetite was "abnormally good," and he talked continually about "something to eat." By now, he was nearly deaf and could carry on conversations only with great difficulty. He had definitely not lost his voice, however, as one visitor who watched him spend almost an entire day singing "Amazing Grace, How Sweet the Sound" could attest. And notwithstanding a failing memory, he was reportedly able one day to give "a fairly intelligible account of his duel with Yancey." When he was not eating or singing or reminiscing about past triumphs, he read his Bible. On numerous occasions, he could be seen going out into the sunshine on the east side of the hospital and with trembling hands raising the book to his lips to kiss a passage that had made a special impression on him.[66]

Some time in October Clingman's condition began deteriorating, and in early November it was reported that "his death may be expected at any time." The end came at about one o'clock in the afternoon of 3 November 1897. At the close of the war, Clingman had entrusted his Confederate uniform to Jenny Kerr and had told her that he wished to be buried in it. She had promised her uncle that "you shall be if I am living when you die." After Clingman was committed to Morganton, she sent the clothes to Dr. P. L. Murphey, the superintendent, and he saw to it that the general's wishes were carried out.[67]

By request of Bettie Gibson, Clingman's body was sent to Concord, where it lay in state the next day in the Episcopal church. On 5 November the church was filled to overflowing as Rev. J. C. Davis conducted the memorial service. Six members of Clingman's Brigade served as pallbearers, while ninety-four Confederate veterans acted as an escort. After another service at the city cemetery, the veterans participated in filling the grave. A beautiful wreath of flowers was laid atop it, and the mourners "left the hero to sleep."[68]

20 Prince of Politicians

The hero did not sleep long in Concord. Even before Clingman's death, the Confederate veterans of Buncombe County, many of whom had served with him in the 25th Regiment, had expressed the desire that he be buried in Asheville. After learning of Clingman's death, William H. S. Burgwyn, who had served as adjutant in Clingman's Brigade, communicated their wish to the family. By that time, arrangements had already been made for his interment at Concord, and the family was unwilling to disappoint the old soldiers who were coming, many from long distances, to serve as pallbearers.[1]

The Buncombe County veterans remained persistent. Together with the Asheville City Council and other interested citizens, they passed resolutions conveying their "deep sense of appropriateness that Asheville should be his last resting place" and memorialized the family to that end. The councilors appropriated one hundred dollars to help defray the expenses of disinterring the remains and transporting them to Asheville. That sum was quickly matched by an identical appropriation from the Buncombe County Board of Commissioners.[2]

The veterans' request was formally conveyed to Bettie Gibson, who agreed that Clingman's enduring love of the mountains made Asheville a more fitting location for his final resting place. The other members of the family were consulted, and in mid-November they sent a letter of approval to Mayor J. E. Rankin. The letter was turned over to James M. Ray, commander of the Zeb Vance camp of the United Confederate Veterans, who made arrangements for a memorial ceremony to take place in Asheville on 7 December. A committee consisting of Ray, Burgwyn, and three others visited Riverside cemetery and purchased a plot overlooking the French Broad River, just a short distance from the grave of Clingman's great rival Zebulon B. Vance, who had passed away three years earlier.[3]

On the appointed day, a funeral procession formed on Church Street and, shortly after noon, began moving toward the courthouse. The space between the courthouse and the speaker's stand was filled with citizens who had come to pay their last respects to Asheville's most distinguished resident. The casket, which had been escorted to Courthouse Square by veterans of the 25th Regiment, rested directly in front of the speaker's stand, draped in the old regimental flag.[4]

The ceremony began with the singing of "America" and an invocation from the Book of Psalms, followed by eulogies from Ray, Burgwyn, Allen T. Davidson, Bishop T. U. Dudley of Kentucky, and Col. V. S. Lusk. The speakers emphasized Clingman's incorruptibility as a politician and his gallantry as a soldier. In the life of Clingman, said Lusk, the historian would find much material "to embellish a chapter in the history of great men. In the annals of North Carolina . . . no man would occupy a more exalted place." After a closing prayer, a procession was formed and the casket was carried to Riverside cemetery. There, Clingman was laid to rest "amid the scenes of his youthful struggles and manhood's triumphs," with the mountains that he had so often explored standing as "sentinels to guard him for eternity."[5]

The obituaries that appeared in the North Carolina newspapers in the weeks after Clingman's death dutifully recounted his political, military, scientific, and literary achievements. He was also the subject of a Memorial Day address by William H. S. Burgwyn in May 1898, which remains the most detailed and accurate brief account of his career. Like most of the other chroniclers, Burgwyn made a distinction between Clingman's prewar career, which was devoted mainly to politics, and the postwar years during which he "disappears forever from the public stage" and "turns his attention to developing the mineral resources of the western part of the state, and . . . [to] scientific investigation."[6]

In fact, Clingman's ambition was too overpowering, and politics too much in his blood, for him ever to have been content with a life dedicated strictly to intellectual pursuits. An obituary published in the *New York Times* presented a more accurate characterization of the man when it noted that he "never lost his infatuation for politics and political life." The *Asheville Citizen* was also closer to the mark eight years earlier when it had assigned him "the title of Prince of Politicians." In Clingman's case, as the *New York Tribune* remarked a few weeks before his death, the old adage "once a politician always a politician" held true. "As in his young days . . . the veteran could still shake hands and crack jokes with the best of them."[7]

The two prizes for which Clingman "strove in every act of his political career"—"the two great desires of his life"—were a seat in the U.S. Senate and the presidency. All other considerations were subordinated to those all-consuming goals. By 1858 he had accomplished his first objective, "and he at least, never doubted that, but for the war, he would have gained the other also."[8] After the war, Clingman most likely realized that no Southerner would ever again occupy the presidency in his lifetime. However, far from eschewing politics, he spent the remainder of his life engaging in a succession of failed schemes to recover the Senate seat he had abandoned at the beginning of the Civil War.

Clingman's prewar success was due, in no small part, to his adeptness at creating an image of himself as a political independent. Reflecting back on his career, he remarked in 1882 that he had been "elected as an independent candidate to both houses of the Legislature of the State, and for fourteen years to the Congress of the United States, besides having been made a Senator three times to the same political body." When he spoke of being an "independent," Clingman did not mean he had never affiliated with a party. He readily acknowledged that he began his career as "a most decided and zealous Whig" and later "steadily supported the Democratic [presidential] candidates." In his own mind, Clingman's status as an "independent" derived from the fact that he was never "the candidate of any political convention." Thus he had never been obligated to subordinate his own principles to the dictates of party. Instead, he had "always told the people that I should, on all occasions, follow my convictions in my votes and speeches."[9]

The political culture in which Clingman grew up was conditioned by the yeoman ideals of autonomy and self-sufficiency. The small-scale farmers who comprised the majority of the population in the Old North State "valued their independence above all else and struggled to maintain a large degree of autonomy as the core of their social identity; they were not accustomed to being told what to do." That attitude necessarily led to a suspicion of elites and faraway governments over which ordinary people had little control. The yeoman ideal was embodied in the ideology of classical republicanism, which emphasized the endemic conflict between liberty and power and stressed the need for constant vigilance on the part of the people to prevent aggressions of power.[10]

Classical republicanism bred an ambivalent attitude toward political parties. In recent years, historians have called attention to "the strength and intensity of the commitment to parties" among antebellum Americans. By the 1830s, according to Joel H. Silbey, the antipartyism so characteristic of late eighteenth- and early nineteenth-century America had given way to a "partisan imperative," as "people came to accept parties and develop partisan commitments and loyalties of tremendous strength, intensity, and vitality." Those loyalties were evidenced by the remarkable stability in voting behavior and by the extraordinarily high voter turnout. Americans would not have flocked to the polls in such staggering numbers, the argument goes, if the parties had not meant something important to them.[11]

There is much to recommend in that viewpoint. Nineteenth-century Americans were, in fact, tenaciously loyal to their parties and to the principles for which each party claimed to stand. At the same time, they were deeply suspicious of the caucuses, conventions, and other mechanisms of central control the parties established to nominate candidates and conduct campaigns. Voters and politicians were expected to subordinate their personal preferences to the will of the party as expressed by those caucuses and conventions—an expectation that ran counter to the republican ideal of an independent electorate. Moreover, party machinery was highly susceptible to manipulation by small groups of politicians in Congress and the state capitals, as well as by "courthouse cliques" at the county seats. In North Carolina, the apparatus established by the parties worked most effectively in districts where the party balance was close and the need to present a united front overrode all other considerations. It worked less efficiently in localities where one party had a heavy majority.[12]

In the mountain district, where the Whigs enjoyed large majorities throughout the 1840s, elections to Congress were contested by rival Whig candidates who ran without benefit of a formal party nomination. Ironically, that situation left the balance of power in the hands of the Democrats and gave the advantage to any Whig who was able to mobilize their support. During the 1850s Clingman "proved himself extraordinarily adept at getting elected as a[n] . . . independent" by combining Democratic votes with those of his own faction of Southern Rights Whigs.[13] He won his first election to Congress a decade earlier not by proclaiming his independentism but by capitalizing on Whig dissatisfaction with the independent course pursued in Congress by longtime incumbent James Graham. It was not Clingman, but rather Graham in 1845, who first demonstrated that it was possible for an "independent" Whig with solid backing from the Democrats to defeat a "regular" Whig who enjoyed the overwhelming support of his own party.

Clingman's transformation from "ultra Whig" to independent was the product of political calculation as much as conviction. After winning back his House seat in 1847, he had initially shown no affinity toward the Democrats but continued to behave as a partisan Whig, much to the consternation of the Polk administration. It was Clingman's determination to challenge incumbent George E. Badger for the U.S. Senate in December 1848 that caused him to reassess his position and strike out as an independent.

Clingman hoped to gain enough support from the Democratic legislators to overcome Badger's overwhelming strength among the Whigs. In order to accomplish that objective, he placed himself "in the position of an independent candidate" whose goal was to "promote the welfare and honor of our common country" rather than to advance the interests of a particular party. By taking a more forceful stand than Badger on Southern Rights and by demonstrating a willingness to accommodate the Democrats on partisan issues unrelated to slavery, Clingman succeeded in rallying a substantial number of Democrats behind his candidacy. At the same time, his disloyal and opportunistic behavior alienated most of the leading Whigs in the Old North State, who had previously been his ardent supporters.[14]

After 1848 Clingman's hopes for a Senate seat rested almost entirely on the Democrats. His speech of January 1850, in which he unabashedly calculated the value of the Union, and his subsequent vote against the key provisions of the Compromise of 1850 were both designed to shore up Democratic support in preparation for another try for the Senate. As Whigs in his own congressional district became increasingly alienated by his course on the Southern Rights issue, Clingman also became more dependent on Democratic votes to retain his seat in the House of Representatives. Until 1857, when he ran for the first time as an avowed Democrat, Clingman managed to win reelection to Congress by adopting the same strategy James Graham had successfully used against him in 1845—combining a solid Democratic vote with the support of a substantial minority of the Whigs.

Clingman's ability to retain the loyalty of many western Whigs even as he opposed the candidates and issues put forward by their party stemmed, in large part, from his self-cultivated image as a champion of western rights and an enemy of the "central managers" who allegedly controlled the party from Raleigh. No antebellum North Carolinian proved more adept than Clingman in tapping the deep vein of popular suspicion against caucuses, conventions, and other mechanisms of party governance. "If for the future you intend to act," he admonished his constituents in 1849, ". . . take such men as will regard themselves as *your* representatives, rather than the servants of the central managers—men, in short, who will dare to tell them if they want *white slaves* they must look for them elsewhere than in the Western reserve." By Clingman's logic, any voter who supported a candidate beholden to the central managers would lose his autonomy and reduce himself to the status of a slave.[15]

Clingman's supporters portrayed him as a crusader "against the corrupt and tyrannical dictates of cabals, caucusses [sic] and cliques."[16] In fact, his opposition to caucuses waxed and waned depending on his own political calculations. In 1840, while still an "ultra Whig," he made a stirring speech in defense of the legitimacy of the legislative caucus. Eight years later, he bitterly condemned the Whig caucus that had nominated Badger as the tool of the "central managers." In 1858 and 1860, however, he secured his own election to the U.S. Senate through his adroit manipulation of the Democratic caucus. Ironically, his failure to win election to the Confederate Senate in 1861 resulted primarily from the breakdown

314 THOMAS LANIER CLINGMAN

of the caucus system he had denounced so vehemently, and used so skillfully, during the 1850s.

Clingman's stridency on the Southern Rights issue also waxed and waned during the 1850s. He was at his most bellicose at the beginning of the decade and far less so by its end. Clingman's aggressive expansionism and his ambition for the presidency served as powerful counterweights to his fire-eating proclivities. The country he wanted to lead was a great and powerful entity extending from the polar icecaps to the tropics—not a rump of a nation centered around the Gulf of Mexico. For that reason, he found the views of Stephen A. Douglas and the national Democrats far more congenial than those of Jefferson Davis and the other Southern sectionalists in the Democratic party.

Clingman never abandoned his commitment to Southern Rights, but he also never gave up hope that those rights could somehow be maintained within the Union. By the end of the 1850s the onetime "independent outsider" had become convinced that the maintenance of the Democratic party as a national institution offered the best prospect for protecting Southern Rights and preserving the Union. Thus he vigorously opposed efforts by Southern sectionalists to pressure the party into endorsing a slave code for the territories or taking other positions that might weaken the Democracy in the North.

During the crisis of 1860–61 Clingman did not lead the secessionist vanguard in the Old North State but lagged behind the majority of his fellow Democrats, hoping to find a compromise that would stem the tide of disunion. Even after formally endorsing secession in February 1861, he regarded it not as a means of securing an enduring Southern nation but as a tactical maneuver to prevent war and buy time for additional negotiations that might lead to the restoration of the Union. To the end of his life, he believed war could have been avoided and the Union eventually restored if the upper South had seceded before the Battle of Fort Sumter.

Clingman's reluctant embrace of disunion made him more inclined than some Southerners to accept the results of the war and, subsequently, to acquiesce in the plan of congressional Reconstruction. As early as December 1865, he was publicly preaching sectional reconciliation. For the remainder of his life, he continued to deprecate sectional politics, whether it be the "bloody shirt" brand practiced by Northern Republicans or the "Negro rule" variety favored by Southern Democrats. In addition to striving for the political reintegration of the South into the nation, Clingman also worked hard to build up his section economically, lending his support to efforts by Henry W. Grady and other apostles of the New South creed to attract immigration and Northern investment.

Clingman's endeavors did not go unnoticed in the North. In 1880 the *New York Tribune,* commenting on his recent application for an electric light patent, remarked that "General Clingman assuredly deserves public recognition for a much more important matter, viz., his efforts to improve the condition of the South since the war. He has foresworn politics and fire-eating, and devoted himself . . . to develop[ing] the natural resources of . . . [the] mountains and to rous[ing] the people to action toward self-improvement." "If the South had a few more leaders like Clingman," asserted the *Tribune*, "her future would be assured." [17]

Clingman had, indeed, foresworn fire eating. But by no means had he abdicated from politics. Although his efforts to reclaim his Senate seat ultimately proved futile, his lack of success does not detract from the considerable amount of time and energy he invested toward achieving that goal. Clingman undoubtedly understood that the obstacles in the way of a political comeback were formidable. Four years of bloody civil war and the abolition of slavery had thoroughly discredited the leaders of the prewar Democratic party throughout the South. In North Carolina the Democrats had lost their majority as early as 1862, when the Conservatives coasted to easy victories in the state elections. The postwar Conservative party continued to be dominated by former Whigs, even after it formally changed its name to "Democrat" during the mid-1870s.

Although old-line Democrats in the Old North State supported the Conservative party because of the perceived need for "maintaining a united front in opposition to the [Republican] party of carpetbaggers, scalawags and negroes," many of them were uneasy about an alliance in which they were consigned to the role of junior partner. As C. Vann Woodward has noted, "the so-called 'Solid South' was weakest along the seams where old Whigs and Unionists had been forcibly joined with Democrats and Secessionists." Clingman's political efforts in the years immediately following the war were directed toward detaching former Democrats from the Conservative party in order to reconstitute the prewar Democratic party or establish a new party under his leadership. The culmination of those endeavors came in 1870 with the publication of his *Address to the Citizens of North Carolina*—a document that his opponents quite accurately characterized as a "letter to dissolve the Conservative party by arousing the prejudices of the old Whigs and Democrats against each other." [18]

Clingman's failure to reestablish the prewar Democratic party, together with his distaste for the hard-money, high-tariff policies of the national Republican party, led him into an uncomfortable alliance with the Conservative-Democrats during the 1870s. By the end of that decade, however, it had become apparent that a party dominated by the "Senatorial-Satrapical" duo of Zebulon B. Vance and Matt W. Ransom was an inadequate vehicle on which to ride back to the U.S. Senate.

Clingman thereupon adopted a strategy similar to the one he had used successfully against the Whigs during the antebellum period. He would remain nominally a Democrat, but an independent one unfettered by the dictates of "packed conventions." He would assail Vance, Ransom, and the other "bosses" in the North Carolina party as furiously as he had once denounced Badger, Graham, and the Whig "central managers." He would call upon the people to "burst to pieces all the present party machinery, break up the rings . . . overthrow the bosses . . . and reassert our right of self-government, by selecting our best men to represent us and manage our business." [19]

Although that strategy had served Clingman well during the antebellum years, it was not as effective in the new political environment created by the Civil War and Reconstruction. According to Kemp P. Battle, Clingman "lost his influence after the war because he was so cold-blooded as to think that the war was like a Presid[ential] campaign. He could not understand the fierce feelings of ex-Confeds & hence his 'Independent party' lost him the confidence of his old friends." [20]

As Battle perceptively observed, Clingman never fully comprehended how drastically the Civil War had changed the rules of the political game in North Carolina. Before the war, high property qualifications for officeholding, a system of legislative apportionment that favored the wealthy plantation counties of the east, and an undemocratic system of local government had placed the reins of power firmly in the hands of the elite. Maintaining a moderate degree of prosperity and desiring primarily to be left alone, Tar Heel farmers "tolerated power realities that were difficult to change, and thus a combination of yeoman independence and aristocratic privilege was usually possible." [21]

Both prewar parties were dominated by slaveholders, and both served the interests of the propertied class. In North Carolina as in other states, partisan competition revolved primarily around national issues such as the Bank of the United States, the tariff, and public land policy. Such issues, although fiercely debated, had little relevance to existing power relationships. By the same token, independent candidates, whatever their impact on the balance of party power, posed little threat to the established racial and socioeconomic order. Under such circumstances, independentism could be presented, and perceived by many voters, as a virtue—the embodiment of the yeoman ideal of autonomy and self-sufficiency.

Certainly no antebellum editor would have presented the scathing characterization of political independentism that appeared in the *Raleigh News and Observer* in 1886. According to that newspaper, "the people understand full well that independentism means a selfish office-seeking. . . . The independent is the same in all lands and in all ages. He is the egotist who would destroy the whole political fabric in order that he may rise upon the ruins. . . . He is always the disorganizer, the iconoclast, who expects to profit for a season by the destruction of what is held sacred. . . . He is therefore sat down upon invariably sooner or later as a public enemy." The *News and Observer* was not alone in its low opinion of independent candidates. Other postwar Democratic presses habitually denounced them as "charlatans," "demagogues," "cheats," and "tricksters"—"detestable subjects" who should be "put . . . 'down and out' without mercy." [22]

The Civil War had, indeed, wrought a profound change in the party system in North Carolina. The poverty, suffering, and dislocation caused by the war had fallen with disproportionate force upon the yeoman farmers and had released the class resentments that had been latent in the antebellum social order. With considerable justification, the politicians who had controlled both antebellum parties viewed the postwar Republican party as a menace not only to white supremacy but also to upper-class rule. The Republican-written Constitution of 1868 had enfranchised the freedmen, reformed the undemocratic system of county government, and abolished the property qualifications for officeholding. Yeoman farmers and artisans, some of them black, came into office as county commissioners, replacing the local notables who had dominated the old county courts. "Prominent men of the old elite saw their worst nightmare—an alliance among the lower classes of both races—materializing under the protection of the federal government."[23]

By appealing to the racist sensibilities of lower-class whites and by capitalizing on the scandals of the Holden administration, the Conservative-Democrats managed to regain control of the state during the 1870s. But redemption did not relieve the anxieties of North Carolina's elite. The balance of parties remained close, and Tar Heel Republicans adopted a strategy of concentrating on local elections and cooperating with dissident Democrats—a strategy that was sanctioned and financially assisted by the Republican administrations in Washington.[24]

Under the circumstances, it is not surprising that independentism came to be associated in the Democratic mind with Republicanism and social disorder. As one party newspaper put it, "Independents are only Republicans in disguise. . . . All roads from the Democratic camp . . . lead to that of our enemies. . . . There is and can be no half-way ground between the two parties." Indeed, according to the Democrats, independents were even more despicable than Republicans. The Republican threat was open and aboveboard, whereas the independents "profess to be Democrats and then stab their party under the cloak of perfidious independentism."[25]

Faced by the need to present a united front against the Republicans, postwar Democratic leaders turned the words "discipline" and "organization" into sacred shibboleths. Party conventions and caucuses became the indispensable tools for maintaining white supremacy and preventing a return to the supposed horrors of Radical Reconstruction and Negro rule. As the *Asheville Citizen* pointed out, "from time immemorial, but specially since the war, have parties settled important matters, either in the selection of persons to fill certain offices, or public measures, through private caucusses [sic] or conventions. . . . Thus only can party supremacy be maintained, and its great principles be carried into effect." In such a political environment, independents like Clingman, instead of being admired as champions of the "right of private judgment," were regarded by many white voters as traitors to their race.[26]

Whereas race was central to the consciousness of most white North Carolinians after the Civil War, it was not an important concern to Clingman. Indeed, the former fire eater's views on race relations were far closer to those of the native white Republicans, or "scalawags," than to the opinions of the Democrats with whom he was nominally associated. Although unwilling to acknowledge blacks as social equals, Clingman had no problem granting them political and legal equality with members of the white race. Noticeably absent from his rhetoric were the blatant appeals to white supremacy so characteristic of most Democratic leaders in the postwar South.

In Clingman's opinion, the black voter was not a political enemy to be put down, but rather a potential ally in his crusade against the "managers" and "bosses" who controlled the North Carolina Democratic party. Like "other liberals who befriended blacks and who wished to alter the centuries-old relationship between the races," Clingman underestimated the tenacity of white racism and the lengths to which the Democratic leadership was willing to go in its efforts to forestall the formation of a biracial alliance of lower-class whites and blacks.[27]

Clingman's critique of the "bosses" may have been self-serving, but his low opinion of the political leadership of postwar North Carolina has largely been sustained by historians. As one scholar has pointed out, "there was genuine dissatisfaction with the [Democratic] party's record." The heterogeneous character of the groups comprising the party forced it "to suppress real issues within their own ranks and rely on the race question and memories of Reconstruction to keep their followers united. . . . In the final analysis, the Democrats imposed upon North Carolina an era of neglect which left the state among the most backward in the nation." While Clingman failed to benefit personally from the widespread dissatisfaction with Democratic rule, he did play a role in sowing the seeds of discontent that led to the party's overthrow in 1894.[28]

Both before and after the war, Clingman was a highly controversial figure. Some regarded him as a man of principle; others denounced him as a self-serving opportunist. It is not begging the question to conclude that both assessments are valid. Clingman did hold some deep-seated political beliefs, and rarely did he consciously act in an insincere manner. "Insincerity," he once remarked, ". . . is always disgusting to me. It is also futile, because subterfuges or stratagems to conceal egotism, only serve to render it more conspicuous." While acknowledging that his opinions on parties and measures had changed over the course of the years, he argued that consistency was not always a virtue. Indeed, "the only consistency worthy of consideration is . . . to be true to the principles recognized as important."[29]

The career of Thomas Lanier Clingman illustrates the adage "politics makes strange bedfellows." In Clingman's case, however, the would-be man of principle had no stranger bedfellow than his own insatiable ambition. At an early stage in his political career, he "deliberately made his choice of ambition for his mistress, and fame for his reward."[30] That demanding mistress impelled him to place his personal advancement at the center of all his political calculations, even at the expense of those "principles recognized as important." His idol Henry Clay supposedly remarked that he would rather be right than president. Clingman, if presented with the same alternatives, would most likely have opted for the presidency.

Opportunism undoubtedly played a major role in guiding Clingman's erratic political course before and after the Civil War. To gratify his ego and his desire for office, he showed no compunction about attacking former friends or courting old enemies. The issues he chose either to champion or to crusade against were all selected with a view to their effect on his own political fortunes. Nonetheless, as Joel Silbey has pointed out, "the very fact that issues could be used for opportunistic purposes by some implies that they served substantive purposes for others." In that regard, the public career of Clingman, whose life spanned almost the entire nineteenth century, offers an interesting and useful window into the political culture of that period in American history.[31]

Despite his enormous intellect and genuine ability, Clingman's egotism, bellicose temperament, and incessant efforts at self-promotion prevented him from attaining true greatness. Regarded by his contemporaries as "one of the most remarkable men who have figured in politics in North Carolina," he is remembered today in his home state primarily as the mountain climber who gave his name to the highest peak in the Smokies. Among historians, his name is associated not with the political leaders whom he genuinely admired—Clay, Webster, Mangum, and Douglas—but with Rhett, Yancey, and the other "fire eaters" who led the South down the path to civil war.[32]

Even at his most strident, Clingman was never a fire eater in the Rhett-Yancey mold. His aim was not to lead the Old North State out of the Union but to develop its vast untapped resources in order to make it "the richest and most prosperous" state within the United States. The challenge he issued his fellow Tar Heels near the end of his life stands as a fitting epitaph to Clingman's noblest ideals. "Let us, then, fellow-countrymen of North Carolina, press forward vigorously, and we can make our State the greatest in the world, and assist in giving our great and glorious Union of States the foremost position that humanity can have on the earth."[33]

Notes

Works and archives frequently cited in the notes or bibliography have been identified by the following abbreviations:

AJSA	*American Journal of Science and Arts*
CG	*Congressional Globe*
DAB	*Dictionary of American Biography*
DNB	*Dictionary of National Biography*
DNCB	*Dictionary of North Carolina Biography*
Duke	Special Collections, Duke University, Durham, N.C.
ENHS	Edison National Historic Site, West Orange, N.J.
HJ	*Journal of the House of Commons of North Carolina*
NCC	North Carolina Collection, University of North Carolina, Chapel Hill, N.C.
NCDAH	North Carolina Division of Archives and History, Raleigh, N.C.
NCHR	*North Carolina Historical Review*
O.R.	*The War of the Rebellion: A Compilation of the Official Records of the Union and Confederate Armies*
Pack	Pack Memorial Library, Asheville, N.C.
S&W	*Selections from the Speeches and Writings of Hon. Thomas L. Clingman of North Carolina*, 2d ed.
SHC	Southern Historical Collection, University of North Carolina, Chapel Hill, N.C.
SJ	*Journal of the Senate of North Carolina*
WHi	State Historical Society of Wisconsin, Madison, Wisc.

1. A Compound of Incongruities

1. This description is based on the account in *New York Herald*, 5 March 1893.

2. Quoted in *Asheville Citizen*, 16 March 1893. Earlier in the Senate ceremony, Clingman had created another scene by appropriating the seat provided for President Harrison. An attendant quickly procured him another. See *Charlotte Observer*, in *Asheville Citizen*, 9 March 1893. The *Citizen* quipped that "Gen. Clingman had a narrow escape from being either sworn into or out of the presidential chair."

3. Obituary, *New York Times*, 5 November 1897; [Alexander K. McClure], "The Career of T. L. Clingman" (from *Philadelphia Times*, 10 October 1896), in R. A. Brock, ed., *Southern Historical Society Papers* 24 (1896): 307.

4. Obituary, *New York Times*, 5 November 1897; [McClure], "Career of T. L. Clingman," 308; *Raleigh State Chronicle*, 30 March 1888.

5. Jane Puryear Kerr, "Brigadier-General Thomas L. Clingman," *Trinity Archive* 12

(1899): 395. See also Alice Dugger Grimes, "'I'm Going to be President,'" *State* 2 (29 September 1934): 22–23.

6. *Charlotte North Carolina Whig*, 14 August 1860; *Raleigh North Carolina Standard*, 17 April 1861; John H. Wheeler, *Reminiscences and Memoirs of North Carolina and Eminent North Carolinians* (Columbus: Columbus Printing Works, 1884), 74–75.

7. The phrase "unlettered men of the mountains" is from Bayles M. Edney to William A. Graham, 13 May 1844, in J. G. de Roulhac Hamilton and Max R. Williams, eds., *The Papers of William A. Graham*, 8 vols. (Raleigh: Division of Archives and History, 1957–92), 2:498. For the nickname "Handsome Tom," see communication from "H" [Edward J. Hale], in *Charlotte Observer*, 20 March 1885. The characterization of Clingman as a "strange-looking man" is from C. Vann Woodward, ed., *Mary Chesnut's Civil War* (New Haven: Yale University Press, 1981), 114. William H. S. Burgwyn claimed that Clingman's habit of talking to himself was acquired from his mother ("Life and Services of Gen. Thos. L. Clingman," newspaper clipping, ca. May 1898, Clipping File, NCC).

8. Richard B. Creecy to William H. S. Burgwyn, 17 January 1898, William Hyslop Sumner Burgwyn Papers, NCDAH.

9. Burgwyn, "Life and Services of Clingman"; C. S. Wooten, "General Thomas L. Clingman," newspaper clipping, 1917, Clipping File, NCC.

10. Kerr, "Brigadier-General Clingman," 390–91.

11. [McClure], "Career of T. L. Clingman," 307.

12. Kerr, "Brigadier-General Clingman," 389, 395; Elizabeth Puryear Gibson to Jane Puryear Kerr, 14 February 1892, Jane P. Kerr Papers, Duke; Risden T. Bennett to William H. S. Burgwyn, 22 March 1898, Burgwyn Papers; Burgwyn, "Life and Services of Clingman."

13. John C. Inscoe, "Thomas Clingman, Mountain Whiggery, and the Southern Cause," *Civil War History* 33 (1987): 42–62; Marc W. Kruman, "Thomas L. Clingman and the Whig Party: A Reconsideration," *NCHR* 64 (1987): 1–17. Inscoe and Kruman both argue that Clingman's unexpected defeat in 1845 by a rival Whig with a more pro-Southern position played an important role in pushing him in a more radical direction.

14. Thomas E. Jeffrey, "'Thunder from the Mountains': Thomas Lanier Clingman and the End of Whig Supremacy in North Carolina," *NCHR* 56 (1979): 366–95.

15. Eric H. Walther, *The Fire-Eaters* (Baton Rouge: Louisiana State University Press, 1992), 2. See also William J. Cooper Jr., *The South and the Politics of Slavery, 1828–1856* (Baton Rouge: Louisiana State University Press, 1978), 296.

16. The quotation is from Clarence C. Norton, *The Democratic Party in Ante-Bellum North Carolina, 1835–1861* (Chapel Hill: University of North Carolina Press, 1930), 207.

17. The "entrepreneurial spirit" of Clingman and other western North Carolinians is ably examined in John C. Inscoe, *Mountain Masters, Slavery, and the Sectional Crisis in Western North Carolina* (Knoxville: University of Tennessee Press, 1989), chapters 2 and 3. For the argument that the antebellum South was precapitalistic, see Eugene Genovese, *The Political Economy of Slavery: Studies in the Economy and Society of the Slave South* (New York: Pantheon, 1965).

18. "Statesman and Author First Great Booster," clipping from *Asheville Times*, 29 November 1931, Pack. See also Bob Gallimore, "Thomas L. Clingman: Soldier, Explorer,

and One-Man Chamber of Commerce," clipping from *Asheville Citizen-Times,* 23 January 1949, NCC.

19. Burgess S. Gaither, "To the Citizens of the 8th Congressional District of North Carolina," in *Raleigh Register,* 6 July 1853.

20. The quotations are from the titles of two works by Joel H. Silbey: *The Partisan Imperative: The Dynamics of American Politics before the Civil War* (New York: Oxford University Press, 1985); *The Shrine of Party: Congressional Voting Behavior, 1841–1852* (Pittsburgh: University of Pittsburgh Press, 1967).

21. *S&W,* 2.

22. For Clingman's antebellum career, see the articles by Jeffrey, Kruman, and Inscoe, cited above. For the Civil War period, see Frances Harding Casstevens, "The Military Career of Brigadier General Thomas Lanier Clingman" (master's thesis, University of North Carolina at Greensboro, 1984). The most extended discussion of Clingman's postwar career is Clarence N. Gilbert, "The Public Career of Thomas L. Clingman" (master's thesis, University of North Carolina at Chapel Hill, 1946), chapter 5, which is essentially a summary of the essays published in Clingman's *Speeches and Writings.*

23. Kerr, "Brigadier-General Clingman," 394; *DNCB,* s.v. "Clingman, Thomas Lanier."

24. Mark Mayo Boatner III, *Civil War Dictionary* (New York: David McKay, 1959), 159. See also Jon L. Wakelyn, *Biographical Dictionary of the Confederacy* (Westport, Conn.: Greenwood Press, 1977), 140.

25. For example, Clingman is not mentioned in three of the most important and influential studies of this period: David Potter, *The Impending Crisis, 1848–1861* (New York: Harper & Row, 1976); James M. McPherson, *Battle Cry of Freedom: The Civil War Era* (New York: Oxford University Press, 1988); and Eric Foner, *Reconstruction: America's Unfinished Revolution, 1863–1877* (New York: Harper & Row, 1988). There are only a few scattered references to him in Cooper's *South and the Politics of Slavery.*

26. Quoted in Glenn Tucker, "For the Want of a Scribe," *NCHR* 43 (1966): 177.

27. As the *Asheville Citizen* remarked, "his prominence as a statesman, politician and scientist gives interest to any thing relating to him, and weight to every statement regarding [him]" (8 December 1886).

28. Remarks of TLC, in *A Record of the Proceedings of the Alumni Association of the University of North Carolina at the Centennial Celebration* ([Chapel Hill?]: Alumni Association, 1889), 155.

29. "Address Delivered at Davidson College, North Carolina," 25 June 1873, in *S&W,* 43.

30. *Elizabeth City Economist,* 5 November, 3 December 1897.

2. A Promising Young Man

1. *Asheville Citizen,* 30 July 1891. See also ibid., 4 August 1892. Clingman further identified himself with Caesar by claiming they were both born on 27 July.

2. William H. S. Burgwyn, "Life and Services of Gen. Thos. L. Clingman," newspaper clipping, ca. May 1898, Clipping File, NCC; Jane Puryear Kerr, "Brigadier-General

Thomas L. Clingman," *Trinity Archive* 12 (1899): 388; Lewis Shore Brumfield, *Thomas Lanier Clingman and the Shallow Ford Families* (Yadkinville: privately printed, 1990), 1. Brumfield, who conducted an exhaustive search of genealogical sources relating to the Clingman and allied families, was unable to locate a marriage record either in Pennsylvania or in North Carolina.

3. John Hill Wheeler, *Reminiscences and Memoirs of North Carolina and Eminent North Carolinians* (Columbus: Columbus Printing Works, 1884), 72; *DNCB*, s.v. "Clingman, Thomas Lanier." According to Brumfield, "the voluminous reports of immigrant passengers arriving by ship in Philadelphia do not show Alexander and Elizabeth Kayser Clingman arriving." That does not preclude the possibility that "they debarked in America at some place other than Philadelphia" (*Clingman and Shallow Ford*, 5).

4. Augustus H. Jarratt, "The Family History," Jarratt Family File, Yadkinville Public Library, Yadkinville, N.C., typescript, 6. According to Wheeler, the name Clingman "signifies, in German, a swordsman and a fighter" (*Reminiscences and Memoirs*, 72).

5. Robert W. Ramsey, *Carolina Cradle: Settlement of the Northwest Carolina Frontier, 1747–1762* (Chapel Hill: University of North Carolina Press, 1964), 12, 17–22, 146–47; Brumfield, *Clingman and Shallow Ford*, 2. No direct evidence links Alexander Clingman with any of the numerous Clingman families living in Pennsylvania at the time of the Revolution. Possibly, he was the brother of John Michael Clingman (1734–1816), who lived near Philadelphia. See William D. Clingman, *Clingman-Klingman Families & Descendants* (Richmond, Calif.: privately printed, 1931), 7–8.

6. Clarence E. Ratcliff, *North Carolina Taxpayers, 1701–1786*, 2 vols. (Baltimore: Genealogical Publishing Co., 1984–87), 1:41, 2:40; Jo White Linn, *Abstracts of the Deeds of Rowan County, North Carolina, 1753–1785, Vols. 1–10* (Salisbury: privately printed, 1983), 21–22, 124; Jo White Linn, *Abstracts of Wills and Estates Records of Rowan County, North Carolina, 1753–1805 and Tax Lists of 1759 and 1778* (Salisbury: privately printed, 1980), 112; Brumfield, *Clingman and Shallow Ford*, 6–8; Ramsey, *Carolina Cradle*, 87.

7. Ramsey, "Carolina Cradle," 171–78; Brumfield, *Clingman and Shallow Ford*, 9–10; Clingman, *Clingman-Klingman Families*, 39–40; Frances H. Casstevens, ed., *The Heritage of Yadkin County* (Yadkinville: Yadkin County Historical Society, 1981), 322. Jacob Clingman was born on 30 November 1786.

8. Brumfield, *Clingman and Shallow Ford*, 10–11; Wheeler, *Reminiscences and Memoirs*, 72.

9. For Alexander Clingman's postwar land acquisitions, see Brumfield, *Clingman and Shallow Ford*, 11–13; Linn, *Abstracts of Deeds*, 193; Linn, *Abstracts of Wills*, 124. A tax list for 1804 indicates that "Widow Clingman" held 1,120 acres. Only one person in the tax district owned more property. See Rowan County Tax Records, NCDAH.

10. Rowan County Record of Wills, volume E (1800–1805): 234–36, NCDAH, microfilm; Linn, *Abstracts of Wills*, 82. Jacob Clingman received the largest bequest—three hundred acres—on condition that he "shall stay on the plantation & not leave the same untill *[sic]* he shall arrive at the full age of twenty-one years."

11. Brumfield, *Clingman and Shallow Ford*, 13–16; Casstevens, *Yadkin County Heritage*, 322; Lucy H. Houck, *The Story of Rockford* (n.p., privately printed, 1972), 127.

12. Brumfield, *Clingman and Shallow Ford*, 18–20, 44–45; Casstevens, *Yadkin County*

Heritage, 81. A book containing accounts and other records of Jacob Clingman & Co. for the period 1816–29 can be found in Jacob Clingman & Co. Papers, Duke.

13. Brumfield, *Clingman and Shallow Ford,* 21, 44–45, 48–49, 52, 54. The store was still prospering in the early 1830s. See Richard C. Puryear to Isaac Jarratt, 17 February 1832, Jarratt-Puryear Family Papers, Duke.

14. Brent H. Holcomb, *Marriages of Surry County, North Carolina, 1779–1868* (Baltimore: Genealogical Publishing Co., 1982), 37. Peter and Anne were married on 14 January 1806. See Clingman, *Clingman-Klingman Families,* 39.

15. Casstevens, *Yadkin County Heritage,* 550–51; Brumfield, *Clingman and Shallow Ford,* 34–35; Jarratt, "Family History," 2–3; Wheeler, *Reminiscences and Memoirs,* 72. Elizabeth Pledge, the wife of Thomas Poindexter and grandmother of Anne and Jane, was the granddaughter of Donnahoo, a Native American who gained notoriety by saving the town of Edenton from destruction by a hostile tribe.

16. Durward T. Stokes, "Henry Pattillo in North Carolina," *NCHR* 44 (1967): 373–91; Brumfield, *Clingman and Shallow Ford,* 25–28, 43; Wheeler, *Reminiscences and Memoirs,* 72.

17. Brumfield, *Clingman and Shallow Ford,* 28–31, 34; Casstevens, *Yadkin County Heritage,* 535; Wheeler, *Reminiscences and Memoirs,* 72. For the children of Joseph Williams, see John Hill Wheeler, *Historical Sketches of North Carolina from 1584 to 1851,* 2 vols. in 1 (Philadelphia: Lippincott, Grambo, 1851), 2:409–10. Thomas Lanier Williams was the great-grandfather of the playwright Tennessee Williams, whose given name was also Thomas Lanier. See Tennessee Williams, *Memoirs* (Garden City: Doubleday, 1972), 12.

18. For Thomas Lanier (1776–1800), see Casstevens, *Yadkin County Heritage,* 535. Elizabeth, the only other child of Robert Lanier and Jane Pattillo, died in childhood. For the children of Jacob and Jane, see Brumfield, *Clingman and Shallow Ford,* 49, 50, 54–55; Casstevens, *Yadkin County Heritage,* 322. John Pattillo Clingman (1814–94) became a physician and practiced in Huntsville and other North Carolina towns. Elizabeth Ann Clingman (1816–50) married Richard C. Puryear in 1835. For the children of Peter and Anne Clingman, see Brumfield, *Clingman and Shallow Ford,* 35, 49, 51, 63; Casstevens, *Yadkin County Heritage,* 322–23. Alexander Brandon Clingman (1806–81) moved to Tennessee and then to Arkansas; according to family tradition, he was disinherited for marrying his first cousin, Anne Martha Clingman. Francis Poindexter Clingman was the only Clingman child to follow in the family's mercantile tradition. After the death of his father in 1845, he inherited the family home and later moved to Alabama. Henry Pattillo Clingman (1813–1906) became a physician and practiced in Mocksville before moving to Arkansas. Elizabeth Lanier Clingman, born in 1809, died in 1814.

19. William E. Rutledge Jr., *An Illustrated History of Yadkin County, 1850–1980* (Yadkinville: privately printed, 1981), 12, 30; Agnes M. Wells and Iris M. Harvey, *Surry County, North Carolina Tax List, 1815* (Mount Airy, N.C.: privately printed, 1990), 42; Brumfield, *Clingman and Shallow Ford,* 47, 50.

20. Brumfield, *Clingman and Shallow Ford,* 50–51. The quotation is from Peter Clingman to Jacob Reese, 16 June 1817, Jacob Clingman & Co. Record Book. Little is known about Thomas Clingman's youngest brother, Jacob Alexander, who was born in 1817 after the death of his father. In 1854 he was serving in the U.S. Army at Barrancas Barracks in Pensacola, Florida (Richard C. Puryear to [?], 15 April 1854, Jarratt-Puryear Papers).

21. Although Peter became the sole proprietor of the Red Store after Jacob's death, Jane owned the building and the lot on which it stood (Brumfield, *Clingman and Shallow Ford*, 51). In 1835 she owned five lots in the Huntsville area, comprising 199 acres valued at $725, as well as four slaves. See Carol Leonard Snow, *Taxables in Surry County, North Carolina for the Year 1835* (Toast: privately printed, 1990), 54. Sarah Esther Mitchell was the daughter of Esther Clingman, sister of Peter and Jacob, and her second husband (Brumfield, *Clingman and Shallow Ford*, 13).

22. Richard C. Puryear to Isaac Jarratt, 13 November 1832, Jarratt to Sarah Mitchell, 18 February 1833, Elizabeth Ann Clingman to Jarratt, 19 March, 8 May 1834, 8 January 1835, Jarratt-Puryear Papers. It is unclear whether the relationship between Peter and Jane was ever more than a business arrangement. Peter was only thirty-eight and Jane only twenty-nine at the time she moved into the White House, but neither ever remarried. Peter seems to have had a healthy sexual appetite. Shortly before he moved to Huntsville he had impregnated Elizabeth Davis, a young woman whom the family had taken in as a servant (Brumfield, *Clingman and Shallow Ford*, 17). After the death of his wife, he apparently did make some effort to remarry (Elizabeth Ann Clingman to Isaac Jarratt, 8 May 1834, Jarratt-Puryear Papers).

23. Obituary, *Charlotte Democrat*, 6 May 1873. As late as 1864, when fifty-two-year-old Thomas Clingman was fighting in the trenches around Petersburg, Jane was still providing her "own darling son" with instructions on how to do his laundry. See Jane Clingman to TLC, 1 August 1864, Clingman Family File, Yadkinville Public Library, photocopy. Clingman reciprocated his mother's affections, addressing her as "my dear mother" and signing his letters as "your loving son." See, for example, TLC to Jane Clingman, 22 August 1852, Clingman and Puryear Family Papers, SHC.

24. Henry Pattillo, Jane Clingman's maternal grandfather, had been "a teacher of unusual ability" with a "genuine love of learning" (Stokes, *Pattillo*, 372, 388). After the death of her father in 1802, Jane moved into the home of Pattillo's widow, Mary Anderson Pattillo, and was educated there by her uncle, John Franklin Pattillo, who had followed his father into the teaching profession (Brumfield, *Clingman and Shallow Ford*, 35).

25. Late in her life, Jane Clingman recalled that she had "whipped that boy more for fighting than anything else" but hadn't "broken him yet" (Burgwyn, "Life and Services of Clingman").

26. Richard C. Puryear to Isaac Jarratt, 26 May 1834, Jarratt-Puryear Papers. For clashes between Peter Clingman and his charges over their education, see Puryear to Jarratt, 13 November 1832, Jarratt to Sarah Mitchell, 18 February 1833, Jarratt-Puryear Papers. On the other hand, Peter did have some positive attributes, not the least of which was his generosity. Despite his reservations about the value of a university education, he ultimately subsidized Thomas's college studies.

27. A[ugustus] H. J[arratt], "General Thomas L. Clingman," *University Magazine*, n.s., 18 (1901): 166; TLC to Lyman Draper, 2 June 1885, Daniel Boone Papers (Series C), Lyman Copeland Draper Manuscripts, WHi; Burgwyn, "Life and Services of Clingman."

28. Kerr, "Brigadier-General Clingman," 389. The "present day" to which Clingman's niece referred was the year 1899. By 1910 Huntsville had ceased to function as a town and had become no more than a crossroads.

29. Jarratt, "General Clingman," 166; Brumfield, *Clingman and Shallow Ford*, 51, 54.

Subscription schools, also known as old field schools, taught elementary subjects such as reading, writing, and arithmetic. They generally ran for two or three months during the winter. See Homer M. Keever, *Iredell: Piedmont County* (Statesville: Iredell County Bicentennial Commission, 1976), 204–5.

30. TLC to Lyman Draper, 18 June 1885, Rudolph-Ney Papers (Series RR), Draper Manuscripts; *The Heritage of Iredell County* (Statesville: Genealogical Society of Iredell County, 1980), 66–68; Virginia Fraser Evans, comp., *Iredell County Landmarks: A Pictorial History of Iredell County* (Statesville: Iredell County Bicentennial Commission, 1976), 96; Keever, *Iredell County*, 210–11. The quoted advertisement appears in Charles L. Coon, ed., *North Carolina Schools and Academies, 1790–1840: A Documentary History* (Raleigh: Edwards & Broughton, 1915), 190–91. Although in disrepair, the log building that housed Ebenezer Academy is still standing. See Howard Covington, "History Falling into Poison Ivy Patch: Old Ebenezer Academy Is Iredell Restoration Project," clipping from *Charlotte Observer*, 12 September 1967, Iredell County Public Library, Statesville, N.C.

31. Most antebellum academies emphasized classical languages, literature, and history at the expense of instruction in contemporary literature and the sciences. See Edwin A. Miles, "The Old South and the Classical World," *NCHR* 48 (1971): 258–75. For James Hall and the Academy of Sciences, see *Iredell County Heritage*, 52, 64–66, 96–97, 304; Keever, *Iredell County*, 81–82, 209–10. In 1843 the Ebenezer Academy was offering instruction in astronomy and chemistry. See Francis D. Cash to Leonard B. Cash, 2 July 1843, Jarratt-Puryear Papers.

32. Faculty Minutes, August 1829, University Archives, University of North Carolina, Chapel Hill, N.C. Lists of prerequisites for admission can be found in the advertisements in *Raleigh Register*, 20 January 1835, 12 October 1839.

33. For a description of Chapel Hill and the university campus a few years before Clingman's arrival, see Max R. Williams, "The Education of William A. Graham," *NCHR* 40 (1963): 6–7. For student enrollment from 1804 to 1840, see *Raleigh Register*, 30 July 1841.

34. *DNCB*, s.v. "Caldwell, Joseph"; Kemp P. Battle, *History of the University of North Carolina*, 2 vols. (Raleigh: Edwards & Broughton, 1907–12), 1:110–15, 173–76, 291–94; William Earle Drake, *Higher Education in North Carolina before 1860* (New York: Carlton Press, 1964), 69–71, 97–99. The phrase "renaissance at Chapel Hill" appears in Williams, "Education of Graham," 9.

35. Richard Benbury Creecy, *Grandfather's Tales of North Carolina History* (Raleigh: Edwards & Broughton, 1901), 213. For the nickname "Old Mike," see Creecy, "University Days Seventy Years Ago," *University Magazine*, n.s., 20 (1902): 93. For biographical sketches of Mitchell, see *DNCB*, s.v. "Mitchell, Elisha"; Battle, *History of the University*, 250–53; Drake, *Higher Education*, 99–100.

36. Clingman's performance on his examinations can be found in Student Records, 24 June 1830, 7–14 December 1830, June 1831, 16 June 1832, University Archives. The rankings for 1832 can be found in Faculty Minutes, May 1832, and in Drake, *Higher Education*, 155. The quotation is from John D. Cameron, "Thomas Lanier Clingman," *University Magazine*, n.s., 8 (1889): 252.

37. Except where noted, the quotations in this and the following two paragraphs are from Creecy, "Recollections of Clingman," and Burgwyn, "Life and Services of Cling-

man." Burgwyn's account of Clingman's university days is based on information supplied by Creecy.

38. The characterization of bandy is from Charles Grier Sellers Jr., "Jim Polk Goes to Chapel Hill," *NCHR* 29 (1952): 200. According to Sellers, it was the most popular sport at the university during the early nineteenth century.

39. Albert Coates and Gladys Hall Coates, *The Story of Student Government in the University of North Carolina at Chapel Hill* (Chapel Hill, 1985), 43, 59, 61–63; Hallie S. McLean, "The History of the Dialectic Society, 1795–1860" (master's thesis, University of North Carolina at Chapel Hill, 1949), 35–42, 59–60, 113; Williams, "Education of Graham," 11–12. In addition to instilling proper behavior, the fines levied by the societies also served as an important source of income for their treasuries.

40. Less than a month after being admitted to membership, Clingman received his first fine, for ten cents. Over the course of three years, he was penalized thirty times, mostly for minor infractions. The discussion in this and the following paragraph is based on an examination of the Dialectic Society Minutes, September 1829–June 1832, University Archives.

41. So that as many members as possible might acquire experience in governing, tenure in each office was limited to a period of three or four weeks. Shortly before graduation, Clingman received permission to remove his addresses and papers from the society's archives (Dialectic Society Minutes, 4 April 1832). They have not been found.

42. Gaston's presence at the commencement guaranteed an even larger audience than usual. The *Raleigh Register* commented that the gathering contained "a greater portion of talent, character, wit and beauty, than ever graced any similar occasion at the University" (in *Fayetteville Observer*, 10 July 1832).

43. Creecy, *Grandfather's Tales*, 85–86. For Clingman's concern about his dress and appearance during his last semester at Chapel Hill, see TLC to Jane P. Clingman, 3 February 1832, TLC to Francis P. Clingman, 4 May 1832, Clingman-Puryear Papers.

44. Battle, *History of the University*, 345; diary of David L. Swain, 21 June 1832, David L. Swain Papers, NCDAH.

45. Fannie Memory Farmer, "Legal Education in North Carolina, 1820–1860," *NCHR* 28 (1951): 271–97.

46. Henry P. Poindexter to Thomas Ruffin, 14 January, 3 July 1832, in J. G. de Roulhac Hamilton, ed., *The Papers of Thomas Ruffin*, 4 vols. (Raleigh: Edwards & Broughton, 1918–20), 2: 55, 60; Ruffin to Poindexter, 21 July 1832, Clingman-Puryear Papers.

47. Richard C. Puryear to Isaac Jarratt, 13 November 1832, Jarratt-Puryear Papers. For Clingman's trip to the North Carolina mountains, see TLC to Lyman Draper, 6, 14, 25 August 1884, Boone Papers.

48. Many historians have claimed that Clingman studied under Graham's direction. However, John C. Cameron, who knew Clingman personally, wrote that "he repaired to Hillsboro to read law, without placing himself under any instructor, but using books and authorities kindly lent him by Mr. William A. Graham" ("Thomas Lanier Clingman," 252). That was a common practice during the antebellum era. Even the more formal schools usually "had little system as to curriculum or lecture periods. . . . The students read and studied law by themselves for the most part" (Farmer, "Legal Education," 297).

49. Surry County Court Records, 10 February 1834, in Houck, *Story of Rockford,* 129; Richard C. Puryear to Isaac Jarratt, 29 December 1833, Jarratt-Puryear Papers; Fannie Memory Farmer, "The Bar Examination and Beginning Years of Legal Practice in North Carolina, 1820–1860," *NCHR* 29 (1952): 161.

50. TLC to Isaac Jarratt, 4 February 1834, Richard C. Puryear to Jarratt, 3 March 1834, Elizabeth Ann Clingman to Jarratt, 19 March, 8 May 1834, Jarratt-Puryear Papers; Jane Clingman to TLC, 10 March 1834, in Casstevens, *Yadkin County Heritage,* 322.

51. Elizabeth Ann Clingman to Isaac Jarratt, 8 May 1834, Richard C. Puryear to Jarratt, 20, 26 May 1834, Jarratt-Puryear Papers. The quotation and the reference to Elizabeth Clingman reading law books to her brother are from Kerr, "Brigadier-General Clingman," 390.

52. The quotation is from Kerr, "Brigadier-General Clingman," 390.

53. C. Vann Woodward, ed., *Mary Chesnut's Civil War* (New Haven: Yale University Press, 1981), 115; Richard B. Creecy to William H. S. Burgwyn, 17 January 1898, William Hyslop Sumner Burgwyn Papers, NCDAH.

54. TLC to Willie P. Mangum, 30 January 1835, in Henry T. Shanks, ed., *The Papers of Willie Person Mangum,* 5 vols. (Raleigh: State Department of Archives and History, 1950–56), 2:295; *Raleigh Register,* 2 February 1835. For Clingman's gradual recovery of his health (and an apparent relapse in January 1835), see Elizabeth Ann Clingman to Isaac Jarratt, 9 December 1834, 8 January 1835, Richard C. Puryear to Jarratt, 30 January 1835, Jarratt-Puryear Papers.

55. Thomas E. Jeffrey, *State Parties and National Politics: North Carolina, 1815–1861* (Athens: University of Georgia Press, 1989), chapter 1.

56. Letter of Edward B. Dudley (from *Raleigh Register,* 23 February 1836), in Jeffrey, *State Parties and National Politics,* 77.

57. Wheeler, *Historical Sketches,* 2:409; Brumfield, *Clingman and Shallow Ford,* 58–60, 71; Rutledge, *Yadkin County,* 26.

58. Hugh Talmage Lefler and Albert Ray Newsome, *North Carolina: The History of a Southern State,* 2d ed. (Chapel Hill: University of North Carolina Press, 1963), chapter 20; Jeffrey, *State Parties and National Politics,* 68–69.

59. William Gordon Kornegay, "The North Carolina Institute of Education, 1831–1834," *NCHR* 36 (1959): 143. Clingman's name appears on the "List of Persons Subscribing to the Constitution of the . . . Institute," ibid., 151–52.

60. *Proceedings of the Internal Improvement Convention Held in the City of Raleigh, November 1833* (Raleigh: Joseph Gales & Son, 1834), 5–6; Sarah Mitchell to Isaac Jarratt, 20 December 1833, Jarratt-Puryear Papers; Richard B. Creecy to William H. S. Burgwyn, 17 January 1898, Burgwyn Papers.

61. Jeffrey, *State Parties and National Politics,* 41, 43, 47.

62. Clingman recalled his "first long conversation" with Calhoun in a letter published in the *Asheville News,* 18 July 1882. For the patronage investigation, see John Niven, *John C. Calhoun and the Price of Union: A Biography* (Baton Rouge: Louisiana State University Press, 1988), 211–12; TLC to Willie P. Mangum, 30 January 1835, in Shanks, *Mangum Papers,* 2:296.

63. TLC to Willie P. Mangum, 30 January 1835, in Shanks, *Mangum Papers,* 2:295–96.

64. TLC to William A. Graham, 10 March 1835, in J. G. de Roulhac Hamilton and Max R. Williams, eds., *The Papers of William A. Graham,* 8 vols. (Raleigh: Division of Archives and History, 1957–92), 1:375–76.

65. *Raleigh North Carolina Standard,* 27 August 1835.

66. Harold J. Counihan, "The North Carolina Constitutional Convention of 1835: A Study in Jacksonian Democracy," *NCHR* 46 (1969): 335–64. For the date of Clingman's departure for Raleigh, see Richard C. Puryear to [?], 18 November 1835, Jarratt-Puryear Papers.

67. Snow, *Taxables in Surry County,* 54; Jarratt, "Family History," 19–20; Brumfield, *Clingman and Shallow Ford,* 66.

68. For the slavery resolutions, see *Raleigh Register,* 22 December 1835; *Fayetteville Observer,* 31 December 1835. Clingman's resolution was introduced on 15 December 1835 (*Raleigh Register,* 22 December 1835).

69. *Raleigh Register,* 15, 22 December 1835.

70. During the session of 1834–35, Pleasant Henderson of Surry County introduced distribution resolutions that passed the lower house by a vote of eighty-two to thirty-two; about half the Democrats supported them. However, the proposals were allowed to die in the senate without a formal vote. See William S. Hoffmann, *Andrew Jackson and North Carolina Politics* (Chapel Hill: University of North Carolina Press, 1958), 92.

71. *Fayetteville Observer,* 26 November 1835. A third resolution requested the governor "to transmit copies of these Resolutions to the Senators and Representatives from this State in the Congress."

72. *Raleigh Register,* 15 December 1835.

73. Ibid. See also *Salisbury Carolina Watchman,* in *Raleigh Register,* 19 January 1836.

74. *Raleigh Register,* 8, 15 December 1835; *Fayetteville Observer,* 10 December 1835. Well aware that the Jackson administration's policy of donating the public lands to the western states was not popular in North Carolina, the Democrats were unwilling to speak against Clingman's first resolution. The debate centered, therefore, on the second resolution.

75. The quotation is from the report of the debate of 3 December, in *Raleigh Register,* 8 December 1835. Clingman's second resolution passed the House of Commons by a vote of seventy to fifty-four, with thirteen Democrats voting in the affirmative (ibid., 15 December 1835).

76. *Raleigh Register,* 8, 22 December 1835.

77. Ibid., 22, 29 December 1835.

78. Ibid., 29 December 1835.

79. TLC to William A. Graham, 29 April 1836, in Hamilton and Williams, *Graham Papers,* 1:425.

80. *Raleigh Register,* 23 August 1836.

3. Champion of the West

1. Clingman's recollections of his arrival in Asheville can be found in *Asheville Citizen,* 2 November 1887.

2. For descriptions of Asheville around the time of Clingman's arrival, see the reminiscences of J. M. Israel and A. T. Summey, in *Asheville Citizen,* 31 August 1893, 17 November 1896; J. S. T. Baird, "Historical Sketches of the Early Days," scrapbook of clippings from *Asheville Register,* January–March, 1905, NCC; John Preston Arthur, *Western North Carolina: A History from 1730 to 1913* (Raleigh: Edwards & Broughton, 1914), 146–49. For the slaveholdings of Patton, see John C. Inscoe, *Mountain Masters, Slavery, and the Sectional Crisis in Western North Carolina* (Knoxville: University of Tennessee Press, 1989), 66.

3. Inscoe, *Mountain Masters,* 25, 46–49, 154–56; Ora Blackmun, *Western North Carolina: Its Mountains and Its People to 1880* (Boone: Appalachian Consortium Press, 1977), 215–21.

4. Fannie Memory Farmer, "Legal Practice and Ethics in North Carolina, 1820–1860," *NCHR* 30 (1953): 329–32; Farmer, "The Bar Examination and Beginning Years of Legal Practice in North Carolina, 1820–1860," *NCHR* 29 (1952): 170. In one instance, Clingman had to go all the way to the state Supreme Court in order to make a recalcitrant client pay what he owed. See *George W. Candler et al. v. Jacob Trammell, North Carolina Reports* 29 (1846): 102–3.

5. Over $119,000 worth of Cherokee lands, ceded to the state under the treaties of 1817 and 1819, had been sold to settlers. More than $49,000 of principal and accrued interest remained outstanding in 1835. See "Report of Jacob Siler Agent of the State for Cherokee Lands," 1 August 1844, in *Legislative Documents, 1844–45.*

6. Financial records pertaining to Clingman's activities as state agent can be found in the following sources: Indian Affairs and Lands—Cherokee Nation, and Journals and Ledgers, vols. 40–41, both in Treasurer's & Comptroller's Records, NCDAH; reports of the treasurer and comptroller, in *Legislative Documents, 1838–39, 1840–41, 1842–43, 1844–45.* For the use of the collected monies on the state road, see John L. Smith to Edward B. Dudley, 23 October 1837, Ruben Deaver to Dudley, 17 May 1838, Dudley to Deaver, 24 May 1838, Governor's Papers, NCDAH; Dudley to TLC, 24 May 1838, Governor's Letter Books, NCDAH.

7. Farmer, "Legal Practice," 343–44. The cases argued by Clingman can be found in *North Carolina Reports* 20 (1838–39), 182–88, 190–92, 259–63 (December 1838 term); ibid., 508–12, 527–29, 559–60, 565–69, 572–74, 612–16, 661–66 (December 1839 term); ibid., 25 (1842–43), 1–2, 4–6, 20–22, 27–28, 35–54, 89–93, 185–90 (December 1842 term).

8. The account in this and the following paragraph is derived from *Sutton and Wife v. John C. Moore and others, North Carolina Reports* 25 (1842–43): 42–52. All quotations are from the court case. Clingman represented the defendant in his capacity as state agent appointed to defend the titles of purchasers of Cherokee lands.

9. John E. Patton to Edward B. Dudley, 28 April 1838, David L. Swain to Dudley, 4 May 1838, Governor's Papers. Enclosed with Patton's letter was another letter of recommendation from his brother, James W. Patton, who was one of Buncombe County's most successful and influential businessmen.

10. Inscoe, *Mountain Masters,* 154.

11. *Proceedings of the Stockholders . . . January 1837* (Knoxville: Ramsey & Craighead,

1837), 8–11; Henry D. Capers, *The Life and Times of C. G. Memminger* (Richmond: Everett Waddey, 1893), 555; Burke Davis, *The Southern Railway: Road of the Innovators* (Chapel Hill: University of North Carolina Press, 1985), 101–3.

12. C. G. Memminger to the Governor of North Carolina, in *Raleigh North Carolina Standard,* 4 January 1837. Many North Carolina Democrats opposed granting banking privileges to the LC & CRR on the grounds that the bank would be controlled by South Carolina nullifiers. Nonetheless, the bill passed the general assembly in January 1837. See *Raleigh North Carolina Standard* 11, 18 January 1837.

13. The convention proceedings were published in *Raleigh Register,* 31 December 1838. For the number of delegates and counties, see *Fayetteville Observer,* 12 December 1838.

14. *Fayetteville Observer,* 12, 19 December 1838; *Raleigh Register,* 31 December 1838. Among the proposals considered by the convention were several resolutions to construct a railroad or turnpike that would connect at some unspecified point with the LC & CRR.

15. Clingman himself introduced the resolution requesting the president of the convention to appoint the Committee of Seven (*Raleigh Register,* 31 December 1838). He was the only delegate to serve on all three major committees.

16. *Raleigh Register,* 7 January 1839.

17. *Fayetteville Observer,* 2 January 1839; Thomas E. Jeffrey, *State Parties and National Politics: North Carolina, 1815–1861* (Athens: University of Georgia Press, 1989), 188–91.

18. *Proceedings of the Louisville, Cincinnati, & Charleston Railroad Company, 1839* (Charleston: A. E. Miller, 1839), 10–31; Davis, *Southern Railway,* 103–6. Supporters of the French Broad route were dealt an unexpected blow by the death of the railroad's president, Robert Y. Hayne, in 1839.

19. *Proceedings of an Adjourned Meeting of the Stockholders . . . December 1839* (Charleston: A. E. Miller, 1840), 4–6, 9–12, 15.

20. The quotations in this and the two following paragraphs are from Clingman's speech, in *Raleigh Register,* 3 January 1840. Memminger's comment appears in the first paragraph of that speech.

21. The quotations are from Clingman's obituary in *New York Times,* 5 November 1897. For the importance of the Memminger debate in promoting Clingman's "reputation for ability, courage, eloquence, and large information," see also John D. Cameron, "Thomas Lanier Clingman," *University Magazine,* n.s., 8 (1889): 252–53.

22. *Fayetteville Observer,* 24 December 1839. Similar expressions of approbation can be found in *Raleigh Register,* 3 January 1840. Even the *Charleston (S.C.) Courier* spoke respectfully of Clingman, acknowledging that he had given "some hard knocks to our State and one of her distinguished citizens" (18 December 1839).

23. For the circumstances surrounding the acquisition of the Mount Pisgah property, see Mary Lacy Byrd, "Friend Helped Launch Politician," clipping from *Asheville Citizen-Times,* 30 October 1966, Pack. Candler apparently donated the land to Clingman without charge. A record of the transfer, dated 22 April 1839, can be found in George A. Diggs, *Buncombe County, North Carolina, Grantee Deed Index,* 2 vols. (Asheville: Miller, 1927), 1:C-465. Clingman boasted that "his plantation on the top of Pisgah . . . is the finest huckleberry plantation on the continent" (*Asheville Citizen,* in *Charlotte Observer,* 21 August 1885).

24. The proceedings of the Whig District Convention were published in *Raleigh Regis-*

ter, 8 May 1840. The Asheville senatorial district was composed of the counties of Buncombe, Cherokee, Haywood, Henderson, and Macon. For Rabun, see W. C. Allen, *The Annals of Haywood County North Carolina* ([Waynesville]: n.p., 1935), 141–42. For his narrow victory over Whig James Gudger in 1838, see *Raleigh Register,* 27 August 1838.

25. Voting returns for the Asheville senatorial district were published in *Raleigh North Carolina Standard,* 26 August 1840. For Clingman's campaign activities after the state elections, see *Asheville Messenger,* 2, 16 October 1840. Harrison received 76 percent of the vote in Clingman's congressional district, compared to 71 percent for Morehead. These figures were compiled from the county-level data in W. Dean Burnham, *Presidential Ballots, 1836–1892* (Baltimore: Johns Hopkins University Press, 1955), 646–68, and John L. Cheney, ed., *North Carolina Government, 1585–1979* (Raleigh: North Carolina Department of the Secretary of State, 1980), 1396–97. In 1840 Clingman's congressional district comprised the five counties in his senatorial district, along with Burke, Rutherford, and Yancey Counties.

26. Jeffrey, *State Parties and National Politics,* 112–13; Thomas E. Jeffrey "The Second Party System in North Carolina, 1836–1860" (Ph.D. diss., Catholic University of America, 1976), 214–17.

27. Nicholas W. Woodfin to David L. Swain, 8 November 1840, TLC to Swain, 19 November 1840, David Lowry Swain Papers, SHC; TLC to William Gaston, 13 November 1840, William Gaston Papers, SHC; *Raleigh Register,* 1 January 1841. Badger was subsequently appointed secretary of the navy in Harrison's cabinet.

28. One cynic suggested that much of Graham's support for the senatorship came from aspirants who wanted to succeed him as Speaker of the House of Commons. See Montreville Patton to David L. Swain, 19 November 1840, Swain Papers, SHC.

29. *Raleigh North Carolina Standard,* 9 December 1840, 13 January 1841. Clingman successfully sponsored two other measures to benefit the purchasers of Cherokee lands—a bill authorizing state agents to receive their payments in notes issued by specie-paying banks in South Carolina and Georgia and a bill allowing newly established Cherokee County to purchase the unsold lands adjoining its seat of government at a nominal price of fifty cents per acre. See *Raleigh Register,* 27 November 1840; *Raleigh North Carolina Standard,* 13 January 1841; *Asheville Messenger,* 20 July 1848.

30. On 7 January Clingman made an "admirable speech" on behalf of the Hickory Nut road (*Raleigh Register,* 8 January 1841). Earlier in the session he had "ably advocated" the Blue Ridge road, ibid. In addition, Clingman introduced a bill to incorporate the Hembrick (or Hembic) Turnpike Co. and spoke in favor of endorsing the bonds of the Raleigh & Gaston Railroad (*Raleigh North Carolina Standard,* 6, 13 January 1841).

31. Clingman buttressed his arguments with numerous facts and figures, engineers' reports, his own knowledge of the terrain, and the experience of similar projects in other states and in Great Britain. The speech was published in *Raleigh Register,* 22 December 1840, and was well received by the Whig press. The *Hillsborough Recorder* praised it as a "very able speech" characterized by "a masterly style . . . good common sense and statesmanlike views" (7 January 1841).

32. Shepard's speech can be found in *Raleigh North Carolina Standard,* 6 January 1841. For the importance of the Nags Head issue to easterners, see Jeffrey, *State Parties and National Politics,* 138–39.

33. Shepard's claim that a small number of insiders controlled the Whig caucus was not entirely consistent with his argument that westerners as a group bore responsibility for the nomination of Mangum and Graham. Although both men had pledged themselves to press for a federal appropriation for Nags Head, Shepard cavalierly dismissed their assurances as "promises made on the eve of an election."

34. *Raleigh Register*, 11 December 1840; *Fayetteville Observer*, 16 December 1840.

35. Clingman's speech was published in *Raleigh Register*, 1 January 1841.

36. For Whig opposition to caucuses, see Jeffrey, *State Parties and National Politics*, 92–96. While publicly defending the legitimacy of the legislative caucus, Clingman privately shared Shepard's belief that party leaders in and around Raleigh exercised a disproportionate influence on its deliberations. See TLC to David L. Swain, 19 November 1840, Swain Papers, SHC.

37. Shepard defended his record in an extemporaneous speech on the senate floor immediately after Clingman's address. The speech was published in *Raleigh Register*, 8 January 1841.

38. *Raleigh Register*, 11 December 1840; *Fayetteville Observer*, 16 December 1840. The encounter between Clingman and Shepard resulted in an inspired bit of doggerel by an anonymous correspondent of the *Register* (25 December 1840):

Quoth Senator C., of Improvements the best,

Is surely to make a good Road to the *West;*

To which Senator S. says, "*My Nag's* such a beast

That his *head* will not go any way but due East."

4. Ultra Whig

1. *Fayetteville Observer*, 24 March 1841; *Raleigh Register*, 16, 23 April, 25 May 1841; *Asheville Messenger*, 16 April, 7 May 1841. County-level election returns can be found in *Raleigh North Carolina Standard*, 2 June 1841. During the campaign, friends of both candidates attempted to arrange a settlement whereby one of them would voluntarily withdraw from the race. Clingman offered to step aside, but only if Graham agreed not to run in 1843. Graham spurned the proposition, retorting that he was "no man for political bargain and sale" and "would neither buy out, nor sell out." See communications from TLC and Graham, in *Asheville Messenger*, 7, 14 April 1843.

2. TLC to John M. Morehead, 10 April 1842, Governor's Papers, NCDAH. In reporting the debate at Asheville, the *Asheville Messenger* asserted that Clingman "completely demolished the positions assumed by Mr. Henry" and that his remarks were "greeted with frequent and loud applause" (15 April 1842).

3. *Raleigh Register*, 12 August 1842. Morehead won 73 percent of the vote in Clingman's district—an increase of two percentage points over his 1840 showing. At the same time, his statewide vote declined three percentage points from the previous election. See John L. Cheney, ed., *North Carolina Government, 1585–1979* (Raleigh: North Carolina Department of the Secretary of State, 1980), 1396–97.

4. Graham's remarks about the role of a representative were reported in *Asheville Messenger*, 14 April 1843. For his opposition to the distribution and bankruptcy bills, see

Raleigh Register, 13 July 1841; James Graham to William A. Graham, 25 May 1843, in J. G. de Roulhac Hamilton and Max R. Williams, eds., *The Papers of William A. Graham,* 8 vols. (Raleigh: Division of Archives and History, 1957–92), 2:426.

5. Richard B. Creecy, Clingman's classmate at the University of North Carolina, remembered that "his admiration for Clay . . . was unbounded" (Creecy to William H. S. Burgwyn, 17 January 1898, William Hyslop Sumner Burgwyn Papers, NCDAH).

6. Communications from TLC and Graham, in *Asheville Messenger,* 7, 14 April 1843. As in 1841, efforts were made to persuade Graham and Clingman to submit their claims to a nominating convention. Neither candidate was willing to agree to such a plan. See *Asheville Messenger,* 10, 24 March, 7 April 1843.

7. For the Asheville debate, see *Asheville Messenger,* 14 April 1843. For the controversy over the postmastership, see William Coleman to David L. Swain, 18, 25 February, 15 March 1842, and James Graham to Swain, 19 March 1842, David L. Swain Papers, NCDAH; *Asheville Messenger,* 15 April 1842, 28 April, 19 May 1843. During the 1840s Asheville was the mail distribution center for a wide area that included not only the North Carolina mountain region but also parts of Tennessee, South Carolina, and Georgia. For almost fifty years the postmaster position had been monopolized by George Swain (father of Gov. David L. Swain) and his son-in-law, Coleman.

8. TLC to Jane Clingman, 8 July 1843, Clingman and Puryear Family Papers, SHC. See also John H. Coleman to David L. Swain, 31 July 1843, Swain Papers, NCDAH.

9. Election returns by county can be found in *Hillsborough Recorder,* 17 August 1843; *Asheville Messenger,* 25 August 1843. According to the *Recorder,* "the Democrats in a body voted for Mr. Clingman." That assertion is substantiated by the fact that Graham's vote declined by only seven hundred from the previous election, whereas Clingman's vote increased by more than sixteen hundred.

10. *Hillsborough Recorder,* 17 August 1843; William A. Graham to James Graham, 1 September 1843, in Hamilton and Williams, *Graham Papers,* 2:440.

11. The *Asheville Messenger* (originally called the *Highland Messenger*) began publication in late May or early June 1840 (*Raleigh North Carolina Standard,* 10 June 1840). It was the first North Carolina newspaper published west of the Blue Ridge and, for many years, the only such paper. For opposition to McAnally and Roberts on the part of Clingman's supporters, see William Coleman to David L. Swain, 4 August 1843, Swain Papers, NCDAH; *Asheville Messenger,* 11 August 1843.

12. *Asheville Messenger,* 10 November 1843, 16 August 1844; John Hill Wheeler, *Historical Sketches of North Carolina from 1584 to 1851,* 2 vols. in 1 (Philadelphia: Lippincott, Grambo, 1851), 1:113; Frontis W. Johnston and Joe A. Mobley, eds., *The Papers of Zebulon Baird Vance,* 2 vols. to date (Raleigh: Division of Archives and History, 1963–), 1:18n.

13. For Clingman's arrival in Washington, see *Washington (D.C.) Madisonian,* 27 November 1843; *Washington (D.C.) National Intelligencer,* 29 November 1843. For the freshmen members of the Twenty-Eighth Congress, see Nathan Sargent, *Public Men and Events, from the Commencement of Mr. Monroe's Administration in 1817, to the Close of Mr. Fillmore's Administration, in 1853,* 2 vols. (Philadelphia: Lippincott, 1875), 2:202–9; Leroy P. Graf and Paul Bergeron, eds., *The Papers of Andrew Johnson,* 13 vols. to date (Knoxville: University of Tennessee Press, 1967–), 1:xxvii–xxviii.

14. For the legislative history of the gag rule prior to 1844, see Norman D. Brown,

Edward Stanly: Whiggery's Tarheel "Conqueror" (University: University of Alabama Press, 1974), 41–43, 47–48, 60–61, 70, 75. For the fate of the gag rule during the first session of the Twenty-Eighth Congress, see *Washington (D.C.) Spectator,* 5 January 1844, and *Fayetteville Observer,* 6 March 1844. Although Adams's motion was defeated by a four-vote margin, the gag rule was subsequently repealed at the second session.

15. The quotations in this and the following paragraph are from Clingman's speech, in *Raleigh Register,* 30 January 1844.

16. *New York Tribune,* 8 January 1844; *New York Courier and Inquirer* and *Philadelphia U.S. Gazette,* in *Fayetteville Observer,* 17 January 1844. The *Raleigh Register* reported that Clingman's speech had contributed mightily toward earning him a "high reputation as a bold, prompt, and efficient debater" (30 January 1844). Several weeks before his speech on the gag rule, Clingman had attracted favorable attention in the North Carolina newspapers for his performance in an extemporaneous debate with Henry A. Wise over the credentials of the Democratic delegations from Georgia, Mississippi, Missouri, and New Hampshire. According to the *Raleigh Register,* the veteran congressman from Virginia definitely "came off second best" in the exchange (29 December 1843). For other glowing accounts of the debate, see *Fayetteville Observer,* 20 December 1843; *Greensboro Patriot,* 23 December 1843; *Asheville Messenger,* 12 January 1844.

17. *Fayetteville Observer,* 17 January 1844; *Greensboro Patriot,* 13 January 1844; *Asheville Messenger,* 26 January 1844. See also *Newbernian,* 7 January 1844; *Raleigh Register,* 30 January 1844.

18. *Raleigh North Carolina Standard,* 17 January 1844; *Washington (D.C.) Madisonian,* 6 January 1844; *South Carolinian,* in *Raleigh North Carolina Standard,* 31 January 1844; "Speech on the Principles of the Whig and Democratic Parties," in *S&W,* 157.

19. For Duncan's remarks, see *CG,* 28 Cong., 1 sess., 348–50.

20. "Whig and Democratic Parties," in *S&W,* 152, 161, 163, 165–67.

21. The *Raleigh Register* expressed its hope that Clingman's "admirable Speech will not only be copied by the Whig Press generally, but that Candidates for the Legislature, and others, will well digest its wholesome truths" (5 April 1844). The speech was subsequently published as a twenty-four-page pamphlet by Gales & Seaton, proprietors of the *National Intelligencer.*

22. *New York Tribune,* 9 March 1844; *Baltimore (Md.) Patriot,* in *Raleigh Register,* 15 March 1844; *Raleigh North Carolina Standard,* 3 April 1844.

23. Bayles M. Edney to William A. Graham, 13 May 1844, in Hamilton and Williams, *Graham Papers,* 2:498; Jeffrey, *State Parties and National Politics,* 98, 136–37, 154–55, 177–79, 201–3; Max R. Williams, "William A. Graham and the Election of 1844: A Study in North Carolina Politics," *NCHR* 45 (1968): 23–46.

24. A copy of the Democratic pamphlet can be found in Hamilton and Williams, *Graham Papers,* 2:503–6.

25. TLC to Willie P. Mangum, 25 August 1846, in Henry T. Shanks, ed., *The Papers of Willie Person Mangum,* 5 vols. (Raleigh: State Department of Archives and History, 1950–56), 4:478.

26. *Raleigh Register,* 19 July 1844; *Asheville Messenger,* 12 July 1844; Cheney, *North Carolina Government,* 1396–97. As noted above, Morehead had received 73 percent of the vote in Clingman's district in 1842.

27. Accounts of the Knoxville and Nashville meetings can be found in *Raleigh Register,* 6 September 1844. For a description of the Nashville meeting from a Democratic viewpoint, see Daniel Graham to James K. Polk, 25 August 1844, in Herbert Weaver et al., eds., *Correspondence of James K. Polk,* 9 vols. to date (Nashville: Vanderbilt University Press, 1969–), 7:468–70.

28. *Raleigh Register,* 15 October 1844. For the Rutherfordton and Morganton meetings, see ibid., 25 October, 1 November 1844.

29. Clay received 6,468 votes in the mountain district, compared to 3,063 for Polk—a substantial improvement over the Whig margin of 2,500 votes in the governor's election. See W. Dean Burnham, *Presidential Ballots, 1836–1892* (Baltimore: Johns Hopkins University Press, 1955), 646–68. A sharp drop in turnout among the Democrats accounted for most of the difference. Clay received only 49 more votes than Graham, whereas Polk polled 832 fewer votes than Hoke. For the Raleigh letter, see William J. Cooper Jr., *The South and the Politics of Slavery, 1828–1856* (Baton Rouge: Louisiana State University Press, 1978), 207–8, 212.

30. "Speech on the Causes of Mr. Clay's Defeat," in *S&W,* 173, 179.

31. Ibid., 177, 179.

32. Ibid., 179, 187–88. A "thimble rig" was a type of shell game. For the genesis of the Empire Club, see Isaac C. Pray, *Memoirs of James Gordon Bennett and His Times* (New York: Stringer & Townsend, 1855), 354–55.

33. "Speech on the Causes of Mr. Clay's Defeat," in *S&W,* 174–75.

34. William H. Hammett (Democrat, Mississippi) and William A. Moseley (Whig, New York), quoted in *S&W,* 195; *Greensboro Patriot,* 18 January 1845. Clingman's remarks about his speech can be found in *S&W,* 196. Andrew Johnson claimed the speech was "intended for the elections in North Carolina next summer" ("Speech on the Admission of Texas and Other Matters," 21 January 1845, in Graf and Bergeron, *Johnson Papers,* 1:193). In fact, the Whigs immediately issued thirty thousand copies in pamphlet form (*Raleigh Register,* 31 January 1845).

35. *Raleigh North Carolina Standard,* 15 January 1845. Yancey's speech was published in *CG,* 28 Cong., 2 sess., 100, and reprinted in *Raleigh Register,* 14 January 1845, and *Raleigh North Carolina Standard,* 15 January 1845.

36. TLC to William L. Yancey, 7 January 1845, Yancey to TLC, 8 January 1845, in John M. Huger, *Memoranda of the Late Affair of Honor between Hon. T. L. Clingman, of North Carolina, and Hon. William L. Yancey, of Alabama* (Washington, D.C.: n.p., 1845).

37. Most accounts of the Clingman-Yancey duel have been based on the correspondence published by John Middleton Huger, who served as Yancey's second. Historians have overlooked the account written during the 1880s by Charles Lee Jones, who served as Clingman's second. Jones's narrative, entitled "Reminiscences of the Duello at Washington," was published in the *Washington (D.C.) Star* and reprinted in several North Carolina newspapers. Unless otherwise noted, the quotations in the following paragraphs are from Jones's reminiscences, in *Raleigh State Journal,* 11 January 1883.

38. The first quotation is from Huger, *Memoranda,* 3n.

39. Ibid., 4–7.

40. Communications from "Richelieu," in *New York Tribune,* 13, 14 January 1845. The various rumors were published in *New York Tribune,* 14 January 1845; *Baltimore (Md.)*

American and *Baltimore (Md.) Sun*, in *New York Tribune*, 14 January 1845; *Fayetteville Observer*, 15 January 1845.

41. According to Jones, "every road leading into Delaware was guarded," and the authorities were "so positive . . . of our [imminent] capture that the newspapers announced our actual arrest."

42. John W. DuBose, *The Life and Times of William Lowndes Yancey*, 2 vols. (Birmingham: Roberts & Son, 1892), 1:143; Huger, *Memoranda*, 8.

43. Andrew Johnson to [Blackston McDannel], [January 1845], in Graf and Bergeron, *Johnson Papers*, 1:184; Huger, *Memoranda*, 8.

44. John Fairfield to wife, 15 January 1845, in Arthur G. Staples, ed., *The Letters of John Fairfield* (Lewiston, Maine: Lewiston Journal, 1922), 357; Graf and Bergeron, *Johnson Papers*, 1:206n; Andrew Johnson, "Speech on the Admission of Texas," ibid., 191; Johnson to [Blackston McDannel], [January 1845], ibid., 185.

45. Willie P. Mangum to Tod R. Caldwell, 20 February 1845, in Shanks, *Mangum Papers*, 4:269–70.

46. *Hartford (Conn.) Journal*, in *Raleigh Register*, 7 February 1845; *Asheville Messenger*, 14 February 1845. Pleasant Henderson, the Clingman family doctor, characterized the duel as "a rascally Democratic move to get Tom out of their way" (Henderson to Jane P. Clingman, 17 January 1845, Clingman-Puryear Papers).

47. *Raleigh Register*, 18 April 1845. See also *Fayetteville Observer*, 14 May 1845.

48. *Asheville Messenger*, in *Fayetteville Observer*, 4 June 1845; James Graham to William A. Graham, 19 August 1845, in Hamilton and Williams, *Graham Papers*, 3:63–65; communication from "Richland," in *Asheville Messenger*, 1 August 1845; TLC "to the Public," 13 August 1845, ibid., 15 August 1845.

49. Graham's circular, 17 July 1845, was published in *Asheville Messenger*, 1 August 1845. All four of North Carolina's Whig congressmen voted against Milton Brown's annexation resolution, which passed the House of Representatives by a vote of 120 to 98. See *Raleigh North Carolina Standard*, 29 January 1845; *Raleigh Register*, 31 January 1845.

50. Communications from "A Voter," T. George Walton et al., and "A Burke Whig," in *Asheville Messenger*, 25 July 1845.

51. *Greensboro Patriot*, 2 August 1845; *Fayetteville Observer*, 6 August 1845; *Raleigh Register*, 1 August 1845; Edward W. Johnston to William A. Graham, 11 October 1845, in Hamilton and Williams, *Graham Papers*, 3:77. Reprinting an endorsement from the *Milton Chronicle*, the *Asheville Messenger* remarked that it "could, were it necessary, quote something of a similar character from almost every Whig paper in the State" (22 August 1845).

52. Communication from "A Burke Whig," in *Asheville Messenger*, 25 July 1845; circular from TLC to his constituents, 21 July 1845, in *Asheville Messenger*, 1 August 1845.

53. Graham received 5,244 votes, compared to 4,918 for Clingman. Voting returns by county for 1843 and 1845 can be found in *New York Tribune*, 26 August 1845. For the 1845 vote, see also *Asheville Messenger*, 22 August 1845. A correspondent of the *Raleigh North Carolina Standard* expressed the prevailing view that "the democrats of this District . . . rallied almost in solid column to the support of Mr. Graham, thereby securing his election" (20 August 1845).

54. *Wilmington Journal*, 22 August 1845; communication from a correspondent in

Burke County, in *Raleigh North Carolina Standard*, 20 August 1845. Holden's editorial remarks can be found in the same issue of the *Standard*.

55. *Asheville Messenger*, 15 August 1845. Clingman's letter, dated 13 August 1845, was published in the same issue of the *Messenger*.

56. John C. Inscoe, "Thomas Clingman, Mountain Whiggery, and the Southern Cause," *Civil War History* 33 (1987): 47. A similar analysis can be found in John C. Inscoe, *Mountain Masters, Slavery, and the Sectional Crisis in Western North Carolina* (Knoxville: University of Tennessee Press, 1989), 185; and Marc W. Kruman, "Thomas L. Clingman and the Whig Party: A Reconsideration," *NCHR* 64 (1987): 6–7.

57. *Raleigh North Carolina Standard*, 20 August 1845; *Speech of John Baxter Made in Reply to Hon. T. L. Clingman, at Rutherfordton, 13th November, 1850* (Asheville: Messenger, 1850), 7. According to Baxter, Clingman's "reverse of fortune [in 1845] took him by surprise, and produced . . . a remarkable degree of respect toward the Democratic party."

5. Renegade Whig

1. *Asheville Messenger*, 15 August, 5 September 1845.

2. *Asheville Messenger*, 15 August 1845. Clingman's circular, dated 13 August 1845, was published in the same issue of the *Messenger*. According to the *Messenger*, "almost the entire Whig press of the state had joined us in denouncing the course of Mr. Graham" (29 August 1845).

3. The letter, which Clingman labeled "Confidential," can be found in Henry T. Shanks, ed., *The Papers of Willie Person Mangum*, 5 vols. (Raleigh: State Department of Archives and History, 1950–56), 4:315–17. Whether consciously or unconsciously, Clingman exaggerated Graham's unpopularity in the far west. See James W. Osborne to William A. Graham, 22 October 1845, and John Gray Bynum to Graham, 4 November 1845, in J. G. de Roulhac Hamilton and Max R. Williams, eds., *The Papers of William A. Graham*, 8 vols. (Raleigh: Division of Archives and History, 1957–92), 3:79–80, 84.

4. TLC to Willie P. Mangum, 5 October 1845, in Shanks, *Mangum Papers*, 4:315–17. Clingman believed that by supporting Graham over Michael Hoke in 1844, he had made "many enemies *[sic]* with the fishy whigs, (Hoke's friends of course)." See also TLC to Mangum, 25 August 1846, ibid., 476–79.

5. Asheville resolutions, in *Raleigh Register*, 21 October 1845; *Raleigh North Carolina Standard*, 22 October 1845.

6. *Asheville Messenger*, 31 October 1845; John Gray Bynum to William A. Graham, 4 November 1845, in Hamilton and Williams, *Graham Papers*, 3:84. See also James W. Osborne to William A. Graham, 22 October 1845, ibid., 79–80.

7. Proceedings of meetings in Burke, Haywood, Henderson, Macon, and Rutherford Counties, in *Asheville Messenger*, 21 November, 26 December 1845, 30 January 1846. The proceedings of the Whig State Convention were published in *Raleigh Register*, 16 January 1846.

8. TLC to Willie P. Mangum, 25 August 1846, in Shanks, *Mangum Papers*, 4:478. For Clingman's continuing reservations about Graham after his nomination, see TLC to Mangum, 21 February 1846, ibid., 395–96. For his debates with Shepard, see *Asheville*

Messenger, 24, 31 July 1846. Through an intermediary, Clingman promised Graham that he and his friends would *"all do their best"* on his behalf. See John Cameron to Graham, 21 June 1846, Governor's Papers, NCDAH.

9. *Asheville Messenger,* in *Raleigh Register,* 3 February 1846; communication from "C," ibid., 20 February 1846; Thomas E. Jeffrey, *State Parties and National Politics: North Carolina: 1815–1861* (Athens: University of Georgia Press, 1989), 108–9, 179–83, 203–5. Graham received 6,922 votes in the mountain district, compared to only 3,315 for Shepard. Statistics on the gubernatorial elections discussed in this chapter were compiled from the county-level data in John L. Cheney, ed., *North Carolina Government, 1585–1979* (Raleigh: North Carolina Department of the Secretary of State, 1980), 1398–99.

10. TLC to Willie P. Mangum, 25 August 1846, in Shanks, *Mangum Papers,* 4:476–79. Haywood resigned because of a disagreement with the Polk administration over tariff policy. The "Locofocos" were members of the radical wing of the Democratic party in New York. During the antebellum period the Whigs habitually referred to all Democrats as "Locofocos" or "Locos."

11. The principal contenders for the nomination were identified in *Raleigh Register,* 28 August 1846. Clingman's name was not mentioned—an omission that his supporters were quick to criticize. See *Raleigh Register,* 18 September 1846.

12. *Speech of John Baxter Made in Reply to Hon. T. L. Clingman, at Rutherfordton, 13th November, 1850* (Asheville: Messenger Office, 1850), 8. The "Fair Play" letter may have been written by Thomas W. Atkin of the *Asheville Messenger.* Baxter characterized its author as "a generous youth always willing to gratify a friend."

13. "Fair Play," quoted in Baxter, *Reply to Clingman,* 9, and in *Raleigh Register,* 20 October 1846.

14. *Raleigh Register,* 20, 23 October 1846.

15. "Fair Play," quoted in Baxter, *Reply to Clingman,* 9. Baxter asserted that the original communication to the *Raleigh Register* "was not strong enough to satisfy Mr. Clingman's vanity," so "a copy of 'Fair Play,' with an addition written by Mr. Clingman's own hand" was published in the *Asheville Messenger* on 8 October 1846. That issue of the *Messenger* is not extant, but the contents of the letter can be reconstructed from the excerpts published in Baxter's pamphlet and in the *Raleigh Register.*

16. *Raleigh North Carolina Standard,* 28 October, 11 November 1846.

17. Communication to *Newbernian,* in *Raleigh North Carolina Standard,* 2 December 1846; *Raleigh North Carolina Standard,* 25 November 1846. See also *Fayetteville Observer,* 24 November 1846; *Raleigh Register,* 27 November, 4 December 1846.

18. James Graham to William A. Graham, 10 May 1847, in Hamilton and Williams, *Graham Papers,* 3:193–95. For Clingman's attitude toward Badger, see TLC to Willie P. Mangum, 25 August 1846, 15 January 1847, in Shanks, *Mangum Papers,* 4:476, 5:15.

19. John Hill Wheeler to David S. Reid, 19 April 1847, in Lindley S. Butler, ed., *The Papers of David Settle Reid,* 2 vols. (Raleigh: Department of Cultural Resources, Division of Archives and History, 1993–97), 1:208; *Asheville Messenger,* 1 July 1847; *Raleigh North Carolina Standard,* 14, 28 July 1847; TLC, *The Tobacco Remedy* (New York: Orange Judd, 1885), 6–7. Clingman received 4,550 votes, compared to 3,426 for Bynum, and carried every county except Rutherford and Cleveland. See *Raleigh North Carolina Standard,* 25 August 1847. The *Standard* claimed that the Democrats "took but little part in the contest" (18 August 1847).

20. The quotations are from John C. Inscoe, "Thomas Clingman, Mountain Whiggery, and the Southern Cause," *Civil War History*, 33 (1987): 48; Marc W. Kruman, "Thomas L. Clingman and the Whig Party: A Reconsideration," *NCHR* 64 (1987): 7.

21. *CG*, 30 Cong., 1 sess., 60; "Speech on the Political Aspect of the Slave Question," 22 December 1847, in *S&W*, 198.

22. *S&W*, 197. For the controversy over the Wilmot Proviso, see Eric Foner, "The Wilmot Proviso Revisited," *Journal of American History* 56 (1969): 262–79; David Potter, *The Impending Crisis, 1848–1861* (New York: Harper & Row, 1976), 67–68, 89; Michael F. Holt, *The Political Crisis of the 1850s* (New York: John Wiley & Sons, 1978), 52–56; William J. Cooper Jr., *The South and the Politics of Slavery, 1828–1856* (Baton Rouge: Louisiana State University Press, 1978), 238–44.

23. "Speech on the Slave Question," in *S&W*, 200–204. Clingman rejected the notion that the territorial legislatures had the power to pass laws recognizing or excluding slavery, as Lewis Cass and other proponents of "popular sovereignty" were arguing. "The inhabitants of the territory have no rights of legislation," he asserted. "All the powers that can be exercised belong to Congress alone" (201).

24. Ibid., 214, 217–18.

25. Ibid., 225.

26. Inscoe, "Clingman, Mountain Whiggery, and the Southern Cause," 49; *Raleigh Register*, 30 January 1844.

27. "Speech on the Slave Question," in *S&W*, 223, 225–26.

28. *Washington (D.C.) National Era*, 30 December 1847. The antislavery *New York Tribune* also judged the speech to be "no discreditable production" (24 December 1847). For favorable assessments by North Carolina Whigs, see *Raleigh Register*, 29 December 1847, 4 January 1848; *Fayetteville Observer*, 4 January 1848; *Asheville Messenger*, 6 January 1848 (quoting *Charleston (S.C.) Courier*), 13 January 1848; *Hillsborough Recorder*, 13 January 1848. According to the *Messenger*, the speech had "received the approbation of the southern press generally" (13 January 1848).

29. *Raleigh Register*, 5 January 1848.

30. Communication from "Halifax," in *Raleigh North Carolina Standard*, 5 January 1848. See also Duff Green to William H. Thomas, 17 August 1848, William Holland Thomas Papers, Duke.

31. Hopkins Holsey to Howell Cobb, 31 December 1848, in Ulrich B. Phillips, ed., *The Correspondence of Robert Toombs, Alexander H. Stephens, and Howell Cobb* (Washington, D.C.: American Historical Association, 1913), 91–94. Holsey was editor of the *Athens (Ga.) Southern Banner*.

32. For the failure of efforts to extend the Missouri Compromise line to the Pacific, see Potter, *Impending Crisis*, 54–57, 65–77. Potter has aptly characterized the Missouri plan as "the forgotten alternative of the sectional controversy" (56).

33. Otis Singletary, *The Mexican War* (Chicago: University of Chicago Press, 1960), 116–27, 134–36.

34. *CG*, 30 Cong., 1 sess., 269, 459, 505; Milo Milton Quaife, ed., *The Diary of James K. Polk*, 4 vols. (Chicago: A. C. McClurg, 1910; New York: Kraus Reprint Co., 1970), 3:394.

35. Quaife, *Polk Diary*, 3:394; *CG*, 30 Cong., 1 sess., 514–16, 519, 583, 586, 638, 686–88; *Washington (D.C.) National Era*, 21 March, 13 April 1848.

36. *New York Tribune*, 29 April 1848; *Raleigh Register*, 29 April, 3 June 1848. Clingman

later claimed he had preferred Scott over Taylor in 1848 because the latter "had refused to take any position with reference to the great pending questions of the day." See TLC to Ladson A. Mills, 8 October 1852, in *S&W*, 317.

37. For the campaign of 1848, see Thomas E. Jeffrey, "'Free Suffrage' Revisited: Party Politics and Constitutional Reform in Antebellum North Carolina," *NCHR* 59 (1982): 26–37.

38. Badger opposed the Clayton Compromise because he believed the Supreme Court would sustain his own opinion that "slavery does not exist anywhere . . . independently of law authorizing it." Since slavery had never been explicitly recognized in the Mexican Cession under either Mexican or U.S. law, the Clayton Compromise, in Badger's opinion, would be tantamount to the Wilmot Proviso. See Lawrence Foushee London, "George Edmund Badger in the United States Senate, 1846–1849," *NCHR* 15 (1938): 19; Herbert D. Pegg, *The Whig Party in North Carolina* (Chapel Hill: Colonial Press, 1968), 138–39; *Raleigh Register*, 2 August 1848. Probably for the same reason, two North Carolina Whigs also voted against the Clayton Compromise in the House of Representatives. In March 1848 Clingman had expressed opinions similar to Badger's, remarking that slavery could "never be established . . . [in] new territory [to] be got from Mexico" without the explicit approval of Congress inasmuch as "slavery does not exist there" under Mexican law. See communication from TLC, 22 March 1848, in *Washington (D.C.) National Intelligencer*, 23 March 1848. Nonetheless, Clingman, together with three other North Carolina Whigs, supported the Clayton Compromise in the House, as did Mangum in the Senate. The measure passed the Senate, only to be tabled by the House. See *Raleigh Register*, 5 August 1848.

39. London, "Badger in the United States Senate," 15–20; *Raleigh North Carolina Standard*, 29 November 1848. A month before the convening of the general assembly, Badger regarded his prospects for reelection as "very doubtful." See Badger to J. J. Crittenden, 12 October 1848, in Lawrence Foushee London, "George Edmund Badger and the Compromise of 1850," *NCHR* 15 (1938): 99.

40. David Outlaw to Emily B. Outlaw, 3 March 1848, David Outlaw Letters, SHC; TLC to Willie P. Mangum, 1 September 1848, in Shanks, *Mangum Papers*, 5:109–10. Clingman himself acknowledged that his "difficulty with Mr. Badger" was "personal" rather than political. See *Address of T. L. Clingman on the Recent Senatorial Election* (Washington, D.C.: J. & G. S. Gideon, 1849), 3.

41. TLC, *Address on the Recent Senatorial Election*, 3; *Fayetteville Observer*, 23 January 1849. The other Whig insurgent was William B. Shepard of Pasquotank, who had been Clingman's main antagonist during the legislative session of 1840–41.

42. A breakdown of the votes can be found in Brian G. Walton, "Elections to the United States Senate in North Carolina, 1835–1861," *NCHR* 53 (1976): 184. For the vote on the first ballot, see also *Raleigh North Carolina Standard*, 13 December 1848.

43. Robert G. A. Love to TLC, 16 December 1848, Bayles Edney to TLC, 16 December 1848, Clingman and Puryear Family Papers, SHC. Love, a Democratic legislator from Haywood County, was not the only observer who perceived a movement toward Shepard. David L. Swain also considered Shepard's election "very probable" (Swain to William H. Battle, 16 December 1848, Battle Family Papers, SHC).

44. David Outlaw to Emily B. Outlaw, 16 December 1848, Outlaw Letters. Outlaw, who

seems to have been genuinely fond of Clingman despite his increasingly erratic behavior, predicted that "his ambition will overreach itself."

45. *Fayetteville North Carolinian*, 27 January 1849. According to the *North Carolinian*, the Democrats in the general assembly had "concluded to try how far he would come over the line which divides the two parties."

46. The quotations in this and the following paragraph are from TLC to Calvin Graves et al., 18 December 1848, in *Raleigh North Carolina Standard*, 24 January 1849.

47. Badger received seventy-five votes on the fourth ballot, compared to fifty-five for Clingman. For the plans of some Whigs to support a Democrat "in order to defeat Clingman," see Bartholomew F. Moore to Daniel M. Barringer, 29 December 1848, Daniel Moreau Barringer Papers, SHC. Stanly's speech on behalf of Swain was published in *Raleigh Register*, 27 December 1848.

48. Bartholomew F. Moore to Daniel M. Barringer, 29 December 1848, Barringer Papers. On 21 December Farmer wrote a public letter explaining that he had voted for Badger on the fifth ballot "in compliance with the wish of Mr. Clingman" (*Raleigh Register*, 27 December 1848). See also TLC, *Address on the Recent Senatorial Election*, 4.

49. Victor Barringer to "my dear sister," 1 January 1849, Barringer Papers; Charles Manly to Samuel F. Patterson, 4 March 1849, Jones and Patterson Family Papers, SHC. See also Bartholomew F. Moore to Daniel M. Barringer, 29 December 1848, Barringer Papers.

50. In his letter to the Democratic legislators, Clingman characterized himself as "an independent candidate" (*Raleigh North Carolina Standard*, 24 January 1849). The same phrase appears in TLC, *Address on the Recent Senatorial Election*, 4, 7.

51. After the election, Clingman claimed some Whigs had "intended, if I came near an election, to change their votes from Mr. Badger to me, and thereby elect me" (TLC, *Address on the Recent Senatorial Election*, 7). That may have been wishful thinking. Of the eighty Democratic legislators, sixty-six voted for Clingman on the fifth ballot. According to Brian G. Walton, "it is unlikely that the Democrats could have rallied solidly around Clingman on further ballots. . . . Party ties were too strong" ("Elections to the U. S. Senate," 184). Clingman himself acknowledged that his prospects for defeating Badger were diminished by the fact that "a number of Democrats were averse to voting for any Whig" (TLC, *Address on the Recent Senatorial Election*, 8).

52. TLC to Calvin Graves et al., 18 December 1848, in *Raleigh North Carolina Standard*, 24 January 1849; TLC, *Address on the Recent Senatorial Election*, 7.

53. TLC, *Address on the Recent Senatorial Election*, 10–12.

54. Ibid., 15.

55. *Raleigh Register*, 24 January 1849. See also the lengthy rebuttals published in *Fayetteville Observer*, 23, 30 January, 6, 13 February 1849; *Raleigh Register*, 24 January, 7 February 1849; *Greensboro Patriot*, 27 January, 3 February 1849; *Salisbury Carolina Watchman*, 8 February 1849.

56. Communication from Samuel F. Patterson, in *Raleigh Register*, 7 March 1849. See also the communications from Tod R. Caldwell, John Y. Hicks, and E. P. Miller, ibid., 24, 31 January, 4 April 1849.

57. For the tensions between republican ideology and party politics in antebellum North Carolina, see Jeffrey, *State Parties and National Politics*, chapter 4. For Clingman's skillful

use of the rhetoric of postrevolutionary republicanism, see also Kruman, "Clingman and the Whig Party."

58. Clingman received 7,231 votes in 1849, compared to 4,550 votes in 1847. The remaining 1,146 ballots were scattered among individuals not in the race. See TLC to Daniel M. Barringer, 13 August 1849, Barringer Papers.

6. Champion of the South

1. *S&W*, 274; John Inscoe, "Thomas Clingman, Mountain Whiggery, and the Southern Cause," *Civil War History*, 33 (1987): 48.

2. TLC to Calvin Graves et al., 18 December 1848, in *Raleigh North Carolina Standard*, 24 January 1849; *Fayetteville North Carolinian*, 6 January 1849.

3. *New York Tribune*, 30 January 1849; *Fayetteville Observer*, 23, 30 January 1849.

4. TLC to John M. Clayton, 5 July 1849, John Middleton Clayton Papers, Manuscript Division, Library of Congress, Washington, D.C.; TLC to Willie P. Mangum, 1 September 1848, in Henry T. Shanks, ed., *The Papers of Willie Person Mangum*, 5 vols. (Raleigh: State Department of Archives and History, 1950–56), 5:110; TLC to Daniel M. Barringer, 21 June 1849, Daniel Moreau Barringer Papers, SHC; Norman D. Brown, *Edward Stanly: Whiggery's Tarheel "Conqueror"* (University: University of Alabama Press, 1974), 120–21. Clingman was somewhat assuaged after Graham declined the Spanish mission and it was offered to Barringer. See TLC to Daniel M. Barringer, 13 August 1849, Barringer Papers.

5. TLC to John M. Clayton, 5 July 1849, Clayton Papers. For Whig opposition to Edney's appointment, see David Outlaw to Emily B. Outlaw, 4 March 1850, David Outlaw Letters, SHC; Edward Stanly to William A. Graham, 8 November 1852, in J. G. de Roulhac Hamilton and Max R. Williams, eds., *The Papers of William A. Graham*, 8 vols. (Raleigh: Division of Archives and History, 1957–92), 4:430. For Clingman's efforts on behalf of Edney, see Edward Stanly to William A. Graham, 2 April 1850, in Hamilton and Williams, *Graham Papers*, 3:319; David Outlaw to Emily B. Outlaw, 17 December 1849, 5, 24, 31 January, 24 February, 4 March, 18 April 1850, Outlaw Letters.

6. *S&W*, 230; David Potter, *The Impending Crisis, 1848–1861* (New York: Harper & Row, 1976), 74–75.

7. *S&W*, 230. Clingman left Washington en route to the North in early September (TLC to Daniel M. Barringer, 2 September 1849, Barringer Papers). He was back in the nation's capital by early November. Clingman was correct in his belief that the Northern Democrats had jettisoned popular sovereignty in favor of the Wilmot Proviso. See Michael F. Holt, *The Political Crisis of the 1850s* (New York: John Wiley & Sons, 1978), 72.

8. *S&W*, 231.

9. Henry S. Foote to TLC, 10 November 1849, in *Raleigh North Carolina Standard*, 28 November 1849; TLC to Foote, 13 November 1849, in *S&W*, 231–33.

10. *Washington (D.C.) National Era*, 29 November 1849. Foote himself was no disunionist, as his efforts on behalf of Henry Clay's compromise in 1850 and his election on the Union ticket to the Mississippi governorship the following year testify. See William J.

Cooper Jr., *The South and the Politics of Slavery, 1828–1856* (Baton Rouge: Louisiana State University Press, 1978), 306, 310.

11. *Raleigh North Carolina Standard,* 28 November 1849; *Washington (D.C.) Union,* in *Washington (D.C.) National Era,* 29 November 1849.

12. *New York Tribune,* 4, 5 December 1849; *Raleigh North Carolina Standard,* 12 December 1849; *Greensboro Patriot,* 15 December 1849; *S&W,* 235–36. The other Whigs who withdrew from the caucus were E. Carrington Cabell of Florida, Henry Hilliard of Alabama, Jeremiah Morton of Virginia, and Allen F. Owen of Georgia.

13. The characterization of the Toombs faction as "Southern impracticables" can be found in *Raleigh Register,* 22 December 1849. The recently established Free Soil party had unsuccessfully run Martin Van Buren for president in 1848. Nonetheless, it did manage to elect several of its candidates to Congress. For the vote for Speaker, see *CG,* 31 Cong., 1 sess., 2–66, passim.

14. Cobb was elected by a vote of 102 to 99. Henry Hilliard, who had acted up to that point with the Toombs group, voted for Winthrop on the final ballot. See *CG,* 31 Cong., 1 sess., 66.

15. *CG,* 31 Cong., 1 sess., 33–34.

16. David Outlaw to Emily B. Outlaw, 21 December 1849, Outlaw Letters.

17. "Speech in Defence of the South against the Aggressive Movement of the North," in *S&W,* 235, 237.

18. Ibid., 237, 241, 251.

19. Ibid., 245, 252, 254.

20. *Richmond (Va.) Times,* in *Raleigh North Carolina Standard,* 30 January 1850. See also the comments in *Philadelphia (Pa.) North American,* 29 January 1850, *New York Herald,* 28 January 1850, in *S&W,* appendix, 34–35, 39.

21. *Philadelphia (Pa.) North American,* 29 January 1850, in *S&W,* appendix, 35; communication from Washington correspondent, in *Asheville Messenger,* 6 March 1850. Another eyewitness agreed that "the House, ordinarily as noisy and confused an assemblage of persons as can be met at any public fair . . . was hushed in the deepest silence, and every eye rested on the speaker . . . [whose] clear, distinct enunciation and concentrated calmness of manners [were] more imposing than any exhibition of passion could have been." See *Columbia (S.C.) Telegraph,* 28 January 1850, in *S&W,* appendix, 33.

22. *Charleston (S.C.) Mercury,* 6 February 1850.

23. Ibid.; David Outlaw to Emily B. Outlaw, 22 January 1850, Outlaw Letters; *Asheville Messenger,* in *Raleigh Register,* 23 February 1850. For Democratic reaction to the speech, see *Raleigh North Carolina Standard,* 30 January 1850; *New Bern Republican,* 27 February 1850. For Whig reaction, see *Fayetteville Observer,* 5 February 1850; *Greensboro Patriot,* 9 February 1850 (quoting *Baltimore (Md.) Clipper*); *Raleigh Register,* 13 February 1850 (quoting *Richmond (Va.) Whig*).

24. Communication from Washington correspondent, in *Asheville Messenger,* 6 March 1850; David Outlaw to Emily B. Outlaw, 30 January 1850, Outlaw Letters; *London Chronicle,* 21 February 1850, in *S&W,* appendix, 43.

25. David Outlaw to Emily B. Outlaw, 8 February 1850, Outlaw Letters; James C. Johnston to William S. Pettigrew, 6 March 1850, Pettigrew to Johnston, 14 March 1850,

Pettigrew Family Papers, SHC. Pettigrew told Johnston that his brother Charles, who had recently returned from a trip to Georgia, "says Mr. Clingman is there regarded as one of the first men in the South."

26. Stanly's speech was published in *Raleigh Register*, 27 March 1850. Contrary to Stanly's assertion, Clingman was consistent in his constitutional views on slavery in the territories. As previously noted, his principle of equitable division, first outlined in his speech of 22 December 1847, acknowledged Congress's exclusive jurisdiction over the territories while also affirming its constitutional obligation to apportion the territories fairly between the sections.

27. TLC to *Washington (D.C.) Republic*, 22 March 1850, in *Raleigh North Carolina Standard*, 3 April 1850. The portion of the letter published in *S&W*, 259–67, does not include the initial paragraphs attacking Stanly.

28. TLC to *Washington (D.C.) Republic*, 22 March 1850, in *S&W*, 262.

29. During the crisis of 1860–61, advocates of the right of secession generally argued that the election of a Republican president was in itself a sufficient reason for the South to withdraw from the Union, whereas the revolutionists pushed for a sectional compromise that would avert disunion.

30. *S&W*, 255–59, 271–74.

31. *Richmond (Va.) Times*, in *Salisbury Carolina Watchman*, 17 April 1851; David Outlaw to Emily B. Outlaw, [10 January?], 1 May 1850, Outlaw Letters; William A. Graham to James Graham, 25 August 1850, in Hamilton and Williams, *Graham Papers*, 3:373.

32. *Washington (D.C.) Union*, 25 January 1850; *Fayetteville North Carolinian*, in *Greensboro Patriot*, 27 April 1850. See also *Wilmington Journal*, 25 July 1851.

33. The only full-length study of the Compromise of 1850 is Holman Hamilton, *Prologue to Conflict: The Crisis and Compromise of 1850* (Lexington: University Press of Kentucky, 1964). The best summary of the events leading to the passage of the compromise is Potter, *Impending Crisis*, 63–120.

34. For the conflicting interpretations of nonintervention, see Potter, *Impending Crisis*, 115–17. The generalizations in this and the following paragraph about the position of the North Carolina congressional delegation are based on their votes on the five compromise measures (Hamilton, *Prologue to Conflict*, appendix C). North Carolinians in both parties supported the Fugitive Slave Act and (with the exception of Stanly) opposed the abolition of the slave trade in the District.

35. David Outlaw to Emily B. Outlaw, 15 May 1850, Outlaw Letters.

36. For Clingman's attitude toward the state elections, see William A. Graham to James Graham, 25 August 1850, in Hamilton and Williams, *Graham Papers* 3:373; TLC to William H. Thomas, 15 August 1850, William Holland Thomas Papers, Duke. For Clingman's speculation about a cabinet appointment for Mangum, see David Outlaw to Emily B. Outlaw, 27 July 1850, Outlaw Letters. As early as January, Clingman reportedly had been "daily besieging" Mangum to resign his Senate seat. See Calvin Wiley to David F. Caldwell, 7 January 1850, David Franklin Caldwell Papers, SHC.

37. Clingman's speech was published in *Raleigh Register*, 11 September 1850. He argued that slaves could be profitably employed both in the gold mines of California and on farms producing "sugar, cotton, rice, and tropical fruits."

38. The votes on Clingman's amendment and the Texas–New Mexico bill can be found

in *Raleigh Register*, 11 September 1850. Although Democrats from the Deep South voted against the Texas–New Mexico bill by a margin of nineteen to four, those from the upper South supported it by a vote of twenty-two to eleven. Among the eleven Democrats in opposition were the three in the North Carolina delegation.

39. *Raleigh Register*, 11 September 1850. See also David Outlaw to Emily B. Outlaw, 10 September 1850, Outlaw Letters. For Whig attacks against Clingman, see the communications from "Old Buncombe," in *Raleigh Register*, 16 October, 6 November 1850; *Speech of John Baxter Made in Reply to Hon. T. L. Clingman, at Rutherfordton, 13th November, 1850* (Asheville: Messenger Office, 1850); John Baxter to *Asheville News*, in *Raleigh Register*, 5 February 1851. According to Baxter, "ambition—the sin that has so often beset him" was "the fruitful source of all his errors" (*Speech in Reply to Clingman*, 12).

40. TLC to E. P. Jones et al., 14 November 1850, clipping from *Asheville News*, Scrapbook, George Washington Flowers Collection, Duke; TLC to *Asheville News*, 30 December 1850, in *Raleigh North Carolina Standard*, 8 January 1851.

41. "Speech on the Future Policy of the Government," 15 February 1851, in *S&W*, 276, 279–80.

42. "Difficulty between Messrs. Clingman and Stanley *[sic]*," 4 March 1851, Clingman and Puryear Family Papers, SHC. The encounter was widely reported in the newspapers. See *New York Tribune*, 4 March 1851; *Baltimore (Md.) Patriot*, in *Fayetteville Observer*, 11 March 1851; *Raleigh Register*, 12 March 1851; *Raleigh North Carolina Standard*, 12 March 1851; *Norfolk (Va.) Argus*, in *Raleigh North Carolina Standard*, 12 March 1851.

43. For Gaither's announcement of his candidacy and his first debate with Clingman, see *Rutherfordton Banner*, in *Raleigh North Carolina Standard*, 28 May 1851. For endorsements of Gaither, see *Greensboro Patriot*, 31 May 1851; *Fayetteville Observer*, 24 June 1851; *Raleigh Register*, 25 June 1851; *Asheville Messenger*, in *Salisbury Carolina Watchman*, 24 July 1851. After the election the *Asheville News* claimed Gaither had been supported by "the entire Whig press of the State . . . out[side] of the District," in *Raleigh North Carolina Standard*, 27 August 1851.

44. Atkin resigned as editor of the *Messenger* in March 1849, shortly after Clingman's break with the "central clique." See *Raleigh Register*, 28 March 1849. The *Asheville News*, originally called the *Buncombe Dollar News*, began publication shortly afterward. See *Raleigh Register*, 14 July 1849. For Erwin's role, see *Raleigh Register*, 20 May, 25 October 1848, 28 March 1849, 14 May 1851. For Atkin's efforts on behalf of constitutional reform, see Jeffrey, *State Parties and National Politics*, 230–31.

45. *Fayetteville Observer*, 19 August 1851; communication from McDowell County, in *Raleigh Register*, 22 August 1851.

46. *Rutherfordton Banner*, in *Raleigh North Carolina Standard*, 28 May 1851. See also *Asheville Messenger*, in *Salisbury Carolina Watchman*, 24 July 1851.

47. Returns by county can be found in *Raleigh North Carolina Standard*, 27 August 1851. Clingman received 6,600 votes, compared to only 2,819 for Gaither. Despite the heated nature of the campaign, the total vote in 1851 was only 82 percent of that cast in the governor's election the previous year.

48. *Raleigh North Carolina Standard*, 25 June 1851; *Fayetteville Observer*, 19 August 1851.

49. John C. Inscoe, *Mountain Masters, Slavery, and the Sectional Crisis in Western North*

Carolina (Knoxville: University of Tennessee Press, 1989), 60; Marc W. Kruman, "Thomas L. Clingman and the Whig Party: A Reconsideration," *NCHR* 64 (1987): 17.

50. TLC to E. P. Jones et al., 14 November 1850, clipping from *Asheville News,* Scrapbook, Flowers Collection; *Asheville News,* in *Raleigh North Carolina Standard,* 27 August 1851. According to state senator Nicholas W. Woodfin, Clingman had proved "too cunning" to "make the true issues" and, instead, was "deceiving a large portion of the voters by pretending to be for the Union & Whig policy. He insists that he is a stronger Union man than Gaither." See Woodfin to David L. Swain, 28 July 1851, Walter Clark Papers, NCDAH. For additional comments regarding Clingman's successful exploitation of the Union issue, see *Asheville Messenger,* in *Greensboro Patriot,* 26 July 1851; *Fayetteville Observer,* 5 August 1851; communication from McDowell County, in *Raleigh Register,* 22 August 1851; Woodfin to Calvin Wiley, 27 August 1851, Calvin H. Wiley Papers, NCDAH; *Raleigh Register,* 3 September 1851; A. R. Bryan to Thomas I. Lenoir, 4 September 1851, Lenoir Family Papers, SHC.

51. Joseph Carlyle Sitterson, *The Secession Movement in North Carolina* (Chapel Hill: University of North Carolina Press, 1938), 90–93. Thomas Ruffin (1820–63), who won election to Congress in 1853 and served until the Civil War, should not be confused with Judge Thomas Ruffin (1787–1870) or his son, Thomas Ruffin Jr. (1824–89).

52. Clingman compared Gaither and his supporters to the American Tories who had misled the government of Great Britain into believing the colonists would submit to whatever restrictions Parliament might impose. Had it not been for those earlier submissionists, "the British ministry would never have gone to the point of driving our ancestors to resistance." See TLC to E. P. Jones et al., 14 November 1850, clipping from *Asheville News,* Scrapbook, Flowers Collection.

53. *Raleigh Register,* 22 August 1851. The Eighth District was Stanly's district. In the Third District, Whig Alfred Dockery defeated Democratic challenger Greene W. Caldwell. Like Ruffin, Caldwell advocated the right of secession, although neither Democrat claimed that existing circumstances justified a resort to that right (Sitterson, *Secession Movement in North Carolina,* 85–90).

54. Communication from McDowell County, in *Raleigh Register,* 22 August 1851. The Democrats correctly surmised that Clingman was a far more valuable asset to them as a Whig "than if he was to come out as a democrat." See John M. Dick to David S. Reid, 5 November 1850, in Lindley S. Butler, ed., *The Papers of David Settle Reid,* 2 vols. (Raleigh: Department of Cultural Resources, Division of Archives and History, 1993–97), 1:267.

55. *Fayetteville Observer,* 19 August 1851.

56. Inscoe, *Mountain Masters,* 209. For the relationship between the congressional election of 1851 and the campaign for constitutional reform, see Thomas E. Jeffrey, "Beyond 'Free Suffrage': North Carolina Parties and the Convention Movement of the 1850s," *NCHR* 62 (1985): 406.

57. *Richmond (Va.) Times,* in *Salisbury Carolina Watchman,* 17 April 1851.

7. *A Sort Of Filibuster*

1. *Asheville News,* 19 October 1854; *CG,* 34 Cong., 1 sess., 325.
2. That attitude was best expressed in the Georgia Platform, which was adopted by a

unionist-controlled convention in December 1850. While declaring that they did "not wholly approve" of the compromise, the delegates went on to affirm that they would, nonetheless, "abide by it as a permanent adjustment of this sectional controversy." See James A. Rawley, *Secession: The Disruption of the American Republic, 1844–1861* (Malabar, Fla.: Krieger, 1990), 175–76.

3. *New York Tribune*, 8 April 1852. Clingman, along with the three North Carolina Democrats, also opposed a resolution by Junius Hillyer declaring the compromise to be "a final judgment and a permanent settlement." The characterization of the two "ultra" factions is from *Washington (D.C.) Republic*, in *Fayetteville Observer*, 13 April 1852.

4. For the proceedings of the Whig caucus of 1 December 1851, see *Raleigh Register*, 10 December 1851. The vote for Speaker can be found in *CG*, 32 Cong., 1 sess., 9–10.

5. For the proceedings of the Whig caucus, which met on 20 April 1852, see "Address to the Whigs of the United States," in *Raleigh Register*, 5 May 1852. The "Address" was signed by ten Southern Whigs who had bolted the caucus. Curiously, Clingman did not sign the document itself but, instead, appended a sentence declaring his concurrence "in the statement of facts, as well as the general position of this Address." For Clingman's role in the caucus, see TLC to *Washington (D.C.) Republic*, 10 May 1852, in *S&W*, 309–11.

6. TLC to *Washington (D.C.) Republic*, 10 May 1852, in *S&W*, 314–15. Clingman acknowledged that he had opposed the key provisions of the compromise during the last Congress. However, since "those features of the so-called Compromise which I and others at the South objected to have already been carried into effect," it was not unreasonable for Southerners to demand that "the other party shall pay what was promised" (313).

7. TLC to *Washington (D.C.) Republic*, 10 May 1852, in *S&W*, 316. For Clingman's reconciliation with Webster and his role in the Whig National Convention of 1852, see *S&W*, 257.

8. The ballot-by-ballot totals can be found in *New York Tribune*, 22 June 1852. Like most Southerners, the ten delegates from North Carolina "voted solidly for Fillmore to the end." See Herbert Dale Pegg, *The Whig Party in North Carolina* (Chapel Hill: Colonial Press, 1968), 205.

9. *S&W*, 316. For the Whig platform, see *New York Tribune*, 22 June 1852. Scott's reluctance to endorse the platform resulted from his concerns about the negative impact of such an endorsement on the antislavery Northern Whigs. Realizing that "he could not avoid taking heavy losses in one section or the other," Scott "chose, in effect, to take them in the South." See David Potter, *The Impending Crisis 1848–1861* (New York: Harper & Row, 1976), 234.

10. William J. Cooper Jr., *The South and the Politics of Slavery, 1828–1856* (Baton Rouge: Louisiana State University Press, 1978), 327. The manifesto was published in *New York Tribune*, 7 July 1852.

11. *CG*, 32 Cong., 1 sess., 2054; "Speech on Duties on Railroad Iron and Commercial Restrictions," 21 August 1852, in *S&W*, 288–307; TLC to Jane Clingman, 22 August 1852, Clingman and Puryear Family Papers, SHC.

12. *Address of T. L. Clingman* (n.p., 1853), 12. Pages 10 through 17 of the address are omitted from the version published in *S&W*, 323–34. For Clingman's strategy, see also communication from "A Farmer" (extract from *Asheville Spectator*), in *Raleigh Register*, 9 March 1853.

13. Thomas E. Jeffrey, *State Parties and National Politics: North Carolina, 1815–1861*

(Athens: University of Georgia Press, 1989), 231–32. For the relationship between the Kerr and Clingman families, see Lewis Shore Brumfield, *Thomas Lanier Clingman and the Shallow Ford Families* (Yadkinville: privately printed, 1990), 60, 65.

14. TLC to J. F. E. Hardy, 18 July 1852, Clingman-Puryear Papers.

15. Calvin Graves to Thomas Settle, 10 July 1852, Thomas Settle Papers (Group 1), SHC. See also Settle to David S. Reid, 16 July 1852, David S. Reid Papers, NCDAH. The fourth volume of J. G. de Roulhac Hamilton and Max R. Williams, eds., *The Papers of William A. Graham*, 8 vols. (Raleigh: Division of Archives and History, 1957–92), contains numerous letters from Whigs expressing concern about Kerr's prospects in the mountain district. Statistics on the gubernatorial elections discussed in this chapter were compiled from the county-level data in John L. Cheney, ed., *North Carolina Government, 1585–1979* (Raleigh: North Carolina Department of the Secretary of State, 1980), 1398–99.

16. According to one Whig, "in every instance, the Clingman Candidates were defeated, and in most cases by large majorities." See Samuel F. Patterson to William A. Graham, 2 September 1852, in Hamilton and Williams, *Graham Papers*, 4:386. In Rutherford County, however, Southern Rights Whig Ladson A. Mills did win election by a narrow majority over William M. Shipp. See *Raleigh North Carolina Standard*, 18 August 1852.

17. Communication from a western Whig [John Baxter] to *Asheville Messenger*, in *Raleigh Register*, 20 October 1852; *Raleigh North Carolina Standard*, 20 October 1852.

18. J. A. Caldwell to John Baxter, in *Raleigh Register*, 3 November 1852. See also the communication from Baxter, with certificates from John A. Fagg and David F. Caldwell, in the same issue of the *Register;* communication from a western Whig [John Baxter] to *Asheville Messenger*, in *Raleigh Register*, 20 October 1852; communication from "A Farmer" (extract from *Asheville Spectator*), in *Raleigh Register*, 9 March 1853.

19. Bayles M. Edney to John A. Fagg, 22 September 1852, in *Raleigh Register*, 3 November 1852. Before the election, Marcus Erwin, another close Clingman ally, had warned the congressman about Edney's indiscretions, remarking that "many things which he says & does have, tho not intended perhaps to injure you, do[ne] you no good" (Erwin to TLC, 16 April 1852, Clingman-Puryear Papers).

20. Bayles M. Edney to John A. Fagg, 22 September 1852; communication from John Baxter, with certificates from Fagg, J. A. Caldwell, and David F. Caldwell; communication from TLC, 24 October 1852, all in *Raleigh Register*, 3 November 1852. Edney later claimed he "wrote three or four other letters [from Kentucky] at the same time to different gentlemen in Raleigh, and simply to save postage, enclosed the whole to Mr. Clingman, who I knew would be there at that time." See Edney to Millard Fillmore, 13 February 1853, in *Raleigh North Carolina Standard*, 28 June 1854. A correspondent of the *Asheville Spectator* remarked that "considering Mr. Clingman's insanity on that subject [the senatorship]," it was highly improbable that "he [did] not know the contents of that *open* letter, either by reading it, or by being told by Edney, or by dictating it for the writer, which is more likely." See communication from "A Farmer" (extract from *Asheville Spectator*), in *Raleigh Register*, 9 March 1853.

21. John Baxter expressed the Whig viewpoint, noting that Clingman kept "his long silence upon the Presidential question . . . until the contested seat from the Senatorial District of Camden and Currituck was decided." According to Baxter, "his present zeal in behalf of Pierce and King [can] be accounted for . . . by an over weening desire to be elected

Senator." See communication from a western Whig [John Baxter] to *Asheville Messenger,* in *Raleigh Register,* 20 October 1852.

22. TLC to Ladson A. Mills, 8 October 1852, in *S&W,* 318, 321, 323; *Washington (D.C.) Union,* in *Raleigh North Carolina Standard,* 27 October 1852.

23. *Raleigh Register,* 13 October 1852. For similar comments, see *Fayetteville Observer,* 12 October 1852; *Newbernian,* 15 October 1852; *Greensboro Patriot,* 16 October 1852; *Salisbury Carolina Watchman,* 21 October 1852. The *Patriot* characterized Clingman's letter to Mills as a "labor of love (love of a Senatorship)."

24. *Raleigh Register,* 13 October 1852; communication from "Candor," in *Greensboro Patriot,* 16 October 1852.

25. Potter, *Impending Crisis,* 143. Despite his unpopularity in the South, Scott actually received a higher percentage of the vote in that section than in the North (ibid., 235). In North Carolina, Scott lost by a mere 686 votes. See James R. Morrill, "The Presidential Election of 1852: Death Knell of the Whig Party of North Carolina," *NCHR* 44 (1967): 358.

26. *Address of T. L. Clingman,* 16; *Fayetteville Observer,* 16 November 1852. The *Asheville Messenger* is quoted in the same issue of the *Observer.*

27. *Address of T. L. Clingman on the Recent Senatorial Election* (Washington, D.C.: J. and G. S. Gideon, 1849), 1. Statistics on the presidential elections discussed in this chapter were compiled from the county-level data in W. Dean Burnham, *Presidential Ballots, 1836–1892* (Baltimore: Johns Hopkins University Press, 1955), 646–68. According to James R. Morrill, the decline in the Whig vote in Clingman's district between the August and November elections was "almost five times that of any other district" ("Presidential Election of 1852," 359).

28. Duncan K. McRae to TLC, 16 November 1852, Clingman-Puryear Papers. Clingman's only votes on the early ballots came from Democrat Cornelius R. Bird of Yancey; Southern Rights Whig Ladson A. Mills of Rutherford; and William J. Blow, a maverick Whig from Pitt who would shortly defect to the Democrats. As Burgess Gaither sarcastically remarked, "the Clingman party in the Legislature was composed solely of this *trio,* and they were the only members that, in reality, desired his election." See Gaither's circular in *Raleigh Register,* 6 July 1853.

29. For the number of votes received by each candidate during the course of the fifteen ballots, see the table in Brian G. Walton, "Elections to the United States Senate in North Carolina, 1835–1861," *NCHR* 53 (1976): 186. The *Greensboro Patriot* wondered why Clingman "did not receive a clean nomination, instead of being merely 'recommended'" (8 January 1853). It suggested that the Democrats had introduced his name to fend off Woodfin rather than to elect Clingman.

30. The *Raleigh North Carolina Standard* remarked that "both parties seemed to fear . . . a continuation of the voting for Senator" (29 December 1852). Moreover, with the congressional and legislative districts still not reapportioned and with only a week remaining before adjournment, many members were anxious to get on with the legislative business.

31. *Address of T. L. Clingman,* 13. On the final ballot, Clingman fell ten votes short of a majority. Eight Democrats in the House of Commons (including one who voted for Woodfin) and five Democrats in the state senate refused to support him (*HJ, 1852,* 462–63; *SJ, 1852,* 376). On 25 December the state senate agreed by a vote of twenty-eight

to ten not to make another attempt to elect a U.S. senator. Sixteen Whigs and twelve Democrats supported the motion, while ten Democrats voted against it (*SJ, 1852,* 455–56). Clingman's claim that he would have been elected if another vote had been taken was probably wishful thinking.

32. In typical fashion, Clingman blamed the "central managers" for the redistricting (*Address of T. L. Clingman,* 14–15). The Whigs retorted that the original bill had left Clingman's old district intact and that the Democrats had subsequently decided to transfer Cleveland to the adjoining Charlotte district in order to insure a Democratic majority there. See *Rowan Whig,* in *Fayetteville Observer,* 10 February 1853; *Asheville Spectator,* 27 April 1853.

33. *Address of T. L. Clingman,* 8–9. Clingman also denied that he had bargained with the Democrats to deliver his district to Pierce in return for a seat in the U.S. Senate. Instead, he claimed, his course had been "taken with reference solely to public considerations, and without calculating the consequences to myself personally" (ibid., 12).

34. "To the Citizens of the 8th Congressional District of North Carolina," in *Raleigh Register,* 6 July 1853. Gaither also pointed to Clingman's numerous Democratic supporters as evidence that he really belonged to that party. "If Mr. Clingman is still a whig . . . why is it . . . [that] every Democratic paper in the State is out for him [and] the democracy in the district are running him as their candidate?"

35. *Asheville Spectator,* 11 May 1853. The *Fayetteville Observer* remarked that many Whigs outside the mountain district were "amaze[d] . . . to find that Mr. Clingman still claims to be a Whig" (18 May 1853).

36. Report of the debate between Clingman and Gaither, in *Raleigh Register,* 27 April 1853; *Asheville News,* 28 July 1853.

37. Communication from "A Buncombe Whig," in *Asheville Spectator,* 13 July 1853; *Salisbury Banner,* in *Raleigh North Carolina Standard,* 13 July 1853. The *Asheville News* stated that Clingman would beat Gaither by at least three thousand votes (28 July 1853)—a prediction that proved very close to the mark.

38. County-level returns appear in *Raleigh Register,* 24 August 1853. The *Wilmington Herald* claimed that many voters supported Clingman in 1853 "because he represented himself as 'a better Whig' than his competitor" (in *Raleigh Register,* 5 July 1854).

39. "Speech on Nebraska and Kansas," 4 April 1854, in *S&W,* 339. The vote for Speaker can be found in *CG,* 33 Cong., 1 sess., 2. In casting a complimentary vote for Ashe, Clingman was repaying a debt of gratitude. In the general assembly of 1848–49, the Wilmington Democrat had been one of only four members of that party to support him for the senatorship on all five ballots.

40. *CG,* 32 Cong., 2 sess., 565. Clingman was the only North Carolina member to support the bill. Two North Carolina Democrats and four Whigs voted against it. For the legislative history of the first Nebraska bill, see James C. Malin, *The Nebraska Question, 1852–1854* (Lawrence: privately printed, 1953), 102–12. For Clingman's role, see also *S&W,* 334; and "Speech on Nebraska and Kansas," in *S&W,* 336.

41. *S&W,* 335.

42. "Speech on Nebraska and Kansas," in *S&W,* 337, 343.

43. Potter, *Impending Crisis,* 166–67. Five North Carolina congressmen, including Whig John Kerr, joined Clingman and Sen. George E. Badger in voting for the Kansas-

Nebraska bill. Two other Whigs voted against it. See *Raleigh Register,* 31 May 1854. Clingman may well have doubted his own assurances that Northerners would willingly accept the repeal of the Missouri Compromise. As he acknowledged two decades later, "the repeal . . . had the appearance of extending slavery into territory previously made free, and also violating an old compromise" (*S&W,* 355).

44. *Asheville Spectator,* in *Asheville News,* 4 May 1854; Richard C. Puryear to Isaac Jarratt, 15 April 1854, Jarratt-Puryear Family Papers, Duke. Elizabeth Ann Clingman, who had married Puryear in 1835, died on 9 February 1850. See *Raleigh Register,* 2 March 1850.

45. Richard C. Puryear to Isaac Jarratt, 15 April 1854, Jarratt-Puryear Papers. On 11 May 1854 Erwin temporarily took over the editorship of the *Asheville News* from Atkin, announcing that, henceforth, the paper would be "a thorough going Democratic journal."

46. *Asheville News,* 4 May 1854. For the *News's* endorsement of Bragg, see *Greensboro Patriot,* 20 May 1854. The *Patriot* welcomed the announcement, remarking that "we always prefer an open to a secret foe." For Clingman's disapproval of Dockery, see TLC to William H. Thomas, 19 March 1854, William Holland Thomas Papers, Duke.

47. Communication from TLC, 19 June 1854, in *Asheville News,* 29 June 1854.

48. TLC to William H. Thomas, 19 March 1854, Thomas Papers; *Asheville News,* 22 June 1854. Erwin reiterated that theme throughout the campaign. On 6 July, for example, he editorialized that "Mr. Clingman can easily be elected Senator if his friends will stick together."

49. The quotation is from *Raleigh North Carolina Standard,* 21 June 1854. For Clingman's preference for Southern Rights candidates over regular Democrats, see John B. Woodfin to TLC, 8 June 1854, Clingman-Puryear Papers.

50. *Asheville News,* 10 August 1854; *Raleigh North Carolina Standard,* 16, 23 August 1854. The successful Southern Rights candidates were John Roland of Cherokee, Thaddeus D. Bryson of Jackson, S. J. Neal of McDowell, and A. J. Patton of Macon. With the partial exception of Bryson, the Southern Rights legislators subsequently acted with the Whigs on most political issues. See, for example, the votes for Speaker and U.S. senator in *HJ, 1854–55,* 5–6, 49, 53–54.

51. *Wilmington Journal,* 1, 8 September 1854; *Wilmington Journal,* in *Fayetteville North Carolinian,* 26 August 1854; *Fayetteville North Carolinian,* 19 September 1854. See also *Goldsboro Republican,* in *Fayetteville Observer,* 16 October 1854.

52. For the progressive-conservative split within the North Carolina Democratic party during the 1850s, see Thomas E. Jeffrey, "The Progressive Paradigm of Antebellum North Carolina Politics," *Carolina Comments* 30 (1982): 66–75; Jerry Lee Cross, "Political Metamorphosis: An Historical Profile of the Democratic Party in North Carolina, 1800–1892" (Ph.D. diss., State University of New York at Binghamton, 1975), 58–61.

53. Duncan K. McRae to TLC, 16 November 1852, John B. Woodfin to TLC, 9 June 1854 (quoting Courts), David S. Reid to TLC, 20 June 1854, Clingman-Puryear Papers. Whigs like Kenneth Rayner were also convinced that "Reid & Clingman will be the next Senators." See diary of John Hill Wheeler, 24 August 1854, SHC, microfilm.

54. TLC to David S. Reid, 24 September 1854, Reid Papers.

55. Reid's behavior seems to contradict the Whig accusation that Clingman had entered into a bargain with him to divide the two Senate seats. Those charges had first surfaced in June, when Clingman had announced his opposition to Dockery. See *Raleigh Register,*

28 June 1854. Even some Democrats wondered about a possible "coalition between him [Reid] & Clingman." See Thomas Ruffin Jr. to Thomas Settle Jr., 4 October 1854, Settle Papers (Group 2).

56. Communication from Raleigh correspondent, in *Asheville News*, 30 November 1854. The *News* claimed that the Democratic members from the mountain district had initially refused to go into the caucus and had finally done so only after instructions from Clingman (7 December 1854). According to J. G. de Roulhac Hamilton, Clingman received eleven votes on the first ballot, twenty-one on the third, and the same number on the fourth, with forty-four votes required for election. See *Party Politics in North Carolina, 1835–1860* (Durham: Seeman Printery, 1916), 171. Hamilton does not cite his source, but a contemporary observer agreed that Clingman received about twenty votes in the caucus. See Samuel F. Phillips to David L. Swain, [23 November 1854], David L. Swain Papers, NCDAH, typescript of original in SHC.

57. *Salisbury Carolina Watchman*, 7 December 1854. On 30 November 1854, the *Asheville News* had reported a rumor that the Whigs "would nominate Mr. Clingman, in order to embarrass the Democrats" and had remarked that "some of the old line Democrats opposed to him were terribly frightened" by the prospect. It seems incredible that Clingman would have allowed his name to be brought before the Whig caucus under any circumstances, and the Southern Rights legislators may have acted without his approval. In recounting the episode almost twenty-five years later, however, the *Raleigh News* claimed that Clingman himself had written a letter to the Whig caucus and that there were surviving legislators who still remembered the incident (16 July 1878).

58. Clingman was nominated by A. J. Patton of Macon who "got out of the notion of voting for him before his name was called." See communication from Raleigh correspondent, in *Greensboro Patriot*, 2 December 1854.

59. *Salisbury Carolina Watchman*, 7 December 1854; *Milton Chronicle*, in *Raleigh Register*, 6 December 1854; Samuel F. Phillips to David L. Swain, [23 November 1854], Swain Papers, NCDAH.

8. Not "Locofocoised," but "Clingmanised"

1. Marc W. Kruman, "Thomas L. Clingman and the Whig Party: A Reconsideration," *NCHR* 64 (1987): 17. Technically, a politician's "coattails" means his ability to carry other candidates of his party into office on the basis of his own popularity. Strictly speaking, Clingman could not have had coattails during the early and mid-1850s because (1) his party affiliation was unclear and (2) the North Carolina election cycle, in which congressmen ran in odd-numbered years and other candidates for national and state offices ran in even-numbered years, meant that Clingman's name never appeared on the ballot with the Democratic and Southern Rights candidates he was supporting. By "coattails," Kruman is really talking about Clingman's ability to influence voters. In that regard, his generalization is accurate for the early 1850s but must be qualified for the mid-1850s.

2. Richard C. Puryear to David F. Caldwell, 1 February 1854, David Franklin Caldwell Papers, SHC. See also John B. Woodfin to TLC, 8 June 1854, Clingman and Puryear Family Papers, SHC.

3. "Speech on the Future Policy of the Government," 15 February 1851, in *S&W,* 278; "Speech on Nebraska and Kansas," 4 April 1854, ibid., 351.

4. "Speech in Favor of a Proposition for Mediation in the Eastern War," 3 January 1855, in *S&W,* 373. For the origins of the phrase "Young America," see Robert E. May, *The Southern Dream of a Caribbean Empire, 1854–1861* (Baton Rouge: Louisiana State University Press, 1973; Athens: University of Georgia Press, 1989), 20–21.

5. "Speech on Nebraska and Kansas," in *S&W,* 350.

6. The quotation is from May, *Caribbean Empire,* 56. For the background of the crisis, see ibid., 43–44, 54–55; Larry Gara, *The Presidency of Franklin Pierce* (Lawrence: University Press of Kansas, 1991), 151.

7. *S&W,* 375–76; May, *Caribbean Empire,* 58; Samuel Flagg Bemis, *A Diplomatic History of the United States,* 5th ed. (New York: Holt, Rinehart & Winston, 1965), 321n.

8. "Speech for Mediation," in *S&W,* 373. For the text of Clingman's mediation resolution, see ibid., 363. For press reaction to his speech, see *Washington (D.C.) Union,* 7 January 1855; *Greensboro Patriot,* 13 January 1855; communication from Washington correspondent, in *Raleigh North Carolina Standard,* 17 January 1855. The *Union* expressed the prevailing view when it noted that Clingman's proposal violated the long-standing "principle of non-interference in European politics."

9. Bayly's comments were reported in *Washington (D.C.) Union,* 5 January 1855. The *Union* correctly predicted that the Virginian's statement "will probably settle that question." For the overture to France, see *Asheville News,* 1 February 1855.

10. Clingman's remarks were published in *Washington (D.C.) Union,* 7 January 1855.

11. The quotation is from *Rutherfordton Western Eagle,* in *Raleigh Register,* 18 July 1855. See also the statement of principles in *Asheville Spectator,* 21 April 1855. For the popularity of the Know-Nothings among clergymen, see communication from "Junius," in *Raleigh North Carolina Standard,* 4 July 1855; *Asheville News,* 23 August 1855.

12. The quotation is from the party's national platform, in Thomas E. Jeffrey, *State Parties and National Politics: North Carolina, 1815–1861* (Athens: University of Georgia Press, 1989), 248. See also the statement of principles in *Asheville Spectator,* 21 April 1855. Typical among the Whigs who joined the new party was Dr. C. Lafayette Cook, a two-term legislator from Wilkes County, who reportedly declared in a debate with Clingman that "the old parties are corrupt; I thank my God that I have washed my hands of the old Whig party." See communication from "P. A. T.," in *Raleigh North Carolina Standard,* 20 June 1855.

13. A summary of Clingman's speech at Franklin can be found in *Asheville News,* 22 March 1855. For the phrase "independent outsider," see *Asheville Spectator,* in *Raleigh Register,* 18 April 1855; *Rutherfordton Western Eagle,* in *Fayetteville Observer,* 30 July 1855. For Clingman's early canvass of the mountain district, see *Asheville News,* 22 March, 5, 12 April, 17, 24 May, 7 June 1855. Historians have generally assumed that Clingman waged the campaign as a Democrat. See, for example, Thomas E. Jeffrey, "'Thunder from the Mountains': Thomas Lanier Clingman and the End of Whig Supremacy in North Carolina," *NCHR* 56 (1979): 392, 394; John C. Inscoe, *Mountain Masters, Slavery, and the Sectional Crisis in Western North Carolina* (Knoxville: University of Tennessee Press, 1989), 200. The confusion about the timing of Clingman's defection to the Democracy is understandable in light of the congressman's own ambiguous pronouncements, the charges by

the Whig presses that he had gone over to the enemy, and the claims by Democratic editors outside the mountain district that he was in fact a member of their party. On the latter point, see, for example, *Raleigh North Carolina Standard,* 22 August 1855.

14. The quotation is from *Asheville News,* 17 May 1855. For Carmichael's age, physical characteristics, strengths, and liabilities, see also ibid., 14 June, 12 July 1855; *Raleigh Register,* 23 May 1855; *Asheville Spectator* and *Rutherfordton Western Eagle,* in *Raleigh Register,* 30 May, 18 July 1855; *Fayetteville Observer,* 30 July 1855. For Clingman's "anger and bad temper," see *Asheville Spectator,* in *Raleigh Register,* 4 July 1855. For the debate at Murphey, see *Asheville News,* 14 June 1855.

15. *Raleigh Register,* 1 August 1855; communication from "Anti," in *Asheville News,* 17 May 1855; account of TLC's speech at Franklin and editorial comments, in *Asheville News,* 22 March 1855.

16. Communication from "A Free White Man," in *Asheville News,* 17 May 1855; account of Clingman's speech at Waynesville (communication from "Native of Haywood"), ibid., 5 July 1855; "To the Freemen of the 8th Congressional District," 13 July 1855, ibid., 19 July 1855.

17. *Asheville News,* 9 August 1855; *Asheville Spectator,* in *Raleigh Register,* 15 August 1855. The county-by-county returns were published in *Raleigh North Carolina Standard,* 22 August 1855. Clingman polled 8,079 votes and won majorities in all but four of the fourteen counties, while Carmichael garnered 6,584 votes.

18. *Asheville News,* 16, 23 August 1855; TLC to James L. Orr, 15 September 1855, Orr and Patterson Family Papers, SHC.

19. Thomas E. Schott, *Alexander H. Stephens of Georgia: A Biography* (Baton Rouge: Louisiana State University Press, 1988), 192–94; David Potter, *The Impending Crisis, 1848–1861* (New York: Harper & Row, 1976), 255–56.

20. Remarks of 30 January 1856, in *Asheville News,* 14 February 1856. Clingman's resolution was defeated by a vote of 106 to 110. Only five Democrats supported it. See *Raleigh North Carolina Standard,* 6 February 1856; *Raleigh Register,* 6 February 1856. For Democratic efforts to dissuade Clingman, see *CG,* 34 Cong., 1 sess., 325. Smith's resolution passed by a vote of 113 to 104. See *Fayetteville Observer,* 11 February 1856.

21. Report of the congressional debate, in *Fayetteville Observer,* 11 February 1856; *Greensboro Patriot,* 8 February 1856. Banks received 103 votes on the 133d ballot, compared to 100 votes for William Aiken of South Carolina, whom the Democrats had brought forward in place of Orr. According to the *Observer,* about thirty Know-Nothings voted for Aiken. Clingman's supplementary resolution passed by a vote of 156 to 40, with all the North Carolina delegation voting in its favor.

22. *Asheville Spectator,* 14 February 1856; *Raleigh Register,* 6 February 1856. The *Asheville News* defended Clingman's behavior, claiming that "the wheels of Government would have been stopped and the Union effectually dissolved" if the plurality rule had not been invoked (14 February 1856).

23. Clingman recounted these events in his "Speech against the Clayton-Bulwer Treaty, and In Favor of American Ascendency in the Gulf of Mexico and Central America," 5 May 1858, in *S&W,* 411–12. See also *S&W,* 375–76. For Clingman's rank on the Foreign Affairs Committee, see *Fayetteville Observer,* 18 February 1856.

24. "Speech against the Clayton-Bulwer Treaty," in *S&W*, 412; *Asheville News*, 15 May 1856.

25. "Speech on Nebraska and Kansas," in *S&W*, 345–46; *S&W*, 375. Clingman's plan to unite the country by precipitating a foreign conflict was strikingly similar to the one proposed by Secretary of State William H. Seward during the secession crisis of 1861. For Seward's strategy, see Potter, *Impending Crisis*, 577; Bemis, *Diplomatic History*, 367–68.

26. "Speech against the Clayton-Bulwer Treaty," in *S&W*, 411; *S&W*, 377.

27. "Address to the Freemen of the Eighth Congressional District of North Carolina, on the Political Condition and Prospects of the Country," 16 March 1856, in *S&W*, 381, 383–84.

28. Ibid., 386–87, 389.

29. Ibid., 390; Clarence C. Norton, *The Democratic Party in Ante-Bellum North Carolina, 1835–1861* (Chapel Hill: University of North Carolina Press, 1930), 251–52; *Official Proceedings of the National Democratic Convention Held in Cincinnati, June 2–6, 1856* (Cincinnati: Enquirer, 1856), 39–51. Although Clingman's name appears on the list of North Carolina delegates on page six of the *Official Proceedings*, he was not one of the delegates formally appointed by the Asheville District Convention in April (*Asheville News*, 8 May 1856).

30. For the background and ramifications of the Ostend Manifesto, see Potter, *Impending Crisis*, 190–92; May, *Caribbean Empire*, 67–70. The quotation from the Democratic platform is from May, *Caribbean Empire*, 101. See also Potter, *Impending Crisis*, 262; Schott, *Alexander H. Stephens*, 208–9.

31. "Letter of Hon. T. L. Clingman to His Constituents," 20 June 1856, in *Raleigh North Carolina Standard*, 2 July 1856. Once again, Clingman made the argument that Whig voters could in good conscience support a "democratic party, purified by losing its free-soil elements and strengthened by the accession of patriotic and intelligent whigs."

32. *Asheville News*, 13 March, 10, 17 April, 8 May 1856; Jeffrey, *State Parties and National Politics*, 249–51. Vance, who had represented Buncombe County in the House of Commons of 1854–55, was now running for the state senate.

33. The quotations are from the resolutions adopted by the Anti-Know-Nothing meeting in McDowell County, in *Asheville News*, 8 May 1856. Similarly, the delegates at the Anti-Know-Nothing meeting in Rutherfordton acknowledged that their organization was "composed of Whigs and Democrats" (ibid., 24 July 1856).

34. Bragg received 8,651 votes in the mountain district, compared to 7,063 for Gilmer. Bragg's 55 percent of the vote in the far west was identical to the share won by Clingman in 1855. Statistics on the gubernatorial election were compiled from the county-level data in John L. Cheney, ed., *North Carolina Government, 1585–1979* (Raleigh: North Carolina Department of the Secretary of State, 1980), 1400–1401. For the legislative elections, see *Raleigh North Carolina Standard*, 13, 20 August 1856; *Asheville News*, 14 August 1856.

35. *Asheville News*, 28 August 1856.

36. Ibid., 11 September, 2, 9, 30 October, 13 November 1856; *Raleigh North Carolina Standard*, 29 October 1856.

37. "Address to the Freemen," in *S&W*, 384, 389; "Letter of Hon. T. L. Clingman," in *Raleigh North Carolina Standard*, 2 July 1856.

38. During the crisis of 1860–61, a number of politicians who had earlier acquired reputations as militant Southern Righters actively opposed the secession movement, while others offered passive resistance. Among those in the former category were William W. Holden of North Carolina and Andrew Johnson of Tennessee. For the difficulty of using a politician's pronouncements during the 1850s to accurately predict his behavior in 1860–61, see Robert E. May, "Psychobiography and Secession: The Southern Radical as Maladjusted 'Outsider,'" *Civil War History* 34 (1988): 51–54.

39. The quotations in this and the following paragraph are from TLC to William Phifer et al., 10 October 1856, in *Charlotte Democrat*, 21 October 1856. The letter was widely reprinted. See, for example, *Asheville News*, 30 October 1856.

40. Joseph Carlyle Sitterson, *The Secession Movement in North Carolina* (Chapel Hill: University of North Carolina Press, 1939), 136.

41. On 20 May 1775 a convention of delegates from Mecklenburg County met in Charlotte and supposedly declared independence from Britain. The authenticity of the Mecklenburg Declaration of Independence was a matter of intense controversy in North Carolina during the antebellum era. See William H. Hoyt, *The Mecklenburg Declaration of Independence* (New York: G. P. Putnam, 1907).

42. "Address Delivered at Davidson College, North Carolina," 25 June 1873, in *S&W*, 48; TLC to William Phifer et al., in *Charlotte Democrat*, 21 October 1856. During the campaign of 1860, Clingman elaborated on some of the ideas contained in his Charlotte letter, expressing regret that "the framers of the Constitution made no provision for the expulsion of a State." If Massachusetts "had been expelled from the Union" after it nullified the Fugitive Slave Act, he hypothesized, that action "might possibly then have arrested the anti-slavery movement when it was comparatively feeble." See "Speech against the Revolutionary Movement of the Anti-slavery Party," 16 January 1860, in *S&W*, 474.

43. *New York Day Book*, in *Asheville News*, 27 November 1856; *Asheville News*, 16 July 1857. The *News* went so far as to affirm that "Mr. Fillmore's language is even more emphatic and pointed than Mr. Clingman's." The *New York Times*, on the other hand, printed the letter under the heading "Another Disunion Patriot" (4 November 1856).

44. *Raleigh North Carolina Standard*, 19 November 1856; *New York Times*, 27 November 1856. Buchanan won 53 percent of the vote in the mountain district. See W. Dean Burnham, *Presidential Ballots, 1836–1892* (Baltimore: Johns Hopkins University Press, 1955), 646–68. For the outcome nationally, see Potter, *Impending Crisis*, 264–66.

45. "Speech on British Policy in Central America and Cuba," 5 February 1857, in *S&W*, 404; *S&W*, 391. For speculation that Clingman might be appointed secretary of the navy, see *Asheville News*, 29 January 1857. According to the *Washington (D.C.) States*, Clingman could have had any federal office he wanted under the Buchanan administration, but he preferred his seat in Congress "to any other honor or the emoluments of office" (in *Raleigh North Carolina Standard*, 15 July 1857).

46. "Speech on British Policy," in *S&W*, 397. For the Clayton-Bulwer Treaty, see Gara, *Presidency of Pierce*, 139; Bemis, *Diplomatic History*, 246–52, May, *Caribbean Empire*, 86–88.

47. "Speech on British Policy," in *S&W*, 406, 408. For the distinction between national Democrats and Southern sectionalists, see Joel H. Silbey, "The Southern National Dem-

ocrats, 1845–1861," in *The Partisan Imperative: The Dynamics of American Politics before the Civil War* (New York: Oxford University Press, 1985), 116–26.

48. *Wilmington Herald,* in *Asheville News,* 26 February 1857.

49. *Asheville News,* 26 February 1857.

50. Ibid., 28 May, 4 June 1857; *Yorkville (S.C.) Chronicle* and *Warrenton News,* in *Asheville News,* 23, 30 April 1857.

51. William Hicks to William H. Thomas, 15 April 1857, William Holland Thomas Papers, Duke; *Asheville Spectator,* in *Asheville News,* 23 July 1857.

52. *Asheville News,* 20 August 1857. The vote by county in Clingman's district can be found in the same issue of the *News.*

53. Clingman's appointment was, at least in part, compensation for the vigorous support he gave James L. Orr in the Speaker's contest. See TLC to Orr, 3 October 1857, Orr-Patterson Papers.

54. Appointed to the court by Thomas Jefferson in 1801, Potter died on 20 December 1857 at age ninety-three. See *Charlotte Democrat,* 29 December 1857.

9. The Bubbling Cauldron

1. TLC to Thomas Bragg, 7 May 1858, Governor's Papers, NCDAH; *Fayetteville Observer,* 10 May 1858; *Greensboro Patriot,* 14 May 1858.

2. *Asheville News,* 7 January 1858; *Richmond (Va.) South,* in *Asheville News,* 7 January 1858; *S&W,* 409.

3. For Buchanan's attitude toward the Clayton-Bulwer Treaty, see Elbert B. Smith, *The Presidency of James Buchanan* (Lawrence: University Press of Kansas, 1975), 68–71.

4. *S&W,* 409. Clingman's resolutions were published in *Asheville News,* 11 February 1858.

5. "Speech against the Clayton-Bulwer Treaty, and in Favor of American Ascendency in the Gulf of Mexico and Central America," in *S&W,* 415, 417–18.

6. *Washington (D.C.) National Intelligencer,* 8, 13 May 1858; *Fayetteville Observer,* 24 May 1858.

7. Clingman was the first U.S. senator from North Carolina to take his seat through an interim appointment by the governor. Even though Congress was still in session at the time of Biggs's resignation, Bragg could have allowed the Senate seat to remain vacant until the general assembly convened in the fall, just as Gov. William A. Graham had done following the resignation of William H. Haywood Jr. in July 1846. Similarly, Biggs could have waited until the end of the session before submitting his resignation. Clingman's appointment actually diminished the Democrats' strength in Congress, since it created a vacancy in the House that was not filled until after the session had ended.

8. TLC to William H. Thomas, 8 January 1857, William Holland Thomas Papers, Duke.

9. *Fayetteville Observer,* 4 January, 19 April 1858. See also *Greensboro Patriot,* 8 January 1858; *Asheville News,* 14 January 1858.

10. Henry M. Shaw to Thomas Bragg, 13 January 1858, Governor's Papers; *Fayetteville Observer,* 18 January 1858.

11. TLC et al. to James Buchanan, 23 December 1857, Autograph File, Houghton Library, Harvard University, Cambridge, Mass.; Henry M. Shaw to Thomas Bragg, 13 January 1858, Governor's Papers; diary of John Hill Wheeler, 1 March 1858, SHC, microfilm; *Asheville News,* 7 January, 18 February 1858. Although also bearing the signatures of Reid, Warren Winslow, Burton Craige, and Thomas Ruffin, the letter to Buchanan is in Clingman's hand. Reid cautiously added that he was offering his endorsement "without knowing the feelings or wishes of my colleague (Mr. Biggs) on the subject."

12. Asa Biggs to David S. Reid, 21 February 1858, David S. Reid Papers, NCDAH.

13. The roll-call vote on the English bill can be found in *Wilmington Journal,* 7 May 1858. For the relationship between the judicial appointment and the Kansas issue, see *Fayetteville Observer,* 5 April 1858, *Raleigh Register,* 12 May 1858. The announcement of Biggs's appointment to the U.S. Circuit Court, along with his letter of resignation from the Senate, can be found in *Raleigh North Carolina Standard,* 12 May 1858.

14. *Greensboro Patriot,* 19 March 1858; *Fayetteville Observer,* 19 April 1858; *Asheville News,* 1 April 1858. There is no evidence to support the *Observer's* assertion that Clingman deliberately double-crossed Holden at the convention. The *Patriot* claimed he was bitterly opposed to Ellis because of "the unpardonable sin which Ellis committed in not voting for Clingman against Mr. Badger" in the general assembly of 1848. According to William C. Harris, Holden's endorsement of the westward extension of the North Carolina Railroad gained him support among Democrats in the far west but alienated party members in the east. See *William Woods Holden: Firebrand of North Carolina Politics* (Baton Rouge: Louisiana State University Press, 1987), 74.

15. *Raleigh North Carolina Standard,* 12 May 1858; *Washington (D.C.) Union,* 8 May 1858; *Richmond (Va.) South,* in *Raleigh North Carolina Standard,* 19 May 1858.

16. *Fayetteville Observer,* 10 May 1858; *Greensboro Patriot,* 14 May 1858; *Raleigh Register,* 12 May 1858. See also *Charlotte North Carolina Whig,* 18 May 1858.

17. *Fayetteville Observer,* 10 May 1858; *Wilmington Journal,* 14 May 1858; *Washington (D.C.) Star,* in *Asheville News,* 20 May 1858.

18. Johanna Nicol Shields, *The Line of Duty: Maverick Congressmen and the Development of American Political Culture, 1836–1860* (Westport, Conn.: Greenwood Press, 1985), 53. For Clingman's effort to eliminate the duties on railroad iron, see "Speech on Duties on Railroad Iron and Commercial Restrictions," 21 August 1852, in *S&W,* 288–307; "Remarks of Mr. Clingman . . . on the Duties on Railroad Iron," 20 December 1858, in *Raleigh North Carolina Standard,* 12 January 1859. For Britain's increasing willingness to acknowledge American hegemony in the Western Hemisphere, see Smith, *Presidency of Buchanan,* 68–71.

19. Shields notes that the choice of Clingman as chairman of the Foreign Affairs Committee "would appear utterly senseless, if it were assumed that any kind of responsibility to party . . . were a prerequisite" (*Line of Duty,* 53). For Clingman's complaints about excessive expenditures, see "Remarks on the Public Expenditures," 17 April 1854, in *S&W,* 356–62; "Remarks of Mr. Clingman," in *Asheville News,* 15 May 1856; "Valedictory Address of Thomas L. Clingman," *Asheville News,* 2 June 1858. For his opposition to the deficiency bill, see *Fayetteville Observer,* 19 April, 24 May 1858.

20. Communication from Washington correspondent, in *New York Tribune,* 23 April 1858; communication from Washington correspondent (from *Charleston (S.C.) Courier*),

in *Asheville News,* 5 March 1857; communication from M. J. W. (from *Charleston (S.C.) Courier*), in *Asheville News,* 17 June 1858.

21. Communication from Washington correspondent (from *Charleston (S.C.) Courier*), in *Asheville News,* 5 March 1857; *Washington (D.C.) Star,* in *Asheville News,* 20 April 1854; *Raleigh North Carolina Standard,* 12 May 1858. According to the *Asheville Citizen,* "few men in the history of the Union before the war made so remarkable a record as a public debater" (5 November 1897).

22. John S. Bassett, "The Congressional Career of Thos. L. Clingman," *Trinity College Historical Papers* 4 (1900): 50. The phrase "extreme sensibility" is from communication from J. S. Robinson Jr., in *Raleigh North Carolina Standard,* 23 March 1859.

23. TLC to Sidney Webster, 16 March 1856, Webster to TLC, 17 March 1856, Clingman and Puryear Family Papers, SHC.

24. Communication from Washington correspondent (from *Charleston (S.C.) Courier*), in *Asheville News,* 5 March 1857. For Clingman's late hours, see TLC to *New York Herald,* 13 August 1876, in *S&W,* 273. For his sterling attendance record, see *St. Louis (Mo.) Globe-Democrat,* in *Asheville Democrat,* 28 August 1892; *Asheville Citizen,* 29 October 1891; *New York Times,* 5 November 1897.

25. Communication from Washington correspondent (from *Charleston (S.C.) Courier*), in *Asheville News,* 5 March 1857; Alexander K. McClure, *Recollections of Half a Century* (Salem, Mass.: Salem Press, 1902), 358. The intricate maneuvering that led to the passage of the Kansas-Nebraska bill in the House is ably presented in Thomas E. Schott, *Alexander H. Stephens of Georgia: A Biography* (Baton Rouge: Louisiana State University Press, 1988), 169–72. For Clingman's role, see the communication from the Washington correspondent of the *Raleigh North Carolina Standard,* in *Asheville News,* 25 May 1854.

26. The quotations are from communication from Washington correspondent (from *Charleston (S.C.) Courier*), in *Asheville News,* 5 March 1857; Constance McLaughlin Green, *Washington: A History of the Capital, 1800–1950,* 2 vols. (Princeton: Princeton University Press, 1962), 1:49 (quoting Augustus Foster); communication from Washington correspondent (from *Boston (Mass.) Globe*), in *Raleigh North Carolina Standard,* 9 December 1857. For social life in antebellum Washington, see Green, *Washington,* 1:150–51, 226–28; George Worthington Adams, ed., *Reminiscences of the Civil War and Reconstruction by Mary Logan* (Carbondale: Southern Illinois University Press, 1970), 23–37; Roy F. Nichols, *The Disruption of American Democracy* (New York: Macmillan, 1948; New York: Free Press, 1967), 150–55. For descriptions of Clingman's physical features, see communication from Washington correspondent (from *Charleston (S.C.) Courier*), in *Asheville News,* 5 March 1857; *Wilmington Journal,* 14 May 1858. For his dancing, see Lawrence O'Bryan Branch to Nancy H. B. Branch, 1 February 1859, in A. R. Newsome, ed., "Letters of Lawrence O'Bryan Branch, 1856–1861," *NCHR* 10 (1933): 62.

27. Communication from "Herman Husband," in *Raleigh North Carolina Standard,* 29 February 1860; C. S. Wooten, "General Thomas L. Clingman," newspaper clipping, 1917, Clipping File, NCC; Ada Sterling, ed., *A Belle of the Fifties: Memoirs of Mrs. [Clement C.] Clay of Alabama* (New York: Doubleday, 1904), 95. For Clingman's courtship of Harriet Lane, see also Virginia C. T. Clay to [?], ca. April 1858, Clement C. Clay Papers, Duke.

28. C. Vann Woodward, ed., *Mary Chesnut's Civil War* (New Haven: Yale University

Press, 1981), 114–15. The characterization of Harriet Lane as "queenly and gracious" appears in Adams, *Reminiscences by Mary Logan,* 23. Chesnut referred to her as "the very queen of the proprieties."

29. Woodward, *Mary Chesnut's Civil War,* 50, 115; Lawrence O. Branch to Nancy H. B. Branch, 1 February 1859, in Newsome, "Letters of Branch," 62.

30. David Outlaw to Emily B. Outlaw, 17 December 1849, David Outlaw Letters, SHC.

31. Sterling, *Belle of the Fifties,* 120–21; [Alexander K. McClure], "The Career of T. L. Clingman" (from *Philadelphia Times,* 10 October 1896), in R. A. Brock, ed., *Southern Historical Society Papers* 24 (1896): 308; communication from Washington correspondent, in *Raleigh State Chronicle,* 30 March 1888. McClure referred to the courtship of Louise Corcoran as "the only genuine *affaire de coeur* of Clingman's life." See also Glenn Tucker, "Many-Starred Career of Thomas Clingman," *State* 43 (August 1975): 15.

32. North Carolina Whigs favored distributing the proceeds from federal land sales among the states, whereas Tar Heel Democrats opposed homesteads out of the belief that high land prices would allow for a reduction in tariff duties.

33. Clingman's remarks against the homestead bill were published in *Fayetteville Observer,* 31 May 1858. The *Observer* bestowed rare praise upon Clingman in an editorial entitled "Good for Mr. Clingman" (24 May 1858). See also *Raleigh Register,* 2 June 1858. For the defeat of the bill, see *Asheville News,* 2 June 1858. For Clingman's opposition to the homestead bill in 1852, see *CG,* 32 Cong., 1 sess., 1281.

34. "Valedictory Address of Thomas L. Clingman," 16 May 1858, in *Raleigh North Carolina Standard,* 2 June 1858. Clingman praised his constituents for their "independence of thought" and ability "to decide the issues presented, without being influenced by past party associations or personal prejudices." The characterization regarding Clingman's health can be found in *Asheville News,* 1 July 1858.

35. For Bennett's land bill, see Thomas E. Jeffrey, *State Parties and National Politics: North Carolina, 1815–1861* (Athens: University of Georgia Press, 1989), 236, 263–64. For Clingman's position on distribution during the campaigns of 1855 and 1857, see his communications in *Asheville News,* 5 July 1855, and *Raleigh North Carolina Standard,* 29 July 1857.

36. *Asheville News,* 8 July 1858.

37. The vote by county in the congressional election can be found in *Raleigh North Carolina Standard,* 25 August 1858. The few Distribution Democrats who won election in the far west had all promised during the campaign to support Clingman for senator (*Asheville Spectator,* 3 September 1858).

38. *Asheville News,* 12 August 1858; *Greensboro Patriot,* 3 September 1858. Avery's role in frustrating Clingman's bid to win election to the Confederate senate is discussed in chapter 11.

39. *Greensboro Patriot,* 14 May 1858.

40. For Reid's illness and recovery, see *Charlotte Democrat,* 2 March, 6 April, 4 May 1858; *Raleigh North Carolina Standard,* 24 March 1858; *Fayetteville Observer,* 5 April, 24 May 1858. For rumors about Reid's continued health problems and his alleged intention to retire from the Senate, see William V. Geffroy to David S. Reid, 30 August, 28 September 1858, William J. Yates to Reid, 10 September 1858, Reid Papers. To dispel those rumors, Geffroy wrote an editorial for the *Winston Sentinel,* which was reprinted in other newspapers friendly to Reid. See *Charlotte Democrat,* 5 October 1858.

41. William V. Geffroy to David S. Reid, 28 September 1858, Reid Papers. In 1858 easterners controlled twenty-one of the thirty-two Democratic Senate seats, and forty-three of the eighty-one House seats. Although Clingman and Reid lived two hundred miles apart, Reid's home county of Rockingham in the northern Piedmont lay west of Raleigh and, thus, was considered part of the "west."

42. *Fayetteville Observer,* 22 November 1858. For the vote in the caucus, see John Masten to J. A. Waugh, 22 November 1858, Jones and Patterson Family Papers, SHC; *Charlotte Democrat,* 30 November 1858. On the first ballot Bragg received fifty-five votes, while Holden and Reid each garnered twenty-six votes. On the second ballot Bragg won sixty-two votes, compared to twenty-six for Holden and eighteen for Reid.

43. Communication from "Squiggins," in *New Bern Progress,* 24 November 1858. According to this report, supporters of both defeated candidates afterward complained about "the *lies* told them by Members!"

44. William J. Yates to David S. Reid, 25 November 1858, Reid Papers; John W. Ellis to Reid, 1 January 1859, in Noble J. Tolbert, ed., *The Papers of John Willis Ellis,* 2 vols. (Raleigh: State Department of Archives and History, 1964), 1:212; *Wilmington Journal,* 26 November 1858.

45. Communication from Washington correspondent, in *New York Tribune,* 10 December 1858. Douglas regarded the Lecompton Constitution, which had been drawn up by a convention boycotted by the antislavery majority in Kansas, as a travesty of his doctrine of popular sovereignty.

46. Communication from Washington correspondent, in *New York Tribune,* 10 December 1858; *S&W,* 450. As noted earlier, Northerners believed a local legislature could ban slavery at any point during the territorial stage, whereas Southerners maintained slavery could be prohibited only at the time a territory formally applied for statehood.

47. For speculation about a Douglas-Clingman ticket, see *New Bern Progress,* 6 December 1858, 15 April 1859; *Asheville News,* 14 April 1859; *Raleigh North Carolina Standard,* 20 April 1859.

48. "Speech of Hon. T. L. Clingman," in *Raleigh North Carolina Standard,* 29 December 1858; communications from Washington correspondents in *New Bern Progress,* 21 December 1858, *Raleigh North Carolina Standard,* 22 December 1858, *Raleigh Register,* 22 December 1858, *Asheville News,* 23 December 1858, 3 March 1859; Smith, *Presidency of James Buchanan,* 71.

49. *Asheville News,* 31 March 1859. Clingman may well have crossed paths with Seward and Sumner in Paris, since all three were in that city in July. See *Raleigh North Carolina Standard,* 13 July 1859. The term "runaway session" was used by Roy F. Nichols in *Disruption of American Democracy* as the title for his chapter on the second session of the Thirty-Fifth Congress.

50. Communication from foreign correspondent (from *New York Tribune*), in *New Bern Progress,* 18 May 1859. See also *Raleigh North Carolina Standard,* 30 March, 4 May 1859; *Raleigh Register,* 18 May 1859.

51. Communication from foreign correspondent (from *New York Tribune*), in *New Bern Progress,* 18 May 1859.

52. According to a report in the *Raleigh North Carolina Standard,* Clingman passed through Marseilles on 8 May still "in feeble health, having suffered much from sea-sickness on the voyage from America to England" (18 May 1859).

53. TLC to John D. Whitford, 15 May 1875, in *S&W*, 85; "Address Delivered at Davidson College," 25 June 1873, ibid., 43–44. According to the *Raleigh North Carolina Standard*, about two hundred Americans, including Clingman and Pierce, were registered at the U.S. Consul's office in Rome on 16 May (25 May 1859).

54. A[ugustus] H. J[arratt], "General Thomas L. Clingman," *University Magazine*, n.s., 18 (1901): 167; *New Bern Progress*, 18 November 1859; *Raleigh North Carolina Standard*, 23 November 1859. See also *Raleigh North Carolina Standard*, 14 September, 18 November 1859; *New Bern Progress*, 23 November 1859.

55. *New Bern Progress*, 15 August 1859; *Raleigh Register*, 6 April 1859. Vance defeated David Coleman by a majority of 1,695 votes and carried nine of the district's fifteen counties. See *Greensboro Patriot*, 26 August 1859.

56. "Annual Address Delivered before the North Carolina State Agricultural Society," 21 October 1858, in *S&W*, 101.

10. A One-Man Chamber of Commerce

1. *Wilmington Journal*, 14 May 1858; *Raleigh North Carolina Standard*, 12 May 1858. For the reference to "pioneer press agent," see Alice Dugger Grimes, "'I'm Going to be President,'" *State* 2 (29 September 1934): 22. For his reputation as a booster, see "Statesman and Author First Great Booster," clipping from *Asheville Times*, 29 November 1931, Pack. The "one-man chamber of commerce" characterization has been employed by numerous writers. See, for example, Bob Gallimore, "Thomas L. Clingman: Soldier, Explorer, and One-Man Chamber of Commerce," clipping from *Asheville Citizen-Times*, 23 January 1949, Clipping File, NCC; Fred Hardesty, "Fiery Spokesman for the South," *State* 39 (15 March 1972): 14; Glenn Tucker, "Many-Starred Career of Thomas Clingman," *State* 43 (August 1975): 17.

2. John C. Inscoe, *Mountain Masters, Slavery, and the Sectional Crisis in Western North Carolina* (Knoxville: University of Tennessee Press, 1989), 7, 9, 39, 53.

3. The quotations in this and the following paragraph are from "Speech of T. L. Clingman . . . on the Bill to Construct the Raleigh and Western Turnpike Road," in *Raleigh Register*, 22 December 1840.

4. Kent Schwarzkopf, *A History of Mt. Mitchell and the Black Mountains: Exploration, Development, and Preservation* (Raleigh: North Carolina Department of Cultural Resources and North Carolina Department of Natural Resources and Community Development, 1985), 35.

5. Clingman's letter was ostensibly written in response to a request by Skinner for information about the prospects for sheep husbandry in Yancey County. The version quoted in the following paragraph is from *S&W*, 113–16. For the letter's publication history, see Charles Lanman, *Letters from the Alleghany Mountains* (New York: Putnam, 1849), 173.

6. For Mitchell, see *DNCB*, s.v. "Mitchell, Elisha"; Clark A. Elliott, *Biographical Dictionary of American Science: The Seventeenth through the Nineteenth Century* (Westport, Conn.: Greenwood Press, 1979), 180; Schwarzkopf, *History of Mt. Mitchell*, 20–22. For Shepard, see *DAB*, s.v. "Shepard, Charles Upham"; Elliott, *Biographical Dictionary*, 234–35.

7. The letters can be found in *Asheville Messenger,* 24 January 1845; *Raleigh Register,* 25 March 1845. The quotation regarding their subsequent publication is from TLC, *Measurements of the Black Mountain* (Washington, D.C.: G. S. Gideon, 1856), 5.

8. TLC to *Asheville Messenger* [ca. September 1846], with attached letter from Charles U. Shepard to TLC, 15 September 1846, in *S&W,* 116–20.

9. George H. Daniels, *American Science in the Age of Jackson* (New York: Columbia University Press, 1968), 34; TLC, *Measurements of the Black Mountain,* 15. For the influence of Baconianism on American science, see Daniels, *American Science,* chapter 3.

10. Daniels, *American Science,* 66, 72; Charles U. Shepard to TLC, 15 September 1846, in *S&W,* 120.

11. Sally Gregory Kohlstedt, *The Formation of the American Scientific Community: The American Association for the Advancement of Science, 1848–1860* (Urbana: University of Illinois Press, 1976), 83. For the years of Clingman's active membership, see appendix B.

12. The quotations in this and the following paragraph are from TLC, "About the Minerals of Western N.C. How Certain Mineral Discoveries Were Made," *Asheville Citizen,* 22 October 1886.

13. Interview with *New York Tribune,* in *Raleigh News and Observer,* 3 June 1884; TLC, "About the Minerals of Western N.C."; Charles U. Shepard, "Diamond in North Carolina," *AJSA,* 2d ser., 2 (1846): 253–54.

14. Charles U. Shepard, "Native Platinum in North Carolina," *AJSA,* 2d ser., 4 (1847): 280–81; interview with *New York Tribune,* in *Raleigh News and Observer,* 3 June 1884. Despite the notoriety occasioned by those discoveries, substantial quantities of diamonds or platinum were never found in North Carolina.

15. The quotations are from TLC, "About the Minerals of Western N.C." See also his communications to the *New York Sun,* in *Raleigh News and Observer,* 18 January 1881, and in *Goldsboro Messenger,* 12 December 1881. Unlike diamonds and platinum, corundum was subsequently found in considerable quantities in the North Carolina mountains. It is used commercially as an abrasive.

16. Communication from "Perley," in *Raleigh North Carolina Standard,* 9 December 1857; Benjamin Silliman Jr., "Descriptions and Analysis of Several American Minerals," *AJSA,* 2d ser., 8 (1849): 383; James Dwight Dana, "Observations on the Mica Family," *AJSA,* 2d ser., 10 (1850): 116–17. Silliman characterized Clingman as a "distinguished gentleman . . . who has shown great interest in advancing the study of mineralogy."

17. The quotation is from [Alexander K. McClure], "The Career of T. L. Clingman," (from *Philadelphia Times,* 10 October 1896), in R. A. Brock, ed., *Southern Historical Society Papers* 24 (1896): 307. For the discovery of Clingmanite, see Silliman, "Descriptions and Analysis of Several American Minerals," 383. Clingmanite was listed under the "calcium mica" subgroup in James D. Dana, *Manual of Mineralogy and Petrography,* 4th ed. (New York: Wiley & Sons, 1887), 341. Five years later, however, Edward S. Dana noted that Clingmanite was not a mineral in its own right, since the attribution was "based on an incorrect determination of the silica in the analysis." See *System of Mineralogy of James Dwight Dana: Descriptive Mineralogy,* 6th ed. (New York: Wiley & Sons, 1892), 637.

18. Numerous agreements between Clingman and local landowners for both the antebellum and postwar periods can be found in the Clingman and Puryear Family Papers, SHC. There are also several letters from January and February 1861 regarding copper

investments, written by Clingman's agent, John P. Cunningham, along with related bonds and powers of attorney. Cunningham argued that "any [Northern] Capitalist desirous for safe and tangible investments could not do better . . . [than] to put their money in our mines and wait [for] better times." See John P. Cunningham to TLC, 29 January, 4 February 1861.

19. Fletcher Green, "Gold Mining: A Forgotten Industry of Ante-Bellum North Carolina," *NCHR* 14 (1937): 1–19, 135–55.

20. The quotations in this and the following paragraph are from TLC to Joseph Henry, 8 January 1857, in *Asheville News*, 2 March 1857. Clingman's letter was initially published in the *Washington (D.C.) Globe*. It was reprinted in the *News* under the title "Gold Mining."

21. Agreement between TLC and Marinus H. Van Dyke, 29 October 1856, Van Dyke to TLC, 22 March 1858, list of Chestatee company directors, 23 June 1858, agreement between TLC, Van Dyke, and Benjamin Hamilton, 21 June 1858, D. P. Barhyde to TLC, 28 January 1859, Van Dyke to TLC, 7 February 1859, Chestatee company stock certificates, 18 March 1859, Charles Levi Woodbury to TLC, 15 October 1860, all in Clingman-Puryear Papers; Fletcher M. Green, "Georgia's Forgotten Industry: Gold Mining," *Georgia Historical Quarterly* 19 (1935): 225–26; Andrew W. Cain, *History of Lumpkin County for the First Hundred Years* (Spartanburg: Reprint Co., 1978 [originally published in 1932]), 98. The capital stock of the Yahoola company was later increased to $1 million. See proceedings of the stockholders meeting, 13 October 1859, Clingman-Puryear Papers; Cain, *Lumpkin County*, 98.

22. William P. Blake, *Report upon the Gold Placers of a Part of Lumpkin County, Georgia* (New York: John F. Trow, 1858), 12; Blake, *Report upon the Gold Placers in the Vicinity of Dahlonega, Georgia* (New York: Baker & Godwin, 1858), 4, 14. The characterization of Blake is from Green, "Gold Mining: A Forgotten Industry," 151n.

23. The quotations are from William P. Blake, *The Gold Placers of the Vicinity of Dahlonega, Georgia* (Boston: n.p., 1859), 19, 51. For the financial difficulties of the Yahoola company, see the proceedings of the stockholders meeting, 13 October 1859, Clingman-Puryear Papers. For the Chestatee company, see John Van Nest to TLC, 23 June, 8 October 1860, Clingman-Puryear Papers.

24. T. C. A. Dexter to TLC, 16, 21 April 1860, William P. Blake to TLC, 1 May 1860, agreement with George H. Gordon, 15 October 1860, Clingman-Puryear Papers.

25. C. P. Culver to TLC, 1 April 1861, Clingman-Puryear Papers. Augustus H. Jarratt noted that his cousin "owned a half interest in the battle field" at Manassas. As he entered the battle, Clingman supposedly remarked to one of his comrades that "a cock always fights best on his own walk." See A[ugustus] H. J[arratt], "General Thomas L. Clingman," *University Magazine*, n.s., 18 (1901): 169.

26. Inscoe, *Mountain Masters*, 179, 191–92; C. S. Wooten, "General Thomas L. Clingman," newspaper clipping, 1917, Clipping File, NCC.

27. "Statesman and Author First Great Booster"; David F. Ramsour to William A. Graham, 29 March 1847, Governor's Papers, NCDAH.

28. *Asheville News*, 30 September 1858. The account of the Clingman–Mitchell controversy presented in this chapter is based on Thomas E. Jeffrey, "'A Whole Torrent of Mean and Malevolent Abuse': Party Politics and the Clingman-Mitchell Controversy," *NCHR* 70 (1993): 241–65, 401–29. See also Schwarzkopf, *History of Mt. Mitchell*, 20–72.

29. D. Hiden Ramsey, "Elisha Mitchell and Mount Mitchell," *Journal of the Elisha Mitchell Scientific Society* 73 (1957): 201–2. See also Archibald Henderson, "Elisha Mitchell: Scientist and Man," ibid., 204–10. A notable exception to the pro-Mitchell bias of most accounts is the balanced discussion in Schwarzkopf, *History of Mt. Mitchell.* Schwarzkopf acknowledges that most authors "have portrayed Mitchell as the protagonist in the dispute and Clingman as the villain" (58).

30. "Clingman's Peak" (from *Washington (D.C.) City Spectator*), in *Asheville News,* 19 November 1855; TLC, "Topography of Black Mountain," in *Tenth Annual Report of the Board of Regents of the Smithsonian Institution* (Washington, D.C.: Cornelius Wendell, 1856), 299–305. Clingman calculated that the point he measured was between 140 and 209 feet higher than "Mount Mitchell."

31. Elisha Mitchell to Joseph Henry, 20 November 1855, in TLC, *Measurements of the Black Mountain,* 3–4.

32. Jeffrey, "Clingman-Mitchell Controversy," 245–48; Schwarzkopf, *History of Mt. Mitchell,* 23–33, 49–59.

33. Elisha Mitchell to Joseph Henry, 20 November 1855, in TLC, *Measurements of the Black Mountain,* 3–4.

34. Elisha Mitchell to Joseph Henry, 20 November 1855, TLC to Henry, 1 December 1855, in TLC, *Measurements of the Black Mountain,* 3–8; Jeffrey, "Clingman-Mitchell Controversy," 251–53; Schwarzkopf, *History of Mt. Mitchell,* 54.

35. TLC, *Measurements of the Black Mountain,* 2.

36. The characterization "bear fight" is from Elisha Mitchell, *Black Mountain: Professor Mitchell's Reply to Mr. Clingman* (n.p., 1856), 7.

37. Communication from Elisha Mitchell, in *Asheville Spectator,* 19 June 1856. The issue of the *Spectator* containing Mitchell's second letter is not extant. However, its contents can be reconstructed from the extracts and summaries presented in TLC, *Measurements of the Black Mountain,* 15–16, and in TLC to Thomas W. Atkin, 12 September 1857, in *Raleigh North Carolina Standard,* 7 October 1857.

38. TLC, *Measurements of the Black Mountain,* 1, 12.

39. Mitchell, *Black Mountain,* 3, 5, 7–8.

40. Riddle's statement appears in TLC to Thomas W. Atkin, 22 October 1856, in *Asheville News,* 30 October 1856. The statement was written out by Clingman, signed by Riddle, and witnessed by Isaac M. Broyles, the postmaster at Burnsville.

41. Charles Phillips to Benjamin S. Hedrick, 1 December 1856, Benjamin S. Hedrick Papers, Duke. Mitchell's final communication was published in *Asheville Spectator,* 20 November 1856. Although that issue is not extant, a long extract from his letter appears in TLC to Thomas W. Atkin, 12 September 1857, in *Raleigh North Carolina Standard,* 7 October 1857.

42. Schwarzkopf, *History of Mt. Mitchell,* 61–65.

43. Jeffrey, "Clingman-Mitchell Controversy," 402–13; Schwarzkopf, *History of Mt. Mitchell,* 68–72.

44. *Asheville News,* 30 July 1857; communication from TLC, 8 January 1858, in *Raleigh North Carolina Standard,* 20 January 1858.

45. Zebulon B. Vance to Charles Phillips, 4 Aug. 1857, Elisha Mitchell Papers, SHC; Jeffrey, "Clingman-Mitchell Controversy," 426–27; Schwarzkopf, *History of Mt. Mitchell,* 49.

46. Bishop James H. Otey of Tennessee, who delivered the oration at the re-interment

ceremony, announced to the approving crowd that "by right of prior discovery . . . we con-
secrate this mountain by the name of Mt. Mitchell." However, that name was not officially
assigned to the highest peak in the Black Mountains (which Clingman's supporters always
insisted should be called Clingman's Peak) until the U.S. Geological Survey of 1886. Ironically, the smaller mountain three miles to the south, which was popularly known for more
than fifty years as Mount Mitchell, is today called Clingman's Peak. That peak should not
be confused with Clingman's Dome, the mountain in the Great Smokies that Clingman
and naturalist Samuel B. Buckley ascended in September 1858. That ascent led to a bitter
dispute, which in some ways paralleled the Clingman-Mitchell controversy, over which of
the two men had been responsible for locating and measuring the highest point in the
Smoky mountain range. Although the initial calculations indicated that Clingman's Dome
was about forty feet higher than present-day Mount Mitchell, the accepted elevations
today are 6,642 feet for Clingman's Dome and 6,684 for Mount Mitchell. See Jeffrey,
"Clingman-Mitchell Controversy," 415–16.

47. The quotation is from *Asheville News*, 24 June 1858. The argument that Vance's
defense of Mitchell was an important factor affecting the outcome of the congressional
election of 1858 is made in greater detail in Jeffrey, "Clingman-Mitchell Controversy,"
416–19. County-level voting returns can be found in *Raleigh North Carolina Standard*,
25 August 1858. Vance received 8,321 votes, compared to 6,272 for Avery.

11. Almost a Union Man

1. Clarence C. Norton, *The Democratic Party in Ante-Bellum North Carolina, 1835–
1861* (Chapel Hill: University of North Carolina Press, 1930), 207; John C. Inscoe,
"Thomas Clingman, Mountain Whiggery, and the Southern Cause," *Civil War History* 33
(1987): 48; J. Carlyle Sitterson, *The Secession Movement in North Carolina* (Chapel Hill:
University of North Carolina Press, 1939), 65; *Wilmington Herald*, 11 September 1860;
Greensboro Patriot, 20 September 1860.

2. Joel H. Silbey, "The Southern National Democrats, 1845–1861," in *The Partisan
Imperative: The Dynamics of American Politics before the Civil War* (New York: Oxford University Press, 1985), 119.

3. *S&W*, 449–50.

4. Ibid., 450. For Southern reaction to the *Harpers* article, see David Potter, *The Impending Crisis, 1848–1861* (New York: Harper & Row, 1976), 402; Sitterson, *Secession
Movement*, 147.

5. *S&W*, 451.

6. Ibid.; "Speech against the Revolutionary Movement of the Anti-Slavery Party,"
16 January 1860, in *S&W*, 456, 461, 484.

7. "Speech against the Anti-Slavery Party," in *S&W*, 474, 479.

8. Ibid., 479, 482–84.

9. *New York Tribune*, 17 January 1860; *Raleigh North Carolina Standard*, 25 January 1860; *Washington (D.C.) States*, in *Raleigh North Carolina Standard*, 8 February 1860;
New Bern Progress, 14 February 1860. The *Standard* lauded the speech as "the ablest
effort . . . of Mr. Clingman's long and useful public life."

10. Davis's resolutions were published in *Greensboro Patriot,* 17 February 1860.

11. *S&W,* 484–85; *Raleigh North Carolina Standard,* 22 February, 14 March 1860.

12. Toombs is quoted in Potter, *Impending Crisis,* 404. The *Raleigh Register* characterized Davis's resolutions as "Democratic scaffolding set up for the execution of Douglas at Charleston" (14 March 1860).

13. For the role of the North Carolina delegates in the convention, see Owen M. Peterson, "W. W. Avery in the Democratic National Convention of 1860," *NCHR* 31 (1954): 463–78. Avery served as chair of the Committee on Resolutions. After the walkout, he and the other North Carolinians remained in the convention and cast their votes at various times for Robert M. T. Hunter of Virginia, Joseph Lane of Oregon, and Daniel S. Dickinson of New York.

14. *Raleigh North Carolina Standard,* 9 May 1860. The *Fayetteville North Carolinian* also expressed its opinion that "a triumph awaits us" should Clingman be nominated on the Cincinnati platform (12 May 1860).

15. "Speech on the Subject of Congressional Legislation as to the Rights of Property in the Territories," 7 and 8 May 1860, in *S&W,* 497, 503–4. Once again, Clingman explicitly dissociated himself from those Southerners whom he called "disunionists *per se*"— individuals "who honestly believe . . . that the Union had better be dissolved . . . [and] that if the Democratic party were destroyed, a great step would be taken in that direction" (ibid., 500).

16. *Charlotte Democrat,* 12 June 1860; *Raleigh Register,* 6 June 1860.

17. *S&W,* 507.

18. The quotation is from communication from TLC, 30 November 1865, in *New York Times,* 8 December 1865. For the rally at the Cooper Institute, see *New York Tribune,* 22 May 1860; *New York Times,* 23 May 1860.

19. William B. Hesseltine, ed., *Three against Lincoln: Murat Halstead Reports the Caucuses of 1860* (Baton Rouge: Louisiana State University Press, 1960), 119; communication from Washington correspondent, in *Raleigh North Carolina Standard,* 8 February 1860.

20. For Clingman's role in the convention, see *New Bern Progress,* 11 September, 16 October 1860; *Asheville News,* in *New Bern Progress,* 16 October 1860; *Raleigh North Carolina Standard,* 17 October 1860. The *News* and *Standard* denied that Clingman had lobbied for the vice presidential nomination, but the *Progress* retorted that it had obtained its information "from gentlemen who were in Baltimore at the Convention." Fitzpatrick subsequently declined to run, and Herschel V. Johnson of Georgia was chosen as his replacement.

21. *Fayetteville Observer,* 2 July 1860; *Charlotte Democrat,* 3 July 1860; *Raleigh North Carolina Standard,* 18 July 1860. A few newspapers such as the *Standard* initially called for a state convention to decide between the two sets of candidates but quickly dropped the idea once it became apparent that Breckinridge enjoyed widespread support among North Carolina Democrats.

22. *Wilmington Herald,* 6 September 1860. For opposition within the Democratic party to Clingman's reelection, see *New Bern Progress,* 21, 28 August, 4 September 1860; *Wilmington Herald,* 4, 6 September 1860; *Charlotte North Carolina Whig,* in *Greensboro Patriot,* 14 September 1860. Among the Democrats mentioned as possible challengers were William W. Avery, Bedford Brown, John W. Ellis, and Romulus M. Saunders.

23. Communication from TLC, in *Raleigh North Carolina Standard,* 1 August 1860;

reports of TLC speech at Beaufort, in *Raleigh North Carolina Standard,* 29 August 1860, and *Charlotte Democrat,* 28 August 1860; *S&W,* 513.

24. *Raleigh North Carolina Standard,* in *Fayetteville Observer,* 3 September 1860; *S&W,* 512–13.

25. I am indebted to Jerry L. Cross of the North Carolina Division of Archives and History for the notion of Clingman as a political chameleon.

26. Account of Democratic mass meeting, in *Charlotte Democrat,* 11 September 1860.

27. *Wilmington Herald,* 11 September 1860; *Greensboro Patriot,* 4 October 1860. The Charlotte letter was published in full in *Wilmington Herald,* 11 September 1860, *Raleigh Register,* 19 September 1860, *Greensboro Patriot,* 20 September 1860, *New Bern Progress,* 25 September 1860. It was also excerpted in a widely circulated pamphlet entitled *The Breckinridge Party a Disunion Party* (n.p., 1860). Clingman's position was actually more complex than his enemies were willing to acknowledge. At none of the numerous mass meetings at which he spoke during the month before the election did he call for immediate secession in the event of a Republican victory. In a speech at Charlotte, a hotbed of Southern Rights sentiment, he unequivocally told his audience that "he was no disunionist" (*Charlotte Democrat,* 30 October 1860).

28. Thomas E. Jeffrey, *State Parties and National Politics: North Carolina, 1815–1861* (Athens: University of Georgia Press, 1989), 301–2; Potter, *Impending Crisis,* 442–47.

29. Jeffrey, *State Parties and National Politics,* 302–3; Potter, *Impending Crisis,* 485–500. During late November and early December, secession meetings were held in at least twenty-five North Carolina counties.

30. William K. Scarborough, ed., *Diary of Edmund Ruffin,* 3 vols. (Baton Rouge: Louisiana State University Press, 1972–89), 1:474; "Gen. Clingman's Reply to Hon. Jacob Thompson," 8 October 1877, in *S&W,* appendix, 29.

31. Personal Journal of John W. Ellis, 17 November 1860, in Noble J. Tolbert, ed., *The Papers of John Willis Ellis,* 2 vols. (Raleigh: State Department of Archives and History, 1964), 2:472; *S&W,* 514. Clingman remarked ambiguously that if Lincoln "resort[ed] to coercion against the seceding states," North Carolina should "take ground against him."

32. Communication from Edward J. Hale, in *Fayetteville Observer,* 26 November 1860; communication from John L. Pennington, in *New Bern Progress,* 22 November 1860; *Greensboro Patriot,* 22 November 1860; *Raleigh Register,* 21 November 1860.

33. Communication from Edward J. Hale, in *Fayetteville Observer,* 26 November 1860. Hale reported the caucus vote as follows: Clingman, 40; Person, 16; Avery, 15; Brown, 6. He also noted that seventeen Democrats were absent. Clingman thus received the support of only 43 percent of the Democratic legislators.

34. Ellis Journal, 28 November 1860, in Tolbert, *Ellis Papers,* 2:473; C. B. Harrison to Lawrence O'Bryan Branch, 11 December 1860, Branch Family Papers, Duke; communication from Edward J. Hale, in *Fayetteville Observer,* 26 November 1860; *Wilmington Herald,* 28 November 1860; communication from Raleigh correspondent, in *Fayetteville Observer,* 3 December 1860.

35. Proceedings of 4 December 1860, from *Congressional Globe,* in *S&W,* 517–19.

36. *Raleigh North Carolina Standard,* 12 December 1860. See also *Raleigh Register,* 11 December 1860; *Fayetteville Observer,* 10 December 1860. The *Register* wondered aloud whether the general assembly would be so foolhardy as to "re-elect Clingman to the Senate, and by so doing, endorse his disunion course."

37. For the distinction between immediate secessionists, fast ultimatumists, and extended ultimatumists, see Daniel W. Crofts, *Reluctant Confederates: Upper South Unionists in the Secession Crisis* (Chapel Hill: University of North Carolina Press, 1989), 105.

38. The address of the Southern congressmen can be found in *Raleigh North Carolina Standard*, 19 December 1860. Thomas Ruffin, who served in the U.S. Congress from 1853 until 1861, should not be confused with Judge Thomas Ruffin or his son, Thomas Ruffin Jr.

39. *S&W*, 523; Potter, *Impending Crisis*, 531.

40. Roy Nichols, *The Disruption of American Democracy* (New York: Macmillan, 1948; New York: Free Press, 1967), 416; Crofts, *Reluctant Confederates*, 129, 201; Potter, *Impending Crisis*, 544; diary of Thomas Bragg, 8 January 1861, SHC, typescript. On hearing of the defeat of the Etheridge resolutions, Clingman telegraphed two supporters that the Republicans were "solid against Crittenden's propositions" and that "without their aid no result can be attained." See TLC to Marcus Erwin, 7 January 1861, and TLC to John F. Hoke, 7 January 1861, *O.R.* ser. 1, vol. 51, pt. 2, p. 3.

41. TLC to William H. Thomas, 9 January 1861, in *Raleigh State Journal*, 23 January 1861 (also in *S&W*, 553–54); communication from TLC to *Winston Sentinel*, 15 January 1861, in *Charlotte Democrat*, 29 January 1861.

42. On several occasions in mid-January, Sen. Thomas Bragg privately acknowledged that the prospects for passage of a convention bill were doubtful. See Bragg diary, 10–13, 15 January 1861.

43. Edmund Wilkes to Charles Wilkes, 23 November 1860, Wilkes Family Papers, Duke; Ellis Journal, 28 November 1860, in Tolbert, *Ellis Papers*, 2:473; Jonathan Worth to J. J. Jackson, 29 November 1860, in J. G. de Roulhac Hamilton, ed., *The Correspondence of Jonathan Worth*, 2 vols. (Raleigh: Edwards & Broughton, 1909), 1:124; C. B. Harrison to Lawrence O'Bryan Branch, 11 December 1860, Branch Papers; B. F. Eller to Zebulon B. Vance, 17 December 1860, in Frontis W. Johnston and Joe A. Mobley, eds., *The Papers of Zebulon Baird Vance*, 2 vols. to date (Raleigh: Division of Archives and History, 1963–), 1:74; *Raleigh North Carolina Standard*, 9 January 1861; *HJ, 1860–61*, 186–89, 422–23; *SJ, 1860–61*, 212, 216, 222–23.

44. *HJ, 1860–61*, 452–53; *SJ, 1860–61*, 252–53. Union Democrat Bedford Brown played an important role in engineering the agreement by refusing to challenge Clingman for the senatorship. See *Raleigh North Carolina Standard*, 6 February 1861; *Fayetteville Observer*, 11 February 1861.

45. John J. Crittenden to Sion Rogers, 17 January 1861, in *Charlotte Democrat*, 22 January 1861; "Speech on the State of the Union," 4 February 1861, in *S&W*, 543, 546; Potter, *Impending Crisis*, 545–47. On 31 January 1861 Stephen A. Douglas also wrote an optimistic letter to a Virginia unionist, which was copied in the North Carolina newspapers. See *Raleigh North Carolina Standard*, 6 February 1861.

46. "Speech on the State of the Union," in *S&W*, 533, 547, 549.

47. *Wilmington Journal*, 21 February 1861.

48. Clingman could have indicated his support for secession by resigning his Senate seat. Instead, on 21 February 1861—three days after he formally endorsed disunion—he presented his credentials to the U.S. Senate as "Senator elect for the next term" (*Raleigh North Carolina Standard*, 27 February 1861). Far from being irretrievably committed to secession, Clingman was hedging his bets on the outcome of the convention election.

49. TLC to James W. Osborne, 18 February 1861, in *S&W*, 554–55. See also TLC to

Charlotte Bulletin, 18 February 1861, ibid., 555; TLC to James R. Love, 18 February 1861, in *Raleigh State Journal*, 27 February 1861; communication from TLC, 18 February 1861, in *Asheville News Extra*, 21 February 1861, Broadside Collection, NCC; communication from TLC, 22 February 1861, in *Wilmington Herald*, 23 February 1861; communication from TLC, Thomas Bragg, Warren Winslow, and Thomas Ruffin, 26 February 1861, in *Raleigh State Journal*, 20 March 1861; TLC to Robert G. Rankin, 27 February 1861, in *Wilmington Journal*, 28 February 1861.

50. Inscoe, *Mountain Masters*, 236–46; Jeffrey, *State Parties and National Politics*, 302, 309.

51. *Raleigh Register*, 13 March 1861; Inscoe, *Mountain Masters*, 238.

52. *Raleigh North Carolina Standard*, 13 March 1861.

53. "Remarks on President Lincoln's Inaugural," 6 March 1861, in *S&W*, 556–57; *Raleigh State Journal*, 3 April 1861; *S&W*, 564.

54. Clingman later claimed that he continued to hope "that there might be a union of all the States under a common government" even after North Carolina formally joined the Confederacy in May 1861. See communication from TLC, 30 November 1865, in *New York Times*, 8 December 1865.

55. Roy F. Nichols offers evidence that "there may have been fewer Southern actionists bent on independence for its own sake than has been assumed." See his *Blueprints for Leviathan: American Style* (New York: Atheneum, 1963), 143–47, 160–63 (quotation on p. 146). Daniel W. Crofts takes a more skeptical view, arguing that "as it became clear that the lower South considered disunion irrevocable, reconstruction [through secession] appeared more and more a secessionist subterfuge" rather than a genuine alternative (*Reluctant Confederates*, 135).

56. *Charleston (S.C.) Courier*, 19 April 1861; *Raleigh State Journal*, 22 May 1861. For Clingman's commission as North Carolina's representative to the Confederacy, 6 May 1861, see *O.R.* ser. 4, vol. 1, p. 289.

57. Marc W. Kruman, *Parties and Politics in North Carolina, 1836–1865* (Baton Rouge: Louisiana State University Press, 1983), 223; *Raleigh Register*, 28 August 1861. The reference to Clingman exchanging his "senatorial robes" for "soldier's clothes" is from C. Vann Woodward, ed., *Mary Chesnut's Civil War* (New Haven: Yale University Press, 1981), 192.

58. *SJ, 1860–61, 2nd Ex. Sess.*, 46, 53–54, 57, 89.

59. Ibid., 91, 118–19, 132, 139, 150–52; *HJ, 1860–61, 2nd Ex. Sess.*, 162, 178, 192–93; *Raleigh North Carolina Standard*, 18 September 1861. Seventy-two percent of Davis's vote came from legislators who cast their other ballot for either Clingman or Avery. Seventy-eight percent of those legislators who voted for Clingman also voted for Davis, compared to 61 percent of Avery's supporters. All but nine of the fifty-four legislators in the Clingman-Avery-Davis bloc were Democrats.

60. *SJ, 1860–61, 2nd Ex. Sess.*, 152–53; *HJ, 1860–61, 2nd Ex. Sess.*, 194–95; *Raleigh North Carolina Standard*, 18 September 1861.

61. Clingman received forty-one votes on the twelfth ballot and forty-five votes on the thirteenth ballot, compared to forty votes in the Democratic caucus of November 1860.

62. *Raleigh North Carolina Standard*, 18 September 1861. On the final ballot, Dortch and Clingman each received 31 percent of the Democratic vote, compared to 39 percent

for Avery. On the other hand, 81 percent of the Whigs voted for Dortch. Overall, more than two-thirds of Dortch's vote on the final ballot came from the Whigs.

63. *Raleigh State Journal,* 18 September 1861. See also *Wilmington Journal,* 19 September 1861; *Charlotte Democrat,* 24 August 1861; *Shelby Eagle* and *Asheville News,* in *Raleigh North Carolina Standard,* 9, 16 October 1861. The Whig presses, on the other hand, "hailed the result of the Senatorial Election" as a sign that "mere sectional strife . . . had been merged . . . in a united and efficient action against the common foe" (*Raleigh Register,* 25 September 1861).

12. A Noble Ambition

1. *Fayetteville Observer,* 29 April 1861. Turner's recollection of his speech of 1861 can be found in *Raleigh Sentinel,* 26 April 1870.

2. TLC, "The Battle of Manassas," 21 July 1874, in Walter Clark, ed., *Histories of the Several Regiments and Battalions from North Carolina in the Great War,* 5 vols. (Raleigh: E. M. Uzzell, 1901), 5:33; William H. S. Burgwyn, "Clingman's Brigade," ibid., 481; *S&W,* 512.

3. TLC, "Battle of Manassas," in Clark, *North Carolina Regiments,* 5:32.

4. Garland S. Ferguson, "Twenty-Fifth Regiment," in Clark, *North Carolina Regiments,* 2:291–92, 294. Clingman's desire to demonstrate his patriotism was undoubtedly stimulated by reports in the Northern newspapers that he regretted "his hasty and ill-considered committal to the Secession movement" and was now preparing to organize "a new State Government loyal to the Union" in the mountain counties. See *New York Tribune,* 10 August 1861; *Raleigh Register,* 28 August 1861.

5. Ferguson, "Twenty-Fifth Regiment," in Clark, *North Carolina Regiments,* 2:293; *Raleigh North Carolina Standard,* 25 September 1861. The *Fayetteville Observer* agreed that Clingman "ought to have been with his regiment instead of button-holing members" of the legislature (30 September 1861).

6. Communication from TLC, 13 October 1861 (from *Asheville News*), in *Raleigh State Journal,* 30 October 1861; Ferguson, "Twenty-Fifth Regiment," in Clark, *North Carolina Regiments,* 2:293; *Raleigh North Carolina Standard,* 16 October 1861.

7. *Raleigh Register,* 13 November 1861; *Raleigh North Carolina Standard,* 27 November 1861; Thomas I. Lenoir to Walter W. Lenoir, 12, 13, 14 November 1861, Lenoir Family Papers, SHC; communication from S. S. Satchwell, in *Raleigh North Carolina Standard,* 5 February 1862; communication from T. M. Dula, in *Asheville News,* 2 January 1862; Garland, "Twenty-Fifth Regiment," in Clark, *North Carolina Regiments,* 2:293–94; Frances H. Casstevens, "The Military Career of Brigadier General Thomas Lanier Clingman" (master's thesis, University of North Carolina at Greensboro, 1984), 34–35. The letters of Thomas and Walter Lenoir to their brother, Rufus, and other family members in the Lenoir Family Papers contain many references to sickness in the regiment.

8. Walter W. Lenoir to Rufus Lenoir, 19 January 1862, Lenoir Papers; diary of Thomas Bragg, 10, 11, 14, 15 February, 14 March 1862, SHC, typescript.

9. Walter W. Lenoir to Joseph Norwood, 13 April 1862, Walter W. Lenoir to Rufus

Lenoir, 24 April 1862, Thomas I. Lenoir to Walter W. Lenoir, 30 April 1862, Lenoir Papers.

10. TLC, *Address to the Citizens of North Carolina* (Raleigh: n.p., 1870), 8. For the labels "original secessionist" and "old unionist," see Marc W. Kruman, *Parties and Politics in North Carolina, 1836–1865* (Baton Rouge: Louisiana State University Press, 1983), 228, 231. Ellis died of tuberculosis on 7 July 1861. Clark, the Speaker of the state senate, served as acting governor during the remaining year of his term. See *DNCB*, s.v. "Ellis, John Willis"; "Clark, Henry Toole."

11. Kruman, *Parties and Politics*, 232–38 (quotation on p. 238). Although Clingman did not take an active role in the gubernatorial campaign, the *Raleigh State Journal* announced that he was "decidedly in favor of Johnston's election . . . [and] sternly opposed to Colonel Vance's election, more on account . . . of the support which the latter derives from Holden . . . than of any personal objections to Col. Vance" (6 August 1862).

12. TLC, *Address to the Citizens*, 8; Bragg diary, 1 December 1861; Burgwyn, "Clingman's Brigade," in Clark, *North Carolina Regiments*, 5:482; General Order No. 1, 4 August 1862 (unsigned, in TLC's hand), Thomas Lanier Clingman Papers, SHC.

13. *Raleigh North Carolina Standard*, 25 September 1861, 21 May 1862; *Asheville News*, 29 May 1862; communication from "North Carolina" (from *Raleigh State Journal*), in *Asheville News*, 14 August 1862.

14. John G. Barrett, *The Civil War in North Carolina* (Chapel Hill: University of North Carolina Press, 1963), 128–30; *Raleigh North Carolina Standard*, 19 March, 27 August 1862; *Asheville News*, 29 May, 7 August 1862; TLC to D. H. Hill, 7 August 1862, *O.R.* ser. 1, vol. 9, p. 477; Gustavus W. Smith to Samuel G. French, 29 October 1862, *O.R.* ser. 1, vol. 18, p. 762; TLC to William S. Ashe, 26 August 1862, John W. Cameron to TLC, 12 December 1862, Clingman Papers, SHC.

15. For the early history of these regiments, see H. T. J. Ludwig, "Eighth Regiment," in Clark, *North Carolina Regiments*, 1:387–91; E. K. Bryan and E. H. Meadows, "Thirty-First Regiment," ibid., 2:507–13; A. A. McKethan, "Fifty-First Regiment," ibid., 3:205–6; N. A. Ramsey, "Sixty-First Regiment," ibid., 3:503–7; Louis H. Manarin and Weymouth T. Jordan Jr., *North Carolina Troops*, 13 vols. to date (Raleigh: Division of Archives and History, 1966–), 4:515–16, 8:424–25, 12:258–59. By the time Clingman reported for duty at Wilmington, Cantwell had been replaced as commander of the 51st Regiment by William A. Allen.

16. The 8th Regiment arrived in Wilmington on 24 November; the 31st Regiment, on 8 December. The 61st Regiment did not join Clingman's Brigade until the Battle of Goldsboro.

17. "Report of Brig. Gen. Thomas L. Clingman," 21 December 1862, *O.R.* ser. 1, vol. 18, p. 117; Barrett, *Civil War in North Carolina*, 139–46.

18. "Report of Brig. Gen. Thomas L. Clingman," 21 December 1862, *O.R.* ser. 1, vol. 18, pp. 117–18; James H. Robertson, "Fifty-Second Regiment," in Clark, *North Carolina Regiments*, 3:230; James K. Marshall to TLC, 19 December 1862, in *Our Living and Our Dead* 3 (1875): 452; Barrett, *Civil War in North Carolina*, 139–47.

19. "Report of Brig. Gen. Thomas L. Clingman," 21 December 1862, *O.R.* ser. 1, vol. 18, p. 119; Robertson, "Fifty-Second Regiment," in Clark, *North Carolina Regiments*, 3:231; James K. Marshall to TLC, 19 December 1862, in *Our Living and Our Dead* 3 (1875): 452–53. Clingman listed total casualties as 20 dead, 107 wounded, and 18 missing. Most

of the casualties were sustained by the 51st and 52d regiments during the afternoon counterattack.

20. Burgwyn, "Clingman's Brigade," in Clark, *North Carolina Regiments,* 5:484 (quoting Fuller); Barrett, *Civil War in North Carolina,* 139n, 148.

21. *Fayetteville Observer,* 22 December 1862; *Charleston (S.C.) Courier,* 5 January 1863; TLC to Zebulon B. Vance, 28 January 1863, in Gordon B. McKinney and Richard M. McMurry, eds., *The Papers of Zebulon Vance* (Frederick, Md.: University Publications of America, 1987), microfilm, reel 2, original in Vance Papers, NCDAH. Laudatory accounts of the battle can be found in *Raleigh Progress,* 30 December 1862; *Wilmington Journal,* 8 January 1863; *Raleigh North Carolina Standard,* 20 February 1863. Clingman's defenders exaggerated by giving him credit for forcing the Federals to retreat. Most of the Union troops had already withdrawn from the Goldsboro area before the afternoon engagement.

22. *Raleigh Progress,* 20 December 1862; "Report of Brig. Gen. Thomas L. Clingman," 21 December 1862, *O.R.* ser. 1, vol. 18, p. 118. Clingman later pointed out that Evans had a brigade in Goldsboro within three miles of the railroad bridge (TLC to Zebulon B. Vance, 28 January 1863, in McKinney and McMurry, *Vance Papers,* reel 2). According to the commanding officer, Gustavus W. Smith, reinforcements were delayed by lack of water for the railroad engines. See Smith to Samuel Cooper, 29 December 1862, *O.R.* ser. 1, vol. 18, pp. 109–10.

23. TLC to Zebulon B. Vance, 28 January 1863, in McKinney and McMurry, *Vance Papers,* reel 2. With the permission of his commanding officer, Clingman had given Vance a copy of his report when the governor had visited Goldsboro a few days after the battle.

24. The quotations are from TLC to Zebulon B. Vance, 28 January 1863, in McKinney and McMurry, *Vance Papers,* reel 2. The report first appeared in *Raleigh North Carolina Standard,* 20 February 1863. It can also be found in *Wilmington Journal,* 26 February 1863; *Raleigh State Journal,* 4 March 1863.

25. Manarin and Jordan, *North Carolina Troops,* 4:517; 12:261. Col. William A. Allen resigned as commander of the 51st Regiment around the time the brigade moved to South Carolina. He was succeeded by Hector McKethan.

26. Ramsey, "Sixty-First Regiment," in Clark, *North Carolina Regiments,* 3:510; Ludwig, "Eighth Regiment," ibid., 1:392; communication from "31st NC," in *Fayetteville Observer,* 4 April 1863.

27. Communication from Capt. Co. D, 61st N.C.T. [N. A. Ramsey], in *Raleigh North Carolina Standard,* 20 March 1863. The *Raleigh Progress* asserted that if the people of South Carolina "persist in their insults . . . Governor Vance would be justified in marching every North-Carolina regiment out" (in *Raleigh North Carolina Standard,* 31 March 1863).

28. TLC to Zebulon B. Vance, 19 March 1863, Thomas L. Clingman Papers, Duke; TLC to Thomas Jordan, 14 April 1863, Clingman Papers, SHC; Daniel H. Hill to Pierre G. T. Beauregard, 29 April 1863, *O.R.* ser. 1, vol. 18, p. 1030.

29. W. H. C. Whiting to Daniel H. Hill, 3 May 1863, *O.R.* ser. 1, vol. 18, pp. 1041–42; Hector McKethan to B. Brown Venable, 10 May 1863, Caleb B. Hobson to Venable, 13 May 1863, General Order No. 7, 12 May 1863, Clingman Papers, SHC.

30. Memorandum by Thomas Jordan, 12 July 1863, *O.R.* ser. 1, vol. 28, pt. 1, pp. 60–62.

31. McKethan, "Fifty-First Regiment," in Clark, *North Carolina Regiments,* 3:206–7;

Ramsey, "Sixty-First Regiment," ibid., 511; E. K. Bryan and E. H. Meadows, "Defence of Fort Wagner," ibid., 5:162; Manarin and Jordan, *North Carolina Troops,* 12:262–64.

32. Report of William B. Taliaferro, in Manarin and Jordan, *North Carolina Troops,* 8:427; McKethan, "Fifty-First Regiment," in Clark, *North Carolina Regiments,* 3:208–10; TLC to Zebulon B. Vance, 4 August 1863, Clingman Papers, SHC. After the battle Beauregard praised the 51st Regiment for its "heroic conduct" (Manarin and Jordan, *North Carolina Troops,* 12:264).

33. TLC to Zebulon B. Vance, 4 August 1863, Clingman Papers, SHC. According to Clingman, the 51st Regiment sustained 74 of the 150 total casualties (killed, wounded, and missing), while the 31st incurred 37 casualties.

34. "Occurrences at Battery Wagner during the days of July 29, 30, 31, & Aug 1, 1863, made by Brig. Gen. T. L. Clingman," Clingman Papers, SHC; communication from TLC, in John W. Moore, *History of North Carolina,* 2 vols. (Raleigh: Alfred Williams, 1880), 241n-242n. The Confederates finally evacuated Battery Wagner on 6 September 1863.

35. On 18 July 1863 Clingman had been assigned command of the Second Sub-Division of the First Military District, embracing Sullivan's Island and Christ Church. See Special Order No. 251, *O.R.* ser. 1, vol. 28, pt. 2, p. 209.

36. Communication from TLC, in Moore, *History of North Carolina,* 240n. In a letter to Vance on 18 September 1863, Clingman referred to his position at Sullivan's Island as "the most exposed one in the District" (Miscellaneous Collections, Houghton Library, Harvard University, Cambridge, Mass.). The two generals to whom he referred were William G. Taliaferro and Henry A. Wise.

37. The quotations are from TLC to William F. Nance, 18 September 1863, Clingman Papers, SHC; C. D. Melton to John S. Preston, 25 August 1863, *O.R.* ser. 4, vol. 2, pp. 769–70. For complaints by the North Carolina troops, see *Raleigh North Carolina Standard,* 2 September 1863; E. Mallett to Edward White, 1 September 1863, C. B. Hobson to White, 1 September 1863, White to James D. Radcliffe, 11 September 1863, Clingman Papers, SHC. For Clingman's complaints regarding unequal duty assignments, see "Occurrences at Battery Wagner," Clingman Papers, SHC.

38. TLC to William H. C. Whiting, 28 September 1863, *O.R.* ser. 1, vol. 28, pt. 2, p. 383.

39. William H. C. Whiting to James A. Seddon, 30 September 1863, with endorsements by Jefferson Davis and Seddon, *O.R.* ser. 1, vol. 29, pt. 2, pp. 761–62.

40. William H. C. Whiting to James A. Seddon, 30 September 1863, with endorsements by Jefferson Davis and Seddon, *O.R.* ser. 1, vol. 29, pt. 2, pp. 761–62; Seddon to Pierre G. T. Beauregard, 7 October 1863, ibid., vol. 28, pt. 1, pp. 397–98; Seddon to Whiting, 7 October 1863, ibid., vol. 29, pt. 2, pp. 775–76; Beauregard to Seddon, 12 October 1863, ibid., vol. 28, pt. 1, p. 413.

41. Samuel Cooper to Pierre G. T. Beauregard, 27 November 1863, *O.R.* ser. 1, vol. 28, pt. 2, p. 527; Beauregard to Robert B. Rhett, 12 December 1863, ibid., 547; Special Order No. 252, 28 November 1863, Clingman Papers, SHC; *Petersburg (Va.) Register,* in *Raleigh State Journal,* 18 December 1863.

42. W. H. C. Whiting to Samuel Cooper, 28 December 1863, *O.R.* ser. 1, vol. 29, pt. 2, pp. 892–93; Whiting to Cooper, 4 January 1864, with endorsement by Jefferson Davis, ibid., vol 33, p. 1064; George E. Pickett to Cooper, 8 January 1864, with endorsement by

James A. Seddon, ibid., 1067–68; Pickett to Cooper, 8 January 1864, ibid., 1073; Cooper to Pickett, 9 January 1864, ibid., 1074; Whiting to Pickett, 14 January 1864, ibid., 1091; Seddon to Pickett, 16 January 1864, ibid., 1092. According to Pickett, Clingman was "quite anxious not to go back" to North Carolina.

43. George E. Pickett to Samuel Cooper, 15 February 1864, *O.R.* ser. 1, vol. 33, pp. 92–93.

44. TLC to Major Pickett, 17 March 1864, *O.R.* ser. 1, vol. 33, p. 101; Robert F. Hoke to Major Taylor, 8 February 1864, ibid., 95–96; George E. Pickett to Samuel Cooper, 15 February 1864, ibid., 93. Lt. Col. J. M. Whitson took over command of the 8th Regiment following Shaw's death.

45. Burgwyn, "Clingman's Brigade," in Clark, *North Carolina Regiments*, 5:487–88; George E. Pickett to Robert E. Lee, 15 February 1864, *O.R.* ser. 1, vol. 33, p. 92.

46. *Richmond (Va.) Dispatch*, in *Fayetteville Observer*, 22 February 1864; *Raleigh Confederate*, in *Fayetteville Observer*, 15 February 1864. On the other hand, the *Wilmington Journal* faulted the expedition's leaders for abandoning New Bern "without any effort at all" (in *Raleigh Progress*, 2 March 1864).

47. Herbert M. Schiller, ed., *A Captain's War: The Letters and Diaries of William H. S. Burgwyn, 1861–1865* (Shippensburg, Pa.: White Mane Publishing, 1994), 123; TLC to Zebulon B. Vance, 18 February 1864, in McKinney and McMurry, *Vance Papers*, reel 3 (original in Vance Papers, NCDAH). For Holden's announcement of 2 March and Clingman's appearance in Raleigh two days later, see *Raleigh Progress*, 4 March 1864; *Raleigh Confederate*, 9 March 1864. As founding members of the Conservative party, Holden and Vance had been allies until the editor became convinced that North Carolina should make a separate peace with the federal government. See Kruman, *Parties and Politics*, 249–65.

48. *Raleigh Confederate*, 9 March 1864; TLC to Zebulon B. Vance, 18 February 1864, in McKinney and McMurry, *Vance Papers*, reel 3; communication from TLC, 25 March 1864, in *Raleigh Confederate*, 29 March 1864; TLC, *Address to the Citizens*, 9; Kruman, *Parties and Politics*, 265. Vance's percentage of the vote in Clingman's Brigade was as follows: 8th Regiment, 96 percent; 31st Regiment, 53 percent; 51st Regiment, 76 percent; 61st Regiment, 57 percent. See *Fayetteville Observer*, 4 August 1864.

49. The definitive account of the Bermuda Hundred campaign is William Glenn Robertson, *Back Door to Richmond: The Bermuda Hundred Campaign, April–June 1864* (Baton Rouge: Louisiana State University Press, 1987). For the early phases of the campaign summarized in this paragraph, see chapters 4–10. For the role of Clingman's troops, see Schiller, *Burgwyn Letters*, 139–43; Casstevens, "Military Career of Clingman," 122–130. Until the fighting resumed in May, the brigade had been doing picket duty in the vicinity of Petersburg. A day-by-day account can be found in Schiller, *Burgwyn Letters*, 116–39. Burgwyn joined the brigade in January 1864 as assistant adjutant general.

50. *Raleigh North Carolina Standard*, 18 May 1864; Schiller, *Burgwyn Letters*, 143–44; Casstevens, "Military Career of Clingman," 130–34; Robertson, *Back Door to Richmond*, chapters 12–14.

51. Robert F. Hoke to J. M. Otey, 25 May 1864, *O.R.* ser. 1, vol. 36, pt. 2, pp. 236–38; Bryan and Meadows, "31st Regiment," in Clark, *North Carolina Regiments*, 2:515 (quoting Davis); TLC to Henry K. Burgwyn, 25 June 1864, in Burgwyn Papers, NCDAH (reprinted in Schiller, *Burgwyn Letters*, 150). Casualties in Clingman's Brigade during the

first day of the engagement amounted to 237 men, including 15 officers. See "List of killed, wounded, and missing in the engagement near Drewry's Bluff on Monday, May 16, 1864," *O.R.* ser. 1, vol. 36, pt. 2, p. 205.

52. Clingman's account of the battle can be found in "Second Cold Harbor," 3 June 1874, in Clark, *North Carolina Regiments*, 5:197–202.

53. Ibid.; Schiller, *Burgwyn Letters*, 148.

54. Ludwig, "Eighth Regiment," in Clark, *North Carolina Regiments*, 1:405; TLC, "Second Cold Harbor," ibid., 5:202–4. Contrary to Clingman's orders, Radcliffe's 61st Regiment remained in the trenches until Lt. Col. Devane finally "took out a portion of the regiment" (TLC, "Second Cold Harbor," 203). Burgwyn surmised that Radcliffe had not understood the order (Schiller, *Burgwyn Letters*, 148).

55. TLC, "Second Cold Harbor," in Clark, *North Carolina Regiments*, 5:205; *Raleigh Confederate*, 15 June 1864; Burgwyn, "Clingman's Brigade," in Clark, *North Carolina Regiments*, 5:493. The *Richmond Dispatch* report is quoted in *Raleigh Confederate*, 15 June 1864. The *Confederate*'s editor, Duncan McRae, asserted that the press reporter had meant no injustice to Clingman's troops. He had only communicated a report that he supposed reliable.

56. TLC to *Richmond (Va.) Dispatch*, 5 June 1864, in *Raleigh North Carolina Standard*, 15 June 1864.

57. *Fayetteville Observer*, 9 June 1864. The "statistical details" mentioned by the *Observer* probably referred to Clingman's enumeration of brigade casualties during the previous three weeks of fighting. The *Observer* did not publish the paragraph containing those numbers, although the *North Carolina Standard* and many of the Richmond papers did.

58. Communication from TLC, in *Fayetteville Observer*, 23 June 1864; Burgwyn, "Clingman's Brigade," in Clark, *North Carolina Regiments*, 5:493–95.

59. TLC to Henry K. Burgwyn, 25 June 1864, Burgwyn Papers; John D. McGeachy to [?], 30 July 1864, Catherine McGeachy Buie Papers, Duke; Ludwig, "Eighth Regiment," in Clark, *North Carolina Regiments*, 1:407; Henry S. Puryear to Richard C. Puryear, 31 July 1864, Jarratt-Puryear Family Papers, Duke; Casstevens, "Military Career of Clingman," 154–61.

60. *Raleigh Confederate*, in *Fayetteville Observer*, 19 September 1864. For the engagement at the Petersburg railroad, see also Casstevens, "Military Career of Clingman," 161–63.

61. William H. S. Burgwyn, "Life and Services of Gen. Thos. L. Clingman," newspaper clipping, ca. May 1898, Clipping File, NCC; *Fayetteville Observer*, 19 September 1864; Ann Greenough Burgwyn to TLC, 23 December 1864, Jarratt-Puryear Papers; Ann Greenough Burgwyn diary, in Schiller, *Burgwyn Letters*, 150n; Casstevens, "Military Career of Clingman," 163–65.

62. *Raleigh Confederate*, in *Fayetteville Observer*, 19 September 1864; *Raleigh North Carolina Standard*, 21 September 1864.

63. Communication to Jefferson Davis, 12 February 1864, Daniel M. Barringer to Davis, 8 October 1864, General and Staff Officers Files, War Department Collection of Confederate Records, RG 109, National Archives, Washington, D.C. I am indebted to Lynda Crist of the Jefferson Davis Papers for calling these letters to my attention.

64. *Raleigh Confederate*, in *Fayetteville Observer*, 15 February 1864; Burgwyn, "Life and Services of Clingman"; Richard M. McMurry, *Two Great Rebel Armies* (Chapel Hill: University of North Carolina Press, 1989), 109. According to McMurry, 90 percent of the ma-

jor generals in the Army of Northern Virginia had prewar military education or experience, compared to about half of the brigadier generals.

65. The quotation is from Richard E. Beringer et al., *Why the South Lost the Civil War* (Athens: University of Georgia Press, 1986), 43. A summary of the opinions of contemporaries and historians regarding Clingman's military abilities can be found in Casstevens, "Military Career of Clingman," 169–70.

66. For Clingman's belief in the frontal attack, see his "Speech Delivered at the Charlotte Centennial," 20 May 1875, in *S&W,* 110–12. As Clingman pointed out, the Romans and Greeks had used that tactic very effectively. During the Civil War, however, the substitution of the long-range rifle for the inaccurate smoothbore and the advent of trench warfare gave a decisive advantage to the defense. Inexperience may have accounted for Clingman's preference for frontal assaults over flanking movements. "A direct assault occurs most readily to the uninitiated . . . [whereas] an attack that circumvents the front of an opposing force requires more skill by the commander and mastery of drill by the men" (Beringer, *Why the South Lost the Civil War,* 473).

67. Unlike many North Carolinians, Clingman did not ground his opposition to the Davis administration on civil liberties issues such as conscription and suspension of the writ of habeas corpus. Instead, he faulted the administration for its inept military policies (*S&W,* 512). Shortly after the end of the war, he publicly characterized the Confederate administration as "utterly destitute of practical talent." See communication from TLC, 30 November 1865, in *New York Times,* 8 December 1865.

68. In April 1863 Clingman had requested that North Carolina senator George Davis use his influence to have the brigade transferred to North Carolina. See James A. Seddon to George Davis, 25 April 1863, Clingman Papers, SHC. He also persuaded Nathan G. Evans, who was stationed at Wilmington, to formally request that their brigades exchange stations. See Pierre G. T. Beauregard to Samuel Cooper, 17 April 1863, *O.R.* ser. 1, vol. 14, p. 900. In September, he induced Chase Whiting to lobby the Davis administration for a transfer by telling him that Wilmington was about to be attacked.

69. Burgwyn, "Clingman's Brigade," in Clark, *North Carolina Regiments,* 5:499. Johnston's remark regarding the "Thermopylae business" appears in [Alexander K. McClure], "The Career of T. L. Clingman" (from *Philadelphia Times,* 10 October 1896), in R. A. Brock, ed., *Southern Historical Society Papers* 24 (1896): 308. Clingman presented another version of the conversation in his *Speeches and Writings.* According to Clingman, Johnston had politely told him that if his soldiers "were all like you, I would do it, but there are many young men here who have a future, and I ought not to sacrifice their lives" ("Speech Delivered at the Charlotte Centennial," in *S&W,* 112).

70. *S&W,* 512. According to Clingman's niece, he characterized Lincoln's assassination as "the hardest blow that has been struck at the South yet." See Jane P. Kerr, "Brigadier-General Thomas L. Clingman," *Trinity Archive* 12 (1899): 394.

13. Poor Old "Played Out Clingman"

1. TLC, *Address to the Citizens of North Carolina* (Raleigh: n.p., 1870), 9; communication from TLC, 30 November 1865, in *New York Times,* 8 December 1865.

2. For Clingman's position, see *Wilmington Journal,* in *Raleigh Sentinel,* 4 Decem-

ber 1865. In a debate in the North Carolina Senate on 4 December 1865, Clingman's argument was upheld by Dennis Ferebee and George Howard (*Raleigh North Carolina Standard*, 5 December 1865). On Howard's motion, the matter was referred to the Judiciary Committee, which reported the next day that the seat had been vacated. The second quotation is from the committee's report, in *Raleigh North Carolina Standard*, 6 December 1865.

3. Clingman, along with several other Southern senators, was expelled on 11 July 1861. See Leroy P. Graf and Paul Bergeron, eds., *The Papers of Andrew Johnson*, 13 vols. to date (Knoxville: University of Tennessee Press, 1967–), 4:710. Johnson's amnesty proclamation excluded, among others, generals in the Confederate army and former members of the U.S. Congress. See Jonathan Truman Dorris, *Pardon and Amnesty under Lincoln and Johnson: The Restoration of the Confederates to Their Rights and Privileges, 1861–1898* (Chapel Hill: University of North Carolina Press, 1953), 35, 111–12.

4. The quotations in this and the following paragraph are from the communication from TLC, in *New York Times*, 8 December 1865. As examples of his moderation, Clingman pointed to his support for repeal of the gag rule, his vote for the first Kansas bill in 1853, and his opposition to Jefferson Davis's federal protection resolutions in 1860. On each occasion, he noted, he had voted in opposition to most Southern congressmen.

5. *Raleigh North Carolina Standard*, 13 December 1865. For favorable newspaper reaction to Clingman's letter, see *Wilmington Journal*, 13 December 1865; *Raleigh Sentinel*, 13 December 1865.

6. Communication from TLC, in *New York Times*, 8 December 1865; *Raleigh North Carolina Standard*, 13 December 1865.

7. *Report of the Joint Committee on Reconstruction* (Washington, D.C.: Government Printing Office, 1866), iii; report of the North Carolina Senate Judiciary Committee, in *Raleigh North Carolina Standard*, 6 December 1865.

8. TLC to Andrew Johnson, 3 January 1866, Thomas L. Clingman Amnesty Papers, Records of the Adjutant General's Office, RG 94, National Archives, Washington, D.C. The pardon application also appears in Graf and Bergeron, *Johnson Papers*, 9:569–70. For Clingman's opinion of Johnson, see *S&W*, 523–26. For Johnson's policy on pardons, see Jonathan Truman Dorris, "Pardoning North Carolinians," *NCHR* 23 (1946): 360–65.

9. TLC to Jonathan Worth, 30 January 1866, with endorsement by Worth, 30 January 1866, Clingman Amnesty Papers; Worth to B. S. Hedrick, 7 February 1866, in J. G. de Roulhac Hamilton, ed., *The Correspondence of Jonathan Worth*, 2 vols. (Raleigh: Edwards & Broughton, 1909), 2:498; William W. Holden to Andrew Johnson, 1 February 1866, Clingman Amnesty Papers.

10. *Raleigh North Carolina Standard*, 6 February 1866; *Danville (Va.) Times*, in *Raleigh Sentinel*, 17 February 1866.

11. Jonathan Worth to William A. Graham, 28 January 1866, in J. G. de Roulhac Hamilton and Max R. Williams, eds., *The Papers of William A. Graham*, 8 vols. (Raleigh: Division of Archives and History, 1957–92), 7:25. For similar sentiments, see Kemp P. Battle to Benjamin S. Hedrick, 6 February 1866, Richard H. Battle Jr. to Hedrick, 6 February 1866, Benjamin S. Hedrick Papers, Duke; A. C. Cowles to Isaac Jarratt, 12 February 1866, Jarratt-Puryear Family Papers, Duke.

12. TLC, *Address to the Citizens*, 10; *Raleigh North Carolina Standard*, 19, 28 February 1866. For Holden's attitude toward the secessionists, see William C. Harris, *William*

Woods Holden: Firebrand of North Carolina Politics (Baton Rouge: Louisiana State University Press, 1987), 182.

13. *Wilmington Journal,* 20 February 1866; Kemp P. Battle to Benjamin S. Hedrick, 6 February 1866, Hedrick Papers; *Asheville News,* 16 November 1865.

14. John Hill Wheeler to TLC, 4 February 1866, Clingman and Puryear Family Papers, SHC. The date on which Clingman received his pardon is noted on the docket of his file in the Clingman Amnesty Papers.

15. The exact date of Clingman's return to the mountain region is uncertain. He apparently left Raleigh some time during the first week of February. See Leander S. Gash to Adeline Gash, 11 February 1866, in Otto H. Olsen and Ellen Z. McGrew, eds., "Prelude to Reconstruction: The Correspondence of State Senator Leander Sams Gash, 1866–1867, Part 1," *NCHR* 60 (1983): 61. He was probably in McDowell County on 8 February, when he executed an agreement with Hugh Tate, a local landowner. See Clingman-Puryear Papers.

16. Ora Blackmun, *Western North Carolina: Its Mountains and Its People to 1880* (Boone: Appalachian Consortium Press, 1977), 343–59. Among those killed in the fighting in the mountain counties were Clingman's close associate Bayles M. Edney and his arch rival within the western Democracy, William W. Avery.

17. B. B. Long to TLC, 14 December 1865, Clingman-Puryear Papers. For Butler's investments, see James A. Padgett, ed., "Reconstruction Letters from North Carolina. Part 10: Letters to Benjamin Franklin Butler," *NCHR* 19 (1942): 381–404; 20 (1943): 54–82, 157–80, 259–82, 341–70; 21 (1944): 46–71. For Stevens, see *Charlotte Democrat,* 6 August 1867.

18. Agreements with Hugh A. Tate, 8 February 1866, John C. Hallyburton, 3 April 1866, Joseph Smawley, 5 April 1866, Clingman-Puryear Papers; Peter S. Michie to Benjamin F. Butler, 30 April 1866, in Padgett, "Butler Letters," 403. Several other agreements from 1866 and 1867 are in the Clingman-Puryear Papers. In addition to gold and copper, Clingman was also interested in mica, a heat-resistant mineral used in the manufacture of stoves and lanterns. In 1867 he discovered a promising deposit in one of the western counties and unsuccessfully attempted to interest George W. Swepson in a partnership. See TLC to George Swepson, 28 August 1867, George W. Swepson Papers, NCDAH.

19. Calvin H. Wiley to Jonathan Worth, 16 September 1867, Jonathan Worth Papers, NCDAH; *Charlotte Democrat,* 25 December 1866. Kemp P. Battle, who tried unsuccessfully after the war to run a land office business in New York City, also attributed his failure to the unsettled political situation. See his *Memories of an Old-Time Tar Heel* (Chapel Hill: University of North Carolina Press, 1945), 202.

20. TLC to Jonathan Worth, 16 March 1867, Governor's Papers, NCDAH. For the events leading to the formation of the North Carolina Republican party, see Otto H. Olsen, "North Carolina: An Incongruous Presence," in Olsen, ed., *Reconstruction and Redemption in the South* (Baton Rouge: Louisiana State University Press, 1980), 163–65; Gordon B. McKinney, *Southern Mountain Republicans, 1865–1900: Politics and the Appalachian Community* (Chapel Hill: University of North Carolina Press, 1978), 44–46; Harris, *William Woods Holden,* chapters 10 and 11. In 1866 Worth easily defeated Alfred Dockery, the candidate of the Union party, and the Conservatives also won handily in the legislative elections (Harris, *William Woods Holden,* 209–10).

21. Michael Perman, *Reunion without Compromise: The South and Reconstruction, 1865–1868* (Cambridge, Eng.: University Press, 1973), 277, 327–29.

22. TLC, *Address to the Citizens,* 11. Perman notes that for most of the Southern power elite, "retention of office and power within the State was far more important" than readmission to Congress or the end of military rule. "The self-interest of thousands of individual officeholders" thus acted as a powerful force against cooperation with congressional Reconstruction. See *Reunion without Compromise,* 311.

23. *Raleigh North Carolina Standard,* 26 June 1867; TLC to George Swepson, 29 August 1867, Swepson Papers; *Charlotte Democrat,* 8 October 1867; TLC to Isaac Jarratt, 2 October 1867, Jarratt-Puryear Papers. Clingman's misgivings about the constitutionality of the Reconstruction Acts may also have made him reluctant to speak out publicly on behalf of the convention (see TLC to *Raleigh North Carolina Standard,* 22 April 1870, in *Raleigh Sentinel,* 26 April 1870). On the other hand, some prominent North Carolinians did openly advocate a convention despite expressing doubts about its constitutionality. See, for example, the communication from Daniel M. Barringer, in *Charlotte Democrat,* 7 May 1867; and the remarks of Richmond Pearson, in J. G. de Roulhac Hamilton, *Reconstruction in North Carolina* (New York: Longmans, Green, 1914), 361–62.

24. Richard L. Zuber, *North Carolina during Reconstruction* (Raleigh: State Department of Archives and History, 1969), 14–17; Hamilton, *Reconstruction in North Carolina,* 253–78; Thomas E. Jeffrey, "Beyond 'Free Suffrage': North Carolina Parties and the Convention Movement of the 1850s," *NCHR* 62 (1985): 387–419. The vote on the convention was 93,006 in favor and 32,961 opposed. Among white registered voters, 31,284 approved the convention, 32,961 voted against it, and 42,476 abstained. See Perman, *Reunion without Compromise,* 348.

25. TLC, *Address to the Citizens,* 11–12. For Clingman's whereabouts during the winter and early spring of 1868, see Jane P. Clingman to Jane P. Kerr, 12 February 1868, Jarratt-Puryear Papers; diary of John Hill Wheeler, 7, 10, 13, 17 April 1868, SHC, microfilm; *Washington (D.C.) Express,* in *Charlotte Democrat,* 28 April 1868. Puryear died on 30 July 1867 (*DNCB,* s.v. "Puryear, Richard Clanselle").

26. Communication from TLC, 1 January 1868, in *Wilmington Journal,* 10 January 1868; TLC, *Address to the Citizens,* 12. Clingman was not the only non-Republican who believed in acquiescence to congressional Reconstruction. See the sources cited in Harris, *William Woods Holden,* 217n. However, as Harris points out, "a large number of conservatives bitterly opposed and feared congressional reconstruction" (ibid.).

27. *Raleigh Sentinel,* 6, 7 February, 20 April 1868; *Charlotte Democrat,* 11 February 1868; TLC, *Address to the Citizens,* 12.

28. Hamilton, *Reconstruction in North Carolina,* 286; Zuber, *North Carolina during Reconstruction,* 18; TLC, *Address to the Citizens,* 12.

29. The proceedings of the Asheville District Convention can be found in *Raleigh Sentinel,* 15 June 1868.

30. *New York World,* in *Wilmington Journal,* 14 July 1868; "Remarks of Gen. Clingman," in *Asheville Citizen,* 1 July 1880. Hancock received the unanimous vote of the North Carolina delegation on nine of the twenty-two ballots and secured a majority of its votes on three other occasions. See *Official Proceedings of the National Democratic Convention* (Boston: Rockwell & Rollins, 1868), 77–161.

31. TLC, *To the Voters of N. Carolina* (Asheville: n.p., 1868), 4, 6. For reaction to the

letter on the part of the Conservative presses, see *Raleigh Sentinel,* 21, 23 September 1868. For Clingman's optimism regarding the presidential election, see Wheeler diary, 18 July 1868. The Democratic platform can be found in *Official Proceedings,* 58–60.

32. For charges of inconsistency, see communication from "Citizen of Yancy," in *Raleigh Sentinel,* 21 April 1870. For Clingman's response, see TLC to *Raleigh North Carolina Standard,* 22 April 1870, in *Raleigh Sentinel,* 26 April 1870.

33. TLC, *To the Voters,* 6, 8. Clingman's critique of Republican economic policies is discussed in greater detail in chapter 16.

34. Communication from "Democrat," in *Raleigh Sentinel,* 9 October 1868. See also ibid., 30 September, 7 October 1868; *Rutherfordton Vindicator,* 12 October 1868. For Clingman's health, see TLC, *To the Voters,* 1.

35. McKinney, *Southern Mountain Republicans,* 12, 18–20, 24–26, 44–45.

36. *Rutherfordton Star,* 10 October 1868; Union Republican Congressional Committee, *Record of the New York Democratic Convention* (Washington, D.C., 1868), in Scrapbook, Thomas Settle Papers Group 2, SHC; John L. Cheney, ed., *North Carolina Government, 1585–1979* (Raleigh: North Carolina Department of the Secretary of State, 1980), 1332–33. In this and the following chapters the term "mountain region" (or "mountain counties" or "far west") refers to those counties lying west of Surry, Yadkin, Alexander, Catawba, and Cleveland Counties. Most, but not all, of the mountain counties were embodied within a single congressional district (referred to in the text as the "mountain district"). The boundaries of that district were slightly readjusted after each decennial census. See the maps in Cheney, *North Carolina Government,* 694–702.

37. James Sinclair to Ulysses S. Grant, 15 March 1869, in John Y. Simon, ed., *The Papers of Ulysses S. Grant,* 20 vols. to date (Carbondale: Southern Illinois University Press, 1967–), 19:381; *Raleigh Sentinel,* 5 November 1868. A year after Grant's inauguration, Clingman asserted that the president "has shown himself more liberal to the Southern States than the majority of his party have done." He did not rule out the possibility of endorsing him for reelection. See TLC, *Address to the Citizens,* 16.

38. Blackmun, *Western North Carolina,* 377.

39. Proceedings of stockholders' meeting, 15 October 1868, in *A Record of the Acts and Charter . . . of the Western Division of the Western North-Carolina Railroad* (Asheville: Pioneer Office, 1869), 71; Blackmun, *Western North Carolina,* 377–78.

40. TLC deposition, in *Report of the Commission to Investigate Charges of Fraud and Corruption* (Raleigh: James H. Moore, 1872), 255; Charles L. Price, "The Railroad Schemes of George W. Swepson," *East Carolina College Publications in History* 1 (1964): 32–34, 50.

41. TLC deposition, in *Fraud Commission Report,* 255–58; Price, "Railroad Schemes," 34, 39–42; Charles L. Price, "Railroads and Reconstruction in North Carolina, 1865–1871" (Ph.D. diss., University of North Carolina at Chapel Hill, 1959), 403, 407. For a more detailed account of Clingman's involvement in the Swepson-Littlefield frauds, see Thomas E. Jeffrey, "An Unclean Vessel: Thomas Lanier Clingman and the 'Railroad Ring,'" *NCHR* 74 (1997): 389–431.

42. TLC deposition, in *Fraud Commission Report,* 266–67; Price, "Railroad Schemes," 35–37; Cecil K. Brown, "The Florida Investments of George W. Swepson," *NCHR* 5 (1928): 275–76.

43. Agreement between TLC and Swepson, 5 April 1869, in *Fraud Commission Report,* 336–37; TLC deposition, ibid., 268–71.

44. TLC deposition, in *Fraud Commission Report,* 259–60, 272–74; Price, "Railroad Schemes," 36; Brown, "Florida Investments," 275. According to Brown, Swepson realized approximately $1.9 million from the sale of bonds nominally worth about $6.4 million.

45. TLC deposition, in *Fraud Commission Report,* 266–67; Swepson testimony, ibid., 218; Good M. Roberts testimony, ibid., 240. Clingman never carried through on his threat to resign but, instead, remained on the board until the road was sold in July 1872. See TLC deposition, in *Fraud Commission Report,* 273; Proceedings of the Board of Directors, 25 June 1872, in *Records and Documents Pertaining to the Title of the Western North Carolina Railroad* (n.p., n.d.), 177.

46. *Asheville News,* 29 October, 11 November 1869; *Raleigh Sentinel,* 28 October 1869.

47. Price, "Railroads and Reconstruction," 468–71.

48. TLC, *Address to the Citizens,* 1–2.

49. Ibid., 2, 5. Between January 1869 and February 1870, the price of North Carolina bonds had declined from seventy-three cents on the dollar to only twenty-three cents. See Hamilton, *Reconstruction in North Carolina,* 449.

50. TLC, *Address to the Citizens,* 12–14.

51. Ibid., 12–13, 15.

52. William A. Graham to William A. Graham Jr., 13 April 1870, in J. G. de Roulhac Hamilton and Max R. Williams, eds., *The Papers of William A. Graham,* 8 vols. (Raleigh: Division of Archives and History, 1957–92), 8:89; *Raleigh Sentinel,* 18 March 1870; *Asheville Citizen,* 31 March 1870.

53. *Raleigh Sentinel,* 21 March 1870; F. N. Strudwick to *Hillsborough Recorder,* in *Raleigh Sentinel,* 6 April 1870; *Salisbury Old North State,* 8 April 1870. According to Turner, fifty thousand copies of the address had been printed at the *Standard*'s office (18 March 1870).

54. *Salisbury Old North State,* 8 April 1870.

55. *Greensboro Patriot,* 24 March 1870; *Raleigh Sentinel,* 28 March, 3 May 1870. One correspondent of the *Sentinel* complained that "Mr. Clingman is again eligible to a seat in the United States Senate, while many less rebellious than himself are still under the ban" (communication from "Citizen of Yancy," 21 April 1870).

56. *Raleigh Sentinel,* 25 April, 3 May 1870.

57. TLC deposition, in *Fraud Commission Report,* 270–72.

58. *Raleigh Sentinel,* 1 June, 16 May 1870.

59. *Rutherfordton Star,* 11 June 1870; *Raleigh Sentinel,* 10 June, 9 July 1870; "Address [by Conservative members of the North Carolina General Assembly] to the People of North Carolina," in *Charlotte Democrat,* 5 April 1870.

60. Conservatives captured all five senatorial districts in the far west and won sixteen of its twenty-one seats in the North Carolina House of Representatives (*Raleigh Sentinel,* 7 September 1870). For the competition for U. S. senator, see ibid., 19, 20, 30 August, 7, 14, 15, 16, 21 September 1870; George W. Swepson to Matt W. Ransom, 11 September 1870, Matt Whitaker Ransom Papers, SHC; Zebulon B. Vance to Kemp P. Battle, 27 October 1870, Battle Family Papers, SHC.

61. Communication from "Civis," in *Raleigh Sentinel,* 31 October 1870; *Raleigh Sentinel,* 31 October, 21 November 1870. In characteristic fashion, Turner offered a mock endorsement, praising Clingman as a man upon whom all parties could unite. "He can com-

mend himself to the old Whigs for he was one of them; he can present his claims with confidence to the old Democrats, for he was one of them, also. He is acceptable to the carpet baggers, for he is on terms with Littlefield. He is acceptable to the native scalawag, for he made an address to the people which was published in the *Standard* office."

62. *Raleigh Sentinel,* 31 October, 30 November 1870; Hamilton, *Reconstruction in North Carolina,* 562–64, 571. Despite the entreaties of many Conservatives, Vance did not formally resign his Senate seat until December 1871. Matt W. Ransom was elected in his place in January 1872 and was seated the following April. See Nancy Revelle, "Matthew Whitaker Ransom's Political Career" (master's thesis, University of North Carolina at Chapel Hill, 1959), 35–38.

63. *Raleigh Sentinel,* 3 December 1870. The Welker Committee was established in March 1870 to determine whether illegal means had been used to secure passage of a bill amending the charter of the Western North Carolina Railroad. After testifying that he knew nothing about the particular bill under investigation, Clingman had gratuitously added that he had been "consulted confidentially" by an individual in regard to another bill embracing the same subject matter. However, he "did not feel at liberty" to disclose the substance of the conversation since he had been requested to treat it "as a confidential one between a client and his attorney." See "Report of the Committee to Inquire into the Means Used to Pass An Act Entitled 'An Act to Amend an Act to Incorporate the Western North Carolina Railroad Company,'" in *Executive and Legislative Documents* (Raleigh: Joseph W. Holden, 1870), 3. Turner characterized Clingman's claim of lawyer-client privilege as "altogether preposterous" and "a miserable subterfuge" (*Raleigh Sentinel,* 1 April 1870).

64. The most detailed account of the fight is the one by Turner in *Raleigh Sentinel,* 26 January 1871.

65. *Greensboro North State,* 9 December 1870; *Raleigh North Carolina Standard,* 3, 9 December 1870; *Wilmington Journal,* 4 December 1870; *New York Times,* 4 December 1870; *Raleigh Sentinel,* 26 January 1871, 20 January 1872; Thomas Sparrow to William B. Rodman, 4 December 1870, William Blount Rodman Papers, East Carolina University, Greenville, N.C.; William A. Graham to William A. Graham Jr., 10 December 1870, in Hamilton and Williams, *Graham Papers,* 8:162.

66. Communication from "Citizen of Yancy," in *Raleigh Sentinel,* 16 May 1870; *Raleigh Sentinel,* 1 June 1870.

67. See, for example, *Raleigh Sentinel,* 18 March, 10 June, 14 September, 31 October 1870.

68. As the *Raleigh North Carolina Standard* noted, the venerable William A. Graham had received only ten votes in the Conservative senatorial caucus of 1870 despite expressing a willingness to serve. According to the *Standard,* his poor showing constituted striking evidence that "the Grahams have had their day" (7 December 1870).

69. Communication from "Citizen of Yancy," in *Raleigh Sentinel,* 16 May 1870.

14. Endeavoring to Redeem Himself

1. The quotations are from Mark Mayo Boatner III, *Civil War Dictionary* (New York: David McKay, 1959), 159; *DNCB,* s.v. "Turner, Josiah, Jr." Michael Perman notes that

"from 1868 until about 1873 or 1874, the Republicans' opponents throughout the South referred to themselves as either the Conservative party or else as the Democratic and Conservative party." The term "Conservative" reflected the ambivalence of most anti-Republicans, who wished to identify with Northern Democrats in national politics while retaining the support of former Whigs in their own states. See *The Road to Redemption: Southern Politics, 1869–1879* (Chapel Hill: University of North Carolina Press, 1984), 6. In this and the following chapters, the term "Conservative" is used to characterize the anti-Republican party in North Carolina during the period before 1875, while the term "Democratic" is used for references to the party during later periods.

2. *Raleigh Sentinel*, 3 December 1870; Richard L. Zuber, *North Carolina during Reconstruction* (Raleigh: State Department of Archives and History, 1969), 41–44. Vance was also concerned that the Republican-controlled U.S. Senate would refuse to seat him if Holden were impeached. That concern proved well founded. See Jerry Lee Cross, "Political Metamorphosis: An Historical Profile of the Democratic Party in North Carolina, 1800–1892" (Ph.D. diss., State University of New York at Binghamton, 1975), 156.

3. John Luther Bell Jr., "Constitutions and Politics: Constitutional Revision in the South Atlantic States, 1864–1902" (Ph.D. diss., University of North Carolina at Chapel Hill, 1969), 225–31.

4. *Asheville Pioneer*, 8 June 1871; TLC, *Address to the Citizens of North Carolina* (Raleigh: n.p., 1870), 11–12.

5. *Salem People's Press*, in *Asheville Pioneer*, 22 June 1871.

6. TLC, "To the Voters of North Carolina," 7 June 1871, in *Wilmington Journal*, 14 June 1871.

7. *Wilmington Journal*, 16 June 1871; *Raleigh Sentinel*, 12 June 1871.

8. *Asheville Pioneer*, 31 August 1871; Bell, "Constitutions and Politics," 231–34. According to the *Pioneer*, the total vote was 86,607 in favor of a convention and 95,252 opposed. In the mountain counties, the vote was 11,049 for and 10,128 against.

9. *Report of the Commission to Investigate Charges of Fraud and Corruption* (Raleigh: James H. Moore, 1872); Charles L. Price, "Railroads and Reconstruction in North Carolina, 1865–1871" (Ph.D. diss., University of North Carolina at Chapel Hill, 1959), 472–73.

10. TLC deposition, in *Fraud Commission Report*, 257, 259, 262, 272–74.

11. TLC deposition, in *Fraud Commission Report*, 257, 265–66, 271–73. For Clingman's efforts to collect from Littlefield, see Thomas E. Jeffrey, "An Unclean Vessel: Thomas Lanier Clingman and the 'Railroad Ring,'" *NCHR* 74 (1997): 410–12, 417–19, 421–25.

12. *Raleigh News*, in *Wilmington Journal*, 10 May 1872; *Raleigh Sentinel*, 3 May 1872; communication from correspondent of *Raleigh Carolina Era*, in *Asheville Pioneer*, 9 May 1872.

13. For the Conservative platform, see *Raleigh Carolina Era*, 9 May 1872. For Clingman's alleged authorship of the platform, see ibid., 30 May, 4 July 1872; *Raleigh Carolina Era*, in *Asheville Pioneer*, 23 May 1872.

14. *Raleigh Carolina Era*, 13 June 1872. A more detailed account of the role of the railroad fraud issue in the campaign of 1872 can be found in Jeffrey, "An Unclean Vessel," 412–17.

15. *Raleigh Carolina Era,* 13 June 1872; Price, "Railroads and Reconstruction," 475–77; TLC deposition, in *Fraud Commission Report,* 273; agreement signed by Robert R. Swepson and Rufus Y. McAden, 22 April 1871, with attached acceptance by the Western Division Commissioners, 29 April 1871, in *Raleigh Carolina Era,* 20 June 1872.

16. *Raleigh News,* 5 June 1872; *Asheville Pioneer,* 6 June 1872.

17. *Charlotte Democrat,* 16 July 1872; communication from "C," in *Wilmington Journal,* 19 July 1872. For Fitzhugh Lee, see *DAB,* s.v. "Lee, Fitzhugh."

18. James B. Beck to TLC, 8 July 1872, in *Charlotte Democrat,* 23 July 1872.

19. For Republican charges that Clingman was the author of the letter, see *Raleigh Carolina Era,* 21 November 1872. Beck's letter was dated 8 July 1872. Clingman passed through Washington that day on the way to the Baltimore convention. See diary of John Hill Wheeler, 8 July 1872, SHC, microfilm.

20. *Raleigh News,* 13 July 1872; *Charlotte Democrat,* 23 July 1872; *Raleigh Sentinel,* 16 July 1862; Samuel T. Carrow to James B. Beck, in *Raleigh Carolina Era,* 18 July 1872. J. G. de Roulhac Hamilton uncritically cites the Beck letter as evidence of widespread interference by federal officials in the 1872 elections in North Carolina. See *Reconstruction in North Carolina* (New York: Longmans, Green, 1914), 589.

21. *Raleigh News,* 6, 13 July 1872; *Raleigh Sentinel,* 15, 17, 24 July 1872.

22. *Goldsboro Messenger,* 15 July 1872; *Raleigh News,* 24 July, 13 August 1872. Clingman was accompanied during the final days of the campaign by W. P. Wood, a Liberal Republican from New York, whom the Republicans characterized as a "detective," "spy," and "informer" who "means to stuff ballot-boxes, destroy registration lists, and to do anything and everything to carry the State for the Democrats." See *Raleigh Carolina Era,* 1 August 1872.

23. *Raleigh News,* 3, 8, 19 August 1872. Caldwell received 98,630 votes compared to 96,731 for Merrimon. See John L. Cheney, ed., *North Carolina Government, 1585–1979* (Raleigh: North Carolina Department of the Secretary of State, 1980), 1402–3.

24. Communication from TLC, in *Raleigh News,* 4 September 1872.

25. Augustus S. Merrimon to D. Franklin Caldwell, 20 August 1872, David Franklin Caldwell Papers, SHC; *Raleigh News,* 27 August, 12 September 1872, 4 January 1873; Douglass C. Dailey, "The Elections of 1872 in North Carolina," *NCHR* 40 (1963): 350–54; Cross, "Political Metamorphosis," 177–79.

26. *Raleigh Sentinel,* quoted in Perman, *Road to Redemption,* 123; Thomas J. Jarvis to Edward J. Warren and D. M. Carter, 21 October 1872, in W. Buck Yearns, ed., *The Papers of Thomas Jordan Jarvis,* 1 vol. to date (Raleigh: State Department of Archives and History, 1969–), 1:16; *Raleigh News,* 10 September, 5 November 1872; Dailey, "Elections of 1872," 359. A precipitous decline in voter turnout was the most significant factor behind Greeley's disastrous defeat in North Carolina. The Democrats lost almost twenty-six thousand votes between the August governor's election and the November presidential election, compared to less than four thousand votes for the Republicans.

27. *Asheville Citizen,* in *Raleigh Carolina Era,* 14 February 1872; *Charlotte Democrat,* 18 June 1872; *Greensboro North State,* in *Raleigh Carolina Era,* 24 October 1872; Alfred J. Morrison to William A. Graham, 18 November 1872, in J. G. de Roulhac Hamilton and Max R. Williams, eds., *The Papers of William A. Graham,* 8 vols. (Raleigh: Division of Archives and History, 1957–92), 8:284.

28. *Raleigh News,* 28 November, 1, 3 December 1872; *Wilmington Journal,* 29 November, 6 December 1872; *Salisbury Carolina Watchman,* in *Raleigh News,* 1 December 1872.

29. Communication from "Civis," in *Raleigh Sentinel,* 31 October 1870; *Raleigh News,* 4 December 1872; *Wilmington Journal,* 6 December 1872.

30. *Wilmington Journal,* 6 December 1872. Extracts from numerous Democratic newspapers denouncing Merrimon can be found in *Raleigh Carolina Era,* 12 December 1872. Merrimon's Conservative supporters denied that any deal had been made with the Republicans: "no pledge, or promise of any kind [was] proposed, given, or accepted." See communication from L. W. Humphrey and W. L. Love, in *Raleigh Sentinel,* 20 December 1872.

31. *Raleigh Sentinel,* 6 October, 7 November 1870; *Proceedings of the Second Annual Meeting of the Stockholders of the Western Division* (Salisbury, N.C.: J. J. Bruner, 1870); William D. Cotten, "Appalachian North Carolina: A Political Study, 1860–1889" (Ph.D. diss., University of North Carolina at Chapel Hill, 1954), 227.

32. Wallace W. Rollins to Rufus Y. McAden, 6 June 1872, George W. Swepson Papers, NCDAH; Proceedings of the Board of Directors, 26 June–9 July 1872, in *Records and Documents Pertaining to the Title of the Western N.C. Railroad* (n.p., n.d.), 177–81; McAden to Thomas L. Clayton and John C. Smathers, 8 July 1872, ibid., 176; McAden to the president and directors of the Western Division, 8 July 1872, ibid., 180. The legislative committee examined Clingman, McAden, Woodfin, Merrimon, and several others involved in the affairs of the Western North Carolina Railroad but was unable to discover any evidence to support allegations that there had been fraud and collusion in the sale of the road. See *Report of W. A. Smith, Legislative Document No. 15* (Raleigh: Josiah Turner, 1875), 2–3.

33. *Asheville News,* 18 November 1869; *Asheville Citizen* 3 July 1873.

34. *Asheville Citizen,* 19 June, 10 July 1873.

35. Ibid., 25 September 1873; *Chicago (Ill.) Inter-Ocean* and *Charleston (S.C.) News and Courier,* in *Asheville Citizen,* 23 October, 20 November 1873. Illinois, Indiana, Kentucky, Tennessee, South Carolina, and Georgia also sent delegates to the convention.

36. *Asheville Citizen,* 3 October 1874, 10 June 1875; *Asheville Pioneer,* 12 June 1875.

37. *Asheville Citizen,* 10 July 1879; *Charlotte Observer,* 6 July 1879; *Raleigh News,* 6 July 1879; *Charleston (S.C.) News and Courier,* in *Raleigh News,* 9 July 1879; *Raleigh News and Observer,* 30 June 1886; Ora Blackmun, *Western North Carolina: Its Mountains and Its People to 1880* (Boone: Appalachian Consortium Press, 1977), 396–97. Hayne was president of the Louisville, Cincinnati, and Charleston Railroad until his death in 1839.

38. TLC to Ross A. Neilson, 7 June 1873, Simon Gratz Autograph Collection, Historical Society of Pennsylvania, Philadelphia, Pa.

39. *The Geneva Award: Argument by T. L. Clingman* (Washington, D.C.: McGill & Witherow, 1876), 1, 5, 16. This was the second of three pamphlets containing arguments by Clingman before the Judiciary Committee of the U.S. House of Representatives.

40. The published pamphlets, in addition to the one cited above, were *The Alabama Claims: A Synopsis by T. L. Clingman, January 18, 1876* (Washington, D.C.: McGill & Witherow, 1876); *The Geneva Award: Argument Made before the Judiciary of the House of Representatives by T. L. Clingman* (Washington, D.C.: McGill & Co, 1877). The arguments in the three pamphlets are basically the same, although each of the latter two was revised

slightly from its predecessor. The Washington correspondent of the *Raleigh Observer* referred to one of the pamphlets as "a legal document of great worth and ability" (8 December 1878). For Clingman's comments to Battle, see William H. S. Burgwyn, "Life and Services of Gen. Thos. L. Clingman," newspaper clipping, ca. May 1898, Clipping File, NCC.

41. *Report of the Committee on the Judiciary,* 48 Cong., 1 sess., 1883–84, H. Rept. 1032, 1, in U.S. Government Publications, Serial Set No. 2256 (New York: Readex Microprint, 1966); communication from "Maxwell," in *Greensboro North State,* 9 September 1880. In 1881 Henry W. Grady of the *Atlanta Constitution* noted that Clingman was "practicing law and doing well" (in *Goldsboro Messenger,* 31 January 1881).

42. [Alexander K. McClure], "The Career of T. L. Clingman" (from *Philadelphia Times,* 10 October 1896), in R. A. Brock, ed., *Southern Historical Society Papers* 24 (1896): 307; *Raleigh State Chronicle,* 30 March 1888; Wheeler diary, 17 December 1873.

43. Risden Tyler Bennett to William H. S. Burgwyn, 22 March 1898, William Hyslop Sumner Burgwyn Papers, NCDAH. The "book" to which Clingman referred was his *Selections from the Speeches and Writings of Hon. Thomas L. Clingman* (see chapter 15).

44. *Raleigh State Chronicle,* 20 October 1883; *Wilmington Messenger,* 17 July 1889; diary of David Schenck, September 1875, SHC, typescript. The phrase "colossal egotism" is from Burgwyn, "Life and Services of Clingman."

45. Schenck diary, September 1875; Wheeler diary, 19 December 1873.

46. *Raleigh News,* 24 July 1878; [McClure], "Career of T. L. Clingman," 307. In regard to Clingman's relations with the Northern press, the *Charlotte Observer* noted that "there has been a notion abroad . . . that when he spoke upon any question whatsoever it was the duty of the State to listen. This . . . has enabled him to occupy more than a fair share of space in the newspapers" (30 July 1878).

47. Communications from "Fred" and "J. C. J.," in *Raleigh Observer,* 9 July, 14 August 1879; TLC to William Frazier, 12 June 1867, in *Letters and Reports on Western North Carolina* (New York: G. E. Sears, 1868), 6.

48. Communication from "Farmer," in *Asheville Citizen,* 17 June 1875; communication from TLC, 10 July 1878, in *Raleigh Observer,* 13 July 1878. Clingman's reluctance to become a candidate stemmed, in part, from a prior commitment to deliver the commencement address at the University of the South in Sewanee, Tennessee—an obligation that would necessitate his absence from North Carolina during the final week of the campaign. See communication from TLC, 26 July 1875, in *Asheville Citizen,* 29 July 1875.

49. *Asheville Citizen,* 8, 22, 29 July, 5 August 1875; communication from TLC, 18 July 1878, in *Raleigh Observer,* 21 July 1878; *Raleigh News,* 16 July 1878.

50. *Raleigh News,* 7 September 1875; Bell, "Constitutions and Politics," 246. The convention election constituted a setback for the Democrats, since a year earlier they had elected ninety-three members to the state House of Representatives from the same districts. Moreover, the Republicans won the popular vote by a majority of at least seven thousand.

51. Bell, "Constitutions and Politics," 246–50; communication from "Sky-Lark," in *Charlotte Southern Home,* 13 September 1875. The Democratic delegates from Robeson County presented sheriff's certificates, while the Republican challengers offered a statement of the poll holders in the various precincts.

52. *Journal of the Constitutional Convention of the State of North Carolina, Held in 1875* (Raleigh: J. Turner, 1875), 7–9; communication from "Sky-Lark," in *Charlotte Southern Home,* 13 September 1875; *Raleigh News,* 7, 8 September 1875; *Raleigh Sentinel,* 6, 7 September 1875; Bell, "Constitutions and Politics," 249–51. After the convention was organized, a committee was appointed to investigate the Robeson election. By a strictly partisan vote, the two Democrats were allowed to keep their seats. The Republicans bitterly protested the convention president's decision to allow the Robeson Democrats to vote on their own case. Had their votes not been counted, "the Republicans would have commanded enough votes to unseat them and to secure a majority" (Bell, "Constitutions and Politics," 250).

53. *Salisbury Carolina Watchman,* 9 September 1875; *Charlotte Democrat,* 13 September 1875; communication from "Sky-Lark," in *Charlotte Southern Home,* 13 September 1875; *Hillsborough Recorder,* in *Raleigh News,* 16 September 1875; Bell, "Constitutions and Politics," 247–49.

54. "Remarks of Hon. T. L. Clingman," in *Raleigh News,* 15 September 1875.

55. Communication from "Sky-Lark," in *Charlotte Southern Home,* 13 September 1875; *Raleigh Constitution,* 15 September 1875; *Raleigh News,* 15 September 1875; *Convention Journal,* 41, 50, 60. Clingman was also a member of the Committee on Revision, which had responsibility for examining and ensuring the correctness of approved ordinances filed with the North Carolina Secretary of State.

56. *Convention Journal,* 73–74, 78–79; *Raleigh Constitution,* 14, 15, 16 September 1875; *Asheville Citizen,* 30 September 1875; *Raleigh News,* 15 September 1875. While supporting measures to reduce the cost of government, Clingman successfully resisted more radical efforts to modify the Constitution of 1868. On two occasions in late September, for example, he spoke out against an ordinance to reduce the number of senators from fifty to twenty-five.

57. Edward Conigland to TLC, 21 September 1875, in William K. Boyd, ed., *Memoirs of W. W. Holden* (Durham: Seeman Printery, 1911), 176–77; *Convention Journal,* 28, 82.

58. *Convention Journal,* 126–27; *Raleigh Sentinel,* 23 September 1875; *Raleigh Constitution,* 22, 23, 25 September 1875; *Raleigh News,* 24 September 1875. The ordinance was defeated by a vote of fifty-three to fifty-six. All but one Democrat voted against it, while all but two Republicans supported it.

59. *Raleigh Constitution,* 2 October 1875; *Asheville Citizen,* 14 October 1875.

60. *Convention Journal,* 188; *Raleigh Constitution,* 2 October 1875; *Raleigh News,* 3 October 1875; *Asheville Citizen,* 14 October 1875.

61. *Convention Journal,* 188, 196–203, 208–9, 241–42, 276–77. So sudden and unexpected was the decision to adjourn that the convention closed without passing the customary resolution of thanks to the presiding officer. The following day, an ad hoc "committee on behalf of the friends of constitutional reform," chaired by Clingman, presented Ransom with an engraved silver service as a "testimonial of their appreciation of your patriotic devotion to the great principles of Constitutional liberty." See TLC et al. to Edward Ransom, 12 October 1875, and Ransom to TLC et al., 12 October 1875, in *Charlotte Democrat,* 18 October 1875.

62. *Charlotte Democrat,* 18 October 1875; *Raleigh Sentinel,* in *Charlotte Southern Home,* 23 October 1875.

63. *Raleigh Sentinel*, in *Charlotte Southern Home*, 23 October 1875. The convention passed thirty amendments, which were ratified in a popular referendum in November 1876. For a synopsis of the amendments, see *Charlotte Democrat*, 18 October 1875; Bell, "Constitutions and Politics," 253–59.

64. *Raleigh News*, 12 October 1875; *Raleigh Sentinel*, 27 October 1875. For Turner's later career, see Samuel A. Ashe et al., eds., *Biographical History of North Carolina*, 8 vols. (Greensboro: Charles L. Van Noppen, 1905–17), 3:425–26; *DNCB*, s.v. "Turner, Josiah, Jr."

65. *Vicksburg (Miss.) Herald*, in *Raleigh News*, 24 September 1875; communication from TLC, 10 July 1878, in *Raleigh Observer*, 13 July 1878. Clingman's niece, Jane Puryear Kerr, referred to him as a "controlling influence" in the convention ("Brigadier-General Thomas L. Clingman," *Trinity Archive* 12 (1899): 394).

15. Champion of the New South

1. Dan T. Carter, *When the War Was Over: The Failure of Self-Reconstruction in the South, 1865–1867* (Baton Rouge: Louisiana State University Press, 1985), 108.

2. The quotations are from *Washington (D.C.) Chronicle*, in *Charlotte Democrat*, 14 May 1867. See also Paul M. Gaston, *The New South Creed: A Study in Southern Mythmaking* (New York: Alfred A. Knopf, 1970), 7, 25–30, 55–63.

3. *Raleigh Sentinel*, 19 April 1871; *Raleigh North Carolina Standard*, 3 February 1869; Carter, *When the War Was Over*, 169; Joseph Flake Steelman, "The Immigration Movement in North Carolina, 1865–1900" (master's thesis, University of North Carolina at Chapel Hill, 1947), 61–73.

4. TLC to Jonathan Worth, 16 March 1867, Governor's Papers, NCDAH; Worth to Englehard and Price, 27 January 1869, in J. G. de Roulhac Hamilton, ed., *The Correspondence of Jonathan Worth*, 2 vols. (Raleigh: Edwards & Broughton, 1909), 2:1274. Clingman expressed doubt in his letter as to whether he would be able to attend the exposition.

5. The quotations are from TLC to William Frazier, 12 June 1867, in American Agricultural and Mineral Land Co., *Letters and Reports on Western North Carolina* (New York: G. E. Sears, 1868), 10. An excerpt from his letter was published in *S&W,* 124–26.

6. *Raleigh North Carolina Standard*, 3 February 1869; *Raleigh Sentinel*, 21 April 1871; Steelman, "Immigration Movement," 38, 68–70. Clingman's testimonial can be found in North Carolina Land Co., *Guide to Capitalists and Emigrants: Being a Statistical and Descriptive Account of the Several Counties of the State of North Carolina* (Raleigh: Nichols & Gorman, 1869), 78–83. It also appears in *S&W,* 121–24. Another promotional piece by Clingman, addressed to Richard Kingsland, was published in *Raleigh North Carolina Standard*, 25 May 1869, and reprinted in *S&W,* 126–30.

7. TLC to *New York Sun*, 2 December 1881, in *Goldsboro Messenger*, 12 December 1881. For other examples of Clingman's efforts to publicize the resources of North Carolina, see "Mount Pisgah, North Carolina," in *Appleton's Journal*, 27 December 1873 (also in *S&W,* 133–35); *Gold Hill Mine, Rowan County, North Carolina: Memorandum by General T. L. Clingman* (Washington, D.C.: M'Gill & Witherow, 1875); "North Carolina's Resources: Gen. Thomas L. Clingman on the Agricultural and Mineral Wealth of the State" (from

New York Sun), in *Raleigh News and Observer,* 18 January 1881. In 1877 Clingman reprinted several of his antebellum and postwar publicity pieces in his collection of speeches and writings under the title, "Articles Relating to the Mountain Region of North Carolina" (*S&W,* 113–47).

8. The quotations in this and the following paragraph are from "Letter to Col. John D. Whitford," 15 May 1875, in *S&W,* 84–90. Clingman's letter also contained a scathing critique of the dietary habits of North Carolinians, particularly their fondness for fried, greasy food. "I am inclined to think," he wrote, "that within ten years as many persons have died prematurely in the State from bad cookery as were slain in the war" (88).

9. Cornelius O. Cathey, *Agriculture in North Carolina before the Civil War* (Raleigh: State Department of Archives and History, 1966), 25–28; Melton A. McLaurin, "The Nineteenth-Century North Carolina State Fair as a Social Institution," *NCHR* 59 (1982): 213–15; McLaurin, "The North Carolina State Fair, 1853–1899" (master's thesis, East Carolina College, 1963), 87–131.

10. *Raleigh Sentinel,* 23 October 1871. The *Sentinel* had earlier announced that Clingman would present a paper entitled "The Native Grasses of Western North Carolina" at the meeting (30 August 1871). It is not clear whether that paper was actually written or read.

11. During the session of 1874–75, for example, the state House of Representatives passed a resolution repealing the annual appropriation (*Raleigh News,* 22 December 1874). The society's supporters managed to defeat the resolution in the senate.

12. *Raleigh Observer,* 17 October 1877.

13. Ibid.; "Address Delivered At Davidson College, North Carolina," 25 June 1873, in *S&W,* 45, 51, 53. For Southern reformers' "indictment of the lazy and traditional South," see Carter, *When the War Was Over,* 119–21; Gaston, *New South Creed,* 29–30.

14. The crop-lien system was a contractual relationship between the farmer and the local merchant, whereby the farmer pledged his unplanted crop in return for fertilizer, implements, and other supplies. Once a lien had been executed, the farmer could not buy from a competing merchant except for cash. If the farmer ended the year still in debt, as was often the case, his contract required him to renew the lien on his next crop with the same merchant. The effect was to reduce many farmers to a state of helpless peonage. The system also encouraged one-crop agriculture since the merchant would generally accept only cotton or some other cash crop as security. See C. Vann Woodward, *Origins of the New South, 1877–1913* (Baton Rouge: Louisiana State University Press, 1951), 180–85.

15. For descriptions of the problems of North Carolina's farmers, see Paul D. Escott, *Many Excellent People: Power and Privilege in North Carolina, 1850–1900* (Chapel Hill: University of North Carolina Press, 1985), 173–79; Jerry Lee Cross, "Political Metamorphosis: An Historical Profile of the Democratic Party in North Carolina, 1800–1892" (Ph.D. diss., State University of New York at Binghamton, 1975), 213–23; Hugh T. Lefler and Albert R. Newsome, *North Carolina: The History of a Southern State,* 2d ed. (Chapel Hill: University of North Carolina Press, 1963), chapter 36. I am grateful to Dr. Cross for calling my attention to the weaknesses in Clingman's critique of postbellum agriculture.

16. "Follies of the Positive Philosophers," in *S&W,* appendix, 25; Lefler and Newsome, *North Carolina,* 498–506.

17. Carter, *When the War Was Over,* 117–19.

18. "Address Delivered at Davidson College," in *S&W,* 40, 45.

19. "Follies of the Positive Philosophers," in *S&W,* appendix, 17, 19–20.

20. *Raleigh Observer,* 27 June 1878; *Raleigh State Chronicle,* 30 March 1888; *Salisbury Carolina Watchman,* in *Asheville Citizen,* 11 July 1878.

21. "Huxley, Darwin, and Tyndall; or, The Theory of Evolution," 31 January 1875, in *S&W,* 60; C. S. Wooten, "General Thomas L. Clingman," newspaper clipping, 1917, Clipping File, NCC; diary of David Schenck, September 1875, SHC, typescript.

22. Communication from "S," in *Raleigh Observer,* 27 May 1877.

23. "The Great Meteor of 1860," 7 January 1871, in *S&W,* 53–54.

24. Ibid., 55. Clingman discussed his essay with Newcomb on 31 December 1867. An entry of that date in the diary of John Hill Wheeler notes that he and Clingman trudged "through a furious snow storm to the National Observatory . . . [where] he read a long article to Professor Newcome *[sic]* on a meteor," SHC, microfilm. For Newcomb's reaction, see TLC, "The Mystery of the Weather" (from *New York Sun*), in *Charlotte Home Democrat,* 13 January 1882. Subsequent investigation has revealed that the atmosphere is considerably higher than even Clingman believed. Its outermost layer, the exosphere, extends from about four hundred miles to six thousand miles above the earth. See *Encarta: The Complete Interactive Multimedia Encyclopedia,* 1995 ed., s.v. "atmosphere."

25. Clingman's essay was published in *Asheville Western Expositor,* 17 April 1873. That issue is not extant, but the impending publication of the essay is noted ibid., 10 April 1873. The essay was reprinted in *Raleigh News,* 20 April 1873, and appears under the title, "Old Diggings for Mica in Western North Carolina," in *S&W,* 130–33. The Mound Builders were an advanced Native American civilization that inhabited southern Ohio and other parts of the Middle West and Southeast before the time of Columbus. See Ashton Chapman, "Hopewell Indians Came Here for Mica," *State* 36 (15 February 1969): 13–14.

26. "Volcanic Action in North Carolina: Lecture Delivered before the Washington Philosophical Society, May 1874," in *S&W,* 80; report of F. W. Clark (from *Asheville Pioneer*), in *Charlotte Democrat,* 26 July 1878.

27. TLC, "The Mystery of the Weather" (from *New York Sun*), in *Charlotte Home Democrat,* 13 January 1882; TLC, "New Light on Meteorology" (from *New York Sun*), in *Raleigh News and Observer,* 21 February 1884; *Van Nostrand's Scientific Encyclopedia,* 4th ed. (Princeton: Van Nostrand, 1968), s.v. "comet"; *Encarta,* s.v. "Krakatau"; "comet."

28. Robert V. Bruce, *The Launching of Modern American Science, 1846–1876* (Ithaca: Cornell University Press, 1987), 343; "Follies of the Positive Philosophers," in *S&W,* appendix, 16, 18. Bruce attributes the lack of attention to science in the postwar South to the "grinding poverty [that] left the Southerners little time for nonpaying science."

29. George H. Daniels, *American Science in the Age of Jackson* (New York: Columbia University Press, 1968), 53.

30. Cynthia Eagle Russett, *Darwin in America: The Intellectual Response, 1865–1912* (San Francisco: Freeman, 1976), 34–35; Herbert Hovenkamp, *Science and Religion in America, 1800–1860* (Philadelphia: University of Pennsylvania Press, 1978), 209; *DNB,* s.v. "Huxley, Thomas Henry"; "Tyndall, John."

31. Hovenkamp, *Science and Religion,* 209. For the scientific reception of Darwinism, see Richard Hofstadter, *Social Darwinism in American Thought,* rev. ed. (Boston: Beacon

Press, 1955), 16–19; Russett, *Darwin in America*, 8–11. For opposition from the non-scientific community, see Russett, *Darwin in America*, 11–14.

32. "Follies of the Positive Philosophers," in *S&W*, appendix, 18–19; "'Hell': Suggestions by Hon. T. L. Clingman" (from *Washington (D.C.) Capital*, 10 March 1878), in *S&W*, appendix, 49.

33. Positivism is a philosophy of science associated with the teachings of Auguste Comte (1798–1857). In its most extreme form, it rejects the cognitive credentials of metaphysics and religion and stipulates that the only valid kind of knowledge is scientific. See *Dictionary of the History of Science* (Princeton: Princeton University Press, 1981), s.v. "positivism." Although Clingman was familiar with the writings of Comte, his attacks on "positivism" and "positive philosophers" centered primarily on the religious skepticism of Darwin's two principal popularizers, John Tyndall and Thomas Huxley.

34. "Science and Christianity: A Lecture Delivered in New York, Washington, Raleigh, and Other Points by T. L. Clingman," in *S&W*, 5–22. Clingman read an early version of the lecture to his friend John Hill Wheeler on 8 February 1873 (Wheeler diary). It was first publicly presented before the Young Men's Christian Association of New York City (*Charlotte Observer*, 14 May 1875) and the YMCA of Asheville (*Raleigh News*, 27 April 1873). The lecture was delivered in Raleigh on 3 December 1874 (*Raleigh News*, 6 December 1874); in Washington on 5 February 1875 (*Washington (D.C.) National Republican*, 6 February 1875); and at Weaverville College near Asheville on 16 July 1875 (*Asheville Citizen*, 29 July 1875). A presentation scheduled in Charlotte for 15 May 1875 was canceled due to inclement weather (*Charlotte Democrat*, 17 May 1875).

35. "Science and Christianity," in *S&W*, 14–15, 20. For the role of natural theology in nineteenth-century science, see Bruce, *Modern American Science*, 122; Daniels, *American Science*, 53; Hovenkamp, *Science and Religion*, ix–x.

36. The quotations about phrenology are from Orson S. Fowler and Lorenzo N. Fowler, *New Illustrated Self-Instructor in Phrenology and Physiology* (New York: Fowler and Wells, [1859]), 123. The other quotations are from "Science and Christianity," in *S&W*, 13. Although regarded today as a pseudoscience, phrenology seemed to many educated nineteenth-century Americans to be "a legitimate attempt . . . to understand how the mind functioned." See Ronald G. Walters, *American Reformers, 1815–1860* (New York: Hill & Wang, 1978), 157. For the role of Scottish common-sense philosophy in nineteenth-century science, see Daniels, *American Science*, 66–67, 75–77.

37. *Charlotte Observer*, 14 May 1875; *Raleigh News*, 5 December 1874; communication from C. H. Brogden et al., in *Raleigh News*, 6 December 1874.

38. "Huxley, Darwin, and Tyndall," in *S&W*, 63, 68. Although he rejected the Darwinian view of the origin of life, Clingman was not a proponent of biblical literalism. He accepted geological evidence that life on earth had developed gradually over a period of millions of years and that simpler organisms had appeared much earlier than more sophisticated ones.

39. "Follies of the Positive Philosophers," in *S&W*, appendix, 4.

40. *Salisbury Carolina Watchman*, in *Asheville Citizen*, 11 July 1878; *Elizabeth City Economist*, 8 October 1878; communication from "F. D. W.," in *Raleigh News*, 28 June 1878; *Raleigh Observer*, 2 October 1878.

41. For the growing acceptance of Darwinism among scientists and liberal theologians in the late nineteenth century, see Hofstadter, *Social Darwinism*, chapter 1.

42. Gaines M. Foster, *Ghosts of the Confederacy: Defeat, the Lost Cause, and the Emergence of the New South, 1865 to 1913* (New York: Oxford University Press, 1987), 80. On the relationship between the New South creed and the cult of the Lost Cause, see also Gaston, *New South Creed*, 153–86. For an interpretation that emphasizes the discontinuities between the two belief systems, see Charles Reagan Wilson, *Baptized in Blood: The Religion of the Lost Cause, 1865–1920* (Athens: University of Georgia Press, 1980), 79–99.

43. "Davidson College Address," in *S&W*, 47–49. Reaction to the address, although limited to the Charlotte newspapers, was highly favorable. The *Charlotte Southern Home*, for example, characterized it as a "masterly effort" and a "magnificent specimen of word painting" (30 June 1873). See also the laudatory comments in *Charlotte Southern Home*, 14 July 1873; *Charlotte Observer*, 26 June 1873; *Charlotte Democrat*, 1 July 1873.

44. "Speech Delivered at the Charlotte Centennial," 20 May 1875, in *S&W*, 111–12.

45. *New York Tribune*, in *Asheville Citizen*, 3 June 1875; *Raleigh News*, 27 May 1873; *Our Living and Our Dead* 3 (August 1875): 165–69; Ray M. Atchison, "*Our Living and Our Dead:* A Post-Bellum North Carolina Magazine of Literature and History," *NCHR* 40 (1963): 423–33.

46. [Cornelia Phillips Spencer?], "The Historical Society," *University Magazine* 2 (October 1878): 85; *Raleigh News*, 8 June 1873.

47. *Wilmington Star*, 3, 8, 25 April 1875; *Charlotte Observer*, 12 May 1875. For Clingman's involvement in efforts to revive the state historical society, see *Charlotte Democrat*, 5 July 1870; "Official Proceedings of the First Meeting of the North Carolina Historical Society," *Our Living and Our Dead* 3 (July 1875): 62–65.

48. "Religious and Popular Orators: An Address Delivered at the Commencement of the University of the South," 5 August 1875, in *S&W*, 38–39.

49. Theodore Kingsbury, in *Our Living and Our Dead* 3 (October 1875): 548; *Raleigh News*, 9 September 1875. The remarks of Bradley and Carpenter can be found in *Raleigh News*, 7, 9 September 1875. For the address's publication in the *New York Tribune*, see *Raleigh News*, 10 August 1875.

50. The quotation is from *Raleigh News*, 7 September 1875.

51. "Religious and Popular Orators," in *S&W*, 38.

52. *S&W*, 1, 4. A North Carolinian who discussed the book with Clingman shortly before its publication predicted that it would serve "as a sort of political text book for our younger men." See communication from "S," in *Raleigh Observer*, 27 May 1877.

53. *S&W*, 4; review in *Nation*, 6 September 1877, 155. The phrase "brief-for-the-defense approach" is from Thomas J. Pressly, *Americans Interpret Their Civil War* (New York: Free Press, 1962), 113.

54. *S&W*, 572.

55. Ibid., 566–67, 572.

56. Ibid., 570–71. For Davis as a symbol of the Lost Cause, see Wilson, *Baptized in Blood*, 25, 50–51; Pressly, *Americans Interpret Their Civil War*, 109–10. It is interesting that the three villains in Clingman's book—Davis, Buchanan, and Andrew Johnson—were all fellow Democrats. Republicans like Charles Sumner and William H. Seward escaped severe criticism. Indeed, the diatribe that Clingman delivered against Sumner shortly after his caning by Preston Brooks in 1856 was the only major congressional speech omitted from his book.

57. *S&W*, 230.

58. Ibid., 514, 564.

59. Ibid., 572–73.

60. *Raleigh News*, 17 July 1877; communication from "Branch's Brigade," in *Raleigh Observer*, 15 August 1877; *Wilmington Star*, 24 August 1877. See also *Raleigh Observer*, 13 July 1877; *Charlotte Observer*, 18 July 1877; *Charlotte Democrat*, 20 July 1877; *Burke Blade* and communication from "H," in *Raleigh Observer*, 24 July, 1 August 1877. Years later, Theodore Kingsbury of the *Wilmington Star* characterized the book as "the best collection of speeches and addresses . . . issued by a native of our State." See *Raleigh News and Observer*, 25 October 1908.

61. *Raleigh News*, 17 July 1877.

62. Ibid., *Raleigh Observer*, 13 July 1877. For the relationship between the Lost Cause mentality and postwar social tensions, see Foster, *Ghosts of the Confederacy*, 6, 79–87; Wilson, *Baptized in Blood*, chapter 4.

63. Communication from "S," in *Raleigh Observer*, 27 May 1877; *Wilmington Star*, 24 August 1877.

16. An Old Dog Who Has Lost His Teeth

1. The quoted phrase is from Mark Mayo Boatner III, *Civil War Dictionary* (New York: David McKay, 1959), 159.

2. Terry L. Seip, *The South Returns to Congress: Men, Economic Measures, and Intersectional Relationships, 1869–1879* (Baton Rouge: Louisiana State University Press, 1983), 171–218.

3. "Scheme of National Currency," communication to Simeon Draper, 8 October 1849, in *S&W*, 574–79; TLC, *To the Voters of N. Carolina* (Asheville: n.p., 1868), 6.

4. *S&W*, 580; Seip, *South Returns to Congress*, 187–88. The essay, dated 1 November 1873, appears in *S&W*, 580–87. In an editorial note, Clingman remarked that "the managers of the paper" to which he submitted the essay "declined to insert it" when he presented it to them in 1873.

5. *S&W*, 583–85.

6. Ibid., 586–87.

7. TLC interview with *New York Herald*, 27 September 1875, in *Raleigh News*, 6 October 1875; Seip, *South Returns to Congress*, 189–94, 201–2. The abbreviated version of the interview published in *S&W*, 587–92, does not contain Clingman's concluding remarks regarding the prospects of the Democratic party in the presidential election.

8. TLC interview with *New York Herald*, in *S&W*, 589.

9. Ibid., 590–91; *Raleigh Constitution*, 30 September 1875.

10. *Raleigh News*, 3, 6 October 1875; William D. Kelley to TLC, in *Raleigh News*, 3 October 1875. The characterization of Kelley is from *DAB*, s.v. "Kelley, William Darrah." For Carey's role in the soft-money movement, see Irwin Unger, *The Greenback Era: A Social and Political History of American Finance, 1865–1879* (Princeton: Princeton University Press, 1964), 50–59.

11. The Democratic platform can be found in *Charlotte Observer*, 18 June 1876. Clingman's characterization of the platform appears in the same issue of the *Observer*. For the heterogeneous character of the North Carolina Democrats and their preference "to attack

Republican misrule rather than put forth specific policies of their own," see Alan Bruce Bromberg, "'Pure Democracy and White Supremacy': The Redeemer Period in North Carolina, 1876–1894" (Ph.D. diss., University of Virginia, 1977), 5–6; Jerry Lee Cross, "Political Metamorphosis: An Historical Profile of the Democratic Party in North Carolina, 1800–1892" (Ph.D. diss., State University of New York at Binghamton, 1975), 162–63.

12. Democratic platform, in *Charlotte Observer,* 18 June 1876.

13. *New York Herald,* 23 June 1876. Interviews with Clingman and the other members of the North Carolina delegation regarding prospective Democratic presidential candidates can be found in the same issue of the *Herald.* For the views of North Carolinians on Tilden, see also *New York Herald,* 27 May 1876; *Raleigh News,* 5 July 1876. The *News* claimed that Thomas A. Hendricks had been the early favorite in North Carolina but that by April "the tide began to turn toward Tilden" on account of "his unrivalled capabilities of winning in the fight."

14. *Official Proceedings of the National Democratic Convention* (St. Louis: Woodward, Tiernan & Hale, 1876), 144–46; *New York Herald,* 27 May 1876. For Clingman's vote, see his interview with the *New York Star,* in *Raleigh Observer,* 29 January 1878. Clingman most likely voted for Hancock out of a belief that the nomination of a Union general would defuse the "bloody shirt" issue that Republicans had effectively used against the Northern Democrats in previous campaigns. See "Remarks of Gen. Clingman," in *Asheville Citizen,* 1 July 1880.

15. "Speech Delivered at Hendersonville, North Carolina," 12 September 1876, in *S&W,* 612. Clingman's speech was printed in the *Asheville Citizen* and distributed as a campaign tract. The *Raleigh News* characterized it as "an able address . . . [that] merits a wide circulation among those who need enlightenment upon the great issues of the day" (26 September 1876). For his address at Mills Springs in Polk County, see *Charlotte Observer,* 4 November 1876. The *Observer* described that address as "a powerful speech . . . one of his best efforts."

16. *New York Tribune,* 3 August 1876; *Charlotte Observer,* 4 November 1876; *New York Herald,* 24 October 1876; *Wilmington Star,* 7 November 1876.

17. *Raleigh News,* 8 November 1876. For the election results, see John L. Cheney, ed., *North Carolina Government, 1585–1979: A Narrative and Statistical History* (Raleigh: North Carolina Department of the Secretary of State, 1981), 1332–33, 1402–3; *Raleigh Observer,* 2 January 1877. For the use of Reconstruction issues by Vance and his supporters, see Sandra Porter Babb, "The Battle of the Giants: The Gubernatorial Election of 1876 in North Carolina" (master's thesis, University of North Carolina at Chapel Hill, 1970), 51–68. Clingman would later point to Vance's disappointing showing as evidence of his unpopularity. An argument can be made, however, that he faced tougher competition than the other candidates on the Democratic ticket. Settle, the scion of a prominent North Carolina family, was "a handsome man of magnetic personality" and a "well-informed and persuasive debater." See Otto Olsen, "North Carolina: An Incongruous Presence," in Olsen, ed., *Reconstruction and Redemption in the South* (Baton Rouge: Louisiana State University Press, 1980), 193; Jeffrey J. Crow, "Thomas Settle Jr., Reconstruction, and the Memory of the Civil War," *Journal of Southern History* 62 (1996): 716–26.

18. The standard account of the crisis of 1876–77 is C. Vann Woodward, *Reunion and*

Reaction: The Compromise of 1877 and the End of Reconstruction (Boston: Little, Brown, 1951). Woodward's argument that the crisis was resolved through a bargain between Hayes and conservative Southern Democrats is challenged in Allan Peskin, "Was There a Compromise of 1877?" *Journal of American History* 60 (1963): 63–75, and Michael Les Benedict, "Southern Democrats in the Crisis of 1876–1877: A Reconsideration of *Reunion and Reaction,*" *Journal of Southern History* 46 (1980): 489–524.

19. *New York Herald,* 24 October 1876; Thomas D. Johnston to Zebulon B. Vance, 21 November 1876, Zebulon Baird Vance Papers, SHC; *Raleigh Observer,* 23 November 1876; *Raleigh News,* 23 November 1876.

20. *Raleigh Observer,* 23 November 1876; *Raleigh News,* 23 November 1876.

21. The quotations are from Allan Nevins, *Abram S. Hewitt* (New York: Octagon Books, 1967), 334; Irving Katz, *August Belmont: A Political Biography* (New York: Columbia University Press, 1968), 228. See also Benedict, "Southern Democrats in the Crisis of 1876–1877," 497–502, 506–10. Democrats expected that the swing vote on the commission would come from Supreme Court Justice David Davis, an independent. Davis, who had just been elected to the U.S. Senate, refused to serve on the commission. His replacement, Justice Joseph P. Bradley, voted with the Republicans.

22. TLC interview with *New York Star,* in *Raleigh Observer,* 29 January 1878. Similar remarks can be found in his interview with *New York World,* in *Raleigh Observer,* 1 December 1878.

23. "An Open Letter to the Congress of the United States," in *S&W,* 614, 618. The *New York Tribune,* 24 February 1877, notes that the letter was originally published in the *Washington (D.C.) Union.* According to Clingman, there would be no danger of the life-tenured electors becoming an "oligarchy," because they would serve for only one week a year and because their advanced ages would guarantee an annual turnover of twenty or thirty electors.

24. *Raleigh News,* 25 February 1877; *New York Tribune,* 24 February 1877. Clingman's proposal was briefly noted in *Charlotte Observer,* 27 February 1877; *Raleigh Observer,* 25 March 1877; *Charlotte Democrat,* in *Raleigh Observer,* 25 March 1877.

25. Bromberg, "Redeemer Period," 7–8; *Raleigh News,* 12 December 1876.

26. *Raleigh News,* 12 December 1876; communication from TLC, 13 January 1877, ibid., 18 January 1877.

27. Communication from TLC, 13 January 1877, and editorial, in *Raleigh News,* 18 January 1877.

28. The account in this and the following two paragraphs is based on the recollections in "Letter of Gen. Clingman on Political Parties," in *Asheville News,* 18 July 1882.

29. For the date of Clingman's visit to Hayes, see diary of John Hill Wheeler, 16 July 1877, SHC, microfilm. For newspaper comments about the similarity between the two executive orders, see Charles Richard Williams, *The Life of Rutherford Birchard Hayes,* 2 vols. (Boston: Houghton Mifflin, 1914), 2:79–80. The two documents are reprinted in Williams's book.

30. TLC interview with *New York Star,* in *Raleigh Observer,* 29 January 1878. For the feud between Hayes and Conking, see Ari Hoogenboom, *Outlawing the Spoils: A History of the Civil Service Reform Movement, 1865–1883* (Urbana: University of Illinois Press, 1961), 155–67.

31. *Raleigh News,* 26 April 1878; *Raleigh Observer,* 27 April 1878.

32. Communication from "H" [Edward J. Hale], in *Raleigh Observer,* 2 May 1878. On 17 May the House of Representatives appointed a committee under Clarkson N. Potter to inquire into the alleged frauds in Florida and Louisiana. The Potter Committee found abundant evidence of election tampering but implicated Democrats as well as Republicans in the wrongdoing. See *Raleigh News,* 18 May 1878; Ari Hoogenboom, *The Presidency of Rutherford B. Hayes* (Lawrence: University Press of Kansas, 1988), 71–74.

33. For the rivalry between Vance and Merrimon, see Bromberg, "Redeemer Period," 25–30. Merrimon's letter announcing his candidacy for reelection can be found in *Raleigh News,* 8 June 1878. The *Raleigh Observer* was the leading editorial supporter of Merrimon, while the *Raleigh News, Asheville Citizen,* and *Charlotte Observer* were among the most notable advocates of Vance. Some papers, like the *Charlotte Democrat* and the *Elizabeth City Economist,* remained neutral.

34. *Elizabeth City Economist,* 13 June 1878; *Charlotte Democrat,* 21 June 1878; *Wilmington Star* (quoting communication from Raleigh correspondent of *Norfolk Virginian*), in *Raleigh News,* 4 July 1878.

35. The quotations in this and the following paragraph are from the interview with TLC, in *Raleigh Observer,* 20 June 1878.

36. *Raleigh News,* 22 June 1878. See also *Asheville Citizen,* 27 June 1878.

37. T. J. Boykin to Zebulon B. Vance, 25 June 1878, Vance Papers; *Charlotte Observer,* 22 June 1878; *Raleigh News,* 25 June 1878.

38. The "interview" was first published in *Raleigh News,* 25 June 1878. It subsequently appeared in *Charlotte Observer,* 28 June 1878, and *Raleigh Observer,* 17 July 1878. The quotations in the following paragraphs are from the version published in the *Raleigh Observer.* Clingman's claim about Vance's authorship appears in his communication, 10 July 1878, in *Raleigh Observer,* 13 July 1878.

39. *Raleigh News,* 14 July 1878; communication from TLC, 10 July 1878, in *Raleigh Observer,* 13 July 1878.

40. Communication from TLC, 10 July 1878, in *Raleigh Observer,* 13 July 1878.

41. *Raleigh News,* 14 July 1878. See also ibid., 16, 18, 23 July 1878; *Asheville Citizen,* 19 July 1878.

42. *Raleigh News,* 18 July 1878; *Asheville Citizen,* 25 July 1878. On 14 July the *News* reported that Clingman's letter had been "printed and circulated as a Senatorial campaign document throughout the State."

43. *Asheville Pioneer,* in *Asheville Citizen,* 11 July 1878; *Charlotte Observer* and *Greensboro Patriot,* in *Raleigh News,* 16 July 1878. The *Asheville Pioneer* denounced Merrimon for the "ingratitude" displayed toward Republicans during his six years in the U.S. Senate (in *Charlotte Observer,* 11 August 1878). See also *Charlotte Democrat,* 24 January 1879. For the prevalence of independent candidates in 1878, see Bromberg, "Redeemer Period," 33–38; *Charlotte Democrat,* 5, 12, 19 July 1878; *Raleigh Observer,* 6 July 1878; *Asheville Citizen,* 18 July 1878.

44. Communication from TLC, 10 July 1878, in *Raleigh Observer,* 13 July 1878; *Raleigh News,* 14 July 1878.

45. Communication from TLC, 18 July 1878, in *Raleigh Observer,* 21 July 1878. Clingman claimed that by endorsing Vance for reelection in 1864 he had prevented the Democrats from nominating their own candidate—a move he said would surely have thrown Vance into the arms of Holden.

46. *Raleigh News,* 24 July 1878; *Wadesboro Pee Dee Herald,* in *Raleigh News,* 4 August 1878; communication from "G. E. M.," in *Raleigh Observer,* 30 July 1878. See also communications from "Calypso" and "W. A. P.," in *Raleigh Observer,* 24, 28 July 1878; *Hendersonville Courier, Salisbury Carolina Watchman, Charlotte Observer,* in *Asheville Citizen,* 8 August 1878.

47. TLC to *Raleigh Observer,* in *New York Times,* 18 July 1878; interview with TLC, in *Washington (D.C.) Post,* 26 July 1878. For Southern newspaper reaction to the senatorial contest, see *Norfolk Virginian* and *Mobile (Ala.) Register,* in *Raleigh News,* 4 July 1878; *Atlanta Constitution, Augusta (Ga.) Chronicle,* and *Galveston (Tex.) News,* in *Charlotte Observer,* 7, 30 July, 30 October 1878; *New Orleans (La.) Democrat,* in *Raleigh News,* 5 December 1878.

48. Interview with TLC, in *Washington (D.C.) Post,* 26 July 1878.

49. *Charlotte Observer,* 30 July 1878; *Concord (N.C.) Register,* in *Asheville Citizen,* 15 August 1878.

50. Augustus S. Merrimon to D. Frank Caldwell, 3 August 1878, David Franklin Caldwell Papers, SHC; *Charlotte Democrat,* 9 August 1878. For the number of independents elected, see *Raleigh Observer,* 3 August 1878. For the number of legislative candidates pledged to Vance and their fate in the general election, see *Raleigh News,* 20 July 1878; communication from "Senex," in *Raleigh Observer,* 30 August 1878.

51. For Clingman's remarks about his candidacy, see *Raleigh Observer,* 21 November 1878. For the "dark horse" characterization and the distribution of his book among members of the general assembly, see *Charlotte Observer,* in *Asheville Citizen,* 21 November 1878; *Raleigh News,* 17 November 1878.

52. TLC interview with *New York World,* in *Raleigh Observer,* 1 December 1878; Merrimon interview, ibid., 25 December 1878.

53. Augustus S. Merrimon to D. Frank Caldwell, 11 December 1878, Caldwell Papers; *Raleigh Observer,* 25 December 1878, 14 January 1879.

54. *Charlotte Democrat,* 24 January 1879; communication from "W. H. M.," in *Raleigh Observer* 16 January 1879; *Charlotte Observer,* 17 January 1879.

55. *Charlotte Observer,* 7 July 1878.

56. According to the *Raleigh News,* the majority of counties had instructed their Democratic candidates to stand by the caucus nominee (20 July 1878).

17. The Mahone of North Carolina

1. Interview with TLC, in *New York Tribune,* 18 March 1879.

2. The quotations in this and the following paragraph are from the interview with TLC, in *New York Herald,* 22 November 1879.

3. *Raleigh Observer,* 25 November 1879; *Asheville Citizen,* 4 December 1879.

4. Communications from "H" [Edward J. Hale], in *Raleigh Observer,* 4, 20 May 1879; diary of John Hill Wheeler, 17 May 1879, SHC, microfilm. For the rumor that he had sailed for Europe, see also *Asheville Citizen,* 15 May 1879.

5. Wheeler diary, 17 December 1873; TLC interview with *New York World,* in *Raleigh Observer,* 1 December 1878; *Raleigh Observer,* 15 October 1878.

6. *Concord (N.C.) Sun,* in *Raleigh News,* 19 November 1879; Wheeler diary, 17 May 1879; *Raleigh Observer,* 26 June, 3 August 1879; *Asheville Citizen,* 7 August 1879.

7. *Asheville Citizen,* 7 August, 11 September, 9 October 1879; William E. Hidden to Thomas A. Edison, 27 August 1879, Document File, ENHS. For Clingman's attempt to interest Edison in purchasing his zircons, see chapter 18.

8. Communication from "Correspondent," in *Raleigh News,* 26 September 1879.

9. Wheeler diary, 18 November 1879; communications from Washington correspondent, in *Asheville Citizen,* 11 December 1879, 5 February, 3 June 1880.

10. *International Dictionary of Medicine and Biology* (New York: John Wiley & Sons, 1986), 1914–15. Possibly, the neuralgia had first afflicted Clingman in the late winter and early spring of 1877. He was ill for several weeks during that period, although there is no evidence of the nature of his complaint. See National Bank of Commerce to TLC, 21 March 1877, Clingman and Puryear Family Papers, SHC; Wheeler diary, 7 April 1877.

11. TLC, *The Tobacco Remedy* (New York: Orange Judd, 1885), 12–13. Blistering was popularized in the late eighteenth century by Benjamin Rush, who believed that disease resulted from the accumulation of bodily poisons that could be removed through bleeding, purging, and blistering. Rush's teachings had long since fallen into disfavor among orthodox physicians, but the medicines available to them were, in many cases, no more effective than the treatments pursued by self-practitioners like Clingman. See James Bordley III and A. McGehee Harvey, *Two Centuries of American Medicine, 1776–1976* (Philadelphia: W. B. Saunders, 1976), 34–42.

12. TLC, *Tobacco Remedy,* 6–9. For the development of the idea of self-limited disease, see Bordley and Harvey, *American Medicine,* 36.

13. For Clingman's return to North Carolina, see *Asheville Citizen,* 24 June 1880. The *Citizen* reported that he had "spent the past six months in Washington and New York."

14. Interview with TLC, in *New York Herald,* 11 June 1880.

15. Interviews with TLC, in *New York Herald,* 22 November 1879, 11 June 1880; TLC interview with *Washington (D.C.) Star,* in *Raleigh Observer,* 5 December 1879. For Grant's status as front runner for the Republican nomination, see William B. Hesseltine, *Ulysses S. Grant: Politician* (New York: Dodd, Mead, 1935; New York: Frederick Ungar, 1957), 431–36; Herbert J. Clancy, *The Presidential Election of 1880* (Chicago: Loyola University Press, 1958), 45–51.

16. *Raleigh Observer,* 18 June 1880; *Asheville Citizen,* 1 July 1880.

17. "Remarks of Gen. Clingman," in *Asheville Citizen,* 1 July 1880. Selections from his speech were also published in *Raleigh News,* 3 July 1880.

18. Communication from "W. M. D.," in *Raleigh News,* 11 September 1880. The Bland-Allison Silver Coinage Act, enacted in 1878, required the federal government to purchase from $2 million to $4 million worth of silver each month and then to coin it into silver dollars. However, because of the hard-money policies pursued by the successive secretaries of the treasury, the act did not result in an appreciable increase in the money supply. See John D. Hicks, *The Populist Revolt: A History of the Farmer's Alliance and the People's Party* (Minneapolis: University of Minnesota Press, 1931), 305–6.

19. Communication from "H" [Edward J. Hale], in *Charlotte Democrat,* 12 November 1880; *New York Tribune,* 2 November 1880; *New York Times,* 2 November 1880; *New York Herald,* 2 November 1880. For Clingman's departure for Washington in mid-

September, see TLC to Jane P. Kerr, 11 September 1880, Thomas L. Clingman Papers, Duke; *Asheville Citizen,* 16 September 1880; Wheeler diary, 16 September 1880. The "business engagements" to which Clingman referred involved the upcoming session of the Supreme Court of the District of Columbia, which was scheduled to rule on his patent application for an electric light. See chapter 18.

20. Wheeler diary, 16 September 1880; Clancy, *Presidential Election of 1880,* 242–43. In North Carolina, Hancock received 124,746 votes, compared to 115,879 for Garfield. See John L. Cheney, ed., *North Carolina Government, 1585–1979* (Raleigh: North Carolina Department of the Secretary of State, 1980), 1333.

21. Wheeler diary, 5 November 1880; *Asheville Citizen,* 4 November 1880; *Raleigh Republican,* 12 November 1880; Cheney, *North Carolina Government,* 1332–33, 1402–4.

22. For the sale of the Western North Carolina Railroad, see Elgiva D. Watson, "The Election Campaign of Governor Jarvis, 1880: A Study of the Issues," *NCHR* 48 (1971): 281–86; Margaret W. Morris, "The Completion of the Western North Carolina Railroad: Politics of Concealment," *NCHR* 52 (1975): 256–82. Clingman reportedly remarked that he had "no doubt but there is a fraud in the sale of the Western North Carolina Railroad" (*Asheville News,* 20 October 1880).

23. *New York Tribune,* 8 January 1881; *Louisville (Ky.) Courier-Journal,* in *Goldsboro Messenger,* 24 February 1881; *Raleigh News and Observer,* 21 May 1881.

24. Communications from "H" [Edward J. Hale], in *Charlotte Democrat,* 25 March, 27 May 1881; Jane Puryear Kerr to Sarah Puryear Jarratt, 29 August 1881, Jarratt-Puryear Family Papers, Duke.

25. For Clingman's return to Asheville, see *Raleigh News and Observer,* 18 June 1881. The only full-length biography of Mahone is Nelson Morehouse Blake, *William Mahone of Virginia: Soldier and Political Insurgent* (Richmond: Garrett & Massie, 1935). For the Readjustor period, see pp. 147–274.

26. During the session of 1879 the Democrats had repudiated the special-tax bonds used to finance the Western North Carolina Railroad and had drastically scaled down the state's other antebellum and postwar debts. Thus, even if Clingman had been inclined toward repudiation, the debt was not available as an issue around which to organize an independent movement in North Carolina. See B. U. Ratchford, "The Adjustment of the North Carolina Public Debt, 1879–1883," *NCHR* 10 (1933): 157–67.

27. *Raleigh News and Observer,* 29 June 1881; *Asheville Citizen,* 1 September 1881. The quotations in this and the following paragraphs are from the version of the essay published in the *Citizen.*

28. For Riddleberger, see Blake, *William Mahone,* 213n, 219. Despite the solid backing of Riddleberger by the Republicans, the Democrats in the U.S. Senate blocked his nomination as sergeant-at-arms by refusing to bring it to a vote.

29. Daniel J. Whitener, "North Carolina Prohibition Election of 1881 and Its Aftermath," *NCHR* 11 (1934): 71–93.

30. Ibid., 82–84; *Raleigh News and Observer,* 9 August 1881.

31. Whitener, "Prohibition Election," 80; communication from Raleigh correspondent of *New York Times,* in *Raleigh News and Observer,* 24 November 1881; *Charlotte Observer,* in *Asheville News,* 28 June 1882.

32. For Garfield's disabilities and the ensuing issue of presidential inability, see John D. Feerick, *From Failing Hands: The Story of Presidential Succession* (New York: Fordham

University Press, 1965), 133–39; Ruth C. Silva, *Presidential Succession* (New York: Greenwood Press, 1968), 52–57.

33. The quotation is from Feerick, *From Failing Hands*, 133.

34. TLC interview with *New York Express*, in *Raleigh News and Observer*, 23 August 1881; communication from TLC to *New York Herald*, 31 August 1881, in *Raleigh News and Observer*, 6 September 1881.

35. TLC interview with *New York Express*, in *Raleigh News and Observer*, 23 August 1881; communication from TLC to *New York Herald*, 31 August 1881, in *Raleigh News and Observer*, 6 September 1881.

36. Communication from Kenneth Rayner, in *New York Herald*, 29 August 1881; communication from "X. Y." and editorial comments, in *Raleigh News and Observer*, 23 August 1881.

37. Communication from TLC to *New York Herald*, 31 August 1881, in *Raleigh News and Observer*, 6 September 1881. Ironically, Clingman's pride in his memory proved stronger than the memory itself. The presidential succession bill had not been introduced in Congress in 1789, as he asserted, but a year later (Feerick, *From Failing Hands*, 57–62).

38. *Asheville Citizen*, 22 September 1881.

39. *Raleigh News and Observer*, 14 October 1881.

40. Communication from "C. W. H.," in *Goldsboro Messenger*, 31 October 1881; *Asheville Citizen*, 10, 17 November 1881, [day obscured] July 1882; *New York Herald*, in *Greensboro North State*, 1 December 1881; *Goldsboro Messenger*, 19, 23 January 1882.

41. *Raleigh News and Observer*, 18 January, 3 May 1882; Justus D. Doenecke, *The Presidencies of James A. Garfield and Chester A. Arthur* (Lawrence: Regents Press of Kansas, 1981), 114–15; *DNCB*, s.v. "Johnston, William"; "Price, Charles."

42. *Charlotte Observer*, in *Charlotte Home and Democrat*, 27 January 1882; *Washington (D.C.) Star*, in *Raleigh News and Observer*, 10 February 1882; *Asheville Citizen*, 15 February 1882; *Goldsboro Messenger*, 9 February 1882.

43. Communication from TLC, 17 February 1882, in *Washington (D.C.) Post*, 20 February 1882; *Salisbury Carolina Watchman*, 23 February 1882. See also *Raleigh News and Observer*, 22 February 1882. The *New York Tribune* argued that a substantial part of Clingman's dissatisfaction with the party system resulted "from his own enforced retirement from active and prominent participation in public affairs. The shelved politician is apt to be critical always, and sometimes even cynical" (21 February 1882).

44. At a state convention held on 7 June 1882, the Liberals adopted a platform calling for the restoration of local self-government, opposition to prohibition, and a liberal system of public education. Republican Oliver H. Dockery was nominated for congressman-at-large, and Democrat George N. Folk was selected as the party's candidate for Supreme Court judge. See *Raleigh News and Observer*, 8 June 1882; *Charlotte Home and Democrat*, 9 June 1882; *Raleigh State Journal*, in *Greensboro North State*, 22 June 1882; Whitener, "Prohibition Election," 88–89. Despite the similarity in names, there was no relationship between the North Carolina Liberal party of 1882 and the national Liberal Republican party of 1872. Indeed, most of the support in North Carolina for the earlier party had come from regular Democrats.

45. "Letter of Gen. Clingman on Political Parties," in *Asheville News*, 18 July 1882. The quotations in the following paragraphs are from Clingman's letter.

46. *Oxford Torchlight*, in *Raleigh News and Observer*, 28 July 1882; *Wilmington Star*,

4 August 1882; *Raleigh News and Observer,* 8 August 1882. See also *Asheville Citizen,* 30 August 1882. Of the leading Liberals, only Charles Price, at age thirty-six, could legitimately claim to be a "young" man.

47. *Charlotte Observer,* 8 August 1882. The *Observer* estimated the number attending at two thousand. The Democrats claimed that the rally attracted between five hundred and eight hundred spectators, of whom a substantial number were blacks and revenue officials. See *Raleigh News and Observer,* 8 August 1882; *Salisbury Carolina Watchman,* 10 August 1882; *Greensboro Patriot,* in *Charlotte Home and Democrat,* 11 August 1882.

48. Remarks of Isaac Young, in *Charlotte Observer,* 8 August 1882; *Greensboro Patriot,* in *Charlotte Home and Democrat,* 11 August 1882. The quotation about the "Vance dynasty" is from the account presented by Charles R. Jones, in *Charlotte Observer,* 24 April 1886. Jones's recollection of events is supported by a communication from a correspondent of the *Raleigh News and Observer,* who reported that Clingman was overheard saying after the meeting, "well, upon the whole we have managed very badly. If we continue to disagree in this way . . . the Vance dynasty will remain in power" (8 August 1882).

49. *Raleigh News and Observer,* 8 August 1882; *Greensboro Patriot,* in *Charlotte Home and Democrat,* 11 August 1882; *Reply of Gen. Clingman to "Truth"* (Asheville: n.p., 1882).

50. For the race issue, see *Raleigh News and Observer,* 29 August 1882; *Goldsboro Messenger,* 14 September, 26 October 1882. For the bond issue, see *Raleigh News and Observer,* 16 July 1882; *Asheville News,* 23 August 1882.

51. *Raleigh News and Observer,* 8, 18 August 1882; *A Card from William M. Cocke Jr.* (Asheville: n.p., 1882); *Asheville Citizen,* 27 September 1882.

52. *Asheville Citizen,* 27 September 1882.

53. Ibid., 14 October 1882.

54. *Raleigh News and Observer,* 3 May 1882. In deference to their Republican allies, Liberal candidates in the congressional and legislative races formally ran on Liberal-Republican "coalition" tickets. In districts with heavy Republican majorities, the Liberals refrained from making nominations, allowing the Republicans to run under their own name.

55. Communication from "R. O. P.," in *Greensboro North State,* 5 October 1882; *Greensboro North State,* in *Raleigh News and Observer,* 23 September 1882.

56. Communication from "X," in *Raleigh News and Observer,* 18 October 1882; *Raleigh State Journal,* 26 October, 9 November 1882; *Salisbury Carolina Watchman,* 2 November 1882; *Asheville Citizen,* 4 November 1882. For Clingman's complaints about lumbago, see *Salisbury Carolina Watchman,* 2 November 1882. It is likely that he was actually suffering from sciatica, a form of neuralgia that would afflict him even more severely the following year. See chapter 18.

57. *Charlotte Home and Democrat,* 1 December 1882; *Asheville News,* 20 December 1882. In the second congressional district, which had a large Republican majority, the Liberals refrained from making a nomination, and Republican James E. O'Hara ran unopposed. The other successful opposition candidates were Walter F. Pool in the first district and Tyre York in the seventh district.

58. *Raleigh News and Observer,* 29 August 1882. The Republican *Greensboro North State* ruefully acknowledged the effectiveness of racial appeals among lower-class whites. "To rally the last of these poor, ignorant electors to the polls," it remarked, "it is only needed to resort to the oft-repeated cry of 'nigger rule,' 'nigger equality,' [and] 'amalgamation'" (27 July 1882).

59. Communication from "Qui Vive," in *Raleigh News and Observer*, 8 August 1882. Liberals were, in fact, elected in 1882 from the normally Democratic counties of Cherokee, Jackson, and Transylvania.

60. *Asheville Citizen*, 4 November 1882; *Greensboro Patriot*, 24 November 1882; *Raleigh News and Observer*, 26 November 1882.

61. Wheeler died on 7 December 1882. The following day, Clingman presided over a memorial meeting attended by Senators Vance and Ransom and other prominent North Carolinians. See *Washington (D.C.) Post*, 9 December 1882; *Raleigh News and Observer*, 15 December 1882.

18. Benefactor of the Human Race

1. *Raleigh News and Observer*, 8 August 1882, 8 September 1883.
2. *Asheville Citizen*, 11 October 1884; *Raleigh Register*, 15 October 1884.
3. Remarks of TLC, in *A Record of the Proceedings of the Alumni Association of the University of North Carolina at the Centennial Celebration* ([Chapel Hill?]: Alumni Association, 1889), 160. The following account of Clingman's involvement in incandescent lighting is based, in part, on Thomas E. Jeffrey, "Thomas Lanier Clingman and the Invention of the Electric Light: A Forgotten Episode," *Carolina Comments* 32 (1984): 71–82.
4. According to Clingman, before the discovery of the Henderson County deposits, zircons "were regarded as such rare and curious minerals that large prices were paid for the crystals." See remarks of TLC, in *Proceedings of the Alumni Association*, 160.
5. *Argument of T. L. Clingman . . . before the Examiners in Chief* (n.p., 1880), 4, in Application File 276,133, Records of the Patent Office, RG 241, National Archives, Washington, D.C.; TLC to Thomas A. Edison, 17 May, 8 September 1879, Document File, ENHS; Frederick Penzel, *Theatre Lighting before Electricity* (Middletown: Wesleyan University Press, 1978), 56–57, 100–101.
6. *Argument of T. L. Clingman*, 4; Robert Friedel and Paul Israel, *Edison's Electric Light: Biography of an Invention* (New Brunswick: Rutgers University Press, 1986), 7–8.
7. *Raleigh Observer*, 18 September 1878; *Raleigh News*, 20 September 1878; Friedel and Israel, *Edison's Electric Light*, 13–14, 23–26, 63, 75–76.
8. TLC to Thomas A. Edison, 26 March 1879, Document File; Edison to TLC, 27 March 1879, in *Argument of T. L. Clingman*, 5; Friedel and Israel, *Edison's Electric Light*, 8, 76–78. The major technical problem with platinum was the difficulty of raising its temperature to the incandescing point without allowing it to heat up further past the melting point. Also, platinum is a rare metal, and it would have been difficult for Edison to find sufficient quantities to produce a commercially marketable lamp.
9. Charles Batchelor Notebook, 23 March 1879, Charles Batchelor Collection, ENHS; Friedel and Israel, *Edison's Electric Light*, 78–79.
10. Thomas A. Edison to TLC, 15, 19, 28 May 1879, in *Argument of T. L. Clingman*, 5–6; TLC to Edison, 16 May [misdated 16 April], 29 May 1879, Document File.
11. TLC to Thomas A. Edison, 12 June 1879, Document File; Edison to TLC, 16 June, 31 July 1879, in *Argument of T. L. Clingman*, 6.
12. William E. Hidden to Thomas A. Edison, 31 July 1879, with draft reply by Edison, 5 August 1879, Document File.

13. TLC to Thomas A. Edison, 21 August 1879, Document File. According to the docket on this letter, Edison did not reply until 3 September.

14. William E. Hidden to Thomas A. Edison, 28 August 1879, Document File.

15. William E. Hidden to Thomas A. Edison, telegram, copy in Edison's hand, 29 August 1879, Document File. Edison's reply appears at the bottom of Hidden's telegram. For the experiments on zirconia coating, see Menlo Park Notebook, N-79-07-31, Laboratory Notebooks, ENHS, particularly the entries of 1, 10, 12, 13 August 1879.

16. Thomas A. Edison to TLC, 3 September 1879 (marginal notation on TLC to Edison, 21 August 1879), Document File; Edison to TLC, 10 September 1879, in *Argument of T. L. Clingman*, 7; TLC to Edison, 13 September 1879, Document File.

17. TLC to Thomas A. Edison, 20 November, 6 December 1879, Document File; Edison to TLC, 9 December 1879, in *Argument of T. L. Clingman*, 7.

18. Clingman's initial patent application file is not extant, but the reaction of the Patent Office is characterized in *Argument of T. L. Clingman*, 1–3, 10–11.

19. Specification, 20 March 1880, in Patent Application File 276,133.

20. *Spartanburg (S.C.) Spartan*, in *Asheville Citizen*, 25 March 1880. The correspondence with the patent examiner is in Application File 276,133. The appeal is in Case File 58, Appeals from Decision of the Commissioner of Patents, Records of the District Courts of the United States, RG 21, National Archives.

21. Examiner's Answer to Reasons of Appeal, 19 April 1880, in Case File 58. Townsend was unaware of Edison's discovery that zirconia becomes a conductor when heated to sufficiently high temperatures.

22. Thomas A. Edison, "Improvement in Electric Lights," 16 September 1879, U.S. Patent 219,628, in *Specifications and Drawings of Patents Relating to Electricity Issued by the United States Prior to July 1, 1881*, 16 vols. (Washington, D.C.: Government Printing Office, 1881), vol 1.

23. *Answer of T. L. Clingman*, 7–8.

24. Ibid., 8. Tessie and Stern had applied for their patent on 2 December 1878—one week before Edison's application. It had been granted on 4 March 1879, more than six months before Edison received his patent. See Cyprien M. Tessie du Motay and Edward Stern, "Improvement in Electric Lights," U.S. Patent 212,860, in *Specifications and Drawings of Patents Relating to Electricity* , vol 1.

25. *Answer of T. L. Clingman*, 9.

26. Decision of the Examiners-in-Chief, 27 April 1880, in Case File 58.

27. Appeal to the Commissioner of Patents, 8 May 1880; *Additional Suggestions by T. L. Clingman before the Commissioner of Patents* (n.p., 1880), 2, in Application File 276,133.

28. Decision of the Commissioner of Patents, 5 June 1880, in Case File 58.

29. TLC to the Supreme Court of the District of Columbia, 12 June 1880, in Case File 58; *New York Times*, 31 August 1880.

30. *Wilmington Star*, 6 May 1880; communication from "F," in *Asheville Citizen*, 13 May 1880. See also *Raleigh Observer*, 6 May 1880; *Greensboro North State*, 3 June 1880. According to the *Citizen's* correspondent, "Edison pretended the [zirconia] process was an entire failure, but took care to slip in and have it patented in his name."

31. *Conclusion by T. L. Clingman in Answer to the Commissioner of Patents* (n.p., 1880), 2–3, in Case File 58.

32. "In the Matter of the Application of Thomas L. Clingman for Improvement in Electric Lights," *Washington Law Reporter* 9 (26 October 1881): 678–79, in Application File 276,133.

33. Communication from "H" [Edward J. Hale], in *Charlotte Democrat,* 12 November 1880; *Asheville Citizen,* 28 October 1880. See also *Raleigh News and Observer,* 23 October 1880. For the specifications and application date of the British patent, see the clippings from *Engineer,* 10 December 1880, and *Telegraphic Journal,* 1 January 1881, in Scrapbook, Cat. 1013, Scrapbook Collection, ENHS. For the specifications and application date of the French patent, see *Brevets D'Invention,* n.s., 35, pt. 2 (1880): 148. For the issue dates of the British and French patents, see affidavit of TLC, 27 March 1883, in Application File 276,133.

34. Affidavit of TLC, 9 March 1883, in Application File 276,133.

35. Affidavit of William J. Green, 9 March 1883, in Application File 276,133. A copy of the issued patent can be found in the application file.

36. *Greensboro North State,* 6 September 1883; *Raleigh News and Observer,* 8 September 1883. See also communication from "C. W. H.," in *Goldsboro Messenger,* 10 May 1883; *Asheville Citizen,* 20 September 1883.

37. *Asheville Citizen,* 16 September 1880; *Raleigh Farmer and Mechanic,* in *Charlotte Observer,* 19 October 1883.

38. TLC to Thomas A. Edison, 6 April 1883, Document File; *Raleigh Farmer and Mechanic,* in *Charlotte Observer,* 19 October 1883. The contract with Willis, dated 27 December 1883, is summarized in Edward A. Oldham to Thomas A. Edison Company, 3 June 1939, Archivist's Files, ENHS. According to Oldham, the contract was in the possession of "an old gentleman down in North Carolina who was a grandson of General Thomas L. Clingman." Oldham may have been referring to Henry A. Jarratt, who was sixty years old at that time. For Potter and Willis, see *Trow's New York City Directory for the Year Ending May 1, 1884* (New York: Trow, 1883), 1346, 1809.

39. TLC interviews with *New York Tribune,* in *Charlotte Observer,* 11 March 1884, and in *Raleigh News and Observer,* 3 June 1884.

40. Digest of Assignments, C13:201, Records of the Patent Office; *Raleigh News and Observer,* 7 January 1886. The New York City directory for 1884–85 lists Baldwin as "president" and Miller as "vice-president" of an unnamed company located at 58 Broadway. However, there are no electric light companies listed at that address. See *Trow's New York City Directory for the Year Ending May 1, 1885* (New York: Trow, 1884), 73, 1215.

41. An excellent discussion of the various technical problems that had to be surmounted before the arc light could become a commercial success can be found in W. James King, "The Development of Electrical Technology in the Nineteenth Century: The Early Arc Light and Generator," *United States National Museum Bulletin* 228 (1962): 333–407.

42. TLC interview with *New York Tribune,* in *Charlotte Observer,* 11 March 1884. Clingman's U.S. patent of 24 April 1888, along with references to his French and German patents, can be found in Application File, Patent 381,614, Records of the Patent Office.

43. TLC to International Patent Co., Ltd., 28 Nov. 1888, Jarratt-Puryear Family Papers, Duke; William Hadden to TLC, 26 March 1890, Clingman and Puryear Family Papers, SHC.

44. *Raleigh News and Observer,* 7 January 1886, 28 December 1888. There was a grain

of truth in Clingman's complaint. By the late 1880s the electric lighting industry in the United States was, in fact, controlled by three large corporations—Edison General Electric, Thomson-Houston, and Westinghouse. The odds against an independent entrepreneur like Clingman setting up a new company to compete with them were very high. On the other hand, if any of those companies had genuinely believed in the superior qualities of Clingman's lamp, they would have attempted to purchase his patent rights rather than bribe electrical engineers to present false reports.

45. *Atlanta (Ga.) Dixie*, in *Asheville Democrat*, 24 October 1889; *Hendersonville Times*, in *Asheville Citizen*, 14 September 1887; *Asheville Citizen*, 15 December 1887, 7 April 1888; Arthur A. Bright Jr., *The Electric-Lamp Industry: Technological Change and Economic Development from 1800 to 1947* (New York: MacMillan, 1949; New York: Arno Press, 1972), 126–27.

46. Bright, *Electric-Lamp Industry*, 166–73. Unlike the invention patented by Clingman in 1883, the Nernst lamp did not combine zirconia with carbon but, instead, used rare earths such as yttrium and cerium. Nernst was able to surmount the technical problems that had bedeviled Clingman by adding a heater coil of platinum to raise the rod's temperature to the point of incandescence and a ballast of iron wire to maintain proper current flow. Ironically, the work of Welsbach also inspired Edison to reconsider his earlier attitude toward zirconia. In June 1899 he received a patent on a filament incorporating a mixture of carbon and zirconia—the same substances that Clingman had used in the 1880s (U.S. Patent 626,460). I am indebted to Paul B. Israel of the Thomas A. Edison Papers for calling Edison's patent to my attention.

47. Jerome E. Brooks, *Tobacco: Its History Illustrated by the Books, Manuscripts, and Engravings in the Library of George Arents Jr.*, 5 vols. (New York: Rosenbach, 1937–52), 1: 236–37; Brooks, *The Mighty Leaf: Tobacco through the Centuries* (Boston: Little, Brown, 1952), 36–44. Some country doctors, at least in North Carolina, were still receptive to the use of tobacco for medicinal purposes.

48. TLC, *The Tobacco Remedy* (New York: Orange Judd, 1885), 6–14; *Raleigh News and Observer*, 31 July, 16 October 1883; communication from "C. W. H.," in *Goldsboro Messenger*, 23 August 1883. Clingman's niece, whom he visited on his way to Asheville, remarked that "he looks and seems very well" (Jane P. Kerr to "my dear Crafford[?]," 22 August 1883, Jarratt-Puryear Papers). See also *Asheville Citizen*, 23 August 1883.

49. TLC, *Tobacco Remedy*, 9–11.

50. Ibid., 17–18.

51. Ibid., 17–20; *Asheville Citizen*, 14 August 1884. Between 1883 and 1885, the quantity of tobacco handled at Asheville increased from 400,000 pounds to 3.4 million pounds (*Asheville Citizen*, 14 April 1887).

52. TLC to W. H. Hale, 6 September 1884, and clipping from *Asheville Citizen*, in TLC, *Tobacco Remedy*, 20–21. A month later, Clingman followed up with another communication in which he provided additional testimonials and case histories to establish the power of tobacco to cure tubercular laryngitis, orchitis, and dropsy. He also suggested that scarlet fever, diphtheria, and other forms of throat disorders could be successfully treated with tobacco. See TLC, *Tobacco Remedy*, 23–29.

53. *Asheville Citizen*, 11 October 1884; J. S. T. Baird to TLC, ibid., 19 November 1884; *Health and Home*, in *Raleigh Register*, 19 November 1884.

54. *Asheville Citizen,* 19 November 1884; *Raleigh Farmer and Mechanic,* in *Charlotte Observer,* 30 January 1885; Brooks, *Tobacco,* 5:306. The promise to "reduce suffering 90 percent" appears in Clingman's interview with the *New York Tribune,* in *Charlotte Observer,* 6 January 1885. In *The Tobacco Remedy,* Clingman more modestly claimed that "much more than half of the bodily suffering of humanity will be prevented" if the facts about tobacco became generally known (42).

55. TLC, *Tobacco Remedy,* 42; *Charlotte Observer,* 3 February 1885; Trademark 11,909, in *Official Gazette of the United States Patent Office* 30 (1885): 453.

56. Digest of Assignments, C13:252, Records of the Patent Office; *Charlotte Observer,* 26 May 1885; William K. Boyd, *The Story of Durham: City of the New South* (Durham: Duke University Press, 1925), 61–76. See also *DNCB,* s.v. "Blackwell, William Thomas"; "Carr, Julian Shakespeare"; "Parrish, Edward James."

57. There are no references to Clingman or his company in the correspondence in the William T. Blackwell Papers, Duke, or in the Julian Shakespeare Carr Papers, SHC.

58. *New York World,* in *Raleigh News and Observer,* 12 March 1885; *New York Sun,* in *Charlotte Observer,* 15 April 1885.

59. *New York World,* in *Raleigh News and Observer,* 12 March 1885; *Health and Home,* in *Raleigh Register,* 22 April 1885; *Greensboro Patriot,* in *Charlotte Observer,* 27 May 1885.

60. *Charlotte Home and Democrat,* in *Raleigh News and Observer,* 2 August 1884; *The Clingman Tobacco Cure Company* ([Durham?]: n.p., 1885), 19.

61. The quotations are from the four-page pamphlet, *Clingman's Tobacco Remedies: The Greatest Medical Discovery of the Age* (Durham: n.p., [1885?]), NCC. One of Clingman's tobacco plasters is filed with the pamphlet. The prices of the remedies can be found in an advertisement by the company in *Charles Emerson's North Carolina Tobacco Belt Directory, 1886–1887* (Raleigh: Edwards, Broughton, 1886), 119.

62. *Asheville Citizen,* in *Charlotte Observer,* 22 April 1885; *Raleigh News and Observer,* 15 August 1885. Hale's comment can be found in the advertisement in *Tobacco Belt Directory,* 119; the druggist's endorsement appears in *Clingman's Tobacco Remedies.*

63. Bank of Durham Account Book, 1886–88, 107–8, William T. Blackwell Journal, 1886–88, 282, Blackwell Papers. In 1889 an effort was made by several Asheville businessmen, including John Evans Brown and his son W. Vance Brown, to purchase the Clingman Tobacco Cure Company. Clingman was willing to go along with the arrangement, but the prospective purchasers eventually concluded that the enterprise was "going to take more money than we first thought." The sale was never consummated. See diary of W. Vance Brown, 6, 7, 10, 14, 16, 17, 18 September, 26 October, 26 November 1889, W. Vance Brown Papers, NCDAH.

64. A few testimonials continued to be published until the end of the 1880s. The latest one I have been able to locate appears in *Asheville Citizen,* 2 May 1889.

65. The definitive study of the patent medicine business is James Harvey Young, *The Toadstool Millionaires: A Social History of Patent Medicines in America before Federal Regulation* (Princeton: Princeton University Press, 1961). Young makes only brief mention of tobacco as a curative (171). For the relationship between patent medicines and the temperance movement, see pp. 129–34. Even a cursory examination of the North Carolina newspapers will reveal the number and variety of available patent medicines. The examples mentioned in this paragraph appear in various issues of the *Asheville Citizen* for April 1887.

66. *Asheville Citizen,* 16 April 1891; [Alexander K. McClure], "The Career of T. L. Clingman" (from *Philadelphia Times,* 10 October 1896), in R. A. Brock, ed., *Southern Historical Society Papers* 24 (1896): 307.

67. [McClure], "Career of T. L. Clingman," 307. For Jarratt's debt, see TLC to Isaac A. Jarratt, 21 August 1875, Jarratt-Puryear Papers. The numerous letters written by Elizabeth Puryear Gibson to Jane Puryear Kerr during a family crisis in 1886 illuminate Clingman's role as financial adviser (Jarratt-Puryear Papers).

68. TLC to Isaac A. Jarratt, 16 March, 8 May, 19 August 1885, TLC to Jane Puryear Kerr, 31 July 1886, Jarratt-Puryear Papers.

69. Communication from "C. W. H.," in *Goldsboro Messenger,* 10 May 1883; *Asheville Citizen,* in *Raleigh Register,* 5 November 1884.

19. A Candidate for Matrimony

1. For the currency reform convention, see *Washington (D.C.) Post,* 8 February 1883; *Charlotte Observer,* 15 February 1883; communication from "C. W. H.," in *Goldsboro Messenger,* 15 February 1883. Clingman's essay on the tariff, published under the title "Protection in Parable," can be found in *Washington (D.C.) Post,* 10 February 1883. In an accompanying editorial, the *Post* noted that Clingman "has a happy faculty of illustrating his ideas on the tariff question so that plain and simple people may understand it." The essay also received favorable notice in *Goldsboro Messenger,* 19 March 1883; *Asheville Citizen,* 6 September 1883.

2. Ari Hoogenboom, *Outlawing the Spoils: A History of the Civil Service Reform Movement, 1865–1883* (Urbana: University of Illinois Press, 1961), 236–52. Initially, about 14,000 of the 130,000 federal employees were covered by the Pendleton Act.

3. *Charlotte Observer,* 1 February 1884; interview with TLC, in *New York Tribune,* 11 February 1884. The North Carolina presses were considerably less optimistic than Clingman about the prospects for reform. The *Raleigh State Chronicle* characterized his proposal as "the most improbable of all schemes" (9 February 1884). See also *Raleigh News and Observer,* 2 February 1884.

4. Interview with TLC, in *New York Tribune,* 11 February 1884. For the cotton claims, see communications from "C. W. H.," in *Goldsboro Messenger,* 17 April, 10 July 1884. Those claims related to North Carolina's efforts to seek reimbursement for five hundred bales of cotton seized by U.S. treasury agents in Georgia and New York in 1865 and 1866.

5. *Raleigh News and Observer,* 20 March, 2 May, 13 August 1884; communication from "C. W. H.," in *Goldsboro Messenger,* 24 April 1884. Clingman had refused two years earlier to endorse unequivocally the Liberal demand for a change in the system of county government.

6. Communication from "C. W. H.," in *Goldsboro Messenger,* 8 May 1884; *Asheville Citizen,* 5 June 1884.

7. *Asheville Citizen,* in *Raleigh News and Observer,* 26 July 1884. See also *Raleigh News and Observer,* 16 July, 21 August 1884; *Charlotte Observer,* 18 July 1884; *Goldsboro Messenger,* 4 August 1884; *Raleigh Register,* 6 August 1884; *Raleigh State Chronicle,* 8 November 1884.

8. *Asheville Advance,* in *Raleigh State Chronicle,* 2 August 1884; *Asheville Citizen,* in *Raleigh News and Observer,* 26 July 1884.

9. *Raleigh Register,* 6 August 1884; interview with TLC, in *Raleigh State Chronicle,* 8 November 1884. The third-party candidates that Clingman specifically mentioned were Benjamin F. Butler, the nominee of the Greenback and Anti-monopoly parties, and John P. St. John, who was running on the Prohibition ticket.

10. Returns by county for the presidential and gubernatorial elections can be found in John L. Cheney, ed., *North Carolina Government, 1585–1979* (Raleigh: North Carolina Department of the Secretary of State, 1980), 1332–33, 1404–5. For the legislative elections, see *Asheville Citizen,* 19 November 1884.

11. Communications from "Llewxam" [Maxwell], in *Raleigh News and Observer,* 28 December 1884, 1 February, 26 March 1885; *Raleigh News and Observer,* 4 January, 7 February 1885; communication from "H" [Edward J. Hale], in *Charlotte Observer,* 8 February 1885; *Goldsboro Messenger,* 9 February 1885; communication from "C. W. H.," in *Goldsboro Messenger,* 12 February 1885. The copy of Clingman's *Speeches and Writings* in the Princeton University Library bears Cleveland's signature on the flyleaf.

12. *Asheville Citizen,* 30 April 1885; TLC to Lyman C. Draper, 6, 14, 25 August 1884, 2 June 1885, Daniel Boone Papers, Series C, Lyman Copeland Draper Manuscripts, WHi. For Draper's unsuccessful efforts to write a biography of Boone, see William B. Hesseltine, *Pioneer's Mission: The Story of Lyman Copeland Draper* (Madison: State Historical Society of Wisconsin, 1954; Westport, Conn.: Greenwood Press, 1970). As Hesseltine points out, Draper was far more adept at collecting voluminous quantities of information than he was at putting pen to paper.

13. TLC to Lyman Draper, 11, 18 June 1885, Rudolph-Ney Papers, Series RR, Draper Manuscripts. For Draper's interest in Ney, see Hesseltine, *Draper,* 307–9.

14. *Asheville Citizen,* 24 July 1885. See also *S&W,* 525. As early as 1870, Clingman had publicly expressed his opinion that "President Grant has shown himself more liberal to the Southern States than the majority of his party have done." See TLC, *Address to the Citizens of North Carolina* (Raleigh: n.p., 1870), 16.

15. *Asheville Citizen,* 28, 29 July 1885; *Tarboro Southerner,* in *Asheville Citizen,* 10 August 1885. Organized in 1877 after the Democrats took complete control of the state government, the State Guard was designed to protect the white citizens of North Carolina from civil unrest. After several years of relative inactivity, it was reorganized in 1883 as a volunteer service. From 22 until 30 July 1885 the troops drilled at Fort Scales, an encampment near the French Broad on the north side of Asheville.

16. *Asheville Citizen,* in *Charlotte Observer,* 21 August, 2 October 1885; *Asheville Citizen,* 24 October 1885.

17. Communication from "Unaka," in *Greensboro North State,* 12 November 1885.

18. Communications from "H" [Edward J. Hale], in *Charlotte Observer,* 5 December 1885, 15 January 1886; communication from "C. W. H.," in *Goldsboro Messenger,* 18 January 1886; Richard E. Welch Jr., *The Presidencies of Grover Cleveland* (Lawrence: University Press of Kansas, 1988), 81–82.

19. *Raleigh News and Observer,* 26 March 1886; communication from "Llewxam" [Maxwell], ibid., 28 March 1886. Like many Southerners, Clingman was also miffed by Cleveland's appointment of James C. Matthews, a wealthy black attorney from Albany,

N.Y., as recorder of deeds for the District of Columbia—a lucrative patronage position that had been highly coveted by several white residents of the District. "If I were a member of Congress," Clingman reportedly told a number of Democrats, "I would introduce a resolution . . . 'that in the opinion of this House the President of the United States would do a wise and patriotic act in resigning his high office forthwith.'" See communication from "C. W. H.," in *Goldsboro Messenger*, 11 March 1886.

20. Clingman's essay was reprinted in *Asheville Citizen*, 22 October 1886, under the title, "About the Minerals of Western N.C. How Certain Mineral Discoveries Were Made, by T. L. Clingman." The characterization of *The Land of the Sky* is from *Raleigh State Chronicle*, 24 May 1884.

21. *Asheville Citizen*, 2 November, 4 December 1886; *Raleigh News and Observer*, 30 November, 5 December 1886; communications from Asheville correspondent, *Raleigh News and Observer*, 25 November, 2, 8, 10 December 1886.

22. *Richmond (Va.) Dispatch*, in *Concord (N.C.) Times*, 16 December 1886; *Asheville Citizen*, 8, 11 December 1886; communications from Asheville correspondent and from "C," in *Raleigh News and Observer*, 16 December 1886.

23. *Charlotte Chronicle*, 19 December 1886; *Asheville Citizen*, 23 December 1886.

24. The quotations from the *Sun* interview in this and the following paragraph are from the abridged version published in *Asheville Citizen*, 23 December 1886.

25. For Cleveland's position on the tariff, see Welch, *Presidencies of Grover Cleveland*, 83.

26. *Concord (N.C.) Times*, 30 December 1886; *Raleigh News and Observer*, 2 January 1887; *Asheville Citizen*, 11, 21, 25 October 1887.

27. Clingman's conversation with the *Citizen* is summarized in *Raleigh News and Observer*, 28 December 1888. For his patent and his agreement with the International Patent Company, see chapter 18.

28. *Charlotte Chronicle*, in *Raleigh News and Observer*, 9 December 1888.

29. The account in this and the following paragraph is based on the following sources: *Asheville Citizen*, 8, 9, 10, 15, 16 January 1889; *Raleigh State Chronicle*, 11, 18 January 1889; *Raleigh News and Observer*, 16 January 1889; *Wilmington Messenger*, 16 January 1889.

30. On 22 January 1889 Ransom was elected to a fourth term in the U.S. Senate, defeating Republican Oliver H. Dockery by a vote of 113 to 47 (*Asheville Citizen*, 23 January 1889).

31. For the Asheville banquet, see *Raleigh News and Observer*, 16 March 1889; *Raleigh State Chronicle*, 15, 22 March 1889. For Clingman's interest in Vance's seat, see communication from Washington correspondent, in *Raleigh State Chronicle*, 11 March 1890; *Asheville Citizen*, 5 June 1890 (quoting Washington correspondent of "the Winston daily").

32. *Raleigh News and Observer*, 18, 22, 23 January 1889; *Asheville Citizen*, 24 January 1889.

33. *Asheville Citizen*, 5 September 1889; *Raleigh News and Observer*, 3 September 1889. Clingman was also invited to a reunion of the Fifty-first Regiment in Fayetteville, scheduled for November, but apparently he did not attend. See *Raleigh News and Observer*, 30 August 1889.

34. *A Record of the Proceedings of the Alumni Association of the University of North Car-

olina at the Centennial Celebration ([Chapel Hill?]: Alumni Association, 1889), 139–43; *Raleigh News and Observer,* 29 May, 6 June 1889; *Asheville Citizen,* 13 June 1889.

35. Remarks of TLC, in *Proceedings of the Alumni Association,* 157, 161–62.

36. *Raleigh State Chronicle,* 14 June 1889.

37. Diary of David Schenck, 7 September 1877, SHC, typescript; *Asheville Journal,* 7 December 1889.

38. *Asheville Democrat,* 12 December 1889; *Asheville Journal,* 7, 11 December 1889; *Asheville Citizen,* 12 December 1889. For the earlier comments about Davis and Clingman, see *Asheville Citizen,* 13 August 1887.

39. Homer E. Socolofsky and Allan B. Spetter, *The Presidency of Benjamin Harrison* (Lawrence: University Press of Kansas, 1987), 56–57.

40. *General Clingman's Message to the Senate and House of Representatives* [Washington, D.C.: n.p., 1890], 4, 6. For the pamphlet's date of publication, see *Raleigh State Chronicle,* 8 March 1890.

41. *Raleigh News and Observer,* 9 March 1890; *Asheville Democrat,* 13 March 1890.

42. Communication from Washington correspondent, in *Raleigh State Chronicle,* 11 March 1890.

43. *Asheville Citizen,* 5 June 1890 (quoting Washington correspondent of "the Winston daily"); diary of John Hill Wheeler, 7 April 1877, SHC, microfilm; remarks of TLC, in *Proceedings of the Alumni Association,* 155. As early as 1875 the *Asheville Citizen* had reported the rumor that Clingman was "courting a rich and distinguished lady in Washington, with most flattering prospects for success" (23 December 1875).

44. W. Weston to TLC, 22 May 1890, Clingman and Puryear Family Papers, SHC.

45. *Asheville Citizen,* 5 June 1890 (quoting Washington correspondent of "the Winston daily"). Regarded as one of the most influential Democratic senators, Beck died at the Baltimore and Potomac Railroad station in Washington, D.C., on 3 May 1890, just after arriving there from Kentucky. On 6 May a memorial service was held in the Senate chamber. See *Raleigh News and Observer,* 4, 7 May 1890.

46. *Asheville Citizen,* 21 October 1887, 10 July 1890.

47. Charles A. Webb, *Asheville, North Carolina: Forty-Six Years in Asheville, 1889–1935* (Asheville : n.p., 1935), 4–7. Webb recalled that Clingman was "a familiar figure upon the streets of Asheville. Tall, slender, gray haired, with a long gray beard, he was a most picturesque individual and attracted attention wherever he went" (14–15).

48. Webb, *Asheville,* 7; *Asheville Citizen,* 23 April, 7 May 1891.

49. *Asheville Citizen,* 28 August, 4 September, 9, 16, 23 October 1890; *Raleigh State Chronicle,* 24 August 1890; *Asheville Democrat,* 9, 16 October 1890.

50. *Asheville Democrat,* 16 October 1890.

51. Ibid., 16 October, 4 December 1890. Ewart's defeat probably resulted more from the unpopularity of the Lodge bill, which provided for federal supervision of elections, than from Clingman's clever campaigning. Although Ewart was one of the few Republican congressmen to speak out against the bill, the proposed law, which passed the House but was defeated in the Senate, probably cost him votes among the whites in the mountain district. See Gordon B. McKinney, *Southern Mountain Republicans, 1865–1900: Politics and the Appalachian Community* (Chapel Hill: University of North Carolina Press, 1978), 135–37.

52. *Asheville Citizen,* 25 December 1890, 25 June, 30 July, 22 October 1891; *Asheville Democrat,* 7 May 1891; TLC to *Washington (D.C.) National View,* 4 July 1891, in *Asheville Citizen,* 6 August 1891; *Raleigh State Chronicle,* 18, 21 October 1891. Elected lieutenant governor in 1888, Thomas M. Holt became governor upon the death of Daniel G. Fowle in April 1891 (*DNCB,* s.v. "Holt, Thomas Michael").

53. *Asheville Democrat,* 12 November 1891; Elizabeth Puryear Gibson to Jane Puryear Kerr, 2 February 1892, Jane P. Kerr Papers, Duke. For James Turner Morehead (1840–1908), see *DNCB,* s.v. "Morehead, James Turner." Two years earlier, Clingman had tried unsuccessfully to sell the baryta mine to certain "parties in Lynchburg." See W. M. Enloes to TLC, 27 March 1890, Clingman-Puryear Papers.

54. Elizabeth Puryear Gibson to Jane Puryear Kerr, 11, 14 February 1892, Kerr Papers.

55. Elizabeth Puryear Gibson to Jane Puryear Kerr, 2, 11 February 1892, Kerr Papers.

56. Communication from Washington correspondent of *New York World,* in *Asheville Citizen,* 24 March 1892.

57. *New York Tribune,* 24 September 1897. The same incident is related more briefly in communication from Washington correspondent of *New York World,* in *Asheville Citizen,* 24 March 1892.

58. *Asheville Journal,* in *Wilmington Messenger,* 30 July 1892; *Asheville Citizen,* 15 September 1892; *Raleigh News and Observer,* 15 September 1892; *Wilmington Messenger,* 16 September 1892.

59. *Asheville Gazette,* in *Wilmington Messenger,* 21 December 1892. For the sale of Mount Pisgah, see Lewis Shore Brumfield, *Thomas Lanier Clingman and the Shallow Ford Families* (Yadkinville: privately printed, 1990), 147.

60. *Asheville Citizen,* 8 February, 23 March 1893; *Charlotte Observer,* in *Asheville Citizen,* 9 March 1893; *New York World,* in *Asheville Citizen,* 16 March 1893. The *New York World*'s account is described more fully in chapter 1.

61. *Asheville Citizen,* 16 March 1893; *Wilmington Messenger,* in *Asheville Citizen,* 23 March 1893.

62. Obituary, *New York Times,* 5 November 1897; TLC to Jane Puryear Kerr, 11 July 1893, Kerr Papers.

63. *Concord (N.C.) Standard,* 1 December 1893, 7 July, 22 August 1894; *Asheville Citizen,* 7 December 1893, 9 August 1894; A[ugustus] H. J[arratt], "General Thomas L. Clingman," *University Magazine,* n.s., 18 (1901): 170.

64. Augustus H. Jarratt, "The Family History," Jarratt Family File, Yadkinville Public Library, Yadkinville, N.C., typescript, 8.

65. *Charlotte Observer* and *Salisbury World,* in *Asheville Citizen,* 14, 21 September 1897; Jarratt, "Family History," 8. For the Morganton hospital, see *Raleigh State Chronicle,* 3 March 1891, 29 December 1892, 19 January 1897. William Holland Thomas, a close political ally of Clingman during the antebellum years, was also confined to the Morganton hospital, where he died in 1893. See *DNCB,* s.v. "Thomas, William Holland."

66. *Asheville Citizen,* 24 September 1897; *Elizabeth City Economist,* ca. September 1897, Clipping File, NCC; *Charlotte Observer,* in *Asheville Citizen,* 19 October 1897; J. E. Walker to William H. S. Burgwyn, 16 April 1898, William Hyslop Sumner Burgwyn Papers, NCDAH.

67. *Asheville Citizen,* 2, 5 November 1897; Jane Puryear Kerr to William H. S. Burgwyn, 15 March 1898, Burgwyn Papers.

68. *Asheville Citizen,* 9 November 1897; *Concord (N.C.) Standard,* in *Asheville Citizen,* 9 November 1897.

20. Prince of Politicians

1. *Asheville Citizen,* 29 October 1897; Hal S. Puryear to William H. S. Burgwyn, 4 November 1897, William Hyslop Sumner Burgwyn Papers, NCDAH.
2. *Concord (N.C.) Standard,* in *Asheville Citizen,* 9 November 1897; *Asheville Citizen,* 16 November 1897.
3. *Asheville Citizen,* 16, 17 November 1897; communication from James M. Ray, ibid., 19 November 1897.
4. *Asheville Citizen,* 10 December 1897.
5. Ibid.; William H. S. Burgwyn, "Life and Services of Gen. Thos. L. Clingman," newspaper clipping, ca. May 1898, Clipping File, NCC.
6. Burgwyn, "Life and Services of Clingman." For similar statements, see *Asheville Citizen,* 5 November 1897; "Gen. Clingman is Dead," newspaper clipping, ca. November 1897, Clipping File, NCC; Jane Puryear Kerr, "Brigadier-General Thomas L. Clingman," *Trinity Archive* 12 (1899): 394. The dichotomy between a political prewar and a nonpolitical postwar career appears as early as 1887 in the biographical sketch published in James Grant Wilson and John Fiske, eds., *Appleton's Cyclopaedia of American Biography,* 6 vols. (New York: D. Appleton, 1887–89), 1:658–59.
7. Obituary, *New York Times,* 5 November 1897; *Asheville Citizen,* 13 June 1889; *New York Tribune,* 24 September 1897.
8. Kerr, "Brigadier-General Clingman," 395.
9. "Letter of Gen. Clingman on Political Parties," in *Asheville News,* 18 July 1882.
10. Paul D. Escott, *Many Excellent People: Power and Privilege in North Carolina, 1850– 1900* (Chapel Hill: University of North Carolina Press, 1985), 149; Thomas E. Jeffrey, *State Parties and National Politics: North Carolina, 1815–1861* (Athens: University of Georgia Press, 1989), 118–21.
11. Joel H. Silbey, "'The Salt of the Nation': Political Parties in Antebellum America," in *The Partisan Imperative: The Dynamics of American Politics before the Civil War* (New York: Oxford University Press, 1985), 56–57.
12. Jeffrey, *State Parties and National Politics,* 91–92, 99–105.
13. Marc W. Kruman, "Thomas L. Clingman and the Whig Party: A Reconsideration," *NCHR* 64 (1987): 18.
14. *Raleigh North Carolina Standard,* 24 January 1849. In defending his behavior to his constituents, Clingman avowed that he had committed "no impropriety" in soliciting Democratic support since he had been "standing . . . in the attitude of an independent candidate." See *Address of T. L. Clingman on the Recent Senatorial Election* (Washington, D.C.: J. & G. S. Gideon, 1849), 7.
15. TLC, *Address on the Recent Senatorial Election,* 15.
16. *Asheville News,* 28 July 1853.
17. *New York Tribune,* 10 September 1880.
18. *Raleigh News,* 17 February 1876; C. Vann Woodward, *Origins of the New South, 1877–1913* (Baton Rouge: Louisiana State University Press, 1951), 27. The division within

the North Carolina Conservative party between old-line Democrats and former Whigs is ably discussed in Jerry Lee Cross, "Political Metamorphosis: An Historical Profile of the Democratic Party in North Carolina, 1800–1892" (Ph.D. diss., State University of New York at Binghamton, 1975), chapters 4–7.

19. "Letter of Gen. Clingman on Political Parties," in *Asheville News,* 18 July 1882.

20. Kemp P. Battle to William H. S. Burgwyn, 23 May 1898, Burgwyn Papers.

21. Escott, *Many Excellent People,* 81.

22. *Raleigh News and Observer,* 1 August 1886; *Charlotte Chronicle,* in *Raleigh News and Observer,* 1 August 1886; *Raleigh News,* 16 May 1876.

23. Escott, *Many Excellent People,* 139, 144–45, 167.

24. Alan Bruce Bromberg, "'Pure Democracy and White Supremacy': The Redeemer Period in North Carolina, 1876–1894" (Ph.D. diss., University of Virginia, 1977), vi–vii, 71–72, 264–67; Escott, *Many Excellent People,* 160–70; Justus D. Doenecke, *The Presidencies of James A. Garfield and Chester A. Arthur* (Lawrence: Regents Press of Kansas, 1981), 50–53, 114–25.

25. *Goldsboro Messenger,* 16 October 1884.

26. *Asheville Citizen,* 4 July 1878.

27. The quotation is from Cross, "Political Metamorphosis," 192.

28. Bromberg, "Redeemer Period," 130, 147, 227. Other studies that take a negative view of North Carolina's postwar Democratic leadership include Escott, *Many Excellent People,* 171–95; Cross, "Political Metamorphosis," chapters 4–8; Hugh Talmage Lefler and Albert Ray Newsome, *North Carolina: The History of a Southern State,* 2d ed. (Chapel Hill: University of North Carolina Press, 1963), 507–16. A more general critique of postwar Southern Democratic leadership can be found in Edward L. Ayers, *The Promise of the New South: Life after Reconstruction* (New York: Oxford University Press, 1992), 34–54.

29. *S&W,* 2–3.

30. Kerr, "Brigadier-General Clingman," 390–91.

31. Joel H. Silbey, "The Southern National Democrats, 1845–1861," in *Partisan Imperative,* 125 (quoting William O. Aydelotte). I am indebted to Jerry L. Cross of the North Carolina Division of Archives and History for the notion of Clingman as his own strangest bedfellow.

32. The quotation is from *Wilmington Messenger,* 17 July 1889.

33. Remarks of TLC, in *A Record of the Proceedings of the Alumni Association of the University of North Carolina at the Centennial Celebration* ([Chapel Hill?]: Alumni Association, 1889), 158, 162–63.

Bibliography

I. PRIMARY SOURCES

A. Manuscript Collections

Duke University, William R. Perkins Library, Special Collections, Durham, N.C. William T. Blackwell Papers. Branch Family Papers. Catherine McGeachy Buie Papers. Clement C. Clay Papers. Jacob Clingman & Co. Papers. Thomas L. Clingman Papers. Benjamin S. Hedrick Papers. Jarratt-Puryear Family Papers. Jane P. Kerr Papers. William Holland Thomas Papers. Wilkes Family Papers.

East Carolina University, Greenville, N.C. William Blount Rodman Papers.

Edison National Historic Site, West Orange, N.J. Archivist's Files. Charles Batchelor Collection. Document File. Laboratory Notebooks. Scrapbook Collection.

Harvard University, Houghton Library, Cambridge, Mass. Autograph File. Miscellaneous Collections.

Historical Society of Pennsylvania, Philadelphia, Pa. Simon Gratz Autograph Collection.

Library of Congress, Manuscript Division, Washington, D.C. John Middleton Clayton Papers.

North Carolina Division of Archives and History, Raleigh, N.C. Asa Biggs Papers. W. Vance Brown Papers. William Hyslop Sumner Burgwyn Papers. Walter Clark Papers. David S. Reid Papers. David L. Swain Papers. George W. Swepson Papers. Calvin H. Wiley Papers. Jonathan Worth Papers.

State Historical Society of Wisconsin, Madison, Wisc. Lyman Copeland Draper Manuscripts. Daniel Boone Papers. Rudolph-Ney Papers.

University of North Carolina, Chapel Hill, N.C.

Southern Historical Collection. Daniel Moreau Barringer Papers. Battle Family Papers. Thomas Bragg Diary. David Franklin Caldwell Papers. Thomas L. Clingman Papers. Clingman and Puryear Family Papers. William Gaston Papers. Jones and Patterson Family Papers. Lenoir Family Papers. Elisha Mitchell Papers. Orr and Patterson Family Papers. David Outlaw Letters. Pettigrew Family Papers. Matt Whitaker Ransom Papers. Diary of David Schenck. Thomas Settle Papers. David Lowry Swain Papers. Zebulon Baird Vance Papers. Diary of John Hill Wheeler, Microfilm.

University Archives. Dialectic Society Minutes. Faculty Minutes. Student Records.

Yadkinville Public Library, Yadkinville, N.C. Clingman Family File. Jarratt Family File.

B. Government Documents

National Archives, Washington, D.C. Records of the Adjutant General's Office. RG 94. Records of the District Courts of the United States. RG 21. Records of the Patent Office. RG 241. War Department Collection of Confederate Records. RG 109.

North Carolina Division of Archives and History, Raleigh, N.C.
 Governor's Letter Books. Edward B. Dudley, 1837–40.
 Governor's Papers. Edward B. Dudley, 1837–40. John M. Morehead, 1841–44.
  William A. Graham, 1845–48. Thomas Bragg, 1855–58. Jonathan Worth,
  1866–68.
 Rowan County Record of Wills, Microfilm.
 Rowan County Tax Records.
 Treasurer's and Comptroller's Records.

C. Broadsides, Pamphlets, and Other Primary Printed Material

Unless otherwise noted, repository locations for printed material can be found in *The National Union Catalog Pre-1956 Imprints*.

American Agricultural and Mineral Land Co. *Letters and Reports on Western North Carolina*. New York: G. E. Sears, 1868.
American Journal of Science and Arts.
Asheville News Extra. [Asheville], 1861. Broadside Collection, NCC.
Baxter, John. *Speech . . . at Rutherfordton, 13th November, 1850*. Asheville: Messenger Office, 1850.
Blake, William P. *The Gold Placers of the Vicinity of Dahlonega, Georgia*. Boston: n.p., 1859.
———. *Report upon the Gold Placers in the Vicinity of Dahlonega, Georgia*. New York: Baker & Godwin, 1858.
———. *Report upon the Gold Placers of Lumpkin County, Georgia*. New York: John F. Trow, 1858.
The Breckinridge Party a Disunion Party. N.p., 1860. Broadside Collection, NCC.
Clark, Walter, ed. *Histories of the Several Regiments and Battalions from North Carolina in the Great War*. 5 vols. Raleigh: E. M. Uzzell, 1901.
Clingman, Thomas L. *Address of T. L. Clingman*. N.p., 1853.
———. *Address of T. L. Clingman on the Recent Senatorial Election*. Washington, D.C.: J. & G. S. Gideon, 1849.
———. *Address to the Citizens of North Carolina*. Raleigh: n.p., 1870.
———. *The Alabama Claims: A Synopsis by T. L. Clingman, January 18, 1876*. Washington, D.C.: M'Gill & Witherow, 1876.
———. "The Battle of Manassas." In *Histories of the Several Regiments and Battalions from North Carolina in the Great War*, edited by Walter Clark, 5:29–33. 5 vols. Raleigh: E. M. Uzzell, 1901.
———. *General Clingman's Message to the Senate and House of Representatives*. [Washington, D.C.: n.p., 1890].
———. *The Geneva Award: Argument by T. L. Clingman*. Washington, D.C.: McGill & Witherow, 1876.
———. *The Geneva Award: Argument Made before the Judiciary of the House of Representatives by T. L. Clingman*. Washington, D.C.: McGill & Co., 1877.
———. *Gold Hill Mine, Rowan County, North Carolina: Memorandum by General T. L. Clingman*. Washington, D.C.: M'Gill & Witherow, 1875.

————. *Measurements of the Black Mountain.* Washington, D.C.: G. S. Gideon, 1856.

————. *Reply of Gen. Clingman to "Truth."* Asheville: n.p., 1882.

————. Scrapbook. Newspaper clippings. George Washington Flowers Collection, Duke.

————. "Second Cold Harbor." In *Histories of the Several Regiments and Battalions from North Carolina in the Great War,* edited by Walter Clark, 5:197–205. 5 vols. Raleigh: E. M. Uzzell, 1901.

————. *Selections from the Speeches and Writings of Hon. Thomas L. Clingman of North Carolina.* 2d ed. Raleigh: John Nichols, 1878.

————. *The Tobacco Remedy.* New York: Orange Judd, 1885.

————. "Topography of Black Mountain." In *Tenth Annual Report of the Board of Regents of the Smithsonian Institution,* 299–305. Washington, D.C.: Cornelius Wendell, 1856.

————. *To the Voters of N. Carolina.* Asheville: n.p., 1868. Pamphlet Collection, WHi.

Clingman Tobacco Cure Co. *Clingman's Tobacco Remedies: The Greatest Medical Discovery of the Age.* Durham: n.p., [1885?].

————. *The Clingman Tobacco Cure Company.* [Durham?]: n.p., 1885. Duke.

Cocke, William M., Jr. *A Card from William M. Cocke Jr.* Asheville: n.p., 1882. NCC.

Democratic Party. National Convention. *Official Proceedings.* Cincinnati: Enquirer, 1856.

————. *Official Proceedings.* Boston: Rockwell & Rollins, 1868.

————. *Official Proceedings.* St. Louis: Woodward, Tiernan & Hale, 1876.

Emerson, Charles. *Charles Emerson's North Carolina Tobacco Belt Directory, 1886–1887.* Raleigh: Edwards, Broughton, 1886.

Huger, John M. *Memoranda of the Late Affair of Honor between Hon. T. L. Clingman, of North Carolina, and Hon. William L. Yancey, of Alabama.* Washington, D.C.: n.p., 1845.

Internal Improvement Convention, Raleigh. *Proceedings of the Internal Improvement Convention Held in the City of Raleigh, November, 1833.* Raleigh: Joseph Gales & Son, 1834.

Lanman, Charles. *Letters from the Alleghany Mountains.* New York: Putnam, 1849.

Louisville, Cincinnati, and Charleston Railroad. *Proceedings of an Adjourned Meeting of the Stockholders . . . December, 1839.* Charleston: A. E. Miller, 1840.

————. *Proceedings of the Louisville, Cincinnati & Charleston Railroad Company, 1839.* Charleston: A. E. Miller, 1839.

————. *Proceedings of the Stockholders . . . January, 1837.* Knoxville: Ramsey & Craighead, 1837.

Mitchell, Elisha. *Black Mountain: Professor Mitchell's Reply to Mr. Clingman.* N.p., 1856.

North Carolina Convention. *Journal of the Constitutional Convention of the State of North Carolina, Held in 1875.* Raleigh: J. Turner, 1875.

North Carolina Fraud Commission. *Report of the Commission to Investigate Charges of Fraud and Corruption.* Raleigh: James H. Moore, 1872.

North Carolina. University. *A Record of the Proceedings of the Alumni Association of the University of North Carolina at the Centennial Celebration.* [Chapel Hill?]: Alumni Association, 1889.

North Carolina Land Co. *Guide to Capitalists and Emigrants: Being a Statistical and Descriptive Account of the Several Counties of the State of North Carolina.* Raleigh: Nichols & Gorman, 1869.

Trow's New York City Directory for the Year Ending May 1, 1884. New York: Trow, 1883.

Trow's New York City Directory for the Year Ending May 1, 1885. New York: Trow, 1884.

U.S. Congress. House of Representatives. *Report of the Committee on the Judiciary,* 48 Cong., 1 sess., 1883–84, H. Rept. 1032. In U.S. Government Publications, Serial Set No. 2256. New York: Readex Microprint, 1966.

U.S. Congress. *Report of the Joint Committee on Reconstruction.* Washington, D.C.: Government Printing Office, 1866.

U.S. Patent Office. *Official Gazette of the United States Patent Office.*

———. *Specifications and Drawings of Patents Relating to Electricity Issued by the United States Prior to July 1, 1881.* 16 vols. Washington, D.C.: Government Printing Office, 1881. ENHS.

Western North Carolina Railroad Co. Western Division. *Proceedings of the Second Annual Meeting of the Stockholders of the Western Division.* Salisbury: J. J Bruner, 1870.

———. *A Record of the Acts and Charter . . . of the Western Division of the Western North-Carolina Railroad.* Asheville: Pioneer Office, 1869.

———. *Records and Documents Pertaining to the Title of the Western North Carolina Railroad.* N.p., n.d. NCC.

D. Newspapers

Asheville Citizen.
Asheville Democrat.
Asheville Journal.
Asheville Messenger.
Asheville News, 1851–69, 1880–82.
Asheville Pioneer.
Asheville Spectator.
Asheville Western Expositor.
Charleston (S.C.) Courier.
Charleston (S.C.) Mercury.
Charlotte Chronicle.
Charlotte Democrat.
Charlotte Home and Democrat.
Charlotte North Carolina Whig.
Charlotte Observer.
Charlotte Southern Home.
Concord (N.C.) Standard.
Concord (N.C.) Times.
Elizabeth City Economist.
Fayetteville North Carolinian.
Fayetteville Observer.
Goldsboro Messenger.
Greensboro North State.

Greensboro Patriot.
Hillsborough Recorder.
Newbernian.
New Bern Progress.
New Bern Republican.
New York Herald.
New York Times.
New York Tribune.
Raleigh Carolina Era.
Raleigh Confederate.
Raleigh Constitution.
Raleigh News.
Raleigh News and Observer.
Raleigh North Carolina Standard.
Raleigh Observer.
Raleigh Progress.
Raleigh Register, 1832–61, 1884–85.
Raleigh Republican.
Raleigh Sentinel.
Raleigh State Chronicle.
Raleigh State Journal, 1861–63, 1882–83.
Rutherfordton Star.
Rutherfordton Vindicator.
Salisbury Carolina Watchman.
Salisbury Old North State.
Washington (D.C.) Madisonian.
Washington (D.C.) National Era.
Washington (D.C.) National Intelligencer.
Washington (D.C.) National Republican.
Washington (D.C.) Post.
Washington (D.C.) Spectator.
Washington (D.C.) Union.
Wilmington Herald.
Wilmington Journal.
Wilmington Messenger.
Wilmington Star.

E. Published Sources

Adams, George Worthington, ed. *Reminiscences of the Civil War and Reconstruction by Mary Logan.* Carbondale: Southern Illinois University Press, 1970.
Boyd, William K., ed. *Memoirs of W. W. Holden.* Durham: Seeman Printery, 1911.
Burnham, W. Dean. *Presidential Ballots, 1836–1892.* Baltimore: Johns Hopkins University Press, 1955.
Butler, Lindley S., ed. *The Papers of David Settle Reid.* 2 vols. Raleigh: Department of Cultural Resources, Division of Archives and History, 1993–97.

Cheney, John L., ed. *North Carolina Government, 1585–1979*. Raleigh: North Carolina Department of the Secretary of State, 1980.

Coon, Charles L., ed. *North Carolina Schools and Academies, 1790–1840: A Documentary History*. Raleigh: Edwards & Broughton, 1915.

Diggs, George A. *Buncombe County, North Carolina, Grantee Deed Index*. 2 vols. Asheville: Miller, 1927.

Graf, Leroy P., and Paul Bergeron, eds. *The Papers of Andrew Johnson*. 13 vols. to date. Knoxville: University of Tennessee Press, 1967– .

Hamilton, J. G. de Roulhac, ed. *The Correspondence of Jonathan Worth*. 2 vols. Raleigh: Edwards & Broughton, 1909.

———. *The Papers of Thomas Ruffin*. 4 vols. Raleigh: Edwards & Broughton, 1918–20.

Hamilton, J. G. de Roulhac, and Max R. Williams, eds. *The Papers of William A. Graham*. 8 vols. Raleigh: Division of Archives and History, 1957–92.

Hesseltine, William B., ed. *Three against Lincoln: Murat Halstead Reports the Caucuses of 1860*. Baton Rouge: Louisiana State University Press, 1960.

Holcomb, Brent H. *Marriages of Surry County, North Carolina, 1779–1868*. Baltimore: Genealogical Publishing Co., 1982.

Johnston, Frontis W., and Joe A. Mobley, eds. *The Papers of Zebulon Baird Vance*. 2 vols. to date. Raleigh: Division of Archives and History, 1963– .

Linn, Jo White. *Abstracts of the Deeds of Rowan County, North Carolina, 1753–1785, vols. 1–10*. Salisbury: privately printed, 1983.

———. *Abstracts of Wills and Estates Records of Rowan County, North Carolina, 1753–1805 and Tax Lists of 1759 and 1778*. Salisbury: privately printed, 1980.

McKinney, Gordon B., and Michael M. McMurry, eds. *The Papers of Zebulon Vance*. Frederick: University Publications of America, 1987. Microfilm.

Manarin, Louis H., and Weymouth T. Jordan Jr., comps. *North Carolina Troops*. 13 vols. to date. Raleigh: Division of Archives and History, 1966– .

Newsome, A. R., ed. "Letters of Lawrence O'Bryan Branch, 1856–1861." *NCHR* 10 (1933): 44–79.

Olsen, Otto H., and Ellen Z. McGrew, eds. "Prelude to Reconstruction: The Correspondence of State Senator Leander Sams Gash, 1866–1867, Part 1." *NCHR* 60 (1983): 37–88.

Padgett, James A., ed. "Reconstruction Letters from North Carolina. Part 10: Letters to Benjamin Franklin Butler." *NCHR* 19 (1942): 381–404; 20 (1943): 54–82, 157–80, 259–82, 341–70; 21 (1944): 46–71.

Phillips, Ulrich B., ed. *The Correspondence of Robert Toombs, Alexander H. Stephens, and Howell Cobb*. Washington, D.C.: American Historical Association, 1913.

Quaife, Milo Milton, ed. *The Diary of James K. Polk*. 4 vols. Chicago: A. C. McClurg, 1910; New York: Kraus Reprint Co., 1970.

Ratcliff, Clarence E. *North Carolina Taxpayers, 1701–1786*. 2 vols. Baltimore: Genealogical Publishing Co., 1984–87.

Scarborough, William K., ed. *Diary of Edmund Ruffin*. 3 vols. Baton Rouge: Louisiana State University Press, 1972–89.

Schiller, Herbert M., ed. *A Captain's War: The Letters and Diaries of William H. S. Burgwyn, 1861–1865*. Shippensburg, Pa.: White Mane Publishing, 1994.

Shanks, Henry T., ed. *The Papers of Willie Person Mangum*. 5 vols. Raleigh: State
Department of Archives and History, 1950–56.

Simon, John Y., ed. *The Papers of Ulysses S. Grant*. 20 vols. to date. Carbondale:
Southern Illinois University Press, 1967– .

Snow, Carol Leonard. *Taxables in Surry County, North Carolina, for the Year 1835*.
Toast: privately printed, 1990.

Staples, Arthur G., ed. *The Letters of John Fairfield*. Lewiston, Maine: Lewiston Journal,
1922.

Sterling, Ada, ed. *A Belle of the Fifties: Memoirs of Mrs. [Clement C.] Clay of Alabama*.
New York: Doubleday, 1904.

Tolbert, Noble J., ed. *The Papers of John Willis Ellis*. 2 vols. Raleigh: State Department of
Archives and History, 1964.

U.S. War Department. *The War of the Rebellion: A Compilation of the Official Records of
the Union and Confederate Armies*. Washington, D.C.: Government Printing Office,
1880–1901.

Weaver, Herbert, et al., eds. *Correspondence of James K. Polk*. 9 vols. to date. Nashville:
Vanderbilt University Press, 1969– .

Wells, Agnes M., and Iris M. Harvey. *Surry County, North Carolina Tax List, 1815*.
Mount Airy: privately printed, 1990.

Woodward, C. Vann, ed. *Mary Chesnut's Civil War*. New Haven: Yale University Press,
1981.

Yearns, W. Buck, ed. *The Papers of Thomas Jordan Jarvis*. 1 vol. to date. Raleigh: State
Department of Archives and History, 1969– .

II. SECONDARY SOURCES

Allen, W. C. *The Annals of Haywood County North Carolina*. [Waynesville]: n.p., 1935.

Arthur, Billy. "The Cure-All of General Clingman." *State* 50 (July 1982): 9–10.

Arthur, John Preston. *Western North Carolina: A History from 1730 to 1913*. Raleigh:
Edwards & Broughton, 1914.

Ashe, Samuel A., et al. *Biographical History of North Carolina*. 8 vols. Greensboro:
Charles L. Van Noppen, 1905–17.

Atchison, Ray M. "*Our Living and Our Dead:* A Post-Bellum North Carolina Magazine
of Literature and History." *NCHR* 40 (1963): 423–33.

Ayers, Edward L. *The Promise of the New South: Life after Reconstruction*. New York:
Oxford University Press, 1992.

Babb, Sandra Porter. "The Battle of the Giants: The Gubernatorial Election of 1876 in
North Carolina." Master's thesis, University of North Carolina at Chapel Hill, 1970.

Baird, J. S. T. "Historical Sketches of the Early Days." Scrapbook of clippings from
Asheville Register, January–March, 1905. NCC.

Barrett, John G. *The Civil War in North Carolina*. Chapel Hill: University of North
Carolina Press, 1963.

Bassett, John Spencer. "The Congressional Career of Thos. L. Clingman." *Trinity
College Historical Society Papers* 4 (1900): 48–63.

Battle, Kemp P. *History of the University of North Carolina.* 2 vols. Raleigh: Edwards & Broughton, 1907–12.

———. *Memories of an Old-Time Tar Heel.* Chapel Hill: University of North Carolina Press, 1945.

Bell, John Luther, Jr. "Constitutions and Politics: Constitutional Revision in the South Atlantic States, 1864–1902." Ph.D. diss., University of North Carolina at Chapel Hill, 1969.

Bemis, Samuel Flagg. *A Diplomatic History of the United States.* 5th ed. New York: Holt, Rinehart & Winston, 1965.

Benedict, Michael Les. "Southern Democrats in the Crisis of 1876–1877: A Reconsideration of *Reunion and Reaction.*" *Journal of Southern History* 46 (1980): 489–524.

Beringer, Richard E., et al. *Why the South Lost the Civil War.* Athens: University of Georgia Press, 1986.

Blackmun, Ora. *Western North Carolina: Its Mountains and Its People to 1880.* Boone: Appalachian Consortium Press, 1977.

Blake, Nelson Morehouse. *William Mahone of Virginia: Soldier and Political Insurgent.* Richmond: Garrett & Massie, 1935.

Boatner, Mark Mayo, III. *Civil War Dictionary.* New York: David McKay, 1959.

Bordley, James, III, and A. McGehee Harvey. *Two Centuries of American Medicine, 1776–1976.* Philadelphia: W. B. Saunders, 1976.

Boyd, William K. "Clingman, Thomas Lanier." *DAB.*

———. *The Story of Durham: City of the New South.* Durham: Duke University Press, 1925.

Bright, Arthur A., Jr. *The Electric-Lamp Industry: Technological Change and Economic Development from 1800 to 1947.* New York: Macmillan, 1949; New York: Arno Press, 1972.

Bromberg, Alan Bruce. "'Pure Democracy and White Supremacy': The Redeemer Period in North Carolina, 1876–1894." Ph.D. diss., University of Virginia, 1977.

Brooks, Jerome E. *The Mighty Leaf: Tobacco through the Centuries.* Boston: Little, Brown, 1952.

———. *Tobacco: Its History Illustrated by the Books, Manuscripts, and Engravings in the Library of George Arents Jr.* 5 vols. New York: Rosenbach, 1937–52.

Brown, Norman D. *Edward Stanly: Whiggery's Tarheel "Conqueror."* University: University of Alabama Press, 1974.

Bruce, Robert V. *The Launching of Modern American Science, 1846–1876.* Ithaca: Cornell University Press, 1987.

Brumfield, Lewis Shore. *Thomas Lanier Clingman and the Shallow Ford Families.* Yadkinville: privately printed, 1990.

Burgwyn, William H. S. "Life and Services of Gen. Thos. L. Clingman." Newspaper clipping, ca. May 1898. Clipping File, NCC.

Byrd, Mary Lacy. "Friend Helped Launch Politician." Clipping from *Asheville Citizen-Times,* 30 October 1966. Pack.

Cain, Andrew W. *History of Lumpkin County for the First Hundred Years.* Spartanburg: Reprint Co., 1978.

Cameron, John D. "Thomas Lanier Clingman." *University Magazine,* n.s., 8 (1889): 249–57.

Capers, Henry D. *The Life and Times of C. G. Memminger.* Richmond: Everett Waddey, 1893.

Carter, Dan T. *When the War Was Over: The Failure of Self-Reconstruction in the South, 1865–1867.* Baton Rouge: Louisiana State University Press, 1985.

Casstevens, Frances Harding. "The Military Career of Brigadier General Thomas Lanier Clingman." Master's thesis, University of North Carolina at Greensboro, 1984.

———. "A Raid They Blamed on Clingman." *State* 53 (January 1985): 11–12, 30.

———. "Thomas Lanier Clingman: General, Statesman, and Explorer." In *The Heritage of Yadkin County,* 172–74. Yadkinville: Yadkin County Historical Society, 1981.

———, ed. *The Heritage of Yadkin County.* Yadkinville: Yadkin County Historical Society, 1981.

Cathey, Cornelius O. *Agriculture in North Carolina before the Civil War.* Raleigh: State Department of Archives and History, 1966.

Chapman, Ashton. "Hopewell Indians Came Here for Mica." *State* 36 (15 February 1969): 13–14.

Clancy, Herbert J. *The Presidential Election of 1880.* Chicago: Loyola University Press, 1958.

"Clingman, Thomas Lanier." In *Appleton's Cyclopaedia of American Biography,* 1:658–59. 6 vols. New York: D. Appleton, 1887–89.

Clingman, William D. *Clingman-Klingman Families & Descendants.* Richmond, Calif.: privately printed, 1931.

Coates, Albert, and Gladys Hall Coates. *The Story of Student Government in the University of North Carolina at Chapel Hill.* Chapel Hill, 1985.

Cooper, William J., Jr. *The South and the Politics of Slavery, 1828–1856.* Baton Rouge: Louisiana State University Press, 1978.

Cotten, William D. "Appalachian North Carolina: A Political Study, 1860–1889." Ph.D. diss., University of North Carolina at Chapel Hill, 1954.

Counihan, Harold J. "The North Carolina Constitutional Convention of 1835: A Study in Jacksonian Democracy." *NCHR* 46 (1969): 335–64.

Covington, Howard. "History Falling into Poison Ivy Patch: Old Ebenezer Academy Is Iredell Restoration Project." Clipping from *Charlotte Observer,* 12 September 1967. Iredell County Public Library, Statesville, N.C.

Creecy, Richard Benbury. "General Clingman." Newspaper clipping, ca. 1897. Clipping File, NCC.

———. *Grandfather's Tales of North Carolina History.* Raleigh: Edwards & Broughton, 1901.

———. "Recollections of Clingman" (from *Elizabeth City Economist*). In *Asheville Citizen,* 5 November 1897.

———. "University Days Seventy Years Ago." *University Magazine,* n.s., 20 (1902): 89–96.

Crofts, Daniel W. *Reluctant Confederates: Upper South Unionists in the Secession Crisis.* Chapel Hill: University of North Carolina Press, 1989.

Cross, Jerry Lee. "Political Metamorphosis: An Historical Profile of the Democratic

Party in North Carolina, 1800–1892." Ph.D. diss., State University of New York at Binghamton, 1975.

Crow, Jeffrey J. "Thomas Settle Jr., Reconstruction, and the Memory of the Civil War." *Journal of Southern History* 62 (1996): 689–726.

Dailey, Douglass C. "The Elections of 1872 in North Carolina." *NCHR* 40 (1963): 338–60.

Dana, Edward S. *System of Mineralogy of James Dwight Dana: Descriptive Mineralogy.* 6th ed. New York: Wiley & Sons, 1892.

Dana, James D. *Manual of Mineralogy and Petrography.* 4th ed. New York: Wiley & Sons, 1887.

Daniels, George H. *American Science in the Age of Jackson.* New York: Columbia University Press, 1968.

Davis, Burke. *The Southern Railway: Road of the Innovators.* Chapel Hill: University of North Carolina Press, 1985.

Dictionary of the History of Science. Princeton: Princeton University Press, 1981.

Doenecke, Justus D. *The Presidencies of James A. Garfield and Chester A. Arthur.* Lawrence: Regents Press of Kansas, 1981.

Dorris, Jonathan Truman. *Pardon and Amnesty under Lincoln and Johnson: The Restoration of the Confederates to Their Rights and Privileges, 1861–1898.* Chapel Hill: University of North Carolina Press, 1953.

———. "Pardoning North Carolinians." *NCHR* 23 (1946): 360–401.

Drake, William Earle. *Higher Education in North Carolina before 1860.* New York: Carlton Press, 1964.

DuBose, John W. *The Life and Times of William Lowndes Yancey.* 2 vols. Birmingham: Roberts and Son, 1892.

Elliott, Clark A. *Biographical Dictionary of American Science: The Seventeenth through the Nineteenth Century.* Westport, Conn.: Greenwood Press, 1979.

Escott, Paul D. *Many Excellent People: Power and Privilege in North Carolina, 1850–1900.* Chapel Hill: University of North Carolina Press, 1985.

Evans, Virginia Fraser, comp. *Iredell County Landmarks: A Pictorial History of Iredell County.* Statesville: Iredell County Bicentennial Commission, 1976.

Farmer, Fannie Memory. "The Bar Examination and Beginning Years of Legal Practice in North Carolina, 1820–1860." *NCHR* 29 (1952): 159–70.

———. "Legal Education in North Carolina, 1820–1860." *NCHR* 28 (1951): 271–97.

———. "Legal Practice and Ethics in North Carolina, 1820–1860." *NCHR* 30 (1953): 329–53.

Feerick, John D. *From Failing Hands: The Story of Presidential Succession.* New York: Fordham University Press, 1965.

Foner, Eric. "The Wilmot Proviso Revisited." *Journal of American History* 56 (1969): 262–79.

Foster, Gaines M. *Ghosts of the Confederacy: Defeat, the Lost Cause, and the Emergence of the New South, 1865 to 1913.* New York: Oxford University Press, 1987.

Friedel, Robert, and Paul Israel. *Edison's Electric Light: Biography of an Invention.* New Brunswick: Rutgers University Press, 1986.

Gallimore, Bob. "Thomas L. Clingman: Soldier, Explorer, and One-Man Chamber of

Commerce." Clipping from *Asheville Citizen-Times,* 23 January 1949. Clipping File, NCC.

Gara, Larry. *The Presidency of Franklin Pierce.* Lawrence: University Press of Kansas, 1991.

Gaston, Paul M. *The New South Creed: A Study in Southern Mythmaking.* New York: Alfred A. Knopf, 1970.

Genovese, Eugene. *The Political Economy of Slavery: Studies in the Economy and Society of the Slave South.* New York: Pantheon, 1965.

Gilbert, Clarence N. "The Public Career of Thomas L. Clingman." Master's thesis, University of North Carolina at Chapel Hill, 1946.

Green, Constance McLaughlin. *Washington: A History of the Capital, 1800–1950.* 2 vols. Princeton: Princeton University Press, 1962.

Green, Fletcher. "Georgia's Forgotten Industry: Gold Mining." *Georgia Historical Quarterly* 19 (1935): 93–111, 210–28.

———. "Gold Mining: A Forgotten Industry of Ante-Bellum North Carolina." *NCHR* 14 (1937): 1–19, 135–55.

Grimes, Alice Dugger. "'I'm Going to Be President.'" *State* 2 (29 September 1934): 22–23.

Hamilton, Holman. *Prologue to Conflict: The Crisis and Compromise of 1850.* Lexington: University Press of Kentucky, 1964.

Hamilton, J. G. de Roulhac. *Party Politics in North Carolina, 1835–1860.* Durham: Seeman Printery, 1916.

———. *Reconstruction in North Carolina.* New York: Longmans, Green, 1914.

Hardesty, Fred. "Fiery Spokesman for the South." *State* 39 (15 March 1972): 7–8, 14.

Harris, William C. *William Woods Holden: Firebrand of North Carolina Politics.* Baton Rouge: Louisiana State University Press, 1987.

Henderson, Archibald. "Elisha Mitchell: Scientist and Man." *Journal of the Elisha Mitchell Scientific Society* 73 (1957): 204–12.

The Heritage of Iredell County. Statesville: Genealogical Society of Iredell County, 1980.

Hesseltine, William B. *Pioneer's Mission: The Story of Lyman Copeland Draper.* Madison: State Historical Society of Wisconsin, 1954; Westport, Conn.: Greenwood Press, 1970.

———. *Ulysses S. Grant: Politician.* New York: Dodd, Mead, 1935; New York: Frederick Ungar, 1957.

Hicks, John D. *The Populist Revolt: A History of the Farmer's Alliance and the People's Party.* Minneapolis: University of Minnesota Press, 1931.

Hoffmann, William S. *Andrew Jackson and North Carolina Politics.* Chapel Hill: University of North Carolina Press, 1958.

Hofstadter, Richard. *Social Darwinism in American Thought.* Rev. ed. Boston: Beacon Press, 1955.

Holt, Michael F. *The Political Crisis of the 1850s.* New York: John Wiley & Sons, 1978.

Hoogenboom, Ari. *Outlawing the Spoils: A History of the Civil Service Reform Movement, 1865–1883.* Urbana: University of Illinois Press, 1961.

———. *The Presidency of Rutherford B. Hayes.* Lawrence: University Press of Kansas, 1988.

Houck, Lucy H. *The Story of Rockford.* N.p.: privately printed, 1972.

Hovenkamp, Herbert. *Science and Religion in America, 1800–1860.* Philadelphia: University of Pennsylvania Press, 1978.

Inscoe, John C. "Clingman, Thomas Lanier." In *Encyclopedia of the Confederacy,* edited by Richard N. Current, 1:354–55. 5 vols. New York: Simon & Schuster, 1993.

———. *Mountain Masters, Slavery, and the Sectional Crisis in Western North Carolina.* Knoxville: University of Tennessee Press, 1989.

———. "Thomas Clingman, Mountain Whiggery, and the Southern Cause." *Civil War History* 33 (1987): 42–62.

International Dictionary of Medicine and Biology. New York: John Wiley & Sons, 1986.

Jarratt, Augustus H. "The Family History." Typescript, n.d. Jarratt Family File, Yadkinville Public Library, Yadkinville, N.C.

———. "General Thomas L. Clingman." *University Magazine,* n.s., 18 (1901): 166–70.

Jeffrey, Thomas E. "Beyond 'Free Suffrage': North Carolina Parties and the Convention Movement of the 1850s." *NCHR* 62 (1985): 387–419.

———. "'Free Suffrage' Revisited: Party Politics and Constitutional Reform in Antebellum North Carolina." *NCHR* 59 (1982): 24–48.

———. "The Progressive Paradigm of Antebellum North Carolina Politics." *Carolina Comments* 30 (1982): 66–75.

———. "The Second Party System in North Carolina, 1836–1860." Ph.D. diss., Catholic University of America, 1976.

———. *State Parties and National Politics: North Carolina, 1815–1861.* Athens: University of Georgia Press, 1989.

———. "Thomas Lanier Clingman and the Invention of the Electric Light: A Forgotten Episode." *Carolina Comments* 32 (1984): 71–82.

———. "'Thunder from the Mountains': Thomas Lanier Clingman and the End of Whig Supremacy in North Carolina." *NCHR* 56 (1979): 366–95.

———. "An Unclean Vessel: Thomas Lanier Clingman and the 'Railroad Ring.'" *NCHR* 74 (1997): 389–431.

———. "'A Whole Torrent of Mean and Malevolent Abuse': Party Politics and the Clingman-Mitchell Controversy." *NCHR* 70 (1993): 241–65, 401–29.

Katz, Irving. *August Belmont: A Political Biography.* New York: Columbia University Press, 1968.

Kearney, H. Thomas, Jr. "Clingman, Thomas Lanier." *DNCB.*

Keever, Homer M. *Iredell: Piedmont County.* Statesville: Iredell County Bicentennial Commission, 1976.

Kerr, Jane Puryear. "Brigadier-General Thomas L. Clingman." *Trinity Archive* 12 (1899): 388–96.

King, W. James. "The Development of Electrical Technology in the Nineteenth Century: The Early Arc Light and Generator." In United States National Museum *Bulletin* 228 (1962): 333–407.

Kohlstedt, Sally Gregory. *The Formation of the American Scientific Community: The American Association for the Advancement of Science, 1848–1860.* Urbana: University of Illinois Press, 1976.

Kornegay, William Gordon. "The North Carolina Institute of Education, 1831–1834." *NCHR* 36 (1959): 141–52.

Kruman, Marc W. *Parties and Politics in North Carolina, 1836–1865.* Baton Rouge: Louisiana State University Press, 1983.

———. "Thomas L. Clingman and the Whig Party: A Reconsideration." *NCHR* 64 (1987): 1–17.

Lawrence, R. C. "General Thomas Clingman." *State* 12 (14 April 1945): 6–7, 21.

Lefler, Hugh Talmage, and Albert Ray Newsome. *North Carolina: The History of a Southern State.* 2d ed. Chapel Hill: University of North Carolina Press, 1963.

London, Lawrence Foushee. "George Edmund Badger and the Compromise of 1850." *NCHR* 15 (1938): 99–118.

———. "George Edmund Badger in the United States Senate, 1846–1849." *NCHR* 15 (1938): 1–22.

Mahler, Fred G. "The Man for Whom They Named Clingman's Dome." Clipping from *Raleigh News and Observer,* 29 September 1957. Clipping File, NCC.

Malin, James C. *The Nebraska Question, 1852–1854.* Lawrence: privately printed, 1953.

May, Robert E. "Psychobiography and Secession: The Southern Radical as Maladjusted 'Outsider.'" *Civil War History* 34 (1988): 46–69.

———. *The Southern Dream of a Caribbean Empire, 1854–1861.* Baton Rouge: Louisiana State University Press, 1973; Athens: University of Georgia Press, 1989.

McClure, Alexander K. "The Career of T. L. Clingman" (from *Philadelphia Times,* 10 October 1896). In *Southern Historical Society Papers,* edited by R. A. Brock, 24 (1896): 303–8.

———. *Recollections of Half a Century.* Salem, Mass.: Salem Press, 1902.

McKinney, Gordon B. *Southern Mountain Republicans, 1865–1900: Politics and the Appalachian Community.* Chapel Hill: University of North Carolina Press, 1978.

McLaurin, Melton A. "The Nineteenth-Century North Carolina State Fair as a Social Institution." *NCHR* 59 (1982): 213–29.

———. "The North Carolina State Fair, 1853–1899." Master's thesis, East Carolina College, 1963.

McLean, Hallie S. "The History of the Dialectic Society, 1795–1860." Master's thesis, University of North Carolina at Chapel Hill, 1949.

McMurry, Richard M. *Two Great Rebel Armies.* Chapel Hill: University of North Carolina Press, 1989.

Miles, Edwin A. "The Old South and the Classical World." *NCHR* 48 (1971): 258–75.

Moore, John W. *History of North Carolina.* 2 vols. Raleigh: Alfred Williams, 1880.

Morrill, James R. "The Presidential Election of 1852: Death Knell of the Whig Party of North Carolina." *NCHR* 44 (1967): 342–59.

Morris, Margaret W. "The Completion of the Western North Carolina Railroad: Politics of Concealment." *NCHR* 52 (1975): 256–82.

Murphey, Walter. "Thomas Lanier Clingman." *State* 11 (2 October 1943): 4–5.

Nevins, Allan. *Abram S. Hewitt.* New York: Octagon Books, 1967.

New York Times, 5 November 1897. Obituary.

Nichols, Roy F. *Blueprints for Leviathan: American Style.* New York: Atheneum, 1963.

———. *The Disruption of American Democracy.* New York: Macmillan, 1948; New York: Free Press, 1967.

Niven, John. *John C. Calhoun and the Price of Union: A Biography.* Baton Rouge: Louisiana State University Press, 1988.

Norton, Clarence C. *The Democratic Party in Ante-Bellum North Carolina, 1835–1861.* Chapel Hill: University of North Carolina Press, 1930.

Olsen, Otto H. "North Carolina: An Incongruous Presence." In *Reconstruction and Redemption in the South,* edited by Otto H. Olsen, 156–201. Baton Rouge: Louisiana State University Press, 1980.

Pegg, Herbert Dale. *The Whig Party in North Carolina.* Chapel Hill: Colonial Press, 1968.

Penzel, Frederick. *Theatre Lighting before Electricity.* Middletown: Wesleyan University Press, 1978.

Perman, Michael. *Reunion without Compromise: The South and Reconstruction, 1865–1868.* Cambridge, Eng.: University Press, 1973.

———. *The Road to Redemption: Southern Politics, 1869–1879.* Chapel Hill: University of North Carolina Press, 1984.

Peskin, Allan. "Was There a Compromise of 1877?" *Journal of American History* 60 (1963): 63–75.

Peterson, Owen M. "W. W. Avery in the Democratic National Convention of 1860." *NCHR* 31 (1954): 463–78.

Potter, David. *The Impending Crisis, 1848–1861.* New York: Harper & Row, 1976.

Pray, Isaac C. *Memoirs of James Gordon Bennett and His Times.* New York: Stringer & Townsend, 1855.

Pressly, Thomas J. *Americans Interpret Their Civil War.* New York: Free Press, 1962.

Price, Charles L. "Railroads and Reconstruction in North Carolina, 1865–1871." Ph.D. diss., University of North Carolina at Chapel Hill, 1959.

———. "The Railroad Schemes of George W. Swepson." *East Carolina College Publications in History* 1 (1964): 32–50.

Ramsey, D. Hiden. "Elisha Mitchell and Mount Mitchell." *Journal of the Elisha Mitchell Scientific Society* 73 (1957): 199–204.

Ramsey, Robert W. *Carolina Cradle: Settlement of the Northwest Carolina Frontier, 1747–1762.* Chapel Hill: University of North Carolina Press, 1964.

Ratchford, B. U. "The Adjustment of the North Carolina Public Debt, 1879–1883." *NCHR* 10 (1933): 157–67.

Rawley, James A. *Secession: The Disruption of the American Republic, 1844–1861.* Malabar, Fla.: Krieger, 1990.

Revelle, Nancy. "Matthew Whitaker Ransom's Political Career." Master's thesis, University of North Carolina at Chapel Hill, 1959.

Robertson, William Glenn. *Back Door to Richmond: The Bermuda Hundred Campaign, April–June 1864.* Baton Rouge: Louisiana State University Press, 1987.

Russett, Cynthia Eagle. *Darwin in America: The Intellectual Response, 1865–1912.* San Francisco: Freeman, 1976.

Rutledge, William E. *An Illustrated History of Yadkin County, 1850–1980.* Yadkinville: privately printed, 1981.

Sargent, Nathan. *Public Men and Events, from the Commencement of Mr. Monroe's Administration in 1817, to the Close of Mr. Fillmore's Administration, in 1853.* 2 vols. Philadelphia: Lippincott, 1875.

Schott, Thomas E. *Alexander H. Stephens of Georgia: A Biography.* Baton Rouge: Louisiana State University Press, 1988.

Schwarzkopf, Kent. *A History of Mt. Mitchell and the Black Mountains: Exploration,*

Development, and Preservation. Raleigh: North Carolina Department of Cultural Resources and North Carolina Department of Natural Resources and Community Development, 1985.

Seip, Terry L. *The South Returns to Congress: Men, Economic Measures, and Intersectional Relationships, 1869–1879.* Baton Rouge: Louisiana State University Press, 1983.

Sellers, Charles Grier, Jr. "Jim Polk Goes to Chapel Hill." *NCHR* 29 (1952): 189–203.

Shields, Johanna Nicol. *The Line of Duty: Maverick Congressmen and the Development of American Political Culture, 1836–1860.* Westport, Conn.: Greenwood Press, 1985.

Silbey, Joel H. *The Partisan Imperative: The Dynamics of American Politics before the Civil War.* New York: Oxford University Press, 1985.

———. "'The Salt of the Nation': Political Parties in Antebellum America." In *The Partisan Imperative: The Dynamics of American Politics before the Civil War,* 50–68. New York: Oxford University Press, 1985.

———. *The Shrine of Party: Congressional Voting Behavior, 1841–1852.* Pittsburgh: University of Pittsburgh Press, 1967.

———. "The Southern National Democrats, 1845–1861." In *The Partisan Imperative: The Dynamics of American Politics before the Civil War,* 116–26. New York: Oxford University Press, 1985.

Silva, Ruth C. *Presidential Succession.* New York: Greenwood Press, 1968.

Singletary, Otis. *The Mexican War.* Chicago: University of Chicago Press, 1960.

Sitterson, Joseph Carlyle. *The Secession Movement in North Carolina.* Chapel Hill: University of North Carolina Press, 1938.

Smith, Elbert B. *The Presidency of James Buchanan.* Lawrence: University Press of Kansas, 1975.

Socolofsky, Homer E., and Allan B. Spetter. *The Presidency of Benjamin Harrison.* Lawrence: University Press of Kansas, 1987.

"Statesman and Author First Great Booster." Clipping from *Asheville Times,* 29 November 1931. Pack.

Steelman, Joseph Flake. "The Immigration Movement in North Carolina, 1865–1900." Master's thesis, University of North Carolina at Chapel Hill, 1947.

Stokes, Durward T. "Henry Pattillo in North Carolina." *NCHR* 44 (1967): 373–91.

Tucker, Glenn. "Eagle Forgotten: The Career of Thomas Lanier Clingman." Three draft chapters of an unfinished biography. Glenn Tucker Papers, Special Collections, Western Carolina University.

———. "For the Want of a Scribe." *NCHR* 43 (1966): 174–85.

———. "Many-Starred Career of Thomas Clingman." *State* 43 (August 1975): 15–17.

Unger, Irwin. *The Greenback Era: A Social and Political History of American Finance, 1865–1879.* Princeton: Princeton University Press, 1964.

Van Nostrand's Scientific Encyclopedia. 4th ed. Princeton: Van Nostrand, 1968.

Wakelyn, Jon L. *Biographical Dictionary of the Confederacy.* Westport, Conn.: Greenwood Press, 1977.

Walters, Ronald G. *American Reformers, 1815–1860.* New York: Hill and Wang, 1978.

Walther, Eric H. *The Fire-Eaters.* Baton Rouge: Louisiana State University Press, 1992.

Walton, Brian G. "Elections to the United States Senate in North Carolina, 1835–1861." *NCHR* 53 (1976): 168–92.

Watson, Elgiva D. "The Election Campaign of Governor Jarvis, 1880: A Study of the Issues." *NCHR* 48 (1971): 276–300.

Webb, Charles A. *Asheville, North Carolina: Forty-Six Years in Asheville, 1889–1935.* Asheville: n.p., 1935.

Welch, Richard E., Jr. *The Presidencies of Grover Cleveland.* Lawrence: University Press of Kansas, 1988.

Wellman, Manly Wade. "Duel Paper Work Heavy." Clipping from *Raleigh News and Observer,* 31 January 1954. Clipping File, NCC.

Wheeler, John Hill. *Historical Sketches of North Carolina from 1584 to 1851.* 2 vols. in 1. Philadelphia: Lippincott, Grambo, 1851.

———. *Reminiscences and Memoirs of North Carolina and Eminent North Carolinians.* Columbus: Columbus Printing Works, 1884.

Whitener, Daniel J. "North Carolina Prohibition Election of 1881 and Its Aftermath." *NCHR* 11 (1934): 71–93.

Williams, Charles Richard. *The Life of Rutherford Birchard Hayes.* 2 vols. Boston: Houghton Mifflin, 1914.

Williams, Max R. "The Education of William A. Graham." *NCHR* 40 (1963): 1–15.

———. "William A. Graham and the Election of 1844: A Study in North Carolina Politics." *NCHR* 45 (1968): 23–46.

Wills, George. "Thomas Lanier Clingman." Manuscript. Charles Leonard Van Noppen Biographical Sketches, Duke.

Wilson, Charles Reagan. *Baptized in Blood: The Religion of the Lost Cause, 1865–1920.* Athens: University of Georgia Press, 1980.

Woodward, C. Vann. *Origins of the New South, 1877–1913.* Baton Rouge: Louisiana State University Press, 1951.

———. *Reunion and Reaction: The Compromise of 1877 and the End of Reconstruction.* Boston: Little, Brown, 1951.

Wooten, C. S. "General Thomas L. Clingman." Newspaper clipping, 1917. Clipping File, NCC.

Young, James Harvey. *The Toadstool Millionaires: A Social History of Patent Medicines in America before Federal Regulation.* Princeton: Princeton University Press, 1961.

Zuber, Richard L. *North Carolina during Reconstruction.* Raleigh: State Department of Archives and History, 1969.

Index

campaigns for congressional seat of
(1841), 41, 334 (n. 1); loses seat to TLC
(1843), 42–43, 55, 312, 335 (nn. 6, 9);
reclaims seat (1845), 52–55, 58, 312–13,
338 (n. 53); criticized by Whig presses,
53, 56–57, 339 (n. 2); withdraws from
congressional race (1847), 60–61
Graham, William A., 27, 41, 43, 197, 200,
210, 249, 315, 344 (n. 4), 359 (n. 7), 385
(n. 68); as TLC's mentor, 20, 24, 28,
142, 328 (n. 48); TLC writes to, 24, 28;
and senatorial election of 1840, 37, 39,
333 (n. 28), 334 (n. 33); and election of
1844, 47; TLC's attitude toward, 47,
57, 65, 73, 339 (n. 3), 339–40 (n. 8);
TLC blames for defeat in 1845, 57, 339
(n. 4); and election of 1846, 57–58, 340
(n. 9); nominated for vice president,
89; opposes a state convention, 189;
denounces TLC, 196; death of, 216;
TLC eulogizes, 217
Grant, Ulysses S., 247; in Civil War, 177,
179, 182; and election of 1868, 192–93;
TLC's attitude toward, 193, 242, 260,
295, 383 (n. 37), 411 (n. 14); and election
of 1872, 207, 223, 243; financial policies
of, 241–43; and election of 1880, 260;
illness and death of, 287–88, 295
Great Britain: and Crimean War, 104;
TLC's confrontational policy toward,
109–10, 114–15, 118, 122, 129–30;
TLC visits, 130; and *Alabama* claims,
213–14
"Great Meteor of 1860," 227, 393 (n. 24)
Greeley, Horace, 207, 209–10, 223, 387
(n. 26)
Green, William J., 282
Greenback movement, 260
Greenbacks, 240–41, 304. *See also* Banks
and Currency
Gudger, James, 332–33 (n. 24)
Guiteau, Charles Julius, 265
Guyot, Arnold, 142

Hadden, William, 284
Hagood, Johnson, 178
Hale, Edward J., 84–86, 121, 156, 370
(n. 33)
Hale, John P., 44
Hale, W. H., 286, 288

Hall, Hugh Roddy, 16, 135
Hall, James, 16
Hall, Robert Sloan, 16
Hall, William Alexander, 16
Hamilton, Benjamin, 140
Hamlin, Hannibal, 44
Hammond, James H., 156
Hancock, Winfield Scott, 191, 243, 260–
62, 382 (n. 30), 397 (n. 14), 402 (n. 20)
Hanson, Charles C., 51
Hardy, J. F. E., 91, 137
Harper's Magazine, 149
Harrison, Benjamin, 1, 301–4, 306–7, 321
(n. 2)
Harrison, William Henry, 36–37, 41, 247,
333 (nn. 25, 27)
Hatch, Col., 223
Hayes, Rutherford B., 244–45, 247–48,
398 (n. 18)
Hayne, Robert Y., 213, 332 (n. 18), 388
(n. 37)
Haywood, William H., Jr., 58, 340 (n. 10),
359 (n. 7)
Hembrick (Hembic) Turnpike Co., 333
(n. 30)
Henderson, Leonard, 20
Henderson, Pleasant, 20, 330 (n. 70), 338
(n. 46)
Hendricks, Thomas A., 288, 293, 397
(n. 13)
Henry, Joseph, 139, 142–44
Henry, Louis D., 42, 334 (n. 2)
Hickory Nut Gap Turnpike, 38, 40, 333
(n. 30)
Hidden, William E., 276–77
Highland Messenger, 335 (n. 11)
Hilliard, Henry, 345 (nn. 12, 14)
Hillyer, Junius, 349 (n. 3)
Hoke, John F., 191
Hoke, Michael, 47, 339 (n. 4)
Hoke, Robert F., 176, 178
Holden, William W., 55, 163, 317, 358
(n. 38), 374 (n. 11), 386 (n. 2); de-
nounces TLC, 46, 54, 57–58, 60, 63,
157, 184; fuels TLC's resentment
against "central clique," 60; declines
to endorse TLC for U.S. Senate, 100;
candidate for gubernatorial nomination,
119–21, 360 (n. 14); praises TLC, 121,
131; candidate for U.S. Senate, 127–28,

Mining, gold: TLC's interest in, 139–41, 187

Missouri Compromise line: proposed extension of, 63–64, 77, 81–82, 341 (n. 32). *See also* Slavery in territories

Mitchell, Elisha: as TLC's scientific mentor, 17, 135–36, 138; discovers Mount Mitchell, 135, 142; writes about mountain region, 135–36; TLC's controversy with, 141–47, 367 (n. 29), 368 (n. 47); death of, 142, 146–47; re-interred on Mount Mitchell, 147, 367–68 (n. 46)

Mitchell, Sarah Esther, 14, 326 (n. 21)

Morehead, James Turner, 305

Morehead, John M., 21, 36–37, 42, 47, 59, 333 (n. 25), 334 (n. 3), 336 (n. 26)

Morganton Hospital for the Insane, 2, 307–8, 414 (n. 65)

Morton, Jeremiah, 345 (n. 12)

Mound Builders, 227, 393 (n. 25)

Mountain region: TLC's influence among voters in, 3, 133, 141, 147, 258–59; and slavery, 5, 78, 84–85; and the Union, 5, 85, 160–61; bourgeois character of, 6, 133–34, 141; TLC writes promotional articles about, 6, 133–36, 222–23, 296–97; entrepreneurial elite in, 32, 134; Democrats hold balance of power in, 55, 84, 312; provides winning margin for Whigs in state elections, 69, 93; Democrats become majority party in, 102, 111; impact of Civil War on, 187; Republican party in, 192, 199; dissatisfaction with Democratic party in, 246, 262, 304, 318; definition of, 383 (n. 36)

Mount Mitchell, 135, 142–43, 367 (n. 30), 367–68 (n. 46)

Mount Pisgah, 36, 295, 306

Murphey, Archibald D., 22

Murphey, P. L., 308

Nags Head inlet, 38–40, 334 (nn. 33, 38)

Nash, Frederick, 20

Nashville Convention, 74

National Banking Act of 1863, 240

National Democrats, 103, 115, 129, 149, 151, 314

National Republican party, 21–22, 315

Natural theology, 229–30

Neal, S. J., 353 (n. 50)

Nebraska bill (1853), 97, 352 (n. 40), 380 (n. 4)

Nernst, Walther, 285, 408 (n. 46)

New Bern: Battle of, 175–76, 181, 233

Newcomb, Simon, 227, 393 (n. 24)

New Echota: treaty of, 31, 37. *See also* Cherokee lands

New Mexico bill, 77, 81–82, 97, 346–47 (n. 38)

New South creed, 221, 224, 228, 314

New York Hotel, 215, 265

Ney, Peter S., 295

Nicaragua, 114

Nonintervention, 81–83, 103, 129, 149–52, 363 (nn. 45–46). *See also* Slavery in territories

North Carolina Agricultural Society, 131, 216, 223–24, 297

North Carolina Historical Society, 233

North Carolina Institute of Education, 22–23

North Carolina Land Co., 222

North Carolina Railroad, 32, 99, 360 (n. 14)

North Carolina State Guard, 295, 411 (n. 15)

Nullification crisis, 19, 21

Nuttall, Thomas, 137, 274

O'Hara, James E., 404 (n. 57)

Oldham, Edward A., 407 (n. 38)

Origin of Species, 228

Orr, James L., 108, 356 (n. 21), 359 (n. 53)

Ostend Manifesto, 111, 114

Otey, James H., 367–68 (n. 46)

Our Living and Our Dead, 232

Ousley, Sir William Gore, 118

Outlaw, David, 66, 77–79, 81, 88, 125, 342–43 (n. 44)

Owen, Allen F., 345 (n. 12)

Page, Walter Hines, 215

Panama, 109, 115

Panic of 1837, 34, 36

Panic of 1873, 212, 222, 239–41

Paris Exposition, 222

Parker, J. H., 19

Parrish, Edward J., 287